MISCELLANEA

GENEALOGICA ET HERALDICA

EDITED BY

JOSEPH JACKSON HOWARD

THIRD SERIES

Volume 5

Elibron Classics
www.elibron.com

Elibron Classics series.

© 2005 Adamant Media Corporation.

ISBN 1-4021-9409-9 (paperback)
ISBN 1-4212-9730-2 (hardcover)

This Elibron Classics Replica Edition is an unabridged facsimile
of the edition published in 1904 by Mitchell Hughes and Clarke,
London.

Miscellanea

Genealogica et Heraldica.

EDITED BY

W. BRUCE BANNERMAN, F.S.A.

VOLUME V.

THIRD SERIES.

LONDON:

MITCHELL HUGHES AND CLARKE, 140 WARDOUR STREET, W.

1904.

MITCHELL & HUGHES

YE WARDOVR PRESS

ESTABLISHED 1797

140 WARDOVR STREET LONDON W

PREFATORY NOTE.

IN bringing forward the present Volume the ACTING EDITOR of the MISCELLANEA GENEALOGICA ET HERALDICA feels that he cannot forget to notice the devout attention which the late Dr. HOWARD paid to the authenticity of documents and the dates committed to his judgment and approval, and how, in any case submitted to him, his decision was always on the right side, and his opinion at all times cheerfully given without any ulterior gain to himself.

The EDITORS have to acknowledge with pleasure the various contributions made by Mr. A. F. G. LEVESON GOWER, F.S.A., of H.B.M. Legation, The Hague, as it is their duty to again thank him for the transcriptions of the Monuments in the Church of St. Giles-in-the-Fields. To our able contributor Mr. MAXWELL ADAMS, B.A., we were indebted for the History of the Family of Adams, which included an interesting account of the Family of Viscount Iveagh. To Mr. CECIL T. DAVIS they are much indebted for his ample account of the Inhabitants of Wandsworth. The genealogical history of the Family of Savage of Warwickshire is also interesting, the pedigree shewing the maternal relatives of Walter Savage Landor. To Mr. EVERARD GREEN, F.S.A., Rouge Dragon, they owe their best thanks for the pedigree he contributed, and also to Mr. GEORGE GRAZEBROOK, F.S.A., for his " Physiological Curiosity," which has aroused a good deal of attention in the medical world.

By the advice of Subscribers we shall issue the forthcoming Volume as Volume I., Fourth Series; it will enable many new Subscribers to join at the beginning of a Series, and will contain a transcription of the Monumental Inscriptions in the British Cemeteries of the Ionian Islands by Mr. LEVESON GOWER, which he had done previous to their demolition by the municipal authorities. We have also had copied all the monuments in St. Anne's Church, Soho, for publication.

The EDITORS trust to be favoured with contributions appertaining to family history, grants of arms, etc.; and any other matter of a genealogical nature will be always cheerfully acknowledged.

12th March, 1904.

CONTENTS.

Miscellanea Genealogica et Heraldica.

The Family of Savage of Warwickshire.*

CHESTERTON REGISTER.

Marriages.

1558	June 10	Rowland Griffin & Annis Savage.
1578	Oct. 18	Richard Hill, Vicar of Tachbrooke, & Alice Granger.
1712	Dec. 11	George Commander & Maria Savage, both of Tachbrooke ; by Licence.
1724	Oct. 1	John Savage & Sarah Smith, widow ; by Licence.

Buried.

| 1750 | Oct. 19 | Sarah wife of John Savage. |

* Communicated by Rev. R. E. H. DUKE, Rector of Maltby, Lincolnshire—continued from Vol. IV., p. 288.

CHILD'S WICKHAM, CO. GLOUCESTER, REGISTER.

Married.

1678 Dec. 13 John Savage, gent., of Warwick, & Anne Murcott of Willersey; by Licence.*

BUDBROKE REGISTERS.

Married.

1723 Oct. 20 Willm Smith & Cath. Savage, both of St Mary's, Warwick; by Licence.

HAMPTON LUCY REGISTER.

Married.

1610 Nov. 5 Willm Clarke & Patience Savage.

LADBROKE REGISTER.

Married.

1592 Dec. 28 Thos Savage & Hope Pratt, wydow.

KINGTON OR KINETON REGISTERS.

Baptisms.

1538	Oct. 18	John Savage.
1547	Dec. 8	John Savadge.
1548	July 28	Thomas Savadge.
1550	April 11	Alicia Savadge.
1550	June 13	Leonard Savadge.
15—	April 5	Christopher Savadge.
1577	June 14	Christopher Savadge.
1582	July 24	Thomas s. of Thomas Savadge.
1583	Mar. 2	Elinor d. of Leonard Savadge.
1585	Aug. 4	Prudence d. of Francis Savadge.
1586	May 21	Leonard s. of Thomas Savadge.
1587	Feb. 15	John s. of Francis Savadge.
1595	Feb. 12	Agnes d. of Richard Savage.
1596	April 4	Walter s. of Francis Savage.
1600	Dec. 14	Kath^e d. of Richard Savadge.
1601	Feb. 27	Kath^e d. of William Savadge.
1602	Feb. 6	Kath^e d. of Edmond Savadge.
1603	Oct. 20	Willm. s. of Richard Savadge.
1604	July 15	Maria d. of William Savadge.

* This Licence is thus entered in the Book of Marriage Allegations at Gloucester :—
1678 Nov. 25 John Savage of the Town of Warwick to marry Ann Murcott of Willersey, dio Gloucester, coram Geo. Sandys, Rector of Willersey.

1606	Jan. 25	Anne d. of William Savadge.
1608	June 26	Richard s. of Richard Savage.
1609	June 4	Jane d. of William Savage.
1612	May 1	Elizabeth d. of William Savage.
1612	May 31	Dority d. of Richard Savage.
1614	Oct. 21	Richard s. of Leonard Savage.
1615	Jan. 15	Leonard s. of William Savage.
1616	Aug. 4	Anne d. of Richard Savage.
1616	Jan. 29	Leonard s. of William Savag.
1616	Mar. 15	Kathᵉ d. of Leonard Savag.
1617	April 12	Richard s. of Jhon Savage.
1618	Oct. 25	Edmund s. of John Savage.
1618	Mar. 14	Maria d. of Leonard Savage.
1619	Nov. 8	Kathᵉ d. of John Savage.
1620	April 29	Rebecka d. of William Savage.
1621	Dec. 25	Elizabeth d. of Leonard Savag.
1621	Jan. 13	Alice d. of Jhon Savage.
1622	Nov. 17	Anne d. of Leonard Savage.
1622	Dec. 27	Henry s. of Thomas Savage.
1624	Sep. 19	Edward s. of Thomas Savage.
1624	Dec. 15	Ezechiell s. of John Savage.
1626	Feb. 26	Alice d. of Leonard Savage.
1633	Feb. 13	William s. of George Savage.
1634	Nov. 17	Blachea [sic] d. of William Savage.
1635	Feb. 26	John s. of William & Joane Savage.
1636	Sep. 29	Elizabeth d. of Geo. & Elizabeth Savage.
1638	Jan. 6	Humphry s. of William & Blanch Savage.
1643	April 16	Maria d. of William & Elizabeth Savage.
1646	April 18	Anne d. of John & .... Savidge.
1647	Aug. 12	Hannah d. of William & Elizabeth Savage.
1651	June 17	Mary d. of Edward & Susannah Savage.
1652	Nov. 9	Thomas s. of Edward & Susannah Savage.
1654	July 1	Elizabeth d. of Edward & Susannah Savage.
1660	Oct. 26	Jonah s. of William & Elizabeth Savage.
1661	July 7	Moses s. of William & Elizabeth Savage.
1669	Jan. 6	John s. of Wᵐ & Elizabeth Savage.
1674	Dec. 3	Elizabeth d. of Henry & Sarah Savage.
1686	Jan. 16	Mary d. of Richardson Savage.
1686	Feb. 16	Elizabeth d. of Jonah & Deborah Savage.
1689	Sep. 13	William s. of Richard & Mary Savage.
1694	July 4	John s. of Richard & Mary Savage.
1697	Sep. 18	Moses s. of Richard & Mary Savage.
1699	June 4	Elizabeth d. of Edward & Elizᵗʰ Savig.
1704	Nov. 17	Richardson s. of Thomas & Mary Savage.
1721	Oct. 26	Elizabeth d. of Wᵐ & Eliz. Savage.
1722	Nov. 18	Richard s. of Wᵐ & Eliz. Savage.
1724	Jan. 6	Mary d. of Wᵐ & Eliz. Savage.
1727	Feb. 25	William s. of Wᵐ & Eliz. Savage.
1728	July 9	Hester d. of Wᵐ & Eliz. Savage.

Marriages.

1545	Jan. 26	Thomas Sale & Margaret Savag.
1546	Nov. 21	William Wagstaf & Elizabeth Savadge.
[Blank]	Nov. 20	Thomas Savage & Isabella Chamberlen.
1588	Nov. 17	Thomas Wilkes & Anne Savage.
1589	Oct. 4	Thomas Wilkes & Kathᵉ Savage.

1589	Nov. 29	Giles Elliot & Margaret Savadge.
1589	Feb. 14	Nicholas Wise & Margery Savadge.
1597	Oct. 6	Edmond Savadg & Elisth Hill.
1600	Aug. 11	Richard Rogers & Alice Savadge.
1602	Oct. 3	John Kirdoll & Anne Savadge.
1608	Nov. 5	Willm More & Prudence Savage.
1614	Sep. 10	Leonard Savage & Anne Pigeon.
1683	Aug. 3	George Savage & Elisabeth Coles.
1683	Aug. 4	Peter Clarke & Maria Savage.
1683	Oct. 10	Edward King & Anne Savage.
1663	Aug. 27	John Westly & Widow Savage.
1687	Feb. 19	William Avis & Mary Savage, both of Combrook.
1713	June 7	Robert Moor of Combrooke & Mary Savage of Little Kington.
1736	May 19	Edward Clifford of Alkerton & Elizabeth Savage ; by Licence.

Burials.

1588	April 5	Leonard Savage.
1589	Dec. 22	Jhon Savadge.
1598	June 5	Christopher s. of Thomas Savag.
1598	Feb. 20	Richard Savadge.
1602	Nov. 10	Thomas s. of Richard Savadg.
1607	Oct. 9	Leonard s. of Leonard Savage.
1608	July 15	Richard Savage.
1614	Aug. 19	Mary d. of Wm Savage.
1615	Sep. 3	Thomas Savage.
1615	Sep. 16	Richd Savag.
1615	Nov. 28	Leonard s. of Wm Savage.
1620	Dec. 7	Mary Savage.
1621	Jan. 15	Elisabeth Savage.
1623	Aug. 13	Elisabeth Savag, widdowe.
1639	Aug. 25	Richard Savage.
1639	Feb. 25	William Savage.
1649	Dec. 13	Anne Savage of Great Kington.
1652	May 25	Blanche Savage, widow, of Great Kington.
1652	Oct. 28	Elizabeth wife of Edward Savage.
1654	May 17	Anne Savage, widow.
1669	Oct. 29	Widow Savage.
1672	Sep. 18	Widow Savage.
1672	Jan. 13	Cath^e Savage.
1698	Feb. 7	Alis Savage.
1699	Nov. 23	Henery Savage.
1708	June 5	Thomas Savage.
1709	Mar. 25	Mary Savage.
1727	Oct. 14	Mary Savige.
1729	April 8	Hester d. of Wm Savidge.
1729	June 20	William s. of Wm Savige.
1729	June 24	William Savage.
1729	Sep. 19	Mary d. of Wm Savage.
1736	April 14	Richardson Savage.
1736	May 13	Mary Savage.
1738	Oct. 8	Margaret Savage.
1740	Mar. 15	Mary Savage.

(To be continued.)

A GENEALOGICAL HISTORY

OF THE

Family of Adams of Cavan, etc.*

INTRODUCTION.

THE following History has been very carefully compiled from the most authentic sources, viz., information from members of the family, monumental inscriptions, parochial and family registers, wills, deeds, family manuscripts, published works in the libraries of Trinity College, Dublin, the Royal Irish Academy, the Royal Dublin Society, etc.

The original surname of the family was "Adam,"† and they appear to have been the constant and steady friends of the Red Douglases, Earls of Angus, ever ready to unite their followers either to repel an inroad of the English or in turn to become the invaders ; and though they have never obtained a more permanent title than knighthood, they have reached to the highest position in the different professions, and have formed matrimonial alliances with the noble houses of Douglas, Leslie, O'Neill, Magennis, Cosby, etc., ever maintaining their position in that class of society so happily described by Sir Bernard Burke, Ulster King-of-Arms, "as holding the next place to the Nobility, the untitled Country Gentlemen, a class, though be it remembered, not one degree below the other in antiquity of descent, personal accomplishments, and national usefulness ; nay, the Chiefs of the Houses from which the Nobility spring are generally to be found in this division of the Aristocracy, and for the simple reason that the eldest son and heir being already provided for, the field of adventure belongs almost exclusively to the junior members of the family, who, thus forced upon the arena, achieve by their prowess or their talents—the sword or the pen—fame, wealth, and eminence." (Preface to Burke's "Landed Gentry," 1846.)

The following description of Northlands, the seat of the senior branch of the family, is from the pen of the same talented author :—" Northlands, in the county of Cavan, the seat of the Very Rev. Samuel Adams. This mansion was built in the year 1822 by the present proprietor, the estate itself having been in the family for the last 150 years. The house, which is of moderate size, is in the plain English style of building. In front of the hall door is a porch of cut-stone such as may still be seen in many parts of this country. Above forty acres of underwood was planted here in 1817." (Burke's "Visitation of Seats and Arms," vol. ii., p. 93.) Several acres of plantation, with Cornalaragh Lough, have since been added to the demesne, which is now the residence of Samuel Allen Adams.

---

* Communicated by MAXWELL ADAMS, Esq., Barrister-at-Law. From a MS. by the late Rev. B. W. ADAMS, D.D.

† It would seem that inattention to spelling first caused the alteration of the name from *Adam* to *Adams*, for we find that Jane Adams *née* Allen (see p. 8), wife of James Adams of Monaghan, is called *Adams* in the will of her mother, Margaret Allen of Kilmore, dated 5 December 1694, and *Adam* in that of her brother, Richard Allen of Kilmore, co. Monaghan, dated 14 October 1724, in which her son also is called Allen *Adam*. Both wills are in the Probate Office, King's Inns, Dublin. See also the extracts given in the APPENDIX, where Colonel Adams is also called *McAdam*.

THE ARMS OF THE FAMILY OF ADAMS.

The Arms borne by the family of Adams are : *Gules, a heart between three crosses-crosslet fitchée or ;* and for Crest : *On a mount vert a cross-crosslet fitchée or, charged with a bleeding heart,* as registered in the Office of Arms in Dublin.

Richard Adams of Wainsford, Hants, however, used as a crest *a wyvern gules,* and his descendants still use the same. It is not known how this crest came to be assumed by this branch of the family, but there is a tradition that Richard Adams adopted his mother's crest, she being a Leslie.

Another branch of the family used as crest *a cross-crosslet fitchée gules, surmounted by a sword in saltire proper, hilted and pommelled or,* which is the crest of the family of Adam of Blair Adam, from whom the Adamses are descended.

The descendants of Richard Adams of Wainsford also quarter the arms of Peers, viz., *Azure, on a fesse argent between three pelicans or, vulning themselves proper, as many Ogresses*—the said Richard having married Louisa, daughter and coheir of Newsham Peers of Alveston in Warwickshire, who died 1803.

THE FAMILY HISTORY.

The first authentic account of the family is recorded in Scotland, in the reign of Alexander II. (1214—1249), when

SIR DUNCAN ADAM, Knt., affixed his signature, as a witness, to a donation to the church of Wemyss (Burke's "Visitation of Seats and Arms," vol. ii., p. 31) by a progenitor of the Earl of Wemyss. His successor,

ALEXANDER ADAM, lived in the reign of Alexander III. (1249—1286) (Burke's "Visitation of Seats and Arms," vol. ii., p. 31), and is traditionally reported to have married into the illustrious house of Douglas. His son,

DUNCAN ADAM, lived during the eventful reign of Robert Bruce (1306—1329) (Burke's "Visitation of Seats and Arms," vol. ii., p. 31) ; he married and left four sons, Robert, John, Reginald, and Duncan (Burke's "Landed Gentry," 1846, vol. i., p. 4), from whom all the Adams, Adamses, Adamsons, and Addies in Scotland are descended. The third son was very likely the Right Rev. Reginald Adam, Bishop of Brechin, Scotland, one of the most influential men of his time, and was frequently employed by the Estates of the Nation in foreign negotiations during the troubled reign of David Bruce (1329—1371), in all of which he acquitted himself ably and honourably (Burke's "Visitation of Seats and Arms," vol. ii., p. 31). The youngest son,

DUNCAN ADAM, with several other brave Scottish gentlemen, accompanied James, Lord Douglas, in the expedition which he undertook in order to convey, in a golden casket, the embalmed heart of King Robert Bruce to the Holy Sepulchre at Jerusalem (Burke's "Visitation of Seats and Arms," vol. ii., p. 31). On arriving there, Douglas solemnly buried it before the High Altar, and on his voyage home, being forced by a storm to land at Valencia in Spain, he found Alphonsus, King of Arragon, preparing to march against the Saracens or Moors. Lord Douglas joined his forces and was slain in an ambush, 20 August 1330, on the bloody field of Theba in Andalusia (Hume's "Hist. of the Houses of Douglas and Angus"). Another version of this tragic event is given by Thomas Smibert in his "Hist. of the Clans of Scotland," that it was on the journey out Douglas was obliged to land at Valencia, and that when he came up with the Saracens he tossed the casket containing the heart of his royal master into the thickest of the enemy, bidding it "Go first as it was wont, and Douglas would follow or die." Douglas was slain, but his faithful followers, recovering possession of the casket and heart, conveyed them to Jerusalem and there buried them (Smibert's "Hist. of the Clans of Scotland," p. 323). It is believed that the heart and crosses-crosslet in the armorial bearings of the family are derived from the part this Duncan Adam took in this expedition (Burke's "Visitation of Seats and Arms," vol. ii., p. 31). His son,

REGINALD ADAM, in 1385, took part in an invasion of Northumberland, conducted by Sir James Douglas (eleventh Baron and second Earl of Douglas) and John de Vienne, Earl of Valentinois and Admiral of France (Burke's "Visitation of Seats and Arms," vol. ii., p. 31) ; "they took the castles of Wark, Foord, and Cornwall, and spoiled and burned the country between Berwick and Newcastle." Under the walls of the latter Douglas defeated, in personal encounter, Sir Henry Percy, better known as Harry Hotspur, and carried off in triumph his pennon. "But when the Scottish Chiefs intended to march farther, the continual rain that fell in great abundance, it being autumn, did so spoil the roads, raise the waters and wet the soldiers in their armour, that they were forced to return home" (Hume's "Hist. of the Houses of Douglas and Angus"). It was to redeem his pennon thus taken that Percy, invading Scotland in 1388, was defeated and taken prisoner at the Battle of Otterbourne, 15 August 1388, where Douglas, though victorious, was slain (Smibert's "Hist. of the Clans of Scotland"). This is the battle celebrated in the old Border ballad of "Chevy Chase." Reginald Adam's lineal descendant,

SIR JOHN ADAM, Knt., accompanied James IV. in his invasion of England August 1513, and fell at the Battle of Flodden Field 9 September 1513 (Burke's "Visitation of Seats and Arms," vol. ii., p. 31),

> " In that undaunted ring
> That fought unbroken round their King "

while vainly striving to shield their Sovereign from a similar fate. The conclusion of this battle is graphically described by Sir Walter Scott in "Marmion" :—

> " When skilful Surrey's sage commands,
> Led back from strife his shattered bands ;
> Then did their loss his foemen know ;
> Their king, their lords, their mightiest low,
> To tell red Flodden's dismal tale,
> And raise the universal wail.
> Tradition, legend, tune and song,
> Shall many an age that wail prolong ;
> Still from the sire the son shall hear
> Of the stern strife and carnage drear
>   Of Flodden's fatal field,
> When shivered was fair Scotland's spear,
>   And broken was her shield."

> "Marmion," canto vi.

Sir John Adam's son,

CHARLES ADAM, proprietor in 1549 of the estate of Fanno, co. Forfar, married Margaret Ferguson, and had issue two sons, Charles, his heir, and David, progenitor of the Adams of Kingsbarn, co. Fife, and two daughters (Burke's "Landed Gentry," 1846, vol. i., p. 4). The elder son,

CHARLES ADAM of Fanno, married Isabel Bisset, a descendant of the ancient family of Lissendrum (Burke's "Landed Gentry," 1846, vol. i., p. 4), and had issue several sons and daughters.* One of the former left a son,

JAMES ADAMS, a Colonel in the Army, who, affixing the letter " s " to his patro-nymic† and settling in the North of Ireland, probably in the county Down, in the early part of the seventeenth century, married the Hon. Catherine Magennis, dau. of Arthur Magenis, first Viscount Iveagh, by his wife Lady Sarah O'Neill, dau. of Hugh, Earl of Tyrone (Burke's "Landed Gentry," 1862). In 1641 Sir Phelim Roe O'Neill, Commander-in-Chief of the Insurgent Army, and cousin of Mrs. Adams, was breakfasting at Colonel Adams', and overhearing one of his sentries ask Mrs. Adams, who was leading by the hand down stairs her little son James, "Whose little heretic brat that was?" rushed out of the room, and, plunging his sword through the soldier's body, exclaimed, "Let him serve as a warning to all how they speak disrespectfully of the blood of the O'Neill!" Colonel Adams was succeeded by his son,

JAMES ADAMS, Captain in the Army of William III., who distinguished him-self at the Battle of the Boyne 1 July 1690 ; married about 1672, and dying left two sons, James his heir, and another, father of Samuel Adams of Monaghan, who was executor in 1755 to his cousin Allen Adams of Corranearry House, co. Cavan (see below), and progenitor of the (now extinct) family of Adams of Monaghan. The elder son,

JAMES ADAMS of Monaghan, afterwards of Corranearry House, co. Cavan, born 1673, married 1694 Jane, daughter of William and Margaret Allen of Kilmore, co. Monaghan, and died 19 November 1744, aged 71. Mrs. Adams died 17 March 1752, aged 75, and both were interred in Knockbride churchyard, co. Cavan,‡ where their tomb still remains outside the south wall of the old church. They were succeeded by their only son,

ALLEN ADAMS of Corranearry House, co. Cavan, born 1708; married about 1735 Martha (born 1702), daughter of William Higenbotham, Esq. (who died 1760), and granddaughter of Captain Thomas Higenbotham (who died 1737) by his wife Miss Williams, Maid of Honour to Mary II., and daughter of General Scurlog Williams of Clongill Castle, co. Meath.§ He died 15 December 1755, aged 47, and was interred beside his parents. His will, signed 13 May 1755, was proved

---

  * From Robert, the second but eldest surviving son, is descended the family of *Adam* of Blair Adam, Kinross-shire, Scotland.

  † See footnote on p. 5. For some of Colonel Adams' exploits see APPENDIX.

  ‡ Knockbride Churchyard, enclosing both the present and the old churches, is situated on the road from Shercock to Stradone, about four miles from the former village. Corranearry Lough bounds two sides of the churchyard, and on a hill, on the opposite side of the Lough, stand the remains of Corranearry House, the original residence of the Adamses in Cavan. A short distance from it is Castletown House. In the old church, at the south-west corner, is a spacious vault belonging to the family of Richard Adams of Shercock House (see p. 9); but he himself lies with his ancestors in the cemetery adjoining. The old church is the place of burial of the Rev. Benjamin Adams and his descendants.

  § By the marriage of Allen Adams with Miss Higenbotham, the Adams family enjoy the privilege of being hereditary freemen of the Borough of Drogheda, which had been granted to General Scurlog Williams and his descendants for ever, for the prompt and efficient aid afforded by him to the inhabitants of the town in 1690.

in Dublin 24 January 1756 (Probate Court, Dublin). Mrs. Adams continued to reside at Corranearry House with her second son James, and dying there 1807, aged 105, was interred in Knockbride, having had issue five sons and two daughters, namely : 1, RICHARD (see below); 2, JAMES ; 3, WILLIAM ; 4, SAMUEL ; 5, BENJAMIN ; 6, MARGARET ; 7, JANE.

THE DESCENDANTS OF RICHARD ADAMS, ELDEST SON OF ALLEN ADAMS AND MARTHA HIGENBOTHAM.

I. RICHARD ADAMS, J.P., of Shercock House,* co. Cavan, born 1736 ; was High Sheriff of Cavan in 1783 and of Monaghan in 1785 (Walker's " Hibernian Magazine "); married 13 April 1761 (Bailieborough Par. Reg.) Amelia, daughter of Thomas Cosby, Esq., of Beeks Court, co. Cavan, nephew of the Right Hon. Dudley Cosby, Lord Sydney, of Stradbally Hall, Queen's County ; died 1789, aged 53. His will, signed 11 July 1789, with a codicil, dated 22 September 1789, was proved in Dublin 4 February 1790 (Probate Court, Dublin). He and his wife (who survived him some years) were interred in Knockbride, having had issue five sons and four daughters, viz. :—

i. STUART ADAMS, J.P. (Watson's " Gentleman's and Citizen's Almanack "), of Annalee, co. Cavan, born 1763 ; entered the Army as Ensign in the 96th Regiment 13 April 1780 ; Lieut. 28 May 1782, and was placed on half-pay when the Corps was disbanded, 31 May 1783 (Letter from the Horse Guards). He afterwards became Major and Paymaster of the Cavan Regiment ; married 10 May 1789 (St. Peter's, Dublin, Par. Reg.) Catherine, daughter of Henry Leslie, Esq., of Dublin ; was High Sheriff of Cavan in 1790 (Walker's " Hibernian Magazine "), and died at Shercock House 1809. His wife died in Dublin August 1814, and both were interred in Knockbride, leaving issue two sons and two daughters, namely :—

1. RICHARD STUART ADAMS of Ackworth, near Pontefract, co. York, born 2 May 1790 ; entered the Army as Ensign in the 24th Foot 27 November 1806 (Letter from the Horse Guards); Lieut. 11 May 1809 ; was present at the Battle of Talavera in Spain 27 July 1809 ; Captain in the 3rd Battalion of the 14th Foot 13 January 1814, which Battalion was disbanded March 1816 (" Army List ") and its officers placed on half-pay. He married 1827 Jane Guest, daughter of Richard Hazelwood, Esq., of Bridgewater, co. Somerset, and died s.p. August 1837, aged 47, and was interred 11 August 1837 in Ackworth Churchyard beside his wife, who had died July 1837, aged 34, and was buried 8 July 1837 (Ackworth Par. Reg.).

2. HENRY ADAMS, born January 1798 ; baptized in Killersherdiny Church, co. Cavan, 27 January 1798 (Killersherdiny Par. Reg.) ; died unmarried in Liverpool 9 March 1862, aged 63.

---

* Shercock House was situated near the present village of that name. It was the residence of the Piers family, to whom Queen Elizabeth granted the manor of Pierscourt. Some of the garden wall still remains on the lake shore, to the rear of the market house, next which at the end of the town was the entrance-gate and lodge, the avenue corresponding in part to the modern road from Shercock to Canning's town. The house occupied the site of the present Roman Catholic Chapel. In the townland of Leix the boundaries of the Deer Park can still be traced, but its extensive woods, which within the memory of the past generation extended far around, have now their existence only in tradition. The mansion was allowed to go to ruin early in the nineteenth century.

3. CATHERINE, born 1791 ; married 24 July 1821 (Par. Reg. St. Thomas',
Dublin) William Shepard, Esq., of La Vallée, Bray, co. Wicklow,
who died 31 May 1867, aged 83. She died 22 October 1868, aged
77, having had issue one son and one daughter, viz. :—

(1) RICHARD SHEPARD of Islington, London, born 13 January 1826.

(2) ELIZABETH, married 21 June 1858 James Roberts, Esq., of
Castletown, Mountrath, Queen's County, and has issue two sons
and three daughters, viz. :—

    1. JAMES ADAMS ROBERTS, born 22 May 1861.

    2. WILLIAM SHEPARD ROBERTS, born 24 January 1867.

    3. KATHLEEN.

    4. ELIZABETH.

    5. CONSTANCE.

4. HENRIETTA MARIA LESLIE, married 1 January 1817 (Par. Reg.
St. Thomas', Dublin) William Young, Esq., of Copenagh, Tullow,
co. Carlow, who died 4 December 1863, aged 77. She died at
7 Pembroke Place, Merrion Avenue, Blackrock, co. Dublin, 1 Oct.
1874, having had issue three sons and eight daughters, viz. :—

(1) WILLIAM YOUNG of Gayville, Carlow, born 3 December 1821 ;
married 8 August 1861 Ellen, daughter of Thomas Buckley,
Esq., an officer in the 42nd Regiment, and has issue an only
son, viz. :—

WILLIAM ADAMS YOUNG, born 31 May 1862.

(2) STEWARD ADAMS YOUNG of Copenagh, Tullow, co. Carlow, born
7 April 1826.

(3) RICHARD YOUNG, born 20 February 1829.

(4) CATHERINE, born 1819 ; married 25 February 1840 William
Morley Perfect, Esq. (son of George Perfect, Esq., a Banker in
Pontefract, co. York), who died 28 January 1856, aged 42.
She died 30 January 1841, aged 22, leaving an only son—

WILLIAM GEORGE PERFECT, born 24 January 1841.

(5) HANNAH, married 4 February 1845 William Leonard, Esq., of
Hill View, Moone, Ballytore, co. Kildare (son of George
Leonard, Esq., of Belan Lodge, co. Kildare), who died 26 Oct.
1862, aged 65. She died 3 May 1876, having had issue six
sons and two daughters, viz. :—

    1. GEORGE LEONARD, born 25 March 1846 ; died 25 July 1846.

    2. WILLIAM LEONARD, born 24 June 1848; married 15 May
1878 (St. Andrew's, Dublin, Par. Reg.) Ellen, daughter of
John Valentine, Esq., Rathsallagh, co. Wicklow.

    3. MAINWARING LEONARD (a twin), born 1 October 1851 ; died
15 November 1863.

    4. JOHN LEONARD (twin with last), born 1 October 1851.

5. STEWARD ADAMS LEONARD, born 18 December 1853.

6. RICHARD LEONARD, born 9 May 1855.

7. CATHERINE, married 7 December 1880 John Valentine, Esq. (Christ Church, Bray, Par. Reg.).

8. HENRIETTA, born 27 March 1850 ; died 25 March 1853.

(6) CAROLINE.

(7) JANE, married 24 February 1857 Thomas Pilsworth, Esq., of Springfield, The Grange, Athy (son of George Pilsworth, Esq., of Graney, co. Kildare), and has issue five sons and two daughters, viz. :—

    1. GEORGE PILSWORTH (a twin), born 24 March 1858.

    2. WILLIAM PILSWORTH (twin with last), born 24 March 1858.

    3. THOMAS EDWARD PILSWORTH, born 27 June 1866.

    4. JOHN LEONARD PILSWORTH, born 31 March 1868.

    5. DAVID H. LESLIE PILSWORTH, born 8 November 1871.

    6. MARY GATES.

    7. HENRIETTA MARIA.

(8) HENRIETTA.

(9) JOYCE ELIZABETH, born 1820 ; died unmarried at 7 Pembroke Place, Merrion Avenue, Blackrock, co. Dublin, 21 April 1874, aged 46.

(10) AMELIA DOROTHEA.

(11) ADELAIDE.

II. REV. ALLEN NOBLE ADAMS, A.B., of Shercock House, J.P. for the counties of Cavan and Monaghan (Watson's "Gentleman's and Citizen's Almanack") ; Rector of Killan (now called Shercock), Diocese of Kilmore ; born 1765 ; entered Trinity College, Dublin, and took his A.B. degree at the spring commencements 1787 ; married June 1791 (Walker's "Hibernian Magazine") by special licence, dated 8 April 1791, Isabella, daughter of John Battersby, Esq., of Lakefield, co. Meath ; appointed, 26 April 1793, Chaplain to the Cavan Regiment (List of Officers of the Militia, 1799 ; Library Royal Dublin Society, Pamphlets, vol. 93) ; died at Shercock House March 1805, aged 40, and was interred at Knockbride. His will, signed 30 November 1803, was proved in Dublin 20 April 1805 (Probate Court, Dublin). After his decease Mrs. Adams removed to No. 2 Russell Street, Dublin, where she resided until 1846, when she took up her residence with her youngest son, Rev. James Adams, at Castlecor Rectory, co. Meath, where she died 20 June 1852, aged 84, and was interred in Mount Nugent Churchyard, co. Cavan (Castlecor Par. Reg.), having had issue six sons and three daughters, viz. :—

(To be continued.)

Huguenot Refugee Family of Ourry.*

ARMS.—*Azure, in base, upon a mount proper, a chameleon vert spotted sable, in chief the sun in splendour or.*

Jaques Ourry, of Blois══Magdeleine . . . . .

Louis Ourry,[1] b. at Blois 1682; naturalized by Act of Parliament (No. 48, 12 Anne) 1718; held a Commission in the English Army from 1707 to 1771; d. 4 Jan. 1771, and bur. at Bethnal Green. Adm'on 31 July 1771.

══ Anne Louise,[1] dau. of Louis Beauvais; m.² at St. Martin's-in-the-Fields 16 Dec. 1714. D. 22 April 1732. 1st wife.

══ Françoise Tremblé, widow of Simon Beauvais; m. 15 July 1734; d. s.p. 15 July 1746. 2nd wife.

Paul Henry Ourry, b. 3 and bapt. in Jersey, 18 Oct. 1719; Commissioner of the Dockyard, Plymouth, and M.P. for Plympton 1770; d. 31 Jan. 1783. Will dated 10 Feb. 1757 and proved 16 April 1783. (P.C.C., 193, Cornwallis.)

══ Charity, eldest dau. and coheir of the Right Hon. George Treby, Secretary-at-War, and M.P. for Plympton, by Charity his wife, dau. and coheir of Roger Hele; b. 1727; m. 26 Aug. 1749; d. 17 Oct. 1805.

[B]   [O]

Anne Catherine, d. 15 April 1801, having m. Ed. Ricard.

Louis Simon Ourry, b. 21 Feb. 1717; Major in the Army; d. at Kinsale 1779. Will (undated) pr. by the widow 14 July 1779. (P.C.C., 315, Warburton.)

══ Elizabeth, dau. of . . . . Mott. Adm'on granted 30 Sep. 1786.

[A]

---

* Communicated by HENRY WAGNER, Esq., F.S.A.

1 He or she appear to have had a sister Susannah, widow of . . . . Fournier. This lady in her will, dated 23 Sep. 1766 and proved 5 Oct. 1768 (P.C.C., 375, Secker), names her beloved nephew Captain Lewis Ourry, his wife Elizabeth, and daughter Anne, nephew Captain Paul Ourry, niece Anne Ricard, niece Magdalen Susan Ourry, a niece Elizabeth Beuzeville, and appoints Captain Lewis Ourry, of Hammersmith, her sole executor.

The Stepney Register records the marriage on 3 Dec. 1696 of Lewis Dusautoy, weaver, and Fleurimonde Ourry.

M.I. in Bethnal Green Churchyard :—Here | lies Interred | Lieutenant Louis Ourry | who was born at Blois in France A.D. 1682 | and died at London 4 January 1771. | In the year 1707 | He quitted his native Country | for the sake of his religion | and entered into the English army | in which he bore a Commission | from that time to his death. | He left behind him four sons | all of them engaged in the service | of their King & Country | One in the Army | and | Three in the Navy. | Elizabeth Beuzeville | widow of the late | Rev. Samuel Beuzeville | has caused this stone to be erected | as a small | token of her pious regard for the | memory of her Father.

Anne Sarah, b. 11, and bapt. in Jersey 21, Feb. 1748-9; d. 11 Dec. 1820, having m. May 1794 James Furzer, Capt. Royal Marines.

Elizabeth Susanne, bapt. in Jersey 17 Aug. 1751 (?) d. young.

Charity, b. 10 Aug. 1752; m. 1775; d. 1786. = Montagu Edmund Parker of Whiteway, co. Devon, b. ; d. Jan. 1818. (Brother to John, 1st Lord Boringdon.)

(See "Landed Gentry.")

Paul Treby Ourry, d. infant.

Paul Treby Treby, b. 6 Nov. 1758; M.P. for Plympton 1784; took the name of Treby in lieu of his patronymic in 1785; d. 29 Feb. 1832. = Lætitia Anne, dau. of Sir William Trelawny, 6th Bart., of Trelawny, co. Cornwall, and Governor of Jamaica; m. 14 June 1785; d. 1 Dec. 1845.

Caroline Treby, b. 26 June 1761; m. 29 May 1786; d. at Cobham 10 Dec. 1842. = Sir William Molesworth of Pencarrow, 6th Bart., b. 30 June 1758; M.P. for Cornwall 1784—90; d. 22 Feb. 1798.

George Treby Ourry, b. 16 April 1763; d. at Portsmouth 16 Nov. 1774.

Trewlawny Treby, b. 1788; d. at sea 13 Sep. 1801.

Paul Ourry Treby, b. 29 May 1786; of Goodamoor and Plympton House, Devon, J.P. and D.L.; d. unm. 12 Sep. 1862.

Henry Hele Treby, b. 28 May 1800; of Goodamoor; d. unm. 5 April 1867.

Lewis Montagu Treby, d. infant 25 Oct. 1805.

Katharine, m. 6 Nov. 1817; d. 26 May 1823. 1st wife. = Rev. William Molesworth, Rector of St. Breoke and St. Evan, Cornwall, b. 5 Nov. 1792; d. 28 March 1851, having remar. 1829 Frances Susannah, dau. of James Buller, of Downes.

Others. (See "Baronetage.")

Montague Treby Molesworth, Lieut. R.N., killed by natives off the coast of Madagascar in 1844.

Sir Paul William Molesworth, 10th Bart., b. 1821; d. 23 Dec. 1889. = Jane Frances, eldest dau. of Gordon William Francis Gregor of Trewarthenick, co. Cornwall; m. 25 Sep. 1849; d.

(See "Baronetage.")

Walter Hele Molesworth, b. 26 May 1823; d. 11 Jan. 1885. = Frances Mary, only dau. of Rear-Admiral Henry Duncan Twysden by Mary his wife and cousin-german, dau. of Sir William Jervis Twysden, 7th Bart.; m. 10 March 1849; d. 17 July 1892.

Rev. Sir Hugh Henry Molesworth, 9th Bart., Rector of St. Petroc Minor, Cornwall, b. 13 Oct. 1818; d. 6 Jan. 1862, having m. 15 July 1856 Beatrice Anne, dau. of Charles Prideaux Brune of Prideaux Place, Cornwall, who d. 3 March 1902.

¹ A frequent contributor to the "Old Sporting Magazine." One of the four Rangers of Dartmoor.

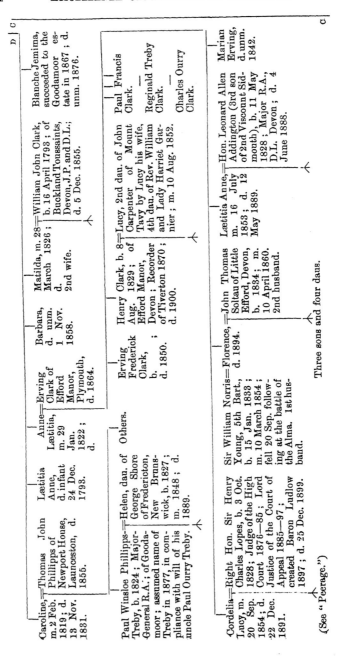

Caroline, m. 2 Feb. 1819; d. 13 Nov. 1831. — John Thomas Phillipps of Newport House, Launceston, d. 1855.

Lætitia Anne, d. infant, 24 Dec. 1793.

Anne, m. 29 Jan. 1822; d. = Erving Clark of Efford Manor, Plymouth, d. 1864.

Barbara, d. unm. 1 Nov. 1858.

Matilda, m. 28 March 1826; d. 2nd wife. = William John Clark, b. 16 April 1793; of Buckland Toussaints, Devon, J.P. and D.L.; d. 5 Dec. 1855.

Blanche Jemima, succeeded to the Goodamoor estate in 1867; d. unm. 1876.

Paul Winsloe Phillipps-Treby, b. 1824; Major-General R.A.; of Goodamoor; assumed name of Treby in 1877, in compliance with will of his uncle Paul Ourry Treby. = Helen, dau. of George Shore of Fredericton, New Brunswick, b. 1827; m. 1848; d. 1889.

Others.

Erving Frederick Clark, b. ; d. 1850.

Henry Clark, b. 8 Aug. 1829; of Efford Manor, Devon; Recorder of Tiverton 1870; d. 1900. = Lucy, 2nd dau. of John Carpenter of Mount Tavy by Lucy his wife, 4th dau. of Rev. William and Lady Harriet Garnier; m. 10 Aug. 1852.

Paul Francis Clark.

Reginald Treby Clark.

Charles Ourry Clark.

Cordelia Lucy, m. 20 Sep. 1854; d. 22 Dec. 1891. = Right Hon. Sir Henry Charles Lopes, b. 3 Oct. 1828; Judge of the High Court 1876—85; Lord Justice of the Court of Appeal 1885—97; created Baron Ludlow 1897; d. 25 Dec. 1899.

Sir William Norris Young, 5th Bart., b. 15 Jan. 1833; m. 10 March 1854; fell 20 Sep. following at the battle of the Alma. 1st husband. = Florence, d. 1894. = John Thomas Soltau of Little Efford, Devon, b. 1834; m. 10 April 1860. 2nd husband.

Lætitia Anne, m. 16 July 1853; d. 12 May 1889. = Hon. Leonard Allen Addington (3rd son of 2nd Viscount Sidmouth), b. 11 May 1828; Major R.A., D.L. Devon; d. 4 June 1888.

Marian Erving, d. unm. 1842.

Three sons and four daus.

(See "Peerage.")

o

William De la Garde,=Anne, dau. of Major John Gonin,=Isaac Florimond Ourry, b. 9 April 1721; Magdalen Susanna, Marie Anne, some time Member latterly of Laleham. Will dated d. in India Will dated b. 4 and bapt. 10 b. 17 Dec. of Council of Bombay, d. Oct. 1760. 10 April and proved 12 Dec. 1786. 12 March 1771; proved 2 Jan. 1775. April 1722; d. unm. 1728; d. 5 1st husband. (P.C.C., 629, Norfolk.) (P.C.C., 28, Alexander.) 16 Oct. 1805. Feb. 1723-4.

John Wallace,=Anne Gonin (Ourry), in 1786 Lieut. m. at St. George's, 22nd Foot. Hanover Square, 15 June 1786.

Henrietta or Harriet De la Garde, 3rd dau. and=George Hartwell, b. 22 April Mary coheir, m. 13 July 1778; d. 1753; d. De la . Garde.
(See Foster's "Baronetage.")

Benjamin Jervis.=Louisa Ellen De la=David Scott of Dunninald, N.B.; 1st husband. Garde, d. 23 March M.P. for co. Angus, b. 1803. d. 4 Oct. 1805.
(See "Baronetage.")

Elizabeth De la=Sir James Sibbald of Sillwood Park, Susanna Martha, George Ourry,=Amelia Newton (a Frances, Garde, m. May Berks; created a Baronet in 1806, bapt. in Jersey b. 15 Aug. Maid of Honour to bapt. 1772; d. s.p. with remainder to his wife's nephew 16 April 1728; 1730; Rear- Queen Charlotte), dau. 10 April 12 April 1809. David Scott; d. s.p. 17 Sep. 1819. (?) d. young. Admiral R.N.; of . . . Newton of and bur. d. s.p. at Bath Crabaton, Devon; b. 12 April 3 Jan. 1800. 1730; d. 1800. 1732.

Elizabeth, b. 22=Rev. Samuel Beuzeville, b. at Bolebec 16 April Feb. and bapt. in 1718; educated at Merchant Taylors' School; Jersey 9 March Minister at French Church of St. Jean, Swan- 1724-5; m. 1764; fields, 1758; d. 1782. Will dated 12 Feb. d. 1811. 1772; proved 28 Jan. 1782. (P.C.C., 4, Gostling.)

Elizabeth Charity Beuzeville, only child, heir to her=Thomas Lempriere, Commissary-General of Jersey and Guernsey, Seigneur of uncle George Ourry; m. 1788; d. Chesnel, Col. R.I.M.; d. 30 June 1828.

E

B

George Ourry Lempriere, b. 11 March 1787; Admiral R.N.; Seigneur of Cheanel and Diélamont, Jersey; j.u. of Pelham Place, Hants; d. 16 Jan. 1864. = Frances, dau. and heir of William Dumaresq of Pelham, Alton, Hants; b. 2 Aug. 1809; m. 8 Aug 1833; d. at Pelham 2 May 1887.

Thomas Lempriere, Lieut. R.E., b. 13 June 1796; d. at Alicante 26 Dec. 1820.

Samuel Lempriere, R.N., b. 30 Aug. 1802; d. at Sierra Leone 24 Sep. 1824.

Charles Lempriere, b. 8 Oct. 1792; Lieut. 58th Regt. Fell near Bayonne 10 Dec. 1813.

Harriet, d. unm. 5 Nov. 1901.

Ellen, of Pelham, Hants.

Algernon Thomas Lempriere, b. 17 Dec. 1835; Barrister, J.P., and Captain of Hants Militia; d. 18 Nov. 1874.

Jane, b. 18 May 1803; d. at Montreal 13 Nov. 1881. = George Deacon Lewis, Major R.A., of Milton, Kent.

Marianne, b. 18 June 1800; m. 2 Aug. 1830; d. 7 Aug. 1870. = Hon. Algernon Herbert (5th son of Henry, 1st Earl of Carnarvon), b. 12 July 1792; d. 11 June 1855.

Audley Lempriere, b. 18 July 1834; Captain 77th Regiment; fell before Sebastopol 19 April 1855.

Elizabeth Sophia, d. unm.

Anne Ourry, d. unm.

Amelia, = Charles Pipon. m.

Maria, d. unm.

Julia, d.

Caroline Charity, d.

Elizabeth Alicia Maria, m. 31 Dec. 1857. = Rev. William Lempriere Lewis, b. 22 Nov. 1829; Scholar and Fellow of Trinity College, Oxford; d. 18 Jan. 1872.

Sir Robert George Wyndham Herbert, G.C.B., D.C.L., LL.D., etc., b. 12 June 1831; Premier of Queensland 1860—66; Permanent Under-Secretary of State for Colonies 1870—92; of Ickleton, Cambs.

Jane Caroline.

TOUJOURS PROPICE

DARTREY

Bookplate of "Dartrey."

This bookplate, the date of which is between 1770 and 1785, represents the arms of Thomas Dawson, who was created, 28 May 1770, BARON DARTREY OF DAWSON'S GROVE, co. Monaghan, in the peerage of Ireland. He was subsequently, 19 June 1785, created VISCOUNT CREMORNE in that peerage, and finally, with in that case a special remainder, 11 Nov. 1791, BARON CREMORNE OF CASTLE DAWSON, co. Monaghan, also in that peerage. He was born 25 Feb. and baptized 2 March 1725 ; was M.P. for co. Monaghan 1749—68, being raised to the peerage in 1770, as above stated. His second wife, whom he married 8 May 1770, and whose arms (being those of the family of Freme of Lippiat, co. Gloucester) are here given in an escutcheon of pretence, was Philadelphia Hannah, daughter of Thomas Freame, of Philadelphia in North America, by Margaretta, daughter of the well-known William Penn, founder of that city. He died, without surviving issue, 1 March 1813, in his 88th year, when the *Barony of Dartrey* and the *Viscountcy of Cremorne* became extinct, but the *Barony of Cremorne* devolved (according to the special remainder) on his great-nephew, Richard Thomas Dawson, whose son, the 3rd Baron, was created, 12 July 1866, EARL OF DARTREY.

The arms, (*Azure*, three torches erect, *argent*, inflamed *gules*) quartered (in the 2nd and 3rd quarters) with those of Dawson, are not given in Archdall's "Lodge's Peerage of Ireland" (1789) under the Viscountcy of Cremorne. They are presumably* those of Dawson of Dawson's Grove, the heiress of which family married, in Nov. 1672, Walter Dawson, of Armagh, by whom she was grandmother of the first Peer. They are continued as a quartering by the present [1902] Peer.

The supporters, ("Two weavers, habited *proper*, each holding in his exterior hand a shuttle,") are entirely different from those of the present Peer.

G. E. C.

---

* Mr. G. D. Burtchaell, of the College of Arms, Dublin, writes on this point as under : "The quarterly coat is somewhat puzzling. When the first Lord was raised to the Peerage, his arms, in THE LORDS ENTRIES, have the 2nd and 3rd quarters *blank*, which looks as if William Hawkins, Ulster, was not satisfied with them. The only explanation seems to be, that they are intended for Dawson of Dawson's Grove. The seals on wills before the marriage with that heiress have only the plain coat."

Monumental Inscriptions

IN

Marylebone Parish Church.*

ABOVE EAST GALLERY.

In a Vault beneath this Church | repose the Mortal Remains of | JAMES BLAIR Esq : | of Penninghame, Wigtonshire, | which county he for some years represented in | Parliament with Honor and Fidelity. | He departed this life 9th Sept 1841, aged 54 Years. | To a well cultivated understanding, a sound judgment | and manly firmness of purpose, were united | gentleness of disposition and humility of mind. | His affections were warm and durable, | his benevolence was unbounded, | and being actuated by the purest principles of integrity | in the performance of every duty, he lived a highly | valued member of society, | and died lamented by all who knew him.

Sacred | to the memory of | PHILADELPHIA MITFORD, | daughter of | JOHN MITFORD, Esqr, of Newtown and Exbury, | in the County of Southampton, | and sister of the late | Colonel MITFORD and LORD REDESDALE, | who departed this Life 21st January 1837, | in the 86th Year of her age.

A window, having beneath a brass plate inscribed :—To the dearly loved Memory of ISABEL PEEK who died 20th August 1885.

To the Memory of | ROBERT ALEXANDER, Esqr | formerly of Seamount in the county of Dublin, | who departed this Life | at his house in Sussex Place, Regent's Park | on the 14th July 1827, Aged 79 years. | Also | to that of HENRIETTA JUDITH, relict of | the above, who departed this Life | at the same residence on the 14th of January 1839 | in the 78th Year of her age. | Their Remains are deposited in a vault | beneath this Church.

To the Memory of | DÓNA MARIA BRIGIDA DO FARIA | E LACERDA | wife of | Sir JOHN CAMPBELL, K.C.T.S. | Lieut Coll in the British, and Majr Genl in the Portuguese Service. | She died much lamented | on the 22nd Jany 1821, in the 24th Year of her age ; | Her remains are deposited in a vault of this Church.

Also of | JOHN DAVID CAMPBELL | Son of the above who died 28th May 1824, | aged 3 Years and 9 Months.

To the Memory of | the Honorable | WILLIAM FULLERTON ELPHINSTONE, | many years a Director of the | East India Company. | He was equally remarkable | for sound judgment and decision | united the highest firmness | to the utmost kindness of heart, | and retained | to the latest period of human life | the warmth of his benevolence, | and the serenity of his temper. | Died the 2nd of May 1834, | in the 94th Year of his age.

Also of | ELIZABETH FULLERTON ELPHINSTONE, | wife of the above | who died May 27th, 1840, | Aged 84 Years.

A window, having beneath a brass plate inscribed :—In Memory of EDWARD LAMBERT of York Terrace, Regent's Park, who died 4th March 1884. The gift of his Widow ANN ALDERSON LAMBERT.

To the Memory of | Captain CHARLES ELPHINSTONE, R.N. | Son of the | Honorable WILLIAM FULLERTON ELPHINSTONE. | In returning from India, | where he greatly distinguished himself | by the capture of force of the enemy | very superior to his own, | he was lost in H.M.S. "Blenheim" in 1807, | in the 27th Year of his Age.

Also of | ELIZABETH ELPHINSTONE, | his sister, | who died the 30th of October 1802, | in the 19th Year of her age.

Sacred to the Memory of | AUGUSTA ELIZABETH, | Wife of JOHN KIRKLAND, Jun*, Esq*, of Baker Street, Portman Square, | and eldest Daughter of Major General J. A. VESEY, | (who died in Sicily on the 2nd December 1811). | She died 5th August 1824, in the 25th Year of her age. | This tablet was erected by her afflicted husband.

In Memory also of | CHARLOTTE FRANCES, | fourth daughter of Major General J. A. VESEY, | who died 3rd July 1824, aged 18 Years. | And of MARGARET, youngest daughter | of JOHN KIRKLAND, Esq*, of Glasgow. | She died in London 26th February 1823, aged 15 Years.

In Memory also of EDWARD AGMONDISHAM VESEY, Esq. | of His Majesty's Treasury | (only son of Major General J. A. VESEY) | who died 13th October 1830, aged 23 Years.

Sacred | to the Memory of | JANE, LADY STAUNTON, | relict of | Sir GEORGE LEONARD STAUNTON, Bart | of Cargin | in the County of Galway, Ireland, | and eldest daughter of the late | BENJAMIN COLLINS, Esq* | of Milford, near Salisbury, | by his second wife, MARY, | daughter of JOHN COOPER, Esq* | of that City ; | She died on the 16th June 1823, | in the 71st Year of her age, | and was buried | on the 24th of the same month, | in a Vault of this Church. | "Her crown of happiness is gained | by an integrity of purpose, a purity | of heart, a benevolence and kindness | of disposition, which were displayed | in all her actions."

A window, having beneath a brass plate inscribed :—This window was dedicated to the Glory of God, and in loving Memory of SUTTON SHARPE, Esq**, of 12 Devonshire Place in this Parish, by his wife and sons. Died August 23d, 1889.

Sacred | to the Memory of | ROBERT FULLERTON, Esq., | late Governor of Prince of Wales's | Island, | who passed many Years | of his life in the Service of the | Honble East India Company, with | the utmost honor and integrity, | in public life most affectionate, | he died on the 6th of June 1831, | Aged 58 Years, | and is interred in a Vault | of this Church. | Also | to the Memory of | HARRIET, | wife of ROBERT FULLERTON, Esq. | who died at Prince of Wales's | Island | on the 30th of June 1830, | leaving her family to deplore | the loss of a most inestimable | and attached mother.

Sacred | to the Memory of | DAVID LYON, Esq** | whose remains are deposited | in a vault beneath this Church ; | Born 5th August 1754. | Died 26th June 1827.

In Memory of | ALEXANDER CAMPBELL | of Queensferry, Argyleshire, N.B. | A Major in the 84th Regiment | or Duke of Cumberland's American Rangers | he served during the American War | was wounded at the battle of Bunker's Hill June 11, 1775 | and Brandy Wine | in Sept 1777 | and lost his life | while serving on the Spanish Main | in the 41st Year of his Age. | Also of | MARY CAMPBELL | of Bercaldine in Argyleshire, N.B. | relict of the above | born in 1745, died July 8, 1831 | and was buried in this Parish. | They had two Sons and four Daughters | the youngest and last surviving of whom | LUCY CAMPBELL | was buried in this Parish. | She died 14 July 1831 Aged 64 Years.

This tablet was erected by the only Grandson of | the above named ALEXANDER and MARY CAMPBELL | in testimony of his affectionate respect | as well for their memory | as for the memory of their children.

A window, having beneath a brass plate inscribed:—This window was placed to the Memory of HENRY TAYLOR of 2 York Gate in this Parish by his son and daughter, in loving remembrance of a good Father. Died 5th July 1886, Aged 82.

In a vault beneath | are deposited the mortal remains of | HENRIETTA, | eldest daughter of JAMES FISHER, Esqr, of Great Yarmouth, | and relict of JAMES RIVETT CARNAC, Esqr, of Derby, | late of the Civil Service of the Honble East India Company, | and Member of Council at Bombay from 1796 | to the period of his death in 1802. | She died on the 23rd Day of December 1837, | Aged 72 Years, | having passed through a long life, | beloved and esteemed by those to whom | her many estimable qualities were best known. | This tablet is erected by her surviving children, | in affectionate remembrance of her piety, | and many virtues ; | and in thankfulness to Almighty God for | the blessings of an exemplary mother.

To the Memory of | GEORGE WEGUELIN, Esquire, | (brother of | Colonel THOMAS MATTHIAS WEGUELIN) | who died on the 1st Day of April 1858, | aged 91 Years. | His Remains | are deposited in a vault No. 6808, | in the Highgate Cemetery.

Sacred to the Memory of | Colonel THOMAS MATTHIAS WEGUELIN, | of the Honble East India Company's Service | Bengal Establishment. | He departed this Life on the 23rd of May 1828, | aged 64 Years, | and his mortal Remains are deposited in a private vault | beneath this Church. | Wherein also rest those of GEORGE ST. CLAIR, | third Son of the above ; | who died on the 4th of March 1829, | in the 8th Year of his age.

Sacred to the Memory of | ANNA MARIA, | wife of HENRY SHANK, Esqre | of Castlerig, County of Fife ; | who died at Hastings, | on the 5th of August, 1835. | Also | their Daughter | DIANA HENRIETTA, | who departed this Life in Gloucester Place, | Portman Square, | on the 1st of March 1836, | in the 23 Year of her Age. | Their remains are deposited in the | vaults under this Church. | Also of the above named | HENRY SHANK, | who died at his residence | 62 Gloucester Place, | on the 4th of January 1860, Aged 82.

Sacred to the Memory of | HENRY MORETON-DYER, Esqre | who died on the 16th of May 1841, in the 66th Year of his age, and whose | mortal remains are deposited in the family vault under this Church. | Exemplary in all the relations of life, eminently distinguished for | his high public character, his true Christian piety, remarkable urbanity of manners, | benevolent disposition and great mental acquirements, | he must ever live in the hearts of his afflicted relatives and friends, | and in the memory of all who knew him.

ABOVE NORTH GALLERIES.

Sacred to the Memory of | FANNY ELIZABETH CARRUTHERS, | second daughter of the late | DAVID and MARY CARRUTHERS,* | of 5, Cornwall Terrace, Regent's Park, | in this Parish, | who departed this Life 9th October 1845, | Aged 26 Years. | Her remains are deposited in the vaults | beneath this church.

Sacred | to the Memory of | STEPHEN CLEASBY, Esquire, | of Cornwall Terrace in this Parish, | who died 31st August 1844, Aged 69 Years. | Also of MARY, his wife, who died 8th December 1844, | Aged 73 Years. | Their remains are placed in one of the vaults in | the Churchyard of old Mary-le-bone Church. | This tablet is erected by their | three surviving children as a token of | affectionate remembrance.

* A monument to David and Mary Carruthers is above West Gallery, see p. 22.

To the Loved Memory of | ARTHUR JAMES CALDWELL, | whose earthly remains | repose below. | This tablet is erected by his Widow. | He was late Captain in Her Majesty's | 2nd Dragoon Guards, and the only son | of Majr Genl Sir JAMES L. CALDWELL, K.C.B. | He died on the 11th of June 1843, | Aged 44.

In this Church | are deposited the remains of | The Right Honourable Sir ROBERT DALLAS, | late Lord Chief Justice of the Court of Common Pleas ; | who departed this Life December 25th, 1824, Aged 70. | And of JUSTINA, his wife, | who died December 1st, 1847, Aged 72. | Their daughters have erected this tablet, | with the deepest love and veneration | for their Memory.

In Memory of | BUXTON KENRICK, Esq. | formerly of Alwalton, Hunts ; | who died on the 23rd of November 1832, | Aged 63 Years, | Deeply lamented by affectionate relatives.

In Memory of | CHARLES CELARIUS FITZGERALD, Esqre | an amiable and affectionate youth, | who departed this Life | January 14th, 1822, | Aged 18 Years.

ABOVE WEST GALLERY.

Sacred to the Memory of | Vice Admiral Sir JOHN TREMAYNE RODD, K.C.B. | who died on the 4th October 1838. | His high character, and universal benevolence, | endeared him to all who knew him : | he was distinguished in his profession | and exemplary in all his duties. | This tablet is erected by his much afflicted widow | in affectionate remembrance | of the best of husbands.

Sacred | to the Memory of | JOHN MORRIS, Esqr | of Baker Street, Portman Square, | formerly of the Bombay | Civil Service, | and for many years | a Director of the East India | Company. | Born 16th August 1763, | Died at Leamington, Warwickshire | on the 27th July 1840.

Sacred to the Memory of | JAMES SUTHERLAND, Esqr | formerly of Bombay, | who departed this Life | the 3rd of December 1828, | in the 80th Year of his age, | whose remains are deposited | in a vault beneath this Church.

Sacred to the Memory of | ALEXANDER GEORGE MACKAY, Esqr | of the Parish | and of Bagthorpe Hall, in the County of Norfolk | who expired after a very short illness | the 25th of July Anno Domini 1827 | in the 63rd year of his age. | Beloved, respected and deeply lamented | by his family, friends and all who knew him, | this tablet is erected to his memory | by his affectionate relatives as a tribute to his worth | and a memorial of their individual regard | and esteem.

Sacred | to the Memory of | SARAH, wife of JOHN MORRIS, Esqre | who departed this life | October 1st, 1831 | in the 59th year of her age.

A window, having beneath a brass plate inscribed :—To the Glory of God, and in Memory of FRANCIS BLACKBURN GRIFFIN and EMILY STEPHENSON GRIFFIN, this window is dedicated by their Sister.

In a vault of this Church | are deposited the remains of | EDWARD PELHAM BRENTON, Esqre, C.B. | a Captain in the Royal Navy. | He obtained his rank and honours in the service | by his distinguished conduct in action | with the enemy, off the Island of Martinique, | on the 13th of December 1808. | In peace he became the historian | of the Naval Services of Great Britain ; | and his energies were also devoted | to the relief of his suffering fellow creatures. | The establishment of the Children's Friend Society | will be a lasting monument of his ardent | and indefatigable Christian charity. | His deeply afflicted Widow erects this tablet | in memory of his uniform kindness | and affection, during a period of thirty-six years. | He lived respected, | and died on the 6th of April 1837, | beloved and lamented by his numerous friends.

The Remains also of his beloved wife | MARGARETTA DIANA BRENTON repose by his side | in the blessed hope of being reunited in the | kingdom of heaven. | She died on the 6th of November 1843, Aged 74.

Sacred to the Memory of | MARY SWINNEY, | (Spinster) | Who died on the 11th of July 1826, | Aged 54 Years | and buried in the vault | of this Church.

Also | to the memory of | FRANCIS SWINNEY, | of Hyde Street, Bloomsbury, | who died on the 18th of August 1837, | Aged 68 Years | and buried in the vault | of this Church.

In memory of | JAMES BISHOP, Esqr | who departed this Life 18th of June 1836, | Aged 54 Years.

Also | EMILY BISHOP | wife of the above | who departed this Life 15th of May 1837, | in the 45 Year of her age. | This tablet is erected to the memory of the best of parents, | by their only and affectionate daughter.

A window, having beneath a brass plate inscribed:—In memory of EMMA WILD BURGOYNE, a loving wife and mother, taken to her rest Christmas Eve 1881, the gift of JOHN CHARLES BURGOYNE.

Sacred to the Memory of | HENRY BARRE BERESFORD, | of Learmount, County Londonderry, | Son of the Right Honble JOHN BERESFORD, | who departed this Life the 15 Decr 1837 | in the 54th Year of his age.

Also | ANNE JANE | Daughter of the above, who died in Baker Street | Decr 18th, 1824, Aged 11 Years.

Sacred | to the Memory of | General ROBERT MORSE, | who after having served his country gallantly | in the field in France, Germany, Holland, | the West Indies and America, | discharged with equal honour during the | latter years of his life | the important duties of Inspector general of | fortifications. | He died 28th January 1818, Ætat. 75.

Also | to that of his beloved Wife | SOPHIA, daughter of PETER GODIN, Esqr | of Southgate; | who died 11th January 1818, | Ætat. 68.

Sacred | to the Memory | of the | Revd GEORGE AUGUSTUS THURSBY | who died at his house | in Wimpole Street | January 17th, 1836, | Aged 64 Years.

A window, having beneath a brass plate inscribed:—To the glory of God and in memory of GEORGE HOLGATE FOSTER, Died Dec. 1st, 1858, and of MARIA ISABELLA FOSTER, Died May 25th, 1871.

Within these walls lie the Remains of | DAVID CARRUTHERS, Esqre | of this Parish, | a representative in Parliament | for the Town of Kingston upon Hull, | who died on the 9th of June 1835, | Aged 55 Years. | This marble, | sacred to his name, | may recall him to his friends, | but a far deeper memorial is engraven | in the hearts of his family.

Sacred also to the memory of | MARY CARRUTHERS, | relict of | the above named DAVID CARRUTHERS, | who died on the 20th of January 1845, | Aged 65 Years. | Her remains are deposited in a vault | beneath this Church.

MARIA MACKENZIE, vidva, fæmina irreprehensa, | matrum tenerissima, | provecter ætate obiit | Feb. XVIII, Anno Domini MDCCCXXI.

Sacred | to the Memory of | THOMAS ALEXANDER OAKES, Esqʳ | of the Madras Civil Service | who departed this Life | in Hinde Street | on the 12ᵗʰ of Septʳ 1840, | in the 54ᵗʰ Year of his Age, | and lies interred | in the vault beneath | old St. Marylebone Church.

A window, having beneath a brass plate inscribed:—Presented by FRANCIS HICKS, Crown Sidesman of this Parish, and GRACE CAROLINE His Wife A.D. 1885.

Within the vault near this place rest the remains of | MARGARETTA, | the only child of the Revᵈ THOMAS EWBANK of Stockton upon Tees, | Rector of Elton in the County of Durham | and of FRANCES his Wife | who died greatly beloved and deeply deplored | at a seminary in this Parish May 20ᵗʰ, 1833, aged 16 Years | in the expectation of the reunion of pious friends | through the merits of the Redeemer.

Sacred | to the Memory of | ELIZA, | relict of the late Captⁿ JAMES BRADSHAW, R.N. | who departed this life | May 26ᵗʰ, 1839. | Also of | WILLIAM RIGBY BRADSHAW, Esquire, | who died November 25ᵗʰ, 1842, | Aged 58 Years. | Their remains are deposited | in the vault beneath.

The Registers of Inkberrow, co. Worcester.* †

PAROCHIA DE INKBORROUGH.

No'i'a eoru' qui Sepulti fuere hoc Anno Dni. 1628.

Mar. 30	Johanna Webb.
April 10	Edwardi Smyth.
April 17	Johes. Boutes.‡
April 17	Jana uxor Edwardi Browne.
May 2	Willia. Harvey.
May 8	Johes. Harrets.
May 14	Jana uxor ffrancisci Tanner.
June 20	Anna uxor Thomæ Jannings.‡
July 10	Johannes Hieron.
Aug. 25	Alicia uxor Henrici Poole.
Aug. 30	Margareta Smith, vidua.
Sep. 6	Thomas Darbee.‡
Sep. 27	Brigitta Robberts.
Jan. 4	Johanna Ellets, vidua.
Feb. 6	Robert fil. Will. Harbage.
Mar. 24	Edwardus fil. Anthonii Wilmor de Kington.

Concordat cum Registro apud Inkborrow testimus:

HUGH GLOUER, Vic.   JOHN PHILLIPPS, } Churchwardens.
                        FFRANCIS BROOKE, }

* From the Transcripts in "Edgar Tower," Bishop's Register.
† Communicated by WILLIAM BRADBROOK, M.R.C.S.—continued from Vol. IV., p. 295.
‡ The entries throughout marked with a double-dagger [thus, ‡] are very indistinct.

INKEBORROW.   ANNO DNI. 1630.

The names of all such as were Baptized in this year, with the day of the month.

—   27   Anna the daughter of Hen. Griffin.
April   8   .... John Tandy.
April   11   .... Knight son of Tho. Knight.
April   25   .... and Willia. sonns of Edw. Eaton.
May   2   .... son of Edw. Rudy.‡
May   2   .... son of John Stile.
May   18   .... son of Arthur Ellins.
May   21   .... son of John Sawndes.
May   30   .... daughter of John Yate.
May   30   .... son of Will. Wyndle.
June   6   .... daughter of Rich. ffrancis.
June   13   .... of Rich. Page.‡
June   20   .... son of Will. King.
June   27   .... son of James Higgons.
Aug.   22   .... daugh. of Edward Howes.
Aug.   22   .... son of John Churchley.
Sep.   6   .... son of Will. Reddill.
Sep.   12   .... son of Tho. Eden, Junior.
Sep.   12   .... dawghter of Hen. Goar.
Oct.   24   .... dawghter of Will. Rand.
Oct.   24   .... dawghter of .... Netherton.
Nov.   7   .... sonne of Tho. Hunt.
Nov.   7   .... Harison sonn of John Harison.
Nov.   28   .... dawghter of Jo. Staples.
Dec.   4   .... dwgh. of Tho. Whyte.
Dec.   16   .... dawght. of Tho. Browne.
Dec.   16   .... sonne of John Harbag.
Jan.   13   .... er dawght. of Tho. al's Phillips.
Jan.   19   .... cis dawgh. of ffrancis ffreeman.
Feb.   2   Mary dawght. of Robert Bidell.
Feb.   10   Edward sonne of Rich. Harret.
Feb.   10   Anne dawght. of Edmond Barcroft.
Feb.   16   Susanna dawght. of Tho. Rudy.
Feb.   25   Tho. sonne of Tho. Wilson.
Mar.   8   Robert the sonne of Rich. Marchall.
Mar.   9   Anne dawght. of ffrancis Darbe.
Mar.   16   Ann dawght. of John Higgs.

[*Married.*]

Jan.   20   Thomas Noxon & Ellenor Clark.

Hæc copia concordat cum Registro reservat apud Inckborrow Transcript. et missa per :

HUGH GLOUER, Vic. ib'em.   THOMAS DISON, junior, } C'wardns.
                                WILLIAM BOWLTON,   }

The names of all such as were Buried in this year, 1630.

May   14   Isabel Hunt, wid.
May   17   Ellenor Huntley, wid.
May   17   Joan wife of Charles Wynnett [?].
May   24   Ellenor ffreeman, wid.
July   20   Georg Layt.
Aug.   14   Rich. Harbage, a young man.

Sep. 15   Ellenor Bromfield, wid.
Sep. 19   Thomas Rowson.
Sep. 30   Tho. Payn of Dormston.
Oct. 10   ffrancis Darbee.
Oct. 12   Ann wife of Hewe Griffin.
Oct. 18   Anne wyfe of Will. Smyth.
Oct. 27   Margaret Poole, wid., of Dormston.
Oct. 30   Charles Wincott.
Nov. 3   Widdow Heynes of Dormst.
Nov. 5   Willia. Poole of Dormston.
Nov. 6   Anne Paynton of Kington.‡
Nov. 22   Tho. Payne of Dormston.
Nov. 24   Will. Bullock.
Nov. 27   Margaret Stevens, wid.
Nov. 28   Willia. Groves.
Dec. 6   John Poole of Dormst.
Dec. 6   Henry Dison, gent.
Dec. 11   John Godwyn.
Dec. 28   Will. Baylis of Kington.
Dec. 28   Joyce Awsoll of Dormston.‡
Feb. 2   Rich. Fisher of Kington.
Feb. 8   ffrancis wyfe of Rich. ffarr of Kington.
Feb. 12   Anne Brock.
Feb. 16   Rich. Hobson.
Feb. 28   Henry Bristo of Cladsoll.

Hæc est vera copia concordat cum Registro reservat apud Inckbor. transcript et missa per:

HUGH GLOUER, Vic. ibid.   THOMAS DISON, jun., ⎫ C'wardns.
                                 WILLIA. BOWLTON,   ⎭

INKBORROW. ANNO DNI. 1631.

Copia Registri reservat apud Inkborrow et transmissa per THOMA' RAVEN et RICH. STEWARD, Gardianos ibid. hoc anno.

Nomina eoru' qui Baptizati hoc anno.

Mar. 25   Joan Oswald populi filia.
April 7   Anne Yong fil. Anthon Yong.
April 17 Jana fil. Willm. Weaver.
April —   Elizabeth fil. Tho. Hieron.
May 1   Willia. fil. Willia. Parsons.
May 1   Isabel fil. Joh'es Nale [?].
May 16   . . . . filius populi.
May 25   Ursula fil. Henrici . . . .
May 26   Jana filia Hugo' Horwood.
June 2   . . . . filia Rich. Payne.‡
June 6   Johes. filius Hen. Layt.
June 12   Ann filia Tho. Perks.
June 17   Ann filia Tho. Heming.
June 20   Mary Blick.
July 24   Ann filia Henr. Griffin.

July	24	Alicia filia Willms. Willis.
July	25	Mary filia Thoma. Knight.
Oct.	26	. . . . Johis. Phillipps.
Nov.	24	Tho. fil. Johis. Dison.‡
Nov.	—	Joan filia Henr. Harvey.
Feb.	5	John filius Mathias Whoman.
Feb.	25	Joan filia Hen. Ellets.
Mar.	—	Thomas fil. Thoma. Rudge.
Mar.	4	Elizabetha filia Arthuri Hemes.
Mar.	11	Richard fil. Joh'es Harbag.
Mar.	14	ffranciscus fil. Robti. Bristo.

Ita est : HUGH GLOUER, Vic.   THOMAS RAVEN, } C'wards.
                                  RICH. STEVENS, }

Nomina eoru' qui in Matrimonio copulati fuere hoc anno 1631.

May	1	Willimus. Smyth et Margaret Yate, vidua.
May	2	Robert Brook & Mary Darbee.
May	4	William Heming & . . . . Goar.
June	2	Richard Marchall & Amphilis Askew.
Aug.	—	Thomas Dison of Holborrow & Jane Russell, widow, of . . . .
Oct.	—	John Boond & Elizabeth Roberts.‡
Oct.	2	Thomas Peer [?] & Alice Hughes.‡
Oct.	7	John Merrell of Flivord [?] & Joan Heming of this parish.
Dec.	—	Arthur Bagshaw & Anne Barcroft.
Dec.	15	Robert Dison & Sarah Brook.‡

Ita est : HUGH GLOUER, Vic.   THOMAS PHILLIPS, } C'wards.
                                  RICHARD STEWARD, }

Nomina eoru' qui Sepulti fuere hoc anno 1631.

Mar.	28	Henry Askew.
April	8	Jane uxor Jobes. Harvy.
May	3	Margaret uxor Thomæ Dison.
May	5	Margery Trevis.
May	29	John Showler.
June	2	Alice Harvy, vidua.
July	8	. . . . uxor Jacobi Heming.
Sep.	9	Felix uxor Cookrell.
Sep.	13	Margery Bowtes, vidua.
Sep.	15	Joan Moore, vidua.
Sep.	—	Joan Makins of Kington.
Sep.	29	Anne Hobson uxor . . . . Hobson.
Oct.	7	Katherine uxor Johis. Smyth.
Oct.	22	Lawrence Harvey.
Dec.	23	Johannes Savage, Armiger, was buryed from Egiok house. Beati mortui in domino.
Jan.	7	Ann Davis of Dormston.
Jan.	9	Mary uxor Willia. Gower, gent.
Jan.	12	Richard Higgins.
Feb.	10	ffrancis Brook.

Ita est : HUGH GLOUER, Vic.   THOMAS RAVEN, } C'wards.
                                  RICHARD STEVENS, }

A Copy of the Register of the Parish of Inkborrow, 1632.

[*Baptisms.*]

June 7 .... son of Will. Heming .... borrow.
June 11 .... sonne of Thomas Dison.
June 17 John, a base son of Anne Bowtes.
June 23 Ellenor the daughter of John Hunt of Treylane.
July 3 Ralph the son of Henry Lawgher of Cookhill.
July 8 Elizabeth dawghter of John Higgs of Egiok.
Aug. 3 Henry & Alice the children of Thomas Smyth of ....
Aug. 20 John the son of John Robinson of Egiok.
Sep. 2 .... dawghter of Edward ....
Sep. 9 .... dawghter of Robert Dison [of Holb]orrow.
Sep. 16 .... sonne of Richard ffarre of [Morton] under Hill.
Sep. 23 Ri .... the sonne of Robt. Haynes of Old ....
Sep. 23 Thomas & Willia. the sonnes of John Hale of Bowtes.
Sep. 23 Joan the daughter of ffrancis ffreeman of Inckborrow Magna.
Sep. 27 .... the base child of Margaret ffigget by one Tho. Dison.‡
Sep. 30 Margaret, a base child of Anne Netherton by John Hunt of Egiok.
Oct. 11 Elizabeth ....
Oct. 11 Arthur the sonne of Arthur Bagshawe of Rush.
Nov. 15 Hugh Bowtes.
Nov. — Anne dawghter of Thomas Dison of ....
Nov. 21 Jane daughter of John Phillipps of Great Inkborrow.
Nov. 25 Willia., a base child of Anne Hobbins begat by ....
Nov. 28 Mary dawghter of Robert Banes [?].
Dec. 28 Richard sonne of Richard Marchall of Great Inkborrow.
Jan. 5 Ellenor dawghter of John Boond.
Jan. 6 Henry sonne of Henry Griffin.
Jan. 13 John sonne of Richard ffrancis.
Jan. 13 Elizabeth dawghter of John Oakes.
Jan. 20 Thomas sonne of Thomas Dowler.
Jan. 27 Elizabeth dawghter of Richard Harvey.
Jan. 31 Elizab. dawghter of ffrancis Darbee of Bowtes.
Feb. — John sonne of Richard Harrets of Cookhill.
Feb. 17 Margery dawghter of Hugh Horwood of Egiok.
Feb. 17 Ellener dawghter of Edward Rudge.
Feb. 24 Anne dawghter of John Hasteler.‡
Mar. 3 Thomas sonne of Richard Hunt of Bowtes.
Mar. 3 Anne dawghter of Thomas Morgan.
Mar. 17 Thomas sonne of Richard Windle of Nowberry.

Ad numerii 40.*

The names of such as were maryed this year 1632.

Mar. 26 William Rogers & Margaret Wigget of Towston (?).
May 27 John Hasterley & ffrancis Croftes.
May 28 John Cockrell & Elizabeth Sheppey.
June 14 Thomas Willets of Chadsley & Katherine Whoman.
June 19 Edward Smyth & Ursula Tayler.
June 28 Robert Pope & .... Heminge of North Pidle.

(*To be continued.*)

* Transcript much torn.

Marriages of Wandsworth Inhabitants.*

EXTRACTS FROM REGISTERS IN VARIOUS PARISHES.

1619, May 31.   JOHN CARTER de Wandsworth & JOANE SLAWTER. (Battersea.)
16$\frac{19}{20}$ Mar. 12   John, son of John Carter, bapt.
1624   April 11   Robert, son of John Carter, bapt.
1625   Oct. 23   Robert, son of John Carter, plague, bur.

1622, Aug.   Mʳ HENRY CAMPION & Mʳˢ ANN WILLET. (Putney.)

1656. May 19.   According to An act Jntituled an Act touching marriages and the Regestering thereof, etc., THOMAS WEBSTAR of Saint Martains in Middellsex & MARGERY SETTEN of Wandsworth in Surry were Married Each to Other in the 19ᵗʰ of May 1656 ; by mee, Jo. Rushworth. (Battersea.)

1656, July 28.   According to An act intituled an act touching Marriages And The Regestering there of, etc., THOMAS LUDLY of the parrish of Wandesworth & ELIZABETH WINNE of the parrish of Battersay, Both in the County of Svrrey, weare Married Each to other on the 28 day of July 1656 ; by mee, Sam. Highand. (Battersea.)

1660, Oct. 8.   MICHAEL TOWNSEND & ELLIN MASON, both of Wandsworth. (Putney.)
1675 Nov. 26   Michaell Townsend, husbandman, bur.

1662-3, March 9.   GERIE PIERRE, fils d'Andrieu, natif de Londres, et ANNE HAULFOTE, natiue de Wansor in Surry. Annonce.

1668, May 21.   WILLIAM CHINER & ELIZABETH COOKE. (Battersea.) [See *ante*, Vol. III., p. 232.]

1686, Sep. 24.   LOUIS GROLLEAU of Sᵗ Margaret's, Lothbury, London, Citizen and Cook, Bachelor, about 24, & Mʳˢ MARY DUFAY of Sᵗ Stephen's, Colman Street, London, Spinster, about 24, at own disposal ; at the French Chapel of the Savoy, Middlesex. (Marriage Allegations, Vicar-General.)
[They are both buried in Mount Nod, Wandsworth, and over them is this inscription : "Here Lyeth the Body of | Mʳ Lewis Grolleau, | who died Decr. 16ᵗʰ, 1715 | Aged 53 Years. | Also the body of | Mʳˢ Mary Grolleau (his wife) | who died Feb. 5ᵗʰ, 1729, | Aged 69 years."
Two daughters were also buried in Mount Nod : Susan, wife of Paul Fourdrinier, died 15 Nov. 1746, and Judith Grolleau, died 3 Nov. 1750, aged 61.]

1686-7, Feb. 21.   THO. MOUSLEY, b., & ELIZ. POTTER, w., of Wansworth, Surry. (St. James, Duke's Place, London.)

1692, Dec. 1.   NICH' MEADE of this parish & SUSAN HAUKINS of Wandsworth, maried by lycence. (Putney.)

1695, Nov. 28.   RICHARD [? S]ISEAGER of Egham & MARY CRISP of Wansworth. (Battersea.)

---

* Communicated by CECIL T. DAVIS, Esq.—continued from Vol. IV., p. 283.

1697, Aug. 31. JOHN MALLARD, b., & AVIS PARSONS, w., of Wandsworth in Surrey. (St. James, Duke's Place, London.)
1698 June 12 Thomas, son of John Mallard, bapt.

1697-8, Jan. 20. JOHN MEERS, b., & HANNAH HEDLY, s., of Wansworth in Surrey. (St. James, Duke's Place, London.)
1675 Sep. 12 Hannah, daughter of Andrew Headley, fisherman, bapt.

1697-8, Feb. 22. RICHARD HILL, b., & SARAH COOK, s., of Wansor and Kinson in Surrey. (St. James, Duke's Place, London.)

1698, Aug. 14. JACOB MONEAU, hatter, w., & MADELAINE NORTIER, w., in Wandsor in Surrey. (St. James, Duke's Place, London.)

1698-9, Jan. 1. FRANCIS HOAR, w., a wheelwright, in Wandsor in Surrey, & JOAN SHEPPARD, s., ditto. (St. James, Duke's Place, London.)
1699 Nov. 26 Mary, daughter of Franc. Hoare, bapt. [She was married to
            Robert Prisnal at Clapham on 10 June 1721.]
1701 May 18 William, son of Francis Hore, bapt.

1699, April 14. DAVID LE PRUVE, b., 27, at the "Red Lyon" in Wandsor in the county of Surey, & SARAH LOVEDAY, w., 40, ditto. (St. James, Duke's Place, London.)

1699, June 8. NICHOLAS BLUNDEL, w., 44, of the parish of Wandsworth, near the "Ship," in the county of Surrey, a waterman, & ELICE KEY, s., 24, of Sᵗ Bride's. (St. James, Duke's Place, London.)
1624 Nov. 24 Nicholas, son of John Blundall, bapt.
1729 Dec. 25 Nicholas Blundell, 75, bur.

1699, Aug. 1. THOMAS CHILD, b., 22, near the "Black Spread Eagle" in Wandsworth in Surrey, a blacksmith, & ANNE GOSWELL, s., 23, ditto. (St. James, Duke's Place, London.)
1676 July 16 Anne, daughter of Richard Goswell, carpenter, bapt.
1700 April 10 Lawrence, son of Thomas Chiles, bapt.
1702 Mar. 30 Thomas, son of Thomas Chiles, bapt.

1700, April 3. ICHABUD CUMB, —, & KATHERINE PHILPOT, —, both of Wansworth in Surrey. (St. James, Duke's Place, London.)

1700, April 30. XTMAS BANTALL, b., & SUSANNA HARVEY, —, both of Wandsworth. (St. James, Duke's Place, London.)

1700, May 22. WILLIAM NORTH, b., of Kingstone, & ELIZ. WINNINGTON, w., of Wandsworth in Surrey. (St. James, Duke's Place, London.)

1700, June 8. WM. GEORGE of Wandsworth, Surrey, b., & ELIZ. MUNDAY, s., of the same. (St. James, Duke's Place, London.)
167⅔ Jan. 19 William, son of Ralph George, bapt.
1700 Oct. 13 Jane, daughter of Willm. George, bapt. [She was married to
            George Blackburn at Clapham 10 Oct. 1719, see *ante*, Vol. IV.,
            p. 235.]
1704 Aug. 21 { Ralph,
             { William, } twins of William George, bapt.
1705 Aug. 25 { Rebecka,
             { Mary, } twins of William George, bapt.
170⅘ Jan. 19 Ralph, son of William George, bapt.

1710 Oct. 22 William, son of Wm. George, bapt.
1714 July 4 Alice, daughter of William George, bapt.
17$\frac{14}{15}$ Jan. 3 Nathaniel, son of William George, bapt.
1717 Dec. 1 John, son of William George, bapt.
1720 Sep. 11 John, son of William George, bapt.
1725 Aug. 1 Edward, son of William George, bapt.
1727 April 30 Elizabeth, daughter of William and Elizabeth George, bapt.
172$\frac{8}{9}$ Feb. 27 Rebecca, daughter of William and Elizabeth George, bapt.
1728 April 5 Elizabeth, inf. daughter of William George, bur.
1745 May 5 Elisabeth, wife of William George, bur.
1762 Feb. 24 William George, 82, bur.

1701-2, Feb. 16. SOMERSET DRAPER of Wandsworth, Surrey, b., & ANN THOMPSON of this parish, s.; licence. (Chiswick.)

1681 Aug. 29 Summersett, son of Mr Edmond Draper, bapt.
170$\frac{2}{3}$ Jan. 30 Anne, daughter of Mr Somerset Draper, bapt.
1704 Sep. 22 Geffery, son of Mr Somerset Draper, bapt.
1706 April 1 Somerset, son of Mr Draper, bapt.
1707 July 8 Jeffery, son of Mr Somerset Draper, bapt.
17$\frac{11}{12}$ Feb. 21 Nightingale, son of Mr Somerset Draper, bapt.
1713 Aug. 31 Mary, daughter of Mr Somerset Draper, bapt.
173$\frac{4}{5}$ Feb. 14 Mary, daughter of Mr Somerset Draper, 21, bur.
1736 May 20 Mr Somerset Draper, 54, bur.
1756 Feb. 7 Somerset Draper, bur. [Aged 49. M.I. in Church. 15s. 4d. burial fee; 10s. bell.]
1764 Nov. 21 Nightingale Draper, 52, bur.

1703, Oct. 16. WRIGHT, JOHN, & ROSHIER, MARTHA. (Faculty Office.)
1703, Oct. 19. JOHN WRIGHT & MARTHA ROSIER, both servants, of the parish of St Martin-in-the-Fields; licence; at Wandsworth.

1706, June 4. KEY, JOHN, & WANHAM, JANE. (Faculty Office.)
1706, June 11. JOHN KEY & JANE WANHAM; licence; at Wandsworth.

1711, May 6. THOMAS EDSELL & JANE SNELLING, both of y^e p^sh of Wandsworth; by banns. (Putney.)

173$\frac{3}{4}$ Jan. 20 Thomas Edsall, 76, bur.
1739 July 17 Jane Edsall, widow, aged, bur.

1717, May 7. JOHN HARRISON of y^e parish of Wandsworth & ANN HADLEY of this Parish; by banns. (Putney.)

1719, April 13. JOHN BARBER & ELIZABETH PICK, both of Wandsworth; licence. (St. Paul, Covent Garden.)

1720-21, Jan. 5. RICHARD NEWMAN of Wansworth & ELIZABETH MORRALL of Husborn Prior. (St. Mary Bourne, Hants.)

172$\frac{1}{2}$ Jan. 14 Elizabeth, daughter of Richard Newman, bapt.
1725 Sep. 16 Edward, son of Richard Newman, bapt.
1728 Aug. 16 Edward, son of Richard Newman, bur.
1745 June 30 Richard Newman, 57, bur.

1721, May 4. RALPH CAVE of Wandsworth & ANNE OSGOOD of Chelsea, co. Middx.; licence. (St. Paul, Covent Garden.)

1721, Sep. 21. JOHN CARTER of Wandsworth, Surrey, & REBECCA PARKER of this parish. (Chiswick.)

1722-3, Jan. 14. RICHARD DAVIS of the parish of St Saviour's, Southwarke, Labourer, & ELIZABETH HUNTINGFORD of the parish of Wandsworth, Spinster; by banns in our said parish this 14th day of January 1722, but the said banns was published & declared in the parish of Wandsworth, but by request was married here. (Putney.)

1723, April 23. ANDREW STANTON of Wandsworth, Surrey, & ELIZABETH TEER of this parish. (Chiswick.)

172$\frac{6}{}$	Jan. 17	Elizabeth, daughter of Andrew Stanton, bapt.
172$\frac{1}{3}$	Jan. 2	Samuel, son of Andrew and Elisabeth Stanton, bapt.

1729, Aug. 17. THOMAS MARSDEN of the parish of St Martin in the fields & JANE SIMONDS of Wandsworth in the County of Surry; by licence; by me, Geo. Osborne, Vicar. (Battersea.)

1709 Oct. 25 Jane, daughter of William Symonds, bapt.

1730, March 31. NICOLAS ADAMS & FRANCES EDWARDS, both of Wandsworth in Surry; by licence. (Clapham.)

1702	Sep. 13	Nicholas, son of Nicholas Adams, bapt.
173$\frac{3}{4}$	Feb. 28	William, son of Nicolas and Frances Adams, bapt.
173$\frac{1}{2}$	Feb. 27	Anne, daughter of Nicolas and Frances Adams, bapt.
173$\frac{3}{4}$	Jan. 2	Mary, daughter of Nicolas and Frances Adams, bapt.
1735	Aug. 23	William, son of Nicolas and Frances Adams, bapt.
1736	Nov. 20	Margaret, daughter of Nicolas and Frances Adams, bapt.
1741	Oct. 9	Loving, son of Nicolas and Frances Adams, bapt.
1743	Aug. 20	Elisabeth, daughter of Nicolas and Frances Adams, bapt.
174$\frac{4}{}$	Feb. 19	Jane, daughter of Nicolas and Frances Adams, bapt.
174$\frac{6}{}$	Jan. 6	Noah, son of Nicolas and Frances Adams, bapt.
1731	Nov. 2	William, inf. son of Nicolas Adams, bur.
173$\frac{1}{2}$	Mar. 11	Anne, inf. daughter of Nicholas Adams, bur.
1741	Oct. 29	Loving, inf. son of Nicolas Adams, bur.
1785	Dec. 1	Noah Adams, 40, bur.

1730, May 25. RICHARD BEAL & ELIZABETH WEBB, both of Wandsworth in y^e County of Surry; by y^e Revd Mr Edgely, Vic^r of Wandsworth; by licence. (Clapham.)

1731	April 13	Elisabeth, daughter of Richard and Elisabeth Beal, bapt.
1732	Oct. 16	Sarah, daughter of Richard and Elisabeth Beal, bapt.
1734	Dec. 27	William, son of Richard and Elisabeth Beal, bapt.
1735	Dec. 18	Richard, son of Richard and Elisabeth Beal, bapt.
173$\frac{7}{}$	Feb. 17	Mary, daughter of Richard and Elisabeth Beal, bapt.
1739	April 5	Hannah, daughter of Richard and Elisabeth Beal, bapt.
174$\frac{1}{3}$	Mar. 7	Fanny, daughter of Richard and Elisabeth Beal, bapt.
174$\frac{3}{4}$	Mar. 19	Susanna, daughter of Richard and Elisabeth Beal, bapt.
1745	Mar. 26	Hester, daughter of Richard and Elisabeth Beal, bapt.
174$\frac{6}{}$	Jan. 29	John, son of Richard and Elisabeth Beale, bapt.
173$\frac{7}{}$	Feb. 2	William, inf. son of Richard Beal, bur.
1743	Oct. 2	Fanny, inf. daughter of Richard Beal, bur.
174$\frac{8}{}$	Mar. 5	William, inf. son of Richard and Elizabeth Bele, bur.
1749	July 31	Richard Beal, bur.
1772	April 12	Richard Beal, 36, bur.

1730, June 14. MICHAEL CHRISTMAS & REBECCA STABLES, both of Wandsworth in y^e County of Surry; by licence. (Clapham.)

1710	April 23	Michael, son of John Christmas, bapt.
17$\frac{13}{14}$	Jan. 24	Rebekah, daughter of Richard Stables, bapt.

1732 July 12 Richard, son of Michael and Rebecca Christmas, bapt.
1733 July 15 John, son of Michael and Rebecca Christmas, bapt.
1735 Aug. 30 Rebecca, daughter of Michael and Rebecca Christmas, bapt.

1730, July 5. MICHAEL SAVAGE & ANNE STOCKER, both of Wandsworth in ye County of Surry; by ye Revd Mr Edgely, Vic^{r} of Wandsworth; by licence. (Clapham.)

1731, July 23. JOSEPH SPARKE & ELIZABETH NEWMAN, both of Wandsworth in ye County of Surry; by ye Rev. Mr Edgely, Vicar of Wandsworth; by licence. (Clapham.)
1743 July 26 Elisabeth, wife of Joseph Sparks, 57, bur.

1731-2, Jan. 20. WILLIAM HULL & ANNE HUCKLEY, both of Wandsworth in ye County of Surry; by licence. (Clapham.)

1732-3, Jan. 10. THOMAS FIELDER & SARAH NURSE, both of ye Parish of Wandsworth in ye County of Surry; by licence. (Clapham.)
1755 June 15 Sarah, daughter of Thomas and Sarah Fielder, 21, bur. (Bell, 5s.)
1765 Sep. 6 Thomas Fielder, 83, bur.
1766 Feb. 14 Sarah, wid. of Thomas Fielder, 73, bur.

1733, Nov. 24. JOHN DOBSON of the Parish of Wandsworth in the County of Surry, Widower, & ANNE DE LEGE of the same Parish, Spinster; by the Revd Mr Cawly of Wandsworth; by licence. (Clapham.)
16$\frac{89}{90}$ Mar. 19 { Judeth, Anne, } daughters of Paul de l'Age, bapt.
1692 Nov. 29 John, son of Robert Dobson, bapt.
1752 Dec. 19 Anne, wife of John Dobson, 64, bur.

1733-4, Feb. 3. BENJAMIN ELLY of the Parish of Wandsworth in the County of Surry, Batchelor, & MARY NELSON of the same place, Spinster; by the Revd Mr Cawley of Wandsworth; by licence. (Clapham.)
173$\frac{4}{5}$ Mar. 11 Elisabeth, daughter of Benjamin and Mary Elly, bapt.
1736 May 30 Brigid, daughter of Benjamin and Mary Elly, bapt.
1737 Oct. 23 Mary, daughter of Benjamin and Mary Elly, bapt.
1738 Nov. 8 { Joseph, Benjamin, } sons of Benjamin and Mary Elly, bapt.
17$\frac{39}{40}$ Mar. 23 Jame- Slater, son of Benjamin and Mary Elly, bapt.
1741 Nov. 1 Anne, daughter of Benjamin and Mary Elly, bapt.
1738 Nov. 13 Joseph and Benjamin, inf. sons of Benjamin Elly, bur.
1741 Dec. 2 Benjamin Elly, bur.
174$\frac{1}{2}$ Feb. 27 Anne, inf. daughter of Widow Elly, bur.

1737, April 12. EZEKIEL EDMONDS of the Parish of Wandsworth in the County of Surry, Batcheler, & ELIZABETH TAYLOR of the same Parish, Spinster; by the Revd Mr Cawley, Vicar of Wandsworth; by licence. (Clapham.)
1709 Oct. 26 Ezekiel, son of Ezekiel Edmonds, bapt. [Ezekiel Edmonds the elder was married at Clapham 14 Oct. 1701, see *ante*, Vol. IV., p. 145.]
17$\frac{39}{40}$ Mar. 2 Ezekiel, son of Ezekiel Edmonds by Elisabeth his wife, deceased; bapt.
17$\frac{39}{40}$ Mar. 2 Elizabeth, y^{e} wife of Ezekiel Edmonds, bur.
1740 Mar. 30 Ezekiel, inf. son of Ezekiel Edmonds, bur.

[He married again. He died 25 Oct. 1788, aged 80 years, and was buried in Wandsworth Churchyard. *Errata:* The last four entries in Vol. IV., p. 145, belong to this entry.]

1737, April 17. JAMES LLEWELLIN of Wandsworth in the County of Surry, Batchelor, & ELIZABETH STANFORD of the same Parish, Spinster; by licence. (Clapham.)

1737-8, Jan. 28. HUMPHREY WEBB of Wandsworth in the County of Surry, Batchelor, & ELIZABETH EXALL of the said County, Spinster; by the Rev⁴ M˙ Sampson, Curate of Wandsworth; by licence. (Clapham.)

1712	Dec. 28	Humphrey, son of William Webb, bapt.
173⁴⁄	Feb. 18	Christopher, son of Humphrey and Elisabeth Webb, bapt.
17³⁵⁄₄₀	Mar. 18	William, son of Humphry Webb, bapt.
1744	Oct. 17	Mary, daughter of Humphrey and Elisabeth Webb, bapt. [She married William Jupp, and is mentioned in her brother's will.]
1743	Nov. 30	Christopher, a child of Humfrey Webb, bur.
1747	May 5	Elisabeth, wife of Humfrey Webb [aged 31], bur. [M.I. in Wandsworth Churchyard.]
1779	Mar. 7	William Webb, 39, bur. [M.I. in Mount Nod. Will: Warburton, 135.]

1738, April 8. SAMUEL WELLDEN of Wandsworth in the County of Surry, Widower, & HANNAH LEE of the same Parish, Spinster; by the Reverend M˙ Cawley, Vicar of Wandsworth; by licence. (Clapham.)

1738, April 10. The Reverend THOMAS CAWLEY of the Parish of Wandsworth in the County of Surry, Batchelor, & ANNE MOSS of the same Parish, Spinster; by licence. (Clapham.)
[He was Vicar of Wandsworth, and his marriage is also entered in the Wandsworth Registers as follows: 1738, April 10. THOMAS CAWLEY, Vicar of this parish, & ANNE MOSS of yᵉ same parish, were married at Clapham Church by M˙ Goodwin, Rector of Clapham; licence.]

1739	April 10	John, son of Thomas Cawley, Vicar of this parish, by Anne his wife, bapt. by M˙ Goodwin, Rector of Clapham; born on Sunday, March yᵉ 25ᵗʰ, 1739.
1740	Aug. 19	Anne, daughter of M˙ Thomas Cawley (Vicar) and Anne his wife, bapt.
1743	Mar. 26	Elisabeth, daughter of Thomas Cawley (Vicar) and Anne his wife, bapt.
1775	Sep. 14	James Shaw of Hinton Sᵗ George, co. Soms., bachelor, and Ann Cawley of Wandsworth, spinster; licence. [Their first-born was baptized at Wandsworth.]
17³⁴⁄₄₈	Feb. 18	John, infant son of Thomas Cawley, bur.
1748	May 16	The Rev. Thomas Cawley, Vicar of this parish, bur.
1795	Mar. 9	Ann Crawley, 76, bur.

[He, his wife, and son buried at Mount Nod, where are their epitaphs. For his life, see "Wandsworth Notes and Queries," p. 47.]

(To be continued.)

𝕸𝖊𝖒𝖔𝖗𝖆𝖓𝖉𝖆 of 𝖂𝖎𝖑𝖑𝖎𝖆𝖒 𝕮𝖚𝖗𝖙𝖔𝖞𝖘,

1670—1752.*

[NOTE.—These Memoranda are contained in a very small note-book, measuring
4½ by 3 inches, which has been carefully preserved. The writing is usually clear
and good, but occasionally much cramped. The order, it will be seen, is not always
strictly chronological. The entries printed first are entirely of a family nature ;
those beginning at the other end of the book and printed second are more general,
though they begin with the solemn and interesting record of the renewal of the
baptismal vow and reception of the Holy Eucharist by the writer on the twenty-
first anniversary of his baptism. That and the earlier entries are in Latin, the rest
in English. The Rev. W. F. CURTOYS will be glad to communicate with any
reader who can throw light upon persons or families herein alluded to.]

[ONE END.]

(Page 1).—Memo. Ego W^{mus} Curtoys natus eram Augusti 4to die Jovis Anno
D'm'ni 1670 inter sextam et septimam noctis horam in loco dicto Nelsons-court in
vico Drury Lane in S^{tt} Martini in agris paroch'.
Signum Zodiacum erat in Leone.

Mariam Viduam Ro. Watson magistri mei, 21mo die Decembris 1691 pro uxore
accepi et in matrimonio in Sacello Cartophylaceorum conjuncti sumus.

Et multos annos unà nos in hoc mundo vivere permittat Deus secundum verbum
et in honore ejus.

(Page 2).—Pater meus Annam uxorem ejus secundam Aprilis 29mo 1680
ducebat.

4to Januarii an. 1683 obligatus sum meo Auctoramento Rowlando Watson de
S^{tt} Martini in agris L'ndin^{io} in Spatium 8to annorum.

Dom^{nus} Rowl^{dus} Watson 26mo die Augusti mortem obiit 27mo '91 in Cæmeterio
S^{tt} Martini in agris sepultus.

Jan. 15th, 1697-8, Broth^r Byby was arrested (?) ; went off then to sea.†

(Page 3).—Margaretta mater mei Octobris 29mo die anno 1679 mortem obiit
31mo die sepulta in S^{tt} Clementis Danes cæmeterio, in.

Johannes Pater mei Novembris 23mo die 1685, mortem obiit 24mo sepultus in
eodem cæmeterio juxta matrem.

Anna noverca mea uxor Patris Aprilis 18mo die 20mo sepulta juxta patrem 1689.

Johannes Curtoys de Claycoton meus patruelis die Julii undecimo obiit Anno
Dmni. 1697° sepultus apud Wilford.‡

---

* Communicated by the Rev. W. F. CURTOYS, Coleby Vicarage, Lincoln.
† Ink faded, added in very small writing.
‡ John Curtoys (of Christ's College, Cambridge) was Rector of Claycoton (inducted 1692),
born at Wilford, at Nottingham School.—(Rev. A. Curtois.)

(Page 4).—Memorand. me 7ᵐᵒ die 7ᵇʳⁱˢ 1691 incipere Scholam intrare ut instituerem post Dmni. Watson mortem in Viduæ vicem.

Me' 7ᵇʳⁱˢ 8ᵗᵒ '92 die terræ motus erat in Londino et locis finitimis, qui mausit circa 1 minutium.

Mem. Elizabetham Alford filiam Richᵈⁱ et Elizᵗʰ Alford natam esse anno 1652 baptizatam 18° die Janʳⁱ sicut Registerio Sᵗⁱ Martini notum erit . . . . et vulgo dictum est, quod Maria soror ejus, mea uxor, est 5 annos natu minor nata 17° Januarii 1657.*

(Page 5).—Edvardus filius meus natus est Januarii decimo septimo die inter Nonam horam et Decima' Annoq' D'm'ni 1692-3 in Nelson's Court.

Baptizatus fuit 2ᵈᵒ die Februarii.

Edvar. Rolt, ⎫
Alex. Biby, ⎭ Compatres.†

1693. Obiit mortem Edvardus filius Novembris 21° die ('93) sub 3ᵐ hora' mane, sepultus 23° die in Calvaria Sᵗⁱ Martini in agris juxta parietem prope officinam in angulo Caurino ejusdem æt. 10 mens. 4 dies.

1702. Obiit mortem charissima mihi uxor Maria 1° Sepᵇʳⁱˢ sub 3ᵃᵐ horam mane, sepulta 2ᵈᵒ die 1702, in Calvaria Sᵗⁱ Martini in agris juxta parietem prope officinam posita' in angulo Caurino ejusdem 45 Nat.   ad caput filii.

(Page 6).—Mem'. Avunculus meus Whitehal Wᵐᵘˢ mortuus est 22° die Febʳⁱ 1697-8 sepultus in Sti. Martini cæmeterio 25° die.

Mea amita Silverwood mortua est ante Nativitatem X'ti 1698 sepulta apud Gunniston [? Gamston] in Com' Nottingham.

Consobrina mea Frances Whitehall ob. die 10ᵇʳⁱˢ 18° sepult' in Calvaria Sᵗ Martini in agris prope monumentum situm exadverso Bibliothecam 10ᵇʳⁱˢ, 20°, 1702.

(Page 7).—Amita Harvey obiit 12° die Maii, mane, sepulta in Calvaria de Aldgate 13°, 1699.

Uxor avunculi Alford obiit die 20° Augusti sep' 24° die *Woolwich* Ecclesiâ, 1699. Thema funeralis orationis 27° Psalmo. 13°, 14° ver., ætat. 52.

Affinis Rᵈᵘˢ Hays obᵗ 28° Martii, sepul' 1° Aprilis 1702 in Cæmeterio Sᵗⁱ Martini in agris.

Avunculus Edvardus Alford obiit die 13° 9ᵇʳⁱˢ Sepul. 17° ejusdem de Woolwich Ecclesia 1701 in eodem sepulchro cum uxore. Thema idem erat ut supra, ætatis anno 72.

80, Brother Bibby dyed Jan. 11ᵗʰ, 1719 ; buried at Harrow 10 Jan.
68, Sistʳ Bibby dyed Mar. 6, 1720 (?) ; buried at Harrow.

* He naturally seems interested in his wife's age! When he married her he was 21 and she was "ut vulgo dictum est" 34, within a month of 35, perhaps a little older. Note that her maiden name was *Alford*, and that John Curtoys's first wife and William's mother was Margaret Alford.
† Word for Sponsors.

(Page 8).—1710, Wife godmother to Mr Pollexfin Daugh^r 18 6
1711, Self, godfather to Mr Tyler's Son. . . 20 0
1712, Wife godmo^r to Mr Tyler's daughter . . 17 6
1714, Self godfath^r Mr Tyler's Daught^r. . . 18 0

(?) 1745, August 2nd. Mane H. W.* me opprobavit indecenter, eodem die Ibamus ad Hackney visum filiam et amicum Ch. et dilacerabat notam datam ab eo filio Geor. 18 12^s 9^d debitam mihi. July 28th, 1749, verbis me opprobavit ; deinde Supplicavit mihi condonare, *at Green Man.*

1749, July 27. A Bricklayer kill'd by falling off Mr Stacie's house, then repairing. Daught^r much out of order about it.

(Page 9).—Annam Spicer al's Helder de paroch. S^{ti} Martini in agris soluta' duxi pro uxore, et matrimonio conjuncti eramus, in paroch' Ecclesiâ prædict', die Julii 17°, 1703, a Domino Yates Curato ejusdem.

Et multos annos una nos in hoc mundo, in honore ejus, et unitate secundum verbum vivere permittat Deus.

Joannes Filius meus ex ea natus est 24° die Aprilis 1704 37^{is} minut' post 2^{dam} horam tempore postmeridiano anno 1704 Baptiz. 13° die Maii.
Do. Joannes Welles, } compat.
Alex. Bibby,
Dom. Allen, commat.,
Nelson C^t.

Obiit mortem filius 29° Junii anno 1705 sub 12^{mam} horam mane sepult' Julii 1° in Calvario S^{ti} Martini in agris juxta parietem prope officinam in Angulo Caurino sitam, ætat. 1^{an} 2me 5^d.†

(Page 10).—Elizabetha filia nata 28° die July 1705 ad 6 tam horam mane ; Baptiz^s 5to die Augusti.
Mr Maddox, } Suscept.
Mrs Monk, } compatres.

Obiit mortem illa 20° die Augusti 1705 Sep^{ts} in eodem sepulchro cum filio. Eta. 23 days.

Will'us Welles. Filii nati sexto die Augusti 1706 mane, alter ¼ h. post 9, alter 10 a.m. ; baptiz^{tt} 19°.
Suscep' { Mr Tho. Welles.
Mr Woodroffe.
Sist^r Mary.
Mrs English.

Will'us fi. obiit mortem 30° die 8^{bris} 1706, Sep^{tus} 1° die 9^{bris} in Calvaria St Martin juxta liberos, ætat. 12 septimanas.

(Page 11).—Maria filia nata 25° die 7^{bris} 1707, ¼ post 2^{dam} horam pomeridianam, Baptizata Octobris die 16°.
Suscep. { Mr Monke.
Mrs Ashcombe.
Mrs White.

* No doubt his son-in-law Henry Webster, who married his daughter Edith 1732.
† Sad that he should lose both his little sons: (i) in 1693 ; (ii) in 1705.

Will'us fi^s natus 23° die 7^{bris} 1708, nona hora nocte, baptiz^{tus} die 12° die Octobris.
Suscep. Mr Peeke, sen.
Mr Collins, sen.
M^{rs} Ch. Monke.

Maria filia mortem obiit 9° die Martii 1709, sep^a 12° juxta liberos in Calvar. S^{ti} Martini, ætat. 2^{an} 5^m 12^d.

Will^{us} Filius obiit 11° die Martii 1709 (10) Sep. 12° juxta liberos in Calv. St Martini ætat. 1^{ann} 5^m 16^d.

(Page 12).—Carolus Filius nat. 31° die Maii 1710 10^a hora nocte. Baptiz. 11° die Junii 1710.   Suscep. Mr Bibby.
Mr Monk, dep.
Mrs Salter.

Editha filia nat. 24° die Octobris, 2da hora mane. Bapt. 11° die Novembris 1711.
Sus. Mr Pollexfin.
Mrs Bibby (dep. Mrs E. Spicer).
Mrs Tyler.

Georgius filius Nat. 30° die Junii 1714 3^a hora mane. Baptiz. 11° die Julii.
Sus. Mr Monk.
Mr Pollexfin.
Mrs Culbert.

Son Welles married to Mrs Mary Meadows 13 May 1731, aged 18^y 10mo.

(Page 13).—1723, obiit mortem charissima mihi uxor Anna 2° die Julii sub 6^{am} horam vesperi Sep. 5° die juxta officinam in Calvaria S^{ti} Martini prope filios, ætat. 49.

Daug^r Edith married to Mr Hen. Webster 30 Sep. 1732 at St Cath^{ne}, by Mr Prissett [? Bissett].

Jo^h Curtoys, son of Welles, born 18 July 1732 [*sic*] 18 : 6.
Compr. Mr Mead^s.
Mrs Mead^s.
Self.

Mary, Daught. d°, born 8th No^r 1733 ; baptized 18 d° [*sic*] 18 : 6 ; died
Com. Ch. Curtoys.
Dau. Webster.
Mrs Pharoe.

W^m, son of Welles, born 26 March 1735 ; bapt. 16 Ap. ; 18^s.   Self.
Mrs Bartlet.

(Page 14).—Filius Carolus ordinatus erat Diaconus 23° die Decembris 1733° ab R R° Dom Benjam° Hoadly Episc. Sarum in Sacello juxta Grosven^r Square. Junii 9° 1734 ordinatus est Presbyter ab eodem.

(*To be continued.*)

Reviews.

The Journal of the Ex Libris Society. Vol. XI., Parts 11, 12, 13, and 14, for November 1901
to February 1902. London : A. and C. Black, Soho Square, W.

THE November Part enlarges upon the number of foreign journals following the footsteps of our
English product ; thus the Editor complains of his German colleague " Ex Libris Zeitschrift "
not sending Numbers in collective order ; then he notices the journal of the French collectors,
and gives us a good account of its contents ; then the October Number of " Zeitschrift für
Bücherfreunde " he reviews, and again its November Number ; lastly, from Switzerland in its
" Archives Heraldiques Suisses " for 1901 ; and from the German Bookplate Society the Editor
is going to cull, from the pen of Count Leiningen-Westerburg, the blocks of all the Royal plates,
which will keep alive the memory of her late Most Gracious Majesty. In the " Queen " for
November 1901 is an able Paper by Sir Arthur Vicars, and the " Studio " is also referred to for
its lengthy article, well illustrated, of the " Art of Gordon Craig," with many examples. Last,
not least, in the " American Printer " for November, with its own notes on bookplates, three of
which are represented, is a review by the Editor of a new periodical entitled " Acadiensis,"
published at St. John, New Brunswick. The Part has as an introduction the arms of C. Ellis
Stevens of Philadelphia, and is a good example of engraving and mantling ; and there are also
some excellent examples of skill by Mr. William Edgar, delicate and *apropos*, the sporting plate
of Silvanus Macy being full of good drawing. The plates for identification now reach 485.

The December Number is well illustrated by the arms of Her late Majesty, as reproduced by
Count Leininген-Westerburg, which makes it a valuable one, as the arms are elaborately drawn.
The life of William Hewer, begun by Mr. Arthur J. Jewers in the November Part, is here continued by Mr. Cecil T. Davis, and his arms given. The writer makes the account very interesting
by his associating Pepys and John Evelyn of Wotton with it, and by his knowledge of Hewer's
connections. There is the plate drawn for the Lowell Memorial Library, and with it a good
description ; and also the bookplate of William Hugh Patterson of Belfast, having a smaller one
suspended from it. The plate has the portrait of the gentleman given, and is surrounded by a
shamrock border. This practice had better not be indulged in too much in heraldry, as every
tinker and tailor will have his arms to give away, if even procured from 'Appy 'Ampstead for
a sixpenny photograph. An article by Mr. Charles Dexter Allen, with the plate of Dr. Van
Dyke's shewn, and in which he announces a " College of Heraldry in America," is interesting.

The Part for January has for frontispiece the two plates of the Empress Frederick of
Germany, and also a small oval label which the Empress might place on it, possibly made
adhesive. Each is very chaste, worthy of the illustrious lady so esteemed in England. There is
a letter also from Mr. W. F. Prideaux, completing the account of Hewer Edgley Hewer commenced by Mr. A. J. Jewers in the November Part. The writer also draws the attention of his
readers to the error of coupling the Latin " Ex Libris " with English names, and he instances
" Ex Libris Sylvanus " as one which would meet with correction in any school. As he says, why
should Latin be employed on English bookplates any more than on modern tombstones ? The
Editor closes this Part with the usual Title and Contents, and a painstaking Index.

The February Part (which has been delayed until the middle of March, more through the
Editor having a giant's task to perform monthly with barely any assistance from his compeers)
opens with a Paper on Sir Philip Sydenham by Carnegy Johnson, and the frontispiece is a large
arms of Sydenham with profuse mantling ; there are six other arms of his also given. The
account of Hewer is next taken up by Mr. Alfred A. Bethune-Baker, F.S.A., who gives another
coat to him while he was at Clapham, and while he kept up a London establishment between
1710—1726. The Part still carries on the Bookplates of Medical Men, and the plates for
identification now reach 497. Its other contents are but meagre.

The Virginia Magazine of History and Biography. No. 3, Vol. IX. January 1902. Virginia
Historical Society, Richmond, U.S.A.

THIS Part commences with the letters of William Bird of Westoner, Virginia, and many
instances are given of the original animals which were found on the native soil when first
settlements were made, there being in Georgia plenty of cattle and hogs, sheep and goats, and
particularly a large creature of the beef kind, being the buffalo, which may be bred up tame,
and is good both for food and labour. Besides these there are vineyards which twist round
every tree, and where from the mulberry trees they could produce silk to any extent, and also as
fine a flax as any in the universe for linen manufacture. Hemp also can be raised for cordage, and
there is also a silk grass which is much stronger than hemp. Of oil from nuts there could be
produced any quantity, and there is also what is called a sugar tree, from which could be drawn
spirits equal to arrack. Such was North Carolina about 1735. Other interesting Papers
follow. In one entitled Henry County is a table giving the quantity of tobacco each paid
towards the County Rate; thus the Clerk was assessed at 1248 "thyables" of 27 lbs. tobacco
per poll, and it comes down to 25 for one day's guard, shewing what a powerful agent tobacco
was then, as 500 were paid for maintaining a prisoner thirteen days. There are the genealogies
of the families of Adams, Brookes, Herndon, Farrar, and Fowler given, as well as Notes and
Queries respecting other families.

Fenland Notes and Queries. Vol. V., Part 52. January 1902. Peterborough : George C. Caster,
Market Place.

THIS Part commences with a short account of Raimond Guches, a Huguenot, the bold and
earnest champion of the cause in 1660, who single-handed stood out among the mass of
corruption gathered round Louis XIV. Another Paper by Henry Peet, Esq., gives an account
of Mr. James Coleman, a Tottenham bookseller, who had purchased a bundle of parchments,
among which was a leaf containing 200 entries of marriages solemnized in St. Mary's Church,
Whittlesey, dated 1662 to 1672. How such a practice of tearing up registers should have been
going on in modern days, when such a scholar as Dr. Henry Burgess was vicar at St. Andrew's,
Whittlesey, a neighbouring church to St. Mary's, from 1861 to 1870 upwards, we cannot understand, as he was a scholar of vast ability, and published a work in Coptic, besides being
editor of the "Journal of Sacred Literature" for some years, during which time he must have
had such documents under his care. Mr. Peet says the registers are virtually destroyed, consisting
now of about thirty-six loose fragments of portions of parchment leaves, gall-stained, mildewed,
and moth-eaten, and almost undecipherable. Not a page is perfect. Only one thin folio volume
is saved, covering the years 1683, 1688—1694.

THE REGISTER SOCIETY.

WE are pleased to see the progress this Society is making in printing the smaller registers of
English counties. Since 1896 there were five a year issued, and in 1899 as many as ten
registers, some only making twenty-four pages, while others extended to hundreds of pages, and
each supplied with an Index Locorum and an Index Nominum. We thus see that with few
exceptions there is a fair chance of every register being published. Our own Magazine began it
when nothing of the kind had been attempted ; our Publishers published several at their own
cost, and then the Harleian Society, with its separate funds and membership, printed every year
one or two, and combatted what a weaker society could not venture upon, by printing the
Registers of St. James, Clerkenwell, in six volumes. There are some still requiring to be
printed, but the expense of transcribing and printing have hitherto stood in the way. The most
valuable we know of are the Registers of St. Anne, Soho, making possibly six volumes, and
containing as they do the birth of a Royal Prince, besides being the home of so many of the
aristocracy, these being followed by the historians, speakers, musicians, and the general art
world of 1700 and 1800, the fashionable world still going westward, beginning with St. George's
in the Bayswater district about the middle of 1700. The parish churchyard is also the last
home of hundreds of Huguenots, who fled from France and settled in Soho about 1500 until

1700. A member of the Vestry of Soho has done great service in saving its registers from mildew and damp by adopting a separate iron safe instead of having them enclosed between brick walls with iron back and front, which the Rector soon found was no improvement upon a wooden cupboard. Each book has been preserved with tissue paper at the edges where at all giving way, thus preserving the writing, and the whole registers now make thirty-seven large folio volumes, half-bound in green vellum, and each book lettered on the back whether baptisms, marriages, or burials, and dated consecutively. Thus the little parish of Soho has done single-handed what even the wealthy parish of St. George's or St. Martin's have not yet begun, beyond one volume published by the latter parish in conjunction with the Harleian Society, and this has all been done in Soho by gentlemen who were in the Vestry, and who knew the task they had undertaken, seconded as they were by the public spirit of the Rector and their fellow members. A case in point where disaster has been almost complete is the parish of Whittlesey, Cambridgeshire, where the registers about 1690 are in a most deplorable state, and have also suffered from ill-usage by some irresponsible meddler. It was first discovered by Mr. Coleman, a Tottenham bookseller, among an odd lot of parchments which he bought, who found a leaf containing 200 entries of marriages in St. Mary's Church between 1662 and 1672. He kindly returned the leaf to the then Vicar of Whittlesey, and besides published a pamphlet of eight pages of these marriages. The Rev. W. D. Sweeting, the Editor of "Fenland Notes and Queries," a notice of which we give above, writes: "The oldest register is 1560; for upwards of 100 years they are unbound, detached leaves much worn, and in many cases illegible." Some leaves are torn from top to bottom, and this must have been done since 1827, for a note written then by a churchwarden is also itself torn in half. If the Register Society will rescue what is still left of these registers, now is the time to do it, and may success attend their labours, both in this case and in many others.

Genealogical Notes and Queries.

HOBSON PEDIGREE.

ADDENDA ET CORRIGENDA.

In Vol. IV., p. 276, last line, *for* "A daughter, born 1894," *read* "Irene Helen, born in London 30 March 1895, christened at St. Mary Abbott's, Kensington."

And for "A son, born 1897," *read* "Percy Arthur, born at Caunton 22 Oct. 1897, christened at Caunton."

BEALE FAMILY.

Can any reader of the "Mis. Gen. et Her." state to what branch of the above family belonged the Rev. John Beale, instituted to the Rectory of North Wraxall 8 September 1676? His first wife Ann died there in 1681, and (possibly) his second wife Elizabeth in 1738. He died August 1697 and was buried there.

F.

LANGSTROTH OR LANGSTRETH FAMILY.

During the preparation of my Work on "The Langstaffs of Teesdale and Weardale," I have collected a good deal of information relative to the family of Langstroth or Langstreth. This I will be happy to place at the disposal of any one interested in that family. The name seems to be quite distinct from Langstaff, whereas Langstraffe is certainly, Langstrop probably, a mere variant of Langstaff.

G. B. LONGSTAFF,
Highlands, Putney Heath, S.W.

*** *Books for Review and Notices of Forthcoming Works should be addressed to the Publishing Office, 140 Wardour Street, London, W.*

CREDO CHRISTI CRUCE

EX
LIBRIS
J J HOWARD

L L D
F S A

MAL
TRAVER
S HERALD

EXTRA
ORDINARY

S S S S

In Memoriam.

JOSEPH JACKSON HOWARD, LL.D., F.S.A.,

MALTRAVERS HERALD EXTRAORDINARY.

THE Subscribers to the "Miscellanea Genealogica et Heraldica" will have heard with much regret of the death of Dr. Joseph Jackson Howard, who originated this Magazine in 1866, and has edited it with such marked ability ever since. It seems therefore fitting that a short memoir of his life should appear in the first issue after his death.

Joseph Jackson Howard of Mayfield, Blackheath, was born on the 12th of April 1827, being the only son of Peter Howard of Woodside in Cheshire by Jane Hayston, daughter of Ralph Prince of Mount Vernon Priory, Edge Hill, Liverpool. He was christened at St. Mary's, Edge Hill, on the 14th of June in the same year, and married on the 26th of July 1862, at St. Mark's, Kennington, Ellen Clara, daughter of Joshua West and Mary Ann his wife. He died on the 18th of April 1902 at the residence of his son, Fairlight, Hampton Hill, and was buried on the 22nd of the same month at Twickenham Cemetery. His widow survives him, as also an only son, Dr. A. Dashwood Howard. He was admitted Pensioner at Trinity Hall, Cambridge, on the 17th of June 1845, graduated LL.B. in 1854, and took his LL.D. degree in 1859.

Dr. Howard's business life was spent in the Civil Service, which he entered as a junior clerk in the Accountant-General's Office at the General Post Office on the 10th of October 1851, rising to be a principal clerk on the 13th of May 1867. He retired in April 1888, after thirty-seven years' continual service. He was popular in the Office, and was a much respected Civil Servant. He was also one of the Pioneers of Civil Service Co-operative Stores, and started the "Post Office Supply" in the Receiver and Accountant Generals' Offices at the Post Office, and was made Chairman of the Society. Persons from other offices were allowed to join, and this eventually developed into the Civil Service Supply Association, Limited, of which he was Chairman.

Very early in life he acquired a taste for heraldry and genealogy, spending nearly all his leisure on these pursuits. He became a Fellow of the Society of Antiquaries on the 2nd of February 1854, and at the time of his death was eighth in seniority of such Fellows. For several years he made frequent contributions to their Meetings, principally by exhibiting ancient pedigrees, grants of arms, and heraldic seals from ancient deeds, all of which are very fully recorded in the printed Proceedings of that Society and in the "Archæologia." He was instrumental in 1860 (in conjunction with the late Sir A. W. Franks) in collecting materials for an Exhibition of Civic Plate, which was held in the Society's Rooms then at Somerset House, and the year following he contributed a similar Exhibition of Seals. In May 1862 (in conjunction with T. W. King, Esq., F.S.A., York Herald) he collected materials for an Exhibition of Heraldry, which was also held in the Society's Rooms, and for which he received the especial thanks of the Society.

To the more recent Heraldic Exhibition, held at the Society's present Rooms in Burlington House in 1894 (of which an illustrated catalogue was published), Dr. Howard was a considerable contributor, and was also a member of the Committee.

He was an indefatigable collector, and was one of the earliest, if not the first, who commenced a collection of Armorial Bookplates, which collection it is believed is unique, being valuable not only for its magnitude, but for the scarcity and brilliancy of most of the specimens it contains. He also made a splendid collection of Armorial China, not improbably the choicest in existence.

He was, however, best known to the readers of the "Miscellanea" as a prolific writer. No correspondent ever wrote to him in vain, and he spared neither time nor trouble to give to all, whether acquaintances or strangers, the best inform-ation he had on genealogical and heraldic subjects, without expecting or receiving any recompence whatever. His charming manner and readiness to help in any investigation endeared him to all who came in contact with him, either personally or by correspondence. He might well be called the leader of a new school of genealogists, who sought for truth and accuracy and for evidence of all their state-ments. The desire to spread these principles led him to initiate the publication of this Journal so long as thirty-six years ago, and fortunate are those Subscribers who possess a complete set of the Work, the two volumes which complete the original series being extremely rare. Some idea of the daily labour devoted to this task may be realized by looking back on the earlier Numbers, which are full of every kind of information, embellished by facsimiles of numerous illuminated grants of arms and hundreds of bookplates, mostly from his own collection. It has been announced that the publication of this Journal will be continued.

He had a great taste for heraldic engraving, and would never employ a second-class artist for any work. Some of his happiest hours were spent in discussing with his friends the respective merits of the best heraldic artists.

It is, however, by Dr. Howard's connection with the Harleian Society that perhaps he is best known to genealogists. He was one of the founders of that Society, and acted as Honorary Treasurer from the day of its foundation in 1869 to the end of last year. He edited for the Society (in conjunction with his co-founder the Honorary Secretary) the first volume of its publications, "The Visitation of London in the Year 1568, taken by Robert Cooke," and he also edited (in conjunction with the late Colonel Chester) "The Visitation of London, 1633-35, made by Sir Henry St. George." This work, in two volumes, was illustrated with over 800 coats of arms engraved by Cleghorn and Utting. In 1861 he edited for the Kent Archæological Society (and also printed privately), pedigrees from "Philipot's Visitation of Kent in 1619." In 1866 he edited for the "East Anglian" and also printed separately, two volumes of "Harvey's Visitation of Suffolk in 1561," containing twenty-one pedigrees of the families of Chetham, Clopton, Colt, Cordell, Crane, Daniell, Eden, Fultneby, Hervey, Heigham, Holt, Kempe, Kytson, Lucas, Martin, Payne, Peyton, Poley, Smyth, Spring, and Warburton, all of which are annotated.

In July 1866 he commenced the issue of the "Miscellanea Genealogica et Heraldica" in Quarterly Numbers at 2s. 6d. each. This, however, subsequently became a monthly publication at 1s., and so continued until it was concluded in four volumes, entitled the "New Series," a title not to be confused with the "Second Series" which followed in January 1884, and was completed in five volumes. A Third Series was begun in March 1894, reverting to the Quarterly Numbers, and is still in progress, being now in its fifth volume.

In 1887 he commenced a collection of Privately Printed Pedigrees, illustrating the History of Roman Catholic Families in England, based on the Lawson Manuscript. This most valuable and elaborate work, which contains, however, but six large and fully annotated pedigrees, viz., Fermor, Petre, Hunloke, Phelips, Arundell, and Hornyold, was discontinued in 1895.

In 1887 (in conjunction with Mr. Robert Hovenden) he printed "Some Pedigrees from the Visitation of Kent, from 1663 to 1668." There are, however, but twelve of these pedigrees, all with copious annotations, viz., Dade, Edolph, Gokin, Jordan, Kitchell, Langworth, Lynch, Petley, Scott, Seyliard, Sheafe, and Turner. He also edited in 1888 Sir Edward Bysshe's "Visitation of the County of Essex, 1664—68."

In 1893 he embarked with F. A. Crisp, Esq., F.S.A., on a joint work (privately printed for Subscribers only), entitled "The Visitation of England and Wales," of which nine volumes have been issued with three volumes of notes, and which is still in progress. It contains very full pedigrees of existing families carried out on the principle of the older Visitations, the evidence being confined to no more than two generations older or younger than the informant. This work is embellished with many engravings of arms and signatures.

In 1897 Dr. Howard and Mr. Crisp commenced a similar publication relating to Irish families.

It is satisfactory to know that these Visitations and Notes will be continued.

He printed in 1894 (in conjunction with H. F. Burke, Esq., F.S.A., Somerset Herald), for private circulation, a book called "Theydon Mount : its Lords and Rectors " (notably of the family of Smith, of Hill Hall, Baronets), with a complete transcript of the Parish Registers and Monumental Inscriptions.

He issued in 1895 a volume of facsimiles of Baronets' Bookplates from his own collection, called the "Wardour Press Series."

Dr. Howard was on the Council of the Kent and Surrey Archæological Societies from their foundation. He was a constant contributor on Antiquarian subjects to "Notes and Queries," "The Athenæum," and many other periodicals.

On the 26th of November 1887 "the Queen was graciously pleased, on the nomination of His Grace the Earl Marshal, to appoint Joseph Jackson Howard, Esq., to be Maltravers Herald Extraordinary," a distinction well earned and deserved by one of the most painstaking and energetic of our genealogists.

G. J. A.

NOTICE TO OUR SUBSCRIBERS.

As ANNOUNCED in the Prefatory Note appended to the Fourth Volume, and published early this year, Mr. W. BRUCE BANNERMAN, F.S.A., has kindly undertaken to co-operate in the Editorship in future, and trusts to be favoured by Contributors with Papers on Genealogy, Family History, and Bookplates, also copies from Monumental Inscriptions, both abroad and at home. All correspondence to be addressed to the Publishing Office, 140 Wardour Street, W.

Alice, Duchess Dudley.

In the note at p. 283, in continuation of the account of the "Family of the Dudleys" (Vol. IV., pp. 259—263), it is suggested that an abstract of the will of this lady, giving all relations named, would be interesting. The will is a very long one, taken up for the most part by charitable bequests, of which particulars are given in the above account; but the will is disappointing as regards the lady's relations, as shewn by the following abstract, which gives the chief points omitted in that notice, and mentions all relations named. It may be mentioned here that the copy of her epitaph printed in the "New View of London" is incorrect in many minor details, as shewn by a careful copy of all the inscriptions in the church of St. Giles-in-the-Fields, which it is hoped will be printed before long, but the second part of the inscription, with the arms, etc., has entirely disappeared.

ARTHUR J. JEWERS.

ABSTRACT OF PART OF THE WILL OF ALICE, DUCHESS OF DUDLEY.

"I, Lady Alicia, Dutchess Duddeley, of the parish of Saint Giles-in-the-fields." Will dated 2 November 1668. To be buried in the chancel of the parish church of Stoneleigh, co. Warwick. Nephew the Rt Hon. Thomas, Lord Leigh, or his successors, giveng permission By an Act of Parliament, is "enabled to bee a feme sole to all intents and purposes." £1500 for her funeral, her body to be wrapped in lead. Nephew the Rt Hon. Thomas, Lord Leigh of Stoneleigh, and his wife, each £50 for a ring. Godson Thomas Leigh, grandson of the said Lord Leigh, £100. Goddaughter, daughter of nephew the Hon. Charles Leigh, viz., Alicia Leigh, £100. Faithful waiting woman Jane Hughes £600. Servant Andrew North, gent., for faithful services, £150. Servant Jane Mison £20. Servant Alice Thurle £15, and other servants £5 each above what is due. Has settled a messuage, etc., called the Whitehouse, as a residence for the parson of St. Giles. Trustees for charitable purposes nephew Lord Leigh, Sir Thomas Leigh, son and heir of Lord Leigh, Charles Leigh, Esq., second son of the said Lord Leigh, Robert Leigh of Nunnin, co. Warwick, Esq., and others. Late dear daughter the Lady Alicia Duddeley. To daughter Lady Katherine Leveson the manor of Foxley, co. Northampton, purchased in the name of nephew Thomas, Lord Leigh, nephew Sir Thomas Leigh, cousin the Rt Hon. Lord Lexington, by the name of Robert Sutton, Esq., etc., from John Foxley, Esq. Has an interest for life in the manor of Sembley or Sembleigh, the estate of the late Lord Arundell of Wardour, etc. Daughter Lady Katherine Leveson to be executrix.

Proved (P.C.C.) 9 March 1668-9. (30, Coke.)

A GENEALOGICAL HISTORY

OF THE

Family of Adams of Cavan, etc.*

THE DESCENDANTS OF RICHARD ADAMS, ELDEST SON OF ALLEN ADAMS AND MARTHA HIGENBOTHAM.

1. RICHARD ADAMS of Drumelton, co. Cavan, born 1792; entered the Cavan Regiment as Ensign 28 November 1808 (Watson's "Gentleman's and Citizen's Almanack," 1809); Lieutenant 8 September 1810 (*ibid.*, 1811); Captain 1 September 1815 ("Army List"); married 12 April 1814 (St. Anne's, Dublin, Par. Reg.) Elizabeth Sophia, daughter of the late John Brabazon Lyster, Esq. (who had died 1803), of 29 North Great George's Street, Dublin; died May 1827, and was interred in Knockbride 29 May 1827 (Knockbride Par. Reg.). Mrs. Adams died aged 35, and was interred in St. Mary's, Dublin, 22 January 1831 (St. Mary's, Dublin, Par. Reg.), having had issue two sons and five daughters, viz. :—

(1) ALLEN NOBLE ADAMS, born 12 January 1822 (Killersherdiny Par. Reg.); entered the 7th Dragoon Guards as Cornet 27 June 1845; was engaged in the Kaffir War, for which he obtained a medal; placed on half-pay June 1846; Lieut. 3 September 1847; appointed to the 12th Lancers July 1851; exchanged September 1851, first into the 18th Foot, and then into the 76th Regiment; Captain 10 March 1858 in the 18th Foot, and exchanged September 1858 into the 20th Foot; Major 1 April 1870; placed on half-pay 11 November 1870; Lieut.-Colonel 1 October 1877 ("Army List"); died unmarried 29 August 1879, and was interred in Nunhead Cemetery, Surrey, 2 Sep. 1879.

(2) WILLIAM EDMUND ADAMS, born 11 March 1824 (Killersherdiny Par. Reg.); appointed Paymaster 31st Regiment 10 March 1857; Hon. Captain 10 March 1862; served in the campaign in North China in 1860 and received the medal; served also during the operations against the Taepings in the vicinity of Shanghai in April and May 1862, including the capture of the stockade of Nanksiang, the walled cities of Kadin, Tsinpoo, and Isolin, and the fortified town of Najow ("Army List"); died unmarried in China 22 September 1863 (Letter from the Horse Guards).

(3) LETITIA THOMASINA, married 22 September 1838 David Beatty, Esq., of Heathfield, co. Wexford, Lieut. 99th Regiment, who was appointed 27 February 1846 Adjutant of the Wexford Militia, and died 18 January 1872. Mrs. Beatty died 8 March 1878, having had issue five sons and six daughters, viz. :—

1. EDWARD BEATTY, born 27 February 1842; married 16 Nov. 1865 Catherine Selina, daughter of Henry Charles B.

* Communicated by MAXWELL ADAMS, Esq., Barrister-at-Law. From a MS. by the late Rev. B. W. ADAMS, D.D.—continued from p. 11.

MacMurrogh Murphy, Esq., of Hume Street, Dublin, and had issue one son and two daughters, viz. :—

    1. HORACE EDWARD BEATTY, born 17 January 1876.

    2. LETITIA EVA GERALDINE, died 15 May 1872 (" Daily Express " Newspaper).

    3. CHARLOTTE ELIZABETH FREDERICA.

2. RICHARD CARDEN ALLEN BEATTY, born 6 October 1845 (Killurin Par. Reg.) ; entered the Army as Ensign in the 39th Regiment 30 January 1866 ; Lieut. 9 April 1870 ; Captain 2 November 1879 (" Army List ").

3. THOMAS CHARLES EDWARD BEATTY, born 4 August 1848 (Killurin Par. Reg.); entered the Wexford Militia as Lieut. 22 April 1871 ; Captain 15 June 1874 ; died 17 November 1876.

4. DAVID WILLIAM BEATTY, born 6 April 1850 ; died September 1856 and was buried at Killurin, co. Wexford, 15 September 1856 (Killurin Par. Reg.).

5. WILLIAM JOHN BEATTY, born 2 January 1854 and has since died (Killurin Par. Reg.).

6. ELIZABETH SOPHIA, married 16 February 1871 (Monkstown Par. Reg.) Lewis John Roberts Riall of Old Conna Hill, Bray, Captain in the 15th Regiment, and eldest son of Phineas Riall, Esq., D.L., of the same place, and had issue one daughter.

7. MARY FRANCES, married 5 January 1882 (Rathmichael Par. Reg.) the Rev. Richard Adams (see *post*).

8. OLIVIA CONSTANCE, married 7 September 1876 (Monkstown Par. Reg.) Thomas Haines Revington, Esq., of Kyle Court, co. Wexford.

9. HENRIETTA LOFTUS.

10. JEANETTA LETITIA KATHERINE.

11. LETITIA ELEANOR.

(4) ISABELLA, born about 1817 ; died about 1822 at Drumelton and was interred at Knockbride.

(5) ELIZABETH, born 1820 ; died unmarried 13 May 1841 and was buried 16 May 1841 at Knockbride (Knockbride Par. Reg.).

(6) MARTHA JANE SOPHIA, married 23 July 1839 (Wexford Par. Reg.) Rev. John Keefe Robinson, A.M., Prebendary of Whitechurch, Diocese of Ferns, who died 7 April 1862 and was buried at Rathaspect Church, co. Wexford (Rathaspect Par. Reg.). Mrs. Robinson died 1 May 1874 at Farnogue House, co. Wexford, having had issue two sons and seven daughters :—

    1. JOHN KEEFE ROBINSON, born 28 October 1845 (Whitechurch Par. Reg.) ; died 31 March 1859 and was buried at Rathaspect (Rathaspect Par. Reg.).

2. RICHARD ADAMS ROBINSON, born October 1850 ; baptized
   7 October 1850 (Whitechurch Par. Reg.) ; died 6 November 1850 and was interred at Rathaspect (Rathaspect
   Par. Reg.).

3. ELIZABETH EVARINA S., married first, 31 July 1863, Henry
   Scott Smith, Bengal (now Indian) Civil Service, Registrar
   of the University of Calcutta, and son of Rev. James
   Smith, Rector of Upper Cumber, Diocese of Derry, who
   died s.p. 26 June 1864.   She married secondly, 3 January
   1870 (Wexford Par. Reg.), William Luis Home, M.D.,
   Deputy Inspector-General of Army Hospitals, Bengal.

4. MARTHA JANE SOPHIA, born 29 November 1842 (Whitechurch
   Par. Reg.) ; married 19 May 1864 (Wexford Par. Reg.)
   Charles Smith, M.D. (another son of the above-named
   Rev. James Smith), and died 29 September 1872, having
   had issue four sons and one daughter.

5. LOUISA MARY GERTRUDE, married 3 November 1869 (Wexford
   Par. Reg.) Francis Bland Herbert, R.N. (promoted to rank
   of Commander 11 September 1865), and has issue one
   daughter.

6. LETITIA EMILY LYSTER, born 1848 ; baptized 20 December
   1848 (Whitechurch Par. Reg.) ; married 21 July 1870
   John Talbot Kellett, Esq., and died 23 May 1874, having
   had issue one son and one daughter.

7. ANNIE CLARA, died unmarried 14 December 1871.

8. EDITH ISABEL MARY, born 30 September 1854 (Whitechurch
   Par. Reg.) ; died unmarried 26 June 1871.

9. AMY RICHARDA.

(7) ANNA MARIA, born 1826 ; baptized 29 January 1826 (Killersherdiny Par. Reg.) ; married 27 January 1845 (Killeagh Par.
Reg.) Richard Ridgeway, Esq., M.D., F.R.C.S., etc., of Castlecor,
Oldcastle, co. Meath ; died 22 October 1851, aged 25, and was
interred at Mount Nugent, co. Cavan (Castlecor Par. Reg.),
leaving issue two sons and two daughters :—

1. WILLIAM ADAMS RIDGEWAY, born 27 June 1847 ; entered the
   Army as Ensign in the 14th Foot 12 September 1865 ;
   Lieut. 12 June 1870 ; died unmarried 10 March 1874,
   aged 27, on his voyage home from India, and was buried
   at Point-de-Galle, Ceylon.

2. RICHARD KIRBY RIDGEWAY, V.C., born 26 August 1848 ;
   entered the Army as Ensign in the 96th Foot 8 January
   1868 ; Lieut. 14 February 1870 ; joined the Bengal Staff
   Corps 6 January 1872 ; Captain 8 January 1880 ; Major
   8 January 1888.   Appointed Deputy-Assistant Quarter-
   Master-General 23 June 1885 ; served in the operations
   against the Nagas 1875 and 1879-80 ; was wounded and
   mentioned in despatches (Governor-General's Orders, India,
   574 of 1875 and 123 of 1880) ; medal and clasp and V.C. ;

married 12 July 1870 Amy, daughter of Dr. Fallon, I.M.S., by whom he has had issue three sons and one daughter.

3. ISABELLA, born 29 December 1845; died 29 October 1850 and was buried in Mount Nugent Churchyard (Castlecor Par. Reg.).

4. ANNETTE LETITIA ELIZABETH, married 17 August 1876 Eben Henry Rowe, Esq., only surviving son of John Rowe, Esq., D.L. of Ballycross, co. Wexford, and has issue one son and one daughter :—

    1. EBEN JOHN RADFORD ROWE, born 11 September 1881.

    2. ANNIE MARGARET RADFORD.

2. JOHN ADAMS, R.N., Rear-Admiral of the White ; born February 1793 ; entered the Royal Navy 8 June 1806 as a first-class Volunteer on board the " Scout, 18," Captain William Raitt, under whom during a period of three years and a half he saw much active service, bore a part in many gun-boat actions, and among other vessels assisted in destroying, after a sharp engagement, a notorious privateer, the " Fort of Gibraltar." He was also present as a Midshipman in a very gallant encounter off Genoa between the boats of the " Scout " and a French Squadron, consisting of a brig of 20 guns, one of 18, and seven gun-boats protected by a heavy fire from several batteries on shore, in face of which the largest of the enemy's vessels was sunk and the remainder beaten off, with a loss, however, to the British of the Master and eleven men killed and upwards of thirty wounded. On the night of 31 October 1809 Mr. Adams further served in the boats of the " Scout " and of a squadron under Lieut. John Tailour* at the capture and destruction, after a fearful struggle and a loss to the assailants of 15 men killed and 55 wounded, of the armed store-ship " Lamproire " of 16 guns and 116 men, the bombards " Victoire " and " Grondeur," and the armed zebec " Normande," with a convoy of seven merchantmen defended by numerous strong batteries in the Bay of Rosas. Removing next in succession to the " Voluntaire " and " Cambrian " frigates, both commanded by Captain Charles Bullen, he joined in various cutting-out affairs, witnessed the reduction of the Island of Pomégue near Marseilles, and co-operated in the defence of Tarragona in May and June 1811 until the receipt of his Lieutenant's Commission, dated 15 February 1815 ; appointed to the " Ajax, 74," Captain George Mundy, 31 May 1815, and the " Hind," Captain Sir Charles Burrard, 17 April 1819 (O'Byrne's " Naval Biography "). He joined the " Ajax,"† and in her was present at the bombard-ment of Algiers 27 August 1816 by the British Fleet under Lord Exmouth (Family Reg.). He afterwards served in the Channel and Mediterranean, on board the " Bulwark, 74," Captains Sir Richard King and Thomas Brown, the " Christian VII., 80,"‡ Captain

---

* Of the Swords family.

† Launched in 1808, and replaced the " Ajax " which had been burnt in 1807 (James' "Naval History," 1847, vol. v., p. 3).

‡ This line of battleship was pierced for eighty-four guns and was added to the British Navy, the result of the siege of Copenhagen in 1807. She measured 2,131 tons, and was built in 1803 by the Danes. The model of the " Christian VII." was so much admired that a ship in every respect the same was immediately ordered to be built for the British Navy. That ship was the " Cambridge " of 2,139 tons, launched in 1815 (James' "Naval History," vol. iv., p. 295. London, 1847).

Henry Lidgbird Ball, and the "Grasshopper, 18," Captains Henry
Robert Battersby and Sir Charles Burrard; appointed 24 September
1822 to the "Windsor Castle, 74," Captain Charles Dashwood, of
the tender belonging to which ship he was for some time entrusted
with the command; 12 January 1824 as First Lieutenant to the
"Grasshopper, 18," Captain John George Aplin; 3 November 1824
to the command, on the Newfoundland station, of the "Pelter"
gun-brig; 1 March 1826 to the "Ramillies, 74," Captain Hugh
Pigot, by whom he was also invested with the charge of a tender;
20 October 1826 and 17 September 1828 as Senior to the "Harrier"
and "Childers" sloops, both commanded by Captain William Morier
(for his exertions in saving the latter, which was nearly wrecked in
a violent gale off Yarmouth, he received the approbation of the
Admiralty); 4 May 1829 in a similar capacity to the "Atholl, 28,"
Captain Alexander Gordon, on the coast of Africa; 6 January 1830
to the command of the "Plumper, 12," on the same station, where
in a small gig with only five men he gallantly effected the capture,
7 November 1830, of the "Maria" of six guns and forty-four men,
having on board 512 slaves, and was otherwise very successful;
23 July 1831 as First Lieutenant to the "Alfred, 50," Captain
Robert Maunsell, in the Mediterranean, and 17 November 1834 to
the command of the "Waterwitch, 10," in which vessel he served
under the orders of Lord John Hay on the north coast of Spain, and
was again successful in his anti-slavery exertions on the African
station, attaining the rank of Commander 10 January 1837. He was
appointed 19 January 1839 to the "Acorn, 16," destined for the
same service, as was latterly the "Waterwitch." Returning therefore to the coast of Africa, he renewed his operations against the
negro traffic during a prolonged service of four years and eight
months, during part of which period he had charge of the station
and squadron at Mozambique, cruising with wonderful activity and
good fortune. Among the prodigious number of prizes made by the
"Acorn" we may instance the capture, 6 July 1841, after a three
days' chase and a running fight, of the "Gabriel," a piratical slave-
brig, notorious for its injury to commerce and the frequency of its
insults to the British Flag. His long, arduous, and highly useful
services were at length rewarded, on his return to England, with a
Post Commission, dated 18 December 1843. In 1849 he held the
Civil appointment of Slave Commissioner at Loango (O'Byrne's
"Naval Biography," p. 4); was appointed 4 January 1850 Captain
of the "Gladiator, 6" on the African coast, and 10 April 1854 to
the "Scourge, 6," and Commodore of the African Squadron,
Governor of Ascension Island, etc. In 1862 was offered but declined
the Governorship of Greenwich Hospital. Became Rear-Admiral
of the Blue 6 February 1863, and of the White 5 March 1864.
Received the Naval Silver Medal and nine clasps, a good-service
pension, and medals from the Royal Humane Society for saving on
different occasions eleven persons from drowning. Married first,
21 September 1838 (Ardbraccan Par. Reg.), Mary Anne, daughter
of Thomas Gerrard, Esq., J.P., of Liscarton Castle, co. Meath, who
died s.p. August 1843 at Bettystown, co. Meath, aged 27, and was
interred 25 August 1843 at Donaghpatrick, co. Meath (Donaghpatrick Par. Reg.); secondly, 22 April 1846, Elizabeth Hurst,
daughter of Henry Ellis, Esq., of Mount Steward, co. Dublin, and
Eccles Street, Dublin, who died at Folkestone in Kent 11 May 1891
suddenly from the effects of influenza, aged 70. Admiral John
Adams died 17 December 1866, and was interred at Weston-

super-Mare. By his second marriage he had one son and two
daughters :—

(1) HENRY ELLIS ADAMS, born 28 January 1847 ; entered the Army
from Sandhurst College 22 June 1867 as Ensign in the 87th
Regiment ; Lieut. 23 March 1870 ; Captain 29 September
1883 ; died unmarried 6 September 1888, aged 41.

(2) ISABELLA EMILY, married 12 August 1875 (St. Saviour's, Paddington, Par. Reg.) Francis Frederick Ditmas, Royal Artillery
(Lieut. 1 September 1863, Captain 21 February 1876), eldest
son of Lieut.-Colonel Ditmas, R.H.A., and has issue one son
and one daughter :—

    1. FRANCIS IVAN LESLIE DITMAS, born 12 August 1876.

    2. ISABEL EBENA LESLIE.

(3) EVERINE FRANCES ELIZABETH, married 18 April 1885 T. R.
Johnson-Smyth, who was born 12 June 1857. He entered the
Army from the Militia as a Second Lieut. in the 106th Foot
(Bombay Light Infantry), now the 2nd Battalion Durham Light
Infantry, 14 September 1878 ; Lieut. 30 April 1879 ; Captain
12 February 1885 ; served in the Soudan with the Frontier
Field Force 1885-86 ; was present at the Battle of Giniss
(Medal and Khedive's Bronze Star) ; Adjutant of Militia
1887—92 ; Major 25 August 1896 ; Commandant of School of
Instruction for Militia and Volunteers at Aldershot 25 April
1889. He was killed in the action at Potgeiter's Drift, Natal,
6 February 1900, and left issue one son and one daughter :—

    1. ROGER HENRY ELLIS JOHNSON-SMYTH, born 17 April 1889.

    2. EVERINA ELIZABETH ADAMS, born 31 December 1894.

3. STUART ADAMS, born 1796 ; held an appointment in the Receiver-
General's Office, Custom House, Dublin ; died unmarried 23 June
1820 and was interred in St. Michan's, Dublin (St. Michan's,
Dublin, Par. Reg.).

4. ALLEN NOBLE ADAMS, born May 1800 ; baptized 2 June 1800 (Shercock
Par. Reg.) ; entered as Ensign 25 January 1816 (" Army List ") the
Glengarry Light Infantry Fencibles, commanded by his uncle Lieut.-
Colonel Francis Battersby, C.B. (vide Burke's "Landed Gentry,"
1862), but died unmarried March 1817 in Russell Street, Dublin,
from injuries received while hunting, and was interred 28 March
1817 in St. Michan's, Dublin (St. Michan's, Dublin, Par. Reg.).

5. COSBY ADAMS of Laurel Lodge, co. Cavan, born 1801 ; married
23 February 1833 Catherine, daughter of John Brabazon Lyster, Esq.
(who had died 1803, of North Great George's Street, Dublin), and
sister of his brother Richard's wife (see p. 45) ; died 9 December
1834, aged 33, at Laurel Lodge, and was interred in Knockbride
Old Church (Knockbride Par. Reg.). Mrs. Adams removed to
Jersey, where she died 12 November 1866, and was there interred,
leaving issue one daughter :—

(1) LETITIA EMILY, a Deaconess of Salisbury.

(To be continued.)

Pedigree of Mallet and Peyton.*

FROM ADD. MS. 5523.

William de Mallett a nobleman of Normandie whoe came into England w^t William the Conqueror, slayne at Yorke in kepinge the Cytie against the Daynes.

- Gilbert de Mallet.
- William de Mallett, Lord of Cory Mallett.
- Walter de Mallett the 3^d son, Lord of the Manner of Sibton and Horham in com. Suffolke.
  - Reynolde, 2^d sonne, Sewer to Hughe Bygod, Earle of Norffolke, Lord of the Manners of Payton Hall in Ramsholt & of Payton Hall in Stoke Naylonde.
    - John, sonne and heire, Lorde of the Manners of Payton hall in Ramsholt and Payton hall in Stoke.
      - Robart de Ufforde, eldest sonne, so surnamed of his mannor of Ufforde in com' Suffolke.
      - Peter de Payton, 2^d sonne, so surnamed of his Mannor of Payton hall in Ramsholte.
        - Sir John de Payton of Stoke Neylonde, Knight, sonne & heire=Clementia, syster to Gernon de Boceter.
          - Sr John de Payton of Payton in Stoke Neylonde in com' Suffolke, Knight, sonne and heire, had 3 wyfis but by Clementia, Lady of Weylonde, he had
            - Walter de Payton, 2^d sonne.
            - James de Payton, 3^d sonne.
            - 3 Daughters.
      - John de Payton, 3^d sonne, so surnamed of the mannor of Payton hall in Stoke Neyland and Boxford in com' Suffolke.
  - Robart the Eldest sonne, Lord of the Manners of Sybton and horham in com. Suffolke, mar' the Daughter and heire of Raylfe de Casineto.
- Robart de Mallett, Vicount de York, obijt sine p'le.

* Communicated by Rev. W. E. LAYTON, M.A., F.S.A.

A

Sir Robart de Payton of Stoke in com' Suffolke, Knight, sonne & heire, by his first wyfe he had much Issue all which died w^{thout} issue, by his 2^d wyfe he had

John de Payton, 2^d sonne.

Peter de Payton, 3^d sonne.

Egidia de Payton, a Nonnent Mullingos.

William Payton of Wyken.

Sr John Payton of Payton in Stoke Neylonde, Knight, sonne & heire, obijt tempore Richard the Second. == Margaret, daugh. & heire of John Genuonne, Esqre.

John Payton of Payton hall & Wyken, Esquier, sonne & heire, died under King Henry the fifth. == Jonne, daugh^r & solle heire of Sr Humonde Sutton, Knight, widowe to .... Drury, Knight.

John Payton of Payton hall & Wyken, Esquier, sonne and heire, died tempore King Henry 6. == Grace, dau. & solle heire of S^r .... Langley, Knight.

Margaret, daugh. & Coheire of Sr John Barnard of Islam in com. Cambridg, Knight, first wyfe. == Thomas Payton of Payton hall, Wyken, & Islam, the which he had in right of his first wyfe, sonne & heire, died a° 2^d of K. Rich. 3^d, 1484. == Margarett, 2^d daugh. & coheire of Sr Hugh Frauncis, Knight, whoe died 26 Marche 30 of Henry 6, a° dn' 1452, wydowe to Thomas Garnishe of Kenton in com' Suffolke, Esquior.

Francis Payton of Bery St Edmond in com' Suffolke, Esquier, 3^d sonne. == Elizabeth, dau. to Reynolde Brooke in com' Suffolke, Esquier.

Christopher Payton, 2^d sonne [sic], died before his father, s.p., & mar' Elizabeth, dau. to John Hyde (she after mar' to y^e Lo. Hunsdon).

Edmond Payton, 2^d sonne, mar' first Joane, daugh. to Nicholas Granham, Esqre, & his heire, 2dly Ann, dau. to .... Poyns.

Elizabeth, died yonge.

Ann, mar' to Richard Moore.

Christopher Payton of Bery St Edmond in com' Suffolke, Esqre, sonne & heire. == Jayne, dau' to Thomas Milenny of Chelmsford in Essex, ar'.

B

C

B

C

Thomas Payton of Bery St Edmonds in com' Suffolke, Esquier, sonne & heire. = Ceeyley, dau' to John Bourcher, Erle of Bathe.

Christopher P., mar' Anne, dau' to William Palmer of Warwicksh'.

Sir Henry Payton of Bery, Kt, sonne and he. = Mary,* dau. to Edward Semer, Duke of Somersett.

Thom. — Will'm.

Robart. — Christopher.

Francisca, mar' to Arthur Fortiscute of Deuenshire.

Presella. — Jayne.

Elinor.

Walter. — Thomas.

Elizabeth. — Cecylie.

Henry P. of London, mar' Mary, daugh' to .... Pickering.

1. Martha, mar' to Will'm Kirkham.

2. Frann', mar' to John Hare.

3. Margarett, mar. firste to Richard Eden ; 2odly to Sr William Worthington, Knt; 3dly to Bryan Tuke of Layer Marney in Essex, Esquier.

4. Mary, mar' to Tobyt Hawghton.

5. Elizabeth, mar' to Robart Bentlee.

6. Ann, mar' to John Kinge.

7. Rosse, mar' to Thomas Lewgor.

Richard, 1st sonne. — Henry, 2d sonne, obijt s.p. — Walter, 3d sonne. — Hester. — Myrabell. — Elyzabeth. — Jayne. — Martha. — Margarett.

Sir Robert Payton of Islam in com. Cambridge, Knight, sonne and heire. = Elizabeth, dau. to Sr Robart Cleere of Ormsby in com' Norffolke, Knight.

Thomas, ffirste sonne, obijt yonge.

Edward, 3d sonne. — Thomas, 4 sonne. — John, 5 sonne.

Dorothy. — Margarett. — Grace.

Ann, mar' to .... Ashby.

Jane, mar' to .... Langley.

Elizabeth, mar' to .... Langley.

John Payton of Knolton in com' Kente, Esqre, 2d sonne. = Dorathe, dau. to Sir William Tyndall, Knight.

Margarett, mar' to Francis Jenney of Knatshall in com' Norffolke, ar'.

Elizabeth, mar' to Sir William Wigston, Knight.

D

E

[* In a different and later handwriting : "Mary, mar' to Sr George Le Hunto of Lyttel Bradley in Suffolke, Knight."]

E

D

Sir Robart Payton of Islam in com' Cambridge, Knight, sonne and heire. = Frances, daugh. & heire of Frann' Haselden, Esquier (of Chesterford p'va Essex, Stepley Gulden, com', com'.... et Oxford Shillings [? Okeford Shilling], 1580 ; bur' at Isleham. She built Morden, the Hospital there).

- Robart Payton of Islam in com' Cam', Esquire, sonne & heire. = Elizabeth, daughter to Robart, the firste Lord Riche.
- Richard Payton, 2d sonne, mar' Mary, dau' to Lawrance Hyde.
- Anne, mar' to Thomas Wrenne.
- William Payton.
- Thomas. — John.
- Christopher. — Edward.
- Katherin. — Elizabeth.

- Sir John Payton of Islam in com' Cambridge, Knight & Barronett, Lord Mayor 1583. = Alice, dau' to Sir Edward Osborne, Kt, of London.
- Wynifred, mar' to Edward Osborne, Gent.
- Frann', mar' to John Haggarde.
- Mary, 3d daugh', mar' firste to Charles Balan, 2dly to Sr Richard Cope, Knight.

- Sir Edward Payton of Iselam in com' Cambridg', Knight and Barronett, sonne & heire, liuinge a° 1625. = Alice, dau' & heire of Robart Liuesey of Surrey, Esqr.
- John P., 2d sonne, Captain in the lowe Cuntreys. — Robart, 3d sonne.
- Anne, mar' to Robart Bacon, Esquier.
- Elizabeth, mar' to Sr Anthony Eresby of Lincolnsh., Knight.
- Alice, mar' to Sr John Payton of Dynnington in the Ile of Elley, Knight.

- Sir John Payton, Knight, Lientenante of the Tower of London, sonne & heire. = Dorathie, dau' & coheire of Edmond Beaupree of Well in com' Norffolke, Esquier.
- Thomas Payton. — Edward Payton.
- Sir Thomas Payton of Kente, Knight, 2d sonne. = Anne, daugh. to Sr Martin Calthrope of London, Lord Mayor a° 1588.
- Elizabeth, mar' to Thomas Munnings of Kent, Esquier.

- Sir John Payton, Knight, of Dynnington in ye Ile of Elley, sonne & heir, mar. Alice, daugh. to Sir John Payton of Islam, Knight.
- Samuell, sonne & heire.
- Mary, eldest dau. — Judyth, 2d dau.
- Elizabeth, 3d daugh.
- Anne, 4th dau'. — Alyce, 5th daugh'.

The Registers of Inkberrow, co. Worcester.*†

A COPY OF THE REGISTER OF THE PARISH OF INKBORROW, 1632.

The names of such as were Maryed this year 1632.

July 30   Christopher Clifton & Anne Ellets.
Aug. 2   John Oakes & Jane Higgons, wid.
Nov. 22   Thomas Gowld of Upton, Snodsbury, & [Alice] Powndrell.
Nov. 28   Samuel Hobday & Katherine Dison.
Feb. 7   John ffreeman & Alice Briscoe [?].

The names of such as were Buried in the year 1632.

April 3   Alice wife of Georg Niblet.
April 13   Mary wife of ffrancis Wilson the elder.
April 17   Anne wife of John Ellins.
April 20   Henry Haynes of Dormston.
July 7   John Lawgher of Cladsell.
July 20   Joan Barley.
July 22   Willia' Yeardly of Kington.
Aug. 2   Nicholas Hobday.
Aug. 11   Robert Wilson.
Oct. 20   Katherine wife of William Page.
Nov. 12   Raph Baker.
Nov. 19   Anne wife of Tho. Bowtes.
Dec. 7   John Yate.
Dec. 9   Henry Hunt.
Dec. 25   Widdow Partady.‡
Feb. 17   Henry sonne of Henry Dison of Holloway, gent.
— —   John Okeley of Kington.
Mar. 5   Anne dawghter of Widdow Harison [?].
Mar. 10   John sonne of John Smith.

Hæc est vera copia concordans cu' Registro reservat apud Inkborrow teste :

HUGH GLOUER, Vic. ibid.   HENRY GOORE, } Wardens.
                                   FFRANCIS SMITH, }

INKBERROW.   COPIA REGESTRI BAPTIZATORUM, SEPULTORUM, ET IN MATRIMONIO CONTRACT HOC ANNO D'NI 1634.

[*Baptisms.*]

Mar. 30   John the son of John Harbage.
April 2   Mary the daughter of ffrancis Darbee.
April 10   Thomas the sonne of Henry Hunt.
April 20   Richard ye sonne of John Robbinson [?].
April 30   Alice the daughter of Henry Goar.
April 30   Thomas the sonne of John . . . . [?].
May 13   Richard the sonne of Tho. Perkes.

---

* From the Transcripts in "Edgar Tower," Bishop's Register.
† Communicated by WILLIAM BRADBROOK, M.R.C.S.—continued from p. 27.
‡ The entries throughout marked with a double-dagger [thus, ‡] are very indistinct.

May	24	ffrancis ye sonne of ffrancis ffreeman.
June	1	James ye sonne of James Hemming.
June	1	Ann ye daughter of John James [?].
June	1	Sibell ye daughter of Henry Grasier.
June	15	Anne ye daughter of John Dison.
June	29	Mary ye daughter of Tho. Eden.
July	6	Edward ye sonne of Edward Eaton.
July	27	.... daughter of Edward Boone.
Aug.	3	Henry ye sonne of Tho. Phillipps.
Sep.	7	Willia' filius populi by Eliz. ffiggett.
Sep.	14	Henry sonne of Henry Newman.
Sep.	28	Elizabeth dawghter of Tho. Browne.
Oct.	19	William sonne of William Willis.
Oct.	26	Nicholas sonne of Tho. Dison.
Oct.	26	Joane dawghter of Rich. Marshall.
Nov.	9	John sonne of Willia' Parsonne.
Nov.	9	Elizabeth daughter of Richard Marshall, farmer [?], of Cladsell.
Nov.	27	Jane daughter of John Parsons.
Nov.	27	Jane the dawghter of Henry Lawgher.
Dec.	3	Robert sonne of Armel Hunt.
Dec.	15	George [?] the sonne of William Hemming.
Dec.	29	Jane daughter of Humfrey Heming.
Jan.	3	John sonne of John ffortenham.
Jan.	11	John the sonne of John Hatherley [?].
Jan.	12	Joan the daughter of Henry Griffin.
Jan.	23	John sonne of John Phillip.
Feb.	12	Ursula daughter of George Blick.
Feb.	19	Joan daughter of John Piper.
Mar.	6	Elizabeth daughter of John Boone.
Mar.	10	John sonne of ffrancis Smyth.
Mar.	22	Richard sonne of Richard Steward.
Mar.	22	Thomas sonne of Thomas Hieron.
Mar.	22	Edward sonne of Christopher Clifford.

The names of such as were Marryed in the year of our Lord 1634.

April	13	Henry Griffin & Dorothy Mosse, both of this parish.
May	1	Thomas Harry & Anne Rand, both of this parish.
May	1	Thomas Barth & Elizabeth Grasier.
June	24	John ffortenham of Barvorde in com. Oxon & Margery Harwood [or Horward].
July	23	Roger Tandy of Abbotts Morton & Elizabeth .... of this parish.

[Burials.]

Mar.	—	ffu [?] Oake.
April	—	Joan Smyth.
April	—	John Stevens.
April	23	Richard Trindar.
June	—	Mary Harvey, widow.
June	20	Anna Whoman.
June	27	ffortuna wife of Edward Beard [?].
Nov.	5	Anne Bowtes.
Nov.	17 [?]	Alice Hawes.
Dec.	—	Anna ux. Rich. Johns.
Dec.	—	Joan ux. John Haines.
—	—	Tho. ....

Jan. 1 Margaret ux. John Hobbins.
Feb. — Elizabeth ux. John . . . .
— — Margaret daughter of Thomas . . . .
Mar. — Thomas Heming of Kington [or Knighton].
Mar. 16 Judith ux. ffrancis Ellins.
Mar. — Mary ux. Will'm Raven.

HUGH GLOUER, Vic.   RICHARD HUBAND, } Churchwardens.
                        JOHN WOOLMER,

COPIA REGESTRARII LIBRI EOR'M QUI BAPTIZATI, VEL MATRIMONIO CON . . . . CTI,
VEL MORTUI ET SEPULTI IN PAROCHIA DE INKBERROW IN ANNO D'NI 1635.

Nomina eoru' qui Baptizati.

Mar. 3 An Smyth fil. ffrancis Smyth.
April 12 Edward sonne of Anthony Yong.
April 20 Thomas sonne of Willia' Rand & Alice his wife.
May 2 Grisill Beele, a child born of a wandering Beggar.
June 12 Edward sonne of Edward Rudge & Ellener uxor.
June 18 Willia' sonne of Richard Harvy & Elizabeth his wife.
July 19 Richard the sonne of Richard Bennet.
Aug. 9 Sarah the daughter of Robert Dison & Sarah his wife.
Aug. 9 John the son of Robert Richards.
Oct. 4 John sonne of John Hunt of Egioke.
Oct. 4 Michael sonne of John Blick & Margaret his wife.
Oct. 4 Elizabeth dawghter of Richard Harrett & Alice his wife.
Nov. 1 John the posthumous sonne of James Heming & Joan his wife.
Nov. 1 Ellenor dawghter of Hugh Horwood.
Nov. 3 Susanna fil. Thomas Bartley et Elizabeth uxor.
Nov. 22 Elizabeth dawghter of ffrancis Heming of Thorn.
Dec. 2 Thomas the sonne of Richard Huband *al's* Hibbots & Ann his wife.
Dec. 13 Henry fil. Henr. Page.
Dec. 20 John fili's Thomas Dowter et Ellenor uxor.
Dec. 31 ffrancis filia ffrancisci Darbe et Anne ux.
Jan. 27 Henry fili's Joh'es ffreema' et Aliciæ uxor.
Jan. 31 Ann filia Tho. Beddow.
Feb. 14 Ellizab. fil. Richardi Steward.
Feb. 17 Robert filius Henrici Hunt.
Feb. 21 John fil. Henrici Speerpoyt.
Feb. 28 Tho. fil. Arthur Hemes.
Mar. 23 Gualter fil. Richardi Steward.

Ita est: HUGH GLOVER, Vic.   THOMAS DISON, } C.-ward.
                                  JOHN HARBAGE,

Nomina eoru' qui Matrimonio copulati 1635.

May 25 Edward Bovey & Ursula Yate.
Aug. 24 Thomas Willis & Elizabeth Bird.
Sep. 22 Richard Wedgbury et Ellener Clymer.
Sep. 29 Henry Page & Mary Corbet.
Oct. 28 Edward Pierce & Margery Blick.
Jan. 19 Willia' Willis & Ursula Whoman,

Jan. 24 Willia' Boone & Sibill ffigget.
Feb. 2 John Merrell of ffliford & Mary Bowtes, vid.
Feb. 11 John Gunne & Katherine Heming.

Ita est: HUGH GLOUER, Vic.   THOMAS DISON, } C.-ward.
                                      JOHN HARBAGE, }

Nomina eoru' qui Sepulti 1635.

Mar. 30 Elizabeth Smith.
April 5 Mary ye wife of Will'm Raven.
April 10 Elizabeth Steward.
April 13 James Smith of Kington.
April 13 ffrancis Heines of Dormston.
April 19 Margaret Brown.
April 29 Robert Horwood.
May   8 Margery wife of Henry Page.
May 14 Richard Steward the elder of Cladsell.
May — Ann Green of Kington.
June 6 ffrancis dawghter of ffrancis Smith of [Kington] Bowtes.
June 10 Thomas Boond of Nowbery.
June 23 John ffarre.
July 4 James Heming the yonger.
July 4 ffrancis Heming the yonger.
July 18 Elizabeth Harbag.
July 19 Margaret Baylis.
July 20 Tabitha dawghter of Thomas Smyth.
July 28 Phillip Browne.
Aug. 13 Margaret Smyth.
Aug. 25 Edward Chambers.
Sep. 11 Thomas Rudg.
Sep. 14 Margaret Ballard uxor Henrici Ballard.
Oct. 15 Richard Windle.
Oct. 18 Elizab. Webb de Kington.
Nov. 13 Mary Tilley.
Dec. 17 Jane uxor Rob'ti Smyth.
Jan. 7 Sibill ux. Rogeri Cox.
Feb. 20 Richard fil. Tho. Ballard.
Mar. 17 fflorence uxor Mathei Greene de Dormston.
Mar. 19 Margeria fil. Hugh Horwood.

1636.

[Baptisms.]

April 3 Anna . . . .
—   —   Elleonora . . . .
—   —   William filius . . . .
—   —   Thomas fil. Tho. . . . .
—   —   Anne fil. Henry . . . .
—   —   Sibella fil. Hugh . . . .
—   —   Elizabeth fil. Joh's Harbag [?].
June — Anne filia Tho. James.
Aug. 23 Anna fil. Edward Pierse & Margaret.
Sep. 3 Guielmus fil. Willmi. Boond et Sibilla uxor eius.
Sep. 15 Henricus fil. Joh'is Phillips et Mariæ uxoris eius.
Sep. 20 Anna fil. Tho. Smith.

Oct.   9   Ursula fil. Tho. Rudg et Phillippa ux.
Oct. 30   Richard fil. Richard Petford.
Oct. 30   Jana fil. Guielm. Bowlts et Jana uxoris.
Nov.   6   Guielmus fil. Johes. Weston et Diana uxoris.
Nov.   6   Ellenora fil. Henr. Ellets et Tabitha uxoris.
Nov. 27   Ægidius fil. Joh'is Ganderton.
Jan.   1   Anna fil. Tho. Eden.
Jan.   8   Gratiamus fil. Henri Grasier.
Jan. 15   Joh'es fil. Joh'es Hunt.
Jan. 15   Maria fil. Richardi Jannings [?].
Feb. 18   Ursula fil. Humfredi Heming.
Feb. 26   Joh'es et Roberty gemilli fil. Edwardi Bovy et Ursula uxoris.
Feb. 26   Thomas filius Tho. Robinson.
Feb. 26   Joanna fil. ffrancisci ffreeman et uxoris eius.
Mar. 12   Russellus fil. Henry Lawgher et ffranciscæ uxoris.

Ita testamur : Hugh Glover.   John ff . . . .
                                               ffran. . . . .

Nomina Sepulti 1636.

May   21   Gulielmus Marshall.
June 13   Francis . . . . vidua.
July 20   John . . . .
July 30   . . . . Ballard.
Aug. 27   . . . . Netherton.

Copia Registri reservat apud Inkborrow Anno Dom. 1637.

Nomina Baptizat.

April 8   Elizabeth the daughter of ffrancis Tomkins.
April 19   Willm. ye sonne of Henry Griffin & Dorothy his wife.
April 23   Katherine ye daugh. of Tho. Dyson & Eliz. uxor prior of Morton Hall.
May   7   Alice ye daugh. of Edward Smith.
June 29   Henry ye sonne of Henry Edkins & Christian uxor of Aston Cantloe in
           com. Warwick.
July   9   ffrancis ye daugh. of Robt. Richards.
July 23   John ye sonne of Armill Hunt.
Aug.   6   Mary ye daught. of John Dyson of Holberow.
Aug. 20   Tho. ye sonne of Henry Spearpoint.
Oct.   1   Anthony ye sonne of William Bromesgrove & Ann his wife of Kingham
           in com. Oxon.
Oct.   1   Tho. son of Robert Pope.
Oct.   8   Tho. son of Hugh Horwood.
Oct. 15   Johanna the daugh. of Tho. Perks.
Oct. 28   Tho. son of Lewis ffiggott.
Nov.   6   Henry the son of John Hasterley.
Nov. 12   Anne daugh. of Joseph Hobday.
Nov. 24   Mary the daugh. of Henry Hobbins.
Dec.   3   Elinor daugh. of Francys Heming.
Dec. 14   Rich. son of Rich. Steward, inino [?] of Cookhill.
Dec. 17   Will'm son of Richard Harriott.
Jan. 14   Aramina or Anna daugh. & bastard child of Ann Churchly & Tho. Smith.
Jan. 21   Elinor the daughter of Tho. James &.Ann uxor.
Feb.   2   Thomas son of Thomas Bennet.
Feb.   4   John son of Robert Brook & Mary uxor.

Feb. 18 Sarah daugh. of Henry Goar.
Feb. 22 Mary daugh. of Richard Marshall.
Mar. 4 Sarah daugh. of William Willis.
Mar. 9 Robert son of Robert Banes & Jane uxor.
Mar. 11 Thomas son of ffrancis Darby & Ann his wife.
Mar. 11 Ann, a bastard child of Ann Boutes by Tho. Pardoe, as she affirmed.
Mar. 18 Samuell son of Henry Hunt of Linsy.
Mar. 18 John son of John Wilson of Wellinton, neere Kington, comit. Heref., & Elizab. uxor.

Nomina Matrimonio contraxit.

May 4 Roger Sale & Margaret Bond.
June 8 John Shailer & Martha Cartwright.
Sep. 3 Edward Peirce & Cassandra Court.
Oct. 7 Henry Symonds & Ann Sturdy.
Nov. 10 Will'm Cartwright & Joan Ballard.
Dec. 21 Henry Ballard & ffrancis Hunt.
Feb. 6 Thomas Dison of Morton Hall & Elizabeth the daughter of Mr Hugh Glouer, the vicar, were maried at Doderhill.

Ita testamur: HUGH GLOVER. JOHN DISON, ROBERT JAMES [?], } Churchwardens.

Nomina Sepultoru'.

April 14 Widdow Reason.
April 19 Tho. Hunt, senior.
April 22 Tho. Ballard of Kington.
April 22 Ursula Heming.
May 6 Tho. Hale.
May 13 Elizabeth Dyson.
June 5 Widdow Chooler.
June 5 Wife of Edward Barnes of Darmpson.
June 7 Ann Ballard.
June 30 Wife of John Woolmare.
Aug. 13 Tho. Butler of Darmpson.
Sep. 6 Georg Heming.
Sep. 20 Tho. Bailis.
Nov. 15 Phillip Goldicote.
Nov. 17 Will'm Hierne, of the plague.
— — Nicholas Goldicote.
Nov. — Isabell Hierne.
Nov. — Isabell Goldicote.
Dec. 6 Thomas Hierne.
Dec. 14 ffrancis Cook, son of Francis.
Dec. 24 William Cook, son of ffrancis.
Dec. 27 ffrancis Cook the father.
Jan. 8 Joan Hierne.
Jan. 10 Katherine Clifford.
These 12 last died of the plague.
Jan. 3 Thomas Davis.
Jan. 6 Alice Parsons.
Jan. 16 A child found in the highway.
Jan. 28 Joan Higgins, a criple.
Feb. 4 Isabell Neale.
Feb. 20 Edward Shacle.
Feb. 20 Will'm Page.

(*To be continued.*)

Will of Sir Nathaniel Riche, 1635.*

A Breife conteyning my resoluc'on for the disposing of my estate according to the substance whereof I intend if God give me life and leisure to drawe upp my last Will and Testam^t wch if I should be disappointed in I appoint that this shalbe in the nature of a Will and that all my lands goods and chattels shalbe disposed according to the tenor of the particulers hereunder menconed. This being made this second daye of December 1635.

First I will that all form^r Wills heretofore by me made shalbe utterly voyd for that the same are not according to my minde & meaning. My soule I bequeath and comend to God my Father in Jesus Christ, my body to be·privately buried in the night without any fun'alls pompe or mourning, the place I leave to the discretion of my Executors the R. ho'ble the Lord Mandehill whome I nominate and appoint sole Executor of my last Will & Testament, but if conveniencie yt maye be I would be buried at Stondon in Essex in the Parr'ish Church there, ouely I would have my Executor erect some monument forme where ever I be buryed the same not exceeding the some of fyftie pounds or a hundred markes. I would onely haue my sisters and brothers in lawe and their childeren and all my servantes to have mourneing suites of black clothe. My manor of Stondon and all my lands in Essex I give to my nephew Nathaniel Riche when he comes to the age of one and twentie years, in the meantime my Executor to receave the rent and to allowe him fowerscore pounds p' ann' for his educac'on for sometyme at the Universitie of Cambridge and then at Lincolnes Inne yt being my desire that he should study and professe the lawe. I give the proffit of seaven of my shares in the Barmudaes now called the So'mer Islands to my sister Grimsdiche and her husband dureing their lives if they will goe and inhabit uppon them and One hundred and fyftie pounds in money for the transporting of themselves and such of their children as they shall thinke fitt to carry with them. I give one other share to my nephue Robert Browne now residing in the said So'mer Islands he haveing one other share there already uppon the guift of my Sister Wroth lately deceased. I give one other share there to . . . . Browne one other of the Sonnes of my sister Browne deceased, whoe hath beene hetherto educated by my noble frend the Countesse of Leicester, mother to Sir John Smith. The residue of my shares there being fyve I give for the mainten'nce of a free schoole in those islands wch my desire is should first be erected out of the proffits of the said fyve shares by the direcc'on of my Executor and then layed for ev^r to the said Schoole. The Schoole Master to be nominated and chosen by my Executor and his noble ladye and after their decease by such religious and discreete feoffees as they shall appoint. My desire is that some of the Indian children to be brought either from Virginia or New England or some other continent of America such as my Executor shall thinke fittest maye be brought over there to be instructed in the knowledge of true religion. And to the end that my Executor may better p'forme the trust com'itted to him in the disposing of all the said shares I doe give the inheritance and freehould of them all to his lo^pp prayeing the Honorable Court of Adventurers for those Islands that im'ediately after my decease he may be admitted to them To have and to hould for him and his heires for ev' Nev'theles upon the trust formerly menc'oned and not any wages to his owne use. But in case my said brother in lawe Mr Grimsdich and his wife will not wth in one yeare after my decease goe thither in their owne p'sons to lyve there then I will not that either of them have any benefit by this guift unles by the hand of God they shalbe hindered. But that in that case my Executor take the yearly p'ffitt of those shares and imploy raysed thereby for three yeares towards the erecc'on of the said free schoole and then passe over the inheritance of the said seaven shares to such childe or children of my said brother and sister Grimsditch as he shall conceave to be most worthy, as alsoe I com'itt the guift of the inheritance of the said shares to be disposed of for the benefit of such childe or children by my Executor in case they

* Communicated by J. R. Brown, Esq., F.R.G.S.

shall goe and lyve there after their decease my meaneing being that my said brother in lawe and his wife should have the use of those seaven shares during their lyves in case they lyve there else not, but in noe case to dispose of the inheritance the care whereof I leave wholly to my Executor for the good and benefit of their children especially such as by their vertue, diligence, and good course of life shall deserve best. I give to Nathaniell Browne now in New England wth Mr Hooker the two hundred pounds wch by my sister Morgan's Will was bequeathed unto him and fyftie pounds more as my owne guift wch two hundred and fyftie pounds I would have Mr Hooker imploye dureing the minority of the said Nathaniel Browne for and towards his educac'on, payeing himself for his charges. This I would have done within one yeare after my decease. Item I give unto Samuell Browne one other sonne of my said sister Browne one hundred pounds in money The same to be imployed during his minority for his benefit as my Executor shall thinke most fitt. The Rectory of Nevorne in Pembrokeshire in Wales I give to my said Executor and heires for ev^r upon the trust and confidence that he shall make sale thereof assoone as conveniently he can and dispose the money arising by sale thereof and of the rents till yt be soulde for the p'formance of this my last Will and Testament. I give unto Thomas Grimsditch the eldest sonne of my brother Grimsditch whoe is now in the Isle of Providence the fourtie poundes p' ann. anuity which my lorde of Warwicke is to paye dureing the life of the said Thomas. I give to Thomas Allaby my servant One hundred pounds. To Jonas Anger tenn pounds p' ann. dureing his life. The said tenn pounds p' ann. to be yssueing out of my mannor of Stondon wth power to distreyne and a nomine pene of six pence per diem every daye that yt shall be unpayed within thirty daies after Michaelmas and our Lady day, my meaning being that yt shalbe payed him half yearly at the said Feasts and I give him tenn pounds in money. I give unto John .... my footeman tenn pounds in money and fourtie shillings a yeare during his life yssueing out of my said mannor to be payed half yearly as the other and with like power of distress and nomine pene not of vi^d a daye but of twelve pence a weeke for every weeke that yt shalbe behinde unpayed. All my goods, chattells, leases of what kinde or nature soever not formerly disposed of other then such legacies as hereafter I shall expresse either by worde before two credible witnesses or by handwriteing I give to my said Executor and his most noble Lady in testimony of my thankfullnes unto them for all their favours and of the humble and harty affecc'on I iustly beare unto them. I give unto William Jesopp more than formorly in my life tyme I have given him fyftie pounds. All my weareing lynnen and apparell I desire my Executor to distribute amongst my brother Grimsditch and my Servants according to his owne discretion wherein I would have Thomas Allabie that waites on me to be especially respected, onely one suite such as my Executor shall thinke fitt I give to Willm Jesopp. And whereas here is in Mr Goffes hands that was some tyme Steward to my lorde of Warwicke a Statute taken in his name for a thousand pounds debt are to my said Lord and myself fyve hundred pounds whereof being the one half belongs to me I doe hereby give unto that my deare and noble Lord the sayd fyve hundred pounds as a testimoney of my humble affection to him and thankfullnes for his love and favour towards me. Item I give unto the R^t Honoble my very noble Lord the Earle of Holland One hundred pounds and another hundred pounds to his noble Lady part of the money wch his lo^pp oweth me and fyftie pounds p'cell of the said debt to my noble Ladye the Lady Essex Cheek. The Drumond Ring wch I usually weare it being my sister Wrothes legacie to mee I give to my brother Wroth. My Emerod Ring wch I usually weare I give to my dear and most vertuous frend M^ris Mary Moore, Widdowe. I doe p'ticulerly give to my deare most noble and religious Lady the Lady Mandeville all that an'uity of One hundred and four score pounds and wch I purchased of my Lord of Warwicke yssuing out of certain lands in Norff. dureing the minority of Mr Hatton Riche for all the terme of years wch are yet to come. My Library bookes and papers I give to my said noble Lord the Lord Mandevill the sole Executor of this my last Will and Testament praying him that at least wth part of them he would furnish a

Library to be sett upp in the free Schoole at the Somer Islands as formerly I have appointed. The late Lady Warwick's picture I give unto my Lord Riche her Sonne. Item I give unto my worthy frend Mr Wharton Minister at Felsted in Essex thirtie pounds as a testimony of my spetial love unto him and thankfullnes for his care bestowed in the educac'on of my nephue Nathaniell Riche. Item I give unto my deare frend Mr John Pym my best gelding and a ring of twenty pounds wch I desire him to weare for my sake. I give unto my very loveing cosen Mrs Martha Willford twenty pounds to bestowe in a ring or what shee please as a remembrance of my love unto her. And to the end that my noble Lord whome I make sole Executor of this my last Will and Testament may be subject to the lesse trouble in the p'formance of this my Will I doe hereby declare my will and meaning to be that none unto whome I have given anything by this my Will shall take any benefitt thereby or have anything thereby bequeathed unles at the same time that my Executor doe affor payment unto any such person of any such legacie according to the expresse words of this my Will he or shee to whome the sayd legacie is tendered doe uppon demand of my said Executor tender likewise a generall acquittance and discharge to my said Executor of all further claymes and demaunds whatsoever for or concerning myself or anything p'tended to be further claymed by from or under me or my said Executor as Executor of this my last Will and Testament. In witness whereof and that this is my last Will and Testament though written in much hast I have subscribed to every page my name and all the p'misses are written wth my owne hand s'c'do Decembris 1635.

NA. RICHE.

This and noe other was acknowledged by the said Sr Nathaniell Riche, Knight, being in full and p'fect memory to be his last Will and Testament about the twenty eight of October 1636 before us vizt Thomas Wolrych, Carey Wolrych.

Mem°. That on Thursdaie the tenth daye of November Anno D'ni 1636 after the sealing and publishing of the Will and Testament of Sir Nathaniel Riche, Knight, dated the second daye of *November* 1635 the said Sir Nathaniel Riche did in the presence of the R^t Hono'ble the Lord Viscount Mandevill Executor of the last Will and Testam^t of the said Sir Nathaniel Riche as alsoe in the p'nce of William Jesopp and Thomas Allaby Servants of the said Sir Nathaniel Riche give and bequeath unto the said William Jessopp all the adventure that he the said Sir Nathaniel Riche then had in the Stocke of the Company of Marchants of the cittye of London tradeing into the East Indies. And he the saide Sir Nathaniell Riche did alsoe graunte unto the said William Jessopp the Tennancy of all that ferme lyeing in Stondon in the said Will menconed called Brooks tenement wch had beene purchased by the said Sir Nathaniel Riche since his purchase of the mannor of Stondon the said William Jesopp payeing for the same fortie shillings p' ann. and the quitt rent due from thence to the manno^r of Stondon aforesaid desireing the said L. Viscount Mandevill to make a lease thereof unto the said William Jessopp at the rents aforesaid. And did further expresse his intenc'on to graunt him interest in the said ferme upon the said rents dureing the naturall life of the said William Jessopp by saying that he would fayne have him the said William Jessopp to lyve there and the said Sir Nathaniell Riche did alsoe signifie his will to be that all the weareing apparell of him the said Sir Nathaniell Riche shalbe distributed unto Mr Thomas Grimsdich in the said Will menc'oned and unto the said Thomas Allaby and William Jessopp indifferently.

Probatum fuit testamentum sup'scriptum unacum Codicillo eidem annex apud London coram ven'li viro m'ro Thoma Eden legum d'core Surro^{to} ven^{lls} viri d'ni Henrici Marten Militis legum etiam doctoris Curiæ Prerogative Cant. m'ri Custodis sive comissarij etime constituti primo die mensis Decembris Anno D'ni mill'mo sexcen'mo tricesimo sexto juramento Honorandi viri Ed'ri D'ni Vice comitis Mandevill ex^{ris} in hu'mo'i testo nominat cui com'isa fuit administraco om' et singulor' bonor' jurin' et creditor' d'ci def't de bene et fideliter administrando eadem ad sancta Dei Evangelia Jurat.

[123, Pile.]

Family of Savage of Warwickshire.*

WILLS, GRANTS, ETC.

..nas Savage of Tachbrok Malory grants to John Olney and William nder one messuage in Tachbrok and another with a croft and four acres. ses : John Savage of Kyngton, Ric^d Savage of the same, Willm. Jennings same. Dated 17 March, 7th year of K. Hen. VII.

ohanna Gibbons of Ashorn, formerly wife of Richd Gibbons, quits claim to iam Savage of Ashorn, son and heir of John Savage, formerly of Bp's Tach- :e, of all claims which she had on the death of Henry Bate her brother in iorn. Witnesses : Richd Savage of Ashorn, John Savage of the same, Willm. mscote of the same, Willm. Smyth, Nicho. Andrews, Ric. Forster of the same. ited Thursday after the feast of the conception of the Blessed Virgin Mary,) year of King Edward the fourth.

William Savage son of John Savage of Tachbrok ep'i grants to William Com- mander of Chesterton half a messuage in Chesterton, in which the said William Commander now lives, and which came to the said William Savage after the death of his mother Juliana of Tachbrok. Witnesses : William White of Chesterton, John Robyns and John Beels of the same. Dated Thursday before the feast of Holy Trinity, 1461.

John Savage of Tachbroke Malory grants to Thomas Savage his son and to Matilda his wife all his lands in Tachbroke Malory and Tachbroke ep'i. Witnesses : Thomas Olney of Tachbroke ep'i, John Savage & Thos. Malory of the same, Robert Commander of Warwick. Dated Sunday after the feast of Tibunt & Valer. martyrs in the 37th year of K. Henry 6th.

Thomas Savage son and heir of Thomas Savage of Tachbroke ep'i, son & heir of John Savage of the same, confirms to Thomas Brynknell, Clerk, Thomas Blenkow, Robert Savage, William Jenens, and John Brynknell, as trustees, a messuage with half a virgate of arable land, together with meadows and pastures in Tachbroke aforesaid, to hold the same to the use of "Benedict Savage my heir," Robert Savage and Margaret Savage & their heirs. Witnesses : Ric^d Frenche, "Thomas Byshopp, Capellani," Richd Wylson. Dated 19 October, 7 year of K. Hen. VIII.
[N.B.—Though Thomas Savage calls Benedict Savage his heir, he does not state the relationship.]

John Mallore of Walton on the Wold in the County of Leicester, son & heir of John Mallore, armiger, deceased, & Joice my wife, quits claim to Benedict Medley of two messuages, one called Hancocks, the other Cadmans, in Tachbroke Mallore, now in the tenure of Matilda Savage, widow, and Richard Savage. Witnesses : Robert Savage, Ric^d Savage & Willm. Commander of Tachebroke ep'i, Willm. Wheler and Thos. Savage of Tachbroke Mallore. Dated 16 May in the ninth year of K. Hen. the seventh.

Richard Savage son of Thomas Savage, dead, lately of Tachbroke Mallore, grants to Benedict Medley of Whitenash a tenement in Tachbroke Mallore bounded by lands of the Abbey of Kenelworth & by lands of Benedict Medley. Witnesses : Robert Malbushe, Rich. Bradshaw, John Mason, & Wm Wheler. Dated 13 March in the eleventh year of K. Hen. the seventh.

* Communicated by Rev. R. E. H. DUKE, Rector of Maltby, Lincolnshire—continued from p. 4.

Matilda Savage, lately wife of Thomas Savage, dead, formerly of Tachbroke Mallore, quits claim to Benedict Medley of Whitnash of a tenement in Tachbroke Malore, which was once John Savage's and afterwards Thomas Savage's my husband. Witnesses : Rob[t] Malbushe, W[m] Wheler, John Mason. Dated 15 March in the eleventh year of K. Hen. the seventh.

Will of W[m] Savage of Newbold Pacye, dated 15 October 1546 ; proved the same year. To his sons Lawrence & Richard Savage £3 6s. 8d. each ; to his daus. Agnes Ingrame & Katherine Wirrall 40s. each ; to the two sons of his son John Savage 40s. each ; to the daus. of his son John Savage, Jane & Ellen, 40s. each ; to his sisters Agnes & Jane 10s. To Moreton Morrell Church, to Wellesburne Church, to Charlecote Church, 3s. 4d. each. To be buried at Newbald among his children & kinsfolk. Residue to his wife Jane. Debts owing to testator, Leonard Savage 8s., etc. Inventory £64. (Testamenta Vetusta, Worcester Probate Court, vol. 5, p. 155.)

Will of Jane Savage of Neubald Pacy, dated 8 July 1548 ; proved 8 Nov. 1548. To Laurence Savage my son £3 ; to Agnes Ingram & Kath. Wyrrall my daus. £3 each ; to the two sons of my son John, now deceased, 20s. over & above my husband's will ; to daus. of the said John, Jane & Ellen, 6s. 8d. each. My son Richard my residue & I make him executor. Debts, Leonard Savage of Kington 40s. Inventory £18 7s. (*Ibid.*, vol. 5, p. 247a.)

John Savage of Mooreton Morrell, yeoman, son & heir of Thomas Savage formerly of Newbald Pacye, yeoman, now dead, in execution of the will of his late father the said Thomas Savage, grants to William Frecleton of the town of Warwick & to Alice his wife, formerly the wife of Edward Savage, deceased, younger son of the said Thomas Savage and also brother to John Savage, and he grants to Agnes Savage daughter to the said Edward Savage and Alice one messuage & nine virgates of land in Buttelers Marston, now in the tenure of John Tubb, to have & to hold the said messuage and nine virgates to W[m] Frecleton & Alice his wife during the life of Alice Frecleton, and after the death of the said Alice Frecleton then to Agnes Savage and her issue, failing such issue to the heirs of John Savage aforesaid. Dated 14 January 1563 in the sixth year of Q. Elizabeth.

Thomas Savage of Cotteruppe in the parish of Banbury in the county of Oxford grants for £45 to John Savage of Moreton Morell, yeoman, a tenement messuage with pastures & meadows in Bishop's Tachbrook alias Fysher's Tachbroke in the tenure of Robert Mawbushe. Dated v[th] March in the fourteenth year of Q. Elizabeth.

Thomas Fysher of the town of Warwick, Esquire, bargains to sell to John Savage of Moreton Morrell a barn and a close in Fysher's Tachbroke in the tenure of Richard Cootes. Dated 1 July in the fourteenth yeare of Queen Elizabeth. [Autograph signature of Tho. Fisher with heraldic seal, a griffin segreant within a bordure vair.]

A fine at Westminster 8 Hillary, 15 year of Queen Elizabeth, between John Savage the demandant and Thomas Savage and Margaret his wife, and Robert Savage son & heir of the said Thomas the tenant, of one messuage, garden, orchard, 20 acres of arable, and 20 acres of pasture in Bp's Tachbrooke, £40.

Articles of Agreement made & set down 20 April in foure & fourtieth yere of Queen Elizabeth, between William Savage of Tachbrooke ep'i, gent., on the one part, & Richard Lane of Brydgetown & Richard Vener of Wellesborne Hastings, gentlemen, of the other part, in consideration of a marriage to be solemnized betwixt William Savage and Alice Faukener of Tiddington in the parish of Alveston, widow. William Savage covenants to bring up and school William Faukener son & heir of Wm Faukener, deceased, late of Tiddington, and also to maintain Marye Faukener sister of Wm Faukener during their nonage. Also the said Wm Savage will keep in repair all buildings in the tenure of Alice Faukener during the minority of the heir.

Fine dated 15 days from S. Martin, 39 Queen Elizabeth, between Thomas Savage, Edmond Hudson & Thomas Ladbrok, qu., and John Stamp & Isabella his wife, def., of 3 messuages, 3 gardens, 3 orchards, 120 acres of arable, 15 acres of meadow, 50 acres of pasture in Teddington, Alveston, Stoneley, & Cubbington. The Court recognized that it was the property of Thomas Savage and that land which Thos., Edmond, & Thomas Ladbroke had by gift of the said John & Isabella, who quit claim in the same for £160.

John Eydes of Ashorne, gent., & Margaret Eydes his wife grants to Thomas Savage of Tachbrooke ep'i, yeoman, a messuage with garden adjoining and 20 acres of land in Tachbrooke in the occupation of Hugh Fletcher, Vicar of Tachbrooke. Dated 20 Sept. in thirty-eighth of Queen Elizabeth.
Peaceable possession was given in the presence of Roger Reading, Will. Reading, William Savage, John Savage, Thomas Pratt, and Thomas Savage, junior, son of the said Thomas Savage.
The deed is endorsed: The deed of the messuage & xx acres of lande in Tachbrooke wch I bought of Mr John Eydes.

Articles agreed upon between William Savage of Tachbrooke ep'i, yeoman, and Richard Savage his son and heir, on the one part, and Ralphe Lees of Lightorne, Clerk, on the other part. In consideration that the said Ralphe Lees did pay the sum of Two hundred Pounds to the said William Savage and Richard his son for the portion of Marie Lees daughter of the said Ralphe, who did become wife to the said Richard, the said William Savage & Richard his son doth grant to the said Ralphe Lees that the said Ralphe Lees shall have liberty to pass over that ground of William Savage's and Richard Savage's called Cleatthill. Dated 20 January in the 10 year of K. Charles, 1634.

Indenture between Humanitas Jackson the elder, of Ashorne, husbandman, of the first part, William Jackson of Ashorne, eldest son of the said Humanitas Jackson, & Alice Savage of Tachbrook ep'i, spinster, one of the daughters of William Savage of Tachbrook, gent., of the second part, and the said William Savage of Tachbrook and Richard Jackson of Whitnash, husbandman, of the third part, witnesseth that whereas the said Humanitas Jackson the elder in consideration of a marriage to be solemnized between the said William Jackson and the said Alice Savage. Her portion was £150. Dated 11 June in the eighteenth year of K. Charles, 1642.

Indenture between Daniel Eyres of Whitnash, Clerk, on the one part, and Richard Savage of Bp's Tachbrooke and Mary his wife, William Savage son and heir apparent of the said Richard Savage, on the other part, in consideration of a marriage intended to be solemnized between the said William Savage and Elizabeth Eyres eldest daughter of the said Daniel Eyres. Dated 16 April 1656.

Indenture between Elizabeth Randoll of Preston Bagot, widow, late wife of Robert Randoll, of the first part, William Randoll of Preston Bagot, gent., one of the sons of the said Robert Randoll, and Robert Randoll, Thomas Randoll, James Randoll, and Joseph Randoll, brothers of the said William Randoll, of the 2nd part, and Richard Savage of Tachbrooke, gent., and William Knight of the Midle

Temple, London, gent., and Mabell Savage daughter of the said Richard Savage, of the 3rd part, witnesseth in consideration of a marriage to be solemnized between the said William Randoll and Mabell Savage.   Her portion was £280.   Dated 18 June in the two & thirtieth year of Charles II., 1680.

Indenture dated 1 June 1656 between William Savage the younger of Bp's Tachbrooke, on the one part, and Richard Savage of Bp's Tachbrooke, father of the said William Savage, relates to a yearly rent.

[DRAFT COPY.]   Between William Savage the elder of Bp's Tachbrooke, gent., of the one part, and George Commander, yeoman, of the other part.   Whereas by an indenture tripartite dated 22 October 1688, being the fourth year of K. James II., made between James Bullock of Pelshall in the county of Stafford, yeoman, & Anne his wife, of the first part, Wm Savage the elder of Bp's Tachbrooke, gent., since dead, and the said Wm Savage, party to this indenture by the then name of Wm Savage the younger, son & heir of the said Wm Savage the elder, & Mary the wife of the said Wm Savage the younger, being sole daughter & heir of the said James Bullock, of the 2nd part, and Thomas Wagstaffe of Tachbrooke Mallory, Esqre, and John Fowler of Pelsall, yeoman, of the third part, the said Wm Savage the elder, dead, & the said Wm Savage parts to these presents did grant to Thos. Wagstaffe & John Fowler the draft proceeds to recite the above mentioned deed whereby power was given to raise portions for the younger children on lands in Hampton Lucy & Tachbrooke not exceeding £400, & it now raises £100 for the portion of Elizabeth Savage one of the daughters of Wm Savage.   Dated 1712.

Articles agreed upon between George Commander of Bp's Tachbrooke, yeoman, of the one part, and William Savage the elder & William Savage the younger, both of Bp's Tachbrooke, gentlemen, of the other part.   Whereas a marriage is intended to be solemnized between the said George Commander and Elizabeth Savage one of the daughters of the said William Savage the elder.   Her portion £120.   Dated 5 Dec. in the eleventh year of Q. Anne, 1712.

I, George Bryers of Rowington in the county of Warwick, yeoman, have received of William Savage of Bp's Tachbrook the sum of £100, being part of the marriage portion of Anne Savage one of the daughters of the said Wm Savage.   Dated 19 July in 12th year of K. Charles, 1636.

A bond of Wm Savage's of the town of Warwick, Blacksmith.   The condition is such that whereas Anne Savage of the town of Warwick, widow, mother of the above-mentioned William Savage, hath delivered to the said William Savage by her deed, bearing date with these presents, all such goods now in the custody of the said Anne Savage to hold to him the said William that he shall on the death of the said Anne Savage deliver unto William Savage, Thomas Savage, Anne Savage, and Alice Savage, four of the children of the above mentioned William Savage, etc.   Witness : Edward Savage.   Dated 22 January 1629.

The will of Humanitas Jackson, dated 5 May, 33 K. Chas. II., 1681, but with no probate ; apparently an original will, signed with his mark and seal, On a chevron three garbs on a canton.   Crest : A Stag.   Humanitas Jackson of Bp's Tachbrooke gives to his cousin William Savage, senr, all his freehold house & land about 43 acres in Tachbrooke ; to his brother Wm Jackson £20 and household goods ; to his sister Elizabeth Comley wife of Clement Comley 40 shillings yearly, to be paid by Wm Savage.   Executor Wm Savage.

Charles Savage of London, Merchant Taylor, nominates my father William Savage of Bp's Tachbrooke to take possession of one tenement & forty acres of land in Bp's Tachbrooke.   Dated 20 April in 6th year of K. Wm & Q. Mary, 1694.

Samuel Carte, Prebendary of Bp's Tachbrooke, grants letters to administer the goods of Mary Savage, widow, late of Bp's Tachbrooke, to her son Charles Savage. Dated 9 August 1733.

Will of Richard Savage of Tachbrooke ep'i, dated 20 Dec. 1682 ; proved 3 Dec. 1684 (Somerset House, Hans, 167). Richard Savage of Tachbrooke, gent., to his eldest son William Savage all his corn on his estate at Tachbrooke ; to his grandson Wm Savage the younger his land in Hampton Lucy, but said William to pay £50 to his younger brother Richard Savage. To his wife Mary all his interest in the lands of his son-in-law John Chebsey of Ladbrooke in trust for his dau. Hester wife of said John Chebsey. Mary his wife & Sarah Savage his dau. to be executrices. His son-in-law Wm Randle & Joseph Trebell, Vicar of Tachbrook, to be overseers.

Will of William Savage, dated 8 April, 12 K. George, 1726 ; proved at Doctors' Commons by Charles Savage 3 October 1726. William Savage of Tachbrook ep'i, gent., devises to his brother Charles Savage all his tenement in Tachbrooke where he dwells in, all his lands in that parish, & to the heirs male of the said Charles Savage, & for want of such issue then to his brother John Savage & his issue male, & for want of such issue then to his own heirs-at-law ; to his sister Mary Savage £100 ; to his sister Hannah Savage £100 ; to his brother John £100 ; to his honoured mother Mary Savage some furniture. Sole executor his brother Charles Savage.

Admission to Guild of Holy Cross, Stratford-on-Avon.

9 Edw. IV.   Thomas Savage, Tachbrooke, & Matilda his wife.
—   —   John Savage, Tachbrooke Mallory, & Joan his wife.
10 Edw. IV. John Savage, Kington, & Alice his wife.

10 October 37 Eliz. [1595]. Indenture tripartite bet^n Thos Savage, Bishoppes Tachebroke al's ffishers Tachebroke, co. War., yeoman, 1st pt., John Murcott, Lemyngton Priors, co. War., yeoman, & Edward Murcott, Tachebroke Malory, co. War., yeoman, 2nd pt., & Thomas Sewell, Byfeild, in co. Northampton, yeoman, 3^d pt. In consideration of a marriage already had & solemnized bet^n s^d Thos Savage and Hope his now wife & for a competent & sufficient jointure to be had or made sure to the s^d Hope, And for & in consideration of the natural good will, fatherly love & affection wh. the s^d Thos Savage beareth unto his several sons hereafter named & for their better preferm^t & maintain^e in living after the decease of the s^d Thos S. & for the continuance of s^d lands, etc., hereafter ment^d in the name, blood stock & kindred of the s^d Thos S., it is fully agreed by & bet^n all the s^d parties to these present Ind^s as follows : Thos S. covenants for himself & heirs, etc., with s^d John Murcot, Edw. Murcot, & Thos Sewell that he will on this side & before 1st March next ensuing above date suffer the s^d J. M., E. M. & T. S. in a writ of "Entrie sur disseisin in le post" to be had & prosecuted ag^t s^d T. S. according to the usual form of common recoveries for assurance of lands, etc., to recover ag^t him the s^d Thos Savage all & singular the messuages, cottages, lands, etc., of the s^d Thos S. whatsoever being in the several towns, parishes, hamlets, & fields of Bp's Tachebrooke al's Fisher's Tach^{ke}, Bradwell, Alveston, Tidington, Barton, & Lemington in co. War., by such name or names as shall be devised or appoint^d by s^d T. S. or his counsel learned .... viz., a mess^{ge} & close adj^g in Bp's Tach^{ke} occup^d by T. S., & in the uppermost lot in Bp's T. called Cotepeeces, 2 closes in Bp's T. called Clete Hill, one half of the meadow in Bp's T. in tenure of s^d T. S. for his life, after his death to use of Hope his wife for life if she lives sole & unmarried ; after her death or marriage to the use of Wm Savage, son & heir appar^t of s^d T. S., & the heirs male of his body ; for default to John Savage, second son of s^d T. S. ; for default to Thos Savage, 3rd son ; for default to s^d Thos S. the

father & his heirs for ever. In all o'r mess^{ges}, etc., in Tach^{ke} not limited to s^d Hope to the use of s^d Thos the father for his nat^l life & after to s^d W^m ; for def^t to John ; for def^t to Thos & for def^t to s^d father & heirs for ever . . . . & of & in one half deale of messuages, etc., in Alveston, Tidington, to s^d Thos the father for life, then to Hope his wife for life if she lives unmarr^d (repitition of above conditions) & of & in the other half moiety of mess^{ges}, etc., in Alveston, etc., to use of s^d Thos S. for life, then to John S. his son ; for default to W^m ; for def^t to Thos ; for def^t to s^d father & heirs . . . . & of & in the half of mess^{ges}, etc., in Lemington & Bradwell to use of s^d Thos, then Hope his wife (as before), at her death to Thos the son, & for def^t to W^m, & for def^t to s^d John ; for def^t to Thos the father & his heirs . . . . & of & in the o'r half in Lemington & B. to use of father Thos, then to Thos the son & heirs ; in def^t to W^m & h^s ; in def^t to John & h^s ; for def^t to father & his heirs . . . . & of & in mess^{ges}, etc., in Barton to s^d Thos the father & his heirs for ever. Proviso that T. S. can alter above arrangem^t if he chooses on certain usual conditions.

Signed by John & Edwd Murcott & Thos Sewell. Seals [not armorial].

Witnesses: Fra. Levinge, John Eyres, Willm Briscooe, Tho. Master's mark, Roger Reding's mark.

[This deed is in the possession of Mr. Richard Savage, Librarian of Shakespeare's Birthplace.] (To be continued.)

Memoranda of William Curtoys,

1670—1752.*

[NOTE.—These Memoranda are contained in a very small note-book, measuring 4½ by 3 inches, which has been carefully preserved. The writing is usually clear and good, but occasionally much cramped. The order, it will be seen, is not always strictly chronological. The entries printed first are entirely of a family nature ; those beginning at the other end of the book and printed second are more general, though they begin with the solemn and interesting record of the renewal of the baptismal vow and reception of the Holy Eucharist by the writer on the twenty-first anniversary of his baptism. That and the earlier entries are in Latin, the rest in English. The Rev. W. F. CURTOYS will be glad to communicate with any reader who can throw light upon persons or families herein alluded to.]

Mr Lamplugh died No^r 3^d, 1737.
10^{br}, 31, 1733, Charles went to Alton, and in 1737-8 to Wott.†
Came up June 1, 1734.
21 July, went down ; ret^d Aug. 10 ; went out town 27 Nov^r.
Sepr 1734. Mr Balls in town.
27 June 1736. Din'd at Paddington.
Mrs Wilson with Mr Reeks.
23, at Daugh^r, 5 . 6 ; ano^r, 2 . 6.

(Page 15).—Son Charles married, May ye 1st, 1739, to Elizath, Daug^r of Mr Hunt of Wooton Rivers.
His Daug^r Ann born Aprill ye 5th, 1740.
June 16th, 1745. In night Charles' son Charles born ; died 21st, and Daug^r Elizabeth died 22nd, and both buried in one Coffin. June 19th, 1750, at 5 aft^r noon was his son born and nam'd Charles.
Son Charles, wife, & daug^r came to town 11 Oct. 1743 ; went out of town 15 No^r 1743.

* Communicated by the Rev. W. F. CURTOYS, Coleby Vicarage, Lincoln—continued from p. 37.
† Is this for Wootton (Rivers) ?

1748, Ap^ll 21. Charles daug^r in town with her Aunt Cook; went home May 6th, '48.

Son George married to Mrs Ann Davis, Daug^r of Widow Davis, 27 Novr 1744, and I hope God will give them an happy life together in Love and Unity.

(Page 16).—29 March 1745. Died son George's wife's mother, of an apoplexy, aged 61; bur^d 3 Ap^l at St Bart^w's, Smithfield-great.

Charles Churchill, son of d^o, born 2^d of May 1746, ¾ aft^r 7 in ye morning; Bap. 26th.

Comp. {
Mr Chas. Davis.
Mr Branch.
Mrs Churchill.

Peter, son of d^o, born 28th of November 1747 at 11 at night; died Dec. 6th, aged 8 days.

11th July '48. Mrs Davis, grandmother to son Geo. wife, died ætat. 88; Buried in St Andrew's, Holborn, Churchyard.

Mr Branch died Ap^l 19, 1750.

(Page 17).—July ye 30, 1751, ½ hour past 8 morning, Ann Daug^r of Son Georg. was born; bapt. Aug. 5th, 1751.

Com.   Mr Pratt.
Mrs Branch.
M. Davis.

[In another hand.] William Curtoys, the writer of these observations, died Nov. 13th, 1752, aged 82. Buried at Paddington [pencilled out by someone].

[BEGINNING AT OTHER END.]

(Page 1, on fly-leaf*).—

Christ's Hospital. Mem.: 1739, July 20th.

Mr Heatherly, m^r, Mr Shipton, 2nd m^r, Gram^r School. Mr Durnford, writing master. Mr Morris, w. master, Hertford.

Nurse Notier's ward.

Trustees of Lady Nevil's Charity: The Archbp. of Cant.; Sr Thomas Hanmer; Dr Hutchinson, D.D.; Dr Smith, provost Queens; Hon. Edwd Digby; .... Hulls, Esqre, Han^r St.; D^r P(?)elling, St Ann's.

For violent looseness: 15 drops of liquid Laudinum in a dram cinnamon water.

(Page 2, really page 1).—Memorandum me 20mo die 7^bris anno d'm'ni 1691 solemniter meum votum et fœdus baptismale renovare accipiendo Sanctam Eucharistiam et tunc meipsum in Dei latram devovere ab quâ haud unquam discedere (gratiâ ejus adjurante) stat mihi sententia, sed semper servum Salvatoris mei Jesu Christi fidelem manere in cujus rei memoriâ idem descripsi; et nomen adposui.

Ita juvet me Deus.

W^m C̄o Curtoys

(Page 3).—Memorand^m. Novembris 5to, 1688. King W^m landed in England Feb^{ry} 13°, '88. Kg. W^m & Q. Mary were proclaimed.

10^{br} ye 11th, '88. An Alarm was throughout England at which time King James abdicated his Throne and went to France.

June ye 10th, '88. The Prince of Wales (as so said) was born at St James.

Ap^l ye 11th, '89. King Willm & Queen Mary were crowned.

Queen Mary died 28 Decr 1694 ; buried at Westm^r Abbey March 5, '94-5.

———

(Page 4).—Mem. Feb^{ry} ye 6th, '84-5. King Charles ye 2^d dyed ; King James 2^d was proclaimed ye same day.

1683-4. The great frost from November till March, in all 6 weekes, at wh. time ye River Thames was frozed over.

1685. The Rebellion in ye west by ye Duke of Monmouth, who was beheaded 15° Julii 1685.

June ye 8th, 1688. The A.-B. of Cant. and 6 other Bishops were sent to ye Tower because they would not read the Declaration.

———

(Page 5).—July 24, 1689. W^m, Duke of Gloucester, son to Prince George & Princess Ann, was born ; dyed August 9th, 1700, æt. 11 yrs. 16 days.

August 7, 1714, died Queen Anne. King George proclaimed ; crown'd 20 Oct. 1714.

July. King George dyed at his Brot^r's June 11, 1727, in Germany. July ye 15 King George 2nd proclaimed.

20 No^r 1737 died Queen Caroline, ab^t 11 at night ; buried at Westm^r.

———

(Page 6).—Tuesday, Feb^{ry} ye 7th, 1698. A great Wind which did much damage, in blowing up trees and down chimnies and killd many and hurt many.

Feb. 28th, a Fire in St Paul's Church.

March ye 16th, '98. A great Fish brot^t up the river, 50 foot long, 12 feet broad, & 6 thick.

March 8th, 1701, King William ye 3^d dyed. Queen Ann proclaimed rgⁿ ; crowned April 23^d, 1702.

Nov^{br} 27th, 1703. A great Wind, S.S.W., which did more mischief than any in ye memory of Man.

Ap. 8 (?), 1715. A remarkable Eclipse of the Sun, almost total.

———

(Page 7).—1704, 9^{br} ye 2nd. Y^e Chappell in Russell C^t was taken for 70 7 years. Opened May 27, 1705.

Mr English died March 31st, 1712.

Mrs English died March 3^d, 1717-18 ; buried at Barnes.

Mr J^{no} Edwards dyed 29 Feb. ; buried at Wickham 1723-4.

Mrs Ann Power, Daughter of Sist^r Hulbert, dyed 11th July 1725 ; buried at St George's, South(? wark), July 16th, 1725.

Mr Richd Nelson dyed July 14th, 1725 ; buried at Marylebone.

Coz' The. Wells died at Earl Soham Feb. 1727.

———

(Page 8).—Aunt Whitehal died Jan. 17, 1715-16.

Sist^r Edith Spicer died Augt 4, 1713 ; buried·in St Bride's.

Sist^r Hulbert died Xmas 1714 ; buried St George's, Southwark.

Uncle Tho. Welles died Augt 3rd, 1716 ; buried at Br . . . . dish,* Suffolk. Sist^r Bartlet died May 26th, 1751.†

Brot^{hr} Bartlet died March 1st, 1716-17 ; buried Cov^t Garden. Sister Bartlet died 26 Feb. 1752.†

* There is Brockdish, Norfolk (?).
† Inserted later.

Coz[n] John Welles dyed August y[e] 28th, 1721 ; buried in S[t] Peter's Church, Ipswich, y[e] 31st, 1721, north side next wall, Chancel end.

Brother Richard Spicer br' al's Helder, ob[t] 28th [sic] 1724 ; sep. at S[t] Andrew Wardrobe Churchyard.

(Page 9).—1721. Tabernacle built and preached in August 1st, 1721.

S[t] Martin's Church 1721-2, first stone laid March y[e] 26th, 1721-2 ; weath[r] cock erected 10[br] 1724 ; consecrated 26th Oct[r] 1726.

Sep. 8th, 1725. A fire at London Bridge that burnt down M[r] Usborn's house and 40 more.

Coz[n] Theod[e] Welles dyed Feb. 1727 at Earl Soham.

Sister Mary Spicer died Jan[ry] 7th, 1730, at night ; buried at S[t] Martin's.

Novr 7th, 1747. Mr Prisset died, age 78.

(Page 10).—Ann Meadows, Daught[r] of Son Welles, born June 21, 1736 ; bap. 11 July.   Mr Cammalt.

                                                                                              Mrs Meadows.

Died 14 July, buried at Paddington 15th, ætat. 23 dies.   Mrs Rogers.

Mary wife of my Son Welles died 26 No[r] 1736 ; buried at Paddington 30th, aged 24 years 4 months 11 days.

Mary her Daug[r] died 27th of Augt 1741 ; buried at Paddington 30, ætat. 7 years 9 mon. 19 days.

Jo. Meadows died Lady [sic] '45.

Mrs Ward died Jan. 11, '45-6.

Son Welles died May 16, '46 ; buried Paddington 19th, aged 39 y[rs].

(?) 15 . 3 . 6, charges by George.

(Page 11).—Daughter went to Bury August 30th, 1738 ; in town & here Oct. 1st. 6th, Charles and she came.

He preached 8th ; 16th took leave.

Jo[h] Curtoys bound ap. Lady Day '47 ; went aboard for Spain No[r] 3, '48.

W[m] Curtoys bound Apprentice to M[r] Brown July 19th, 1749.

Daug[r] went to Bury June 25th, 1742 ; returned July 29th.

Daug[r] went to Wootton '45, July y[e] 17th ; '45, returned Aug[t] 23.

1746, son Charles came to see me Aug[t] 26th ; tar[d] to 5 Sep. ; ill.

Daught. Web[r] went to Bury 3 July 1747 ; lay at son Geo. ; ret[d] Aug. 4 ; slept at Son's . . . . ; chicken & duck bro[t] up with her.

Mrs Meadows died Mar. 11, '47-8 ; buried at S[t] Giles' 15th, ætat. 60 & ½.

(Page 12).—June 20th-1st, 1721. Stone laid in the new Church by Hanover Square ; consecrated East[r] 1725 and divided from S[t] Martin's.

Coz. Eliz. Curtoys died No[r] 5th, 1718, Wilford.[*]

Coz[n] Dorothy Curtoys died at Wilford August ye 4th, 1728 ; buried at Wilf'd 6th.

Coz[n] Jacob Silverwood died y[e] 1st August 1728 ; buried at Epperston.

Coz[n] James Graves died y[e] . . day of Oct[r] 1728 at Yarmouth.

M[rs] Balls died Ap[l] 1750 [added].

Coz[n] Rebecca Janes died 22nd July 1731 ; bu. 25 Epper[n].

(Page 13).—Jan. 8th, 1734. A great storm of wind, W.S.W., which did great Damage.

Coz. Mary Glass died 20 March 1735-6 ; buried 22 at the grand new Church, Broadway, West[r].

Bp. of Eley died 18th May 1738.[†]

---

* This entry is wrongly dated, for Wilford Register has: "Buried M[rs] Elizabeth Curtoys, Oct. 11, 1717 ;" and tombstone : "M[rs] Eliz. Curtoys, Oct. y[e] 10th, 1717."

† Thomas Green, Bishop of Ely 1723-38.

Mrs Larmouth died 20th May 1738 ; buried at St Cath^{ns} 25 d°.
Mr Larmouth died March 20, 1740 [added later].
Octo^r 23, 1739. War declared ag^t Spain.
31 May 1744. War dec^d ag^t France [added later].
A Frost began 26th of Decr and lasted to ye 26th of Feb^{ry} 1739. The Thames froze over.
(July, a great eclipse of Sun.)
Sat^{day}, 1st No^r, 1740, at night a great hurricane of Wind, and blew down ye Garden Wall ; 6th, and a Fire near us in ye Borough.

(Page 14).—Mrs Webster, wife of Mr Wm Webster, died 25th March 1743 ; buried at St Martin's.
Mr Wm Webster died 28th of June 1744 ; buried ye 1st of July at St Martin's.
Mr Geo. Webster died May 26th, '48 [added later].
29 Ap. 1745. A man rode from Stilton in Huntingdonshire and back again and ret^d to London, being 213 miles, in 12 hours 20 minutes.
In Augt 1745 some men landed in the Isle of Skey in Scotland ; and the Clans in the highlands joynd and a Rebellion broke out ; and march'd into Edinburgh and other Towns and proclaimed the Pretender, and took Carlisle and march'd into England as far as Lancaster and Chesh^{re} and Staffordsh^{re} and proceeded to Derby, ec^t.

(Page 15).—16 April 1746. Near Inverness a great Battle at Cullodon heath, and were defeated.
July 15. Began to try some of y^{em} taken. Townley found guilty.
16. 3 more d°.
27th. More tried after and found guilty, in all 17 ; rec^d Sentence and ordered to be executed.
Feby 2nd, 1748. A gen^l peace proclaimed wth France and Spain and Italy.
March 20, 1750-51, the Prince of Wales died ; buried Ap. 6th, '51.

(Page 16).—July 28, 1746. The 3 Lds. tryal began in Westm^r Hall.
Aug. 18. Ld. Kilmarock and Ld. Balmerino were beheaded.
Mar. 20, '46. Simon, Ld. Lovat, rec. Sentence of Death.
Mr Radclif beheaded '47, Jan.
Ap. 9. Ld. Lovat beheaded.
25 March 1748. A great fire in Exchange Alley in Cornhill, and burnt to St Michael's Church ; wind S.W., high.
14 July '48. Eclipse of Sun.
Feb^{ry} 8th, 1749. About noon a Shock of an Earthquake was felt about London and parts adjacent, and a star like a comet seen in the west.
March 8th, about 6 in morn^g, another Shock.

(Page 17).—Daught^r Webster went out of town wth Mr Robert Webster in his Chase to Mr Haws in Berks^r May ye 16th, 1750 ; from thence to Charles ; 19th at Wooton ; returned 30th June.
Sept^r '50. Grandson Wm Curtoys came home to Mr Meadows ill of a cold and exchanged Ind^{rs}, and Mr Brown paid him back the money, being 20^l ; his mast^r prison^r in Fleet ; went again July 1751 to Mr Brown.
Sepr 1751. Granddaug^r came to town wth Mr Webster, after a month's stay at son Charles, Wilts.
Rec^d Octr ye 25th, 1751, a lett^r from son Charles y^t he had got the Curacy of Hewish to hold with Wootton.
July 16th, 1752. Daug^r Webster and her niece went into Wilts to her Brot^{rs}.
21, rec^d a L^r.

Marriages of Wandsworth Inhabitants.*

EXTRACTS FROM REGISTERS IN VARIOUS PARISHES.

1738, May 15.   JOHN GREEN of Wandsworth in the County of Surry, Batchelor, & CATHERINE CLEAR of Clapham in the County aforesaid, Spinster ; by licence. (Clapham.)

173⅜	Jan. 25	Henry, son of John and Catherine Green, bapt.
1740	July 22	Richard, son of John and Catherine Green, bapt.
1741	Nov. 9	Mary, daughter of John and Catherine Green, bapt.
1743	April 21	John, son of John and Catherine Green, bapt.
1745	Sep. 10	Elisabeth, daughter of John and Catherine Green, bapt.
1747	April 30	Rebecca, daughter of John and Catherine Green, bapt.
174⁹⁄₁₀	Jan. 22	Thomas, son of John [altered from Thomas] and Catharine Green, bapt.
1754	April 1	Catherine, daughter of John and Catherine Green, bapt.
1740	Nov. 11	Richard, inf. son of John Green, bur.
1745	Sep. 11	Elisabeth, inf. daughter of John Green, bur.
1747	Nov. 29	Henry, son of John Green, 8, bur.
1757	Nov. 11	Catherine, inf. daughter of John and Mary [sic] Green, bur.

1738, Nov. 28.   RICHARD HUGHES of the Parish of Saint Saviour, Southwark, in the County of Surry, Batchelor, & ELIZABETH ESSINGTON of Wandsworth in the same County, Spinster ; by the Reverend Mr Cawley, Vicar of Wandsworth ; by licence. (Clapham.)

1714	Oct. 19	Elizabeth, daughter of Mr John Essington, bapt.
1751	Sep. 15	Thomas, son of Richard and Elizabeth Hughes, bapt.

1738, Dec. 14.   WILLIAM HEATH of the Parish of Wandsworth in the county of Surry, Widower, & SARAH COMMINS of the same Parish, Spinster ; licence. (Clapham.)

[Burial of first wife.]

173⁴⁄	Mar. 5	Frances, wife of William Heath.

[Children of second marriage.]

17³⁹⁄₄₀	Mar. 19	Thomas, son of William and Sarah Heath, bapt.
1741	July 3	Sarah, daughter of William and Sarah Heath, bapt.
1743	Oct. 23	Mary, daughter of William and Sarah Heath, bapt.
1745	July 14	William Heath, bur.

1740, July 6.   WILLIAM NELSON of Wandsworth in the County of Surry, Batchelor, & MARY BULL of the Parish of St Botolph, Bishopsgate, London, Spinster ; by the Rev. Mr Cawley, Vicar of Wandsworth ; by licence. (Clapham.)

174¹⁶	Mar. 19	William, son of Thomas Nelson, bapt.
1742	June 22	Mary, daughter of William and Mary Nelson, bapt.
1743	Oct. 11	Fanny, daughter of William and Mary Nelson, bapt.
1747	June 2	Thomas, son of William and Mary Nelson, bapt.
1743	May 18	Mary, daughter of William Nelson, senr., bur.
1747	Sep. 11	Thomas, inf. son of William Nelson, bur.
1747	Nov. 19	Mary, wife of William Nelson, bur.

[His parents were married at Clapham 29 Jan. 1711-12, see ante, Vol. IV., p. 172.]

---

* Communicated by CECIL T. DAVIS, Esq.—continued from p. 33.

1741, June 27. THOMAS WILLIAMSON of Wandsworth in the County of Surry, Batchelor, & CHRISTIANA STEPHENSON of the Parish of Saint Edmund the King, London, Widow ; by licence. (Clapham.)

1744 Mar. 11 Thomas an inf. son of Thomas Williamson, bur.
1761 Nov. 1 Thomas Williamson, bur. [His will in P.C.C., Cheslyn, 413.]
1785 Oct. 15 Christiana Williamson, 89, bur.

[Tomb in Mount Nod :—Thomas Williamson, | late of this Parish, Esq., | Citizen of London & Scarlet Dyer, | Died the 20ᵗʰ of October 1761, | Aged 48 years.

Thomas, son of the above | Died the 21ˢᵗ of March 1744 | Æt. 11 months.

Mʳˢ Christiane Williamson, | Wife of the above Thomas Williamson, Esq., | Died the 8ᵗʰ of October 1785 |·Aged 79 years. (See " Mount Nod," by J. T. Squire.)]

1741, July 12. JESSE TREDWELL of Wandsworth in the county of Surry, Batchelor, & ELIZABETH WHITMORE of the same Parish, Spinster ; by the Revᵈ Mʳ Cawley, Vicar of Wandsworth ; licence. (Clapham.)

1745 June 13 Joseph, son of Jesse and Elisabeth Tredwell, bapt.
1747 June 21 William, son of Jesse (deceased) and Elisabeth Tredwell, bapt.
1747 May 27 Jesse Tredwell, bur.

1741, Sep. 29. JOHN OVER of the Parish of Wandsworth, Batchelor, & ANN CLAPHAM of this parish, Widow ; by licence ; by Thoˢ Church, Vicar. (Battersea.)

1741, Dec. 14. JOHN DAVIS of Battersea in the County of Surry, Batchelor, & SUSANNA DOBSON of Wandsworth in the said County of Surry, widow ; by the Revᵈ Mʳ Cawley, Vicar of Wandsworth ; by licence. (Clapham.)

1743, Sep. 18. BENJAMIN PHILLIPS of the Parish of Wansworth in the County of Surry, Batchelor, & ANNE CUTTER of the same Parish, Spinster ; by the Revᵈ Mʳ Cawley, Vicar of Wandsworth ; by licence. (Clapham.)

1716 April 25 Benjamin, son of William Philips, bapt.
1744 Aug. 14 Samuel, son of Benjamin and Anne Philips, bapt.
1745 Aug. 28 Anne, daughter of Benjamin and Anne Philips, bapt.
1746 Oct. 28 James, son of Benjamin and Anne Philips, bapt.
1749 Oct. 17 Elizabeth, daughter of Benjamin and Ann Phillips, bapt.
1751 Dec. 11 George, son of Benjamin and Anne Phillips, bapt.
1758 Mar. 23 Anne, daughter of Benjamin and Anne Phillips, bapt.
1744 Jan. 13 Samuel, inf. son of Benjamin Philips, bur.
1746 Nov. 23 James, inf. son of Benjamin Philips, bur.
1752 June 5 Anne, daughter of Benjamin and Anne Phillips, bur.
1770 Feb. 8 Anne Philips, 52, bur.
1783 Nov. 26 Benjamin Phillips, 68, bur.

1743, Oct. 31. WILLIAM WILKINS of Wandsworth in the County of Surry, Widower, & CATHARINE HIGHAM of the same Parish, Widow ; by the Reverend Mʳ Cawley, Vicar of Wandsworth ; by licence. (Clapham.)

1742 April 18 Thomas Higham and Catherine Sheffils, both of this parish [Wandsworth] ; banns.
1743 Sep. 13 Mary, daughter of Thomas Higham (deceased) by Catherine his wife, bapt.
1745 Aug. 16 Anne, daughter of William and Catherine Wilkins, bapt.
1744 Jan. 11 John, son of William and Catherine Wilkins, bapt.
1748 Jan. 17 George Sheffields, son of William and Catherine Wilkins, bapt.
1751 Jan. 4 William, son of William and Catherine Wilkins, bápt.
1753 Dec. 23 Catherine, daughter of William and Catherine Wilkins, bapt.
1758 Feb. 25 Lucy, daughter of William and Catherine Wilkins, bapt.

1760 June 21 Elizabeth, daughter of William and Catherine Wilkins, bapt.
1766 April 26 George, son of William and Catherine Wilkins, bapt.
1741 Oct. 11 Anne, [first] wife of William Wilkins, bur.
1743 May   3 Thomas Higham, bur.
1745 May 10 William, a child of William Wilkins, bur.
1752 June 9 George Sheffield, son of William and Catherine Wilkins, bur.
1763 June 28 Elizabeth, inf. daughter of William and Catherine Wilkins, bur.
1774 May   4 William Willking, 59, bur.

1743, Nov. 8. ARTHUR HONYWOOD of Cobham in the County of Surry,
Batchelor, & ELIZABETH TRUGLER of Wandsworth in the same County, Spinster;
by the Rev. M\u1d63 Cawley, Vicar of Wandsworth; by licence. (Clapham.)
1753 June 8 Elizabeth, wife of Arthur Honeywood, 37, bur. [He appears to
               have married again.]
1763 Jan. 31 Mary, wife of Arthur Honeywood, 38, bur.
1765 Mar. 8 Arthur Honeywood, 46, bur.
               [A tomb to their memory in Mount Nod.]

1744, Oct. 17. THOMAS CROSS of Tooting-Beck in the County of Surry,
Batchelor, & ANNE MACKUEN of the Parish of Wandsworth in Surry, Widow; by
the Rev\u1d48 M\u1d63 Brady, Rector of Tooting; by licence. (Clapham.)

1745, April 16. SIMON SMITH of Wandsworth in the County of Surry, Batchelor,
& REBECCA DRAKE of the same Parish, Spinster; by the Rev. M\u1d63 Cawley, Vicar of
Wandsworth; by licence. (Clapham.)
172⅞ Mar. 24 Rebecca, daughter of William and Elizabeth Drake, bapt.
1756 July 20 Elizabeth, daughter of Simon and Rebekah Smith, bapt. [*Trans-
               ferred from the Burials, where it had been by mistake inserted.*—
               H. Whitfield.]
1767 Feb. 18 Rebeccah Smith, 39, bur.

1745, June 5. THOMAS FUNNEL of the Parish of Wandsworth in the County of
Surry, Batchelor, & SUSANNAH LANGLEY of Tooting Beck in Streatham in the
county aforesaid, Spinster; by the Rev. M\u1d63 Brady, Rector of Tooting; by licence.
(Clapham.)

1745, Nov. 23. RICHARD LIDGETT of Wandsworth in the County of Surry,
Batchelor, & ANNE TURNER of the same place, Spinster; by the Rev. M\u1d63 Cawley,
Vicar of Wandsworth; by licence. (Clapham.)
174⅚ Mar. 8 George, son of Richard and Anne Lidgett, bapt.
174⅐ Mar. 3 Anne, daughter of Richard and Anne Lidgett, bapt.
17⅘₀ Jan. 20 Jane, daughter of Richard and Anne Lidget, bapt.
1754 June 23 Margaret, daughter of Richard and Anne Lidgett, bapt.
1759 Jan. 27 Richard, son of Richard and Anne Lidgett, bapt.
1772 Jan. 19 Ann Lidget, 54, bur.

1746, Oct. 9. THOMAS MATTOX of Wandsworth in the County of Surry,
Batchelor, & ANNE SOUTHERN of the same parish, Widow; by the Rev\u1d48 M\u1d63 Cawley,
Vicar of Wandsworth; by licence. (Clapham.)
1764 Jan. 8 Thomas, son of Thomas and Anne Mattocks, bapt.
1767 June 14 Thomas, son of Thomas and Anne Mattocks, bapt.
1770 Feb. 16 Charlotte, daughter of Thomas and Anne Mattocks, bapt.
1765 May   3 Thomas, inf. son of Thomas and Anne Mattocks, bur.
1768 Oct. 9 Thomas, inf. son of Thomas and Anne Mattex, bur.
1771 May 23 Ann, wife of Thomas Mattocks, 40, bur.
1782 Nov. 24 Ann Mattocks, 73, bur.

1748, May 6. JOHN PICKERING of Wandsworth in the County of Surry, Batchelor, & MARY MOAD of the same Parish, Widow; by the Revd Mr Cawley, Vicar of Wandsworth; by licence. (Clapham.)

1750, April 3. SAMUEL MASSEY & DORCAS TROTMAN of Wandsworth, Surry. (St. George's Chapel, Mayfair.)
1751 June 9 Samuel Massey, 58, bur.

1750, May 1. CLAPHAMSON ESSINGTON of the Parish of Wimbleton in the County of Surry, Widower, & ANN HILL of the Parish of St Lawrence Jewry, London, Spinster; by the Rev. Mr Castelfranc; by licence. (Clapham.)
1725 Oct. 18 Claphamson, son of Mr John Essington by Elizabeth his wife, bapt.
17$\frac{29}{30}$ Feb. 28 Anne, daughter of Claphamson and Anne Essington, bapt.

1750, Sep. 16. THOMAS BLOWER of Wandsworth, Surry, & ELIZABETH HALL of Battersea in s^d co. (St. George's Chapel, Mayfair.)

1750, Sep. 17. PHILLIP GAREY & SARAH PERT of Wandsworth, Surry. (St. George's Chapel, Mayfair.)
1751 April 27 Elizabeth, daughter of Philip and Sarah Garey, bapt.
1752 June 7 Charles, son of Phillip and Sarah Gearey, bapt.
1753 July 6 Phillip, son of Phillip and Sarah Geary, bapt.
1755 Jan. 19 Mary, daughter of Philip and Sarah Geary, bapt.
1760 July 21 Anne, daughter of Phillip and Sarah Geary, bapt.
1761 Nov. 14 Frances, daughter of Philip and Sarah Geary, bapt.
1763 Oct. 19 Francis, son of Philip and Sarah Geary, bapt.
1768 Sep. 11 Anne, daughter of Philip and Sarah Garey, bapt.
1751 Sep. 5 Elizabeth, inf. daughter of Philip and Sarah Gearey, bur.
1753 June 30 Charles, inf. son of Philip and Sarah Gearey, bur.
1755 May 22 Mary, inf. daughter of Philip and Sarah Geary, bur.
1760 Sep. 17 Anne, daughter of Phillip and Sarah Geary, bur.
1761 Nov. 25 Frances, inf. daughter of Philip and Sarah Geary, bur.
1769 June 29 Anne, inf. daughter of Philip and Sarah Geary, bur.
1773 Sep. 7 Sarah Geary, bur.
1778 April 5 Philip Geary, 63, bur.

1750, Oct. 31. ALEXANDER FAIRLIE of Wandsworth, Surry, & ANNE SHARRATT of Whimblenton [sic] in s^d co. (St. George's Chapel, Mayfair.)

1750, Nov. 6. WILLIAM PERT & MARY RANDALL of Wandsworth, Surry. (St. George's Chapel, Mayfair.)
1751 July 5 William, son of William and Mary Pert, bapt.
1759 Jan. 28 Anne, daughter of William and Mary Pert, bapt.

1750-51, Jan. 14. YEATES THOMAS & HARRIOT MOTT of Wandsworth, Surry. (St. George's Chapel, Mayfair.)

1750-51, Feb. 10. ABRAHAM BRISCOE & HANNAH GRAHAM of Wandsor [sic], Surry. (St. George's Chapel, Mayfair.)
1751 Nov. 5 Abraham Samuel, son of Abraham and Hannah Briscoe, bapt.

1751, May 5. EDWARD EVELYN & PHŒBE RUTTER of Wandsworth, Surry. (St. George's Chapel, Mayfair.)
1727 Dec. 31 Phebe, daughter of John and Phebe Rutter, bapt.
1752 May 20 John, son of Edward and Phebe Evelyn, bapt.
1753 Nov. 3 Charles, son of Edward and Phebe Evelyn, bapt.

1756	Nov. 20	George Rutter, son of Edward and Phebe Evelyn, bapt.
1752	Nov. 5	John, inf. son of Edward and Phebe Evelyn, bur.
1757	Sep. 9	George Rutter, son of Edward and Phœbe Evelyn, bur.
1759	July 7	Edward Rutter, son of Edward and Phœbe Evelyn, bur.

1751, May 14. WILLIAM WILSON & DEBORAH TANNER of Wandsworth, Surry. (St. George's Chapel, Mayfair.)

1752	July 20	William, son of William and Deborah Wilson, bapt.
1756	Jan. 30	John, son of William and Deborah Wilson, bapt.
1758	Mar. 26	Richard, son of William and Deborah Wilson, bapt.
1761	Aug. 17	William, son of William and Deborah Wilson, bapt.
1764	Aug. 5	James, son of William and Deborah Wilson, bapt.
1756	Aug. 18	John, son of William and Deborah Wilson, bur.
1757	Nov. 14	William, inf. dau. [sic] of William and Deborah Wilson, bur.
1764	Aug. 15	James, inf. son of William and Deborah Wilson, bur.
1785	Sep. 25	Deborah Wilson, 63, bur.

1751, June 14. THOMAS TODD & MARY PIPER, Wandsworth, Surry. (St. George's Chapel, Mayfair.)

1752	Mar. 30	Thomas, son of Thomas and Mary Todd, bapt.
1754	July 25	Anne, daughter of Thomas and Mary Todd, bapt.
1753	Dec. 9	Thomas Todd, 30, bur.
1754	Oct. 5	Anne, inf. daughter of Thomas and Mary Todd, bur.

1751, June 17. CHARLES YOUNG & MARGARET MIDDLETON of Wandsworth, Surry. (St. George's Chapel, Mayfair.)

| 1752 | Mar. 31 | Anne, daughter of Charles and Margaret Younge, bapt. |
| 1752 | May 23 | Anne, inf. daughter of Charles and Mary [? Marg.] Younge, bur. |

1751, Sep. 1. JOHN MUNDAY & MARY TOWNE of Wandsworth, Surry. (St. George's Chapel, Mayfair.)

1751	Mar. 23	John, son of John and Mary Munday, bapt.
1754	Jan. 12	Mary, daughter of John and Mary Monday, bapt.
1758	Oct. 17	George, son of John and Mary Monday, bapt.
1760	Sep. 6	George, son of John (originally George) and Mary Monday, bapt.
1763	June 18	Anne Elizabeth, daughter of John and Mary Munday, bapt.
1765	July 7	Richard, son of John and Mary Mary [sic] Munday, bapt.
1757	June 11	Elizabeth, inf. daughter of John and Mary Munday, bur.
1758	Oct. 20	George, inf. son of John and Mary Munday, bur.
1767	Jan. 29	Mary, inf. daughter of John and Mary Monday, bur.
1778	Dec. 13	John Monday, 26, bur.

1751, Sep. 1. TIMOTHY MARI [should be MARR] & MARY PALMER of Wandsworth, Surry. (St. George's Chapel, Mayfair.)

1731	Jan. 21	Mary, daughter of Robert and Elisabeth Palmer, bapt.
1752	July 18	Elizabeth, daughter of Timothy and Mary Marr, bapt.
1754	Aug. 25	Robert, son of Timothy and Mary Marr, bapt.
1756	May 17	Timothy, son of Timothy and Mary Marr, bapt.
1758	June 17	Robert, son of Timothy and Mary Marr, bapt.
1759	Aug. 5	Anne, daughter of Timothy and Mary Marr, bapt.
1762	Aug. 18	Mary, daughter of Timothy and Mary Marr, bapt.
1752	Oct. 8	Elizabeth, inf. daughter of Timothy and Mary Marr, bur.
1757	May 2	Robert, inf. son of Timothy and Mary Marr, bur.
1759	April 19	Robert, son of Timothy and Mary Marr, bur.
1759	Oct. 14	Anne, inf. daughter of Timothy and Mary Marr, bur.
1775	Nov. 29	Timothy Marr, bur.

(To be continued.)

𝕽𝖊𝖛𝖎𝖊𝖜𝖘.

Fenland Notes and Queries. Vol. V., Part 53.   April 1902.   Peterborough : George C. Caster,
                                                                  Market Place.

THIS Part contains some interesting documents respecting the drainage of the Fens, which
seems to have required a great deal of attention and vast sums.   During Charles I. and
Charles II.'s reigns the taxation was large, and in James's time the second tax was a double one,
and a third was called for, and even Londoners were assessed at £80.   The King had a great
aversion to the Commons on account of supplies he was continually wanting.   He wanted
£150,000 a year and looked to the Fens to obtain it.   The Whittlesey Parish Marriage Registers
are next given where they can be decipherable. on one leaf of 100 entries only ten being
legible.   The Registers of St. Mary's in Whittlesey are added for 1683 ; in many cases
leaves are missing, some are torn across with one half leaf, and others are detached, lying quite
loose.   The book only consists of eighteen leaves of paper in leather, and contains entries of
baptisms and of burials from 1683 to 1694.   Surely the Parish Register Society ought to make
a visit to Cambridgeshire a special one, so as to embrace the county, except a Local Society is
started, such as is being done for the county of Surrey at the present time.   The Editor is enabled
to announce that the Duke of Bedford is going to defray the cost of printing the Thorney French
Registers under the auspices of the Huguenot Society, with Mr. Henry Peet, F.S.A., as editor.

The Journal of the Ex Libris Society.   Vol. XII., Parts 3, 4, and 5, March to May 1902.
                                            London : A. and C. Black, Soho Square, W.

THE March Part is embellished by two separate plates, which render it very acceptable.   The
one forming the frontispiece shews a circular library with the symbols of the arts and sciences
shewn on the foreground, and at the top the portrait of the celebrated Dr. J. C. W. Moehsen,
hung with tapestry on both sides ; it is dated 1 September 1753.   The whole forms a massive
and well proportioned bookplate, and the portrait is in that Georgian style which was so
popular a century ago.   There is an article on Musical Bookplates by J. F. Verster, and the Editor
has another on "Art in Modern Bookplates," in which he ably combats the opinion of
Mr. Dennis in *The Artist.*   The Ireland Bookplates are next given, with a brief account of the
gifted young man allowed to go wrong, the son of a man " Shakespere mad," who cast him off
when not yet nineteen years old only for his own selfish sake after the son's confession.   When
pondered on, what a sacrifice of talent to imitate ink, parchment, time-stained vellum, and all
to deceive, whereas it is said he was going to write dramas on history from William the
Conqueror downwards !   The wonder is that in that grand period of English literature from
1800 to 1835 there was no one found to have given the misdirected young man advice so as to
have utilized his talents in a more successful way, as he seems to have passed away unnoticed
about 1835.   He wrote on one occasion, " I was for twelve months at Dr. Barrow's Academy in
Soho Square, and the dismal play performed by the scholars at the breaking up was Shakespere's
tragedy of King Lear."   Years after he wrote on old paper and in a disguised hand the spurious
manuscripts concocted at the time.   The arms of the Rev. W. B. Barrow, LL.D., are given,
addressed at foot, "Academy, Soho Square, 1789."

    The April Part opens with a good account of the late Cecil John Rhodes, with his plate, a
rarity which very few have.   Had an artist designed it for a drawing-room picture it might
have been engraved like that of the death of Moore, but to utilize it as a bookplate is merely
a subterfuge, as it represents him trading with the natives on the first landing of the Dutch at
the Cape.   There is a pleasing account by Mr. Cecil T. Davis of Dr. Andrew Colteé Ducarel
with his arms given, who was appointed Librarian of the Lambeth Palace Library ; and a good
impression is given of the bookplate of the Right Hon. Arthur J. Balfour, designed by
Miss C. Helard.   The plates of Medical Men are still continued, and the arms for identification
now number 505.

    The May Part being upwards of a month late prevents us going into any detail of its con-
tents, only to remark that it may be called the Royal Number, having King Edward's Arms as

the frontispiece, and the two smaller ones for the Royal Library, all etched by Mr. George W. Eve, in his usual dexterous manner, marking him out as a draughtsman second to none. We congratulate the Editor of the "Ex Libris Journal" upon having the privilege of publishing these coats at such an opportune time. The other contents comprise an article on Exeter Cathedral Library, with two representations of its seal, one of 1749, another of 1822; and there follows a short account of Lord Nelson's bookplates.

The Virginia Magazine of History and Biography. No. 4, Vol. IX. April 1902. Virginia Historical Society, Richmond, U.S.A.

THE Number begins with an interesting account of the Germans in the Shenandoah Valley, and what a magnificent aspect the whole bore after the fatigue of days travelling. The Virginia Legislative documents are next treated of, and abridgement of the Laws in 1694. The interest in the Part is the publication of the John Brown letters, long looked for but only found in the Virginia State Library in 1901. Mr. Scott the Librarian had made enquiries about these letters in 1894, but was told that every librarian since the war had exhausted all means of finding them, but without success. It was only a final searching for a state document, which had been missing, that the dust-covered bundle of John Brown's papers came to light. To Americans the papers will be very interesting, as well as the account of the battle of Point Pleasant, when the first troops were raised after the cargo of tea had been thrown into the sea by the people of Boston. A distinguished writer, who saw the troops, said they were the finest set of men that were ever got together on this continent. An account of Henry County from 1776, Notes and Queries, and several genealogical entries and accounts of families, likewise the Title and Index, close the Part.

⚔️ Genealogical Notes and Queries.

GENEALOGY OF THE SIMKINS FAMILY.

... ⚮Charles Simkins of Devizes, co. Wilts ; ⚮Dorothy, da. of Henry Portal 1st wife. | owned Poulshot Manor Farm and Avebury Farm, Wilts. | of Treefolk, co. Hants. 2nd wife.

Sir John Hopkins, Knt.,⚮Anne, on the death | Sir John William Anderson⚮Dorothy, ob. s.p.
Lord Mayor of London | of her sister, sole | of Mill Hill, Bart., Lord 9 Dec. 1817; bur.
1791-2; ob. 14 Oct. 1796; | heir; ob. 5 Sep. | Mayor of London 1797-8; at Hendon.
bur. at Wanstead. | 1806, æt. 78. | ob. 21 May 1813, æt. 77.

"Mis. Gen. et Her.," Second Series, Vol. III., p. 262.

The arms borne by Charles Simkins were : *Argent, on a fesse sable, between three lions passant guardant gules, a white rose between two fleurs-de-lys or.*

I should be much obliged for any information as to the parentage of Charles Simkins and his first wife. He also had a son Charles, but by which wife I do not know, who ob. s.p. I have portraits of Charles Simkins and his daughters.

JOSEPH A. BRADNEY, Talycoed, Mon.

⁎⁎ Books for Review and Notices of Forthcoming Works should be addressed to Messrs. Mitchell and Hughes at the Publishing Office, 140 Wardour Street, London, W.

Pedigree of the Family of Du Prié.*

Christophe Du Prié of Valenciennes, settled in Wentworth Street,=Marie Boutelie, alive Stepney, as a weaver by 1609; bur. at Stepney 20 April 1628. 19 Aug. 1688.

Marie, dau. of=Jacques Lescail-let, bapt. at Nor-wich 5 June 1603; mar. at Thread-needle Street 13 July 1619; bur. at St. Bo-tolph's, Bish-opgate 30 May 1687. 1st wife.

Daniel Du Prié=Jeanne, dau. of Mar-tin Droeshondt, bapt. of Stepney and Bishopsgate, weaver, born about 1598 at Valenciennes; bur. at St. Bo-tolph's, Bish-opsgate, 16 Feb. 1668. | at Dutch Church, Austin Friars, 29 Sep. 1605; mar. at Threadneedle Street 14 Jan. 1688; bur. at Stepney 2 Sep. 1640. 2nd wife.

Jeanne Du Prié, born at Valen-ciennes; mar. at Threadneedle Street, 26 Dec. 1626, Pierre Aerts of Stepney, weaver, born at Tournay.=

Marie Du Prié, bapt. at Thread-needle Street12 March 1609.

Michael Lescail-let (son of Jacques L.) of Stepney, weaver, bapt. at Nor-wich 1605.=Susanna Du Prié, bapt. at Threadneedle Street 11 Nov. 1610; mar. there 7 Aug. 1628; bur. at Step-ney 2 May 1694. Will dated 2 Feb. 1692; proved 10 May 1694 in the Com-missary Court of London.

François de la Fon-taine dit Wicart (son of Michael), born in Valenci-ennes 1606; bur. at St. Botolph's, Bishopsgate, 16 July 1639. 1st husband.=Marie Du Prié, bapt. at Threadneedle Street 2 July 1620; mar. 1st, at Stepney 28 May 1638; 2ndly, at.... (?) 25 March 1643; 3rdly, at Threadneedle Street 20 May 1666; dead in 1686.

Deric Petit=Jean Blondel of Petti-cont Lane, weaver, born in Barleduc; bur. at Step-ney 24 Sep. 1665. 2nd husband. | (son of Moyse B.), bapt. at French Church, Canterbury, 15 Nov. 1618; bur. at Whitechapel 8 Jan. 1686. 3rd husband.

Pierre Du Prié, bapt. at Thread-needle Street 16 Dec. 1621; bur. at Stepney 15 June 1637.

Jean Drigue(son=Judith Du Prié, of Jean D.) of Spitalfields, bapt. at Thread-needle Street 19 Aug. 1627; bur. at St. Bo-tolph's, Bishope-gate, 18 March 1706. | bapt. at Thread-needle Street 18 July 1628; mar. there 3 March 1650; bur. at St. Botolph's, Bishopsgate, 18 Nov. 1692.

Daniel Du Prié of Bishopsgate, merchant, bapt. at Thread-needle Street 16 Jan. 1625; bur. at St. Botolph's, Bishops-gate, 4 May 1694. Will dated 28 Aug. 1688; proved 9 May 1694. (P.C.C. 98, Box.)=Susanna, dau. of Abra-ham Des Quiens, bapt. at Threadneedle Street 17 Feb. 1638; mar. there 8 July 1650; bur. at St. Botolph's, Bishopsgate, 10 May 1677.

Hester Du Prié, bapt. at Thread-needle Street 21 Sep. 1628; bur. at Stepney 4 Jan. 1680.

Jean Du Prié, bapt. at Threadneedle Street 12 Dec. 1680; dead in 1665.=Elizabeth, dau. of ..... Parker and widow of John Weyden of Essex; mar. at St. Bo-tolph's, Bishops-gate, 19 Feb. 1655.

Susanne Du Prié, bapt. at Thread-needle Street 1 July 1632; bur. at Stepney 2 Aug. 1632.

* Communicated by T. Colyer Ferguson, Esq.

Elizabeth Du Prié, bapt. at Threadneedle Street 11 May 1656.

Jean Du Prié, bapt. at Threadneedle Street 20 March 1659.

Abraham Petit (son of Derio P. by his 1st wife Mary Forbo), bapt. at Threadneedle Street 25 Oct. 1629 ; bur. at St. Botolph's, Bishopsgate, 16 Oct. 1658. 1st husband.

=Abraham Sy or Six (son of Thomas S.), bapt. at the French Ch., Canterbury, 29 March 1619. 2nd husband.

Sara Du Prié, bapt. at Threadneedle Street 2 Sep. 1660.

=Susanne Du Prié, bapt. at Threadneedle Street 15 June 1634 ; mar. 1st, at Threadneedle Street 1 July 1654 ; 2ndly, at St. Botolph's, Bishopsgate, 1 May 1664 ; 3rdly, at Aldgate 13 March 1665-6 ; 4thly, at St. Mary Magdalen, Old Fish Street, 29 Aug. 1698.

Isaac Du Prié, bapt. at Threadneedle Street 27 Oct. 1661.

=John Taverner (son of Annan T.) of Stepney, weaver, born at Amsterdam 1628 ; bur. at St. Botolph's, Bishopsgate, 24 June 1692. 3rd husband.

Anne Du Prié, bapt. at Threadneedle Street 9 Aug. 1663.

Ester Du Prié, bapt. at Threadneedle Street 13 Sep. 1665.

Hester Du Prié, bapt. at Threadneedle Street 28 Feb. 1636 ; mar. at St. Botolph's, Bishopsgate, 17 Nov. 1657, Isaac Du Monchant (son of Jacques Du M. of Canterbury), bapt. at Canterbury 7 Dec. 1634.

=Rev. George Topham (son of William T. of London), born about 1646 ; Vicar of Deeping St. James, co. Lincoln ; bur. there 3 Jan. 1694. 4th husband.

Anthony Jenkins, of Southampton. Will dated 20 Nov. 1684 ; proved 6 Feb., 1684-5. (P.C.C. 22, Cann.)

=Susanna Du Prié, bapt. at Threadneedle Street 15 Feb. 1652 ; dead in 1684.

Rev. David Primerose (son of Rev. David P. of Ronen), Pasteur of the French Church in Threadneedle Street, born at Ronen 2 June 1639 ; bur. at St. Stephen's, Coleman Street, 17 Aug. 1713.

=Judith Du Prié, bapt. at Threadneedle Street 17 Sep. 1654 ; mar. there 21 April 1677 ; bur. at St. Botolph's, Bishopsgate, 8 March 1683-4.

Vide PRIMEROSE Pedigree, "Mis. Gen. et Her.," Third Series, Vol. II., p. 78.

Marie Du Prié, bapt. at Threadneedle Street 17 Feb. 1656 ; bur. at St. Botolph's, Bishopsgate, 10 July 1658.

Hester Du Prié, born 16 and bapt. at St. Botolph's, Bishopsgate, 29 Dec. 1657 ; bur. there 28 Nov. 1658.

James Rayner of Bishopsgate, born about 1658 ; bur. at St. Botolph's, Bishopsgate, 28 Sep. 1688. 1st husband.

=Ann Du Prié, born 2 and bapt. at St. Botolph's, Bishopsgate, 14 Oct. 1659 ; mar. 1st, at St. Dunstan's-in-the-East 14 Dec. 1680 ; 2ndly, at Stepney 15 Sep. 1692 ; bur. at Stepney 10 Jan. 1716.

=Rev. Isaac Sharpe of Stepney, bapt. at Sundridge, Kent, 29 April 1659 ; bur. at Stepney 13 Feb. 1735. 2nd husband.

Sarah Du Prié, bapt. at St. Botolph's, Bishopsgate, 8 Aug. 1661 ; bur. there 10 Oct. 1676.

Marie Du Prié, bapt. at Threadneedle Street 8 Feb. 1663 ; bur. at St. Botolph's, Bishopsgate, 19 Dec. 1668.

A | D

John Fuller of Red Lion Sq., Sheriff of London, born about 1663; died 29 March 1737 ; bur. at East Barnet 5 April. = Hester Du Prié, bapt. at Threadneedle Street 8 Jan. 1664 ; mar. lic. dated 18 Feb. 1687-8 ; died 30 Oct., bur. at East Barnet 6 Nov. 1734.

Daniel Du Prié, bapt. at Threadneedle Street 24 Feb. 1667 ; mentioned in his father's will.

Marie Du Prié, bapt. at Threadneedle Street 26 Sep. 1669 ; bur. at St. Botolph's, Bishopsgate, 29 Jan. 1671.

Rachel Du Prié, bapt. at Threadneedle Street 29 Oct. 1671 ; bur. at St. Botolph's, Bishopsgate, 10 Jan. 1681.

Elizabeth Du Prié, bapt. at Threadneedle Street 8 June 1673 ; mar. .... Pitt.

John Du Prié, citizen and haberdasher of London, bapt. at Threadneedle Street 21 Oct. 1675; died Aug. 1734 ; bur. at East Barnet. Will proved 15 Aug. (P.C.C. 179, Ockham.)

Deborah Du Prié, bapt. at Threadneedle Street 3 May 1612.

Jean Du Prié, bapt. at Threadneedle Street 13 Feb. 1614.

Samuel Du Prié, bapt. at Threadneedle Street 21 Dec. 1615. (A Samuel Dupree bur. at Bishopsgate 14 July 1666, æt. 56.) = Elizabeth, dau. of Jean de Rantre, born in Valenciennes ; mar. at Threadneedle Street 25 May 1640.

Pierre Du Prié of Stepney, bapt. at Threadneedle Street 20 June 1619. (A Peter Depree bur. at Bishopsgate 20 May 1671, æt. 51.) = Ester, dau. of Baudewin Moular ; bapt. at Threadneedle Street 19 Sep. 1619; mar. at Stepney 23 Sep. 1639.

Samuel Du Prié, bur. at Stepney 30 July 1641.

Elizabeth Du Prié, bapt. at Threadneedle Street 7 May 1643 ; bur. at Stepney 7 Oct. 1646.

Rachel Du Prié, bapt. at Threadneedle Street 12 Jan. 1645; died infant.

Ester Du Prié, bapt. at Threadneedle Street 1 March 1646.

Rachel Du Prié, bapt. at Threadneedle Street 24 July 1648.

Jacob Du Prié, bapt. 28 Aug., bur. 4 Sep. 1640 at Stepney.

Ester Du Prié, bapt. 8 Dec. bur. 31 Dec. 1641 at Stepney.

James Du Prié, alive 1692 ; mentioned in will of Mrs. Susanna Lescaillet.

A GENEALOGICAL HISTORY

OF THE

Family of Adams of Caban, etc.*

THE DESCENDANTS OF RICHARD ADAMS, ELDEST SON OF ALLEN ADAMS AND MARTHA HIGENBOTHAM.

6. Rev. James Adams, born 22 November 1804, A.B. (T.C.D.) ; took his A.B. degree Æst. 1832 ; Rector of Castlecor (or Kilbride), Diocese of Meath ; married first, 24 December 1835, Elizabeth, daughter of James Denham, Esq., of Fairwood Park, co. Fermanagh, and by her (who died 7 June 1839, aged 25, and was interred in Ballanaleck Churchyard, parish of Cleenish, Diocese of Clogher) he had one son and one daughter :—

(1) Allen Cosby Adams, R.N., born 12 October 1836 ; entered the Royal Navy as Midshipman in the "Gladiator, 6," Captain John Adams, R.N., his uncle (see p. 49), in 1850 ; was present in the "Sans Pareil, 70" at the siege and capture of Sebastopol 1854-55 ; served also on board the "Scourge, 6," the "Hecla, 6," the "Dauntless, 31," the "Doris, 32," the "Salamander, 6," and the "Childers" ; became Lieut. 23 August 1859 ("Navy List"), and died unmarried 12 January 1860 of yellow fever at Tower Hill, Sierra Leone, while Lieut. of the "Arrogant, 47," and was interred in the cemetery of St. George's parish, Freetown, Sierra Leone (St. George's, Sierra Leone, Par. Reg.).

(2) Elizabeth Emily, married 28 April 1864 Edward Roper, Esq., of 33 Adelaide Street, Kingstown (Monkstown Par. Reg.), who died 29 January 1885, and had issue three sons :—

1. Edward Allen Cosby Roper, born 14 November 1866.

2. James Henry Leslie Roper, born 13 March 1868.

3. Campbell Rowley Roper, born 15 June 1870.

The Rev. James Adams married 2ndly, 14 April 1841, Frances, daughter of Rev. Richard Bevan, A.B., Rector of Carne, co. Wexford, (vide line VII., post), and died 21 April 1889, aged 84, and was interred at Mount Nugent (Castlecor Par. Reg.), having had issue one son and two daughters. Mrs. James Adams died 30 December 1878, aged 73, and was also interred in Mount Nugent (Castlecor Par. Reg.) :—

(1) Rev. Richard Adams, A.M., born 23 January 1844 ; took his A.B. degree at Trinity College, Dublin, Hiem. 1866 ; ordained 12 January 1868 for the Curacy of Quarry Bank, Diocese of Lichfield ; Chaplain in the Royal Navy 3 December 1870, on board the "Volage, 18," one of the flying squadron ; visited Brazil, Cape of Good Hope, East Indies, Norway, etc. ; retired

in 1873 and accepted a curacy near Cheltenham ; was Curate of St. Andrew and St. Philip, Notting Hill, Middlesex, and Curate of St. Stephen's, South Lambeth, Surrey ; was appointed Assistant Chaplain of St. Bartholomew's Hospital, London, January 1881 ; married 5 January 1882, in Rathmichael Church, co. Dublin (Rathmichael Par. Reg.), Mary Frances, daughter of David and Letitia Thomasina Beatty (see p. 46).

(2) MARY LOUISA, died 26 February 1894 at Kingstown, aged 52.

(3) FRANCES AUGUSTA.

7. MARTHA, born 1800 ; married 30 October 1818 (St. George's, Dublin, Par. Reg.) Smith Massey Berry, Esq., of Clooneen, King's County. He died at the age of 75, 2 February 1863. She died 7 March 1833, aged 33, and was interred in Eglish, King's County (Eglish Par. Reg.), leaving issue three sons and one daughter :—

  (1) THOMAS BERRY, born 1820 ; died unmarried and was interred 4 January 1852 in Eglish, King's County (Eglish Par. Reg.).

  (2) ALLEN NOBLE BERRY of Irishtown, near Dublin, born 1823 ; baptized 11 September 1823 (Eglish Par. Reg.).

  (3) MARLBOROUGH PARSONS BERRY, J.P., of Clooneen, Parsonstown ; born 1 July 1825 ; married 18 September 1862 Louisa, daughter of John Robert Hewston, Esq., and has issue two daughters.

  (4) ISABELLA ADAMS, born 1821 (St. George's, Dublin, Par. Reg.) ; died unmarried January 1850, aged 29, and was interred in Eglish, King's County.

8. SARAH, born 1801 ; married 4 December 1821 (St. George's, Dublin, Par. Reg.) Robert Jaffray Hautenville of Dublin, who died 14 August 1874, aged 88. Mrs. Hautenville died 25 April 1832, aged 31 (Saunder's "News Letter "), and was interred in St. Anne's, Dublin (St. Anne's, Dublin, Par. Reg.), leaving issue an only son :—

  (1) RAWDON JAFFRAY HAUTENVILLE, born November 1823 ; baptized 2 December 1823 (St. George's, Dublin, Par. Reg.).

9. EMILY, born 1802 ; died unmarried March 1842 in Russell Street, Dublin, and was interred 5 March 1842 in St. Anne's, Dublin (St. Anne's, Dublin, Par. Reg.).

III. JAMES ADAMS of Down Lodge, born about 1767 ; appointed 1 October 1797 Captain in the Cavan Regiment (Watson's "Gentleman's and Citizen's Almanack," 1805) ; was High Sheriff of Cavan in 1810; died unmarried October 1815 suddenly at Fairmount, co. Cavan, and was interred in Knockbride.

IV. COSBY ADAMS of Drum, co. Monaghan, born about 1768 ; married March 1799 (marriage settlement dated 14 March 1799) Dorothea, daughter of David Tighe Winslow of co. Fermanagh ; died s.p. 1805. He resided in the latter part of his life in Dorset Street, Dublin, where he died, and was interred in Knockbride. His will signed 9 January 1805, with a codicil dated 8 August, was proved in Dublin 4 October 1805 (Probate

Court, Dublin). His widow married December 1806 Sterling Berry, Esq.,
who died April 1828 and was interred 13 April 1828 in Eglish, King's
County, beside his wife, who had died 1826 and was buried 3 August 1826
(Eglish Par. Reg.), having had issue several children.

v. WILLIAM ADAMS, born about 1775 ; appointed 1 October 1796 First
Lieutenant of the Clonmahon Cavalry (" Army List ") ; afterwards
joined the Cavan Regiment as Ensign 1 April 1805 (Watson's "Gentleman's and Citizen's Almanack," 1806) ; Lieutenant 9 January 1806
(*Ibid.*, 1807) ; retired from the regiment July 1809 (*Ibid.*, 1810) ; died
unmarried about 1823 in the Isle of Man.

vi. JOYCE, born 1761 ; married 25 November 1806 (St. George's, Dublin,
Par. Reg.) John Adams, Esq., J.P., of Shinan House, co. Cavan (see
post) ; died s.p. 31 December 1835, aged 75, at Leamore Lodge, co.
Wicklow, the residence of her brother-in-law John James Archbold
Leonard, Esq., J.P. (see *post*), where she had resided for several years,
and was interred in Newcastle Churchyard, co. Wicklow (Newcastle,
Par. Reg.).

vii. AMELIA, born 1772 ; married 23 August 1802 (Family Reg.) Captain
Robert Molloy Minnitt (who had assumed the surname of Minnitt in
accordance with the terms of the will of his uncle Paul Minnitt, Esq., of
Annabeg, Nerragh, co. Tipperary) of the Monaghan Regiment, who died
April 1831, aged 60, at Newry, where he was interred 20 April 1831
(Newcastle Par. Reg.). Mrs. Minnitt died 8 June 1844 at Derrygooney
Lodge, the residence of her son Richard, and was interred at Knockbride
(Knockbride Par. Reg.), having had issue three sons and three daughters,
viz. :—

1. REV. ROBERT MINNITT, T.C.D., A.B. Vern. 1831 ; born 23 December
    1804 ; Incumbent of Healy in Lancashire ; married 9 May 1844
    Helen Mary, daughter of Michael Smith, Esq., of Northampton-
    shire, who was a son of the Rev. Thomas Smith, Rector of Clay
    Colon, Northamptonshire, and Mary his wife, daughter of John
    Maling, Esq.   Robert Minnitt died 27 February 1884, aged 79, and
    was interred at Christ Church, Healy.   She died 11 March 1883,
    aged 68, and was also interred at Christ Church, Healy, having had
    issue four sons and one daughter :—

    (1) REV. FRANCIS ALLEN MINNITT, A.B. Cantab 1867 ; A.M. 1871 ;
        born 16 September 1845 at Heywood, Lancashire ; entered
        Holy Orders 1868 ; Curate of the united parishes of Holy
        Trinity and St. Mary, Guildford, Surrey, Diocese of Winchester,
        1869 and 1870 ; Curate of Boldre, Hants, 1870 to 1873.

    (2) RICHARD PAUL MINNITT, born 3 July 1847 ; died 5 September
        1855.

    (3) REV. ROBERT MINNITT, B.A. Cantab, born 25 May 1852 ;
        matriculated at Trinity College, Cambridge, July 1870 ;
        graduated by the Mathematical Tripos as Senior Optime
        January 1874 ; obtained Theological Certificate 1875 ; entered
        Holy Orders as Curate of Healy, Lancashire.

    (4) EDWARD WILLIAM MINNITT, born 11 June 1856 ; died 20 March
        1857.

    (5) HELEN MARY, born 24 June 1849 ; died 26 June 1849.

2. RICHARD ALLEN MINNITT of Derrygooney Lodge, Cortubber, Ballybay, co. Monaghan, J.P. for the counties of Cavan and Monaghan; born 4 August 1806; died unmarried 30 October 1877 and was interred at Knockbride (Knockbride Par. Reg.).

3. PAUL WILLIAM MINNITT, born 24 October 1807; died an infant.

4. AMELIA, born 4 January 1804; died unmarried 17 January 1824 at the residence of Surgeon James Adams (see *post*) at Athboy, and was interred in the Churchyard there (Athboy Par. Reg.).

5. ABIGAIL JANE, born 12 December 1811 (Family Reg.); died unmarried 26 August 1843 at Derrygooney Lodge and was interred at Knockbride (Knockbride Par. Reg.).

6. ALICIA, born 14 February 1813 (Family Reg.); died in Newry about 1815 and was interred in the Old Church there (Family Reg.).

VIII. ALICIA, born 1777; married 11 September 1806 (St. Michan's, Dublin, Par. Reg.) Francis Berry, J.P., of Eglish Castle, King's County, who died 31 October 1864, aged 84, and was interred in Eglish beside his wife, who had died 20 May 1833, aged 56 (Eglish Par. Reg.), having had issue two daughters, viz. :—

1. FRANCES, born 1809; died unmarried 12 July 1832, aged 23, at Bellair, King's County, the seat of her uncle Thomas Homan Mulock, Esq. (Saunder's "News Letter"), and was interred in Eglish (Eglish Par. Reg.).

2. ALICIA, married 28 February 1834 William Fetherstonhaugh, J.P. for the counties of West Meath and Sligo, of Carrick, Mullingar, co. West Meath, who died 1 August 1879, aged 72. She died 15 May 1883 ("Daily Express" Newspaper), and had issue three sons and five daughters, viz. :—

   (1) FRANCIS BERRY FETHERSTONHAUGH of Ballinderry, Mullingar, born 7 October 1837; died unmarried 25 February 1878, aged 40.

   (2) WILLIAM FETHERSTONHAUGH, born 27 February 1840.

   (3) THOMAS ORME FETHERSTONHAUGH, born 16 April 1843; died 21 April 1878.

   (4) ALICIA FRANCES, married 5 June 1860 Arthur Gambell, Esq., of Washbrook, co. Mayo; died 1866, leaving, with other issue, a daughter Susanna Olive, who died unmarried 15 April 1880 ("Daily Express" Newspaper).

   (5) SUSANNA, married to George Roe Bogue, Esq.

   (6) FRANCES MARIA.

   (7) LOUISA MARIA JANE.

   (8) ANNA MARIA.

IX. JANE, born 1786; died unmarried 13 January 1801 at Fairmount, co. Cavan, and was interred in Knockbride (Knockbride Par. Reg.).

II.

JAMES ADAMS, THE SECOND SON OF ALLEN ADAMS AND MARTHA HIGENBOTHAM.

II. JAMES ADAMS of Corranearry House, born 1745 ; died unmarried 15 June 1809, aged 64, and was interred at Knockbride, where there is a tombstone to his memory. His will, dated 2 January 1809, was proved in Dublin, 16 August 1809 (Probate Court, Dublin).

III.

THE DESCENDANTS OF WILLIAM ADAMS, THE THIRD SON OF ALLEN ADAMS AND MARTHA HIGENBOTHAM.

III. WILLIAM ADAMS of Castletown House, co. Cavan, born 1746 ; married first, about 1769, Olivia, daughter of Neason Wildridge, Esq., and by her, who died 1781 and was interred at Knockbride, had issue three sons and one daughter :—

I. ALLEN ADAMS, born 1770 ; married Jane, daughter of Edward King, in 1798 (marriage licence dated 18 April 1798), and sister of Stuart King, Esq., Master in Chancery ; held the appointment of Examiner to Stuart King, A.M., Master in Chancery ; died October 1808 in Temple Street, Dublin, and was interred 27 October 1808 in St. Michan's, Dublin (St. Michan's, Dublin, Par. Reg.). His widow married 30 November 1814 Captain John Blundell (St. Mary's, Dublin, Par. Reg.), son of the Very Rev. Dixie Blundell, D.D., Dean of Kildare, and died 6 November 1846, having had issue by her first husband Mr. Adams two sons and two daughters, viz. :—

1. STUART KING ADAMS, born about 1803 ; died unmarried 1825 in India.

2. WILLIAM O'BRIEN ADAMS of Adelaide Street, Kingstown ; T.C.D., A.B. Vern. 1826, M.B. Vern. 1828, A.M. Æst. 1858, F.K.Q. C.P.I. ; born 24 December 1804 ; married first, 30 September 1835 (St. George's, Hanover Square, London, Par. Reg.), Louisa Jane, daughter of Captain Richard Adams of Wainsford, Hampshire (see post). She died 15 August 1840 and was interred at Athboy, co. Meath, leaving issue :—

   (1) EDMUND PEERS ADAMS, born 24 July 1836 ; died 14 March 1838 and was interred at Milford, Hants, 20 March 1838 (Milford Par. Reg.).

   (2) LOUISA JANE, married 11 August 1864 Rev. Benjamin William Adams, D.D., Rector of Santry, Dublin, formerly of Cloghran, Swords (see post).

   Dr. W. O'Brien Adams married 2ndly, 18 November 1845, Elizabeth Bury (St. George's, Dublin, Par. Reg.), cousin of the Earl of Charleville and daughter of John Berry of Clooneen, King's County, who died 30 November 1861, aged 50, and was interred in Stillorgan Churchyard, co. Dublin (Stillorgan Par. Reg.). He died 1 December 1879 and was interred in Dean's Grange Cemetery, having had issue four sons :—

   (1) ALLEN NEASON ADAMS, born 9 November 1846 ; entered the Army from Sandhurst College as Ensign in the 25th Regiment

(King's Own Scottish Borderers) 21 August 1866 ; Lieut.
30 March 1870 ; Captain 2 March 1878 ; Major 23 September
1885 ; Lieut.-Colonel 1892 ; Adjutant of the 1st Volunteer
Battalion Worcestershire Regiment 15 December 1885 ; married
21 June 1883 Anne Melian, only daughter of The O'Donovan,
D.L., of Liss Ard, Skibbereen, co. Cork (Abbeystrewry Par.
Reg.) ; died 31 December 1893 at Plymouth, while in command of the 1st Battalion King's Own Scottish Borderers,
and was buried at Dean's Grange, Dublin (Dean's Grange
Reg.). He left issue one son—

HENRY WILLIAM ALLEN ADAMS, born 13 June 1884; entered
H.M.S. " Britannia " May 1899 ; appointed to the
"Diadem" (Channel Squadron) 15 September 1900 ;
Midshipman 15 November 1900 ; to the "Illustrious"
19 August 1901.

(2) WILLIAM O'BRIEN ADAMS, T.C.D., A.B. Æst. 1873 ; born
2 July 1850.

(3) CHARLES BURY ADAMS (twin with John James), T.C.D., A.B.
Vern. 1875 ; born 4 June 1854 ; entered the King's County
Rifles as Sub-Lieut. 11 February 1874 ; Lieut. in the 66th
(the Berkshire Regiment) 20 November 1875 ; resigned his
Commission 24 January 1882 ; married 15 October 1877, at
Bombay, Mary Alice, daughter of P. Ryan, Esq., Barrister-at-
law Inner Temple, of Bombay, and has issue :—

1. CHARLES EDWARD ADAMS, born 29 July 1879.

2. WILLIAM BURY ADAMS, born 20 January 1882.

3. JOHN SEWELL ADAMS, born 31 May 1889.

(4) JOHN JAMES ADAMS (twin with Charles Bury), T.C.D., A.B.
1874, M.D. ; born 4 June 1854 ; died 29 October 1878 by a
fall from his horse, and was interred in Dean's Grange Cemetery
(Dean's Grange Reg.).

3. ELLEN, born 1799 ; married 16 December 1814 (St. Mary's, Dublin,
Par. Reg.) Henry Forde, Esq., who died 13 January 1863, Examiner
to the Lord Chief Baron and third son of Robert Forde, Esq., of
Johnstown House, co. Meath, and grandson of Mathew Forde, Esq.,
of Seaforde, co. Down (vide Burke's " Landed Gentry," 1862).
Mrs. Forde died 12 December 1849, aged 50, and was interred in
Mount Jerome (Mount Jerome Reg.), having had issue seven sons
and ten daughters, viz. :—

(To be continued.)

Marriages of Wandsworth Inhabitants.*

EXTRACTS FROM REGISTERS IN VARIOUS PARISHES.

1751, Nov. 5. HUGH MEGEE & ELIZABETH FUNSTON of Wandsworth, Surry.
(St. George's Chapel, Mayfair.)

1729	Oct. 30	Elisabeth, daughter of Richard and Elisabeth Funstone, bapt.
1752	Dec. 25	Richard, son of Hugh and Elizabeth Meggee, bapt.
1755	Jan. 5	John, son of Hugh and Elizabeth Megee, bapt.
1757	Jan. 23	Jane, daughter of Hugh and Elizabeth Megai, bapt.
1760	Oct. 29	John, son of Hugh and Elizabeth Megais, bapt.
1763	Mar. 25	Thomas, son of Hugh and Elizabeth Megais, bapt.
1757	May 17	John, inf. son of Hugh and Elizabeth Megai, bur.
1763	Mar. 29	Thomas, inf. son of Hugh and Elizabeth Megai, bur.
1769	June 2	Hugh Megee, 46, bur.
1770	June 17	Eliz. Magee, 42, bur.

1752, Jan. 7. JAMES KING & ANNE WOOD of Wandsworth, Surry. (St. George's Chapel, Mayfair.)

1732	Jan. 22	Anne, daughter of Nicolas and Mary Wood, bapt.
1753	April 27	Elizabeth Anne, daughter of James and Anne King, bapt.
1754	Nov. 16	James, son of James and Anne King, bapt.
1754	Nov. 27	James, inf. son of James and Anne King, bur.

1752, Feb. 18. LOTT WILSON & MARY MILES of Wandsworth, Surry.
(St. George's Chapel, Mayfair.)

1753 Mar. 20 Eliab, son of Lot and Mary Wilson, bapt.

1754 Mar. 30 { Naphthali, David, } twins, sons of Lot and Mary Wilson, bapt.

1754 April 3 { Naphthali, David, } twins, sons of Lot and Mary Wilson, bur.

1752, April 15. JOHN LEMOND & DORCAS MASSEY of Wandsworth, Surry.
(St. George's Chapel, Mayfair.)

1752, May 9. EDWARD TOMKISS & ELIZABETH STRIKE of Wandsworth, Surry.
(St. George's Chapel, Mayfair.)

1723	Aug. 9	Edward, son of Samuel and Joan Tomkist, bapt.
1732	Jan. 7	Elisabeth, daughter of Jeremiah and Anne Strike, bapt.
1755	Jan. 3	Elizabeth, daughter of Edward and Elizabeth Tomkiss, bapt.
1757	Aug. 14	Anne, daughter of Edward and Elizabeth Tomkins, bapt.
1759	Nov. 18	Sarah, daughter of Edward and Elizabeth Tomkins, bapt.
1765	April 17	Sarah, inf. daughter of Edward and Elizabeth Tomkys, bur.
1767	Dec. 22	Edward Tomkys, 43, bur.
1785	Mar. 24	Eliz. Tomkiss, 53, bur.

1752, June 4. JAMES PLATT & ELIZABETH SKINNER of Wandsworth, Surry.
(St. George's Chapel, Mayfair.)

1729 Dec. 11 Elisabeth, daughter of Joseph and Elisabeth Skinner, bapt.

1752, Sep. 17. HENRY STEVENS & MARY STREETS of Wandsworth, Surry.
(St. George's Chapel, Mayfair.)

* Communicated by CECIL T. DAVIS, Esq.—continued from p. 78.

1752, Oct. 6. ROBERT RIDER of Wandsworth, Surry, & ANN BENNETT of Broxburn, Herts. (St. George's Chapel, Mayfair.)

1752, Oct. 8. PHILIP DWIGHT & SARAH HOW of Wandsworth, Surry. (St. George's Chapel, Mayfair.)

1753	July	6	Millecent, daughter of Phillip and Sarah Dwight, bapt.
1755	July	2	Jane, daughter of Phillip and Sarah Dwight, bapt.
1757	April	12	John, son of Philip and Sarah Dwight, bapt.
1757	April	17	John, inf. son of Philip and Sarah Dwight, bur.
1763	Sep.	8	Jane, inf. daughter of Philip and Sarah Dwight, bur.

1752, Nov. 28. MARMADUKE RUTTER & SARAH STANFORD of Wandsworth, Surry. (St. George's Chapel, Mayfair.)

1732	Jan.	8	Sarah, daughter of John and Elisabeth Stanford, bapt.
1755	Mar.	19	James, son of Marmaduke and Sarah Rutter, bapt.
1757	Feb.	8	William, son of Marmaduke and Sarah Rutter, bapt.
1759	Nov.	10	Benjamin, John, } twins of Marmaduke and Sarah Rutter, bapt.
1762	Oct.	30	Elizabeth, daughter of Marmaduke and Sarah Rutter, bapt.
1766	Mar.	29	Mary, daughter of Marmaduke and Sarah Rutter, bapt.
1770	May	12	John, son of Marmaduke and Sarah Rutter, bapt.
1759	Oct.	25	Benjamin and John, inf. sons of Marmaduke and Sarah Rutter, bur.
1760	Dec.	15	William, inf. son of Marmaduke and Sarah Rutter, bur.
1771	Dec.	8	John, inf. son of Marmaduke and Sarah Rutter, bur.

1752, Dec. 27. THOMAS GREEN & REBECCA BLUNDELL of Wandsworth, Surry. (St. George's Chapel, Mayfair.)

1726	Oct.	16	Thomas, son of Thomas Green, bapt.
1728	Jan.	27	Rebekah, daughter of Adam and Catherine Blundell, bapt.
1753	Dec.	29	Rebekah, daughter of Thomas and Rebekah Green, bapt.
1756	June	14	Thomas, son of Thomas and Rebekah Green, bapt.
1758	April	1	Thomas, son of Thomas and Rebekah Green, bapt.
1760	May	25	Rebekah, daughter of Thomas and Rebekah Green, bapt.
1762	Oct.	25	Thomas, son of Thomas and Rebeccah Green, bapt.
1756	June	19	Thomas, son of Thomas and Rebekah Green, bur.
1759	Jan.	5	Rebekah, inf. daughter of Thomas and Rebekah Green, bur.
1762	Nov.	4	Rebeccah, wife of Thomas Green, 34, bur.
1762	Dec.	4	John, inf. son of Thomas and Rebeccah Green, bur.
1763	Sep.	8	Rebeccah, inf. daughter of Thomas and Rebeccah Green, bur.
1771	Oct.	9	Thomas Green, 46, bur.

1753, Jan. 30. FRANCIS BAGNELL & ELIZABETH DICKERSON of Wandsworth, Surry. (St. George's Chapel, Mayfair.)

1754	April	8	Sarah, daughter of Francis and Elizabeth Bagnall, bapt.
1755	June	22	Thomas, son of Francis and Elizabeth Bagnall, bapt.
1758	April	9	John, son of Francis and Elizabeth Bagnall, bapt.
1759	May	20	Francis, son of Francis and Elizabeth Bagnall, bapt.
1761	Feb.	28	George, son of Francis and Elizabeth Bagnall, bapt.
1754	Oct.	1	Sarah, inf. daughter of Francis and Elizabeth Bagnell, bur. [2s. 6d. paid for bell.]
1758	May	16	John, son of Francis and Elizabeth Bagnall, bur.
1761	July	19	George, inf. son of Thomas [? Francis] and Elizabeth Bagnall, bur.
1777	May	4	Elizabeth Bagnell, bur.

1753, Feb. 11. CHARLES RUSSELL & MARY KIRBY of Wandsworth, Surry. (St. George's Chapel, Mayfair.)

1728	May	19	Mary, daughter of Robert and Margaret Kirby, bapt.
1753	Nov.	2	Margaret, daughter of Charles and Mary Russel, bapt.
1755	May	1	Mary, daughter of Charles and Mary Russell, bapt.
1757	Oct.	4	Mary, daughter of Charles and Mary Russell, bur.
1778	July	5	Mary Russell, 49, bur.

1753, June 3. ISAAC JACOB of Putney & MARY RICKETTS of Wandsworth, Surry. (St. George's Chapel, Mayfair.)

1753, June 19. JOHN HENLY & MARY TUFFNELL of Wandsworth, Surry. (St. George's Chapel, Mayfair.)

1753	Sep.	30	John, son of John and Mary Henley, bapt.
1754	Aug.	18	John, inf. son of John and Mary Henley, bur. [2s. 6d. paid for bell.]
1782	Dec.	31	Mary Henley, 68, bur.

1753, Aug. 1. WILLIAM STANFORD & MARY MURFITT of Wandsworth, Surry. (St. George's Chapel, Mayfair.)

| 1726 | Jan. | 18 | William, son of John Stanford, bapt. |
| 1754 | Nov. | 14 | John, son of William and Mary Stanford, bapt. |

> [He became a Baptist Minister; emigrated to New York in 1786. The degree of D.D. was conferred on him in 1829. He died 14 Jan. 1834 and was buried at New York. His Memoir, by C. G. Sommers, was issued in 1835 at New York.]

1756	Sep.	1	William, son of William and Mary Stanford, bapt.
1757	July	30	Matthew, son of William and Mary Stanford, bapt.
1759	Feb.	8	Sarah, daughter of William and Mary Stanford, bapt.
1759	Oct.	3	Agnes, Elizabeth, } daughters of William and Mary Stanford, bapt.
1762	Oct.	2	Mary, daughter of William and Mary Stanford, bapt.
1765	June	30	Mary, daughter of William and Mary Stanford, bapt.
1767	July	8	William, son of William and Mary Stanford, bapt.
1770	July	25	Anne, daughter of William and Mary Stanford, bapt. [*inserted*].
1756	Oct.	22	William, inf. son of William and Mary Stanford, bur.
1757	Feb.	26	Lewis, son of [Lewis *deleted*] William and Mary Stanford, bur. [No entry of Baptism.]
1758	Sep.	30	Matthew, inf. son of William and Mary Stanford, bur.
1762	Nov.	28	Mary, inf. daughter of William and Mary Stanford, bur.
1767	Oct.	21	William, inf. son of William and Mary Stanford, bur.
1773	April	1	William Stamford, 50, bur. [In the "Memoir" it is stated William Stamford died 24 March 1772.]
1778	April	17	Mary Stanford, bur.

1753, Sep. 19. JAMES WEBB & SARAH BLAKE of Wandsworth, Surry. (St. George's Chapel, Mayfair.)

1753, Sep. 30. SAMUEL DESMOULINS & MARY ARERISS of Wandsworth, Surry. (St. George's Chapel, Mayfair.)

1754	Aug.	11	Judith, daughter of Samuel and Mary Desmoulins, bapt.
1756	April	11	Sarah Catherine, daughter of Samuel and Mary Desmoulin, bapt.
1755	Oct.	5	Judith, inf. daughter of Samuel and Mary Desmoulins, bur. [In Churchwarden Accounts "Judith Desmoline 2s. 6d."]
1756	Oct.	16	Sarah Catherine, inf. daughter of Samuel and Mary Desmoulin, bur.
1768	June	29	Saml., son of Saml. and Mary Demoulins, 2, bur.
1772	June	10	William Samuel, inf. son of Samuel Desmoulins, bur.

1773 Feb. 7 John, inf. son of Samuel Desmolions, bur.
1774 Aug. 2 Elizabeth, inf. daughter of Samuel Desmulions, bur.

1753, Dec. 25. WILLIAM FORD & SARAH KEEP of Wandsworth, Surry. (St. George's Chapel, Mayfair.)

1754 June 23 Sarah, daughter of William and Sarah Ford, bapt.
1756 July 4 William, son of William and Sarah Ford, bapt.
1761 Aug. 16 George, son of William and Sarah Ford, bapt.
1762 Dec. 11 Thomas Keep, son of William and Sarah Ford, bapt.
1764 May 13 Sarah, daughter of William and Sarah Ford, bapt.
1766 May 25 Thomas Keep, son of William and Sarah Ford, bapt.
1768 Mar. 30 Eliz. Dickerson, daughter of Wm. and Sarah Ford, bapt.
1771 Mar. 3 Avis, daughter of William and Sarah Ford, bapt.
1776 Aug. 25 Elick Edward, son of William and Sarah Ford, born 26 July, bapt.
1778 July 19 Susannah, daughter of William and Sarah Ford, born 20 June, bapt.
1763 July 19 Thomas Keepe, inf. son of William and Sarah Ford, bur.

1754, Feb. 19. JOHN HAWES & PHEBE CHILDS of Wandsworth, Surry. (St. George's Chapel, Mayfair.)

1754, March 6. ABRAHAM BARDIN & MARY HICKMAN of Wandsworth, Surry. (St. George's Chapel, Mayfair.)

1754 Nov. 3 John, son of Abraham and Sarah [sic] Bardin, bapt.
1756 Feb. 1 Hugh, son of Abraham and Mary Bardin, bapt.
1757 Nov. 19 William, son of Abraham and Mary Bardin, bapt.
1759 April 20 John, son of Abraham and Mary Bardin, bur.

1688, Aug. 16. JOHN FLOYD & MARGRETT HULL, from Wandsworth; p' Lycens. (Fulham.)

1695-6, March 15. ABRAHAM WARWICK, b., & MARY SHEPPARD, s., of Wansworth. (St. James, Duke's Place, London.)

1697 Sep. 12 Abraham, son of Abraham Warwick, bapt.
1699 Feb. 18 Mary, daughter of Abraham Warwick, bapt.
173⅟ Feb. 5 Abraham Warwick, bur.
1744 Dec. 13 Mary Warwick, widow, 80, bur.
1745 May 14 Abraham Warwick, bur.
1761 Oct. 23 Elizabeth Warwick, 85, bur.

1700, April 30. CHRISTMAS BOUTAL, b., & SUSANNA HARVE . . . . of Wandsworth in Surrey; shoemaker. (St. James, Duke's Place, London.)

1700, May 22. WILLIAM NORTH of Kingston, b., & . . . . Wandsworth, w. (St. James, Duke's Place, London.)

1700, May (? after 28th). WILLIAM . . . ., b., & ELIZABETH MUNDAY, s., both of ye parish of Wands . . . .; fisherman. (St. James, Duke's Place, London.)

1701, Nov. 25. EDWARD MEESE of Wandsworth, b., & MARY LEMAN of Lambeth, Surrey. (St. James, Duke's Place, London.)

170⅜ Feb. 11 John, son of Edward Meez, Junr, bapt.
1705 April 17 Elizabeth, daughter of Edwd. Meez, Junr., bapt.
170⅘ Mar. 17 Richard, son of Edwd. Meeze, Junr., bapt.
1708 April 8 Edward, son of Edwd. Meeze of Garret, bapt.
1731 May 9 Edward Meeze, 87, bur.

1701-2, Feb. 3. ROBERT THEOBALDS, b., & ELIANOR TIMMS, s., both of Wandsworth, Surrey. (St. James, Duke's Place, London.)

1702	Dec.	2	Andrew, son of Robt. Tiball, whitster, bapt.
170¾	Feb.	28	Thomas, son of Robert Tiball, bapt.
1706	Oct.	14	Penelope, daughter of Robt. Tibbalds, bapt.
170⅝	Jan.	9	Mary, daughter of Robert Tibals, bapt.
1711	Sep.	2	Elener, daughter of Robert Tibbals, bapt.
1713	Aug.	27	Robert, son of Robert Tibbalds, bapt.
1716	Oct.	1	Edward, son of Robert Tibbalds, bapt.
1719	April	13	James, son of Robert Tibbalds, bapt.
1720	Dec.	12	Jane, daughter of Robert Tibbalds, bapt.
172⅝	Jan.	16	Edmund, son of Robt. Tibbalds, born July yᵉ 6ᵗʰ, 1724, bapt.
172⅘	Jan.	16	{ Joseph, Benjamin, } sons of Robt. Tibbalds, bapt.
173¼	Jan.	12	'Edward, son of Robert Theobalds, 18, bur.
1751	May	24	Robert Theobalds, 85, bur.

1702, Aug. 26. ISAAC LEOTT, b., of St. Thomas' Parish in Southwark, & MARGARET VIRGO, s., of Wadsworth in Surrey. (St. James, Duke's Place, London.)
1681 Jan. 20 Margarett, daughter of William Virgo, bapt.

1703, May 27. WILLIAM THOMPSON, b., of Malden, & ROSE RICHBILL of Wansworth, both in Surrey. (St. James, Duke's Place, London.)

1703-4, Feb. 3. EDWARD CROCKFORD, b., & ELIZABETH VIRGO, s., both of Wandsworth, Surrey. (St. James, Duke's Place, London.)

1683	Dec.	20	{ Elizabeth, Sarah, } daughters of William Virgo, bapt.
1705	Aug.	26	John, son of Edward Crockford, bapt.
1730	May	17	Edward Crockford, bur. [M.I. in Wandsworth Churchyard.]
17⁴⁴⁄₆	Mar.	22	John Crockford, bur. [M.I. on father's headstone. He married Isabella Barbaux at Wandsworth 31 Dec. 1730.]
1750	July	31	Elizabeth, widow of Edward Crockford, 67, bur. [Her name is not on her husband's headstone.]

1705, April 12. GEORGE HOPKINS, b., & SARAH JONES, s., both of Wandsworth, Surrey. (St. James, Duke's Place, London.)

1708, Dec. 7. ROBERT GLENTON, b., of Wandsworth, Surrey, & MARGARET RICHARDSON, s., of St. Olave's, Hart Street, London. (St. James, Duke's Place, London.)

1709, June 19. EDMUND FISHER, b., & ELIZABETH SAVAGE, s., both of Wandsworth, Surrey. (St. James, Duke's Place, London.)

1688	Aug.	10	Edmond, son of William Fisher, bapt.
1711	Dec.	3	Edmond, son of Edmond Fisher, bapt.
1719	July	8	Elizabeth, daughter of Edmond Fisher, bapt.
1728	April	28	Edmund Fisher, bur.
1772	Mar.	18	Elizabeth Fisher, 63, bur.

1712, April 29. EDWARD COWDERY, b., & MARY MEES, w., both of Wandsworth, Surrey. (St. James, Duke's Place, London.)

1715, Sep. 21. WILLIAM LANGLEY, w., of Wandsworth, & MARY BAGGALEY, s., of Mitcham, both Surrey. (St. James, Duke's Place, London.)
1728 April 15 William Langley, bur.
1734 Sep. 27 Mary Langley, widow, 63, bur.

1715, Sep. 29. JOHN FREE, b., of Barkin, Essex, & SARAH CROSSLEY, s., of Wandsworth, Surrey. (St. James, Duke's Place, London.)
169⅝ Feb. 26 Sarah, daughter of Joseph Crossley [*inserted*], bapt.
174¾ Jan. 30 John Free, bur.

1726-7, Feb. 10. FRANCIS BOOLER, b., & MARY COWDER, w., both of Wandsworth in Surrey. (St. James, Duke's Place, London.)
1743 Oct. 27 Francis Bowler, 52, bur.

1731-2. Paid the Beadle's Expences for going to Examine the Register Book of Marraiges at the Fleet on Acco^t of THOMAS PHILBEY & ANN JENKINS, 1^s 0^d. (Churchwardens' Accounts, Wandsworth.)
1710 Sep. 20 Anne, daughter of William Jenkins, bapt.
173½ Mar. 6 Thomas, son of Thomas and Anne Philby, bapt.
173¼ Jan. 13 John, son of Anne Philbey (*alias* Jenkins), bapt.
1734 April 17 John Philby, inf., bur.

1731-2. Paid on Acco^t of apprehending THOMAS COWARD and Expences, the Counter Fees, and fees of the Fleet when d° was married, p' Acco^t £3 6 3¼. (Churchwardens' Accounts, Wandsworth.)

1739, Oct. 10. WILLIAM SMITH, Widower, & HANNAH WOOLLNER, spinster, both of the parish of Wandsworth, were (after three days' waiting that I might be satisfied of some doubts) married by Licence the 10th day of October 1739. (Merstham.)
1717 June 10 Joanna, daughter of James Wooliner, bapt.
174⁰ Feb. 15 Johanna, daughter of William and Johanna Smith, bapt.
174⅜ Feb. 17 William, son of William and Johanna Smith, bapt.
174⁰ Mar. 1 Johanna, inf. dau. of William Smith, bur.
1743 July 1 William, inf. son of William Smith, bur.
1748 Aug. 27 Johanna Smith, bur.

1743, Oct. 6. ELLIS THOMAS of Wandsworth in Surry, Batch^r, & ALICE BROOKS of the same place, Spinst^r ; p' Lycense. (Fulham.)

1743-4, Feb. 4. ISAAC HUTSON of Wandsworth in Surry, Batch^r, & ELIZ. DEANS of the same place, Spinst^r ; p' Lycense. (Fulham.)
1745 May 27 William, son of Isaac and Elisabeth Hudson, bapt.
1746 Sep. 4 Mary, daughter of Isaac and Elisabeth Hudson, bapt.
1747 Sep. 16 Sarah, daughter of Isaac and Elisabeth Hudson, bapt.
1749 Mar. 31 Lucy, daughter of Isaac and Elizabeth Hudson, bapt.
1751 Aug. 24 Isaac, son of Isaac and Elizabeth Hudson, bapt.
1754 Mar. 20 Elizabeth, daughter of Isaac and Elizabeth Hudson, bapt.
1746 Sep. 13 Mary, infant dau. of Isaac Hudson, bur.
1749 Aug. 31 Lucy, dau. of Isaac and Elizabeth Hudson, bur.

1744-5, Feb. 21. THOMAS BUNCE of St John ye Evangelist, Westm^r, Middx., Batchelor, & ELIZ. GREEN of Wandsworth, Surry, Spinster ; p' Lyc. (Fulham.)
1746 Nov. 16 John, son of Thomas and Elizabeth Bunce, bapt.
1762 Nov. 10 Elizabeth Bunce, 48, bur.

(To be continued.)

Bookplate of Reb. R. E. H. Duke.

Rev. RASHLEIGH EDWARD HUNGERFORD DUKE, born 23 June 1855 at Church Eaton Rectory and baptized there, Rector of Maltby in Lincolnshire, second but eldest surviving son of Rev. Robert Rashleigh Duke, Rector of Birlingham, by Ellen Savage, youngest daughter of Rev. Charles Savage Landor, Rector of Colton, and a grandson of Rev. Edward Duke of Lake House, Wiltshire; married at Birkin Church, 3 April 1888, Elizabeth Sarah, eldest daughter of Benjamin Hemsworth, Esq., of Monk Fryston Hall, by Elizabeth, sole surviving child and heiress of John Bower of Smeathalls, Yorkshire.

The Family of Savage of Warwickshire.*

WILLS, GRANTS, ETC.

Indent^e tripartite, dated 8 April 44 Eliz. [1602] bet^n Thos Savage, Tachebrooke Epi., co. War., yeoman, 1st pt., Richd Lane, Stratford upon Avon, gent., Richd Venner, Wellisborne Mountford, yeoman, & Wm Savage, son & heir appar^t of s^d Thos S., 2^d pt., & John Savage, second son s^d Thos S., 3rd pt., recites deed of 10 Octr 37 Eliz. [1595] & specially refers to the last clause that if s^d Thos S. the father does at any time during his life by deed, sealed & subscribed in the presence of three credible witnesses, declare that his intent is thereby to alter or make void all or any the uses or estates therein created, limited, etc., of all or any the s^d mess^{ges}, etc., then the same shall become void. Now this Ind^{re} witnesses that in consid^n of a marriage to be shortly had bet^n the s^d Wm Savage, son & heir appar^t of s^d Thos, and Alice Fawkener of Tedington afores^d, widow, late wife of William Fawkener, deceased, & for the advancem^t of s^d Wm S. in same marr^{ge} & for a competent jointure to s^d Alice of & in the lands, etc., of s^d Thos S. in full satisf^n of the dower which the s^d Alice might hereafter challenge, claim, or have out of s^d lands, etc., also for the advanc^t of issue of W^m & Alice & the benefit of s^d John S. party to these presents & of Thos Savage the youngest son & s^d Thos S., it is covenanted, etc., by s^d Thos S. the father with above parties & their heirs, etc., that they shall stand seised of the mess^{ges}, etc., in Tachbroke, Alveston, & Tedington to the use of s^d Thos S. until the s^d marr^ge is solemnised & from & immed^y after of & in one close called the great field in Tachbroke lying next to the ground called Wigerland to the use of s^d W^m & Alice & their heirs; for default to use of Wm S. & his heirs for ever, & of & in the residue of all the mess^{ges}, etc., of s^d Thos Savage in Tachebrooke (other than the great field) to the use of s^d Thos S. the father for life & after his decease (if Hope now his wife shall be living) of & in the half part of s^d mess^{ges}, etc., in Tachb^{ke} accounting the great field part of s^d moiety to the use of s^d W^m & Alice during the life of s^d Hope, & after the decease of s^d Thos the father & the s^d Hope then of & in the half part of all the mess^{ges}, etc., of s^d Thos the father in Tachb^{ke} to the use of s^d W^m & Alice for their lives & the longer liver & after the decease of both then s^d moiety to the use of the heirs of s^d W^m begotten on the body of s^d Alice; for default to the use of the heirs males of s^d Wm Savage lawfully

* Communicated by Rev. R. E. H. DUKE, Rector of Maltby, Lincolnshire—continued from p. 69.

DEO DUCENTE

REID

coming; for def^t to use of s^d John Savage & his heirs males lawfully coming; for def^t to use of Thos the 3rd son & the heirs males lawfully coming; for def^t to right heirs of Thos the father for ever. And of & in the other moiety of s^d mess^{ges}, etc., of s^d Thos the father in Tachb^{ke} to the use of s^d Wm S. & the heirs males of the body of s^d Alice; for deft. to heirs males of s^d W^m lawfully coming; for deft. to use of s^d John S. & heirs males coming; for def^t to use of s^d Thos S. & heirs males coming; for def^t to use of right heirs of father Thos S. Of half deal of mess^{ges} in Alveston & Tedington to father Thos for life, then to Hope his wife for life if she remains unmarr^d, then to s^d John & heirs males; def^t to W^m & heirs males; def^t to s^d Thos & heirs males; def^t to right heirs of father T. S. Of & in other half deal of mess^{ges}, etc., in Alveston & Tedington to father T. for life, then to John & heirs males; def^t to W^m & heirs males; default to Thos & heirs males; def^t to right heirs of father. Said John S. covenants with R. Lane, R. Venner, & Wm Savage that he will not by any ways, means, act, or devise whatsoever alter, defeat, bar, extinguish, or make void or frustrate the s^d estate or estates intail in Tachbroke wherby the same will not descend to s^d Wm S. & his heirs males, & for default to the s^d John S. & his heirs males, & for default to s^d Thos & heirs males (same covent^t with regard to Alveston & Tydington estates, that they shall descend by entail to W^m & heirs males, or in def^t to Thos & heirs males; in def^t to right heirs of father). In like manner s^d Wm S. covenants with s^d John S. that he will do nothing whereby the Tachbroke estate cannot descend to s^d John S. & his heirs males, or for default to s^d Thos & his heirs males, or that the Alveston & Tydington estates cannot descend to John & his heirs males, or in def^t to s^d W^m & his heirs males, or in def^t to s^d Thos S. & his heirs males.

Signed: Thomas Savage, Richard Lane, Richard Venar, William Savage, all with seal.

Sealed & del^d by R. Lane, R. Vennar, & Wm Savage unto the within-named John Savage in the pres. of Roger Savage, Richard Yardley, John Evets, Tho. Davenport.

Sealed & del^d by Thos Savage the father in pres. of John Antrobus, minister, Roger Savage, Rich. Yardley, and Jobe Murcott.

[In possession of Mr. Richard Savage.]

James, By the Grace of God Kinge of England, Scotland, ffrance and Ireland, Defender of the faith, etc. To all to whome theis presentes shall come Greeting. Whereas John Savage late of Tachebrooke in our Countie of Warwick, yeoman, being seised in taile to him and the heires males of his bodie lawfully begotten of and in one messuage or tenement and twoe yarde landes and an half, with thappurtenaunces in Alveston alias Auston in our said County of Warwick, and in Tyddington in our said County. And of and in other twoe yarde lande with thappurtenaunces in Alveston and Tyddington aforesaid. The Remainder thereof to one William Savage his elder brother and the heires males of his body lawfully begotten expectant. Hee the said John Savage was purposed to sell the said landes for divers necessary and iust causes. Whereupon the said William Savage of purpose to prevent his said Brother of his said iust and necessary sale by his Indenture bearing date the second day of May in the thirde yeare of our Raigne of England, ffrance and Ireland, and of Scotland the eight and thirtith enrolled in our Court of Common plees at Westminster in Easter Terme in the said yeares did give, graunt and confirme to us our heires and successors the said mesuage or Tenement, and the said fower severall yard land and an half, with their and every their appurtenaunces and all profittes, commodities and hereditamentes whatsoever to the said premisses or any of them belonging or in any wise appertayning. And the reversion and reversions, remaynder and remaynders of the said William Savage of all the said premisses and of every part and parcell thereof. To haue and to holde to vs our heires and successors for and during the naturall life of him the said William Savage to the onely and proper vse and behoofe of vs our heires and successors for and during the naturall life of him the said William Savage. Vpon condic'on nevertheles that if the said William Savage shoulde at any tyme than after during his naturall life paye or cause to be payed or sufficiently tender to be payed or cause to be sufficiently tendered to be payed at the Receipt of our Exchequer the so'me of twenty shillinges of lawfull money of England to the vse of vs our heires and successors That then and ymmediately from thenceforth the said writing bargaine and Sale and all and everie article, sentence, matter and thing therein conteyned to cease, determine and be voide.   And that then it shoulde be lawfull to the said William Savage into the said mesuage and other the premisses with thappurtenaunces to enter and the same to have againe enioye and repossede, the said recited Indenture or any thing therein conteyned to the contrary notwith-standing.   Knowe yee nowe that wee not favoring the said fraude, but willing to doe that which is iust in this behalf and to give meanes to the said John Savage to sell the said landes for such good and necessarie purposes as aforesaid of our especiall grace and favor Haue given, graunted and confirmed and by theis presentes doe give, graunt and confirme vnto our said subiect John Savage all such estate, right, title and interest as we haue or maye haue in the said mesuage and other the premisses with the appurtenaunces by force of the said Indenture made by the said William Savage as aforesaid.   To haue and to holde to the said John Savage his heires and assignees in as free, ample, large and beneficiall manner and forme to all intentes and purposes as wee haue or ought to haue the same by force of the said Indenture of him the said William Savage.   In witnes wherof wee haue caused theis our letters to be made patentes.   Witnes our self at Westminster the twelft day of Aprill in the fifte yeare of our Raigne of England, ffrance and Ireland, and of Scotland the fortith.

(Signed) RIC. CARTWRIGHTE.
p' bre de privitto sigillo, etc.

(Portrait of K. James in Initial Letter ; Great Seal attached, in splendid preservation ; the whole deed in perfect condition.)
Endorsed, " A perpetuity for John Savage."

" CARTWRIGHT."

[This deed in the possession of Mr. Richard Savage, the Librarian of Shakespeare's Birthplace.]

---

1 June, 5 James I.   Conveyance by John Savage of Warwick, yeoman, to Thomas Wells of Alveston, al's Auston, co. Warwick, yeoman, for the sum of £220, of a messuage in Alveston in which the said Thomas Wells was then dwelling, also two yard land and a half with all howses, etc., belonging in Alveston and Tiddington to the said two yard land and a half belonging.   (Usual covenants.)

(Signed) JOHN SAVAGE.   (Seal gone.)

Witnesses : Michl. Gardener, Thomas Townesende, John Skinner (his mark), William Alcox, John Pearse, Fra. Levinge, Thos. Baker, Carolus Saunderson.
[In the possession of Mr. Rich. Savage.]

MARRIAGE SETTLEMENT, DR. LANDOR.

Indenture in three parts dated 12 April 14 King George the third 1774. Between Elizabeth Savage late of Bp's Tachbrooke now of the borough of Warwick, spinster, one of the four daus. and coheiresses of Charles Savage late of Bp's Tachbrooke, deceased, and one of the devisees of his last will of the lands hereinafter mentioned of the first part, Walter Landor, doctor in physic, of the borough of Warwick of the second part, John Norris of Brook Street, and John Loyd, Esq^{res}, of the third part.   Whereas the said Charles Savage, deceased, by his will dated 16 Feb. 1759, devised to his then wife Anne Savage all that messuage wherein he then dwelt for her life, and after her death he devised to his daus. Elizabeth, Mary, Ann, and Susannah all that said messuage as tenants in common in manner hereinafter expressed ; And all the rest of his lands in the parish Tachbrooke, subject to a rent charge of £30 a year to his said wife Anne, as well as the reversion expectant on the death of his wife of all lands in Whitnash, and all his real estate wheresoever situate he devised to John Webb and Robert Hugh for the benefit of his said children till they should attain the age of 23. Then he gave the whole of his estate except as above mentioned to his four daughters as tenants in common. And whereas all four daughters have attained the age of 23 years, and whereas Elizabeth Savage is entitled to £1500 in the 4 per cent. annuities and £3000 in the 3 per cent. annuities, and also £200 in securities, and a Marriage is intended to be solemnized between the said Walter Landor and Elizabeth Savage, and whereas upon treaty of the said intended marriage it was agreed that the said sums of £1500, £3000 and £200 should be transferred to John Norris and John Loyd, for certain purposes which she the said Elizabeth Savage hath done, and it has been likewise agreed as to the her fourth share of land in Tachbrooke and her fourth part of a fifth of land in Whitnash which by this indenture she grants to them also, upon trust for the revenue to be paid to the said Elizabeth Savage during her natural life, and after her death to the use of her husband Walter Landor, and after the death of the survivor of them, to the use as the said Elizabeth Savage shall by deed or will appoint, and failing such appointment, to all their children except the eldest son, in equal shares as tenants in common, and failing any issue to the assigns of Elizabeth Savage. The deed also provides for a dower for Elizabeth Savage in the event of her widowhood.

John Olney of Tachbroke epi. grants to John Savage of Tachbroke lands called Sturtes & Whytemore Closes.

Witnesses : John Savage of Tachbroke Mallore, Rich. Webbe, John Commander, & Henry Symonds. Dated Monday before the feast of the Apostles Philip & James in the third year of K. H. VI.

[Seal attached to the above Deed, being the arms of Olney of Tachbroke. See Berry's "Heraldica."]

Thomas Eyres of Whitnash, senior, grants to John Eyres, the son of Thomas Eyres of the same place, lands in Tachbroke which he had from Thomas Rouse of Ragley.

Witnesses : John Olney, Thomas Savage, Rich. Savage, Thomas Renton, & Robt Savage. Dated 4 June in the second year of K. H. VII.

Thomas Eyres of Whitnash, junr, & Jane his wife grants to William Huggeford, armiger, Ric. Savage, & John Eyres of Whitnash, his son, lands in Tachbroke which he had from John Savage.

Witnesses and date the same as the above Deed.

[This and the previous Deed have this Seal attached to them.]

With the exception of the few in the possession of Mr. Richard Savage, all the above deeds and papers are from the muniment cupboard at Savage's House in Tachbrooke, now the property of Miss C. Landor of Cannington Grange ; there are many more similar deeds, but these extracts are printed for evidence that the Savages were a yeoman family indigenous at and about Tachbrooke from such early times as to argue that they were a family to themselves with no connection with the Savages of Rock-Savage and Elmeley Castle. These deeds do not prove the steps of a pedigree earlier than Queen Elizabeth's time, but they do shew the continued existence of a family dealing with the same fields from the time of King Edward IV. After all its vicissitudes in the Savage family the estate in Tachbrooke was sold by Walter Savage Landor in 1809 to the Earl of Warwick, but the house remained in the family. The arms engraved on page 1, Vol. V., are : (1) Landor, (2) Taylor, (3) Constantine, (4) Unknown.

Pedigree of the Family of Savage of Tachbrooke, Warwickshire,

BEING MATERNAL ANCESTORS OF WALTER SAVAGE LANDOR.

ARMS.—*Argent, on a fesse azure between two pheons sable three roses or,* granted to Walter Savage of Clanfield, Oxfordshire, 16 July, 1574, descended from Sir William Savage of Tachbrooke, Warwickshire. See Berry's "Heraldica" (Appendix); see also "London and Middlesex Illustrated," by John Warburton, Esq., Somerset Herald, 1749.

In 1730 Charles Savage of St. Olave's, Hart Street, had a grant of Crest, viz.: *Two arms embowed in armour proper, issuing out of an Eastern crown or, supporting a pheon sable.*

Thomas Savage of Newbald Pacye, Warwickshire, yeoman (lately dead, 1563).

— Edward Savage, dead before 1563. 1st husband. = Alice . . . . = William Fredston of Warwick. 2nd husband. Agnes.

John Savage of Moreton Morrell, son and heir, buried 18 April 1594.[2] = Joan Smith, married October 1543;[1] buried 17 June 1582.[2]

Roger Savage, baptized 20 April 1555.[1] = Anne, da. of William Commander of Tachbrooke; married 5 Nov. 1576.[2]

Elizabeth, baptized 30 April 1558.[1]

William Murcote of Tachbrooke. = Margaret, baptized 16 Dec. 1559;[1] married 16 July 1579.[2]

Edward Savage, = Jane Greene, baptized 25 married 17 October 1586.[2] Oct. 1614.[2]

Henry Savage, baptized 15 December 1588.[2]

Edward Savage, baptized 4 Feb. 1550.[1]

Richard Savage, baptized 25 Oct. 1553.[1]

Anne, baptized 9 Dec. 1579.[3]

William Savage, baptized 20 September 1582.[2]

Michael Savage, baptized 8 October 1584.[2]

Thomas Savage, baptized 11 October 1577.[2]

Margaret, baptized and buried 1578.[3]

John Savage, baptized 21 April 1581.[2]

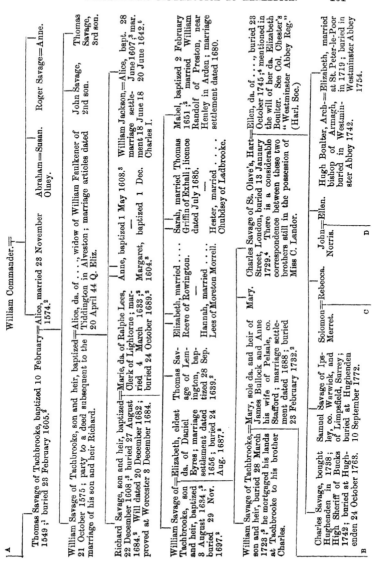

B — C — D

John Norris of Hughenden, High Sheriff of Bucks 1775; buried at Hughenden 1786.

Ellen, only da., married Viscount Conyngham; took possession of Hughenden 1786; buried 1806, aged 92.

William Savage of Tachbrooke, son and heir, baptized 26 March 1689;[2] buried 1 May 1726.[2] Will dated 8 April 1726; proved at Doctors' Commons 8 Oct. 1726.

Richard Savage, baptized 28 Jan. 1697.[2]

Mary, baptized 12 April 1699.[2]

Hannah, baptized 13 June 1704;[2] married 6 June 1785[2] Hewens Cattell of Tysoe.

John Savage, baptized 30 June 1708.[2]

Elizabeth, baptized 12 February 1690;[2] mar. George Commander (articles dated 5 Dec. 11 Q. Anne); she died 1789,[2] he died 1750.[5] M.I. at Tachbrooke.

Charles Savage, baptized 1 June 1696,[2] Merchant=Anne, da. of Henry Eyres of Radford Semale, co. Warwick, married 14 Sep. 1742;[2] Tailor in London; succeeded his brother to buried at Tachbrooke 7 March 1795.[2] This was the grandmother from whom W. S. Tachbrooke; buried 3 June 1759.[2] Landor inherited his leonine appearance.

Walter Landor=Elizabeth, baptized 29 M.D., of War- November 1748;[2] mar- wick. ried at St. Nicolas Church, Warwick, 17 April 1774.

Mary, baptized 3 Sep. 1745;[2] mar. 29 Sep. 1768[2] William Bond of Wolverhampton.

Godolphin William Burs-=Anne, baptized 27 lem of Alton Grange, co. March 1747;[2] Leicester. died 1794.

Sussana, baptized 16 September 1748;[2] married Charles Gregory Wade.

Harry Biggs of Stockton, co. Wilts=Anne, sole da. and heir.

Walter Savage Landor, born 30 January 1775.

Charles Savage Landor, born 7 May 1777, Rector of Colton.

Henry Eyres Landor, born 23 Jan. 1780, coelebs.

Robert Eyres Landor, born 10 May 1781, virgo.

Elizabeth Savage, born 8 May 1776, virgo.

Mary Anne, born 28 June 1778, virgo.

Ellen, born 24 September 1782, virgo.

[I desire to thank Mr. Richard Savage, the Librarian at Shakespeare's birthplace, for the considerable assistance he has given me.—R. E. H. D.]

[1] Moreton Morrell Register.   [2] Tachbrooke Register.   [3] Alveston Register.   [4] Newbald Pacey Register.   [5] St. Olave's, Hart Street, Register.

The Registers of Inkberrow, co. Worcester.* †

INKBARROW, ANNO DNI. 1638.

The names of the Christned of Inkberrow.

April 1   Thomas the sonne of Thomas Bunne.
April 8   ffrancis the sonne of Richard Harvie & Elizabeth his wife.
April 12 Hester the daughter of Richard Steward of Cladsall the elder & Hester
           his wife.
April 22 John the sonne of Thomas Beddowe.
May 24 Mary the daughter of Thomas Rodes & Isabell his wife.
May 28 Anne the daughter of Nicholas ffarre & Marie his wife.
June 10 Anne the daughter of Hugh Court.
July 15 Anne the daughter of William Cartwright.
July 15 Margaret ffreeman the daughter of John ffreeman.
July 16 Elnor Peirce the daughter of Edward Pierce.
Aug. 12 Anne the daughter of Richard Bennet.
Sep. 2   Richard the sonne of John ffreeman.
Sep. 9   Edward Bolton the sonne of William Boulton.
Sep. 16 John the sonne of William Bunne & Sibill his wife.
Sep. 23 Richard the sonne of Richard Hobbins.
Sep. 30 ffrancis the sonne of John Hunt.
Oct. 20 John the sonne of Thomas Perkes & Jane his wife.
Nov. 1   John the sonne of Henry Symmons.
Dec. 10 Hester the daughter of Thomas Rudge & Phillippa his wife.
Dec. 16 Hester the daughter of Thomas Dowty.
Dec. 19 Hugh the sonne of Mr Thom. Dyson of Morton Hall & Elizabeth his
           wife.
Jan. 6   Edward & Robert Chares, gemelli, the children of Thom. Chares.
Jan. 28 Sara the daughter of Edward Ouldaker.
Feb. 17 Anne the daughter of John Harbigg.
Feb. 24 Thomas the sonne of Thom. Edwards.
Feb. 24 Alce the daughter of Arthur Hemues.
Mar. 10 Elizab. the daughter of Edmund Barcroft.
Mar. 13 William the sonne of William Hem'ing & Sara his wife.
Mar. 17 Mary the daughter of William Parsons.
Mar. 21 Alce the daughter of John Phillips & Mary his wife.
Mar. 24 William the sonne of William Reaven & Mary his wife.

ffinis Baptizatorum 1638.

The names of those that were Married in the sayd Parish 1638.

April 28 Thomas Chares & Jane Goodsherry [?].
April 28 Thomas Yates & Margaret Cowley [?] alias Symmons.

ffinis Nuptoru'.

The names of the Buried in Inkborrow.

April 4   Peter Johnson.
— —   Elizabeth Greenhill.
April 20 Ann Horwood.
May 6   Thomas Rudge.
May 13 Sibill Cockerill.

* From the Transcripts in "Edgar Tower," Bishop's Register.
† Communicated by WILLIAM BRADBROOK, M.R.C.S.—continued from p. 60.

June —   William Greene of Keinton.
July 15 Elizabeth the wife of John Cockerill.
July 27 Gyles Morrice.
Aug. 17 Anne the daughter of Thomas Hunt of Keinton.
Sep.   2 ffrancis Alsopp.
Sep. 13 John Brake.
Oct. —   Mrs Elizabeth the wife of Mr Hugh Glover, Vicar of the sayd Church.
Oct. —   John Cobler.
Oct.   8 Anne Bennet.
Oct. 11 Margaret James.
Oct. 17 George Egiocke, gent., of Shernock in the parish of ffeckenham.
Oct. 20 Widdow Hunt-page.
Oct. 27 Katherine Hobbins.
Nov.   4 Jane Briseow, widdow.
Nov. 10 Jane Barley.
Nov. 13 John Cockerill *alias* Gowar.
Nov. 20 ffrancis Wilson.
Dec. 23 Widdow Taylor of the Bowts.
Dec. 25 Henry Hobbins.
Jan.   9 Richard Steward.
Feb. 11 Margery Harbage.
Feb. 18 John Smith of Keinton.
Feb.   2 Grace Hierons.
Feb.   3 Thomas Puttocke.
Feb.   5 Humfrey Hobbins.
Feb. 26 Alce the wife of Robt. Turner of Dormston.
Mar. 11 Jane the wife of Thom. Dyson.
Mar. 24 Edward Webb of Kington.
Mar. 24 Mary the wife of Will'm Reaven.

ffinis Sepultorum.

Hæc copia concordat cu' Registr. reservat apud Inkborrow :

Ita est: HUGH GLOUER, Vic. ibide'.

We believe this is true.

HENRY HUNT,   } Church Wardens.
WILLIAM REAUEN, }

INKBORROW, 1639. A TRUE COPPIE OF ALL THE BAPTIZED, MARRIED, AND
BURIED WITHIN OUR PARISH OF INKBORROW, ACCORDING TO THE REGISTER
THERE KEPT FOR THE YEAR OF OUR LORD GOD 1639.

[Baptisms.]

April 4 ffrancis Hemming the sonne of ffrancis Hemming.
April 8 Thomas Ellins the sonne of John Ellins.
April 15 Richard Jonnings the sonne of Richard Jonnings.
April 15 Elizabeth the daughter of Thomas Eden, Junior.
April 18 Anne the daughter of Alce Daukes, illigitimate.
May   4 ffrancis the sonne of Henry Grasier.
May   19 Elenor the Daughter of Richard Hunt-page.
May   23 John the sonne of Richard Steward, Junior.
June 19 Mary the daughter of Richard Steward the elder.
June 20 Thomas the sonne of Thom. Yate.
July 14 John the sonne of John Hem'ing.

July 29   Elizabeth the daughter of Thomas Bennett.
Sep. 15   Margaret the daughter of Richard Johns.
Oct. 20   Thomas the son of George Windle.
Nov.   2   Martha the daughter of Armill Hunt.
Nov. 22   Ann the daughter of John Smith.
Dec.   1   William the sonne of George Crofts.
Jan. 20   John the sonne of John Boond.
Feb.   2   Anne Cobler the illegitimate child of Anne Cobler.
Feb.   9   John the sonne of Anthony Hem'ing.
Mar.   1   Martha the daughter of Rob'te Richards.
Mar.   8   Elnor. the daughter of Humfrey Hem'ing.
Mar. 14   Constantine the sonne of Edward Rudge.

Omnia baptiz. fu'ere Anno p'dicto.

[Marriages.]

May 11   Robte. Watkins & Mary Smith.
June 10   Ambrose Barley & Anne Layte, Wid.
Oct. 31   Edward Huband & Isabell Dyson.
Nov. 27   Richard Crowme & . . . .
Jan. 20   Edward Heywood & Katherin Ballard.
Feb.   2   John Purser & ffrancis Edwards.

[Burials.]

April 15   Richard Em's of Kington.
April 20   Alce the wife of Richd. Ems.
May   1   Alce Sim'ons, widdow.
May 19   Thom. Paine of Dormston.
May 22   Thomas Crofts.
May 27   Alce Dawkes.
June 2   Joane Weaver of Kington.
June 5   Widdow Cooke.
June 14   Will' Bartley.
June 22   Margaret Petford.
July 22   Thomas Hunt of Bowts.
Aug. 29   John the sonne of Will' Willis.
Sep.   4   Humfrey Ellins.
Sep.   9   Will' Browninge of Dormston.
Sep. 30   Alce the daughter of John Phillips.
Oct.   1   Richard Hobbins.
Oct. 31   A poore traueling woman called Alce Lloyd.
Dec. 14   Alce the daughter of John Willis.
Dec. 22   Widdow Dumbleton.
Dec. 29   ffrancis Yardley of Kington.
Dec. 29   Mary Shakle, widdow.
Jan. 15   Thomas Smith.
Jan. 30   Anne Heynes the wife of Rob'te Heynes.
Jan. 31   Jane ffrancis.
Mar. 13   Elizabeth Taylor the wife of Richard Taylor.
Mar. 15   Ursula Hem'inge the daughter of Humfrey Hem'inge.
Mar. 16   Margery the daughter of John Harbage.

Vera copia teste : HUGH GLOUER, Vic. ibide'.

HENRY LAUGHER.
JOHN PHILLIPS.

A TRUE COPPIE OF ALL THE CHRISTININGS, BURIALLS, AND WEDDINGS W'CH HAPPNED IN THE YEARE OF GRACE 1640.

_____

Vera copia Baptizat.

Mar.	29	Sarah the daughter of John Hasterley.
Mar.	29	Margery the daughter of Rich. Dawks.
Mar.	29	Mary the daughter of Rich. Harrett.
April	12	Anne the daughter of Rich. Woolmer.
April	12	Mary the daughter of Thomas Beddow.
April	19	Elizabeth the daughter of ffrancis Darby.
April	22	Thomas the sonne of John Ganderton.
May	3	ffrancis the sonne of Henry Grasier.
May	7	Tabitha the daughter of Henry Griffin.
May	7	Dorathy the daughter of Thomas Huntley.
May	17	Susanna the daughter of John Dyson.
May	17	Mary the daughter of ffrancis Tomkins.
June	7	Anne the daughter of Henry Elletts.
June	21	Elnor. the daughter of Thomas Robinson.
July	10	Luke the sonne of Henry Page.
July	10	Thomas the sonne of Henry Ballard.
July	19	Charles the sonne of Thomas Dyson of Morton Hall.
Aug.	16	Thomas the sonne of Edward Smith.
Aug.	31	Elizabeth the daughter of John Phillips.
Sep.	9	Mary the daughter of John Hunt.
Sep.	27	Henry Sym'ons the sonne of Henry Symmons.
Nov.	20	Mary the daughter of ffrancis ffreeman.
Dec.	6	Thomas the sonne of Edward Huband.
Dec.	6	Mary the daughter of Rich. Cartwright.
Dec.	20	Thomas the sonne of Hugh Court.
Dec.	27	Thomas the sonne of Thomas Cockerill.
Jan.	6	Mary the daughter of Nicholas ffarre.
Jan.	10	Ursula the daughter of Will' Boonds.
Jan.	17	ffrances the daughter of Edward Smith.
Feb.	21	Thomas the sonne of Elnr [?] Cobler, a bastard child.

Vera copia Nuptoru' 1640.

April	30	George Blicke & Margarett Wilson.
July	29	Richard Hobbins & Margarett Wheeler.
Aug.	31	Symon Ginner & Joane Boults.
Nov.	26	Thomas James & Katherine Marshall.
Dec.	23	Thomas Bristowe & Elizabeth Boulten.
Feb.	15	Richard Hunt & Joane Ransley.

ffinis Nuptoru' habit apud Inkborrow in hoc Anno Doni. 1640.

Vera copia Sepultoru' 1640.

Mar.	27	Richard Hunt of Kington.
Mar.	29	Sarah the daughter of John Hasterley.
Mar.	30	Widdow Gilbart.
Mar.	31	Richard Hunt of Boults.
April	8	ffrances the daughter of Henry Harcott.
May	8	Thomas Garrett of Inkb. Magna, Gent.
May	19	Thomas James.
May	23	Anne the wife of John Blicke.
May	24	Katherine the wife of Nathaniel Showler.

June 18 John the sonne of John Poole.
July 21 Elizabeth ffreeman, virg.
July 21 Elizabeth the daughter of Robt. Wilson.
July 27 Jane the daughter of John Woolmer.
Sep. 1 John Ginner.
Sep. 10 Alce the wife of Thomas Peere.
Sep. — Thomas the sonne of Thom. Boond.
— — A Trauelling Woman's child.*
Dec. — William Chance.*
— — Mary Bristowe, widdowe.*
— — Richard Courte.*
— — Alce the daughter of John Woolm . . . .*
— — Em'e Cobler.*
— — Thomas Perry, who was ser . . . . of Nobury, Gentleman, had s . . . . his
ffellow-servant . . . .*

(*To be continued.*)

The Family of Aldworth,†

ANCESTORS IN THE MALE LINE OF THE BARONS BRAYBROOKE.

RICHARD ALDWORTHE of Tilehurst, co. Berks, clothmaker. He probably came from Wantage, where there were many families of the name. (The entries in the Wantage Registers, 1540—1700, referring to persons of the name of Aldworth, number 422.) His son Thomas in his will mentions his cousin John Aldworth, tanner, of Wantage. Richard Aldworthe married Elizabeth (surname probably Gerying), who survived him, and whose will bears date 4 March, 4 Edward VI. He was buried in "the pyshe churche of Tylhurst in the mydle ylee before the rood," which shews that he was a person of importance. His will is dated 8 November 1543. He had issue :—

I. THOMAS of Reading, clothier, a burgess of Reading from 1541 till his death. He was four times Mayor of Reading, in 1551, when he received King Edward VI. in great state (for the expenses incurred on this occasion see the Reading Records), in 1557, in 1561, and in 1572. He was elected M.P. for Reading in 1557. He died in 1576, and was buried in the Church of St. Law-rence. By his wife Alice (? Symonde), who survived him (will dated 25 Nov. 1585), he had issue :—

    I. THOMAS, mentioned in his grandmother's will 1550 (? bapt. 1538).

    II. ROBERT, who inherited a house at Tilehurst.

    III. SYMONDE or SYMON, Constable of Reading. (See Star Chamber Proceed-ings, temp. Elizabeth, Addenda, Bundle 1, No. 4, "concerning the arrest of Simon Aldworth, Constable, while guarding royal treasure.")

    IV. HENRY, a surety in some Reading municipal money transactions in 1589. Buried in the Church of Arbourfield, near Reading (will dated 29 July 1596). By his wife Katherin he had issue :—

        THOMAS, and six other children (names not mentioned). Thomas inherited a house in Reading.

    V. JOAN DUNSCOMBE.

    VI. ALICE PYLE, executrix of her mother's will.

* Eaten by mice.　　　† Communicated by C. J. AUBERTIN, Esq.

II. WILLIAM, of Sulhampstead Abbot, near Reading. Inherited a house in Tilehurst after his mother's decease. He died in 1552. By his wife Elizabeth
he had issue two sons:—

    I. BARTHOLOMEW.

    II. RALF, godson to his grandfather.

III. RICHARD, clothier, who inherited lands in " Sollomsted and Sheffeld."
Burgess of Reading from 1566 till his death. He was thrice Mayor of
Reading, in 1577, 1585, and 1594. He died in his Mayoralty 12 July 1594.
The churchwardens of St. Mary's paid vj s. and viij d. for his grave and the
tolling of the great bell. He left money towards building the new steeple of
St. Mary's and for " paving the waye and alley that leadeth from St. Lawrence
Church to the Eldehall stayres with pible." His portrait is now in the
Council Chamber at Reading. By his wife Julian or Gelian, who predeceased
him (bur. 18 January 1593), he had issue:—

    I. RICHARD, baptized 13 April 1539. Elected a burgess of Reading in 1573,
    and fined iiij d. " quia venit tarde." He was buried 12 July 1584. On
    28 January 1571-2 he married Jane, daughter of Clement South, by
    whom he had (with two daughters, Alice, born 1578, and Ursula, born
    1580) an only son,

        RICHARD, baptized 10 June 1576, one of the Company of Skinners, to whom
        he left a piece of plate. He is styled in his will (dated 21 December
        1646, with several codicils, the last of which bears date 2 January
        1648-9) as of St. Mary Maudlin, Milk Street. He appears to have
        been extremely wealthy. He left £4000 to Reading and £2000
        to Basingstoke to found a Blue Coat School in either town, after
        the model of Christ's Hospital, with a "godly and learned school-
        master, to teach them to read, write, and cipher, and the Katechisme,"
        the children to have " convenient bedsteades, all of them to be fitted
        with decent and convenient bedds, boulsters, sheets, blanketts,
        coverlettes and all other furniture." They are to be " dyetted " as
        are the children in Christ's Hospital, London, and are to have
        "shoes, hoasen, linnen and woollen—their upper garment to be a
        blue coate with a blue cap." He left also a house in Reading,
        adjoining the Churchyard of " Maries," to provide £20 per annum
        for an " orthodox devine, to preach a lecture every week and visit
        the sick when called upon." There were also charities to provide
        thirty cloth gowns yearly, and thirty loaves every Sabbath day, as
        well as numerous bequests, ranging from £1000 to £5, to kinsmen
        and retainers. He bequeathed the remainder of his fortune (together
        with land at Woollaston, co. Northampton, and at Westham, co.
        Essex) to the governors of Christ's Hospital, " upon condition that
        they provide a convenient place for the children to be educated in
        writing, cyphering, katechising, and the understanding of the Latin
        Tongue." The Skinners' Company were to have five nominations.
        He left money and mourning to the family of his cousin Richard
        Aldworth of London, deceased (of whom later), and also to his
        "kinsman " or cousin Richard Aldworth of Wargrave and Hinton
        Pipard, whom he also releases from a mortgage of £2000. He also
        mentions various members of Richard of Wargrave's family (of whom
        later, as the direct ancestors of Lord Braybrooke). The testator's
        will was not proved till 1654, as there seems to have been some
        dispute raised by the Puritans as to the form of Catechism intended
        to be taught. He apparently married a lady of the name of Charke,
        and had one daughter, who seems to have predeceased him, married
        to Richard Shaxton.

[NOTE.—The number of Richard Aldworths alive at this time makes it some-what difficult to place them. This Richard was almost certainly the son of Richard Aldworth, junior, as has been shewn, for (1) he says he was born in Reading, (2) his executor was Thomas South, and he mentions other members of the South family, whom he calls his kinsmen (his father married Jane South, as above). At any rate it was this Richard who founded the Bluecoat School, and *not* Richard of Ruscombe, ancestor of Lord Braybrooke, to whom this action is ascribed in a published pedigree,* which I have been able to correct and amplify, as well as verify in many particulars. For Richard of Ruscombe, whom we know from the Royalist Composition Papers to have been much impoverished, is mentioned by name (and called kinsman and cousin) in the will of the Richard at present under discussion.]

    II. GILBERT (second son of Richard Aldworth, Mayor), baptized 16 June 1545; elected a burgess of Reading in 1580. Married 21 June 1573 Mary Fittes, and died 1587, having had by her :—

        1. JOHN, born 1576.
        2. GILBERT, born 1580; Surveyor of Highways at Reading 1606.
        3. MARY, born 1574.
        4. ELIZABETH, born 1583.

    III. JOHN, baptized 10 September 1547, his father's executor; inherited lands in Burfield and Sulhampstead; married 3 May 1585 Phœbe Fittes.

    IV. PETER, baptized 1 April 1549. By his wife Alice he left at his death, which occurred in 1580, a son,

        RICHARD, who almost certainly is "my cousin, Richard Aldworth of London," mentioned as already deceased in the will of Richard Aldworth, founder of the Bluecoat School.† He was of St. Augustine's, Paul's Gate, and was a Merchant Taylor. He married Margaret (? Coulson), and in his will dated 1624 (but proved 1638) he states that he was born in Reading, and mentions his children :—

        (1) RICHARD, not yet of age in 1624.
        (2) SUSAN.
        (3) ELIZABETH.
        (4) MARGARET.
        (5) FRANCES.

    V. CATHARINE, married 1579 to Barnabie Hatch.
    VI. ANNE, married 1579 to Peter Hardye.
    VII. ELIZABETH, married to John Austill.
    VIII. ALICE, married to James Matthewes.
    IX. AGNES (youngest daughter), born 1560; married 1588 to Francis Feild of London, Merchant Taylor.

IV. JOHN, the youngest son of Richard Aldworthe of Tilehurst (will 1543). He was a burgess of Reading from 1555-59, when his name drops out of the list, but he and his wife were both living in 1594, as they are mentioned in the will of his brother Richard Aldworth, the Mayor. It is from this John that the Braybrooke Aldworths must have sprung. We know that they were descended from a John Aldworth, from the memorial in Wargrave Church erected by Richard Aldworth of Hinton Pipard (who died 1638-9) to the memory of

* "Miscellanea Genealogica et Heraldica," New Series, Vol. IV., p. 173.
† Quotation in proof: "To Mistris Aldworth, widow, wife of my cousin Richard A. of London, deceased, £5 for mourning, and to *every of her daughters* £5."

Richard Aldworth his father (died 1623), and to John and Alice, "antecessores suos," which must in this case mean grandparents. The published pedigree mentioned above starts boldly with "John Aldworth of West Hagbourne, Lord of the Manor of Garford in 1546, of Wantage in 1597, and latterly of Reading, Merchant"; and not content with this long life and list of honours, the author of the pedigree marries him three times to other men's wives. I have been at some trouble to prove the incorrectness of this statement, viz.:—

(1) There *was* a John Aldworth of West Hagbourne married to an Alice. He was a well-to-do yeoman and died in 1545. He had no son of the name of Richard.

(2) In 38 Henry VIII., *i.e.*, in 1545 or 1546, RICHARD Aldworth purchased the Manor of Garford from the King for £251 8s. 4d. It had formerly belonged to Abingdon Monastery. He left at his death in 1557 a son John, who had a son Richard, but no connection with Reading.

(3) There were a great number of persons named John Aldworth alive in Wantage in 1597, but whether one of them was Lord of the Manor I do not know, though one branch of the family is sometimes honoured with the prefix " Mr." in the registers.

It is obvious then, that our genealogist has selected three John Aldworths and amalgamated them, in order to give a good start to his pedigree. All we can say for certain is that John Aldworth was a burgess of Reading from 1555 to 1559 ; that he was married before 1557, for in that year he pays pew-rent " iiij *d.* for his wyfe's sete " ; that he and his wife were living in 1594, and that he may have lived till 1602, when a person of his name appears in the Churchwardens' Accounts of St. Mary's, Reading, in a list which is entitled " Three and Thertithe of the chefestes and auncientest men in the parish." If this John Aldworth is not the ancestor of the Braybrookes, I cannot see how we can explain the various allusions to kin and cousinship in the will of Richard Aldworth, who founded the Bluecoat School in 1646.

I cannot find any date for the death or will of this John Aldworth. We know from his monument that his wife was named Alice, and that his son was the Richard Aldworth described below, who in his will gives us the names of his sisters. The children born to John and Alice Aldworth therefore were :—

    I. RICHARD, baptized at St. Mary's, Reading, 12 January 1557 (" Visitation of Berks, 1665," says died 1623, aged 66').

    II. ELLEN, ? baptized 26 January 1561 ; married . . . . Rippen.

    III. ALICE, married John Wiseman ; a widow in 1623.

    IV. JOAN, ? baptized 3 April 1553 ; married . . . . Barber.

    V. MARGARET, married . . . . Head ; a widow in 1623.

RICHARD, the only son, is styled in the published pedigree as of St. Mary Magdalen, Milk Street, an obvious confusion with his kinsman Richard of Bluecoat School fame. In his will (dated 14 April 1623) he calls himself " of London, citizen and Grocer." He mentions his house in St. Mary, Aldermanbury, his house at Stanlake, his dwelling in Reading, the moiety of his parsonage of Wargrave, his manor of Hinton Pipard, and his lands in Hinton Pipard, Stanlake, Twiford, Ruscombe, Sonning, and Hurst. He mentions also some barns called Mombury Barnes, which he purchased of Sir Henry Nevill, the elder, and Sir Henry Nevill, the younger, knights—interesting because the purchaser's descendants were to assume the name and represent the family of the vendors. He married firstly, Anne, daughter of Richard May of London, by whom he had (with two daughters, Anne and Alice) an only son,
RICHARD, his heir.

He married secondly, Margaret, daughter of Thomas Deane, clothier, of Reading, by whom he had :—

I. THOMAS, } died before 1623, s.p., as is obvious from their father's will.
II. WILLIAM, }

III. MARGARET, who married 4 September 1623 at St. James's, Clerkenwell, George (afterwards Sir George) Wilmot of Letcombe and Charlton near Wantage, and had issue.

Richard Aldworth died 13 May 1623, and was buried at St. Mary's, Aldermanbury. He was succeeded by his eldest son,

RICHARD, described in the "Visitation of Berks" as of Wargrave. He married 1614 Amy, daughter of Thomas Parsons of Great Milton (who survived him and died in 1672). He died in 1639 and was buried at Ruscombe. His children were :—

I. RICHARD, born in Reading 1614, his heir.

II. THOMAS.

III. ROBERT, who died at Milford on his passage to Ireland in 1652. His goods were administered by his mother.

IV. HENRY, an India merchant. His will was proved 12 August 1664.

V. ANNE, died unmarried at Chievely 14 March 1644.

(All the above were born before 1623.)

VI. JOHN.

VII. GEORGE, }
VIII. WILLIAM, } mentioned in will of their brother Henry 1664.

RICHARD, the eldest son, is stated in the published pedigree to have founded the Bluecoat School, whereas he is mentioned in the will of the real founder as "my cousin, Richard A. of Wargrave, gent.—Mistris Amie A., mother of the said Richard—Five of the bretheren of the said Richard, videlicet, Robert, Henry," etc., as above. He is styled in the Visitation as of Ruscombe. In 1646 he was fined £200 for commanding a troop of horse in the King's service, and describes himself as seised of the Manor of Hinton Pipard, called Stanlakes Farm, which he values at £160 yearly, and pleads poverty. To no purpose, however, for on 4 June 1650 the fine was paid. He was afterwards M.P. for Reading and Auditor of the Exchequer, and died 5 October 1680. He married Anne, daughter of William Gwyn of New Windsor, and had issue :—

I. RICHARD, his heir.

II. WILLIAM of Frogmore. By his wife Anne, who died 1695, he had issue (will proved 23 December 1700) :—

1. CHARLES of Frogmore ; M.P. for Windsor 1710 ; killed in a duel with Colonel Chudleigh, the outcome of a Jacobite dispute, 21 August 1714.

2. SUSAN.

3. ELIZABETH.

III. CHARLES, Vice-President of Magdalen College, Oxford ; expelled by James II., but afterwards reinstated ; died unmarried 15 April 1720 (vide Bloxam's "Register of Magdalen").

IV. JOHN, B.A. of All Souls 1672 ; Rector of Lockinge, near Wantage, 1684 until his death (unmarried) in 1729. He left a curious account book, still extant. It was his custom to have his wine brought up the Thames to Goring, and then carted to Lockinge, thus apparently avoiding duty.

V. HENRY, buried in Ruscombe.

VI. ROBERT.

VII. ANNE, married 14 May 1675 Thomas May.

VIII. AMY.

IX. SUSANNA, married 3 June 1679 Robert Hester of Shiplake ; died 1731.

X. MARGARET, married Thomas Parsons of St. Anne's, Westminster.

XI. ELIZABETH.

XII. DOROTHY.

RICHARD, the eldest son, was born at Lambeth ; B.A. St. John's College, Oxon, 1665 ; M.A. 1668 ; M.P. for Dublin University 1695-99 ; King's Remembrancer in Ireland. He married Mary, daughter of William Crofton, M.P., and had issue :—

   I. JOHN of Stanlake, born 1680 ; matriculated at Christ Church, Oxford, 1696 ; married Mary, daughter of James Tyrrel of Shotover, who died 1760, aged 90. He died s.p. 1710, and was buried at Ruscombe.

   II. RICHARD, heir to his father.

   III. ANNE, married Edward Standen of Arbourfield.

   IV. JANE, married Gilbert Jackson.

   V. MARY, married 1713 James Hayes.

   VI. ROSA.

   VII. ARABELLA.

RICHARD, the second son and heir, born 1685 ; matriculated at Wadham 1701 ; verderer of Windsor Forest. He married 1714 Catharine, daughter of Richard Neville of Billingbere, and on his death in 1738 was succeeded by his only son,

   RICHARD, born 1717, who on the death of his uncle, Henry Neville of Billingbere, became the representative of that family, and assumed the name of Neville-Aldworth, and later of Aldworth-Neville. He was an M.P. from 1747-74 ; Under-Secretary of State and Minister at Paris. He married 1748 Magdalen, daughter of Francis Calandrini. She died 1750. On his own death in 1793 he was succeeded by his only son,

   RICHARD ALDWORTH-NEVILLE, born 1750 ; M.P. for Reading. In 1798 he assumed the name of GRIFFIN only, on succeeding, under the special remainder, to the title of his third-cousin, John Griffin-Whitwell, Lord Howard de Walden and Baron Braybrooke. He married Catherine, daughter of George Granville, and sister of the Marquis of Buckingham. He died 1825 ; the grandfather of the present peer.

SKETCH PEDIGREE.

Richard Aldworth, clothmaker=Elizabeth Gerying,
of Tilehurst, died 1543. | died 1552.

Thomas Aldworth, four times=Alice . . . ,   William Aldworth of=Elizabeth
Mayor of Reading ; M.P. for | died 1585.   Sulhampstead Abbot, | . . . .
Reading ; died 1576.   died 1552.
A   B

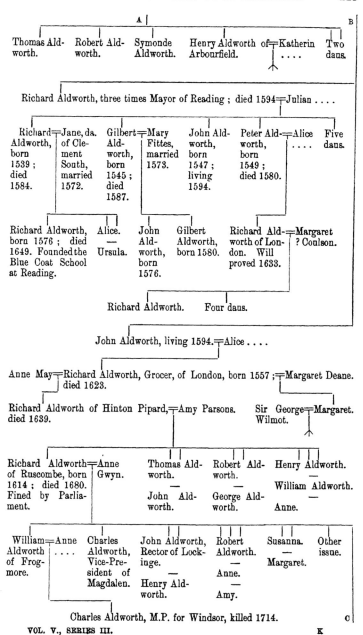

A |
                                                                B

Thomas Ald-   Robert Ald-   Symonde   Henry Aldworth of=Katherin   Two
worth.   worth.   Aldworth.   Arbourfield.   ....   daus.

Richard Aldworth, three times Mayor of Reading ; died 1594=Julian . . . .

Richard=Jane, da.   Gilbert=Mary   John Ald-   Peter Ald-=Alice   Five
Aldworth, | of Cle-   Ald- | Fittes,   worth,   worth, | ....   daus.
born | ment   worth,   married   born   born
1539 ;   South,   born   1573.   1547 ;   1549 ;
died   married 1545 ;   living   died 1580.
1584.   1572.   died   1594.
                    1587.

Richard Aldworth,   Alice.   John   Gilbert   Richard Ald-=Margaret
born 1576 ; died —   Ald-   Aldworth, worth of Lon-   ? Coulson.
1649. Founded the Ursula. worth, born 1580. don. Will
Blue Coat School   born   proved 1633.
at Reading.   1576.

Richard Aldworth.   Four daus.

John Aldworth, living 1594.=Alice . . . .

Anne May=Richard Aldworth, Grocer, of London, born 1557 ;=Margaret Deane.
      | died 1623.

Richard Aldworth of Hinton Pipard,=Amy Parsons.   Sir George=Margaret.
died 1639.   Wilmot.

Richard Aldworth=Anne   Thomas Ald-   Robert Ald-   Henry Aldworth.
of Ruscombe, born | Gwyn. worth.   worth.   —
1614 ; died 1680.   —   —   William Aldworth.
Fined by Parlia-   John Ald-   George Ald-   —
ment.   worth.   worth.   Anne.

William=Anne Charles   John Aldworth, Robert   Susanna. Other
Aldworth | .... Aldworth, Rector of Lock- Aldworth. —   issue.
of Frog-   Vice-Pre- inge.   —   Margaret.
more.   sident of   —   Anne.
           Magdalen. Henry Ald-   Amy.
                 worth.

Charles Aldworth, M.P. for Windsor, killed 1714.   C |

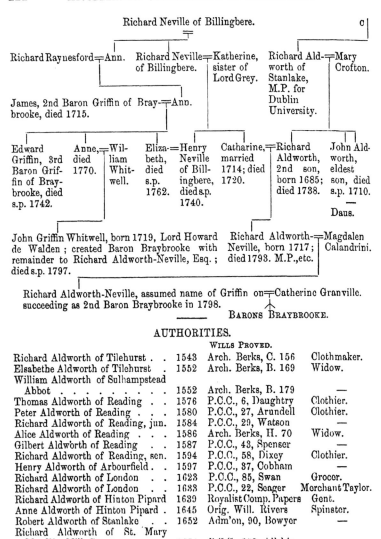

Richard Neville of Billingbere.   c

Richard Raynesford⸱Ann. | Richard Neville⸱Katherine, sister of Lord Grey. | Richard Ald-⸱Mary worth of Stanlake, M.P. for Dublin University. | Crofton.

James, 2nd Baron Griffin of Bray-⸱Ann. brooke, died 1715.

Edward Griffin, 3rd Baron Griffin of Braybrooke, died s.p. 1742. | Anne,⸱Wil- died liam 1770. Whit- well. | Eliza-⸱Henry beth, Neville died of Bill- s.p. ingbere, 1762. died s.p. 1740. | Catharine,⸱Richard married Aldworth, 1714; died 2nd son, 1720. born 1685; died 1738. | John Ald- worth, eldest son, died s.p. 1710. — Daus.

John Griffin Whitwell, born 1719, Lord Howard de Walden ; created Baron Braybrooke with remainder to Richard Aldworth-Neville, Esq. ; died s.p. 1797.

Richard Aldworth-⸱Magdalen Neville, born 1717; Calandrini. died 1793. M.P.,etc.

Richard Aldworth-Neville, assumed name of Griffin on⸱Catherine Granville. succeeding as 2nd Baron Braybrooke in 1798.

BARONS BRAYBROOKE.

AUTHORITIES.

WILLS PROVED.

Richard Aldworth of Tilehurst . .	1543	Arch. Berks, C. 156	Clothmaker.
Elsabethe Aldworth of Tilehurst .	1552	Arch. Berks, B. 169	Widow.
William Aldworth of Sulhampstead Abbot	1552	Arch. Berks, B. 179	—
Thomas Aldworth of Reading . .	1576	P.C.C., 6, Daughtry	Clothier.
Peter Aldworth of Reading . . .	1580	P.C.C., 27, Arundell	Clothier.
Richard Aldworth of Reading, jun.	1584	P.C.C., 29, Watson	—
Alice Aldworth of Reading . . .	1586	Arch. Berks, H. 70	Widow.
Gilbert Aldworth of Reading . .	1587	P.C.C., 43, Spenser	—
Richard Aldworth of Reading, sen.	1594	P.C.C., 58, Dixey	Clothier.
Henry Aldworth of Arbourfield . .	1597	P.C.C., 37, Cobham	—
Richard Aldworth of London . .	1623	P.C.C., 85, Swan	Grocer.
Richard Aldworth of London . .	1633	P.C.C., 22, Seager	Merchant Taylor.
Richard Aldworth of Hinton Pipard	1639	Royalist Comp. Papers	Gent.
Anne Aldworth of Hinton Pipard .	1645	Orig. Will. Rivers	Spinster.
Robert Aldworth of Stanlake . .	1652	Adm'on, 90, Bowyer	—
Richard Aldworth of St. Mary Maudlin, Milk Street	1654	P.C.C., 202, Allchin	—
Henry Aldworth of London . . .	1664	P.C.C., 94, Bruce	Merchant.
William Aldworth of Frogmore .	1700	P.C.C., 175, Noel	Esquire.
John Aldworth of Stanlakes . .	1711	P.C.C., 18, Young	Esquire.
John Aldworth of Lockinge . . .	1729	P.C.C., 239, Abbott	Clergyman.

" Visitation of Berks, 1665 "; Monument in Wargrave Church ; Registers of St. Mary's, Reading. and other places ; Cockayne's Peerage (for the Nevilles) ; Pedigree published in "Mis. Gen. et Her.," New Series, Vol. IV., p. 173 ; Reading Municipal Records ; Churchwardens' Accounts of St. Mary's, Reading ; Foster's "Alumni Oxonienses" (for University Dates).

Pedigree of Butler, Fleming, Byrne, and Delany.*

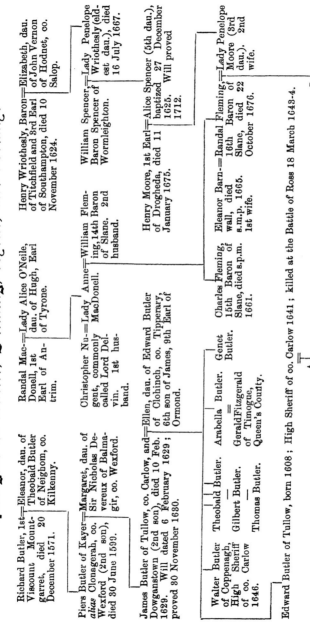

Richard Butler, 1st=Eleanor, dau. of Theobald Butler of Neigbon, co. Kilkenny.
Viscount Mount-garret, died 20 December 1571.

Randal Mac-=Lady Alice O'Neile, dau. of Hugh, Earl of Tyrone.
Donell, 1st Earl of Antrim.

Henry Wriothesly, Baron=Elizabeth, dau. of John Vernon of Hodnet, co. Salop.
of Titchfield and 3rd Earl of Southampton, died 10 November 1624.

Piers Butler of Kayer=Margaret, dau. of Sir Nicholas Devereux of Balmagir, co. Wexford.
alias Clonagerah, co. Wexford (2nd son), died 30 June 1599.

Christopher Nu-=Lady Anne MacDonell.
gent, commonly called Lord Delvin, 1st husband.

Anne=William Flemming, 14th Baron of Slane, 2nd husband.

William Spencer,=Lady Penelope Wriothesly (eldest dau.), died 16 July 1667.
Baron Spencer of Wormleighton.

James Butler of Tullow, co. Carlow, and=Ellen, dau. of Edward Butler of Clohinch, co. Tipperary, 6th son of James, 9th Earl of Ormond.
Dowganstown (2nd son), died 10 Feb. 1629. Will dated 6 February 1629; proved 30 November 1680.

Henry Moore, 1st Earl=Alice Spencer (5th dau.), baptized 27 December 1625. Will proved 1712.
of Drogheda, died 11 January 1675.

Walter Butler of Coppenagh, High Sheriff of co. Carlow 1646.

Theobald Butler.
—
Gilbert Butler.
—
Thomas Butler.

Arabella Butler. = Gerald Fitzgerald of Timogue, Queen's County.

Genet Butler.

Charles Fleming, 15th Baron of Slane, died s.p.m. 1661.

Eleanor Barn-=Randal Fleming, 16th Baron of Slane, died 22 October 1676.
wall, died s.m.p. 1665. 1st wife.

Lady Penelope Moore (3rd dau.), 2nd wife.

Edward Butler of Tullow, born 1608; High Sheriff of co. Carlow 1641; killed at the Battle of Ross 18 March 1648-4.

A

B

* Communicated by J. DELANY, Esq.

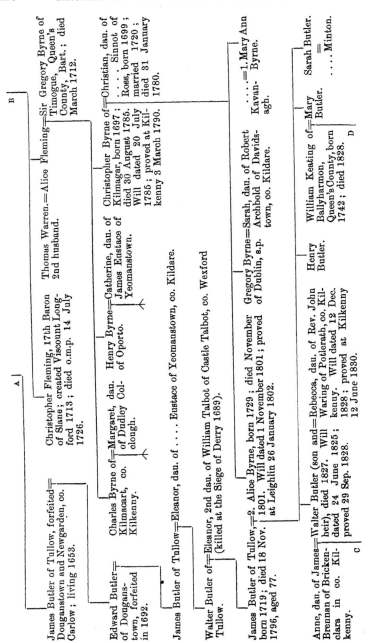

B

Sir Gregory Byrne of Timogue, Queen's County, Bart.; died March 1712.

Thomas Warren.=Alice Fleming=Christopher Fleming, 17th Baron of Slane; created Viscount Longford 1713; died o.m.p. 14 July 1726.
2nd husband.

Christian, dau. of . . . Sinnot of Ross, born 1699; married 1720; died 31 January 1780.=Christopher Byrne of Kilmagar, born 1697; died 30 August 1785. Will dated 20 July 1785; proved at Kilkenny 3 March 1790.

Catherine, dau. of James Eustace of Yeomanstown.=Henry Byrne of Oporto.

Charles Byrne of Kilmacart, co. Kilkenny.=Margaret, dau. of Dudley Colclough.

A

James Butler of Tullow=Eleanor, dau. of . . . Eustace of Yeomanstown, co. Kildare.

Walter Butler of Tullow.=Eleanor, 2nd dau. of William Talbot of Castle Talbot, co. Wexford (killed at the Siege of Derry 1689).

. . . .=1.Mary Ann Byrne.
Kavanagh.

Gregory Byrne=Sarah, dau. of Robert Archbold of Davidstown, co. Kildare.
born 1729; died November of Dublin, s.p.

James Butler of Tullow,=2. Alice Byrne, born 1719; died 18 Nov. 1801. Will dated 1 November 1801; proved at Leighlin 26 January 1802.
born 1719; died 18 Nov. 1796, aged 77.

Henry Butler.

William Keating of Ballyharmon, Queen's County, born 1742; died 1828.=Mary Butler.

Sarah Butler. = ... Minton.

D

Walter Butler (son and=Rebecca, dau. of Rev. John Waring of Potlerath, co. Kilkenny. Will dated 12 Dec. 1828; proved at Kilkenny 12 June 1830.
heir), died 1827. Will dated 24 June 1825; proved 29 Sep. 1828.

Anne, dau. of James Brennan of Brickenclara in co. Kildare=James Butler (son and ...) Kilkenny.

C

Edward Butler of Douganstown, forfeited in 1692.

James Butler of Tullow, forfeited Douganstown and Newgarden, co. Carlow; living 1653.

C |

James Butler of Kilmagar in co. Kilkenny. Will dated 2 Aug. 1854; proved 21 November 1854. = Harriett, dau. of Peter Strange of Aylwardstown in Kilkenny, Esq.

Joanna Butler. = Daniel Murphy.

Maria Butler. = Peter Loughnan.

D |

William Brennan, of Skehena, Queen's County, born 1776; died 1866. = Bridget Keating, born 1790; married 1807; died 1840.

.... Keef of Higginstown, co. Kilkenny. = Mary Ann Keating.

Walter Fleming Butler (only son).

Anne Butler.   Mary Butler.   Julia Butler.

James Delany of Newtown, Queen's County, born 1833; died 1898. = Joanna Brennan of Skehena, born 1828; married 1862; died 1901.

William Delany, M.D., J.P., born November 1862, of Bagnalstown, co. Carlow.

James Delany, born April 1864, of Skehena and Tullamore; County Surveyor, King's County.

Annie Delany, born 1865.   Josephine Delany.   Joanna Delany.   Margaret Delany.   Eliza Delany.

The above Pedigree has been faithfully extracted from Pedigrees, vol. xxvii, pp. 276 and 277, in the Office of Ulster King of Arms. Dated this 24th day of April 1902.

G. D. BURTCHAELL.

Genealogical Notes and Queries.

PEDIGREES OF COPE.

TO THE EDITOR OF "MISCELLANEA GENEALOGICA ET HERALDICA."

DEAR SIR,

The "Salford Priors" Pedigree on page 242 of "Mis. Gen. et Her.," Vol. IV., Third Series, is very defective except in the Osbaston line, so is also the "Birmingham" Pedigree. I enclose these two Pedigrees complete in the hope they may be of some use. The Pedigrees of Cope of Bramshill, etc., with the exception of the exact dates being omitted, which are easily obtainable, contain otherwise only one or two unimportant errors.

Yours obediently,

14 *Great Coram Street, W.C.*   J. R. COPE.

Rev. . . . . Cope, Vicar of Brewood *circa* 1680.

Edward Cope of Brewood Grammar School.

Edward Cope.

Richard Cope.

| Edward Cope. | Charles Henry Cope of Birmingham, died 1863.=Mary Jones | Richard Cope of Malvern, born 1787; died 15 February 1882. | Frederick Cope. | George Cope. |

Edward Cope of Birmingham (Solicitor), born 1814.   Alexander Cope, died 1875.   Charles Henry Cope of Wigginton Park, born 1821.=Mary Minett.

Edward Cope (Bank of England, London), born 1844.   Walter Cope, born 1847.   Charles Henry Cope, born 1854.

Edward Taylor Cope, born 3 May 1870.   Cecil Westall Cope, born 2 October 1879.   Herbert Gordon Cope, born 9 February 1885.

Jonas Cope of Salford Priors, born 1670; died 28 December 1740.=Sarah Haynes, married 1 January 1699.

| Anne Salle,=William Cope,=Martha . . . ., married 1727.   1705—1784.   married 1730. | Thomas Cope,=Mary 1708—1798.   Cope. | Jonas Cope,=Elizabeth 1710—1785.   Hemming. |

Thomas Cope, 1738—1805. 3rd husband=Patience Eleanor (widow).

COPES OF OSBASTON, see "Mis. Gen. et Her.," Vol. IV., Third Series, page 242.

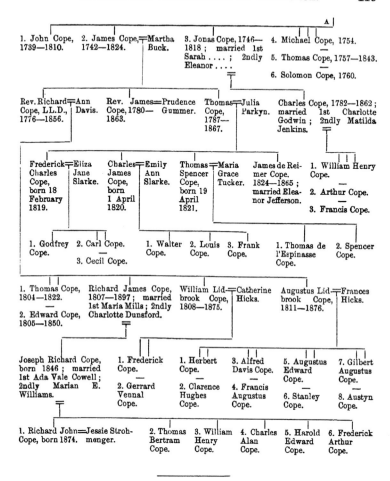

A

1. John Cope, 1739—1810. 2. James Cope,⊤Martha Buck. 1742—1824. 3. Jonas Cope, 1746—1818; married 1st Sarah....; 2ndly Eleanor.... 4. Michael Cope, 1754. 5. Thomas Cope, 1757—1843. 6. Solomon Cope, 1760.

Rev. Richard⊤Ann Davis. Cope, LL.D., 1776—1856. Rev. James⊤Prudence Gummer. Cope, 1780—1863. Thomas⊤Julia Parkyn. Cope, 1787—1867. Charles Cope, 1782—1862; married 1st Charlotte Godwin; 2ndly Matilda Jenkins.

Frederick⊤Eliza Jane Slarke. Charles Cope, born 18 February 1819. Charles⊤Emily Ann Slarke. James Cope, born 1 April 1820. Thomas⊤Maria Grace Tucker. Spencer Cope, born 19 April 1821. James de Reimer Cope. 1824—1865; married Eleanor Jefferson. 1. William Henry Cope. 2. Arthur Cope. 3. Francis Cope.

1. Godfrey Cope. 2. Carl Cope. 3. Cecil Cope. 1. Walter Cope. 2. Louis Cope. 3. Frank Cope. 1. Thomas de l'Espinasse Cope. 2. Spencer Cope.

1. Thomas Cope, 1804—1822. 2. Edward Cope, 1805—1850. Richard James Cope, 1807—1897; married 1st Maria Mills; 2ndly Charlotte Dunsford. William Lid⊤Catherine Hicks. brook Cope, 1808—1875. Augustus Lid⊤Frances Hicks. brook Cope, 1811—1876.

Joseph Richard Cope, born 1846; married 1st Ada Vale Cowell; 2ndly Marian E. Williams. 1. Frederick Cope. 2. Gerrard Vennal Cope. 1. Herbert Cope. 2. Clarence Hughes Cope. 3. Alfred Davis Cope. 4. Francis Augustus Cope. 5. Augustus Edward Cope. 6. Stanley Cope. 7. Gilbert Augustus Cope. 8. Austyn Cope.

1. Richard John=Jessie Strohmenger. Cope, born 1874. 2. Thomas Bertram Cope. 3. William Henry Cope. 4. Charles Alan Cope. 5. Harold Edward Cope. 6. Frederick Arthur Cope.

ANTHONY WARTON, 1581—1661.

I shall be obliged by any clue to his ancestors in Lancashire, where he was born at Walton in 1581; educated at Lincoln College, Oxford, 1596; ordained by the Bishop of London 1607; Curate of Hamsey, Sussex, and in 1626 to 1661 of Breamore, Hants. His will, in P.C.C. 1661, gives no clue to his wife or habitation before the date 1626. His grandson Anthony (1650—1715) of Godalming, etc., was a direct ancestor of Commander Joseph Warton, R.N., 1780—1863, whose will and burial I fail to find.

MS. at Lincoln College gives Anthony Wharton 1596, born 1583; from Lancs.

MS. at Winchester—Anthony Warton, licensed to serve the curacy of Breamore, 1626.

MS. at Doctors' Commons, 1607—Anthony Warton, B.A. of Lincoln College, Oxford, ordained 1607, to be Curate of Hamsey, Sussex; born at Walton, co. Lancaster, 1581.

The registers begin 1586, but give an Anthony, son of Thomas Wharton, baptized 1623. There are no clues at Hamsey or Lewes.

Anthony's sermons were printed in London 1657.   A. C. H.

Reviews.

Fenland Notes and Queries. Vol. V., Part 54. July 1902. Peterborough: George C. Caster, Market Place.

THIS Part gives more particulars of the "Drainage of the Great Level" two hundred years ago, the Commissioners asking for power to tax the country for new works, "to cut off corners and to make crooked rivers straight." Those acquainted with Ely and its neighbourhood at present can appreciate the labour undertaken then, and at a cost of only £1200, to which the country contributed. To shew the schemes undertaken, the River Ouse passed in 1618 to Littleport in a crooked course of ten miles long by water, whereas by land it is only three miles. About £1000 was spent on it, but it was not approved of by the better sort of people, and they found means to stay it. It is rather humoursome to find how civic magnates in 1560, and later, very much approached those of the twentieth century by lavish expenditure on their dinners. At one meal for twelve Commissioners there were drank seven quarts of wine, and for seventeen Commissioners there were five quarts of claret and two quarts of sack, besides sugar in large quantities, so that it was calculated that £100,000 a year was spent on sugar at christenings, at a cost of about £5 each. In 1621 this great waste of money was restricted by Proclamation of the State.

There is given in another Paper an account of the marriages during the Commonwealth, written on loose leaves, now much worn and defaced. The service was before a Justice, and the marriage had to be proclaimed on three several Lord's days; and a short Paper is given of Boston Fair so early as 1282, lasting a month, the citizens resorting to it in great numbers, and all business elsewhere ceasing.

The Journal of the Ex Libris Society. Vol. XII., Parts 6, 7, and 8, June to August 1902. London: A. and C. Black, Soho Square, W.

THE June Part has some interesting plates, among them being the Plates of New College, Oxford, 1702, also those of Sir Horace Mann, Bart., and Lord Walpole.

The July Part for introductory plate has a large one of Mr. Bruce Bannerman's, besides two smaller ones, and other coats are given, all designed by Mr. Graham Johnston, who has the great advantage of being the Herald Painter to the Lyon Office, the arms of Sir James Balfour Paul being given; the plate of Mr. Nevile Reid is also shewn, as well as that of Robert Harley of Bramton Castle, Esq., Speaker and Chancellor of the Exchequer and Lord High Treasurer in Queen Anne's time, and that of his brother, Edward Harley, Esq., both with graceful mantling; and the plate of their father-in-law, Thomas Foley, of Great Witley Court, is also shewn. This is altogether a good Number.

The August Part is chiefly concerned with the President's speech at the Dinner and Annual Meeting, an ample report of which nominally occupies the major part of the Number. Mr. Jewers has an account of the Borlase family, giving three different coats, and Mr. R. Maclay Bull of Brooklyn also has his plate shewn. The plates for identification are now 512.

The Virginia Magazine of History and Biography. No. 1, Vol. X. July 1902. Virginia Historical Society, Richmond, U.S.A.

THIS is an interesting Part, and besides giving the John Brown letters, which are those of a religious fanatic, has a good account of the Battle of Point Pleasant in November 1774 with various tribes of Indians, who heavily outnumbered the troops, under General Lewis, and soon shot three of his best officers while leading on their men, the fighting continuing all day. So eager were the Indians for scalps that three were shot over Captain John Frogge's body while endeavouring to scalp him. Lord Dunmore came with reinforcements and finally effected a treaty with the Indians. The genealogy in the Part is well sustained.

. *Books for Review and Notices of Forthcoming Works should be addressed to Messrs. Mitchell and Hughes at the Publishing Office, 140 Wardour Street, London, W.*

CONFIRMATION OF ARMS TO JOSHUA COLLIN OF LONDON, 1639.

The Armes of the ffamilye of Collin of Laver in the Countye of Essex as is recorded in seuerall Visitations of the saide County remayning in the Office of Armes : From a second Brother of which Family Mr Joshua Collin now of London is descended as appeareth by an affidavit made by Mr John Collyn now of Lincolnes Inne heir Male of that ffamily & Cozen Germayne once remoued to ye sayd Joshua. In testimony hereof I haue subscribed theise presents the 21th day of January : Anno D'ni 1639.

W^M Le Neue, Clarencieux.

ARMS AND CREST OF JOHN RUSSELL OF LONDON, 1552.

The Arms and Crest, viz., " Or on a fesse embattilled azure a starre & twoo cresseants silver between three lions heds caboched gueles vpon his healme on a torse gold & asure a faucons head sables three gutts silver yssuinge out of a rose gueles holding in his beack a compose gold mantled gueles dobled silver," were granted by Sir Gilbert Dethick, Knight, Garter Principal King of Arms, to " John Russell of London, Mr Carpinter to the Kings ma^tie," by Patent, dated at London the 15th day of October 6 Edward VI.

A GENEALOGICAL HISTORY

OF THE

ﬀamilp of Adams of Cavan, etc.*

THE DESCENDANTS OF WILLIAM ADAMS, THE THIRD SON OF
ALLEN ADAMS AND MARTHA HIGENBOTHAM.

(1) ROBERT FORDE, born 1817 ; baptized 24 April 1817 (St. Mary's,
Dublin, Par. Reg.); died 20 December 1836.

(2) WILLIAM ALLEN FORDE, born 1820 ; married 7 April 1851
Isabella Verling, daughter of Alexander Campbell, Esq., of
Mountjoy Square, Dublin. She died 14 January 1875. He died
2 February 1878, aged 57, and was interred in Mount Jerome
(Mount Jerome Reg.), having had issue four daughters:—

    1. ELLEN MARY, married 28 May 1880 Frank D. Hamilton, Esq.
      (Donnybrook Par. Reg.).

    2. ISABELLA HENRIETTA, married 21 June 1880 Stewart F.
      Hamilton, L.K.Q.C.P.I. and L.R.C.S.I., and of the Royal
      Navy (Donnybrook Par. Reg.).

    3. ADA VERLING, married 15 June 1882 (St. Mathew's, Irishtown,
      Par. Reg.) William Lett, Esq., of Kilgibbon, co. Wexford.

    4. ANNIE KATHERINE ALEXANDRINA.

(3) JOHN FORDE, born 17 August 1821 ; married 26 March 1861
(Monkstown Par. Reg.) Elizabeth Dancer, daughter of Rev.
Adderley Campbell, A.M., Rector of Tullycorbet, Diocese of
Clogher, and granddaughter of the late Sir Amyrald Dancer,
Bart., of Modreeny House, Cloughjordan, co. Tipperary, and
died suddenly 3 March 1865 at 2 Vesey Terrace, Garville
Avenue, Rathmines, and was interred in Mount Jerome (Mount
Jerome Reg.), leaving issue two sons, viz. :—

    1. ADDERLEY JOHN FORDE.

    2. JOHN BRABAZON FORDE.

(4) NEASON FORDE, born February 1823 ; died June 1825.

(5) EDWARD FORDE, T.C.D., A.B. Vern. 1851 ; Surveyor-in-Chief of
Harbours and Rivers, Australia ; born 27 November 1827 ;
married 5 April 1864 Helena, youngest daughter of the Hon.
Abraham Scott, A.M., Member of the Legislative Council of
Ash Island, Hexham, Australia ; died s.p. 21 June 1866.

(6) HENRY FORDE, born July 1829 ; baptized 14 August 1829
(Monkstown Par. Reg.). Emigrated to America.

(7) ALLEN FORDE, born 1833 ; baptized 31 January 1833 (Monkstown
Par. Reg.) ; died 19 January 1865 and was buried in Mount
Jerome (Mount Jerome Reg.).

* Communicated by MAXWELL ADAMS, Esq., Barrister-at-Law. From a MS. by the late
Rev. B. W. ADAMS, D.D.—continued from p. 89.

(8) JANE, born 1816 ; baptized 4 February 1816 (St. Mary's, Dublin, Par. Reg.) ; died 13 January 1831, aged 14, at Aubawn, co. Cavan.

(9) OLIVIA, born 1825 ; died 16 October 1826.

(10) CATHERINE ANNE, born 1828 ; baptized 13 July 1828 (Monkstown Par. Reg.) ; died 29 March 1829.

(11) MARCIA HENRIETTA, married 24 May 1870 Rev. Charles Johnson, M.D., of Sydney, Australia, eldest surviving son of Charles Johnson, M.D., of 24 Merrion Square, South Dublin.

(12) ELEANOR SARAH, married 24 August 1854 Robert Francis O'Brien, Esq., J.P., of Rockfield, Killeshandra, co. Cavan, and has issue six sons and one daughter, viz. :—

    1. ROBERT IRWIN O'BRIEN, born 24 August 1855.

    2. HENRY ACHESON O'BRIEN, born 7 September 1857.

    3. WILLIAM FRANCIS O'BRIEN, born 15 June 1860.

    4. EDWARD O'BRIEN, born 9 September 1863.

    5. ARTHUR PERCIVAL O'BRIEN, born 12 Sep. 1868 ; died s.p.

    6. FREDERICK O'BRIEN, born 20 February 1872.

    7. EMILY GRACE.

(13) MARY ANNE, born 1831 ; baptized 24 November 1831 (Monkstown Par. Reg.) ; died 29 October 1857.

(14) ANNE ISABELLA.

(15) SARAH, married 14 July 1881 (Santry Par. Reg.) Henry William Rotheram, Esq., of Castlecor, co. Meath, who died 1890.

(16) EMILY PERCIVAL, married 6 July 1865 James Ramsay, Esq., second son of Dr. Ramsay of Dobroyde, Australia, and has issue three sons and one daughter :—

    1. JAMES ALLEN RAMSAY.

    2. DAVID BRUCE RAMSAY.

    3. EDWARD LORD RAMSAY.

    4. EMILY LOUISA.

(17) ELIZABETH ARMSTRONG, married 8 November 1871 Alexander Campbell Budge, Esq., of Australia, and has issue one son and one daughter, viz. :—

    1. HENRY SINCLAIR CAMPBELL BUDGE, born 12 October 1872.

    2. LOUISA SINCLAIR CAMPBELL.

4. ANNA, born 1805 ; married 2 June 1828 (St. George's, Dublin, Par. Reg.) Lieut. Benjamin Scott, who died November 1847, aged 52, and was interred 29 November 1847 in Mount Jerome beside his wife, who had died 10 October 1845 (Mount Jerome Reg.), having had issue six sons and four daughters, viz. :—

    (1) JOHN BLUNDILL SCOTT, born 1 March 1830 ; died 19 March 1830 and was buried in St. Mark's, Dublin (St. Mark's, Dublin, Par. Reg.).

(2) ALLEN STEWART SCOTT, born 27 January 1832 (St. Mark's, Dublin, Par. Reg.).

(3) SAMUEL BAIRD SCOTT, born 14 December 1836 (St. George's, Dublin, Par. Reg.).

(4) BENJAMIN JAMES SCOTT, born 23 December 1837.

(5) REV. HENRY SCOTT, born 6 January 1840 ; resides in Australia.

(6) EDWARD FORDE SCOTT, born 26 December 1844.

(7) JANE, born 3 March 1829 ; died 4 June 1834 and was interred in St. Mark's, Dublin (St. Mark's, Dublin, Par. Reg.).

(8) ELIZABETH, born 4 March 1831 (St. Mark's, Dublin, Par. Reg.) ; died 1846.

(9) ANNE, born 1833 ; baptized 17 April 1833 (St. Mark's, Dublin, Par. Reg.) ; married 1853 . . . . Simpson, Esq., of Melbourne, Australia, and had issue seven children.

(10) LOUISA, born 19 October 1835 (St. Mark's, Dublin, Par. Reg.) ; married 1853 Captain Vincent of Melbourne, Australia, and died 16 September 1854, having had issue one child, who died with its mother.

II. NEASON WILDRIDGE ADAMS, M.D., born 1777 ; married 2 April 1802 Isabella, daughter of Samuel Adams, Esq. (*vide* p. 129) ; resided in Dublin from 1801 to 20 December 1835, when he retired from practice, giving up his house No. 71 Stephen's Green, and went to live in Achill Island, co. Mayo, where his wife died s.p. 18 December 1855. Afterwards he resided principally in the neighbourhood of Dublin. Died 29 August 1859 at 22 Adelaide Street, Kingstown, the residence of his nephew Dr. William O'Brien Adams (*vide* p. 88), and was interred with his wife in Knockbride (Knockbride Par. Reg.).

III. JAMES ADAMS, M.D., born 1780 ; entered the Army in March 1804 as Assistant-Surgeon ; was attached to the Fourth Ceylon Regiment 20 September 1810 ; Surgeon 15 April 1813 ; retired on half-pay 24 June 1815 ; married 2 September 1816 Maria, daughter of Samuel Adams (see p. 129), and resided at Athboy ; died s.p. 3 September 1840, aged 61, at Kingstown, and was interred in Knockbride (Knockbride Par. Reg.). Mrs. Adams died 31 March 1867, aged 71, at Blackrock, co. Dublin, and was also interred in Knockbride (Knockbride Par. Reg.).

IV. ELIZABETH, born 1767 ; married 1796 Foster Beatty, M.D. (Drumgoon Par. Reg.), of Cootehill, who died 1800, aged 30, and was buried in Cootehill ; she died 30 April 1838, aged 71, and was interred in Knockbride (Knockbride Par. Reg.).

Mr. William Adams of Castletown House, co. Cavan, married 2ndly, 6 July 1783 (Finglas Par. Reg.), Anna, daughter of Robert Smith, Esq., of Finglas, co. Dublin, and relict of George Macdonnell, Esq., uncle of the Rev. Richard Macdonnell, D.D., Provost of Trinity College, Dublin. He died 28 February 1815, aged 69, and was interred with his first wife in Knockbride, where there is a tomb to their memory. His will, signed 14 February 1813, was proved in Dublin 16 March 1815 (Probate Court, Dublin). Mrs. Adams, his second wife, died April 1832, aged 80, in Dorset Street, Dublin, of cholera, and was

interred in Finglas 1 May 1832 (Finglas Par. Reg.), having had issue by
Mr. William Adams one daughter, viz. :—

I. MARTHA SUSANNA, born 1786 ; died unmarried 24 December 1805 (Finglas
Par. Reg.) at Castletown House, co. Cavan, and was interred in the old
churchyard of Finglas. In the present Church there is a mural tablet
to her memory on the north side of the Communion table, which describes
her "as a beloved and dutiful child, endowed with many excellent and
Christian virtues which rendered her an ornament to her sex."

IV.

THE DESCENDANTS OF SAMUEL ADAMS, THE FOURTH SON OF ALLEN ADAMS AND MARTHA HIGENBOTHAM.

IV. SAMUEL ADAMS of Dublin, born 1750 ; married 10 March 1779 (Walker's
"Hibernian Magazine") Elizabeth, daughter of Rev. Alexander Leslie of
Portglenore, co. Antrim, a relation of the Earl of Rothes ; died 7 June 1799,
aged 49. His will, signed 27 May 1799, was proved in Dublin 26 June
1799 (Probate Court, Dublin). His widow removed to Drumgoon House,
co. Cavan, where she died 22 January 1802, aged 50, and was interred beside
her husband at Knockbride, where there is a tomb to their memory, on
which the date of her death, 22 January 1801, is incorrect. Her will, signed
15 September 1801, was proved 27 November 1802 in Dublin (Probate
Court, Dublin). They had issue three sons and six daughters, viz. :—

I. RICHARD ADAMS of Wainsford, Hants, born 1780 ; entered the Army as
Ensign in the 24th Regiment 12 December 1798 ; Lieut. 8 November
1799 ; served in Egypt under Sir Ralph Abercrombie in 1800 ; Captain
in the 59th Regiment 27 June 1805 ; exchanged 24 June 1807 into the
2nd Dragoon Guards (Queen's Bays) ; was present at the siege and
capture of Copenhagen by Lord Cathcart September 1807, and sold out
29 June 1809 ("Army List" and Letter from the Horse Guards) ;
re-entered the Army as Cornet in the 13th Light Dragoons 21 May 1812 ;
Lieut. 15 July 1813 ; was engaged at Waterloo 18 June 1815, and again
sold out October 1816 (ibid.) ; married 4 June 1806 (Alveston Par. Reg.)
Louisa, daughter of Newsham Peers, Esq., of Alveston Park, near
Stratford-on Avon, Warwickshire ; died 11 February 1836, aged 54, at
Wainsford, and was interred 18 February at Milford, Hants (Milford,
Hants, Par. Reg.). His wife died 17 August 1846, aged 74, and was
interred 20 August 1846 beside her husband, having had issue three
sons and two daughters, viz. :—

1. RICHARD GORDON PEERS ADAMS, born 1809 ; baptized 5 July 1809
(Handley Par. Reg.) ; died of measles at school 1820 and was
interred at Handley, Dorsetshire.

2. MAXWELL LESLIE BENJAMIN ADAMS, born 1810 ; baptized 3 November
1810 (Handley Par. Reg.) ; entered the Royal Navy as First Class
Volunteer on board the "Wellesley, 72" 23 April 1824 ; Midshipman
2 December 1825 ; Mate 5 May 1830 ; died unmarried 7 October
1834 on board H.M.S. "Imogene," and was buried in the Sooloo
Sea (Letter from the Admiralty).

3. HENRY AUGUSTUS ADAMS, born 13 December 1814 at Handley House,
Dorsetshire ; entered the Army 1835 ; sold out and entered the
Bombay Army 1836 in the 13th Bombay Infantry ; Ensign

7 February 1836 ; Lieut. 29 June 1841 ; Captain 7 March 1850 ;
Major 20 July 1858 ; Lieut.-Colonel 7 February 1862 ; Colonel
7 February 1867 ; Major-General 1 January 1878 ; Lieut.-General
1 April 1882 ; General 1 December 1888. War service in the Indian
Mutiny 1857-58 in Central India ; capture of Kotah ; with column
in pursuit of Gwallior rebels 1858 ; action at Sunganeer and battle
of the Banass 1858 ; action at Partabgurh 24 December 1858 ;
Brevet of Major; medal and clasp; married 9 June 1840, at Tannah,
East Indies, J. Charlotte (born 3 June 1823), daughter of John
Andrew Rabé, Esq., of Simon's Town, Cape Colony, who died
1 December 1887 at Funchal, Madeira. He died 27 January 1898,
aged 84, and was buried at Salcombe, Devon, having had issue eight
sons and two daughters, viz. :—

(1) HENRY EDWARD ADAMS, born 21 February 1841 ; entered the
Army 8 July 1862, from Sandhurst College, as Ensign in the
15th Foot ; Lieut. 7 April 1865 ; exchanged 13 March 1866
into the 2nd West India Regiment ; exchanged again 11 January
1867 into the 6th Foot, and sold out 8 November 1867 ;
married 9 February 1875 Selina Clayton Elmer, widow, and
died s.p. from wounds received at the battle of Kandahar in
Afghanistan 22 September 1880, having rejoined the Army
24 September 1868.

(2) MAXWELL RICHARD WILLIAM PEERS ADAMS, born 15 January
1849 ; matriculated at King's College, London, Michaelmas
Term 1866 ; Member of the Honourable Society of the Middle
Temple Hilary Term 1870 ; called to the Bar 29 June 1881 ;
entered the Imperial Civil Service of the Government of India,
under nomination by the Secretary of State for India, 30 November 1871 ; married 3 January 1881 (Falmouth Par. Reg.)
Fanny Michell, daughter of William Gay, Esq., H.M.C.S., and
has issue one daughter, viz. :—

FRANCES CHARLOTTE GAY PEERS, born at Umballa, Punjab,
India, 14 September 1882.

(3) JAMES CRAIG-BATE DE LISLE ADAMS, born 20 August 1851 ;
appointed to the Civil Service of the Government of Bombay
3 February 1871; married 14 November 1893, at Baroda,
India, Isabella, eldest daughter of James Richard Naylor, Esq.,
C.S.I., Indian Civil Service, and has issue three daughters,
viz. :—

1. LOUISA PEERS, born 27 August 1894.

2. ELEANOR PEERS, born 30 September 1895 ; baptized at All
Saints' Church, Dharwar, India, 30 November 1895.

3. DOROTHY PEERS, born 18 October 1896 ; baptized at All
Saints' Church, Dharwar, India, 5 December 1896.

(4) ALEXANDER PEERS ADAMS, born 6 September 1855 ; educated at
King Edward VI.'s School, Sherborne, Dorset, St. Bartholomew's
Hospital, London, and Netley Hospital, Southampton ; Surgeon
Indian Medical Service 1880 ; served in the Burma War
1884—87 with distinction, and was rewarded with the decora-
tion of the Distinguished Service Order and Burmese Medal
on account of his services ; died in Madras 12 September 1887

from the results of fever contracted in Burma. He was buried
at Madras. A handsome cross over his grave bears the inscription, " Erected by some of his brother officers as a token of
regard."

(5) NEWSHAM PEERS ADAMS, born 6 June 1861 ; of Corpus Christi
College, Cambridge, B.A. 1899 ; Deacon, Diocese of Norwich,
21 December 1901 ; married 4 June 1892, at St. Thomas'
Mount, Madras, Ada Emily Mary, daughter of Thomas Rowe,
Esq., of Ealing, Middlesex, formerly of Dublin. She died s.p.
20 November 1892, and is buried at St. Thomas' Mount, Madras.
He married 2ndly, 15 August 1895, Catherine Mary, only
daughter of Robert Rouby Oke, Esq., M.R.C.S., of Cumberland
House, Southampton (Baughurst Par. Reg.).

(6) LESLIE PEERS ADAMS, born 27 February 1863 ; married in 1884
Ellen Hardwick, and has issue as follows :—

1. WILLIAM HENRY AUGUSTUS ADAMS, born 29 November 1886.

2. ALEXANDER PEERS ADAMS, born 13 September 1889.

3. JOSEPHINE CHARLOTTE ELLEN, born 19 June 1885.

4. MABEL (a twin), born 14 January 1888.

5. BEATRICE (twin with last), born 14 January 1888.

6. FLORENCE MARY, born 19 December 1890.

7. LESLIE PEERS ADAMS, born 24 August 1892.

8. MAXWELL PEERS ADAMS, born 15 March 1894.

(7) CHARLES WINCKWORTH PEERS ADAMS, born 1 September 1864 ;
died 19 March 1870 and was buried at Colaba, Bombay.

(8) FRANCIS PEERS ADAMS, born 9 December 1866 ; married 25 March
1898, at Brixton, London, Emma Edwards.

(9) KATHERINE LOUISA, born 13 December 1843 ; married 8 July
1864 Rev. Edward Rogers, who died 22 July 1865. She died
at Edgbaston 13 April 1897 and was buried at King's Norton,
Worcestershire (King's Norton Par. Reg.), having had issue
one daughter, viz. :—

CHARLOTTE MABEL, born 8 August 1865.

(10) BEATRICE JULIA, born 14 October 1853 ; died unmarried 26
November 1889, after a painful and lingering illness, at Green-
holme, the residence of her father, General H. A. Adams, at
Kingston Hill, Surrey, and was interred at Kingston-on-
Thames.

4. AMELIA JULIANA PEERS, born 6 March 1807 ; baptized 15 March 1807
(Alveston Par. Reg.) ; died unmarried 3 July 1835, aged 28, at
Wainsford, and was interred 9 July at Milford near Lymington,
Hants (Milford, Hants, Par. Reg.).

5. LOUISA JANE, born 18 July 1808 ; baptized 5 November 1808 (Alveston
Par. Reg.) ; married 30 September 1835 William O'Brien Adams,
M.B. ; died 15 August 1840 of fever, while on a visit to her uncle
Major Benjamin Adams, at Danson Court (see next page), and was
interred in Athboy Churchyard, co. Meath (Athboy Par. Reg.),
where there is a tomb to her memory. [For her children see p. 88.]

II. BENJAMIN ADAMS, born 1784 ; baptized 15 December 1784 (St. Michan's, Dublin, Par. Reg.) ; entered the Army 1 October 1803 as Ensign in the 24th Regiment : Lieut. 22 December 1804 in the 17th Lancers ;* Captain 16 February 1815 ; Major unattached 15 August 1826 ; exchanged 7 May 1829 into the 78th Highlanders ; sold out May 1838 ("Army List") ; married 30 July 1827 (St. Peter's, Dublin, Par. Reg.) Maria Anne, daughter of Thomas Daniell, Esq. She died 10 February 1879 in Dublin, aged 76. They resided for some time at Danson Court near Athboy, then at Glenageary, Kingstown, and finally at 71 Upper Leeson Street, Dublin, where he died 18 November 1847, and was interred in Mount Jerome (Mount Jerome Reg.), having had issue four sons and six daughters, viz. :—

1. SAMUEL ADAMS of Newlands, Ferns, born 27 January 1835 ; entered the Army 19 September 1856 as Cornet in the 12th Lancers ; Lieut. 11 December 1857 ; exchanged into the 15th Foot 24 May 1861 ; sold out 23 August 1864 ("Army List") ; married 31 March 1866 Jane Cannon, daughter of the late B. E. Black, Esq., of Halifax, Nova Scotia.

2. NEASON BENJAMIN JAMES ADAMS, born 5 December 1840 at Monkstown, co. Dublin ; died an infant and was interred in Mount Jerome (Mount Jerome Reg.).

3. BENJAMIN WILLIAM BROWN ADAMS, born 1841 ; died an infant and was interred in Mount Jerome (Mount Jerome Reg.).

4. NEASON ADAMS, T.C.D., A.B. Hiem. 1863 ; born 30 September 1843.

5. ELIZABETH ISABELLA, married 17 January 1851 Rev. Josiah Beatson Lowe, D.D., Incumbent of St. Jude's, Liverpool, where she died 3 October 1871, having had issue fifteen children.

6. EMILY, born 1832 ; died 1 June 1846, aged 13, and was interred in Mount Jerome (Mount Jerome Reg.).

7. LOUISA SUSANNA, married 10 November 1853 Rev. Thomas Sneyd Wallace, LL.D., ex-scholar of Trinity College, Dublin, and Incumbent of St. Paul's, Bolton, who died 13 March 1863 at Southport, and had issue three sons. The second son, the Rev. W. B. Wallace, died 1 May 1897 at Middleburg, Cape Colony, and was buried 4 May at Grahamstown ("Irish Times" Newspaper).

8. ISABELLA.

9. MARIA, married 11 September 1862 John Loyde Peyton, Esq., of Knockvicar, Boyle, co. Roscommon.

10. MARTHA MARY ANNE, born 7 June 1838; baptized 18 July 1838 (St. Peter's, Dublin, Par. Reg.) ; died 30 May 1846, aged 8, and was buried in Mount Jerome (Mount Jerome Reg.).

III. JAMES ADAMS, born 1799 ; was adopted heir by his uncle James Adams of Corranearry House (see p. 88) ; died 1808 at Corranearry House and was buried in Knockbride.

* Major Benjamin Adams saw much service with the 17th Lancers while in India, notably in the Pindaree War, 1817-18. See "Death or Glory Boys : the Story of the 17th Lancers," by D. H. Parry. London, 1899.

IV. ISABELLA, born 1782 ; married 2 April 1802 Neason Wildridge Adams, M.D. (*vide* p. 124) ; died s.p. 18 December 1855 and was interred in Knockbride (Knockbride Par. Reg.).

V. ELIZABETH, born 1783 ; married 2 December 1811 Robert Alexander Wood, Esq., of Castle Cottage, co. Meath, who died March 1848 and was interred 23 March 1848 in Agher Churchyard (Agher Par. Reg.). She died s.p. 2 September 1865 and was interred in Agher Churchyard beside her husband.

VI. AMELIA, born 1787 ; baptized 7 June 1787 (St. Michan's, Dublin, Par. Reg.) ; died October 1788 and was interred 16 October 1788 in St. Michan's, Dublin (*ibid.*).

VII. MARY (a twin), born 1791 ; died an infant and was interred in St. Michan's, Dublin (St. Michan's, Dublin, Par. Reg.).

VIII. AMELIA (twin with last), born 1791 ; married 1812 Henry Potterton, Esq. ; died s.p. 10 June 1840, aged 49, and was interred with her parents in Knockbride (Knockbride Par. Reg.).

IX. MARIA, born 1796 ; married 2 September 1816 James Adams, Esq., M.D. (*vide* p. 124) ; died s.p. 31 March 1867 and was interred with her husband in Knockbride (Knockbride Par. Reg.).

(*To be continued.*)

Tymms.

HERALDS' CERTIFICATE TOUCHING A COAT OF ARMS USED AT THE FUNERAL OF THOMAS TYMMS OF LONDON, PHYSICIAN.*

Whereas there was a Coat of Arms depicted and used at y[e] Funeral of Thomas Tymms or Tymme of the parish of S[t] Mary Aldermanbury London Physitian lately deceased viz[t] Gules two Barrs and three Escallops in Chief Argent : We the Officers of Armes whose Names are hereunto Subscribed do Certifie that we have dilligently Searched the Books and Records of the College of Armes, but do not find that the Armes beforementiond do belong to the name or Family of Tymme or Tymms or that there are any Armes whatsoever belonging to the said Name of Tymme or Tymms ; But on the Contrary We do find That the Armes so made use of at the said Funeral were the Arms of S[r] Walter Bayons or Bayous of Lincolnshire in the time of King Edward the first and of S[r] William Bayons or Bayous tempore Edw : 2 as we are ready to shew. In witnes whereof we have hereunto set Our Names at the College of Armes this 21th day of Novemb[r] 1687.

> THO. S[r] GEORGE, Garter.
> THO. HOLFORD, Windsor.
> JOH. GIBSON, Blew-mantle.
> GRE[ry] KING, R. Dr., Reg'.

* From the original in the possession of W. BRUCE BANNERMAN, Esq., F.S.A.

𝔐onumental 𝔦nscriptions

IN THE

𝔠hurch of 𝔰t. 𝔊iles=in=the=𝔉ields.*

The present fabric of St. Giles' Church was erected in 1733, from the design of Henry Flitcroft, on the site of a church began in 1624 and finished in 1628. This replaced a much older building.

In giving the Inscriptions in this Church we are fortunate in having two separate records of monuments which have now disappeared, for it will be seen that only fragmentary portions of two monuments that were in the Church erected in 1624 remain, and a tablet of the Bertie benefaction, of which parts are gone. These records, which shew what a number of interesting monuments have perished, are, first, a collection of Church Notes, forming Lansdowne MS. 878, in the British Museum. The copies of inscriptions in this MS. (the title-page of which bears the name of William Faldoe) bear evidence of having been carefully made, and the arms are for the most part nicely tricked and coloured, although some towards the end are left unfinished, and in the margin a short note is given setting forth the character and position of many of the monuments. This MS. is undated, but appears to have been written about 1675 from the dates of the inscriptions. Our second source of information is Hatton's "A New View of London." This work corrects what Stowe gives in some points; but on being compared with the MS. and what remains of the actual inscriptions, will be found to vary in many small points, chiefly in the spelling of words and in extending abbreviations. The British Museum copy belonged to B. Grenville, having his name in it, and many pen and ink alterations and notes.

At the West end of the North Aisle an oval marble tablet bears the following :— Deo Votiva | The Honor^ble ROBERT | BERTIE of this Parish, one of | the Son^s of the Right Honble | ROBERT, EARLE OF LINDSEY, Lord | Great Chamberlaine of Englan^d | and Generall of all ye forces of KING | CHARLES the First, who was Slayne in | the Battalle att Edge Hill | hath given | into ye hands of ye Churchwardens, Fifty | pounds, that soe ye Interest thereof may bee | distributed by them from time to time and | for ever, to the poore in bread | (Viz^t) | Twelve peny worth, on every Sunday in y^e | Yeare, & on every New Years day, Five | shillings (if Sunday) otherwise, Four | shillings; & on ye last Sunday of Aug^t | in ye same yeare, Five shillings, | Begun the First day of | January 1677. | Pauperibusqz | Tabula.

[In the "New View" this is given with many variations of spelling, etc., but it adds the arms, now gone, namely: *Three battering rams*, impaling *a bear rampant*. No colours.]

Beneath the first window from the West end of this Aisle is a plain marble tablet, inscribed with the following, and on a ledge beneath it is the recumbent effigy in marble of a lady. The style of the figure might be of a much later date, the form is so well moulded, and shrouded in a robe, the lines of which flow gracefully over the body :—In Memory of the Right Honble LADY FRANCES KNIVETON, (wife of

---

* Communicated by ARTHUR F. G. LEVESON GOWER, Esq., assisted by ARTHUR J. JEWERS.

S[r] GILBERT KNIVETON | of Bradley, in the County of Derby, Baronet,) lyeth buried in the Chancel of this Church. | She was one of the 5 Daughters and Coheirs of the R[t] Hon[ble] S[r] ROBERT DUDLEY, K[t], Duke of the | Empire ; by the LADY ALICE his Wife & Duchess, Which ROBERT was Son of the R[t] Hon[ble] | ROBERT DUDLEY, Late EARLE OF LEICESTER, & his Duchess was Daughter of S[r] THO. LEIGH | & Aunt to the R[t] Hon[ble] THO[s] late LORD LEIGH of Stoneleigh in the County of Warwick, | And the said Honour and Title of DUCHESS DUDLEY was by Letters Patents of his late Majesty | of glorious Memory, KING CHARLES y[e] 1st allowed ; & since graciously confirmed to her by his | now Majesty KING CHARLES y[e] 2[d] and she lived and died worthy of that Honour | Since the rebuilding of this Church, this monument was resett up by the | Hon[ble] CHARLES LEIGH of Leighton in Bedfordshire ; 1738.

[The above is the monument as it now appears, with a careful copy of the inscription, which will be found to vary in minor points from that printed in "A New View of London," which, however, supplies the following inscription, now gone, with the marble on which it was cut :—

" The Right Honourable Lady FRANCES KNIVETON, Wife of Sir GILBERT KNIVETON of Bradley in the County of Derby, Baronet, lyeth buried in the Chancel of this Church. She was one of the Daughters and Coheirs of the Right Honourable Sir ROBERT DUDLEY, Knight, Duke of the Empire, by the Lady ALICE his Wife and Duchess. Which ROBERT was son of the Right Honourable ROBERT DUDLEY, late Earl of Leicester, and his Duchess was Daughter of Sir THO. LEIGH and Aunt to the Right Honourable THO., late LORD LEIGH of Stoneley in the County of Warwick. And the said Honour and Title of DUCHESS DUDLEY was by Letters Patents of his l[a] Majesty of Glorious Memory KING CHARLES the 1st allowed and since graciously confirmed to her by his now Majesty KING CHARLES the 2nd ; and she lived and died worthy of that Honour.

" The Right Honourable Lady ANNE HOLBOURNE, sister of the said LADY FRANCES, another Daughter of the said Duke and Duchess, did will this Monument, which she has provided in her life time, to be erected to the Memory of her dear Sister near to whom herself (who died August 1663) lyes also interred ; and it is placed here for want of convenient room in the Chancel."

The "New View" also gives the following description of the monument and the arms then on it :—

" On the South Side of the Church and at the West End is an Extraordinary Spacious Monument mostly marble, adorned with Cartouches, Cornish, Pediment, Martling, Festoons ; on the Pediment is a Death's Head, having a Laurel Chaplet, and under, the word ' Resurgamus ' between two Boys supporting a large mantling, supposed to let down and cover the whole Monument ; as also Effigies lying at full length, finely carved.

" Here are these arms : *Ruby, a Chevron Verry, on a Canton Pearl a Sinister hand of the first impaled with Topaz, a Lion rampant Diamond which last is also impaled with Pearl on a Fess diamond, 3 Cresents Topaz in Chief 2 Birds rising Diamond*."

The above method of blazon having entirely fallen into disuse as purposeless and confusing, it may be as well to give the modern form. First Shield : *Gules, a chevron vaire* (the badge of a Baronet in chief), KNIVETON ; impaling *Or, a lion rampant double-queued vert*, DUDLEY. This well-known coat is incorrectly given in the "New View," but correctly given in Lansdowne MS. 878. Second Shield : *Argent, on a fess sable three crescents or, in chief two birds rising of the second*, HOLBORN ; impaling DUDLEY, as before. Also two Shields of KNIVETON impaling DUDLEY, both quarterly ; and DUDLEY with quarters and impaling BLAKE (see *post*).

A " Life of Sir Robert Dudley, with notes on the Lives of Alice, Duchess Dudley, and her daughters," states that the present figure in St. Giles' Church was originally part of a very magnificent monument, the figure being under a carved canopy, supported by black marble pillars, which monument is generally supposed to have been erected by Alice, Duchess Dudley, as it closely resembles the monument she erected for herself in Stoneleigh Church ; but this supposition is effectually disposed of by the statement regarding the monument in the will of Dame Anne Holborne, of which the following is an abstract :—

Anne Holborne makes her will in perfect health and memory. Undated. To be buried in the chancel of St. Giles' Church in the fields, as near the body of her sister Lady Frances Kniveton as can be. To the poor of that parish £50 to be distributed at her burial. For the repair and re-edifying of the church adjoyning to the Temple House in Bulsall lane £500, and if that is not sufficient so much more as will build it up in fair and decent manner ; also to that church or chapel £100 a year for ever, out of lands in Bulsall to maintain a preaching minister to the end of the world. Out of lands in Long Itchington £50 a year to be settled upon the church to augment its small income. To the poor of the Parishes of Bulsall and Long Itchington, co. Warwick, £100, to be distributed about the time of her funeral. £200 for a ring and Jewell for her mother the "Lady Duchess Dudley." Cousin Skrimsher, the Lord Viscount Bronker's sister, "my husband's picture set with diamonds," and to her daughter Frances Skrimsher £100 if she live to be twenty years of age. £50 for a ring for cousin Elizabeth Trasie. Cousin Charles Leigh £100 or a ring of that price. To true and faithful friends Thomas Percival, Esq., £100, and his wife Mrs Katherine Percival £500 ; to their daughter "my goddaughter" £500. Cousin Elizabeth Stanley £20. Worthy friend and kinsman Lord Viscount Bronkre £1500 or £100 a year out of lands in Itchington for his care of her and her affairs, and had intended him to be her executor, but for many reasons thinks it not convenient, and therefore ordains her worthy brother Sir Richard Leveson, Knight of the Bath, and dear sister Lady Katherine Leveson his wife to be executors, and the said Lady Katherine Leveson to be residuary legatee, and a ring of £100 to said brother Leveson, and they to see "my deare sister the Lady Frances Leveson's tomb set up in St Gyles church as I have agreed with one Mr Marshall, a stone cutter in Shoe lane, and is to pay him £120 for it, and to be set up under the South window near which her said sister Lady Frances Kniveton is buried." "I desire my owne figure to be added to hers in a winding sheete as my deare sisters is." Goddaughter Anna Howin £20 when she is twenty, and, being much beholden to her parents, gives a ring of £20 to cousin Howin and one of £10 to his wife. "My cozen Andoreus his daughter." Bequests to servants. If brother and sister Leveson are not near at her death and the Lord Viscount Bronnker is, that he will act as Executor.

Proved 27 Aug. 1663 by William Viscount Brouncker as the will of Lady Anna Holborne, late of the parish of St. Paul, Covent Garden, Sir Richard Leveson, K.B., being deceased, and Dame Katherine Leveson, his relict and sister of the deceased, renouncing. (P.C.C., 108, Juxon.)

The following is an exact copy of the inscription as given in Lansdowne MS. 878 :—

"M. S.

"The Right Honorable ye Lady FRANCES KNIVETON, wife of Sr GILBERT KNIVETON of Bradley in com. Derby, Brt, lyeth buried in the chancell of this church. She was one of the five daughters and coheires of the Right Honorable Sr ROBERT DUDLEY, Kt, Duke of the Empire, by the LADY ALICE his wife & dutchess, which ROBERT was sonne of the right honorable ROBERT DUDLEY, late Earle of Leicester, and his dutchess was daughter of Sr THOMAS LEIGH and aunt to the right Honorable THOMAS, late LORD LEIGH of Stoneley in the county of Warwick, and the said Honour and title of DUTCHESS DUDLEY was by Letters Pattent of his Late Majestye of glorious memory KING CHARLES ye first allowed and since graciously confirmed to her by his now Majestye KING CHARLES the second, and she lived and dyed worthy of that honour.

"The right honorable the Lady ANNE HOLBOURN, sister of the said LADY

FRANCIS and an other daughter of the said Duke and Dutchess, did will this monument, which she had provided in her life time, to be erected to the memory of her deare sister, nere to whome her self (who dyed the 6ᵗʰ of August 1663) lyes also interred, and it is placed here for want of convenient roome in the chancell.'']

On a plain marble tablet with an urn at the top, partly hidden by a mantle :— In memory of | Mʳˢ ANN WINTER | formerly of Monmouth Street in this parish and afterwards | of Paradise Row, Chelsea ; died 4ᵗʰ May 1830, aged 80 years. | Also of | EMMELINE HARRIOT WINTER | (Daughter of the above named ANN WINTER) | Died 9 February 1838, aged 52 years. | And of | WASHINGTON COR-NELIUS WINTER | (also daughter of the above named ANN WINTER) | Died 3ʳᵈ July 1850, aged 70 years.
The above named W. C. WINTER bequeathed to the Trustees and | Governors (If any) of the Almshouses in Coal Yard, Drury Lane | in this parish, and in case there were no Trustees and Governors of the | said Almshouse then to the minister and churchwardens of this | parish, Two thousand pounds, three pounds per cent. consolidated Bank | Annuities, upon Trust from time to time to divide the dividends and | interest thereof by monthly payments between and amongst the poor | widows for the time being inhabiting the said almshouses in equal | shares, for the better support and maintenance of such poor widows. | And the above named W. C. WINTER also bequeathed unto the | minister and churchwardens of the parish of Saint Luke, Chelsea, one | thousand pounds three pounds per cent. consolidated Bank Annuities | upon trust to pay and divide the dividens and interest thereof upon | Saint Thomas's day in every year equally between and amongst thirty | poor widows of the said parish of Saint Luke, Chelsea, and who should | have been house-keepers in that parish for ten years at the least.

On a white marble tablet with these arms : *Per bend sinister ermine and ermines a lion rampant or,* impaling *Argent, a fess between three crescents gules.*   Crest : *A lion's head couped per bend sinister ermine and ermines* :—Sacred to the Memory of | THOMAS EDWARDS, Gent. | who died the 9ᵗʰ of July MDCCLXXXXI. | in the LXXIˢᵗ of his Age | And lies in the Vault of this Church ; He lived | Many years a vigilant and useful inhabitant | of this Parish ; esteemed and beloved by all | as an honest and good Man.   He bequeathed | for ever the following Legacies : the Interest of | 500 Pounds 4 per cᵗ Stocks ; to buy Bread for the | Poor of the Parish of St. Giles' in the Fields to be | distributed every Sabbath Day, also the Interest of | 300 Pounds 4 per cᵗ Stocks for the Use of the Charity School | of the said Parish, besides very considerable | Benefactions to several public Charities.
His widow Mʳˢ GRACE EDWARDS | caused this monument to be erected as a | small Tribute of Gratitude and Affection | for one of the best of men and Husbands | as also to Exhibit to Posterity so exemplery | a Pattern of Charity and Goodness in Humble | Hopes that those whom God has blessed with | Abilities and Success may go and do likewise.
The above named | Mʳˢ GRACE EDWARDS | died 23ᵈ November MDCCCXVIII | in the LXXXIIIᵈ year of her Age. | Blessed are the Dead | who die in the Lord | for they rest from | their labours.

Plain white marble tablet :—In Memory of | EDWARD MAWLEY, Esqʳ | many years resident in the | parish of St. Giles in the Fields | ob. 30 Jan. 1826, æt. 65 | And of | ELIZABETH | his wife | ob. 30 Nov. 1838, æt. 68.

Plain white marble on a black tablet:—In memory of | SAMUEL REMNANT, Esqʳᵉ | an old and highly respected inhabitant | of this parish | Whose remains are interred | in the vault beneath this church. | He departed this life at Hampstead | on the 24ᵗʰ December 1838, | In his 82ⁿᵈ year. | His memory will be long revered by | a numerous circle of relations and friends.

[Here is the second window from the West end.]   A large-sized white marble tablet :—Near the body of | WILLIAM JACKSON, Esquire | her former husband | lie the remains of | ELIZABETH | the wife of ISAAC SPENCER, Esquire, | of Poppleton near York. | She died on the eighth of October 1823, | in the fifty fifth year of her age. | This monument | was placed by her husband | in testimony of grief for his loss | her charities | the goodness of her heart | and numerous excellent qualities | acquired the esteem of all | who knew her | in the practise of her many virtues, | she lived affectionately beloved, | by her family and friends, | and she died universally regretted.

An ornamental draped mantle with an antique lamp, cherubs, and Death's head, with scroll shield, but no arms:—Near this | place Lye interred | the Bodies of JOHN HAWFORD of | Clements Inne, gen[t], and ELIZABETH His | wife the daughter of J[no] BANBRIGGE | of Lockington in the County of | Leicester, Esqr. Also their two sons | JOHN and WILLIAM.

JOHN HAWFORD, Senr	} dyed	Decr 1712	ætat. { 69.
ELIZ. His wife		Ap[r] 1714	{ 61.

JOHN their Eldest Son dyed the | 8th of Feby 1713, Ætatis 26 | WILLIAM their young | Son dyed the 19th | of July 1715 | Ætatis 22.

A marble tablet, having carved on it an urn, partly hidden by a mantle :—In the vault | under this Church | are deposited the Remains | of the late | WILLIAM JACKSON, Esqr | Twenty five Years a merchant in | the City of London | who departed this Life | the 21st Day of March 1817 | in the 48th Year of his Age. | This marble is placed here by his | Widow as a Tribute to | the Memory of her revered Husband | her Monitor, and her Friend. | Reader | It may justly be said of him that he was | in Sense a Man, in Innocence a Child. | Them that are meek will God guide in Judgement | And such as are gentle them shall he teach his ways. Also in the same Vault are deposited the Remains | of M[rs] HANNAH SHUTTLEWOOD, Mother of | M[rs] ELIZ[H] JACKSON, who died Feb[y] 9th, 1818, aged 78 | Sincerely beloved by her family | And highly Esteemed by all who knew her.

[Here is the third window from the West end, the subject being Jacob's dream, in coloured glass, with the words " Surely the Lord is in this place."]

A brass, against the wall by the window :—In memoriam A. W. S. H. Dec[r] 15th, 1844, and A. S. Sept[r] 1st, 1867. | " In Thy presence is fulness of Joy."

Marble tablet with a small shield gone :—In memory of | CHARLOTTE | wife of JOSEPH PRENDERGRASS, Esq[r] | of Thorhaugh Street | Bedford Square | whose remains are deposited in the Vault | at S[t] Pancras, belonging to this parish. | She departed this life | on the 18th day of May 1821, | in the 34th year of her age | Sincerely and deservedly lamented.

Black marble slab in gilt capital letters :—Near unto this place lyeth the Body of | ANDREW MARVELL, Esquire, a man so endowed by nature | so improved by education, study & travel, so consummated | by practice & experience, that joining the most peculiar graces | of wit & learning with a singular penetration & strength of | judgement & exercising all these in the whole course of his Life | with an unalterable steadiness in the ways of virtue, he became | the ornament & example of his age ; beloved by good men, fear'd | by bad, admired by all, tho' imitated alas ! by few, & scarce fully | parallelled by any, but a tombstone can neither contain his Character, | nor is marble necessary to transmit it to posterity, it will be always | legible in his inimitable writings.   He served the town of Kingston | upon Hull above 20 years successively in Parliament & that with such | wisdom, dexterity, integrity & courage as becomes a true patriot. | He dyed the 16 Aug. 1678 in the 58th year of his age.

Sacred | To the memory of ANDREW MARVELL, Esqr, as a strenuous assertor of | the constitution, laws & liberties of England, | and out of family affection & admiration of | the uncorrupt probity of his life & manners | ROBERT NETTLETON of London, merchant, his grand nephew | hath caused this small memorial of him | to be erected in the year 1764.

A plain white marble tablet :—Sacred to the Memory of EDWARD WRIGHT, Esq. | more than 40 years an Inhabitant of the Parish | lately of Hendon, Middlesex | where he died on the 7th June 1821 | in the 66th Year of his Age. | As he lived beloved by all who knew him | So was his death by them lamented. | He was indeed one of those Noblest works of God | An honest Man.

Also Mrs MARY WRIGHT | Relict of the above | who died 17th December 1834 in her 72nd Year.

A white marble tablet with a wreath carved on it and a black base :—Sacred | To the Memory of | THOMAS BURROWS, Esqr | late of this Parish | whose remains are deposited | in the Vault of this Church ; | Died June 22nd, 1815 | Aged 72 Years.

If ever truth in Epitaph was told,
Reader, for truth this Character behold :
To act uprightly was through life his Plan,
He lived beloved, and died an honest Man.

An oval of white marble on a black base :—Sacred | to the Memory of | JOSEPH BROWN, Esqr | late of this parish | who departed this life | on the 1st of March 1823 | Aged 78 Years. | CONSTANT BROWN | Relict of the late JOSEPH BROWN. | She departed this life | Feb^{ry} 17th, 1830 | Age 63 Years.

[Here is the fourth window from the West end, the subject being Christ with woman of Samaria at the well, in coloured glass, with the words " I am the Resurrection and the Life."]

A brass, against the wall by the window :—To the beloved Memory of A. P. H. April 7th, 1884. | " Thy brother shall rise again."

Beneath the fourth window stands a very large iron chest, for parish records, and on it are these arms : *Three horses' heads erased.* Crest : *A cubit-arm erect, vested, the sleeve slashed, and in the hand a lance.* The letters R. H. are on either side of the crest (Humphreys or Humphrey, or Heylyn). On another shield : *Three covered cups* (BUTLER) with the initials F. B. There are also the following initials : G. H., J. G., I. W., R. E., I. D., R. S., F. B., R. D., S. B., C. S., C. O., T. E., W. P., W. L. ; also the date (1630) with the Royal arms and those of the City of London.

A black marble tablet with gilt letters :—This stone is to perpetuate the Memory of M^r ROB^T BARNFATHER | late of this Parish, he died Octr 23, 1741, aged 54 years ; and of | Mrs MARY BARNFATHER his wife, who lies near here in the Vault | Underneath, she died Decr 6, 1754, aged 67 Years. | Her life was amiable in all the relations of Wife, Parent, | Friend, &c., neighbour : and she made it so by regulating her | conduct by that precept of Gospel, Of doing to others | what we would they should do unto us. She was | such an example of Piety, Justice, Prudence, & Temperance | as is well worthy of Imitation & tho' her days were soured with | disquietudes & pains, she did not suffer her mind to be oppressed, | but comforted herself with a prospect of being happy thro' the | mercies of Christ after this life. These thoughts enabled | her to meet her dissolution with Cheerfulness and resignation. | Out of a Pious regard to their memories this is | erected by their most Affectionate Son.

A plain white marble tablet:—In the Rector's Vault | near the Stone Coffin of | JOHN BARNFATHER, Esq. | are deposited the Remains of | Mʳ JOHN HUMPHREY | who departed this Life 17ᵗʰ Decʳ 1790 | Aged 50 Years | & of Mʳˢ CATHARINE HUMPHREY | who departed this Life 27ᵗʰ July 1808 | Aged 70 Years, | the Nephew and the Niece | of Mʳˢ MARY BARNFATHER.

A plain white marble tablet:—In pious Memory of | Her Father & Mother & only sister | ARTHUR WILLIAM DEVIS, Artist, | MARGARET DEVIS & ELLIN DEVIS. | (who died in the years 1822, 1818, 1826, | respectively aged 59, 34 & 17) | This Tablet is here placed | in the Church where they worshipped | by ISABELLA, wife of MARTIN F. TUPPER | the Family Tomb having been recently removed.

A large black oval tablet on which, carved in white marble, is a female figure seated, leaning against an urn and holding a balance. Also these arms : *Gules, two chevronels, each charged with three martlets sable ;* and this inscription, also on white marble :—To the Memory of JOHN BARNFATHER, Esqʳ | who died the 17ᵗʰ of September 1793 in the 75ᵗʰ Year of his Age | An active and able Magistrate, who for several Years employed | his Time and Talents without Gratuity or Reward in the strict and | impartial Administration of Justice, nor was his Integrity less | disinterested and useful in many other Publick departments | In private Life he possessed that mildness of temper | and benignity of mind that endeared him to all | his Friends and Relations when Living | and his Memory esteemed and | honoured by them when | Dead.

[Here is the fifth window from the West end, the subject being Christ in the house of Mary and Martha, in coloured glass, with the words " Mary hath chosen that good part which shall not be taken away from her."]

A brass against the wall by the window :—In affectionate remembrance | of a loved sister Nov. 5, 1881.

A white marble tablet in the form of a sarcophagus on a black ground :—In the burial ground of this parish | lie the Remains of | Mʳ JOHN CROSDELL, | he was for more than forty years the chief clerk | of a considerable Banking establishment, | And for the whole of that period enjoyed | the fullest confidence and the highest esteem | of his employers | the last survivor of them | JAMES HALFORD, Esqʳᵉ | has placed this tablet to his memory. | He died respected and beloved | on the 4ᵗʰ of February 1838, | in the 77ᵗʰ Year of his Age.

EAST END OF THE NORTH AISLE.

White and black marble tablet with two reversed torches:—Sacred | to the memory | of | Major General THOMAS SHULDHAM | of the | Honᵇˡᵉ East India Company's Service, | Bengal Presidency, | who died March 14ᵗʰ, 1833, | aged 73 years.

A white marble tablet with these arms carved : *Argent, on a chevron engrailed azure between three martlets sable as many crescents or.* Crest : *A griffin's head erased sable. A knight's helmet beneath the crest.* Colours represented by lines :—H.S.E. | GULIELMUS WATSON eques | Societatis regalis apud Londinum, | et collegii regalis medicorum socius, | regali etiam academiæ madritensi adscriptus, | in universitatibus halæ et virtembergiæ | medicinæ doctor | honoris ergo electus | Vir sui temporis | scientiæ indagator studiosissinus ; | artis medicæ et botanica, nec non philosophiæ naturalis | præcipue quod ad vin electricam attinet | inter primos peritus | obiit die Maii 10 A.D. 1787, ætat. suæ 72. | Hoc marmor nec superbum | nec quidquam habens ornatus ; | præter ipsum ejus nomen, | filio pientissimo legante, testimenti curatores poni jusserunt.

(*To be continued.*)

LLOYD impaling LUMLEY.

Bookplate of Lloyd.

This Bookplate represents the Arms of HUMPHREY LLOYD of Denbigh, a celebrated antiquary, impaling those of his wife BARBARA, sister and coheir of JOHN, LORD LUMLEY. For further particulars of the Pedigree see " Mis. Gen. et Her.," Vol. II., pp. 277—279.

GRANT OF ARMS AND CREST TO FRANCIS DASHWOOD, 1662.

To all and Singular to whom these presents shall come Sr Edward Bysshe Knight Clarenceux Principall Herald and King of Armes of ye South East and West parts of this Realme of England from ye River of Trent Southward sendeth greeting. Wheras antiently it hath been a Custome and to this day is continued that all Estates and Degrees of men have been and yett are distinguished each from other by sundry Markes or Signes in Sheildes comonly called Armes being no otherwise then outward demonstrations and remembrances of ye inward worth of the Bearers atcheived either by their valour in ye ffeild in time of Warr or by ther vertuous Endeavours in ye Com'onwealth in time of peace. Now wheras Francis Dashwood Esqr late an Alderman of London hath requested me to declare and assigne unto him such armes as hee and his posterity may lawfully beare Know yee therfore y^t haveing seriously considered ye Premisses and finding ye said Francis Dashwood to be a man of Ability and faithfullness to ye Crowne and Kingdom reputed worthyly deserving I doe think fitt to assigne unto him and his Posterity ye armes hereunder mentioned Viz. Argent on a fesse between double Cottizes Gules three Griffons Heads Erazed Or and for his Creast on a Helmet and Wreath of his Colours A Griffons Head Erminoys beakt and erazed Gules Mantled Gules doubled Argent as in ye margent more lively is depicted which armes and Creast I ye said Clarenceux by ye authority of my said Office and ye Letters Pattents made unto me under ye great Seale of England doe by these presents assigne give ratifie confirme and grant unto ye said Francis Dashwood and ye Heires of his body lawfully begotten to be by them and every of them borne wth ther due differences according to ye law of Armes for ever in wittnesse whereof I have unto these presents affixed ye seale of my office and subscribed my name.   Dated att ye office of Armes ye Fower and Twentieth day of October An^o D'ni 1662 and in ye Fowerteenth Yeare of ye Raigne of our Soveraigne Lord Charles ye second by ye Grace of God of England Scotland France and Ireland King defender of ye ffaith &c.

EDWARD BYSSHE,
Clarenceux King of Armes.

[N.B.—The above grantee, who was father of Sir Francis Dashwood created a Baronet in 1707, had had a grant of arms in 1655 from Bysshe, who had been put into the office of Garter by the Cromwellian Parliament, but this grant (as were all Cromwellian grants) was declared null and void by a Royal Warrant, dated 4 September 1660.—ED.]

Marriages of Wandsworth Inhabitants.*

EXTRACTS FROM REGISTERS IN VARIOUS PARISHES.

1748-9, Jan. 24. JOSEPH MORRIS of Wandsworth, Surry, Batchelor, & ELIZ. SNOWDON of the same place, Spinster ; p' Lycence. (Fulham.)

1725 May 22 Elizabeth, daughter of George Snowden, bapt.
175½ Feb. 29 Anne, daughter of Joseph and Elizabeth Morris, bapt.
1753 Sep. 16 Mary, daughter of Joseph and Elizabeth Morris, bapt.
1757 June 18 Joseph, son of Joseph and Elizabeth Morris, bapt.
1755 Sep. 3 Margaret [sic], inf. dau. of Joseph and Elizabeth Morris, bur.

1751-2, Jan. 23. WILLIAM HOWELL of St Martin-in-the-Fields, co. Midx., widr, & DOROTHY MOORE of Wansworth, co. Surry, spr ; by lic.; Mr Brady. (Christchurch, Newgate Street, London.)

1752, Sep. 28. JAMES GODDARD of St Andrew, Holbourn, in the County of Middx., Widower, & MARY WINTER of Wandsworth in the County of Surry, Widow, were married by Licence in this Cathedral on the 28th day of September 1752 ; by me Anselm Bayly. (St. Paul's Cathedral.)

1752, Nov. 11. WILLM SMITH of Bow in the County Surry, Widower, & SUSANNAH LUDGILL of Wandsworth in the County aforesaid, Widow ; p' Lycence. (Fulham.)

1754, June 3. JOHN POUMIES, Bachelor, & ELIZABETH GOLDER, Spinster ; Licence of the Bishop of London. (St. George, Hanover Square.)

[They were buried in Mount Nod, Wandsworth, where is their epitaph.]
1769 Feb. 10 John Poumies, Esq., bur.
1771 Mar. 1 Elizabeth, widow of John Poumies, 70, bur.

1755, May 27. EDWARD GEORGE of Wandsworth & SUSANNA GREEN of this parish ; License 27 May 1755 ; by H. Venn, Curate. Witnesses : Richd Green, Mary Guplon. (Clapham.)

1725 Aug. 1 Edward, son of William George, bapt.
1757 July 3 Elizabeth, daughter of Edward and Susannah George, bapt.
1759 June 1 Edward, son of Edward and Susannah George, bapt.
1762 Feb. 27 Henry, son of Edward and Susannah George, bapt.
1764 Feb. 3 Rebeccah, daughter of Edward and Susannah George, bapt.
1767 Sep. 12 Susannah, daughter of Edward and Susannah George, bapt.

1756, Aug. 30. WILLIAM WOOD of Wandsworth in the county of Surrey, Batchelor, & REBECCA CHRISTMAS of this parish ; by lic. ; by Thos. Church, Vicar. Witnesses : Michael Christmas, Will. Marshall. (Battersea.)

1757, April 28. JOSEPH BARTER of Wandsworth, Batchelor, & ANN TAYLOR of this Parish, Spinster ; by Banns ; by Edw. Simons, Curate. Witnesses : Susanna Wilkson, John Stevens, psh Clark. (Battersea.) [The Banns were read at Wandsworth on April 10, 17, 24.]

1758, May —. Mr BENJAMIN ASTERLY of Wandsworth to Miss ELIZABETH ZINCKE of S. Lambeth. ("British Chronicle," May 15-17, 1758, p. 467.)

1726 Dec. 28 Benjamin, son of David Asterley, bapt.
1762 Feb. 21 Elizabeth, wife of Benjamin Asterley, bur. [M.I., Mount Nod, Wandsworth.]
1769 Nov. 12 Benjamin Asterly, 44, bur.

* Communicated by CECIL T. DAVIS, Esq.—continued from p. 95.

1758, July 23. PETER ASHLEY of this Parish & MARIAH TURNER of the Parish of Wandsworth ; Banns ; by Wᵐ Bonner, Curate. (Fulham.)

1758, Aug. 13. JOHN CRUTCHFIELD of Wandsworth in this County, Widower, & MARGARET COLE of this Parish, Widow ; by lic. ; by Edw. Symonds. Witnesses : Wᵐ Harker, John Stevens. (Battersea.)

1759 Mar. 22 Henry, son of John and Margaret Crutchfield, bapt.
1760 Sep. 28 Thomas, son of John and Margaret Crutchfield, bapt.
1762 Oct.   6 Anne, daughter of John and Margaret Crutchfield, bapt.
1763 May   2 Anne, inf. dau. of John and Margaret Crutchfield, bur.
1763 May   6 Henry, inf. son of John and Margaret Crutchfield, bur.
1767 Sep. 26 Thomas, son of John and Margaret Crutchfield, bur.

1759, April 24. LAWS CARRUTHERS & ELIZABETH ROSE of Wandsworth, Surry ; lic. (St. Margaret's, Westminster.)

1760, Jan. 20. JAMES GOLDSMITH of the Parish of Wandsworth & MARY LENNERD of this Parish were married by Banns ; by Wᵐ Bonner, Curate. (Fulham.)

1762 Jan. 17 James, son of James and Mary Goldsmith, bapt.
1762 May 22 James Goldsmith, 22, bur.
1763 April 24 James, inf. son of James and Mary Goldsmith, bur.
            [Second marriage of wife.]

1763, July 2. THOMAS SPILLMAN, Widower, & MARY GOLDSMITH, Widow, mar. by Banns ; at Wandsworth.

1764 Nov. 11 Sarah, daughter of Thomas and Mary Spellman, bapt.
1767 April 6 Sarah, dau. of Thomas and Mary Spillman, bur.
1780 Jan. 27 Thomas Spellman, 59, bur.

1760, May 19. The Hon. THOMAS ARUNDELL of this parish, Esqʳ, B., & MARY PORTER of Sᵗ James, Westmʳ, S. ; L. A. C. (St. George, Hanover Square.)

[Eldest daughter of John Porter of Allfarthing Manor, Wandsworth, great-grandson of Endymion Porter, Groom of the Bedchamber to King Charles I.]

1761, March 22. [No. 62.] ROBERT ATKINSON of the Parish of Sᵗ James, Westminster, Batchelor, & JEMIMA BEATH of this Parish, Spinster, were married in this Church by Licence of the A. B. of Canterbury this Twenty-second day of March in the Year One Thousand Seven Hundred and Sixty One ; By me, Henry Magill, Curate. In the presence of Chas. Gray, Challis Mather. (St. George, Hanover Square.)

1762 April 14 Henry, son of Robert and Jemima Atkinson, bapt. ; by Hen. Whitfield, curate.
1765 Oct. 15 Robert, son of Robert and Jemima Atkinson, bapt.
1769 April 2 Willm., son of Robt. and Jemmina Atkinson, bapt. ·
1774 Aug.   2 John, son of Robert and Jemima Atkinson, bapt.
1780 May 10 Anna-Maria, daughter of Robert and Jemima Atkinson, born April 11, bapt.
1767 Sep. 23 William [?Robert], inf. son of Robert and Jemima Atkinson, bur.
1773 Dec. 20 William Atkinson, inf. son of Robert, bur.

[The first-born, Henry, married Sarah, daughter of James and Mary Greenfield, at Wandsworth on 8 Sep. 1785. He and his wife lie buried in Mount Nod, Wandsworth.]

1761, March 22. JOHN BIRD of Clapham, Batchelor, & CHARLOTTE JONES of Wandsworth, Spinster ; Licence ; J. Mapletoft, Curate. (Clapham.)

1763 May   7 Mary, daughter of John and Charlotte Bird, bapt.
1764 June 22 John, son of John and Charlotte Bird, bapt.

M 2

1763 May 31 Mary, inf. dau. of John and Charlotte Bird, bur.
1764 Aug. 16 John, inf. son of John and Charlotte Bird, bur.
1765 Feb. 13 John Bird, 34, bur.

1761, March 22. RICHARD MUIRHEAD of this parish, B., & SARAH SORSBY of Wandsworth, co. Surrey, S.; L. B. L. (St. George, Hanover Square.)

1761, Aug. 23. EDWARD LINTEN MORGAN of Wandsworth in the County of Surrey & JANE FRANCIS of Battersea in the said County; by lic.; by And. Cheap. Witnesses: Han. Lee and Henry Webb. (Battersea.)

1761, Dec. 14. CHRISTIAN LOAT, Bachelor, of St Martin's-in-the-Fields, Midx., & SARAH LITTLEHALES of Clapham, Surry; J. Mapletoft, Curate.   Witness: Endymion Loat. (Clapham.)
1737 Sep. 11 Christian, son of Endymion and Anne Loat, bapt.

1763, June 30. JOHN BOYCOTT of this parish, Batchelor, & ANNE BRIDGE of the parish of Wandsworth in the County of Surry, Spinster, a Minor, were married in this Church by Licence; by Wm Bounen, Curate. (Fulham.)
1743 June 26 Anne, daughter of Thomas and Sarah-Anne Bridge, bapt.

1763, Oct. 8. SAVAGE BEAR, Bachelor, & ELIZABETH TERWIN, widow; Licence of Bishop of London. (St. George, Hanover Square.)
[Mrs. Bear was buried in Mount Nod, where is her inscription and that of her first husband Mr. John Terwin, who died 9 Jan. 1763, aged 44 years.]
1783 Aug. 17 Elizabeth Bear, 59, bur.

1763, Oct. 29. THOMAS BARTLETT of Wandsworth in the county of Surry, Batchelor, & MARY CHRISTMAS of Battersea, Spinster; by lic.; by W. Fraigneau. Witnesses: Richd Christmass, John Stevens, senr. (Battersea.)
1764 Sep. 26 Thomas, son of Thomas and Mary Bartlett, bapt.
1766 June 1 Rebeccah, daughter of Thomas and Mary Bartlett, bapt.
1766 June 2 Mary, daughter of Thomas and Mary Bartlett, bapt.
1769 Feb. 18 Rebekkah, daughter of Thos. and Mary Bartlett, bapt.
1773 Sep. 30 James, son of Thomas and Mary Bartlett, bapt.
1770 June 27 Rebeccah, inf. dau. of Thomas and Mary Bartlett, bur.

1763, Dec. 14. WILLIAM MILLER of Wandsworth, Bachelor, & REBECCA BROWN of this Parish, Spinster; Licence; J. Mapletoft, Curate. (Clapham.)
1766 Jan. 24 William, son of William and Rebeccah Miller, bapt.
1767 Jan. 11 Henchlow, son of William and Rebecca Miller, bapt.
1770 Nov. 18 William Coleman, son of Willm. and Rebeccah Miller, bapt.
1766 Feb. 2 William, inf. son of William and Rebekah Miller, bur.
1779 Jan. 20 William Miller, 69, bur.

1764, Oct. 18. THOMAS CROSS of the Parish of Wandsworth in this County, Widower, & ELIZABETH STRINGER of this parish, Spinster, were married in this Church by Licence; by me, Thos. Barrow [Curate]. Witnesses: Willm Betts and Mary Betts. (Tooting Graveney.)

1766, Oct. 5. EDMUND PHILLIPS of Wandsworth & ELIZABETH GILBERT of this parish; lic. (St. Margaret, Westminster.)

1768, Sep. 3. HENRY MOTT of this Parish, a Batchelor, & MARGARET EVANS of the Parish of Wandsworth in this County, a Spinster; by Banns; by Moses Porter, Curate. × Mark of Henry Mott, Margret Evens. Witnesses: Thos. Evans, Eliz. Evans. (Clapham.)
[The Banns were also read at Wandsworth.]

1769, April 23. JOHN MARSHALL of this parish & ELIZABETH LEONARD of Wandsworth (Lic. of Bishop of London issued 20 April 1769); by E. Saunders, Vicar. (St. Martin-in-the Fields.)

1770, Feb. 17. THOMAS TAYLOR of Wandsworth, Surry, widower, & MARY LYON of this parish, widow ; lic. (St. Margaret, Westminster.)

1771, Sep. 7. EDWARD HILLER of this parish & MARY BEACHAM of Wandsworth, co. Surry ; by Lic., Bp. of Lond. Witnesses : Rich. Vigo, Wᵐ Russell. (St. James, Westminster.)

1773, June 8. NATHANIEL SAUNDERS of Wandsworth & MARY PRICE of this parish. (St. James, Westminster.)

1774	April 11	Ann, daughter of Nathaniel and Mary Saunders, bapt.
1776	Mar. 6	Mary, daughter of Nathaniel and Mary Saunders, bapt.
1776	Mar. 23	Mary, daughter of Nathaniel and Mary Saunders, born Feb. 24, bapt.
1780	Jan. 29	Nathaniel James, son of Nathaniel and Mary Saunders, born Oct. 24, bapt.
1784	May 30	Sarah, daughter of Nathaniel and Mary Saunders, born May 30, bapt.

1773, June 20. JAMES LEWER of this parish & MARY MACE of Wandsworth ; lic. Bishop of London. (St. James, Westminster.)

1774, March 3. URIAH BROOKS of Wandsworth, Bachelor, & SARAH HOULDEN of this Parish, Spinster ; by Licence 3 March 1774 ; Moses Porter, Curate. (Clapham.)

1776, May 5. The Rᵗ Hon. DAVID, LORD VISCᵀ STORMONT, W., & the Hon. LOUISA CATHCART, S., a minor. Married in the dwelling-house of the Rᵗ Hon. Chaˢ, Lord Cathcart, in Grosvenor Place in this parish by Special Licence and with consent of her Father the sᵈ Lord Cathcart ; by " W. Chester." (St. George, Hanover Square.)

1781	Sep. 16	Charles, son of the Right Honourable David Murray, Lord Viscount Stormonth, and Dame Louisa his wife, born Aug. 22 ; baptized by the Rev. Robert Holt Butcher, LL.B., Vicar of Wandsworth.

[Lady Stormont lost her husband on 1 September 1796 ; she married secondly, 19 October 1797, the Hon. Robert Fulke Greville, son of the first Earl of Brooke and Warwick. She died 11 July 1843. Charles was third son, and became Major. He was born 22 August 1781, and died in Paris 17 September 1859.]

1776, Oct. 27. EDWARD HULL of Wandsworth, Widower, & REBECCA WINGATE of Battersea, Spinster ; by lic. ; by H. S. Cruwys, Curate. Witnesses : Rich. Sparrow, Eleanor Spence ; Robᵗ Munday, Parʰ Clerk. (Battersea.)

1778	Sep. 20	Sarah Eleanor, daughter of Edward and Rebecca Hull, born Aug. 30, bapt.
1780	Sep. 17	William, son of Edward and Rebecca Hull, born Aug. 26, bapt.
1783	Feb. 9	Rebecca, daughter of Edward and Rebecca Hull, born Jan. 13, bapt.
1784	Oct. 27	Rebecca, daughter of Edward and Rebecca Hull, paup., bapt.
1783	April 1	Rebecca Hull, inf., bur.
1783	April 20	Sarah Elizabeth Hull, inf., bur. [? Sarah Eleanor, *see* first entry].
1787	July 23	Rebecca Hull, inf., bur.

1777, Sep. 10. THOMAS LEE of Wandsworth, Bachelor, in y⁰ County of Surry, & SARAH JACKSON, Spinster, of Battersea; by Lic.; by Hen. Sh. Cruwys, Curate. Witnesses: Mary Videon, N. Stride; Robᵗ Munday, Parish Clerk. (Battersea.)
1779 April 28 Thos. Lee, inf., bur.
1779 May   2 Sarah Lee, 34, bur.
[Second marriage of husband.]
1779, Dec. 7. THOS. LEE, Widower, & SARAH BOTTEN, Spinster; lic. mar. at Wandsworth.
1782 Jan. 22 Jane, daughter of Thomas and Sarah Lee, born Jan. 1, 1782, bapt.

1778, Sep. 24. JOHN SQUIRE of Wandsworth, co. Surry, & JANE BRODIE of this parish; by Lic., Bp. of Lond.; by me, J. Fr. Squire, Minister. Witnesses: Thomas Denman, E. Denman, Thomas Abbotts. (St. James, Westminster.)
1779 Aug. 19 John, son of John and Jane Squire, born July 22, bapt.
1780 Oct. 24 Edmund, son of John and Jane Squire, born Oct. 3, bapt.
1782 April 4 Mary Ann, daughter of John and Jane Squire, born Mar. 17, bapt.
1783 May   2 Margaret, daughter of John and Jane Squire, born April 7, bapt.
1784 Nov.   9 Peter, son of John and Jane Squire, bapt.

1779, April 25. JOHN NEALE of Wandsworth, Bachelor, & MARY CHEESEMAN of the same parish, Spinster; by lic.; J. Rennie, Curate. Witnesses: Thoˢ Taylor, Ann Brooks, Ezekiel Penington. (Battersea.)

1780, April 8. CHRISTOPHER GASTON of Wandsworth, Bachelor, & ELIZABETH MULLINAX of this Parish; Licence. Witnesses: Wᵐ Witton, Eliz. Long, Henry Gaston, Eliz. Vidler. (Tooting Graveney.)

1786, April 20. THOMAS SIMPKINS of Wandsworth, Surrey, & ELIZABETH SAUNDERS of this parish; Lic., Bp. of Lond. Witnesses: John Bailey, Thomas Green. (St. James, Westminster.)
1787 Mar. 11 Jane, daughter of Thomas and Elizabeth Simkin, born Feb. 14, bapt.

1786, June 23. WILLIAM GRIEVE of this parish & MARY GRAHAM of Wandsworth; Lic., Bp. of Lond. (St. James, Westminster.)

1788, April 26. JOHN BUTCHER of Wandsworth in Surry & SARAH BENNETT of this parish; Lic., Archbp. of Canterbury. (St. James, Westminster.)

1789, Jan. 31. WILLIAM STEELE of Wandsworth, Widower, & MARY EDMONDS, widow, of this parish; Licence 31 Jan. 1789; by John Sharpe, Assist. Curate. (Clapham.)
[Burial of first wife.]
1785 Aug. 18 Sarah Steele, 40, bur.

1792, Dec. 9. WILLIAM TICHENER & MARY BOXELL. (Mitcham.)
1795 May 10 Charles, of William and Mary Tichener, born April 17.
1796 July 31 George, of William and Mary Titchnear, born July 12, bapt.
1799 July   7 Elizabeth Sarah, of William and Mary Titchnear, born June 17, bapt.
1802 Jan. 24 Mary Ann, of William and Mary Titchnear, born Dec. 30, bapt.
1804 April 15 Sophia, of William and Mary Titchnear, born March 24, bapt.
1812 May   3 Lydia, of William and Mary Titchnear, born April 17, bapt.

MEMORANDUM.—March 19ᵗʰ, 1828. It appears from the Certificate of the Marriage of William Tichener & Mary Boxell on the 9ᵗʰ of Decʳ 1792 at Mitcham,

County of Surrey, that the Name of their Charles Tichener was rightly inserted, but that the One above George was by some mistake registered as George Titchnear instead of Tichener; the same erroneous mode of spelling the Surname occurs also under Date of July 7, 1799, the 24 of Jany 1802, the 15th of April 1804, and May the 3rd, 1812.

(*Signed*) R. H. BUTCHER, Vicar.

Witness: PHILIP ALLWOOD, Curate.

1812, May 18. [No. 160.] JOHN CHAMBERLIN of the Parish of Wandsworth, Bachelour, & ANN BILES of this Parish, Spinster, were Married in this Church by Licence this eighteenth Day of May in the year One Thousand Eight Hundred and Twelve; By me, Willm Marshall, Curate. Witnesses: William Hotton, Elizabeth Grantham, Dinah Baker. (Putney.)

(*To be continued.*)

The Stirling Family.*

A SCOTCH PHYSICIAN'S NOTEBOOK OF THE SEVENTEENTH CENTURY.

There has lately come into my possession "A Register or A Generall Almanack for Every Yeare," printed at London "by William Wilson for the Company of Stationers, 1646," which in itself is a curiosity, with its chapters on Weather, Temperaments, the Planets, Weights and Measures, the Fairs, fixed and moveable, of England and Wales, the Road Highways over England and Wales, and much more information as various as remarkable. Its chief interest, however, lies not only in the fact that it was a notebook of a Scotch physician, apparently a Doctor Stirling, and contains his prescriptions (which are of a weird character, as were the medicines with which unfortunate patients were mercilessly dosed in those days), his patients' names, and the names of some doctors whose special prescriptions he has copied, but also in that there is scattered through its pages the names and obituaries of several persons, probably his patients, mixed with sundry other matters relating to his personal affairs.

It is the genealogical items, however, that are alone suited for the pages of this Magazine, and these I have abstracted and give as below.

The writing is clear and neat on the whole, but it is so small in places that it required a magnifying glass to decipher. Some of it has faded and is partly illegible, but it is all methodical and without signs of haste. It is amazing the amount of matter that is squeezed into the small pages.

Who Dr. Stirling was, or where he practised (if he were a Stirling) I cannot say, but I suspect he was an ancestor of the present Sir John Stirling-Maxwell, Bart., and some of your readers may be able to throw some light on his identification.

The following are the entries recording births and deaths, with an occasional marriage, and some entries relating to property:—

The 10th of May 1660 being Thursday wee be maried near 8 a clocke at night at Baldonocke (?)† Kirke by Mr James Walkinshaw; came in Wensday 23 of May to take ane house & 29 May tuesday I came to dwell in the house.

---

* Communicated by C. M. TENISON, Esq., M.R.I.A., Hobart, Tasmania.
† Baldernock, co. Stirling.—ED.

Elizabeth, born 23 feb. 1661 Saturday a q'rtre past sex at night ; baptized the 3 of March. Witnesses my father & my good brother James Stirlinge. Departed this lyfe the 7 apryll 1662. Mr Ralph Rodger baptised Elizabeth, Saboth, in . . . . [*illegible*] Kirk.

John, born 31 Decer. 1662 being Wensday a q'rtre before 8 in the morninge ; baptised 1 Jan. 1663. Witnesses my good brother and Wm Robertson. Departed the 11 of Jan^r 1665 being Wensday at half 5 afternoone ; buried 12 Januar 1665. Mr Matt. Ramsay baptized John at Kilvarick (?).

Marie, born the 11 of October 1664 being Tuesday, ane q'rter past fyve afternoon ; baptised 13 Octo'r being Thursday by Mr James Hamiltoun . . . . [*illegible*]. Witnesses James Stirlinge and William Robertson. Departed the 23 Octo'r 1664 being Saboth a q'rter befor four afternoon ; buried Moonday 24 October 1664.

John, born 9 Feb. 1666 at half two in the morninge being friday ; baptised Saboth 18 by M^r Wm. Stirlinge. Witnesses my father James Stirlinge & Alexander Woodrop. Departed 25 Agust 1667 being Saboth at half ane in the day ; buried 26 Agust 1667 being Moonday.

William, born 24 Septr 1667 betwixt 8 & 9 at night being tuesday ; baptised 29 Septe'r beinge Saboth. Witnesses Mr George and James Stirlinge and Alex^r Woodrop. Departed 9 March 1670 a litill past two in the morninge being Wensday ; buried thursday the 10th of March 1670. M.V.S. baptized him blakefriars.

James, born the 21 Agust 1670 betwixt one & two in the morninge ; Baptised 25 Agust thursday. Witnesses Mr George and James Stirlinge and Patricke Parke. Departed the 2 of Septre 1673 beinge tuesday & buried the same day. He departed betwixt 2 & 3 in the morninge. Layh (?) Kirk, M.A.R.

Anna, born the 17 October 1671 (beinge tuesday) a q'rtre befor 10 at night ; baptised 29 Octr 1671 Saboth. Witnesses James Stirlinge and Patricke Parke. Departed the 2 October 1672 being Wensday a q'rter befor 5 afternoon ; buried the 3, thursday. Mr William Stirlinge, Laugh (?) Kirke.

Joan, born 6 Janvar 1673 beinge Moonday about half a q'rter befor 10 at night ; baptised the 17 Janvar beinge friday by Mr Bartrum (?) ; departed this Lyf 20 Januar 1673 Moonday at 6 at night ; buried tuesday 21 Januar 1673. Witnesses to baptism James Stirlinge and Patricke Parke.

Marie, born the second of februar 1675 tuesday about half a q'rter past 5 in the afternoon ; baptised (Mr Rob. Max, eld.) near 8 a clocke at night the s^d day. Witnesses James Stirlinge, Patricke Parke, and William Robertson.

Robert, born the 13th of Janvar 1679 beinge Moonday betwixt 6 & 7 a clocke in the morninge ; baptized the 26th of Janvar 1679 beinge the Saboth. Witnesses James Stirlinge and Patricke Parke. Departed 30 Agust 1702 being Moonday betwixt one & two in the morninge.

These ar the wryts underwryten the qich I gave John Poadie : 21 May 1674.
Heugh Eglintoune service as air to his father, 11 June 1647.
Heugh dispositioune to Jon Biscat 10 July 1647.
Heugh, Jon Biscat & his wyfes seasinge 13 July 1647.
Jon Biscat dispositioun to James Braidwood 26 July 1661.
James Braidwood seasing the 8 Agust 1661.
Jon Braidwood & Robert finlay dispositioun 21 agust 1663.
Robert Braidwood ratification to me 18 March 1674.
Robert Braidwoods infestment & myn the 13 May 1674.
John Jacke and James Jack and Andro Braidwood thair ratification anent interdictioun of the daites the 13 and 20 May 1674.
My dispositioune to Jon Poadie 21 May 1674. Also the act counsell of the 26 May 1662 for the discharge of teen shillings qich I bought at seventeen yeares purchase.
John Biskets wyfes ratificatioun 27 July 1661.

Rob. Braidwood extract of service as air to his father.

7 July 1675 I got up the dispositioun that I gave Jon Poadie 21 May 1674 and the said 7 July I renewed the dispositioun for James Hutchosonn, Shoomaker, his name.

26 februar 1680 [*blot*] gibon (?) to lily fleminge of Jake (?) Mabing (?) thursday 26 Feb.*

John Bisset departed the 14th feb. 1683 ; buried 16th feb. 1683.

Patrick boyle, 15 Novr 1683 friday ; buried Moonday 19 Nov. 1683.

Wm Graham departed Saboth 15 febvr 1685 a litle after 12 a clocke in foornoon ; buried tuesday 17 februar.

Joan Craig spous to geo. muirhead departed thursday ye 5 March 1685 and was buried Saturday the 7 March 1685.

John Louke of Claythorn (?) departed friday 12 March 1686 at 12 a clocke the day time ; buried tuesday 16 March.

Ladie Marry Chirstian and a son departed thursday morning ; buried Moonday the 15 March 1686.

Robert Boyle departed this Lyf Sunday the 2 June 1682 betwixt 6 & 7 at night ; buried 4 June Saboth.

Doctor Colhoun the 2 day of Dece'r 1674 ; buried [*blank*] of Decr 1674.

Doctor Hamiltoune departed Saturday 9 of Oct^{re} 1675 ; buried Moonday the 11th Octo'r 1675.

Marion Hamiltoun spous to robert Burnes departed (friday) 27 agust 1686 at 8 in morninge ; buried 29 agust.

Agnes Lindsay relict of Charles Gray departed (friday) 27 agust 1686 ; buried 29 agust.

Andro Scot, elder, departed tuesday the 6 Octo'r 1686 betwixt two & 3 afternoon ; buried by 8 a clocke.

Gavin Hamiltoune thursday 1686 ; buried Saboth 19 Nov^r.

George . . . . [*illegible*] the 18 Nov^r ; buried 20 No^r 1686.

Jon Orr, merchant, departed Saturday 26 March 1687 at 7 in morninge ; buried Moonday 28 March.

Jon Beytoun, young^r, 29 March 1687, tuesday at [*blank*] ; buried 81 March.

Goodwyfe of craigalen departed 30 March 1687 tuesday at 6 a clock at night ; buried Apryll the 2^d Saturday [*sic*].

Lilias Campbell's [*illegible*] daughter departed the [*blank*] of apryll 1687 ; buried Saturday 10 apryll.

Patrick Wilsson, corderer, Kirkloder, departed Saturday 16 apryll Saturday [*sic*] betwixt 10 & 11 a clocke at night ; buried Moonday 18 april 1687.

George Anderson, toun clerk, departed Saboth 28 Jar 1694 ; buried [*blank*].

James Campbell, skiper, departed 10 May betwixt 3 & 4 afternoon ; buried ye 12 May Saturday 1694.

Mgt. Miller spous to umqhle James Boyle departed Saboth the 4th apryll 1686 at 7 in the morninge ; buried the 6th aprylle 1686 tuesday.

James farie (?) departed 20 apryll (tuesday) 1696 ; buried friday the 23 apryll.

Marie hamiltoune, Jon Byset's relict, departed 26th of Apryll 1686 a litle befor three in the morninge ; buried 80 apryll friday.

Ja. lees departed 3 May 1696 Moonday betwixt 5 & 6 at night ; buried the 7th of May being friday.

Lilias fleminge departed this lyf thursday the 5th of Agust 1686 a litle befor 3 in the morninge ; buried the 7th of Agust 1686 at ordinar tyme.

John hall (?), chyrurgion, departed the 26 Sept'r 1697 betwixt 8 & nyne in morninge being Saboth ; buried [*blank*].

Will. Adam departed 16 febr. 1666 beinge friday ; buried [*blank*].

Bessie Adam departed 17 Apryll 1666 being tuesday.

Arthur Kirke 10 Novr 1668 [*sic*].

_____

* This entry may refer to a prescription that follows.

Christian Lindsay 25 Dec[r] 1676 being Moonday ; buried 27 decem[r] Wensday.

M[r] Pat Bell departed thursday the 13 agust 1685 betwixt [blank] ; buried Saboth 16 Agust 1685.

Wm. Walase, Scrivener, departed Saturday 15 Jan. 1687 at [blank] in morninge ; buried Moonday the 17 Janvar.

Mrt. Hamiltonne, Patricke Hamiltounes relict, departed thursday 7 July 1687 at 6 in the morninge ; buried 9 Jul.

22 July 1687 friday Arthur Kirke departed this Lyf betwixt two & three in afternoon ; buried Saboth the 29th of July.

J. Reid, Wm. Hamiltouns relict, departed friday 22 July betwixt 9 & ten at night ; buried Moonday the 25 July.

Elspat Cunyngham, M[t] Charles, moonday the 25 July 1687 at 7 at night ; buried thursday the 28 July.

Mrt. Johnstone, baylie geo. daughter, departed tuesday 26 July ; buried the 28 July 1687.

———

David Adam & Jo. Younge married the 25 of July 1571.

Jon Robertson & Janet Dickson married 11 Dec[r] 1608.

David Adam Adam [sic] & Jo. Younge a lasua (?) daughter Elizabeth the 27 day of December 1588.

John Robertson & Elizabeth Adam maried 12 July 1618.

———

William Robertson son to John Robertson, chyrurgian, departed Saturday the 22 of Oct[re] 1692 ; buried tuesday 25 Octre.

Jon Campbell of Dolban (?) departed tuesday the 3d of Decer. at eight a clock at night ; buried the 7 decbr. Saturday 1695 ; baptized 16 July 1632, aged, in he departed 63 yeares & 20 weeks & a day.

M[r] John Spurell (?) departed the 23 agust (tuesday) a litle after ten in the morninge the year 1687 ; buried 25 of agust.

Mariou Spurell (?) departed thursday 31 July 1690 ; buried 2 agust Saturday.

Ana Spurell (?) departed [blank].

Mrt. Spurell (?) departed Saturday 10 Sept[r] 1692 ; buried 13 Sept. about eight at night ; departed [sic].

James Stirlinge departed this lyf the 12 Nov[r] 1687 betwixt 12 & one in the begininge of the morninge Saturday ; buried the 14 of Nov. being Moonday betwixt 2 & 3 in the afternoone.

Margaret Robertson, george Robertsons wyf, departed this lyfe the 19 March 1688 moonday a litle before 11 a clocke at night ; buried thursday 22 March the 22 day [sic].

Archibald Hamiltoun, wryter, departed this lyfe the 22 of apryll 1688 Saboth at 9 a clock at night ; buried 29 Apryll.

Jon Robertson, chyrurgian, departed moonday the 23 Apryll 1688 at a q'rtre past 9 at night ; buried friday 27 apryll 1688.

Robert Burnes, elder, departed thursday the 26 of apryll 1688 betwixt 11 & 12 a clock fornoon ; buried Saturday 28 apryll.

Jon Warner (?), merchant, departed this lyf the [blank] of May ; buried the 8th of May 1688 tuesday.

John Otterburn departed this lyf May the 18 of May [sic] 1688 friday at 9 in the morninge ; buried the 19 May Saturday, aged 77 years & 2 months.

22 May 1688 tuesday M[r] David Sharp departed this lyf about 4 in the morninge ; buried friday the 25 of May, aged 57 years 7 months.

M[r] Robert Bell, minister at dalway, departed the 23 May 1688 at 11 in fornoon Wensday ; buried the 26 of May.

Jo. Lightbodie spous to Ja. Muray, writer, departed this lyf the 29 May 1688 tuesday [blank] in morninge ; buried 31 May thursday.

M[r] geo. Adam departed tuesday the 13 June about 6 at night; buried friday 15 June 1688. I say the 15th of June 1688.

Margret gilbayre (?) departed the [blank] of agust; buried friday the 10 agust 1685.

James Anderson departed 13 agust moonday at 5 in morninge; buried the [blank] of agust 1688.

M[r] Ralph Rodger departed this lyf the third of Janvar 1689 being thursday at 5 afternoone; buried the 8 Jan. being tuesday [sic].

Elspat Robertson, rob. Dunlop's wyf, departed 5 July 1689 at 4 in morninge; buried 6 July 1689.

My mother departed tuesday the 20 Octre 1646.
My mother in law the 5 apryll thursday 1666; buried 7 apryll.
My father the 28 May friday 1669; buried 29 May 1669.

John Robertson, Dunfries, departed the sexth of dec[bre] 1680 beinge moonday at 9 a clock in morninge; buried 8 december.

Joan Louke his spous departed [sic].

Joan Stirlinge departed Wensday 9 Jan. 1684; buried friday 11 Jan. Shee departed betwixt 5 & 6 in the morninge.

Agnes Robertson departed tuesday the 26 feb. at 12 a clocke of the day; buried 28 februar 1684.

John Robertson, laird, departed 9 Septre 1699 friday at 11 at night; buried 12 Septre.

Jo. Robertson, Ja. robertsons wyf, departed Moonday the 4th of May a q'rtre before 11 a clock at night; buried thursday the 7th of May 1685. James her husband departed the 8 May 1695 betwixt 11 & 12 fornoon; buried 11 May.

John Patersonn (?), bauker (?), departed this lyf tuesday the 5th of May 1685 betwixt 7 & 8 a clocke at night; buried 7 May thursday.

Andro Elphinstoune departed this lyf friday the 4th 1685 of Septre [sic] betwixt 12 & one in the morninge; buried 5 Septre betwixt 2 & 3 afternoon Saturday.

Jet M[c]Kuaon (?) departed the [blank] of Septre; buried 22 Septre tuesday 1685.

Dogald Marcrost (?) departed Moonday 21 Septre 1685; buried 24 of Septre Septre [sic] 1685 thursday.

Marion M[c]Kinlay Saboth the 6 Septre 1685 about 6 a clock at night; buried 8 Septre tuesday.

Anna Stirlinge maried to . . . . [illegible] thursday the 4 of Janu[r] 1666; maried againe to Jon Borland July the 11 July [sic] 1676.

Tuesday the 3 Septre 1695 departed Mistres Langlands at half [blank] forenoon; buried the [blank] of [blank] being [sic].

Margret M[c]taysh (?) spous to Marcus Marshall departed the 20 Octre tuesday; buried 22 Octre 1685.

John Raltoune, maltman, departed the 24 Novr. 1685 tuesday at 10 in the morninge; buried thursday 26 of Novre 1685.

Elizabeth Donaldson spous to Wm. Watestone (?) departed the 2d of Decbre 1685 tuesday; buried friday the 4th of decbre.

Francis Boyd departed Moonday the 28 decbre 1685 at 9 in morninge; buried 30 decbre 1685.

Baylie Caldwell departed tuesday 29 decbre 1685 at 11 at night; buried Saturday the 2 of Janvar 1686.

M^r Wm. Stirlinge my bro. in law departed thursday 31 decbre 1685 ; buried Moonday the fourth of Janvar 1686.   He departed at Ancrum.

Mr James Stirlinge, banker, departed Saboth 3 Janvar 1686 ; buried 4th of Janvar 1686 Moonday.   He died at 9 in the morninge.

Issobell Hunter departed this lyf the 27 februar 1679 at 3 a clock in the morninge being thursday ; buried the 28 Feb. friday betwixt 2 & 3 a clocke afternoon.

Mr Geo. Stirlinge departed the 2 May (friday) 1679 at 7 a clocke at night ; buried the 5 May 1679 betwixt 2 & 3 in afternoon.

Joan Craffurd departed (the laidy W. Pollocke) the 4 of May 1679 being Saboth at half seven in the morninge ; buried 9th of May at the Mains (?) beinge friday.

Thomas Davidson departed 23 decbre 1679 tuesday betwixt 11 & 12 hours fornoon ; buried thursday 25 decbre.

Agnes Stirlinge, Lady garscadon (?), departed the 19 decbr. friday 1679 betwixt 3 & four in the afternoon and was buried the 26 decbr. friday.

John Robertson, writer, departed Saturday the 10 March 1683 at six a clocke at night ; buried the 13 March tuesday.

Wm. Robertson, maltman, departed the 4th of June 1683 Moonday at two a clocke the afternoon ; buried Wensday the 6th of June.

Archbald Kirke departed thursday beinge the 7th of June 1683 betwixt 5 & sex in the morninge ; buried 9 June Saturday.

Rebeka, david Wilkies wyf, departed Wensday 16 May 1683 ; buried [*blank*].

David Wilkie departed Saturday the 23 June 1683 betwixt [*blank*] in afternoon ; buried tuesday 20 June 1683.

James Wadrop (?), son to Alex^r Wadrop (?), departed tuesday the 7th of agust 1683 about eleven a clocke at night beinge tuesday ; buried thursday the 9th agust 1683.

Andro Ralstone died 15 agust friday at [*blank*] 1673 ; buried Saturday 16 agust.

Michall Paterson departed (Saboth) the 3d of agust 1673 betwixt [*blank*] in morninge ; buried Moonday the 4th of agust 1673.

James Armour, elder, departed (Saturday) the 6th of apryll 1678 betwixt 6 & 7 in morninge ; buried (teusday) ye 9 apryll 1678.

Ann Bishet (?), James Armours relict, departed (Saturday) 7th June 1684 betwixt 2 & 3 in afternoon ; buried (tuesday) 10 June 1684.

Marie Stirlinge relict of Jon Govan (?) departed (tuesday) 10 June 1684 ; buried (thursday) 12 June 1684, aged 46 yeares & 21 weeks & 5 days.

Robert Robertson of Stockmellhord (?) departed friday the 12th of february 1686 betwixt 7 & 8 at night ; buried Saboth the 14 februar 1686.

Marion Marshall relict of Ja. Locheid departed Saturday the 20th of feb. at [*blank*] night ; buried 23 of februar 1686.

Agnes Hamiltoun departed (tho. McKinleys wyf) 8 apryll 1693 Saboth ; buried tuesday 10 of aprylle 1693.

John Brownlies wyf buried 11 apryll 1693 Wensday.

MONUMENTAL INSCRIPTIONS FROM THE BURIAL-GROUND OF ST. GEORGE, HANOVER SQUARE, LONDON.*

John Rowe, of Oxford Street, died Jan. . . . . aged 67 years.
Elizabeth Rowe, daughter of the above, died May 5, 1793, aged 17 years.

———

Mrs Ann Cooper, wife of Mr John Cooper, of Little Stanhope Street, Mayfair, who after a lingering & painful illness, etc., died 17 June 1817, in her 38th year.

Mr William Stubble, died Dec. 5, 1828, aged 69.
Mrs Mary McEvoy, late widow of the above Mr William Stubble, died 8 Oct. 1846, aged 86.

———

Nathaniel W . . . ., born at Leeds in Yorkshire, ... years an Officer in his Majesty's Silver Scullery at [Spines ?], who died at Pimlico Oct. . . 1806, in his 51st year.
Mrs Elizabeth Garner, daughter of the above, died Feb. 16, 1841, aged 64.

———

Elizabeth, daughter of Alexander & Ann B . . . ., of Mount Street, in this parish, died 27 March 1794, aged 11 months & 7 days.
Also James, died Oct. 3, 1797, aged 6 months.
Martha, died March 8, 1804, aged 15 months.
John, son of the above, died Sep. 24, 1808, aged 18.

———

Mr John Gregor, died March 9, 1830, in his 29th year.

———

Mr Joseph Waight, died June 27, 1826, aged 36.

———

Mr Bernard Downing, died May 3, 1810, aged 43.

———

Mrs George Fergusson, died 17 June 1798, aged 42.
Miss Barbara Fergusson, died [31 ?] Oct. 1825, aged . . . .
Catherine Henderson, died 8 Jan. 1846, aged 63.

———

David Thomas Gibson, died July 2, 1848, aged 55.

———

George Fisher, of Berwick Street, Soho, died Jan. 9, 1817, aged 56.
Samuel Thomas, son of the above, died 6 Oct. 1838, aged 35.

———

Ann Astley, died 29 June 1775, aged 2.
Mary Astley, died 11 Jan. 1789, aged 19 ; daughters of John & Mary Astley.
The above John Astley, died 8 Jan. 1795, aged 60.
Mary Astley, wife of the above John Astley, died 23 April 1817, aged 79.

———

Mr Richard Sharpus, of Davies Street, Berkeley Square, died Jan. 6, 1827, aged 60.
Mrs Jane Sharpus, relict of the aboue, died July 12, 1827, aged 49.
Their son Mr Richard Sharpus, died Aug. 4, 1832, aged 22.

———

Jane Minter Hart, died 29 Sep. 1825, aged 26.

———

George King, died Feb. 2, 1835, aged 24.
Eleanor King, mother of the above, died 23 Jan. 1840, aged 62.
George King, husband of the above Eleanor King, died 22 May 1844, aged 61.

———

* Communicated by F. S. SNELL, Esq., M.A. Portions of these inscriptions appeared in preceding volumes.

Anne Leigh, born July 19, 1781, died Nov. 20, 1811.
Elizabeth Leigh, mother of the above, died Nov. 6, 1816, aged 74.

Mr Robert Scott, of Great Maddox Street, Painter, died May 27, 1817, aged 37.
James Scott, son of the above, died Aug. 27, 1822, in his 16th year.
Elizabeth Scott, died Aug. 16, 1846, aged 80.

Mr Frederick Finn, died 24 Nov. 1817, aged 74.

John Austin Lines, died June 5, 1815, aged 27.
Mr John Lines, died 28 Feb. 1822, aged 72.

Sarah Carter, widow, died Jan. 9, 1820, in her 46th year.
Her Master and Mistress, to commemorate her Faithful services for nearly 20 years,
    have placed this Tablet as a Token of their Esteem.

Mr Joseph Critchley, died Aug. 29, 1796, aged 74.

Mary Elton, wife of William Elton, died 24 March 1814, aged 59.
Also near is buried the Body of her Niece, who died the following week, after a few
    days' illness, aged 20 years.

Martha Flower, died Nov. 19, 1825, aged 55.

Andrew, the son of James & Margaret Milne, of Lower Grosvenor Street, died
    June 21, 1786, aged 1 year & 7 months.
Isabella Milne, died Oct. 23, 1790, aged 15.
Elizabeth Sarah Milne, died March 24, 1796, aged 20.
Robert Hamilton, died July 18, 1814, aged 77.
Alice Hamilton, wife of the above, died Oct. 30, 1823, aged 87.
James Milne, died Oct. 12, 1834, aged 84.
James Alexander Milne, son of the above, who died in Jamaica (where he had gone
    for the recovery of his health), died 13 May 1808, in his 25th year.

George Champion, died [6th ?] June 1782, in his 45th year.
George Champion, son of the above .... [Rest illegible.]

Sarah, wife of Robert Lewis, of Ebury Street, and daughter of Thomas Ireland, of
    Poole, Dorset, who died of a fever Sep. 14, 1833, five weeks after her
    marriage, aged 20.
William Ireland Lewis, died Sep. 27, 1845, of inflammation of the brain, in his
    9th year.

Robert Evans, died Nov. 18 [1783 ?], in his 69th year.

James Coupland, died Sep. 9, 1795, aged 2.
William Coupland, died Feb. 16, 1809, aged 20.
James Coupland, died June 12, 1812, aged 73.
Mrs Margaret Coupland, died Dec. 13, 1831, aged 83.

Mr Thomas Dempsey, died Feb. 28, 1827, aged 64.
James and Jane Dempsey, children of the above, who died in their infancy.
Mrs Mary Dempsey, wife of the above, died Aug. 18, 1834, aged 64.

Frances Ashe, died Jan. 5, 1795, aged 79.

M[rs] Elizabeth Martin, wife of William Martin, Esq., late Major in the 60th Regiment, died 15 April 1822, aged 50.
William Martin, Esq., died 19 April 1824, aged 67.

Mary Martin, daughter of the late Governor Martin, died 21 March 1820, aged 57.
Miss Sarah Martin, sister of the above, died March 6, 1851, aged 85.
Miss Alice Martin, the youngest daughter of Governor Martin, sister of the above, died May 29, 1852, aged 83.

To the memory of four of the infant daughters of John Fonblanque, Esq., and Frances Caroline, his wife, viz. :—
Elenor, born 3 Sep. 1791, died 17th of the same month, aged 14 days.
Caroline Elenor, born 3 July 1788, died 2 Nov. 1792, aged 4 years & 4 months.
Georgiana, born 3 Dec. 1802, died 23 Dec. in the same year, aged 20 days.
Louisa, born 7th .... 1804, died 8 July ...., aged .... [*Rest illegible.*]

M[r] William Cartwright, late of Bond Street, died April 1, 177[3 or 5 ?], in his 20th year.
Also Dorothy .... Cartwright, his daughter, died Sep. 23, 1779, aged 2 months & 4 days.

Ann, wife of M[r] Thomas Hancock, of Pimlico, died June 12, 1783, aged 47.
M[r] Thomas Hancock, died 9 June 1811, aged 66.

M[r] Richard Tomlinson, Taylor, of this parish, died May 12, 1782, aged 42.
Robert Tomlinson, son of the above, died 29 April 1786, aged 7.
M[rs] Elizabeth Boyd, daughter of the above, died 27 Oct. 1794, aged 25.

Peter Campbell, Gent., of the parish of S[t] George, Hanover Square, died Feb. 17, 1781, aged 90.
Elizabeth Campbell, his eldest daughter, who was born in Oct. 1729 & died Oct. 20, 1805, aged 76.
Sarah Campbell, spinster, died Feb. 3, 1818, aged [81 ?].

Ann, wife of M[r] Thomas L .... [*Rest illegible.*]

Charlotte, wife of M[r] William Hurley, of this parish, died March 27, 1826, aged 53.
Edward, son of the above, died June 16, 1819, aged 17.
Emma, died in her infancy.
The above William Hurley, died 10 June 1835, in his 61st year.
M[rs] Eleanor Hurley, wife of the above-named William Hurley, died .. June 1845, aged 56 years.

M[r] Christopher Wharton, of Davies Street, in this parish, died Aug. 17, 1796, aged 49.
Elizabeth, his wife, died Aug. 6, 1793, in her 48th year.
Joseph Mann, grand child to the above, died Dec. 22, 1805, aged 1 year.
Jane Mann, died Jan. 7, 1812, aged 9 months.

M[r] Richard Hoddle, died June 9, 1782, aged 53.

.... Hansford, of [.... nd ?], in the county of Lincoln, died .... 1st, 1803, aged 43.

M[rs] Ann Palmer, died 4 April 1807, aged 32.

Catherine Rogers, died July 21, 1806, aged 21.

M[r] Henry Castleman, gent., of the parish of S[t] George, Hanover Square, died
    March 17, 1776, aged 72.
Dorothy, widow of the above . . . .   [*Rest illegible.*]

M[rs] Mary Duggin, wife of M[r] John Duggin, of this parish, died 28 June 1770,
    aged 61.

Two children of J. and S. Burrows, of Grosvenor . . . .
Robert, died April 20, 1809, aged 2 years.
William, died April 26, 1819 . . . .
M[r] John Burrows, father of the above, died Oct. 15, 1826, in his 61st year.

M[r] Gilbert Fisher, died Dec. 10, 1782, aged 37.
Gilbert, his son, died March 10 [1764 ?], aged 10 months.
Anna Maria Wilson, died Feb. 11, 1796, aged 65.
M[r] John Wilson, her husband, died May 23, 1790 . . . .
Charles Gilbert Fisher, grandson of the above Gilbert, died 21 June 1815,
    aged 9 months.

Sarah, the wife of M[r] Thomas [Woods ?], of Bolsover Street, S[t] Marylebone, died
    Feb. 1, 1808, in her 72nd year.

M[rs] Ann Burton, died May 21, 1807, aged 27.

Mathew Daly, died March 17, 178[5 ?], aged 7 years.

M[r] Thomas Seaward, died 22 April 1821, aged 55.
His six children, who died infants.
Lucy Seaward, daughter of the above Thomas Seaward, died 13 April 1822, in her
    17th year.
Thomas Seaward, son of the above, died 19 July 1836, in his 29th year.
M[rs] Lucy Seaward, wife of the above M[r] Thomas Seaward, died 4 Nov. 1836,
    aged 70.

M[rs] Mary Cullwick, of this parish, died 2 May 1788, aged 40.

Charles Taylor, son of Jacob and Mary Taylor, of this parish, died April 25, 1794,
    aged 14.
M[rs] Mary Taylor, mother of the above, died 11 April 1808, aged 68.
M[r] Jacob Taylor, died 24 Jan. 1811, aged 68.
M[rs] Ann Rebecca Taylor . . . .   [*Rest in ground.*]

Henry, died April 29, 1774, aged 4 years 5 months & 24 days.
William, died Feb. 10, 177[8 ?], aged 14 years & 5 months . . . . Lockyer . . . .
    [*Rest illegible.*]

Rebecca Horton, died 11 Jan. 1838.

Miss Mary Poole, of Torrington in Devonshire, died Dec. 3, 1803, aged 25.

M[rs] Ann Winlaw, wife of William Winlaw, of Market Street, [Cavendish] Square,
    Engine Maker, died 19 June 1772, in his 39th [or 59th] year.
M[r] Andrew Winlaw, brother of the above William Winlow [*sic*], died 24 May
    . . . . aged 33.
William Winlaw . . . . of the above . . . .   [*Rest illegible.*]

[Obedience ?] Sault, daughter of William and Obedience Sault, of this parish, died
Dec. 24, 1793, aged 13.
Mary Sault, daughter of the above, died Jan. 10, 1797, aged 2.
Margaret Sault, died April 17, 1800, aged 1 year & 7 months.

M⟨r⟩ Thomas Edwards, died March 29, 1823, aged 38.
This stone erected by his brother M⟨r⟩ William Edwards.

Sophia, wife of Eleazar Knapp, died Feb. 11, 1836, aged 33.

M⟨r⟩ Thomas Ryder, surgeon, of Oxford Street, died 13 May 1801, aged 45.

Richard Broome, son of Robert and Hannah Broome, died Feb. 15, 1775, aged
3 weeks & 3 days.
Edward Broome, son of the above Robert and Hannah Broome, died Aug. 29,
1788, aged 14 years & 10 months.
M⟨r⟩ Robert Broome, father of the above, died 24 Dec. 1799, aged 53.
M⟨r⟩ Hannah Broome, wife of the above Robert Broome, died Oct. 17, 1832, aged 87.

Thomas Clarkson . . . . [*Rest illegible.*]

M⟨rs⟩ Mary Goss, wife of M⟨r⟩ Henry Goss, of Park Street, Grosvenor Square, died
8 Feb. 1811, aged 83.
M⟨r⟩ Henry Goss, husband of the above, died Sep. 15, 1814, aged 92.

Elizabeth Bowditch, wife of Thomas Bowditch, of the parish of S⟨t⟩ George, Hanover
Square, died Feb. 2, 1822, aged 60.
The above Thomas Bowditch, died Aug. 9, 1849, aged 64.
M⟨rs⟩ Hester Bowditch, second wife of the above, died Aug. 19, 1849, aged 68.
Joseph Bowditch, died 10 Nov. 1820, aged 14.
Henry Crofts, died Feb. 10, 1836, aged 65.

Joseph Jordan, of this parish, died Dec. 9, 1772, aged 62.

M⟨rs⟩ Ann Tapley, of the parish of S⟨t⟩ Mary-le-bone, died 3 Jan. 1812, aged 21.
M⟨r⟩ Thomas Potts, father of the above, died 1 April [1823], aged . . . . [*hidden by
footstone*] years.
[*Inscription continued on the other side of the stone:—*]
M⟨rs⟩ Ann Potts, died Nov. 30, 1831, aged 75.
The beloved husband and daughter of the above lays [*sic*] in the adjoining grave.
Frances Potts, daughter of M⟨r⟩ Thomas and M⟨rs⟩ Ann Potts, died March 7, 1844,
aged 45.

M⟨r⟩ Henry Holton, late of No. 253 Oxford Street, died 24 Feb. 1847, aged 56.

M⟨r⟩ Joseph Kent, died March 28, 1821, aged 58 ; late Coachman to the Earl of
Aylesbury.
M⟨rs⟩ Ann Kent, widow of the above, a Native of Inverary, Argyleshire, died
Nov. 25, 1824, aged 52.

M⟨r⟩ Thomas Hall, late of Mount Street, of this parish, died 25 Oct. 1797, aged 38.

M⟨r⟩ John Ganerton, died Jan. 4, 1827, aged 52.
N

Mrs Mary Keat, who after a long and severe illness died April 9, 1817, aged 23.
Her four infants who lie interred in and near this spot.
This stone erected by her husband and father 1817.
Sarah, his second beloved wife, died March 17, 1834, aged 39.
Esther, daughter of the above, died March 11, 1840, aged 15.
Mr Richard Waller Keat, husband and father of the above, died Dec. 13, 1844, aged 57.
His third beloved wife has caused this to be erected to his memory.

Mrs Jane Ledbetter, died Nov. 23, 1828 [or 1829 ; *the 8 has been cut across the 9 so as to appear either an 8 or 9*], aged 56.
Mr Frederick Ledbetter, husband of the above, died April 3, 1830, aged 58.

Henry Shepherd, of this parish, died Sep. [17], 1793 [or 1795 ?], aged 45.
Elizabeth Shepherd, wife of the above . . . .
Miss Mary Shepherd, daughter of the above Henry and Elizabeth Shepherd, died July 9, 179[5 ?] . . . . [*Rest illegible.*]

Mr Stephen Taylor, late of this parish, died Feb. 11, 1825, aged 60.

Mr Edward [Powell ?], late of this parish, died Sep. 3 . . . . [aged 53 (?) years].
Mr John Oxley, died 2 Dec. 1827, aged 55.

Mrs Isabella Parker, died Jan. 2, 1845, aged 83.
Mrs Isabella Rooke Hoare, daughter of the above, died Sep. 7, 1847, aged 50.

Edward, son of Lieut. Col. Witherington, of Her Majesty's 9th Regiment of Dragoons, and Eugenia, his wife, died April 8, 1841, aged 13 years & 11 months.

Robert Alexander Hughan, Esq., of Creetown, Kirkcudbright, died Sep. 22, 1844, aged 47.

Charlotte, wife of Hugh Williams, died June 6, 182[5 ?], aged 24.

Mr William Clarke, late of Weston, Staffordshire, died Jan. 2, 1838, aged 48.

Mr Richard Dore, died July 12, 1849, in his 89th year.

Mr Henry [Leggatt] . . . . [1804].
Mr Henry Simpson, nephew of the above, died Nov. . . 1841, aged 36.

George Lambert Baker, son of William and Ann Baker, of Chapel Street West, May-Fair, died Dec. 22, 1831, aged 30.

Henry John William, son of Henry and Virginie Camille Baker, of Chapel Street West, May Fair, born 29 March 1833, died 10 April 1834.
Charles Baker, another son of the above, born 12 Jan. 1840, died 15 March 1841.
The above Virginie Camille Baker, died 22 Feb. 1844, aged 43.

Elizabeth Cole, widow, born 23 Nov. 1750, died 23 April 1808, aged 57.

*(To be continued.)**(To be continued.)*

(To be continued.)

The Registers of Inkberrow, co. Worcester.* †

[A much defaced sheet, ? date.]

Nomina eroru' qui . . . .

— — Joh'is fil. Richardi . . . .
— — . . . . uxor Tho. . . . .
— — Margeria uxor Ric. . . . .
— — . . . . fil. Nicholas . . . .
— — . . . . uxor Henr. Stevens . . . .
— — Guilmus fil. John Sale . . . .
— — Anna fil. John Sale, pred . . . .
— — . . . . Warwick . . . .
— — Elizabeth uxor . . . .
— — Thomas Huband.
— — Joh'es Pearks.
— — Joh . . . . ux. . . . . Rob. B . . . .
— — Maria fil. . . . .
— 29 Joanna Asplin.
— 6 Margareta uxor Tho. Hunt . . . .
— 7 Elizab. fil. Barthol. Ridding.
— 20 Edvardus Rawson.
Sep. 26 Guliel. Griffin.
Sep. 23 Joanna uxor Nicholai Netherton.
Sep. 26 Gulielmus fil. Jacob Asplin.
Oct. 3 Rob'tus Parker.
Oct. 24 Brigett fil. Joh'is Ireland.
Oct. 23 Agnes Edgworth, vid.
— 2 Joanna King . . . . peregrina . . . . caus . . . . inter Charlton et ol . . . .
      Swynford morte obiit apud . . . . -borrow parva.
Nov. 29 Joh'es Huntley.
Dec. 15 Philipp Heynes.
— — Alicia uxor Joh'es par . . . .
Dec. 23 Joh'es Hunt.
Jan. — Edvardus Day de Kington.
Jan. — Joh'es Harison.
— — Anna fil. Tho. Hunt.
Feb. — Joh'es fil. et Nothus . . . .
— — Margeria fil. Tho. . . . .
— — Barthol. Gidding [? Hidding].
— — Elizabeth fil. Tho. . . . .

Concordat cu' original.

HUGONE GLOVER, Vic. ibid.   RICHARD BALLARD,
                                  THOMAS HAYNES, } C-Wardens.

INKBERROW 1661 [?]. TRANSCRIPTUM VERUM OMNIUM .... MATRIMONIORUM,
BAPTIZ .... ET SEPULTORUM CONING .... INTRA P'OCHIAM INCKBERROWE
IN COMITATU ET DIOCES. WIGORN ....

———

[*Married.*]
Mar. — Gwalterus Steward de Inckberrow .... et Alice Hill [?] of ffeckenham.
 .... prius obtent ....

[*Baptisms.*] A.D. 1661.
— 20 .... Glover.
— 4 .... Roberts.
— 14 .... Illegitmus Elianora Huntbac [?] genit. Robtimm .... de Alcester.
April 16 Carolus filius Georgii Windle.
June 4 Jacobus filius Johannes.
— — Johannis filius Johannis Hunt.
April 8 Hester filia Robert Steward.
May 20 Anna filia Johannis Steward.
June — Maria, illegitima Marie Bonds per Georgium Blicke de eadem genita.
June 20 Richardus filius Willielms Walford.
June 23 Jacobus filius Richi. Shekell.
June 26 Laricke [?] filia Armell [?] Hunt.
July 28 Georgius fil. Georgii Wiggett.
July 28 Joh'es filius Joh'is ....
Sep. — Richard filius Richard Marshall.
Sep. 12 Elizebetha filia Henry Grasier [?].
Sep. 12 Maria filia Radulphi Dyson.
Sep. 19 Thomas filius Jacobus Heming.
Oct. 8 Susannah filia Thomas Higgins.
Oct. — Anna filia Johannis (Reic)wood.
— — ....
Oct. — Susanna filia Joh'is Parker.
— — .... Harrits ....
— — .... Hobbins ....
— — ....
— — ffrancis filius ....
— — Elizabetha filia ....
— — ffebe ....
— — Carolus filius ....
— — Martyn ....
Mar. 13 Thomas filius Thomas Hopkins.

[*Burials.*] A.D. 1661.
May — .... Henrici Wilmore de Kington.
May 21 .... Anley, wid.
May 26 .... Humfredi Heming.
June 28 .... uxor. Ricardi Harris.
July 10 .... filius Joh'is Hasterling.
July 16 .... Willimi Boulton.
July 17 .... Thomas [?] Sutton.
Aug. 3 .... Thomas [?] .... son.
July 22 .... Henrici [?] Reeve.
Aug. 4 .... filia Henrici Elliotts.
Aug. 25 ....
Aug. 26 .... ffreeman.
Sep. 28 .... Henrici [?] Reeve.

Oct. 6 ....
— — .... uxor d'ni ffrancisci Edggiocke, militis.
Nov. 15 .... ulielmi Goore [?].
Nov. 15 .... Phillips.
Dec. 21 ....
Jan. 1 .... ci .... vi.
Jan. 3 ....
— 6 Edwardus Pearce.
— — Thomas Phillips.
— — Alicia uxor Richi. Poole.
Mar. — Elizabetha filia Thomas Petford ....
— — Joh'es filius Joh'is Raynolds ....
— — Hester uxor Rich. Pladon ....
Mar. — Rich'us ffarr de Darmston.

(Signed) THOMAS T. R. REAVEN, } Church Wardens.
WILLIAM PHILLIPS,

INKBERROW, 1662.

[*Baptisms.*]

— — ....
— — John and James ....
— — Edmond the sonne ....
— — Elizabeth the daughter of ....
— — Richard the sonne of Henry ...
— — ffrancis the sonne of Henry ....
— — Lewes the sonne of Thomas ....
Mar. — Richard the sonne of ....
This ffor Christ'ings to the 6th day of March Anno d'ni 1662.

[*Married.*]

May 17 ffrancis Hale & Elianor Begley, both of the parrish of Inkborrow.

[*Burials.*]

Mar. — Margery Woodward of Dormston.
Mar. 27 Alice the daughter of Thomas Bennitt.
Mar. 27 Elianor, a bastard child of Bridget Walkers, being gotten by Edward
Rudge the younger.
April 9 Jane the daughter of William Boulton.
April 18 William Boulton.
April 18 Thomas Pettford's daughter.
April 18 John Harritt's daughter.
April 22 Phillipa, a bastard child of Elizabeth Hanthpatch begotten by Robert
Stonhall of Alcester.
April 24 The daughter of the widdow Shouler.
April 24 Edmond Poole's wiffe.
April 27 Thomas Lewes of Dormston.
April 27 The widdowe Pope.
May 4 The widdowe Grasior.
May 12 Thomas Tennant.
May 10 James the sonne of Thomas Edwarde.
May 17 ffrancis the sonne of ffrancis Baskefeild.
June 4 Stephens Baylis.

June —   A poore boy which came ffrom Wicth.
June 30   Thomas Edwarde.
June 30   Elizabeth Moyle.
July   2   William Sale of Sburnocke in the parrish of ffeckenham.
July   8   The sonne of William Sale.
July   8   The sonne of Ann Griffin.
July 15   Ann the wiffe of Richard Steward.
July 21   Mʳˢ Margery Hunt, widdowe.
July —   George the sonne of George Wiggett.
Aug. 12   Alice the daughter of ffrancis Dyson.
Aug. 16   Thomas Beddowes.
Aug. —   A daughter of Richard Collins.
Aug. 26   William Raven.
Aug. 30   Katherine his wiffe.
Aug. —   Joyce the wiffe of Eaven [?] Owding [?].
Sep. —   Richard Steward.
Sep. 18   Ursula the wiffe of Thomas Hunt, gent.
Sep. 25   Richard White, Vicar.
Oct. 21   William the sonne of Thomas ffarr.
Oct. 26   William King.
Oct. 26   William the sonne of William ffiggett.
Oct. 26   Margaret Ellins.
Oct. —   Jane Boulton.
Nov. 11 [?]   Mʳˢ Mary Savage, widowe.
—   —   Ann Smith, widdowe.
Dec. 31   The wiffe of Thomas Yatte.
Jan.   2   Tovey of Kington.
Jan. —   Thomas Pettforde's daughter.

Given in by us—   GEORGE WINDLE,   } Church Wardens of
                    WILLIAM HARUY,   } Inkborrow 166-.

A JUST AND PERFECT TRANSCRIPT GIVEN IN BY THOMAS JAMES, THOMAS HOPKINS, CHURCHWARDENS, OF ALL THE MARRIAGES, CHRIST'INGS, AND BURIALLS THAT HAVE BEEN WITHIN THE PARRISH OF INCKBORROW FROM THE — OF MARCH ANNO D'NI 1663 TO THE 25ᵀᴴ DAY OF MARCH ANNO DOM. 1664, AS FOLLOWETH :—

HENRY JACKSON, Vic.

[Marriages.]

May   1   Thomas Phillips & Jane Leedwooke [?] of . . . .
June 25   Richard ffarwood [?] & Elizabeth Griffin both, of this parish.
Oct. 22   Mʳ Richard ff . . . . erdi [?] of Anne & Alice Huband of Knighton.
Oct. 20   Thomas Hewes or Hemes & Eleanor Cooke of Home Greene in the parrish of ffeckenham.
Nov. 28   John Price & Elizabeth Showle(r), both of this parrish of ffeckenham.
Feb.   3   Anthony Judgins & Susanna Bartlett, both of this parrish.

Christ'nings, Anno Dom' 1663.

Mar. 29   Ann the daughter of John Beeseley.
April 12   Alice the daughter of William Hunt of Cladsall.
May   2   John the sonne of Jerome Rice.
May 24   John the sonne of Richard Herne.
July 19   William the sonne of William Walford of Boults.
July 19   Mary the daughter of Robert Steward of Stockwoode.

Aug.	2	William the sonne of Thomas Marshall of Hollborrowe Greene.
Aug.	15	Bridget the daughter of Thomas Laugher of the Gannow.
Aug.	23	John the sonne of Thomas Attwoode of Little Inkborrow ffarme.
Sep.	7	Elizabeth the daughter of William ffiggett of Stockegreene.
Sep.	—	Thomas the sonne of Thomas Higgins of Cladsall.
Sep.	29	Elizabeth the daughter of Richard Glouer of Inckborrowe.
Oct.	21	Thomas the sonne of Thomas Edwards, shoomaker of Holberrowe Greene.
Oct.	13	ffrancis the sonne of ffrancis ffreman of Inckberrowe and Thomas the sonne of Richard Horne of Egioke.
Oct.	25	Elizabeth the daughter of John Harrett of Cladsall.
Nov.	8	Walter the sonne of Walter Steward of Cladsall and Mary the daughter of George Wiggett.
Dec.	6	Hanna the daughter of Humfrey Domines [?].
Dec.	28	Henry the sonne of William Haruy.
Dec.	29	ffrancis the sonne of Thomas Darby of Boults.
Jan.	31	Ann the daughter of John Goore of Cladsall.
Feb.	2	Thomas the sonne of Christopher Roberts and Joane the daughter of John Steward.
Feb.	20 [?]	Hester the daughter of Richard Williams, tinker.
Feb.	20	ffrances the daughter of Robert Weauer of Holborrowe Greene.
Feb.	21	Ann the daughter of Nicholas Rand [? Ranels] of Morton Under Hill.
Mar.	20	John the sonne of Roger Tandy of Cladsall.
Mar.	21	Ann or a child of Henry Hunt.

(To be continued.)

𝕽𝖊𝖛𝖎𝖊𝖜𝖘.

Some Feudal Coats of Arms. By J. FOSTER, Hon. M.A. Oxon. London and Oxford: James Parker and Co.

THIS is a new book, on a fresh departure, by Mr. Foster, and is well worthy of a place in every gentleman's library. It is a volume complete in itself, and is nicely got up and issued by Messrs. Parker. With other works of Mr. Foster's, half a dozen would be begun in parts, where there was no chance of them being finished for years to come, such as his "Familiæ Minorum Gentium," which has now been issued by the Harleian Society in four volumes, and "Musgrave's Obituary," making six volumes—both works quite out of the reach of private enterprise, and only possible where such a wealthy society such as the Harleian undertakes the printing and issuing for its members. Similarly placed were the Lincolnshire Pedigrees, began by Mr. Foster and relinquished. It has this year been undertaken by the Harleian Society, under the editorship of Canon Maddison, who is adding several pedigrees of his own compilation and that of friends to it; and as it will make three or four volumes, that again was an error of judgment to think of issuing it in sheets with other works, as years would be exhausted before the work was completed.

This present work is rare, in giving so many page illustrations of knights from 1300 upwards. On every other page is a plate given either of arms or figures in full armour, about 130 in all out of a volume of about 300 pp. The smaller coats seem all to be carefully drawn, each with a name attached, and colours given. The facsimiles of the Boroughbridge Roll of 1322 and a tracing from the Camden Roll temp. Edward I. are both given as a double plate on a toned ground, such as we often adopt in this publication. Altogether the work is worthy of its painstaking compiler and publisher, and will prove a boon to many bookplate collectors in corroborating unknown coats.

An Exact List of the Lords Spiritual and Temporal in 1734.   London : Elliot Stock, Paternoster Row, E.C.

THIS is a little book, nicely got up and bound, of the Members of the House of Lords in 1734. It has a Preface by Mr. A. C. Fox-Davies, who gives some interesting summaries of the number of Archbishops, Dukes, Marquesses, Earls, Viscounts, and Bishops.   Each page is a photographed facsimile of a copy found bound up with Goldsmith's Almanack for 1735, which is now in the British Museum.   We note that Lord Palmerston sat for Boffiney, Cornwall, and Sir Rowland Hill for Litchfield, and also that several Lords lived in Soho.   Altogether it is worthy the acceptance or patronage of all members of Parliament.

The Journal of the Ex Libris Society.   Vol. XII., Parts 9, 10, and 11, September to November 1902.   London : A. and C. Black, Soho Square, W.

THE above Parts tend to keep up the Journal to its usual level, and the September one gives some examples of an American draughtsman, which as his narrator, Mr. Truesdell, says, shew some originality in form and shape ; the one of Frank Wood's is a picture in itself, being ably minimized from the Guttenberg plate placed on a pile of books, the open leaf of the one at top shewing his arms.   Another American artist, Mr. Arthur P. Spear, has three plates given, also shewing great care and variety of style, Mr. Lothrop's especially.   The Part also contains a sample of a coat in three colours at one impression, the registering of which is perfect.   The November Part gives the arms of Lord Craven and also two of the Jago family of Cornwall, and of the Borlase family.   The arms for identification now amount to 521.

The Virginia Magazine of History and Biography.   No. 2, Vol. X.   October 1902.   Virginia Historical Society, Richmond, U.S.A.

THIS Part has the article, " The Germans of the Valley," concluded.   It has been very interesting, shewing as it has done the frugal manner and style of living in the early part of 1700.   The Brown papers are also continued, giving an account of events after the scrimmage at Harper's Ferry.   In style John Brown and the Boer Kruger are much alike, each with a Bible in one hand and a death-warrant in the other.   The Part also contains an account of Christ Church, Lancaster, co. Virginia, with two illustrations.

Fenland Notes and Queries.   Vol. V., Part 55.   October 1902.   Peterborough : George C. Caster, Market Place.

THIS Part contains the usual quantity of local matter, including the Drainage question of 1618, and a painstaking article on the liberty of Peterborough, giving an account of the various deeds passed from time to time.   Among other interesting matters given is an advertisement for " Letting the Poor," whereby persons who wished to treat for the same were desired to apply to the Churchwarden or Overseer.   " None but married persons need apply."   We presume their labour was utilized for any purpose the applicants required it for.

** Books for Review and Notices of Forthcoming Works should be addressed to Messrs. Mitchell and Hughes at the Publishing Office, 140 Wardour Street, London, W.

Pedigree of Duguard.*

VISITATION OF WARWICK, ANNO 1682. [College of Arms, K 3, fo. 135.]

At Warwick, 30 Aug. 1682.

Mr. . . . . . Duguard exhibited these armes and sayes he is of the family of
Duguard of Roan in Normandy.

William Duguard of Grafton Fliford in com' Worc.

Henry Duguard, born at Grafton Fliford, but=Elizabeth, dau'r of Mʳ Will.
resided at the Lickey in the p'sh of Broms- | Kimberley of Whitford, near
grove in com' Worcester, obijt a° 1635. | Bromsgrove, gent.

2. Alice, | 1. Margery, w. of | 3. Jane, w. of | 5. Richard Du- | 4. George Du-
died an | Nicholas Orford | John Pettifor | guard, an apothe- | guard of Lon-
infant. | of Bromsgrove in | of London. | cary in London, | dou, stationer.
| com'Wig'orn[sic]. | | obijt cœlebs. |

2. Thomas Duguard,=Hannah, daʳ of=Mary, dau'r of=Anne, dau'r of Hugh
Maʳ of Arts and | Thomas Hanks | John Hage- | Muston of Tibbols
Rector of Barford in | of Stow on the | ford of Hen- | in p'och de Kings-
com' Warwick, æt. | Wold in com' | wood in co. | bury in com' Warr.
75 annor' 1682. | Glocʳ, gent. 1 | Warr', Esq. 2 | 3 w.
| wife. | wife. |

A   B   C

---

* Communicated by W. P. W. PHILLIMORE, Esq., M.A., B.C.L.

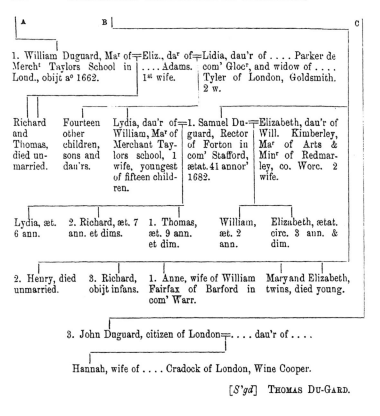

A   B   C

1. William Duguard, Ma^r of=Eliz., da^r of=Lidia, dau'r of . . . . Parker de Merch^t Taylors School in . . . . Adams. com' Gloc^r, and widow of . . . . Lond., obijt a° 1662.   1st wife.   Tyler of London, Goldsmith. 2 w.

Richard and Thomas, died unmarried.

Fourteen other children, sons and dau'rs.

Lydia, dau'r of=William, Ma^r of Merchant Taylors school, 1 wife, youngest of fifteen children.

1. Samuel Du-=guard, Rector of Forton in com' Stafford, ætat. 41 annor' 1682.

Elizabeth, dau'r of Will. Kimberley, Ma^r of Arts & Min^r of Redmarley, co. Worc. 2 wife.

Lydia, æt. 6 ann.

2. Richard, æt. 7 ann. et dims.

1. Thomas, æt. 9 ann. et dim.

William, æt. 2 ann.

Elizabeth, ætat. circ. 3 ann. & dim.

2. Henry, died unmarried.

3. Richard, obijt infans.

1. Anne, wife of William Fairfax of Barford in com' Warr.

Mary and Elizabeth, twins, died young.

3. John Duguard, citizen of London=. . . . dau'r of . . . .

Hannah, wife of . . . . Cradock of London, Wine Cooper.

[*S'gd*] THOMAS DU-GARD.

MONUMENTAL INSCRIPTIONS FROM THE BURIAL-GROUND OF ST. GEORGE, HANOVER SQUARE, LONDON.*

Sarah Elizabeth Moody, daughter of Richard and Sarah Moody, of Burton Street, in this parish, died Jan. 2, 1848, aged 4 years & 5 months.
Richard William Moody, died Jan. 5, 1848, aged 1 year & 4 months.
Also, near this spot, Elizabeth Mary Moody, died Sep. 30, 1841, aged 11 months.

Mrs Sarah Watson, wife of Mr Thomas Watson, of No. 18 James Street, Oxford Street, died 30 Jan. 1826, aged 66.
Also five children, infants, viz.: Henry, William Henry, Harriett, ... Eliza, and John Newton Watson.
The above Mr Thomas Watson . . . . in his 61st year.
Elizabeth Evans Watson, granddaughter of the above, died 31 May 1836, aged 2 years & 5 months.

* Communicated by F. S. SNELL, Esq., M.A.—continued from p. 154,

Mrs Elizabeth Watson, wife of Mr William Watson, and mother of the above, died
31 Aug. 1836, aged 32.
Thomas Edward Watson, son of the before-named W. and E. Watson, died 4 Oct.
1836, aged 11 months & 12 days, and is interred at Wanstead, Essex.

Miss Sarah Halsey, daughter of John and Sarah Halsey, died 5 Jan. 1808, aged 16.
Miss Lucy Halsey, sister of the above, died 23 May 1825, in her 20th year.
John Halsey, father of the above, died 15 May 1838, aged 74.
Sarah Halsey, wife of the above John Halsey, died 1 Oct. 1851, aged 87, deeply
lamented by her family.

Mrs Milborough Clark, wife of Mr William Clark, died Aug. 1, 1830, aged 67.
Frances Mary Killick, granddaughter of the above, died March 11, 1832, aged
1 year & 1 week.
Mr William Clark, died May 12, 1833, aged 62.

[Edward ?] [Cha .... ?], son of [James ?] and Elizabeth [Cha .... ?], died Dec. ....
aged 53 years.

Frances Arabella, wife of John Levett Yeats, Esq., and daughter of Philip
Reinagle, Esq., R.A. She was born 17th July 1786, died 30 Dec. 1831.

Mr Robert Hodgson, of Clarges Street, died May 18, 1822, aged 67.
Robert, son of the above, died Jan. 17, 1831, aged 24.
Elizabeth Hodgson, widow of the above first-named Mr Robert Hodgson, died
May 17, 1849, aged 78.

Samuel Dring, died March 7, 1831, aged 47.

Mrs Mary Oakey, wife of Mr Henry Oakey, late of the parish of St Mary-le-bone,
died 14 May 1802, aged 65.
Mary Ann Oakey, died 29 Nov. 1811, aged 5.
The above Mr Henry Oakey died March 19, 1822, aged 74.

Mary Ann Conway, died Jan. 23, 1850, aged 32.
Henry Gregory, died June 6, 1838, aged 34.

Mr George Lamb, of this parish, died April 29, 1791, aged 53.
Mrs Ann Lamb, wife of the above George Lamb, died March 31 .... [*stone flaked
off*], aged 55 years.

Charles Sharpe, of this parish, died Nov. 12, 1829, aged 48.
Mrs Mary Sharpe, relict of the above, died May 1, 1838, aged 55.
Miss Mary Sharpe, daughter of the above, died July 15, 1838, aged 25.

William Moore, died .... 6, 1799, aged 52.
William Moore, son of the above, died Nov. 2 [1800 ?], in his 16th year.

Mrs Mary Scarman, wife of Mr George Scarman, of Mill Street, Hanover Square,
died Oct. 16, 1825, in her 61st year.
Sarah, daughter of the above, died March 9, 1814, aged 6 years & 6 months.
The above Mr George Scarman died Jan. 15, 1846, aged 80.

Mrs Ann King, wife of Mr Daniel King, of 73 Park Street, Grosvenor Square, died
Aug. 8, 1825, aged 44.
Two daughters and one son died infants.
Mr Daniel King, husband of the above, died Dec. 6, 1833, aged 49.

Charles Birchall, of Northampton, died July 18, 1844, aged 30.

Edward Freake, died April 30, 1822, aged 2 years & 5 months.
Margaret Freake, died July 28, 1822, aged 6 years & 6 months.
M⁎ Margaret Freake, mother of the above children, and wife of M⁎ Charles Freake,
    of Harley Street, died Aug. 8, 1822, aged 37.
Maria Freake, daughter of the above, died Nov. 15, 1822, aged 5 months.
The above M⁎ Charles Freake died June 27, 1837, in his 51ˢᵗ year.

Mary Woodcock, died Nov. 11, 1775, aged 69.

Henry, son of Henry and Sarah Sadler, of New Bond Street, died 6 Oct. 1840, aged
    11 months.

M⁎ Frances Turner, died Sep. 17, 1773, in her 32ⁿᵈ year.

M⁎ Catherine Dight, wife of M⁎ William Dight, of this parish, died 8 Sep. 1785,
    in the 103ʳᵈ year of her age.
M⁎ William Dight, husband of the above M⁎ Catherine Dight, died Nov. 20, 1791,
    aged 88.*

M⁎ Elizabeth Rickards, died Oct. 2, 1805, aged 71.

M⁎ George Stevens, late of New Bond Street, died Oct. 28, 1810, aged 52.

Emma, daughter of Charles Robert and Charlotte Hughes, died Jan. 21, 1834, aged
    5 years & 6 months.

M⁎ James Palmer, died Aug. 14, 1834, aged 86.
M⁎ Johanna Palmer, wife of M⁎ William Palmer, died Aug. 17, 1834, aged 77.
The above M⁎ William Palmer, brother to M⁎ James Palmer, died Aug. 7, 1822,
    aged 77, and whose remains lie interred in Sᵗ John's burial ground,
    Sᵗ Mary-le-bone.
Also two feet south-west of this Stone lie the remains of Mary Ann, wife of
    M⁎ William Hunt, and daughter of the above William and Johanna Palmer,
    died Sep. 7, 1835, aged 45.

.... 1782, aged 78 years.
Also M⁎ Sarah Weightman, sister of the above, died 30 May 1789, aged 72.

M⁎ Thomas Mi[.... ?], of this parish, who died October 1791, in his 40ᵗʰ year.

.... Wiltshire,† died 8 May 1790, aged 6[4 ?].

[A small stone, shaped like a milestone, with date 1773, and the arms of the City
    of London, the latter being much worn.]

M⁎ William Kerry, of Upper Brook Street, died Dec. 22, 1807, aged 77.
M⁎ Elizabeth Kerry, died May 9, 1820, aged 80.
Caroline Kerry, died July 30, 1829, aged 19 months.
Elizabeth Jackson Kerry, died Aug. 4, 1829, aged 6 years & 9 months ; grand-
    children of the above.

---

* The inscription stands thus, and the letters are clearly cut ; the husband was therefore
21 years younger than his wife.
† This is the surname, not the county.

Mⁿˢ Ann Kearsley, of Upper Brook Street, died 21 Nov. 1811, aged 73.

Mʳ Paul Balby, died March 17, 1811, aged 48.
Mⁿˢ Sophia Balby, relict of the above, died Oct. 24, 1853.
Elizabeth Cunnington, niece of the above, died Nov. 27, 1831, aged [68 ?] years.

Mⁿˢ Susannah Johnson, wife of Mʳ John Johnson, of New Bond Street, died
  Aug. 5, 1813, aged 34.
    W. M. J. . . . 1811.   Hʸ J. . . . . 1821.
    Sᵃ J. . . . . 1817.   M. J. . . . . 1826.
    Sᵐ J. . . . . 1817.
The above Mʳ Johnson died March 1, 1845, aged 74.

Elizabeth Weaver, died April 17, 1830, aged 82.

Samuel Spilsbury, died 21 Feb. 1799, aged 70.
Sarah Spilsbury, his wife, died Oct. 1, 1802, aged 73.
Robert Spilsbury, son of the above, died Sep. 3, 1809, aged 44.
Francis Henry Russell, of Sᵗ James's Parish, and Aunt [sic] to the above
  Rᵗ Spilsbury, died 8 Feb. 1811, aged 52.
Dinah Dolby Goodyer Spilsbury, died May 29, 1824, aged 26.
Ann, wife of the above Robert Spilsbury, died 10 Nov. 1833, aged 59.
Robert Spilsbury, died 1 May 1849, aged 56, son of the above Robert and Ann
  Spilsbury.

Jane, wife of Mʳ G. B. Mason, of No. 16 Duke Street, Grosvenor Square, born
  Aug. 29, 1788, died July 14, 1837.
Three of their children died in their infancy.
Sarah, second wife of Mʳ G. B. Mason, died Nov. 18, 1844, aged 32, and their two
  infant children.
Melina Anne, daughter of the above, born April 25, 1823, died May 31, 1853.
Mary Jane, daughter of the above, born April 13, 1815, died Aug. 31, 1853.

Mⁿˢ Mary Ann Barbrook, wife of William Barbrook, of High Street, Sᵗ Mary-le-
  bone, died April 13, 1836, aged 36.
Six children of the above :—
    William, aged 11 months.   Henry, aged 6 months.
    Mary Ann, aged 4½ years.   Elizabeth, aged 9 months.
    Edward, aged 10 months.   Emma, aged 4 years.

Mʳ Thomas Barron, died April 24, 1799, aged 42.
Mⁿˢ Charlotte Barron, died Aug. 16, 1808, aged 49.

Mʳ John Marsh, died March 24, 1810, aged 46, and three of his children.
Mⁿˢ Ruth Marsh, wife of the above, died 23 Dec. 1826, aged 62.
Mⁿˢ Charlotte, wife of Mʳ Daniel Bedborough, and daughter of John and Ruth
  Marsh, died 18 Oct. 1834, aged 41.

. . . . Stanis . . . . De La Rochette, of this parish . . . . 1802, aged 71 years.
Esther Margaret Elizabeth D'Arcy Delia Rochette, daughter of the above, died
  Jan. 6, 1807, aged 28.
Edward Augustus D'Arcy, son of the above, died May 30, 1814, aged 34.
Mⁿˢ Frances D'Arcy, died July 27, 1839, aged 56.

Jane Mellicott, wife of John Mellicott, died 6 July 1775, aged 34.
M[r] John Mellicott, husband of the above, died Jan. 2, 1815, aged 52.

W[m] Cooke, [late ?] of this parish, died .... [1774 ?], aged 82.   [*See next inscription.*]

M[r] William Cooke, died [14] July 177[4 ?], aged 82.
Ann, his wife, died 10 March 1774, aged 67.
.... 1754, aged 61 years.

M[r] Charles [Savage ?] .... 1802 ....
M[rs] Jane Crombie, died July 26, 1811, aged 56.

M[r] William Clayton, died July 22, 1802, in his 30th year.
M[r] George Blackwell, died Dec. 15, 1812, aged 55.
M[rs] Elizabeth Blackwell, wife of the above G. B., died Oct. 21, 1839, aged 8[3 ?].

Edward Johns, of New Bond Street, died .. Aug. 1791, in his 78th year.
His son Edward Johns, of New Bond Street, died 20 Aug. 1795, aged 11.

.... [Ro]bert and Phebe Martin, died Aug. 13, 1776, aged 10 months.
Thomas, died Sep. 18, 1787, aged 4 years and 6 months.
John, died Jan. 17, 1790, aged 17.
William Martin, son of the above, died June 2, 1799, aged 22.
M[r] Robert Martin, father of the above-named, died Feb. .. 1803, in his 64th year.
Phebe Martin, wife of the above, died Feb. .. 180[4 ?], in her 65th year.

M[r] Cadwallader Price, died Aug. 14, 1776, aged 78.

William M[.... ?], of Berkeley Square, in the parish of S[t] George, Hanover
    Square, died Feb. 28, 1776, aged 72.

M[r] Samuel Gou[ld ?], died Oct. 26, 1808, aged 56.

M[r] Henry Joseph Fryer, late of Pimlico, died 12 April 1806, aged 33.

M[r] Emanuel Duhl, died March 26, 1777, aged 69.

M[rs] Elizabeth Bentley, died Dec. 8, 1777, aged 78.

M[r] Samuel Meacher, of this parish, died April 21, 1832, aged 25.

Elizabeth Ellis, wife of Edward Ellis, of the parish of S[t] George, Hanover Square,
    died 10 July 1783, aged 30.
Sophia, their daughter, died 30 July 1783, aged 1 year & 8 months.

. . . .
Also the Ashes of Arthur Savage, late of Boston, America, died 29 March 180-,
    aged .. years.

[*Most of the stone in following has flaked off.*]
[Phil ?]ip Parsons .... New Road, died July .... aged 76 years.
Catherine, infant daughter ....
Mary Sophia .... of South Au [....], great-grand .... of the above.

M[rs] Martha Lay, died 19 June 1821, in her 77th year.
M[rs] Mary Hillhouse, sister of the above, died 14 March 1829, in her 88th year.
M[rs] Lucy Leake, sister of the above, died 19 March 1829, in her 83rd year.
M[rs] Anne Dykes, daughter of the above M[rs] Mary Hillhouse, died 26 March 1830,
      in her 61st year.
M[r] Charles Hillhouse, son of the above M[rs] Mary Hillhouse, died 11 Dec. 1830, in
      his 55th year.
Mary Hillhouse, daughter of the above M[r] Charles Hillhouse, died 27 May 1835,
      aged 31.
Charles Hillhouse, son of the above M[r] Charles Hillhouse, died 4 March 1836,
      aged 30.
Ann Maria Hillhouse, widow of the first-named Charles Hillhouse, died 29 Aug.
      1845, aged 66.

The only and much lamented son of M[r] Thomas and Ann Dykes, of High Street,
      S[t] Giles in the Fields.   His death was sudden, occasioned by an accident in
      Regent Street, 28 Oct. 1839, aged 7.

Margaret Clarke, died 29 Jan. 1810, aged 47.
M[rs] Lucretia Clarke, late mother of the above, died 4 Jan. 1820, aged 86.
Lucretia Collett, died 2 April 1835, aged 65.

M[r] Robert Bancks, Jun[r], of New Bond Street, died Nov. 5, 1830, aged 31.
Martha Bancks, sister of the above, died May 11, 1833, aged 26.
Ann Bancks, sister of the above, died April 9, 1835, aged 29.
M[r] Robert Bancks, father of the above, died Aug. 21, 1841, aged 76.
Martha, wife of M[r] Robert Bancks, died Nov. 20, 1841, aged 74.

M[rs] Elizabeth Finnie, wife of M[r] John Finnie, of this parish, died 19 Nov. 1815,
      aged 56.

M[rs] Mary Griffin, died Dec. 2, 1828, in her 73[d] year.

Jane Cook, died 21 Jan. 1792, aged 71.
John Cook, died 8 Dec. 1801, aged 67.
Amelia Dubochet . . . . 7 Sep. 1815, aged 52.
John Emanuel Dubochet, son of the above, died 4 Aug. 1821, aged 3[4 ?].
George Edward Dubochet, died 27 April 1817, aged 51.

M[r] W[m] White's family vault.
John White, son of William and Frances White, of Oxford Street, died March 8,
      1830, aged 4 years & 4 months.
The above Mr William White died Sep. 6, 1833, in his 44th year.

Lætitia Hardwick Aspinwall, died March 14, 1827, aged 2.
Henry Aspinwall, died Oct. 4, 1833, aged 8 months.
Sarah Elizabeth Aspinwall, died 29 Jan. 1837, aged 5 months.
Margaret Walker Aspinwall, died Oct. 12, 1838, aged 16 years on the 17th inst.
Richard Sykes Aspinwall, died Aug. 13, 1839, aged 11.
Mr James Aspinwall, of Lower Grosvenor Street, father of the above, died 26 Sep.
      1850, aged 56.
Lætitia Hardwick, died 6 Feb. 18[5 ?]2, aged 65.

Sophia Sheward, wife of Samuel Sheward, of this parish, died Jan. 31, 1820,
      aged 20.

A GENEALOGICAL HISTORY

OF THE

Family of Adams of Cavan, etc.*

V.

THE DESCENDANTS OF BENJAMIN ADAMS, THE FIFTH SON OF ALLEN ADAMS AND MARTHA HIGENBOTHAM.

V. REV. BENJAMIN ADAMS, A.B. 3 March 1774, J.P. (Walker's "Hibernian Magazine," May 1783), of Retreat, co. Cavan, Rector of Killinick, Diocese of Ferns; born 1756; married 14 April 1777 Elizabeth, daughter of John Clark, Esq., of Drogheda (Family Records and Castlerock Par. Reg.), grandson of the celebrated Metaphysician Rev. Samuel Clark, D.D., Rector of St. James's, Westminster, and Chaplain to Queen Anne; died 10 June 1840 at Retreat, and was interred in the Old Church of Knockbride (Knockbride Par. Reg.) beside his wife, who had died 28 February 1833, aged 77 (ibid.). A handsome mural tablet of black and white marbles, surmounted with an " Agnus Dei " holding a cross, is erected to his memory in the present Church of Knockbride. He had issue four sons and six daughters, viz. : —

I. WILLIAM ALLEN ADAMS, born 15 May 1783; died 3 March 1784 (Family Records) and was interred in Knockbride.

II. JOHN ADAMS, J.P., of Shinan House, Shercock, co. Cavan, born 16 May 1785 (Family Records); was High Sheriff of Cavan in 1811; married 25 November 1806 (St. George's, Dublin, Par. Reg.) Joyce, daughter of Richard Adams, Esq., J.P., of Shercock House (vide p. 86); admitted by special favour a Freeman of Drogheda Borough 14 July 1814 (vide p. 8, foot-note); died s.p. February 1827 and was interred in Shercock Churchyard. His will was proved in Kilmore (Probate Court, Kilmore).

III. VERY REV. SAMUEL ADAMS, T.C.D., A.B. 15 July 1808, A.M. 6 July 1829, of Northlands, co. Cavan (vide p. 5), J.P. for the counties of Cavan and Monaghan; born 15 February 1788 (Family Records); entered Trinity College, Dublin, October 1803 from Portora School, Enniskillen, and obtained first place; was awarded the Silver Medal for Oratory by the Historical Society; entered Holy Orders 29 November 1812 as Curate of Drumgoon, Diocese of Kilmore; ordained Priest 14 March 1813 on his appointment by the Crown to the Prebend of Tirebrine and Rectory of Aughrim, Diocese of Elphin; admitted by special favour (vide p. 8, foot-note) a Freeman of Drogheda Borough 15 September 1819; presented by the Crown to the Deanery of Cashel 10 August 1829 by a Patent, dated 6 July 1829, and was instituted and installed 29 August 1829; has published, 1st, " A Sermon on the death of Rev. Anthony Edwards, A.M., Curate of Cashel," 8vo, Cork, 1836; 2nd, " A Comparative View of the Anglican and Roman Churches," 12mo, Dublin, 1836 (vide Cotton's Fasti); married 4 January 1809 Frances, youngest daughter of Captain John Hervey of Killiane Castle, co. Wexford; died 7 December 1856 at Northlands and was interred in Knockbride Old Church (Knockbride Par. Reg.). A handsome mural monument of black and white marbles has been erected by his three surviving sons to his memory in Shercock Church. Mrs. Adams died

28 November 1869, aged 76, and was buried in Knockbride (Knockbride Par. Reg.), having had issue four sons and three daughters, viz. :—

1. BENJAMIN WILLIAM ADAMS, born 13 February 1816 (Family Records) ; died 9 March 1822, aged 6 years, and was interred in the Old Church of Knockbride, where there is a handsome monument of white marble, surmounted with the family arms, to his memory.

2. JOHN HERVEY ADAMS, T.C.D., A.B. Vern. 1838, of Northlands, J.P. for the counties of Cavan and Monaghan ; born 28 April 1818 (Family Records) ; entered Trinity College, Dublin, 1834 ; called to the Bar Hilary Term 1842 ; was High Sheriff of Cavan in 1854 ; married first, 30 April 1846 (Killenance Par. Reg.), Elizabeth Frances, third daughter of Ambrose Going, Esq., J.P., of Ballyphilip, co. Tipperary, and by her, who died 25 July 1867, aged 46, had issue two sons and two daughters, viz. :—

    (1) SAMUEL ALLEN ADAMS of Consilla Lodge, Consilla, born 1 March 1847 ; entered the 1st or South Tipperary Artillery as Lieut. 21 January 1869 ; retired January 1871 ; married 13 June 1871 (" Daily Express " Newspaper) Frances Dorothea, daughter of Rev. Decimus William Preston, A.B., Rector of Killinkere, Diocese of Kilmore, and granddaughter of William Preston, Judge of Appeal, and the Hon. Frances Dorothea, daughter of John Evans, 5th Lord Carbery, and has issue three sons and four daughters, viz. :—

        1. JOHN HERVEY STUART ADAMS, born 30 December 1875.

        2. SAMUEL ALLEN ADAMS, born 11 April 1882.

        3. A son, born 9 May 1889 at Northlands, co. Cavan (" Irish Times " Newspaper).

        4. EMILY MAUDE ELIZABETH, died 28 May 1891 of meningitis, aged 18 (" Irish Times " Newspaper).

        5. FELICIA PRESTON, died June 1887.

        6. ANGELINA OLIVE MILDRED.

        7. FRANCES DOROTHEA KATHLEEN, died 5 September 1887, aged 6 months.

    (2) AMBROSE GOING ADAMS of Northlands, J.P. for co. of Cavan ; born 22 March 1850 ; married 3 October 1872 Anne Jane Foster, daughter of Rev. William Watkins Deering, A.M. (see *post*), who was admitted to Holy Orders for the Curacy of Shercock 25 September 1887. Mr. Ambrose Adams died 11 January 1888, having had issue two daughters, viz. :—

        1. CLARA ELIZABETH CHARLOTTE, married 1 June 1893 (St. Stephen's, Dublin, Par. Reg.) James Frederick Foster M'Clintock, M.A., younger son of Alfred Henry M'Clintock.

        2. ETHEL ANNIE.

    (3) MARGARET MAUD ANNE, married 6 April 1871 (Rathmines Par. Reg.) Ormsby Colville McClintock Jones, Esq., J.P., of Mount Edward, co. Sligo, and has issue four sons, viz. :—

        1. PERCY JAMES COLVILLE JONES, born 22 November 1872.

2. JOHN HERVEY COLVILLE JONES, born 28 August 1874.

3. BERKELEY COLVILLE JONES, born 30 May 1877 ; died 10 April 1883.

4. ROBERT CECIL COLVILLE JONES, born 26 November 1882.

(4) ELIZABETH FRANCES, married 3 September 1872 (St. Peter's, Dublin, Par. Reg.) Robert Edward Follett Jones, Esq., her brother-in-law's brother, and has issue four sons and one daughter, viz. :—

1. HERBERT JAMES EDWARD FOLLETT JONES, born 9 July 1873.

2. LINDSEY FOLLETT JONES, born 4 April 1875.

3. GERALD HERVEY FOLLETT JONES, born 19 August 1877.

4. SIDNEY FOLLETT JONES, born 20 June 1879.

5. ELIZABETH NOEL FOLLETT.

Mr. John Hervey Adams married 2ndly, 24 September 1869 (Monkstown Par. Reg.), Sarah Mary, daughter of Lieut.-Colonel Owen Lloyd Ormsby, late of the 88th Regiment (Connaught Rangers) ; died 8 May 1871 and was buried in Knockbride Old Church (Knockbride Par. Reg.). Mrs. Adams married 2ndly, 9 May 1874 (Monkstown Par. Reg.), Edward Gibbs Poingdestre, Esq., of Granville Manor, Jersey, and has issue one son.

3. CHARLES STUART ADAMS of Glynch House, Newbliss, co. Monaghan, J.P. for the counties of Meath and Cavan; born 12 July 1820 (Family Records) ; married 1st, 6 June 1850 (St. George's, Dublin, Par. Reg.), Elizabeth, daughter of Charles McMahon, Esq., of Rockfield, co. Monaghan, and by her, who died 5 May 1860 and was interred in Knockbride, he had issue four sons, viz. :—

(1) SAMUEL STEWART ADAMS, born 21 March 1851.

(2) RICHARD HERVEY ADAMS, born 27 September 1852.

(3) CHARLES ALLEN ADAMS, born 12 June 1857 ; died 22 March 1860 of scarlatina, at Ashfield, co. Meath, and was interred in Knockbride (Knockbride Par. Reg.).

(4) WILLIAM VIGORS ADAMS, born 28 October 1859; died 23 December 1867 and was interred in Knockbride (Knockbride Par. Reg.).

Mr. Charles Stuart Adams married 2ndly, 23 October 1862 (St. George's, Dublin, Par. Reg.), Jane Henrietta, eldest daughter of Rev. Charles Sheridan Young, A.B., and died 30 April 1876. He was buried in Knockbride Old Church. His widow died 21 July 1888 at Cliff Lodge, Bundoran. They had issue three sons and seven daughters, viz. :—

(1) CHARLES SHERIDAN ADAMS, born 29 July 1863; died 19 December 1867 and was buried in Knockbride (Knockbride Par. Reg.).

(2) DOUGLAS GERALD ADAMS, born 20 March 1868 ; married 23 January 1897 Eleanor Mary, second daughter of General Robert Clifford, C.B.   She died 6 December 1897, having had issue one daughter, viz. :—

VIOLET ELEANOR, born 6 December 1897.

(3) CLAUDE STUART ALEXANDER ADAMS, born 16 March 1874 ; died 15 September 1875 and was interred in Knockbride Old Church (Knockbride Par. Reg.).

(4) MARIE (MAY) STUART, married 16 October 1890, in Killeshandra Church, Rev. William Knox, Rector of Killesher ("Irish Times " Newspaper), and has issue :—

1. ARTHUR STUART KNOX, born 11 November 1891.

2. CHARLES WILLIAM KNOX, born 20 February 1894.

3. KATHLEEN NORA, born 22 September 1892.

4. MARIAN FLORENCE, born 18 April 1895.

(5) FRANCES FLORENCE, married 5 August 1897 (Killeshandra Par. Reg.) William Joseph Hamilton, J.P., D.L., and Captain 4th Battalion Royal Irish Fusiliers, of Castle Hamilton, Killeshandra, son of James Hamilton, D.L. ("Irish Times" Newspaper).   They have issue one son, born 12 November 1900 at Dalkey.

(6) EVA ADELINE, married 26 November 1891, in Killeshandra Church, Robert Claude Hamilton, Esq., youngest son of James Hamilton, Esq., D.L., of Castle Hamilton ("Irish Times " Newspaper), and has issue :—

1. ROBERT CLAUDE VICTOR HAMILTON, born 14 June 1897.

2. ANNIE ELIZABETH, born 6 October 1893.

3. EVADNÉE MARIE, born 22 March 1899.

(7) LILIAN MAUDE, born 29 May 1869 ; died 10 September 1875 and was interred in Knockbride Old Church (Knockbride Par. Reg.).

(8) NORAH KATHLEEN.

(9) VIOLET BLANCHE, died 14 September 1875, aged 3 years, and was interred in Knockbride Old Church (Knockbride Par. Reg.).

(10) IRENE GWENDOLINE, married 30 April 1901 (Killeshandra Par. Reg.) the Rev. Herbert Maxwell Carlyle Hughes, B.A., of The Glebe, Mullagh, co. Cavan, eldest son of the Rev. S. C. Hughes, B.D., LL.D., Rector of St. Werburgh's, Dublin ("Irish Times " Newspaper).

4. REV. BENJAMIN WILLIAM ADAMS, entered Trinity College, Dublin, 1 July 1846, A.B. 22 February 1850, A.M. 8 February 1853, B.D.

16 December 1863, D.D. 28 February 1865, M.R.I.A., M.R.D.S.,
M.H.A.A.I., etc.; born 31 March 1827 (Family Records); admitted
to Holy Orders 6 April 1851 for the Curacy of St. Mary-Shandon,
City of Cork ; ordained a Priest 21 December 1851 ; appointed same
year a Life Governor of the Green Coat Hospital, Cork ; promoted
by the Crown 18 February 1854 to the Rectory of Cloghran, Swords,
Diocese of Dubliu, and again promoted 17 March 1876 to the Rectory
of Santry, same Diocese ; author of this History of the Family of
Adams of Cavan, and of " The History and Description of Santry and
Cloghran Parishes, co. Dublin,"* 1883.   Married first, 14 December 1854 (St. Peter's, Dublin, Par. Reg.), Georgina Roberts, second
daughter of John Drew Atkin, Esq., of 5 Merrion Square, East
Dublin, and Castle Park, Dalkey, co. Dublin, and granddaughter of
Sir Thomas Roberts, Bart., of Brightfieldstown, co. Cork (vide
Burke's " Peerage "), and by her (who died 16 May 1863, aged 33,
at Bangor, North Wales, and was interred in Mount Jerome) had
issue one son and two daughters, viz. :—

(1) SAMUEL ARTHUR ADAMS, born 10 September 1857 (St. Peter's,
    Dubliu, Par. Reg.) ; died 10 March 1869 and was interred in
    Mount Jerome (Mount Jerome Reg.).

(2) GEORGINA ROBERTS, married Rev. Adderley Bernard Howard.

(3) FRANCES HERVEY.

   Dr. Adams married 2ndly, 11 August 1864 (Monkstown Par.
Reg.), Louisa Jane, only daughter of William O'Brien Adams, M.B.,
F.K.Q.C.P.I., etc. (see p. 88).   He died 26 June 1886 and was
interred in Mount Jerome, having had issue two sons and one
daughter, viz. :—

(1) WILLIAM AUGUSTUS ADAMS, born 27 May 1865 (St. Peter's,
    Dublin, Par. Reg.) ; educated at Harrow ; matriculated at
    Trinity College, Dublin, Trinity Term 1883 ; First Honourman
    in Classics and in Modern History ; B.A. ; Senior Moderator
    and Gold Medallist in Modern Literature Lent Term 1898 ;
    M.A. 27 June 1901 (conferred in absentia); entered Royal
    Military College, Sandhurst, 10 February 1886 ; appointed to
    the King's Liverpool Regiment (8th Foot) as 2nd Lieut.
    8 February 1887 ; Lieut. 31 July 1889 ; Captain 19 December
    1893 ; exchanged into the 5th Lancers 11 September 1894 ;
    passed into the Staff College 7 November 1898 ; besieged in
    Ladysmith 1900 ; author of poetical works entitled " Rus
    Divinum," 1900, and " Horæ Fugaces," 1902.

(2) HERBERT ALGERNON ADAMS, born 3 January 1872 (Monkstown
    Par. Reg.) ; entered H.M.S. " Britannia " 23 January 1885 ;
    appointed to H.M.S. " Bacchante," Flag-ship on the East Indies
    Station, 15 January 1887, and served in her till 7 November
    1888 ; Midshipman 14 July 1887 ; Acting Sub-Lieut. 14 July
    1891 ; on the " Iron Duke," Channel Squadron, December
    1888 to November 1889 ; " Turquoise," East Indies Station
    (senior officer's ship on East Coast of Africa), December 1889
    to June 1891 ; " Aurora," Channel Squadron, June 1891 to
    August 1891; Lieut. 14 July 1892 ; to the " Banterer " as
    Navigating Lieut. 26 October 1893 ; " Jason " 3 April 1894 ;

* Published by Mitchell and Hughes, 140 Wardour Street, London, W.

"Edgar," Mediterranean Squadron, 20 August 1894; and on the breaking out of hostilities between China and Japan in 1894 his ship was transferred to the China Station to strengthen the British Fleet in those waters; to the "Scout" 23 November 1896; "Revenge," in the Mediterranean Squadron, 23 November 1899; "Victorious" 1900. Married 21 December 1898, at St. Mary Abbots, Kensington, Emily Banner Clough, daughter of Somerset J. Johnstone, Esq., of 11 Glendower Place, South Kensington, and of Alexandria, Egypt (Kaima Kan Somerset Johnstone Bey, of the Egyptian Coastguard Service).

(3) CONSTANCE LOUISA.

5. DOROTHEA ANNE, born 12 November 1810 (Family Register); married 11 November 1833 (Knockbride Par. Reg.) Le Chevalier Charles Augustus Ludolf Zander of Munich, Bavaria (born 12 September 1803), who was knighted by Louis Charles 'Augustus, the King of Bavaria, in 1845; received in 1859 the "Ordre Francis Josef" from Francis Josef, the Emperor of Austria; in 1861 the "Francis Ordre" from Francis II., the King of Naples; and died 24 July 1872. Mrs. Zander died 7 February 1864 and was interred at Munich, having had issue two sons and two daughters, viz.:—

(1) CHARLES ZANDER, born 4 February 1837; entered the Austrian Army 1859 as Lieut. in the 22nd Infanterie Reishach and was present at the battle of Solferino 24 June 1859.

(2) LUDOLF ZANDER, born 22 January 1846.

(3) FRANCES, married 18 February 1860 Kuton Rudolf Marchetti, 1st Lieut. in the 3rd Imperial Regiment of Gendarmes in the Austrian Service.

(4) LEOPOLDINE.

6. ELIZABETH FRANCES, born 11 August 1812 (Family Register); married 21 March 1833 (Knockbride Par. Reg.) John James Duff Hall Macdonald, a descendant of the Lord of the Isles, Lieut. 47th Regiment; died 30 January 1865 in London, and was interred in Kensal Green Cemetery, leaving issue one son and one daughter, viz.:—

(1) JOHN FRANCIS CHARLES MACDONALD, born 26 September 1834 (St. George's, Dublin, Par. Reg.); died 26 October 1834 (Family Register).

(2) GEORGINA FRANCES, married .... Cooper, Esq., who has since died.

7. CAROLINE MATILDA, born 14 June 1814 (Family Register); married 2 May 1837 (Enniskeen Par. Reg.) Thomas Robert Barry, Esq., J.P., of 45 Morehampton Road, Dublin, an Inspector in the Royal Irish Constabulary; died 26 May 1887 and was interred in Mount Jerome, having had issue one son and eight daughters. viz.:—

(1) ROBERT TRISTRAM BERESFORD BARRY, born 22 September 1846; married 28 October 1875 Lucy Moreton, daughter of the late

Stephen Moreton Cox, Esq., of Australia ; died 7 May 1890 at Melbourne, of influenza, after a short illness ("Irish Times" Newspaper), leaving issue two sons, viz. :—

1. BERESFORD ROBERT WILLIAM BARRY, born 26 June 1876.

2. JOHN HARVEY BARRY, born 15 November 1880.

(2) FRANCES DOROTHEA CAROLINE, born 21 April 1838 ; died 21 December 1861 at Sandymount, co. Dublin, and was interred in Mount Jerome (Mount Jerome Reg.).

(3) CAROLINE MATILDA, married 4 July 1867 Rev. William Richardson Weir, A.B., Rector of Sixmilecross, Diocese of Armagh, who died s.p. 16 June 1877, aged 52.

(4) MARGARET ANNE, married 11 July 1871 (St. Thomas's, Dublin, Par. Reg.) Charles Wilson Atkins, Esq., and has issue.

(5) AMELIA JANE.

(6) ELIZABETH FRANCES BUTLER, married 8 February 1869 James Wheeler, Esq.

(7) DOROTHEA ANNE, born 4 December 1852 ; died 27 December 1852 and was interred in Carrickmacross (Carrickmacross Par. Reg.).

(8) CATHERINE SARAH, married 24 July 1873 William Thomas Somerville Limrick, Esq., C.E., son of Thomas Hingston Limrick of Woodview Union Hall, co. Cork. He died 13 February 1893, aged 48, having had issue two sons and one daughter, viz. :—

1. THOMAS HENRY ST. PATRICK LIMRICK, born 17 March 1876 ; died 2 April 1876.

2. ION ST. CLAIR LIMRICK, born 15 May 1877.

3. OLIVE MARY CAROLINE LOUISA.

(9) CLARE ELIZABETH, married 6 December 1879 Theodore Gordon Barclay, Lieut. in the 27th Regiment. She died 28 February 1885 and was interred in Mount Jerome.

IV. CHARLES JAMES ADAMS, R.N., J.P., of Shinan House, co. Cavan, born 29 April 1792 (Family Records) ; entered the Royal Navy 8 May 1807 as First Class Volunteer on board the " Porcupine, 24," Captain the Hon. Sir Henry Duncan, C.B., K.C.H. (son of Viscount Duncan, ancestor of the Earl of Camperdown), with whom he "continued to serve in the ' Mercury, 28,' and ' Impérieuse, 38,' on the Mediterranean Station, until the conclusion of hostilities in 1814. During the time he was serving on the ' Porcupine ' he was instrumental to the cutting out, on the night of 10 July 1808, of a large poleacre ship of 8 guns and upwards of 20 men, moored close to the beach on the coast of Romania, within pistol-shot distance of two batteries, a tower, and three heavy gunboats, to whose conjoined fire, as well as that of a body of troops, he was for a considerable time exposed " (vide " Gazette," 1808, p. 1439).

" He subsequently, when in the 'Mercury' in the spring of 1809, assisted at the capture of Capo d'Istria, a town near Trieste, and in an attack, made in company of the 'Spartan, 38,' on Pesaro and Ceseratico, where the fortifications were destroyed and 25 sail of merchantmen taken. While in the 'Impérieuse' he further participated in the gallant capture and destruction, on 2 November 1811, in conjunction with the 'Thames, 32,' of ten gunboats and twenty-two richly laden felnccas, defended by a strong tower and two batteries in the harbour of Palinuro on the coast of Calabria, at which place the British were opposed by a land force of 700 men. He next contributed, 27 June 1812, to the destruction of a French convoy and of the batteries at Languelia and Alassio ; was also present on 17 August 1812 in a spirited skirmish with a powerful Neapolitan squadron in the Bay of Naples" (O'Byrne's "Naval Biography," p. 4). Appointed mate 15 October 1813 (Letter from the Admiralty), "and in 1813 and 1814 witnessed the capture of Port D'Anzo and the operations against Leghorn and Genoa. He then returned home on board the 'Apollo, 38,' Captain Edward Loyd Graham, and from his promotion to a Lieutenancy, 6 March 1815, remained unemployed on half-pay " (O'Byrne's " Naval Biography," p. 4) ; married 29 September 1821 (marriage settlement dated 28 September 1821) Anne Jane, daughter of William Foster, Esq., of Dowdstown, co. Louth, and cousin of Viscount Ferrard. Admitted by special favour (*vide* p. 8, foot-note) a Freeman of the Borough of Drogheda 23 April 1819 ; was High Sheriff of Cavan in 1833 ; died 23 August 1854 suddenly, while walking before dinner in the garden at Shinan House, and was interred in the Old Church of Knockbride (Knockbride Par. Reg.) beside his wife, who had died 4 March 1834, aged 36 (Knockbride Par. Reg.), having had (with three children who died in infancy) three sons and four daughters, viz. :—

1. BENJAMIN SAMUEL ADAMS of Shinan House, Shercock, J.P. for the County of Cavan, born 22 June 1828 (Family Records) ; entered the Army 31 December 1847 as Ensign in the 12th Foot ; served with distinction in the Kaffir War ; Lieut. 17 August 1852 ; retired May 1856 from the Army by the sale of his Commission ("Army List") ; was High Sheriff of Cavan in 1866 ; married first, 10 September 1856, Georgina Charlotte, youngest daughter of Rev. George Hickson, A.M., Vicar of Magheraclooney, Diocese of Clogher, and by her (who died 21 February 1871 at Corrig Avenue, Kingstown, and was buried in Knockbride Old Church) (Knockbride Par. Reg.) he had issue three sons and four daughters, viz. :—

   (1) CHARLES JAMES STUART ADAMS, born 4 February 1864 ; married 1 August 1900, at St. James's Church, Clapham, Amy Brada, youngest daughter of William Baring Stevenson of Balladoole, Isle of Man ("Morning Post" Newspaper).

   (2) GEORGE HICKSON ADAMS, born February 1868.

   (3) WILLIAM JOHN ADAMS, born 6 July 1870.

   (4) CHARLOTTE, born 15 October 1859 ; died 21 January 1860 and was buried in Knockbride Old Church (Knockbride Par. Reg.).

   (5) CHARLOTTE GEORGINA, died 28 August 1880, aged 20, at the Sycamores, Ballasala, Isle of Man,

(6) ANNA SOPHIA, married 1885 Alexander Nixon Montgomery, M.K.Q.C.P.I., L.R.S.I., of Dublin.

(7) GEORGINA CHARLOTTE, died 18 March 1894, aged 27 ("Irish Times" Newspaper).

Mr. Benjamin S. Adams, J.P., married 2ndly, 17 September 1873 (St. Peter's, Dublin, Par. Reg.), Jeanie Holmes, eldest daughter of the late George Montgomery, Esq., M.D., of York Street, Dublin, and by her (who died 13 June 1876 at La Trecherais, St. Servan, France) he had issue two daughters, viz. :—

(8) AZALINE ELIZABETH MONTGOMERY, died 18 March 1876 and was interred at St. Servan, France.

(9) JANE HOLMES MONTGOMERY, died 5 January 1888, aged 11 years and 6 months.

Mr. Benjamin S. Adams, J.P., married 3rdly, 26 November 1877 (Neuchatel, Switzerland, Reg.), Elizabeth Stanley, daughter of George Montgomery, Esq., who died 21 August 1888, aged 38, at Shinan House, Shercock. Mr. B. S. Adams died 3 June 1899, aged 71, at Shinan House, and was buried at Knockbride ("Irish Times" Newspaper). He had issue two daughters, viz. :—

(10) CAROLINE ELIZABETH STANLEY.

(11) MONA.

2. WILLIAM JOHN ADAMS of Retreat, co. Cavan, born 14 February 1831 (Family Records) ; died unmarried 30 March 1852 at Retreat, and was interred in Knockbride Old Church (Knockbride Par. Reg.).

3. CHARLES JAMES ADAMS, T.C.D., A.B. Vern. 1853, of Farm Hill, co. Monaghan, born 13 February 1832 (Family Records) ; became a medical student, but died unmarried 6 January 1857 at Farm Hill, and was interred in Knockbride Old Church (Knockbride Par. Reg.).

4. REBECCA HORATIA, married 22 April 1841 (St. Andrew's, Dublin, Par. Reg.) Major Thomas Coote, D.L., of Brandrum, co. Monaghan, who had been High Sheriff of Monaghan in 1838, and was appointed Major of the Monaghan Regiment 17 September 1857. He died 17 January 1865. She died suddenly 21 December 1886, aged 63 years, having had issue five sons and two daughters, viz. :—

(To be continued.)

Monumental Inscriptions

IN THE

Church of St. Giles=in=the=Fields.*

The pillars on the North side from East to West :—In Memory of | Sir GEORGE THOMAS SMART, | organist and composer | of Her Majesty's Chapels Royal : | Born May 10th, 1776 | Died February 23rd, 1867, | Aged 90 Years.
There remaineth therefore a rest to | the people of God.—Heb. iv. 9.
MARGARET ROSE SMART, | only child of Sir G. SMART | Died April 13th, 1898.

A white marble with a figure of Hope standing on an anchor above the waves of the sea, all carved in relief :—To the Memory of | Mrs SARAH GOULBURN, | (Relict of HENRY GOULBURN, Esqr | of the Island of Jamaica) | who | closed a long life, | eminently characterized | by unaffected .Simplicity of Manners | and | most active Benevolence of Heart | on the 28th day of Septr | 1803 | Aged 77 Years.

A white marble tablet with a curtain draped over the top and these arms: *Sable, on a fesse or between six arrows bendways, dexter points in base argent, three negroes' heads couped at the neck of the first. Crest : A falcon's wings addorsed, in the beak an arrow, all proper.* Motto: THESAURUS IN FICTILIBUS :—Sacred | to the Memory | of | the Revd WILLIAM WATTS, M.A. | an esteemed and beloved | curate of this parish ; | and minister of Christ church, | Endell Street ; | This tablet is erected | in testimony of | their regard and affection by some of | the many friends | who lament his loss. | He was taken to his rest 11th June 1847, | Aged 39 Years.

A white marble tablet in the form of a curtain with a palm-branch at the top :—Sacred to the Memory of | THOMAS LEVERTON, Esquire, | who departed this life | on the 23rd day of September 1824 | aged 81 years. | He was in the commission of the Peace | for the city of Westminster | and for the counties | of Middlesex, Surrey and Kent. | His remains | are interred in the parish of | Waltham Abbey Holy Cross, Essex, | in which he was born ; | he left by his will the sum of, | 5000 pounds three per cent. consols ; | the interest thereof | to be applied annually for the benefit | of six deserving females, who may have | fallen from affluence into distress | a preference being always given to such | as are widows and inhabitants of the | united parishes of St Giles in the Fields | and St George, Bloomsbury.

A plain white marble tablet :—In Memory of | Mr JOHN BUCKINGHAM, | late of this parish | Died November 5th, 1837 | Aged 44 Years.
Also of | Mrs SARAH BUCKINGHAM, | wife of the above | Died March 30th, 1864 | Aged 64 Years.
Also of | Mr GEORGE WILLIAM BUCKINGHAM | eldest son of the above ; | Died July 14th, 1854 | Aged 31 Years.

A white marble monument with a scroll border decorated with leaves and fruit, and these arms: *Gules, two lions passant argent.* This inscription, in red letters :—In the Middle Isle near | this Place lyeth the Body of | Sr ROGER L'ESTRANGE, | Knt. | Born ye 17th of Decr 1616 | Dyed ye 11th of Decr 1704.

* Communicated by ARTHUR F. G. LEVESON GOWER, Esq., assisted by ARTHUR J. JEWERS—continued from p. 136.

WEST END.

New memorial tablet of gunmetal surrounding copper centre. At the top the City arms and supporters :—V. The City of London Imperial Volunteers. R. | Dulce et decorum (C.I.V.) est pro patria mori. | In memory of | WILLIAM RICHARD GAZZARD | a Private in this Regiment and also in the | 22nd Middlesex Volunteer Regiment, son of | WILLIAM and LOUISA GAZZARD of this parish. | He died at Winchingdon, Bucks, 11th December 1900, | during the South African Campaign, aged 21 years.

This memorial is erected at the $\left\{\begin{array}{c} 1899-1900 \end{array}\right\}$ expense of the Regimental Fund.
The Right Honourable Sir ALFRED NEWTON, Bart., Lord Mayor.

[The dates 1899—1900 are surrounded by scrolls.]

THE SOUTH AISLE FROM WEST TO EAST.

Between the first and second windows, on a black panel on a white marble sarcophagus, with a monogram and Earl's coronet, is this inscription, the lower half in two columns :—Sacred to the Memory of | The Right Honorable MARY, COUNTESS OF KENMARE, who departed this Life | October 16th, 1806, aged 47 Years ; whose Remains are deposited in a Vault beneath this monument | A Lady of uncommon Merit, distinguished by a strong Sense of Religion, an exalted and | dignified Turn of Mind ; the most exemplary Conduct in all the Relative Duties of Life, the most | ardent Charity to the Helpless and the Indigent and a peculiar Glow of Universal Benevolence. | This Monument is raised by the Orders of her truly affected Husband the Right Honourable | EARL OF KENMARE ; and a just and tender tribute of Filial Piety is paid by her Ladyship's | eldest son LORD VISCOUNT CASTLE-ROSSE in the following characteristic lines :—

> This Monument records the honoured name
> Of one who once had Titles, Wealth, & Fame :
> A woman blest with every pleasing Art,
> A mind exalted and a feeling Heart ;
> A constant Advocate in Virtue's Cause,
> She loved her Precepts, and obeyed her laws !   [End of first column.]
>
> The Widow's Comfort, and the Orphan's Friend,
> To all she sought her Bounty to extend,
> Formed to adorn the foremost Ranks of Life,
> A tender Mother, Sister, Friend and Wife ;
> Such was KENMARE, her Sex's Boast and Pride !
> She lived respected, and lamented died !

Requiescat in pace.

On a white marble tablet with arms beneath the inscription, all on a dark slab of pyramid form : *Azure, an oval buckle, tongue upward, between three wolves' heads erased argent; impaling Gules, a dexter hand couped above the wrist, grasping a Latin cross set on three grices, and in chief three mullets, all argent.* Crest : *A naked arm embowed, the hand brandishing a sword, all proper* (lines given for colours). Motto : DEI GRATIA SUMQUOD SUM :—In a Vault beneath | are deposited | the remains of | JOHN LUMSDEN, Esqr, | A Member of the | Bengal Supreme Council, | and a director of the | Honourable the United | East India Company. | He died | on the 4th December 1819, | Aged 57 Years. | His affectionate Widow | consecrates | this Tablet to his | Revered Memory.

Between the second and third windows. A white marble tablet on black with a vase at the top :—In the vault beneath | are deposited the remains of | Mr JOHN BRUCE | late of Denmark Street in this parish | who departed this life March XI ; | M.D.CCCX | Aged XCI Years,

A white marble tablet with a shallow urn at the top :—Sacred to the Memory | of SAMUEL CLEAVER, Esqr | of Gate Street, Lincoln's Inn Fields, | who departed this Life the 22nd Day of December 1805 | in the 56th Year of his age. | A Man whose truly benevolent and Christian Character | endeared him to a large family, | and numerous Circle of Friends | by whom his Death will be long and deeply regretted. | His Remains are deposited in the Vault of this Church.

In the Same Vault are also deposited the Remains of | M^rs ANN CLEAVER, | relict of the above, | who departed this Life the 9th Day of February 1832, | in the 80th Year of her Age.

Between the third and fourth windows. A white marble tablet on a black ground with an ornamental top :—Sacred | to the Memory of | JOHN BYE, Esqr | late of this parish, | who died the 13th day of January 1809, | Aged 70 Years ; | his remains are deposited in the Vault | of this Church. | Reader, seek not his eulogy here, | his Virtues are recorded elsewhere | in the hearts of all who | knew him.

A plain white marble :—My Mother ! ! | as a tribute of filial affection | this tablet is erected to the memory of | THOMAS HAMMOND, Esqr | who died 7th September 1801, | Aged 47 Years.

Also of ANN FRANCES his wife, | who died 3rd May 1831, | Aged 74 Years. | By | FRANCIS W. T. HAMMOND, Esqr.

A white tablet on a black one :—GULIELMO KEDDEN, A.B. | hujus ecclesiæ parochialis curæ | haud ita predem subservienti | illustrissimus JOHANNES CAROLUS WALLOP | COMES DE PORTESMOUTH | hunc lapidem, in pietatus | et memoriæ pigmis urga suum à | sacris domesticis ministrum | sacrum esse voluit. | Obiit die Jany XXVI^mo, MDCCCIV anno, ætatis XXVIII^mo.

ANNÆ | viri reverendi GULIELMI KEDDEN | matris amatissimæ | quod mortale fuit | in eodem tumulo intra hanc ecclesiam | sepultum est | Obiit die XV^mo Junii MDCCCXV anno, ætatis LXI^mo.

Plain white marble monument :—A tribute of paternal affection | to the Memory of | WILLIAM ROBINSON JOHNSTON, Esqr | of the Island of Trinidad, | who died in London, | on the 10th of July 1825 | Aged 35 Years.

A plain white marble tablet :—Sacred to the Memory of | ANNA ELIZA JOHNSTON | youngest daughter of the late | WILLIAM ROBINSON JOHNSTON. | She was born on the 13th of September 1823 | and died on the 19th of April 1835.

Between the fourth and fifth windows. A plain white marble tablet :—Prope hoc Marmor condunter Reliquiæ | SOULDENI LAWRENCE Equitis Aurati | THOMÆ LAWRENCE, M.D., filii | Banci Regis plus quatuor decim annos | Deinde Banci Communis per quatuor annos | Justiciarii | Obiit VIII^vo die Julii A.D. MDCCCIV | Annum agens LXIV.

Near the Remains of Sir SOULDEN LAWRENCE, Knt. | are deposited those of his Sister | Mrs ELIZABETH GIPPS, | Widow of GEORGE GIPPS, Esquire, | Member for the City of Canterbury. | She died on the 29th June A.D. 1814, aged 65.

A white marble tablet on black :—Sacred to the memory of | JOHN SMITH, Esqre | of Bolton Street, St George's, Hanover Square, | who died November the 15th, 1821, | Aged 72 Years, | and lies buried in the West end Vault of this church | with the family of the late HENRY MASON, Esqr | whose daughter CATHERINE he married, | and who in grateful acknowledgement of the happiness | she enjoyed from his affection and kindness to her | during an union of upwards of 41 years | erects this tablet to his memory and Character, | of which it may be truly said, | To act uprightly was through life his plan | he lived beloved and died an honest man.

A white marble tablet with a Cherub's head:—"I know my Redeemer liveth." | Sacred | to the Memory of | CHARLES YARDLEY, Jun[r] | who departed this life | March 30th, 1872, | aged 47 Years. | This tablet is erected | in affectionate remembrance | of him | who in life was beloved | and in death deeply lamented.

A plain white marble:—Sacred to the memory of | M[rs] ELIZABETH AUDINET | who died 13th February 1814, aged 85 years.
Also of SARAH AUDINET, | daughter of the above, | who died 30th June 1832, aged 80 years.
Also of M[r] PHILIP AUDINET, | son of the above, | who died 18th December, 1837, aged 73 years | and of M[r] GABRIEL AUDINET, | son of the above, | who died 3rd December 1847, aged 79 years.

A white marble tablet on black like a roll of parchment :—In Memory of | EMILY | the wife of | METCALFE LARKEN, Esq[re] | of the Bombay Civil Service | who died in India | at Maligaon in the Province of Khandesh | on the 23rd May 1843, | Aged 27 Years. | This tablet is set up in her parish church | by her husband.

EAST END.

Plain white marble tablet :—Sacred to the memory | of | EDMUND LARKEN, Esq[re] | of Bedford Square | in this parish | who died the 8th day of February 1831 | Aged 64 years.
The memory of the Just is Blessed. | Proverbs, chap. x, ver. 7.

A white marble panel on a black slab :—To the memory of | ANNE | the affectionate and beloved wife | of CHARLES JONES of Gower Street | in this parish, Esquire. | She died on the 31st day of January 1838 | in the 57th Year of her age. | Her remains are deposited | in the vault of this church.
In the same vault are deposited the remains of | the above named CHARLES JONES. | He died 27th Sept[r] 1845 | in his 77th year.

A white marble monument with the figures of the husband and three children mourning, carved in relief:—In the Vault beneath is buried | MATTY WOLFF | daughter of EDWARD POORE, of Rushall, in the County of Wilts, Esquire. | She married A.D. 1823 | GEORGE CHILTON, of the Inner Temple, Barrister at Law, | and bore him three children who survive her | EMILY GEORGINA, GEORGE ROBERT COMYN, ROSALIND ELIZABETH. | She died at the age of 31 | on the 11th day of May A.D. 1828.

[The following lines are arranged in two columns :—]

God's will is done, the husband is alone,—
And his young orphans mourn their Mother gone,
Her virtues—tell them not upon the tomb,—
They lov'd the shade of her once happy home ;
There still in memory's fond dream survives
The best of Mothers, and the best of Wives ;
And there through sorrow's desolating storm
A gentle voice is heard—a voice without a form.   [End first column.]

Oh weep not—nor arraign high heaven's decree—
I cannot—it is past—return to thee ;
And thou must tarry—thou our babes must rear
In love to man, and in God's holy fear ;
Must teach their little lips with thine to pray ;
And guide their steps along the narrow way :
So may we meet—Renew'd, Redeem'd, forgiven,
No wanderer lost, a family in heaven.

A white marble tablet:—In memory of | PETER LUDGATE, Esq[r] | many years an inhabitant of | this parish, | and | one of His Majesty's Justices of | the Peace for the county of Middlesex. | Died 1st August 1825, | aged 77 years.

A brass plate with the arms, crest, helmet, and mantling, etc., in relief, all within a heavy dark marble frame. Arms, with lines for the colours : *Argent, a fesse dancettée gules, in chief three crescents of the second; impaling Sable, a dolphin haurient with a fish in its mouth argent.* Crest (on a knight's helmet) : *From a coronet or a plume of five ostrich feathers argent.* Motto : NOSCE TEIPSUM :—In memory of | the Right Honourable | Sir NICHOLAS CONYNGHAM TINDAL, Kᵗ, D.C.L. | for seventeen years | Lord Chief Justice | of the Court of Common Pleas, | and a resident in this parish. | He was born at Chelmsford 12ᵗʰ December 1776, | and died at Folkestone 6ᵗʰ July 1846.

<hr>

PILLARS ON THE SOUTH SIDE GOING FROM EAST TO WEST.

A white marble oval with an urn at the top :—In | Memory of | the Revᵈ RICHARD SOUTHGATE, A.B. | Rector of Warsop | in the County of Nottingham | one of the Sub Librarians | of the British Museum : | and during 30 Years Curate of this Parish | who died Janʸ 21ˢᵗ, 1795 | In the 66ᵗʰ Year of his Age. | In every station of his life | He executed its respective duties, | With Judgement, diligence, & fidelity. | Deep were his Researches, and his learning Various. | Languages & Science acknowledged him a Scholar, | Theology a Divine. | The Purity of his faith the Rectitude of his conduct, | and his unwearied labours in the Pastoral Office | testified his piety, | towards God : | his mildness, humility, and candour, | with his exemplary attention to the wants, | temporal as well as spiritual, | of his fellow-creatures ; | proved his benevolence | towards Man. | Reader | if thou canst, excell him : | it will be well | if thou canst equal him.

A plain white marble slab :—Sacred to the Memory | of | the Revᵈ ROBERT H. FLOWER, M.A. | one of the curates of this parish | to which he had been ordained in 1832, | by the | dispensation of Divine Providence. | His faithful and zealous ministry | was early finished | and after | a few days of severe illness | he departed this life | on Easter day | the 3ʳᵈ April 1836 | in the 29ᵗʰ Year of his age | universally beloved and lamented.

I heard a voice from heaven saying unto me, | Write, from henceforth blessed are the dead | which die in the Lord, even so saith the Spirit, | for they rest from their labours.

A plain white marble on a black tablet :—In Memory of | RICHARD BALSHAW, Esqʳ | of Golden Hill, Leyland, | Lancashire, | who died April 11ᵗʰ, A.D. 1811, | Aged 86 Years | of whom it may justly be said he was | a truly Benevolent and Charitable man.

A white marble tablet :—In memory of | LUKE HANSARD, Esq. | many years printer to the House of Commons, | ob. 29 Oct. 1828, Æ. 77.
Also of | ELIZABETH SUSANNAH | his eldest daughter ; | ob. 27 Sept. 1807, Æ. 28. | And of | ELIZABETH, | his wife, | ob. 18 May 1834, Æ. 78.

<hr>

THE STONE FONT AT THE WEST END.

To the Glory of God this font is dedicated by JOHN MARJORIBANKS NISBET | Rector of this parish, as a thank offering on the occasion of the baptism | of his son HENRY KINGSCOTE NISBET October 24, 1875.

A brass cross on the floor, at the foot of which is the following :—To the Glory of God | and in affectionate remembrance of | The Revᵈ JOHN MARJORIBANKS NISBET, | 25 Years Rector of this Parish, Canon Residentiary of Norwich | Taken to his Rest September 1ˢᵗ, 1892.

Whose faith follow, remembering the end of his conversation, | Jesus Christ, the same yesterday, to-day, and for ever.

[The East window of the Chancel, filled with coloured glass representing the Ascension, bears the following inscription beneath :—]

To the memory of JAMES ENDELL TYLER, B.D., Rector of this parish & Canon | Residentiary of S. Paul's, who was taken to his rest on the 5th of October 1851, this | window is erected by his widow. The Lord gave and the Lord hath taken | away. Blessed be the name of the Lord.

IN THE VESTIBULE GOING FROM SOUTH TO NORTH.

In memory of | Mr JOHN PEARSON, | late of this parish. Who at his | decease An. Do. 1707 left a Gift | of 50¹ a year for 99 years | Viz. 25¹ a year to put out 5 Boys | Sons of poor decayed Houskeep | ers of ye Parish Apprenteses yearly | to handicraft trades | And 25¹ a year to the 20 Women | In the Almeshouses at ye end of | Monmouth Street | { JOHN MARRIOTT / JAMES CANNON } Trustees | And after their decease to ye Care | of the then Rector of the | said Parish.

[This is not given in the "New View," but another to the same name; see under inscriptions from that work.]

[Of the elaborate black and white marble monument, shewn in the engraving in the "Gentleman's Magazine," August 1817, Plate II., p. 113, and reproduced in this Number, only the plain oblong panel near the ground now remains, and is fixed against the wall of the vestibule at the West end of the Church.

The rest of this monument, probably originally within the Church, stood until about the year 1892 at the East end of the Church outside the Vestry wall. It became so ruinous and dangerous that it was taken down by order of the Vestry Authorities, who had applied in vain to the representatives of the family to urge its restoration, and, with the exception of the plain oblong marble panel above mentioned, was buried in the churchyard.]

The inscription on this panel is as follows :—

This Monument was erected in the Year of Our Lord 1736 by the Pious Direction of the Honourable | Dame BARBARA WEBB, wife of Sr JOHN WEBB, of Canford Magna, in the County of Dorset, Bar^t, and the Honourable | CATHARINE TALBOT, wife of the Honourable JOHN TALBOT of Longford in the County of Salop, Esq., Surviveing | Daughters and Coheirs of the Right Honourable JOHN, LORD BELASYSE, Second Son of THOMAS, LORD VISCOUNT | FAUCONBERG, in memory of their most dear Father, his wives and Children. | Who for his Loyalty, Prudence, and Courage was promoted to Several Commands of great trust by their | Majesty's KING CHARLES the First and Second (viz.) Having raised Six Regiments of Horse and Foot in the late Civil Wars | He Commanded a Tertia in His Majesty's Armies at the Battles of Edge Hill, Newbury, and Knaseby ; ye Seiges of Reading | and Bristol. Afterwards being made Governour of York, and Commander in Chief of all his Majesty's Forces in | Yorkshire, he fought the Battle of Selby with LORD FAIRFAX, then being Lieutenant General of ye County's of Lincoln | Nottingham, Darby, and Rutland, and Governour of Newark. He Valiantly defended that Garrison against the English | and Scotch Armies, till His Majesty Came in Person to the Scotch Quarters, and Commanded the surrender of it | At which time he also had the honour of being General of the King's Horse Guards, in all which services dureing | the Wars, and other Atchievements, he deported himself with eminent Courage & Conduct & received many wounds | Sustained Three Imprisonments in the Tower of London ; and after the happy restauration of KING CHARLES the Second | He was made Lord Lieutenant of the East Rideing of the County of York, Governour of Hull, General of his Majesty's | Forces in Africa, Governour of Tangiers, Captain of His Majesty's Guards of Gentleman Pensioners & First Lord | Commissioner of the Treasury to KING JAMES the Second. He dyed the 10ᵗʰ day of September 1689, 'whose remains | are deposited in this Vault. | He married to his first wife JANE, daughter and Sole Heiress of Sʳ ROBERT BOTELER of Woodhall in the | County of Hertford, Knᵗ, by whom he had Sʳ HENRY BELASYSE, Knᵗ, of the Most Honourable Order of the Bath | Interred in this Vault, MARY, VISCOUNTESS DUNBAR, and FRANCES, both deceased | He married to his Second Wife ANN, Daughter and Coheir to Sʳ ROBERT CRANE of Chilton in ye County | of Suffolk, Barᵗ, who also lyes interred here | He married to his third Wife, the Right Honourable the LADY ANN POWLET, second daughter of the | Right Noble JOHN, MARQUIS OF WINCHESTER, Sister to CHARLES, late DUKE OF BOLTON, and is here interr'd the | Issue by that Marriage as above.

The following is a description of the Belasyse monument taken, with the illustration, from the " Gentleman's Magazine," 3 August 1817 :—

" Passing in at the Monmouth-street gate of St. Giles's Church a few Sabbaths ago, some I saw were viewing *Pendril's* tomb, and others the *Belasyse* monument at the East end of this handsome Church ; but neither the one or the other, I found, could easily be decyphered. Time is making rapid progress in the destruction of both these records of memorable events and noble families, and, unless you think them worth a place in your ever-living collection, it is feared their inscriptions may be lost for ever.

" I have endeavoured to decypher the Belasyse monument, and inclose it you. It was, however, the pleasant amusement of three Sabbath mornings' visits ; I hope the record will be of some amusement to all ; and if it meets the eye of any of the family there so highly spoken of, I hope they will take means to restore this not very antient monument to its original beauty."

INSCRIPTION ON A MONUMENT AGAINST THE EAST WALL OUTSIDE OF ST. GILES-IN-THE-FIELDS.

On the sarcophagus :—The Right Honourable JOHN, LORD BELASYSE, had issue by his third marriage | with LADY ANNE POWLET, three sons and nine daughters : whereof | three sons and five of the daughters died in their infancy : | HONNORA, LADY DOWAGER BERGAVENNY, widow and relict of GEORGE, LORD | BERGAVENNY, one of the coheirs of the said JOHN, LORD BELASYSE, who | died without issue the 6ᵗʰ of January 1706, and is interred in this Vault. | The Honourable Dame BARBARA WEBB, and the Honourable | CATHARINE TALBOT, the two surviving Daughters and coheirs now living, | caused this Monument to be erected. | Also the Honourable ISABELLA, the youngest daughter, who married | THOMAS STONOR, of Stonor in the County of Oxon, Esqʳ, one of the coheirs of the | said late LORD BELASYSE, and dyed without Issue the 4ᵗʰ of June 1704.

On the base below :—This Monument was erected in the Year of Our Lord 1736, by the pious direction | of the Honourable Dame BARBARA WEBB, wife of Sʳ JOHN WEBB, of Canford | Magna, in the County of Dorset, Barᵗ, and the Honourable CATHARINE TALBOT, | wife of the Honourable JOHN TALBOT, of Longford in the County of Salop, Esqʳ, | surviving Daughters and Coheirs of the Right Honourable JOHN, LORD BELASYSE, | second son of THOMAS, LORD VISCOUNT FAUCONBERG, in Memory of their most dear | Father, his Wives and Children. | Who, for his Loyalty, Prudence, and Courage was promoted to several Commands | by their Majesties KING CHARLES I. and II. (viz.) having raised six Regiments of | Horse and Foot in the late Civil Wars, He commanded a Tertia in His Majesty's | Armies at the battle of Edge-Hill, Newbury, and Knaseby ; at the sieges of Read- | ing and Bristol ; and afterwards being made Governor of York, and Commander | in Chief of all His Majesty's forces in Yorkshire, He fought the battle of Selby | with the Lord Fairfax, And being Lieutenant General of the Counties of Lincoln, | Nottingham, Derby, and Rutland and Governour of Newark, He valiantly defended | that Garrison against the English and Scotch Armies, till His Majesty came in | person to the Scotch quarters, and commanded the surrender of it. At which | time he also had the Honour of being General of the King's Horse Guards, in all | which services, during the Wars, and other Achievements, he deported himself | with eminent courage and conduct, and received many wounds ; sustained three | imprisonments in the Tower of London ; and after the happy Restoration of KING | CHARLES II., he was made Lord Lieutenant of the East Riding of the County of | York, Governour of Hull, General of his Majesty's Forces in Africa, Governour of | Tangier, Captain of His Majesty's Guard of Gentleman Pensioners, and First Lord | Commissioner of the Treasury to KING JAMES II. He died the 10th of Septem- | ber, 1689, whose remains are deposited in this Vault. | He married to his first wife JANE, daughter and sole heiress of Sr ROBERT | BOTELER, of Woodhall in the County of Hertford, Knight, by whom he had Sr | HENRY BELASYSE, Knight of the Most Honourable Order of the Bath, Interred | in this Vault ; MARY, VISCOUNTESS DUNBAR, and FRANCES, both deceased. | He married to his second wife ANNE, daughter and coheir to Sr ROBERT | CRANE of Chilton, in the County of Suffolk, Bart, who also lies Interred here. | He married to his third wife, the Right Honourable LADY ANNE POWLET, | second daughter of the Right Noble JOHN, MARQUIS OF WINCHESTER, sister to | CHARLES, late DUKE OF BOLTON, and is here Interred.

On two flat stones opposite the Monument :—

Here lyeth the Body of the LADY ANNE, Wife of JOHN, LORD BELASYSE, daughter and coheir to Sr ROBERT CRANE, of Wilton in the County of Suffolk, Bart. She died 11th day of August, 1662.*	Here lyeth the Body of JOHN TALBOT, son of the Honourable JOHN TALBOT, of Longford, in the County of Salop, Esqr, by the Honourable CATHARINE his Wife, one of the Daughters and coheirs of the Right Honourable JOHN, LORD BELASYSE, Baron of Warlaby. He departed this Life the 3rd of June 1710 in the 9th year of his age.

The following is the inscription as it is given in Hatton's "New View of London " :†—

This monument‡ was erected Anno 1670,[1] in memory of the Honourable JOHN, LORD BELASYSE, BARON WORLABY, second son of THOMAS, LORD VISCOUNT FAUCONBERG, his Wives and children.[2] Who for his Loyalty, Prudence, and Courage, was promoted to several commands of great Trust by Their Majesties KING CHARLES the 1st and 2d Viz. Having raised six Regiments of Horse and Foot in the late Civil Wars, he commanded a Tertia in His Majesties Armies at the Battels of Edghill, Newbury and Naseby,[3] the sieges of Redding and Bristol ; afterward being made Governour of York and Commander in Chief of all His Majesty's Forces

---

* This stone was originally within the Church under the communion table, but was here placed when the corpse (which was enclosed in a leaden coffin) was removed with some others to a vault under the North gate. ("Gentleman's Magazine.")

† The following corrections are made in pen and ink :—[1] In the Year 1736. [2] It now is E. end of ch. outside. [3] Naseby spelt Knavesby on the mont. [4] Nottingham. [5] "He " added. [6] "And, etc." more on the monument. [7] In co. Herts. [8] "And Frances, deceased ;" and the sentence from " Bath " to " Mary " struck out. [9] This paragraph is struck out and this added : "dd 11 Aug. 1662." This paragraph is also struck out.

‡ This can hardly be the same monument ; if it is, it must have been considerably altered. The date, 1670, nineteen years before the death of Lord Bellasyse (p. 183, line 3), exactly corresponds with the date of the erection of the monument in Worlaby Church (vide infra, p. 186).

Monument of John Lord Bellasyse,
in the Church-Yard of St. Giles's in the Fields

in Yorkshire. He fought the Battel of Selby with the LORD FAIRFAX; then being Lieutenant General of the counties of Lincoln, Northampton,[4] Derby and Rutland, and Governour of Newark. He valiantly defended that Garrison against the English and Scotch Armies, till His Majesty came in Person to the Scotch Quarters, and commanded the Surrender of it; at which time he also had the Honour of being General of the King's Horse guards: In all which Services, and during the Wars and other Achievements, he deported himself with eminent Courage and Conduct, and received many Wounds, sustained three Imprisonments in the Tower of London; and after the happy Restauration of KING CHARLES the 2[d][5] was made Lord Lieutenant of the E. Riding of the County of York, Governour of Hull, General of His Majesty's Forces in Africa, Governour of Tangier, and Captain of His Majesty's Guard of Gent. Pensioners.[6]

He married to his first Wife JANE, Daughter and sole Heir to Sir ROBERT BOTELER of Woodhall,[7] by whom he had Sir HENRY BELASYSE of the Honourable Order of the Bath who lyes interred in this Choir, and MARY married to the LORD VISCOUNT DUNBAR.[8]

He married to his second Wife ANNE, Daughter and Coheir to Sir ROBERT CRAIN of Chilton in the County of Suffolk, Knight, who lyes also interred in this Choir.[9]

And to his third Wife the LADY ANNE PAULET, Daughter to the MARQUIS OF WINCHESTER, by whom he had issue, besides other children now living, ANN, JOHN, ELIZABETH, and FRANCIS, who all died young, and are also interred in the Choir of this Church.

The following description of a monument to Lord Bellasyse and copy of the inscriptions are taken from Lansdowne MS. 878. The arms in that MS. being also drawn and coloured:—

("A comely monument on y[e] North wall of y[e] chancell. On the East wall of y[e] chancell in a table is y[e] armes of y[e] LORD BELLASIS Depicted with the supporters & motto as over his tombe.)

"Arms at the top: *Argent, a chevron gules between three fleurs-de-lis azure*, BELLASES; impaling *Sable, three swords in pile argent, hilts and pomels or*, PAULETT. On the left side in a lozenge: *Gules, a fesse chequy argent and sable between six cross-crosslets or*, BOTELER OF WEMM; over it a baron's coronet. On the right: *Argent, a fesse between three cross-crosslets fitchée gules*, CRANE; over it a baron's coronet.

"This monument was erected Anno 1670 in memory of the right honorable JOHN, LORD BELASYSE, BARRON WORLABY, second sonne of THOMAS, Lord Viscount FALCONBRIDGE, his wives & children, who for his Loyalty, Prudence, & Courage was promoted to severall commands of greate trust by Theire Majesties KING CHARLES the first & second, viz., Haveing raised six regements of Horse & foote in the Late civill warrs, he commanded a Tertia in his Majesties Armies att the battales of Edghill, Newberry, & Naysby, the seiges of Reading & Bristoll, afterwards being made Governor of Yorke and commander in cheife of all his Majesties forces in Yorke. He fought the Battale of Selbye with the then Lord FAIREFAX, Being Levetenant Generall of the counties of Lincolne, Nottingham, Darby, and Rutland, and Governor of Newarke. He valliantly defended that garrison against the English & Scotch Armies Till his Majestye came in person to the Scotchs quarters and commanded the surrender of itt. At which time he also had the honour of being Generall of the Kings Horse guards, in all which services & dureing the warrs after Atcheivements He deported himself with Eminent courage & conduct & received many wounds, Sustayned three imprisonments in the Tower of London, and after the happy restoration of KING CHARLES the second he was made Lord Levetenant of the East Rideing of the County of Yorke, Governor of Hull, Generall of his Majesties forces in Affrica, Governor of Tanger, and Captaine of his Majesties Gaurds of Gentlemen pensioners.

" He married to his first wife JANE, daughter and sole Heire to Sr ROBERT BOTELER of Woodhall in the county of Hartford, K^t, By whome he had Sr HENRY BELLASIS, K^t, of ye Honorable order of the Bath, who lyes interred in this Quire, and MARY, married to the LORD VISCOUNT DUNBAR. He married to his second wife ANNE, daughter and coheire to Sr ROBERT CRANE of Chilton in the County of Suff., K^t, who lyes also intered in this quire.

" And to his third wife, he married the LADY ANNE PAWLET, daughter to the MARQUESS OF WINCHESTER, by whome he had issue (besides other children now liveinge), ANNE, JOHN, ELIZABETH, & FRANCIS, who all dyed young, and are also interred in the quire of this church.

" Arms below the inscription : *Argent, a chevron gules between three fleurs-de-lis azure*, in a lozenge and surmounted by a baron's coronet.

" On a gravestone within ye railes of ye Communion table :—Here lyeth the bodye of The LADY ANNE, wife to JOHN, LORD BELASYSE, daughter and heire to Sr ROBERT CRANE of Chilton in the county of Suff., Baronet. She dyed the 11th day of August 166–.

" On a gravestone hard by the former. Arms : BELLASYSE as above :—Here lyeth the body of Sr HENRY BELLASIS, Knight of ye honorable Order of ye Bath, who dyed in August 1667, aged about 23 yeares, as also the bodyes of three young children, ANNE, ELIZABETH, & JOHN BELASIS, who dyed in the yeares 1668 & 1669, sonns & daughters of the right honorable JOHN, LORD BELASYS, BARON WORLABY, and of the LADYE ANNE, his third wife, daughter to JOHN, MARQUESS OF WINCHESTER."

The following is a copy of the inscription on a monument erected by the same Lord Bellasyse in Worlaby Church, co. Lincoln :—

This Monvment was errected in memory of ye Sons & Daughters of JOHN, LD. BELASYSE, BARRON OF WORLABYE, Lord Liev^t of ye East Rideing of Yorke Shire, Governo^r of Hull, Generall of His Maj^{ties} Forces in Africk, Governo^r of Tanger & Capt of His Maj^{ties} Band of Gent^t Pentioners to KING CHARLES ye 2^d, besides severall other Comands & Charges wch he possessed in ye late Civil Wars under KING CHARLES ye First.

He Married to his First wife JANE, Daughter & heir to Sr ROBERT BOTELER of Woodhall in ye County of Hartford, K^t, by whome he had issve JOHN (died yovng), Sr HENRY BELASYSE, K^t, of ye Honble Order of ye Bath (marryed to ROGERSA ROGERS, Sister to ye DVCHESSE OF RICHMOND, and afterwards to SVSANA, Davghter & Heir to Sr Wm ARMIN of Osgolbye in this Covnty), THOMAS, FRANCES, & MARY, now wife to ROBERT, LORD VISCOUNT DUNBAR.

He marryed to his second wife ANNIE, Daughter & Coheir to Sr ROBERT GRAINE of Chilton in ye county of Suffolke, Knight, by whome he had noe issve. And to his third wife LADY ANNE, Daughter to JOHN, MARQUISSE OF WINCHESTER, by whome he had issve JOHN, THOMAS, MARY ANN, & ELIZABETH, all dyed young, & HONORA now living.

That their fhort abodf here might be fupply'd by a lafting Monvment their difconfolate Father dedicates thif to their me'ory, fome of them haveing beene borne here though not interred.

An'o 1670.

(To be continued.)

** The reader is requested to observe the alterations noted as below :—P. 130, line 5, *for* " began " *read* " begun." P. 132, line 29, *for* " Lady Frances Leveson's tomb " *read* " Lady Frances Kniveton's tomb."

𝕮𝖍𝖊 𝕽𝖊𝖌𝖎𝖘𝖙𝖊𝖗𝖘 𝖔𝖋 𝕴𝖓𝖐𝖇𝖊𝖗𝖗𝖔𝖜, 𝖈𝖔. 𝕸𝖆𝖗𝖈𝖊𝖘𝖙𝖊𝖗.* †

A JUST AND PERFECT TRANSCRIPT GIVEN IN BY THOMAS JAMES, THOMAS HOPKINS, CHURCHWARDENS, OF ALL THE MARRIAGES, CHRIST'INGS, AND BURIALLS THAT HAVE BEEN WITHIN THE PARRISH OF INCKBORROW FROM THE — OF MARCH ANNO D'NI 1663 TO THE 25ᵀᴴ DAY OF MARCH ANNO DOM. 1664, AS FOLLOWETH :—

HENRY JACKSON, Vic.

[Burials.]

Mar. 20 [?]   Ann .... Thom. Buggins [?].
Mar. —   Thomas ....
April 16   John Ellins [?], a bastard.
— —   .... of Kington.
— —   .... of ....
— —   .... of Dormston.
May 18   John Phillips .... of Inckborrow.
— —   Edward Howse of Stock Greene.
June 18   Thomas the sonne of Thomas Bartlett of Inckborrowe.
July 6   Mary the daughter of Edward Steward [?] of Egioke [?].
Aug. 2   Richard the sonne of William Walford of Boults.
Sep. 25   Lewes the sonne of Thomas ffiggett of Holborrowe Greene.
Oct. —   The widdowe Durham of Knighton.
Oct. —   Richard the sonne of Richard Hobday.
Nov. 22   John the sonne of John Ellins of Salter streete.
Nov. 23   Ann the daughter of Humfrey Hill.
Dec. —   Henry the sonne of Henry Ellins.
Dec. 15   Mʳˢ Ann Hunt, the wife of Mʳ Raphael Hunt of Stock Greene.
Dec. 21   John the sonne of Thomas Attwoode of Little Inckborrowe.
Dec. 22   John Egioke, Esq., of Shurnocke.
— —   William the sonne of Richard Porter.
Jan. —   Mary the wife of Thomas Darby of Boults.
Jan. 28   John Lasey of Knighton.
Feb. 3   Margery the wife of Edward Eaton of Cladsall.
Mar. 12   Margarett the daughter of William Heynes of Knighton.
Mar. 23   The wiffe of William Hill of Egioke.

Subscribed by us—
HENRY JACKSON, Vic.

THOMAS JAMES, his mark. ⎫ Church
THOMAS HOPKINS,   ⎭ Wardens.

THE TRANSCRIPT OF THE P'SH OF INCKBERROWE FOR THE YEAR 1664.

[Baptisms.]

April 11   Richard the sonne of James (Hemynge), sen.
April 17   William the sonne of John Doley.
April 24   Samuel the sonne of Thomas Buggin.
April 24   Elizabeth the daughter of William Groves.
May 1   Richard the sonne of Richard Bennett.

---

* From the Transcripts in "Edgar Tower," Bishop's Register.
† Communicated by WILLIAM BRADBROOK, M.R.C.S.—continued from p. 159.

May   5   Arthur the sonne of Arthur Bagshaw, Jun'.
May   8   Alice the daughter of Thomas Hopkins.
May 11   Henry the sonne of John Hunt.
May 16   Walter the sonne of Walter Shelton.
May 19   Edward the sonne of ffrancis Hall.
June 12   Ann the daughter of John Hooman.
June 18   Sara the daughter of David Hobbins.
July   3   William the sonne of William Goore.
July   3   Deborah the daughter of Nicholas Poole.
July   3   Mary the daughter of Thomas ffiggett.
July   4   John the sonne of James Hemynge, Jun'.
July 14   John the sonne of John Wedgbury.
July 21   Thomas the sonne of Thomas Lambe.
Sep. 15   Geo. [?] the sonne of George Brandon.
Nov. 26   Edward the sonne of Thomas Yate.
Nov. 30   John the sonne of Richard Perkes.
Dec. 28   Ann the daughter of Anthony Juggins.
Feb.   5   Issabell the daughter of Thomas Browne.
Mar. 19   Edward the sonne of Edward Steevens.
Mar. 19   ffrauncis the sonne of ffrauncis Dyson, gen.
Mar. 23   George the sonne of Thomas Ingram.

Marriages.

April 19   John Evett of Badbrooke in the county of Warwick & Margaret Baker
           of Bradley in com' Wigorn.
May   2   Walter Shelton c' Johane Elletts of this p'ishe.
May 14   Henry Hewes of ffeckenham c' Anne Wenderum of Durty Nanton.
June 6   Robert Haye c' Sarah Goare of this p'ishe.
Sep. 19   William Webb c' Ann Smyth of this p'ishe.

Burials.

Mar. 30   Robert the sonne of Robert Eaton.
April 5   Widdowe Hooman.
April 11   ffrauncis the sonne of Thomas Darby.
April 11   The wife of John Shepray.
April 20   Joane the wife of John Cobler.
May   2   Richard the sonne of Henry Glover.
May 20   The wife of John Poundrell.
June 18   Mary the daughter of William Evett of Kineton.
June 19   ffraunces the daughter of Henry Ellins.
July   1   The Widdowe Greene.
July   3   A daughter of the Widdowe Perkes.
July   7   ffrauncis the sonne of Robert Eaton.
July 18   Anne Hale, widdowe.
July 26   Elianor the wife of Thomas Doley.
Aug. 29   Henry the sonne of William Harvey.
Sep.   9   Mary the daughter of Thomas ffiggett.
Sep. 18   Henry Ellett, sen'.
Oct. 17   Dorothy the daughter of John ffiggett.
Nov. 11   Thomas the sonne of Ann Smyth.
Nov. 12   Elizabeth Meele.
Nov. 16   Lewes ffiggett.
Nov. 20   Edward the sonne of Thomas Yate.
Nov. 22   Henry Ballard.
Nov. 28   Thomas Wolmer of Kington, gent.
Dec.   7   William the sonne of the Widdowe Harvey.

Dec. 29   Johane the wife of George Crofts.
Dec. 31   John Stuard.
Jan. 6   Henry Griffin.
Jan. 26   John Mason, gent.
Jan. —   Anne the wife of Thomas Raven.
Mar. —   Thomas the sonne of William Willis (Jun. ?).

THOMAS HUNT [?], } Churchwardens.
ARTHUR BAGSHAW, }

THE TRANSCRIPT OF THE PARISH OF INKBERROW, AN' D'M' 1665.

[*Baptisms.*]

Mar. 26   Francis ye sonne of John Stuward.
Mar. 28   Rebeccha ye daughter of Tho. Atwood.
April 3   Robert ye sonne of Rob. Hay.
April 4   Francis ye daughter of Tho. Phyllips.
April 20 Han'a ye daughter of Francis Freeman.
May 6   Tho. ye sonn of Richard Fullwood.
May 11   Eliz. ye daughter of Wil. Walford.
May 14   Mary ye daughter of Hen. Ellins.
May 25   Elianor ye daughter of John Reynolds.
June 25   Tho. ye sonne of Tho. Petford.
June 29   John ye sonne of Rich. Glouer.
July 3   Francis ye son' of Edward Hubande.
July 6   Cicily ye daughter of Walter Shilton.
July 30   John ye sonn of John Richards.
Aug. 15   Tho. ye son' of Rob. Aston.
Aug. 20   Joseph ye son' of Nich. Brittaine.
Sep. 17   Eliz. ye daughter of James Hem'ing.
Sep. 25   Ann ye daught. of Tho. Yate.
Oct. 15   John ye son' of Tho. Hem'ing.
Oct. 29   Simon & Jude, sons of Jo. Laugher.
Nov. 16   Hester ye daught. of Walter Stuard.
Dec. 3   Alice ye daught. of Ralph Dyson.
Dec. 3   Mary ye daught. of Jo. Harritt.
Dec. 28   Edward ye son' of Tho. Dolphin.
Feb. 9   Tho. ye son of Tho. Figgett.
Mar. 14   John ye son of John Stuard.
Mar. 22   Tho. ye son of John Hunt.
Mar. 22   Wil'ia' ye son of Jo. Harbach.

Marriages.

May 22   John Freeman of Inkberrow & Alice Welsh of Aberton.
Aug. 6   Rich. Maunsell of Claynes & Ann' Dyson of Inkb.
Sep. 7   George Perkes of Aston-Cantloe & Mary Stuard of Ink.
Jan. 13   Tho. Bellett of Ink. & Alice Eades of Coughton.
Feb. 25   Edward Harritt of Ink. & Mary Gibbs of Aston-Cantloe.

Burials.

April 24 Tho. ye son of Tho. Buggins.
May 15   An'e ye daught. of Tho. Huband.
June 2   The Wid. Johns.
July 4   Henry filius populi.
Aug. 9   Tho. Dyson.
Aug. 9   Tho. ye sonne of Tho. Lambe.

Oct. 17   Alice ye wife of Wil. Heynes of Kington.
Oct. 20   James Poole of Dormston.
Oct. 31   Mary Bluck of Dormston.
Nov. 12   Simon & Jude, sons of Jo. Laugher.
Nov. 13   Margery ffarr of Kington.
Dec. 5   Jane ye daugh. of Tho. Poole of Rous-Lench.
Jan. 15   Hester ye wife of Rich. Poole.
Jan. 21   Wid. Trindall.
Jan. 31   Eliz. Greene of Dormstone.

THE TRANSCRIPT OF YE PARISH OF INKBERROW FOR YE YEAR 1667.

[*Baptisms.*]

April 20   Tho. ye son'e of Richard Collins.
May   5   Charles ye son'e of Francis Baskefield.
May   29   Isabell ye daughter of Jo. Laugher.
July   7   William ye son'e of John Harritt.
July 21   Francis ye son'e of Tho. Crace [?].
Aug. 26   Elinor ye daughter of David Hobbins.
Sep.   7   Katherine ye daughter of Tho. Marshall.
Sep. 15   Rob. ye son'e of Jo. Richards.
Sep. 25   Elizab. ye daughter of Jo. Figgett.
Oct.   3   Ann ye daughter of Humfrey Dekins.
Oct. 17   John ye son'e of George Brandon.
Oct. 18   Mary ye daughter of Jo. Reynolds.
Oct. 24   Mary ye daughter of John Care.
Oct. 27   Mary [?] ye daughter of Tho. Heming.
Oct. 31   Alice [?] ye daughter of Walter Stuard.
Oct. 31   Alice [?] ye daughter of Tho. Browne.
Nov.   5   ffrancis ye son'e of John Whately.
Nov. 30   Ann ye daughter of Wil. Walford.
Dec.   4   Alice ye daughter of Richard Fullwood, gent.
Dec. 31   Tho. ye son'e of Tho. Windle.
Jan.   5   Henry ye son'e of Henry Jackson, Cler'.
Jan. 30   Ann ye daughter of Anthony Juggins.
Feb.   1   Margaret ye daughter of Tho. Figgett.
Feb.   6   Mary ye daughter of James Hem'ing, jun^r.
Feb.   9   Mary ye daughter of Wil. Raven.
Feb.   9   Francis ye daughter of Richard Glouer.

Marriages.

April 18   Tho. Parker & Margery Dawkes.
April 20   Tho. Chance [?] & Isabell Perks.
June   3   Moses Mansill & Alice Parker.
Oct.   6   Anthony Baylis & Hester Dowley.
Aug. 28   Tho. Bellett & Sarah Dyson.
Nov. 28   Rob. Savill [?] & Ann Day.
Jan. 13   Tho. Johnsons & Isabell Figgett.
Jan. 15   John Bonde & Ann Garner [?].

(*To be continued.*)

𝔐onumental 𝔍nscriptions

AT

St. Mary's Church, Reading.*

Under the tiling, within the Sanctuary, are stone slabs with the following inscriptions :—

Memento Mori.
Here lyeth ye Body of
GRACE, ye daughter
of RICHARD & ANNE
FROME of the City
of London, who
departed this Life ye
first day of April 1713
Aged 1 year 5 moneths
and 20 days.

Here Under Lyeth
The Body of WILLIAM
KENDRICK, Gent., Late
Mayor of Reading, who
was Buried March 24
1634.

Here Resteth the Body of
WILLIAM REEVES
In Hopes of a Joyfull Resurrection.
He was Chaplain to QUEEN ANN of
Blessed Memory, Vicar of this parish
and Rector of Craneford in Middlesex.
He departed this Life March ye 26
1726 In ye 58th year of his Age.
Here also lies interr'd the Body
of ELIZTH REEVES, Wife of the sd
WM REEVES, who died the 16th
of February 1745, Aged 72.

Here Lyeth ye body of ye late
Reverend Mr ABRA'M BROOKSBANK
Minister of this Parish 34 years
who departed this life ye 14th day
of June Anno D'ni 1711, Aged 79,
and also ye body of MARY his Wife
who departed this life ye 15th day of
May Anno D'ni 1715, aged 66.

* Communicated by Rev. G. P. CRAWFURD, sometime Curate in this parish, now Vicar of Bicester, Oxon.

Also here lyeth in hopes of
a Joyful Resurrection the
Body of JOHN BROOKSBANK
Gentleman, Third Son of ye above
named Mr ABRA'M BROOKSBANK
and MARY his Wife, who departed
this life the 11th December Anno
Salutis 1725 in the 44th year of
his Age.

———

Sacred
to the Memory of
JANE KETURAH HARRISON
Who died
26th January 1837
Aged 66 Years.

———

MARTHA OLIVER
died 14th January 1820,
Aged 58.

———

Sacred
To the Memory of
Mrs CATHERINE SIMON
The affectionate Wife of
J. E. SIMON, Esqr
of Castle Street, Reading
Who departed this life
December 9th, 1822
Aged 57 Years

———

Sacred
To the Memory of
The Revd WILL^m ROMAINE, D.D.
who departed this life
March 11th, 1828
Aged 69 Years.
Also
MARTHA ROMAINE
His Widow
Who died Decr 31st, 1852
aged 97 Years.

———

Under this stone is interred
the Body of
ANNE wife of RICHARD FROME of
London, Merchant, who departed
this Life the 22nd of July 1730
In the 44th Year of her age.
Here also lies the Body of the above said
RICHARD FROME, late Merchant of
London who died the 7th of October
1731 in the 50th Year of his age.

Also the body of JANE FROME
Daughter of RICHARD & ANNE FROME.
She died May ye 29th, 1747
Aged 31 Years.
Also M[rs] GRACE PARKER, Mother of
the aboves[d] M[rs] ANNE FROME, who dy[d]
April ye 12th, 1748, Aged 82 years.

To the Memory of
PENELOPE STURGES
Died July 16th, 1818
Aged 77 years.
Also SARAH
Daughter of the Above
Died Feb[r] 21st, 1846
Aged 78 years.

ANNE 1766.   RICHARD 1770.
CATH[NE] 1769.   CHARLES 1772.

All died in Infancy.

GULIELM' KENDRICKE
Exhinc resurget ad novissimæ tubæ sonitum
Vir felix genere
Aultis ejusdem nominis regibus Saxonicis oriundus,
Fælix consanguineis,
Fratere præserti[m] IOHANNE Meseatore Londinensi cuius in hoc
Oppidum merita, et in pauperes munificentiam nec præsans ætas
Imitata est nec facile credet futura.
Fælix maritus
Matronam post se relinquens castissiman pientissiman
Fælix pater
Natam sertitus cælis paratissiman, ad quos præmesit quiet
In Filio unigenito, nepotibusque pluribus se funeri sensit superstitem
Et ad secula transmissum nascitura.
Fælix magistratu
(Quem sibi ægre quidem ferenti demandatum) sumna cumpenden-
tia, cura, authoritate, decoro administravit
badiquaq demum felix
Nisi quod vesicæ dolores acutissimi autumnum vitæ fecerant
valetudinarium et prorsus afflictissimum : sed et hinc
cessit in exemplum miræ tolerantice.
Naturæ concessit Martii 16° anno salut. 1635 Ætat 56° imen-
sum sui apud bonos inopesq. relinquens desideriu.

IN CHANCEL.

On stone slab on the floor of the choir :—
To the Memory of
M[rs] ANN HUME, Relict
of the late
ALEXANDER HUME, Esquire
of Wimpole St., London, &
Olay Hill, Enfield, Midd.
who died March 3, 1827
aged 77 years.

Also of FREDERICK
Fourth son of
ADOLPHUS WILL^M HUME, Esqre
of this parish
who died March [1 ?] 9, 1828
aged 9 months.

On stone slab on the floor of the choir (with a scutcheon, worn smooth):—

Here lyeth the Body of
MARY FOYLE, wife of EDWARD
FOYLE of the parish of Somer-
ford [Keynes H.M.B.] in the County of
Wilts, Esq., who departed this life
.. July A.D. 16 [*seat covers the rest*].

At the foot of other.   On a slab (with coat of arms) :—

Here lyeth the Body of
ROBERT YONGE, Esqre, fourth
Sonne of Sir JOHN YONGE of
Culliton in the County of
Devon, Knight & Barronett.
He died in this towne on
His way to The Bath
the first day of
April 1684.

On slab lying in choir :—

Here lieth the Body of
THOMAS VELLEY, Esqr
of Bath in the county of Somerset
formerly Lieutenant Colonel
of the Oxfordshire Militia
who departed this life
the 7th of June A.D. 1806
Aged 58 years.

On a stone lying in the choir :—

.... SOUTHGA ..
Died
25th of January 180 [?] [1803 Reg.]
Aged 60 years.
Also
WILL. SOUTHGATE. Esqre
died
.. January 1814
Aged .. Years.
Also
.... KING
.... 1815
Aged 79 years.

On a marble slab on floor of choir :—

Here lyeth the Body of ANNE
Daughter of JOHN THORP, Gent.
And ELEANOR his wife, who departed
This life April 24th Anno Dom. .....
Ætat suæ ....

Here also lyeth the Body of FRANCES
another daughter of the above
named JOHN THORP & ELEANOR
. . . ond wife of THOMAS BLAGRAVE, Gent.
who died the 21 of June 1749, aged 30
with two other of their children.
Here also lyeth the Body of the
above named JOHN THORP, who died
the 18 Nov. 1750, Aged 72
A very eminent Practitioner in
Surgery for 50 Years.
Likewise here lyeth the Body of
the above said THOMAS BLAGRAVE, Gent.
who died the 11ᵗʰ of February 1766
Aged 50 years.

On stone slab in choir :—

Here lyeth the Body of THOMAS
MAPLETON, who died July 5ᵗʰ, 17 . . [1731 Reg.]
Aged 63.
And of ELIZABETH MAPLETON his Mo . . .
who died March 9ᵗʰ, 1726, Aged 87 years.
Also the Bodies of
JONATHAN & ELIZABETH, son & daughter
of . . . . THO. MAPLETON & ELIZ . . . .
his wife.
JONATHAN dyed Feb. 11, 1725, aged . .
and six months. ELIZABETH July 30ᵗʰ
aged 4 years & 8 months.
(To be continued.)

The Stirling Family.*

A SCOTCH PHYSICIAN'S NOTEBOOK OF THE SEVENTEENTH CENTURY.

Alexander Govan, hamerman, departed 18 June 1693 Saboth betwixt 3 & 4 in morninge ; buried 20 June tuesday.

Elizabeth Buchanan, spous to george Dingwall, departed Moonday the 26 June 1693 betwixt [*blank*] afternoon ; buried thursday 29 June.

Bessie Simm relict of Alexander Govan, hamerman, departed the 4 Novʳᵉ of November [*sic*] 1693 beinge Saturday, betwixt 5 & 6 in morninge ; buried Moonday the 6 Novʳᵉ 1693.

Friday 25 Januar 1689 departed provost James Campbell at 11 aclocke fore-noon ; buried Saboth 27 Januar.

Alexander Knox departed the 15 feb. 1689 friday 1689 [*sic*]; buried Saboth 17 Februar.

James Bannatyne departed the 17 March 1689 a q'rtre befor 10 in forenoon beinge Saboth ; buried tuesday 19 March 1689.

Saturday 23 March 1689 departed provost Jon Johnstone betwixt 7 & eight in afternoon ; buried 28 March thursday.

* Communicated by C. M. TENISON, Esq., M.R.I.A., Hobart, Tasmania—continued from p. 148.

Mistres Rodger departed Saboth 24 March Saboth [*sic*] betwixt 5 & 6 after-noon ; buried the 27 of March 1689 Wensday.

baylie Walkinshaw departed [*blank*] of March ; buried Saturday 30 March 1689.

Agnes Hamiltoune, spous to george Anderson, tounclerk, departed the [*blank*] of March ; buried 31 March Saboth 1689.

James Murray, writer, departed [*blank*] ; buried Saboth 14 [*sic*].

John Jack .... buried thursday 23 June 1689.

.... on Boyce departed the 19 Nov^re 1693 betwixt 8 aclocke & ¼ past 8 being Saboth ; buried 22 Nov^re tuesday [*ruled out*] Wensday.

.... Ralstoune departed fryday the 18 Jan^r 1694 betwixt [*blank*] of morninge ; buried Saturday 19 Jan. 1694.

rob. tener (?), gardner, departed Saboth 3 feb. 1695 betwixt 5 & 6 in morninge ; buried tuesday 5 feb^r 1695 aged about 70 years 9 months.

Joh. Jamiesone (?), weaver, departed thys lyf 12 of Decb^re 1692 ; buried 13 Dec. 1692 tuesday.

James Bogle, agnes Sanders husband, departed tuesday 22 March 1692 at 10 aclocke at night ; buried fryday 25 March 1692.

Eleanor Baylie departed thys lyf the fyfth of Agust 1690 being tuesday at [*blank*] aclocke at night ; buried the 7th of agust ; died at ev^g.

Jot. Robertson, spous to Edward Robertson, departed the 3 of Octobre tuesday 1693, betwixt 4 & 5 in afternoone ; buried Octob. 6th beinge fryday.

ERRATA.

The following alterations are required on pp. 143—148, as the proof had not been received from the Compiler before we went to press in December last :—

Page 143, line 11, *for* "is scattered" *read* "are scattered."
,, 143 ,, 19, *after* pages *add* "There is no punctuation in the MSS."
,, 145 ,, 5, *for* "gibon (?)" *read* "given," *and for* "Jake (?) Mabing (?)" *read* "inke-making," to which is a foot-note : "This precedes the formula of ' Doctor Salmon's blak inke.'"
,, 145 ,, 7, *for* "1683" *read* "1682."
,, 145 ,, 15, "Ladie Marry Chirstian and a son" may be "Anderson."
,, 145 ,, 19, *for* "Colhoun" *read* "Collhoun."
,, 145 ,, 35, *after* "[illegible]" *add* "craig's."
,, 145 ,, 37, *for* "corderer" *read* "cordener."
,, 145 ,, 42, *for* "Boyle" *read* "Bogle."
,, 146 ,, 24, *after* "aged" *add* "[sic]."
,, 146 ,, 26, 28, 29, 30, *for* "Spurell (?)" *read* "Spruell."
,, 146 ,, 38, *for* "Archibald" *read* "Archbald."
,, 147 ,, 26, *for* "banker (?)" *read* "weaver."
,, 148 ,, 9, *for* "(the laidy W. Pollocke)" *read* "(the laidy [*illegible*] Polloke)."
,, 148 ,, 24, *for* "Wadrop (?)" *read* "Wodrop."
,, 148 ,, 27, *for* "Andro" *read* "Androw."
,, 148 ,, 29, *for* "Paterson" *read* "Pateson."
,, 148 ,, 37, *for* "Stockmellhord (?)" *read* "Stockwellhord."

VARGAS MACHUCA.

The above book was sold by Mr. Quaritch, and the full title is "Genealogia de la Descendencia de los Sres Don Thomas Rodriguez de Vargas Machuca, de D. Geronimo de Monterde, D. Martin Alberto de Bertodano, y D. Miguel Martines de Velasco, abuelos de D. Ygnacio Rodriguez de Vargas."

It is in four parts in three folio volumes, with MS. on vellum, emblazoned with portraits, arms, etc. Mexico : 1780—82.

The Purchaser of the above will confer a favour on a Gentleman desirous of seeing the book, by communicating with Messrs. MITCHELL and HUGHES, 140 Wardour Street, London, W.

Reviews.

The Carvings and Inscriptions on the Kirkyard Monuments of the Scottish Lowlands, particularly of Perth, Fife, Angus, Mearns, and Lothian. By C. CHRISTISON, M.D. Edinburgh: Neill and Co. 1902. (Only 100 printed.)

THIS is a very neat, small quarto work, amply illustrated throughout with nearly 200 engravings, and well printed. The monuments given, as at Kilmadock, Perthshire, are excellently copied, which shews how carefully they had been cleaned out before photographs of them were taken, and proving beyond a doubt that all were carved by one statuary, both from the similarity of the lettering as well as the words used, such as "Memento Mori," etc. Some stones shew a spade only upon the slab of stone, while others have a plough-share, and some give the date or initials only; on one is a pair of scales, on another a bugle or a funnel—about 1618 to 1741. Taking Angus for example, there are slabs filled with writing in a smaller character entirely than those of 1637, and initials and tools of all kinds, as if they had been masons' marks; figures are sometimes in relief, flowers also, one stone having four clothed figures in buttoned coats, and one with a coronet on his head, each having separate inscriptions, " I do ring," " I shall ring," " I did ring," and " I once rang," with excellently deciphered letters and the date, 1743. Adam and Eve are shewn on other stones, Moses striking the rock, and Aaron with breastplate and his rod, depicted as a round-headed knotty stick; this was built into a cottage years after, and five other stones from Perth were also ready, but the builder, going from home for a few days, found on his return that the blacksmith had carried them off from the builder's cottage and had broken them up to make a hearth for his smithy! The writing on the monuments at Angus and Mearns, again, shews a great similitude, proving that one class of masons had done them all. A large stone at Laurencekirk, Mearns, shews a coat with handsome mantling, and armoured shoulder-piece with helmet on top, and on a slab inside initials of a worthy cobbler and his tools, all depicted in relief underneath. In Fife are shewn Freemasons' signs, saws, initials, ships, etc., and on several is the hour-glass with the age given of the deceased as 80 and the date 1626. In West Lothian also are shewn the hour-glass, hammers, compasses, saws, Death's head and cross-bones, rakes and spades, with " Memento Mori " repeated as in Kilmadock and Angus. Lanark, Peebles, and Dumfries chiefly depict the figures of Adam and Eve in Paradise, with trees and serpents. The Perth figures are mostly given clothed as man and wife, and some shew only the bust of the man. Melrose has several busts of men, and on one slab is an excellently drawn head of a musician, for on the stone, enclosed in a shield, are the violin and bow. At Rosneath is shewn a cobbler's monument, with the motto, " This is for Crispin," and a high boot and shoe with a round-headed knife.

We have thus gone over the various styles given, and our wonder is that so many appear perfect, although 250 years old. The neighbourhood, too, was not subject to a Cromwell's inroads; and even the mischief-makers further south, who cannot allow the nose on a beautiful alabaster monument to remain, found that solid stone triumphantly withstood their dastard tricks. There were not even brass inscriptions or figures of knights to steal.

The compiler, too, has been fortunate in having so many helpers to photograph the monuments; but even in these cases, we know well what a vast amount of cleaning the filth of centuries entails, and the assistance he has had is proved by the scrupulous clearness of all the inscriptions, even where the writing is so small.

The work shews in every way painstaking carefulness, great judgment in the classification of the monuments, and an earnest desire to shew by these records the history and condition of Scotland two centuries ago. What apparently is plain is the respect shewn by the present generation to such monuments, and the care taken by the clergy to preserve all they can. What a different state of things exists in the majority of the churches in England, where to form a passage between the pews the best and the oldest of the stone monuments are made a pavement of: some with small brasses still intact on them, others with the inscriptions and arms only, with all the mantling depicted, and perhaps after a search you find 1600 often inscribed on them.

The value of this work would have been greatly enhanced by a good index.

The Virginia Magazine of History and Biography. No. 3, Vol. X. January 1903. Virginia Historical Society, Richmond, U.S.A.

THIS is an ample Part giving in one article the names of the owners of slaves in Westmoreland in 1782, and the Houses of Burgesses in 1683-4. There are also two plates, one shewing the birthplace of Mary Washington, and the other giving facsimile letters of Sir George Yeardley, Governor of Virginia in 1619, with a good account of him from the Ferrar Papers. " Pioneer days in Alleghany County " shews the hard times the settlers had with the Indians early in 1700, who after being well received would murder the whole of the men, one now and then perhaps escaping, and rushing over the Alleghany mountains would warn the settlements and the nearest fort. So the Indians went from point to point until some spirited Captain went in pursuit, and perhaps having lost half his men in an ambush he came up with a body of them, and then would come across the scalps of the former settlers. Among these was a woman called " Mad Anne," a heroine named Anne Dennis from Liverpool, England, in 1742, she being an immigrant at 13, marrying at 23, and a widow at 32. By her husband she had a son, who his mother left in charge of a neighbour while she sought to avenge her husband's death. Nothing daunted she dressed herself with petticoats and a man's coat over them, and with a rifle, a tomahawk, and a butcher's knife she became a courier. No mountain was too steep for her and her steed, no summer too hot, no enemy too cunning. She spent a year in a hut built by herself, and immortalized herself by a long ride from one fort to another, returning with powder for the besieged garrison. For this valiant act she was given a beautiful and spirited horse which she called " Liverpool." From the ridge which bears the name of " Mad Anne's Ridge " she started for ammunition and was overtaken in a snow-storm and fell asleep, but the horse returning a party was at once despatched in search of her, and finally she was rescued from a hole in the snow, caused by her warm breath. At another time she aroused the garrison at Fort Young by her shouts, and came in bloodstained and haggard, but bearing two Indian scalps as her trophies. She married again a valiant frontiersman and lived up to 1825, her pulseless corpse being found in a rude shanty built by herself on the banks of the Ohio River. Her virtues still echo through the mountain passes where her footsteps are a century old. The above and other interesting papers fill a very good Part.

The Smith Family, being a popular account of most branches of the name from 1300, with numerous pedigrees. By COMPTON READE, M.A. Magdalen College, Oxford, Rector of Kenchester, and Vicar of Bridge Sollars, Author of " A Record of the Redes," etc. London : Elliot Stock, 62 Paternoster Row, E.C.

THIS is a portly volume of 300 pp., and as the author says, " it professes to review the great Fabrician family, whether crisped as Smith, ' smoothed into Smyth,' or ' smidged into Smijth.' " He therefore is not content to give merely a pedigree, but has endeavoured to add a précis of those who have attained celebrity. He makes a joke of how persons born a Smith wriggle out of the name as if it were too common ; and as there is no reason why a butler cannot assume the name of his master, so a Bug will blossom into a Norfolk Howard, or plain John Smith become metamorphosed into a De Montmorency, as the Carringtons, Pauncefotes, etc. As for antiquity, the Smiths, like the poor, have always been with us, and the author says that Professor Mahaffy found a man known as Smith in the twentieth year of the third Ptolemy, B.C. 227, and he was a brewer! The author also pleasingly narrates how a mansion with an ancient rookery was purchased by a man named Smith, and the rooks, whose tenure of the Elizabethan elms was as ancient as the mansion, met in conclave and decided that it would be beneath their dignity to adorn the demesne of anyone with so plebian a patronymic. When about to emigrate one of their tribe arrived post haste to assure them that the name was Smythe and not Smith ! Of course they then remained. The late Mr. Carrington Smith, nursery gardener of Worcester, proved himself a real Carrington, and after that he breathed freely.

The author takes the Heralds' Visitations, beginning with Abingdon, Berks, and going on alphabetically, gives pedigrees in each county down to Yorkshire, and also avails himself of the Harleian Society's " Familiæ Minorum Gentium," and quotes three pedigrees from the work of Smith of Rotherham, Smith of Newark, and Smyth of Colkirk, Norfolk, whose daughter Caroline Smyth of 1678 married Thomas Bendyshe of Gray's Inn, and had a son Ireton B., and from this line possesses a descent from Oliver Cromwell.

Some of the more ambitious Smyths claim a royal descent, such as the Elkington Smyths, who claim descent from Edward I. through Eleanor of Castile, and onward through Sir Robert Drury, Speaker of the House of Commons, whose daughter married Sir Philip Boteler, and from that family into Sir Anthony Chester's, and then finally settled in 1660 into the Smyths family of Elkington Hall.

The whole work is pleasant reading, interspersed as it is with amusing accounts from some of the family histories.

The Journal of the Ex Libris Society. Vol. XII., Part 12, for December 1902, and Parts 1 and 2, Vol. XIII., for January and February 1903. London : A. and C. Black, Soho Square, W.

THE December Part has three coats of arms of Sir Daniel Fleming, Bart., created by the King at Windsor in 1681. He was a notable man in his day, fond of heraldry ; was a great friend of Dugdale the genealogist, who complains of having fallen "into an age wherein matters of antiquity are valued but by few. I often wish myself with you for an hour or two, for I see you both love and understand these things very well." On 11 June 1672 Dugdale informs Daniel that the King's Letters Patent have been issued asking subscriptions toward the new structure "of our College in London commonly called the Heralds' Office." The Paper ends by giving a very good pedigree from Sir Daniel Fleming, born 1633, to Sir Andrew Fleming Hudleston Fleming, 8th Bart. in 1884.—Mr. C. Dexter Allen has an interesting letter on bookplates, and gives one of John Paul Bocock and another of "Willard Lee and his son Jack," a ranchman, in costume, standing beside his horse with lasso and revolver in hand.

The January Part gives the arms of the Speaker, William Court Gully, besides four legal bookplates and two for identification, and the arms with a plate of Mr. E. H. Ebsworth. It also contains a list of Worcestershire Bookplates, and a rough list of legal ones. The Part includes Title of Vol. XII. and Contents, and a General Index.

The February Part gives the arms of the Bristol Law Society, and besides that there are four legal bookplates and three pages of a rough list of them. The Editor's dissertation on bookplates to the members of the Plymouth Institution is noticed, illustrated as it was by a number of slides, and Dr. Peachey's lecture at Abbey Gateway, Reading, before the Berks Archæological Society, is given. There are also shewn the plates for the Gosport and Alvestoke Reference Library and the Limehouse District Public Library. The bookplates for identification number now 536.

Blake Family Records, 1300 to 1600 : *A Chronological Catalogue, with copious Notes and Genealogies, of many branches of the Family of Blake.* By MARTIN J. BLAKE, of Lincoln's Inn. London : Elliot Stock, 62 Paternoster Row, E.C. 1902.

THE Blake Family of Connaught has been blessed with documents proving their right to grants of land from 1315, and in this work we find the appointments under which they received the titles, facsimiles of which are shewn, and from Record No. 1 to No. 173 the deeds of confirmation and mortgage, besides leases. There is an Addendum beginning 1393, after which come the Genealogical Memoirs of various branches of the Blakes of Galway, whose memoirs are given from 1278, to Peter Blake of Corbally, who died in 1851, leaving nine children and twenty-five grandchildren. The work ends with the genealogies of some branches of the Blakes of Galway and Blakes of Canada, who emigrated there in 1832, William Hume Blake becoming Solicitor-General of Upper Canada.

The work is well got up, and makes upwards of 200 pages, and will be esteemed as a most painstaking record of a family well worth resuscitating. We, however, greatly miss an index.

Fenland Notes and Queries. Vol. V., Part 56. January 1903. Peterborough : George C. Caster, Market Place.

THIS Part begins with an account of the Wanty family of Thorney from Mr. Peet's "Memorials of de Vantier," an old Huguenot immigrant supposed to have been driven from France in 1685. For five years after not a single baptism at Thorney is recorded. However, they settled in the neighbourhood, and were successful in reclaiming the fens of Lincolnshire and adjacent counties during the century they settled there, many of them marrying with their English neighbours. The names of these strangers abound in every village and hamlet in the district, but the recollection of the French language has long ceased to be heard in the Fens, and their names are almost beyond recognition through anglicization and corrupt pronunciation. However, the Wantiers between 1586 and 1628 were domiciled at Maidstone and Canterbury, their names appearing in the Registers at Canterbury, and by courtesy the crypt of the cathedral was devoted to them and their companions as a place of worship. It is recorded that they tried to establish themselves at Hatfield Chase in Yorkshire, making overtures to the Earl of Bedford to rent land on his Thorney estate, and drain and cultivate it. This account will be welcomed by the Huguenot Society of London, also the three arms given.

Among other articles there is a reference to the Northampton Free Library disposing of the choice works comprised in the books that had belonged to the Northampton Poet, John Clare. Of course if a poet, like the prophet of old, is not esteemed by his own country his friends may disregard him, but when the collection of books given to him is acquired by his friends and presented to his native library as a record of his memory, it seems to us like a breach of trust for any committee to sell them, because the original donors of the library had a prior claim to them before they were sold, if found valuable. It is a precedent which is just as well stopped at the beginning, else it will ramify through every library in the kingdom. The Part is altogether interesting.

The Dightons of Clifford Chambers and their Descendants. By CONWAY DIGHTON.   London : Elliot Stock, 62 Paternoster Row, E.C.

THIS is a family history, beginning with Job Dighton, Barrister-at-Law of the Middle Temple, who was settled at Clifford about 1639, and bought the manor and advowson in 1649 from the Raynsfords, who were ruined Royalists, for £4450. He died ten years later and was buried in the night by his brother-in-law Mr. William Harewell.

Richard Dighton was his grandson, and his youngest son was John, who bought an estate at Shirburn in 1754, and died intestate in 1761, leaving a widow and eight children. He was the senior partner of a firm of solicitors styled Dighton and Bonnin. His eldest son, James Lucy, who was a minor at his father's death, went to India with his three brothers after the disposal of his father's property. The youngest son, born six months after his father's death, turned out to be a distinguished Indian officer, and became a Lieutenant-General, Hon. East India Company, in 1804. The two surviving sons, David Royd and Richard Henry, who with their father have their portraits given, carried on the Anglo-Indian tradition of their house ; David became First Lieutenant in 1824 and was killed in the Burmese War, and Richard Henry, who was a sickly boy, made a great name for himself in India, being in the banking house of William Palmer and Co., and became mixed up in the finances of Hyderabad, and was named as Commissioner of the District, but the appointment was forbidden by Lord Hardinge. He, however, was chiefly concerned in the care of the Nizam's fortune, and finally got away with all the jewels given to him as security, which were afterwards returned on the Nizam paying interest in 1854, the year Richard died in England.

The eldest brother of Henry was Charles Mein Dighton, who was a short time in the army, but left it to enter Holy Orders. He was soon ordained deacon in the Cathedral of Llandaff, and with a full account of his ministration the writer takes leave of his readers.

The work ends with nine Appendices, which embrace the births, deaths, and marriages of the different branches, and gives an interesting account of this worthy family well worth recording. It, however, loses greatly through the absence of an index. The four portraits and coats of arms are a pleasing feature to the book.

⁎⁎ Books for Review and Notices of Forthcoming Works should be addressed to Messrs. Mitchell and Hughes at the Publishing Office, 140 Wardour Street, London, W.

Peter Sers.

Pedigree of Sirr of Dublin.*

Peter Sers, Lincolnshire fens, as it appears on a MS. pedigree.

Francis Sirr, born 16— ; West India and Silk Merchant of St. Clement Danes ; he was settled there 1722, = Catherine, dau. of . . . .
"before Walpole was made a knight." (Treasury Papers, vol. ccxlviii., No. 69.) A conviction against him │ Judge of . . . . Somerset-
at the Custom House (when a quantity of his rice and silk was illegally seized by officials), without the examina- │ shire (thought to have
tion of evidence or hearing of witnesses, was quashed also. The Treasury document, endorsed "Case of Francis Sirr, Esq²," │ been located near Bath),
is addressed to the Right Hon. Robert Walpole, and sets forth and complains of the irregularities of which Sirr │ of the Judges of co. West-
was the victim, intimating the complaint "is encouraged by some great men." Died 14 December and buried │ meath, and related to the
at St. Clement Danes 16 December 1735. Will dated 1 December 1785 ; mentions Joseph Sirr the son and │ Rochforts and D'Arcys ;
Frances Sirr the daughter, also niece Anne Sirr and Catherine Sirr, and nephew Roger Sirr ; proved 11 Feb. │ bur. at St. Clement Danes
following. │ 8 Sep. 1729. The old
│ spelling of Judge was
│ Brehon in Ireland.

Frances, who reverted to the = Archibald Eliott, 2nd surviving son of Sir Gilbert Eliott, 3rd Bart., of Stobs (and therefore brother to
transitional spelling Seer or │ Lord Heathfield) ; born 14 October 1710 ; a Merchant of Old South Sea House, Broad Street, and
Seers before she married in │ St. Peter-le-Poor, London ; died August 1759. (*Vide* Foster's "Baronetage" and Collins' "Peerage.")
1787.

Vernon Eliott, only son, died s.p.

Joseph Sirr, born 1715 ; equerry, as a young man, to Frederick, Prince of Wales, and spent a = Elizabeth, dau. of William Hall from
large fortune at his Court ; a commissioned officer in British Army upwards of twenty years │ Skelton Castle, Yorkshire, who went
(Home Office Papers, 668, 1787) ; Ensign 1742 (Bicdihell's and Tollicot's) 18th or Royal Regt. │ to Ireland, as a young man, in the suite
of Ireland ; at Waterford and Cork 1745, Lieut. same year ; Adjutant 1747 (Home Office Military │ of the Lord Lieutenant of that day,
Entry Book, vol. xxii.) ; Lieut. and Adjutant Pole's Regt., Castle Island, 1748 ; Reduced Officer │ and who was a Captain in the Army at
1755 ; Lieut. 10th Foot 1756 to 1758 ; Captain Sebright's Regt., 88rd Foot, 1768 to 1761 ; in │ the time of the expedition to Cartha-
suite of John, Duke of Bedford, Lord Lieut., 1756 ; Major in Army 1768 ("Gent. Mag.") ; Town │ gena, under General Wentworth, where
Major of Dublin Garrison and resided at Dublin Castle 1761 to 1768 ; Deputy Advocate-General │ he died from plague, leaving a widow
and Judge-Martial in Ireland 1757, and from 1761 to 1780 ; Prælique Master of the Port of │ at Kinsale in Ireland. [The arms
Dublin 1767 to . . . ; High Sheriff co. Dublin 1770 ; High Sheriff of Fermanagh 1774, Jan. 29 │ used by his descendants : *Argent, a
to February 22 (Hanaper) ; Inspector Royal Hibernian Military School 1776 to 1784 ; also │ chevron between three columbines slipped
served as Assistant Q.-M.-G. and A.D.C. to Lord Halifax on the Irish Army Establishment. │ proper. Crest : A dove, holding an
He stood bail for Father Nicholas Sheehy, who was executed for complicity in Whiteboy pro- │ olive-branch. Motto : *Fide et Amore.*
ceedings, and placed under his keeping while awaiting his second trial (*vide* D.N.B.). His │ Elizabeth Sirr died in Dublin, and
houses in Dublin were in Great Ship Street, Bride Street, and Camden Street. Died in Dublin │ was buried from Great Ship Street in
(Camden Street) November 1799, aged 84 ; buried in family grave, St. Werburgh's, 12 Nov. │ St. Werburgh's graveyard 29 January
1799. Oil portrait with A. E. J. Sirr. Will dated 7 March 1794 ; mentions son Henry Charles │ 1790, aged 60 years. The dates of
Sirr and dau. Catherine Frances Minchin ; administered 8 December 1799 (Diocese Dublin) by │ the births of her nine children are
his dau. last named. │ from her Bible. Skelton Castle passed
│ to the Whartons.

B

A

* Communicated by H. Sirr, Esq.

A

1. Joseph Sirr, born 29 July 1766.

2. Francis Pole Sirr, born 9 Dec. 1757.

3. Gervais Sirr, born 13 June 1760.

4. Dunne Sirr, born 27 July 1763.

Believed to have died young.

5. Henry Charles Sirr, born at Dublin Castle 25 Nov. 1764; Ensign 68th Regt. 6 June 1778; Lieut. 8 March 1780; went with his regiment to relieve Gibraltar 1782, and remained in the garrison some years, and A.D.C. to Lord Heathfield there; retired as Captain in 1792 and resided in Dublin. His houses were in French Street, Dame Street, Leeson Street, Ely Place, and Dawson Street. Acted voluntarily as Adjutant, and organized the St. Stephen's Green Infantry, 800 strong, 1796; Acting Town-Major of the Garrison of Dublin 1796; presented with the Town Majority in 1798 and given a residence in Dublin Castle, which he was allowed to retain for life on his retirement on full pay of £478 14s. 8d. per annum in 1826. Arrested Peter Finnerty 1797, Lord Edward Fitzgerald 1798, Russell, Emmett, and other prominent rebels in 1803, and rendered other services to the Crown. He was offered a Baronetcy, which he declined. Appointed Stipendiary Magistrate, Dublin, 1808, and presided at Head Police Office until his death. Sir Arthur Wellesley employed him to organize the new Dublin Police. He was a Sheriff's Peer of Dublin City, was elected Sheriff 1807, but fined and excused. County Magistrate, Dublin, from 1798 till death; helped to found the Irish Society, 1818, and many other Dublin institutions. Formed collection of Irish Antiquities, deposited in Royal Irish Academy, and other collections of minerals, shells, paintings, etc., all dispersed (Catalogues in B.M. and Trin. Coll. Library, Dublin). His demesne residence with farm, Elm Park, Cullenswood, now built over. Many of his MSS. in Trin. Coll., Dublin; portrait in oils, bust, and cast of face at Hyde Park, co. Westmeath; another portrait in oils with A. E. J. Sirr; ivory relief (W. Ewing, Sc., 1818) with H. Sirr, and miniature in possession of Mrs. Eleanor Brabazon (née Bourne) of Bath, a descendant of his sister Mrs. Minchin; engraved portrait published (J. Martyn, Sculpt.); died at Dublin Castle 8 January and buried in family grave, St. Werburgh's, 14 Jun. 1841. Will dated 2 May 1832; mentions sons Joseph D'Arcy Sirr, Henry Charles Sirr, daus. Alicia Orpen and Catherine, also Dr. Charles Orpen; proved in Prerogative Court, Dublin, 1841. (Vide D.N.B., also Hansard, "Parliamentary Debates," N.S., vol. ix., p. 1309.)

=Elizabeth, eldest dau. of James D'Arcy of Hyde Park, co. Westmeath, and his wife Martha, dau. of William Grierson of Deanstown, co. Dublin, and heiress of Joshua Palin; born at Hyde Park 1767; baptized at Killucan Church; M. I., Prerogative Grant Index, Dublin, 12 August 1791; died in Dublin Castle, aged 62, Dec. 1829, and buried in family grave, St. Werburgh's. Portrait in oils with A. E. J. Sirr (vide Burke's "Landed Gentry").

B

A son, born in French Street, Dublin, 17 Nov. 1793; died young.

Joseph D'Arcy Sirr, D.D. Trin. Coll., Dublin (vide Boase, "Modern Biography"). Will dated 12 December 1867; mentions three daus.; proved at Winchester, 21 July 1868, by J. G. Norman D'Arcy and Louisa Frances Sirr. His children are given in "The History and Genealogy of the Families of Hore and Hoare" (Edward Hoare, 1883). They were: Henry Charles Sirr, born at Dublin Castle 7 September 1818; died at Sutton, Hants, 12 January 1820; Edward Hoare Sirr, was at Dublin Coll., Dublin, and at the Bar, deceased; Joseph D'Arcy Sirr, deceased; Frederick Purefoy Augustus Sirr, deceased; a son, who died an infant a few weeks old; Henry Charles Sirr, deceased; Alfred John Orpen Sirr, deceased; William Shepherd Sirr, deceased; Richard Theodore Howard Sirr, deceased, Captain Royal Indian Navy, the only son who left issue, viz., Edward Joseph Arthur Sirr, who married Agnes, dau. of Major Mate of Sandwich, Kent, and has a son Hubert Hoare Francis Sirr; Elizabeth Lucinda, deceased; Louisa Frances, deceased; Charlotte Henrietta, deceased, married Abbott Trayer, M.D.; Alicia Catherine, deceased; Margaret Theodosia, deceased; Isabella Anne, deceased, married Peter Pearse, Solicitor; Sophia Priscilla, deceased. (Vide also D.N.B.)

Henry Charles Sirr, M.A., etc., Trin. Coll., Dublin (vide "Notable Middle Templars" and Boase, "Modern Biography"). Will dated May 1865; mentions wife Louisa, and sons Harry Sirr, and William Sirr (in Holy Orders), and da. Louisa Catherine; proved by Louisa Sirr the relict 25 January 1873. (Vide also D.N.B.)

B | A

Catherine Louisa, who married John Sauchie Schaw, Royal Artillery. His mother and Sir Walter Scott's mother were both Rutherfurds and were first-cousins. J. S. Schaw's will dated 21 January 1853; proved in London 23 September 1854 by Catherine Louisa Schaw, relict, and Henry Rutherfurd. (Vide Memoir of son, Major-General Henry Schaw, C.B. and Colonel R.E., "Royal Engineers' Journal," 1 November 1902.) Schaw Crest: A demi-savage proper. Motto: I mean well.

Elizabeth M.A., buried at St. Werburgh's, Dublin, 4 Nov. 1792, aged one month.

A dau., died in French Street, Dublin, buried at St. Werburgh's 9 April 1797, aged two months.

Alicia Frances, who married Charles E. Herbert Orpen (vide Orpen of Ardtully and of Glanerough, also Orpen in Burke's "Colonial Gentry"). Hence the Cape of Good Hope family.

Eliza Dorothea, died 1812.

1. Catherine Frances, born 18 Jan. 1759; married 14 January 1775; died at Castle Connel 9 Oct. 1810. Oil portrait with Rev. C. H. Minchin, Pau. She was endowed to the full by her father in his lifetime; he kept sufficient only to live quietly.

= Humphry Minchin of Woodville, co. Tipperary, 4th surviving son of Charles Minchin of Woodville and Elizabeth his wife, dau. of .... Massy of Stoneville, co. Limerick; and aunt of Sir Hugh Dillon Massy; High Sheriff Dublin City 1795; J.P. Dublin and Tipperary; born at Donnybrook 9 November 1750 (o.s.); died in Dublin June 1830 and buried in Sirr and Minchin grave, St. Werburgh's. Oil portrait with Rev. C. H. Minchin, Pau. Minchin arms recorded in Ulster Office.

2. Elizabeth Mory, born 4 April 1762; died at Bride Street, Dublin, and buried at St. Werburgh's 31 March 1770.

Martha

8. Jane, born 17 Mar. 1769; believed to have died young.

6. William Whiteway Sirr, born in Dublin 10 May 1766, Lieut. R.N.; served on "Jason," 1779—82; commanded "The Bush" RevenueCutter, and wrecked in Balinakill Bay 18 Jan. 1786; on "Tremendous," 1793-4; "Amethyst," 1795; Lieut. September 1796; described as "of Portsea" in M. L. Allegation; died — August 1797 (Half-Pay Book).

= Frances Elizabeth, dau. of .... Hewlins; "of Portsea, spinster, and over 21" (M. L. Allegation, Winchester Diocese, 18 Feb. 1797).

B 2

ARMS OF SIRR.—Azure, two chevronels interlaced argent between three estoiles or, in chief a Harp of Ireland, above it the Imperial Crown, both proper.

CREST.—On a wreath of the colours an estoile or as in the arms, within two olive-branches proper. Above, on an escrol, the Motto—NAUTÆ FIDA. Motto beneath the arms—LYRÆ NERVOS APTAVI.

𝕾𝕚𝕣𝕣, 𝕾𝕖𝕣𝕤, 𝕾𝕖𝕙𝕣𝕤, 𝕾𝕖𝕖𝕣, 𝕾𝕖𝕖𝕣𝕤.

NOTES.

The name De Sers lingers in Brittany. Sers in Celtic signifies *Stars*. In the South of France the name has been familiar since the thirteenth century (*vide* "Dictionnaire de la Noblesse," Desbois et Badier).

Many persons named Sers, who left Languedoc apparently at the close of the seventeenth century, were settled in Dublin *circa* 1699—1713, as it appears from Registers published by The Huguenot Society of London. Vol. xvi., "French Refugees," Heralds' College, mentions Pierre Sers and others in extracts, presumably taken from Registers of Foreign Protestant Churches, London, 1720, 1729, 1741.

A transitional spelling of Sirr from Sers was Seer or Seers. This spelling appears to have been used in Germany, and it is known that *Sirr* was altered from a German spelling. "Patronymica Britannica" also connects the two spellings.

Peter Sers, son of John, of St. Martin's, London, matriculated at Christ Church 1720-21, and graduated as Patrick Seers (Alumni Oxonienses).

In Prussia there were persons named Sers in the military service, *vide* "Deutche Biographie" and "Moniteur des Dates," from which it appears that the spelling was also Seers and Sehrs (with or without De or Von), and that General Peter von Seers (spelt also Sehrs in "Deutche Biographie," and with the alternative Sers in "Moniteur des Dates," Tom. iii., Suppl.) left France for the sake of religion, and was probably located at Herford in Westphalia in 1695.

Pass for Samuell Serse for Holland (possibly en route for Prussia) by Marq. de Miremont (Huguenot General in Ireland). (Cal. State Papers, Dom., 1690.)

The will of Peter Sers of Gedney, Lincolnshire (P.C.C.), proved in London 23 March 1812. His sister was included in a grant of arms to Sir George Nayler, York Herald (afterwards Garter), whom she married in 1798.

The arms used in this Lincolnshire family, which is of French origin, accord with the arms for *Seers, Prussia,* given by Rietstrap. The confirmation to Sirr is differenced—*in chief a Harp of Ireland, above it the Imperial Crown, both proper.* (Ulster's Office, Dublin.) The arms were thus differenced for a confirmation a century before the actual confirmation. The difference was allowed, but the crest also was differenced in the confirmation.

A large family Bible, containing all entries relating to Sirr family, the old Baptismal Bowl, and many papers and effects were destroyed by fire at Whiteley's, where they were stored. Many baptisms were private and probably not elsewhere recorded.

It is held that the name Sers is essentially Celtic, and this would imply that the family originated in Brittany, and that the branch which immigrated into Prussia did so *only* after having immigrated into England, where the name Sers was turned into the essentially English spelling Seers.

Sers, Canton de Luz (Hautes-Pyrénées).

MEMORANDA.

Not accounted for in Pedigree :—

Nieces and nephew of Francis Sirr of St. Clement Danes, respectively Anne Sirr, Catherine Sirr, and Roger Sirr.

The following cannot be accounted for :—

Sirr, William, married Celia, dau. of Abraham Marshall, Galway, October 1791. ("Hibernian Mag."—Marriages.)

"In memory of Catherine Ann Sirr, who died April 17ᵗʰ, 1830, aged 25 years." (Stone in churchyard, Denston, Suffolk.)

Thomas Sir of Smithboro', Weaver, Bachelor, and Mary Jane Rogers of Smith-boro', Spinster, 9 November 1829. John Sirr of Golanmurphy, Killievan, Cooper, Bachelor, and Mary Moore of Killalina, Clones, Spinster, both of county of Monaghan, 3 June 1831. (Marriage Licences, Clogher Diocese.)

The spelling Surr has not been connected with Sirr or Sers, but the following are noteworthy examples from Ireland :—

Christoper Surr, Sheriff of Galway. Will July 1668; mentions wife Marrian, son ffrancis Surr, and daughter Elizabeth.

William Surr, Wicklow, 1667. (Hist. MSS. Com. Report 10, Part V., 41.)

"The Major I find to be Major Sirr, who is described by Mr Whitelaw (the Historian of Dublin) as his ' worthy old friend, intimate with the parties mentioned in the song, and particularly with the Earl of Meath.' " .... " Major Sirr went to Ireland in 1757 with the Duke of Bedford. He was then a Captain in Sebright's, the 83rd regiment. Major Sirr was subsequently appointed town-major of the city of Dublin, and pratique master of the port. He was High Sheriff of the County of Dublin, and Deputy Judge-Advocate-General of Ireland ; and Governor of most of the institutions of the Irish metropolis. He was the father of the present well-known Major Sirr of Dublin." (" Popular Songs of Ireland." Crofton Croker : 1839. Re the Kilruddery Hunt.)

Major Joseph Sirr knew Lord Heathfield (the defender of Gibraltar) intimately, and they were very much alike in appearance, so much so, that sometimes one was taken for the other. Heathfield, as General Eliott, was Commander of the Forces in Ireland.

The dates given in their mother's Bible confirm the statements as to age

(a) Of Henry Charles Sirr, in a return to the Lord Lieutenant, dated Dublin Castle, 23 August 1838, wherein he states he is in his 73rd year.

(b) Of William Whiteway Sirr, given in Lieutenants' Certificates, 1795, vol. xix., Record Office, London.

A long correspondence in " The Weekly Irish Times " (9 March to 22 June 1901) followed " Recollections of Major Sirr." Much information was given, popular mendacity refuted, and attention drawn to Sir Robert Peel's reply to Brougham in the House of Commons : " In the whole of the six years during which he had been acquainted with Major Sirr he never knew a milder man, or one less disposed to exert authority unduly." (Hansard, N.S., vol. ix., p. 1309.)

Two autograph letters of Major Sirr are included in the collection of Lord Hardwick's Papers. (B. M.)

Letter of Joseph D'Arcy Sirr from Dublin Castle to Sir William Betham, Ulster King of Arms, re the case of Marquis Clanricarde and the Bishop of Meath, con-cerning the advowson of Killucan, 1834. (Add. MS. 23,683, B. M.)

Joseph D'Arcy Sirr was elected a Member of The Royal Irish Academy in 1829.

A declaration of French Ministers, refugees in England, London, 30 March 1691, is signed by " Sers, formerly Minister in the Church of Montredon." (Hugue-not Society, " Proceedings," vol. iii., p. 337.) It is pointed out in " L'Intermediare des Chercheurs et Curieux," under " Famille de Sirr, Sers, etc." (20 July 1898) : " La famille Sers est, en effet, originaire du haut Languedoc, des montagnes du Tarn, où elle a encore des représentants." Also a pastor of Brassac, Loth Sers, is mentioned as the probable ancestor of General Philip Loth Seers (Sehrs) [the father of General Peter Seers given in " Deutche Biographie "], and several par-ticulars respecting him are enumerated.

There are distinct families with the surname Seer and Seers (of East Anglian and other origin), sometimes erroneously connected with Sirr.

(To be continued.)

Monumental Inscriptions

IN THE

Church of St. Giles-in-the-Fields.*

A plain stone:—The gift of RICHARD HOLFORD | In the yeare of Our Lord God 1658 | R. H. of the parish of St Giles in ye Fields | in the Countye of Middlesex, Esq., did | give ye sume of twentye-nyne poundes | yearelye for ever to bee issueing out | of three messuages, or tenements lyeing | in the sayd parish to bee distributed | quarterlye amongst ye most aged & | necessitated poor people of the said | parish by the minister, Church war | dens & overseers of the said parish | successivelye for ever and to noe | other person or persons or use or uses | whatsoever.

JOHN SEAGOOD ⎫
FRANCIS BREADS ⎬ Churchwar.

[This legacy is mentioned in the "New View," but the inscription is not given *in extenso*. See also the inscriptions from Lansdowne MS., *post*.]

THE NORTH SIDE OF THE VESTIBULE.

To the intent that the poor of this | Parish may for ever hereafter receive | the guift of the donor this following | inscription was here fixed & sett up. | Sr WILLIAM CONY of this parish, Kn^t | hath been pleased to give to the | Poore of the same parish Fifty pounds | To the end that the interest thereof | may be for ever distributed in Bread | to the poore; that is to say twelve | penyworth every Sunday in every | yeare and eight holy dayes in the | same yeare such as are particularly | mentioned in the Act booke of the | said parish remaining in their Vestry. | Given in the yeare of Our Lord 1672.

JAMES PARTURICH ⎫
ROBERT HALCUP ⎬ Church Wardens.

[The "New View" mentions this without giving a copy of the inscription above, but mentions the arms then upon it, viz., *Quarterly:* 1 and 4, *Sable, a fesse cotised or between three conies argent;* 2, *Gules, on a bend cotised or, three torteaux;* 3, *Argent, two bars gemells and in chief three mullets azure.*]

THE NORTH SIDE OF THE GALLERY.

[The first two windows are plain. The third has two subjects: at the top Ruth and Naomi, and this inscription, "The Lord do so to me and more also if ought but death part thee and me. Ruth, 1 chap., 17 verse." Below, Elijah and the Tishbite woman, and the following inscription, "The barrel of meal wasted not neither did the cruse of oil fail according to the word of the Lord which he spake by Elijah. 1 Kings, 17 chap., 16 verse."]

A brass, shaped as a shield:—In Memory of | AGATHA WELLS BRIDGER | the very affectionate much loved | wife of ROBERT HAWTHORN, Esquire | died VIII January MDCCCLXV.

Blessed are the pure in heart | for they shall see | God.

* Communicated by ARTHUR F. G. LEVESON GOWER, Esq., assisted by ARTHUR J. JEWERS—continued from p. 186.

A brass, shaped as a shield :—ROBERT HAWTHORNE | of 68 Gower Street in this parish | Esquire | born XVIII March MDCCXCI | died IV March MDCCCLXIX.

My flesh also shall rest | in hope.   Psalm xvi, verse 9.

A white marble monument with a torch and palm branch at the top:—ALEXANDER HENDRAS SUTHERLAND, Esqre, F.S.A. | of Gower Street, Bedford Square, | died on Whit Sunday May 21st, 1820, aged 67. | His remains | lie in the burial ground belonging to this church. | He bore a long and painful illness, | with Christian submission, and resigned his soul, | in pious and humble hope of acceptance with God | Thro' the merits of Savior [*sic*]. | The souls of the righteous are in the hand of God | They are in peace—their hope is full of immortality.

[The fourth window.   Subject, the Good Samaritan in coloured glass, with the words " Go, and do thou likewise," and the following inscription :—

In memory of HENRY MANNING, died 15th Decr 1871, Aged 74.]

A plain marble tablet :—In the Vault beneath | are deposited the remains of | WILLIAM PHILPOT, Esqre | For many years | a respected inhabitant | of this parish ; | who died on the 10th January 1823 | aged 53 years.

[The fifth window, coloured glass, with these words : " God also to the Gentiles granted repentance unto life.   Neither count I my life dear unto myself."]

Brass:—In memory of | JOHN COLERIDGE PATTESON, D.D., | born in this parish A.D. 1827 | Called to missionary work in New Zealand 1855 | Consecrated first Bishop of Melanesia 1861 | Murdered by natives of Nukapu 1871.

COLOURED GLASS WINDOW EAST END OF NORTH GALLERY.

Below the figures the quotation, " By faith Abraham when he was tried offered up Isaac," and this inscription :—Given by | JOHN and WILLIAM BUCKINGHAM | in memory of their father | 1864.

SOUTH GALLERY.

The first window from West to East, the subject Christ blessing the little children, and this inscription :—Given | by the members | of the | Friday morning | Bible Class | 1863.

The second window, the subject Christ as a child in the temple:—Given by | four parishioners | 1864.

The third window, the subject The miracle of the loaves and fishes :—Given by a member | of the | Congregation, | L. T.

The fourth window, The visit of the wise men to the Virgin and Child:—Dedicated | to the Glory of God | by L. & B.

The fifth window, The miracle of turning water into wine ; no inscription.

Window at the East end of the South side, subject Christ carrying the cross. " Daughters of Jerusalem, weep not for me, but weep for yourselves & for your children ":—Given by | JOHN and WILLIAM BUCKINGHAM | in memory of their mother | 1864.

A table-tomb near the East end of the Church, in the churchyard, has the following :—
On the West end of the tomb : The tomb of | RICHARD PENDRELL | the preserver of the life of | KING CHARLES the Second.
["New View":—Here lyeth (lies) RICHARD PENDRELL, Preserver and conduct (of) to his Majesty KING CHARLES the 2d, etc.]
On the South side : Here lies | RICHARD PENDRELL | Preserver and Conductor | of his sacred Majesty | KING CHARLES | the Second | of Great Britain | after his escape from | Worcester fight 1651 | who died Febrᵞ 8th, 1671.
An inscription at the East end is illegible, while that on the North side is as follows :—

> Hold passenger, here's shrouded in this hearse
> Unparalleled Pendrell thro' the Universe !
> Like when the Eastern star from heav'n gave light
> To three lost Kings ; so he in such dark night
> To Britain's Monarch lost by adverse war,
> On earth appeared a second Eastern Star ;
> A pole, astern in her rebellions main,
> A pilot to her royal soverign came :
> Now to triumph in heav'ns eternal sphere
> He is advanced for his just steerage here
> Whilst Albion's Chronicles with matchless fame
> Embalm the story of great Pendrell's name.

Richard Pendrell of Hubbold Grange in the parish of Tongue, co. Salop, Gent. Will dated 8 Feb. 1671. To eldest son Thomas Pendrell the new built freehold messuage and the lands in the parish of Statherton, co. Salop, called yᵉ Scotts, lately purchased of one Mr Merick, but to pay to testator's son Simon £7 a year for the life of Simon, but executrix to have the profits until the said Thomas is 21, but if he dies then to son Simon. Son Lawrence Pendrell the messuage and garden called Hubbold Grange, co. Salop, for the term of the lease held from William Pierrepont, Esq., after death of executrix. Son William Pendrell a freehold messuage and land in Warsall, co. Staff., in a street there called Russell Street, but executrix to have the profits for her life. Daughter Mary Pendrell £100 when she is 24. Daughters Agatha and Elinor Pendrell £40 each when 21. Residuary legatee and executrix wife Mary Pendrell. Signed with the mark of Richard Pendrell. Witness, the mark of Humphrey Pendrell, etc.
Proved by the executrix 14 Feb. 1671. (P.C.C. Eure 20.)

Against the South wall of the Church, in the churchyard :—GEORGIUS CHAPMAN | Poeta | MDCXXXIV | IGNATIUS JONES | Architectus Regius | ob honorem | Bonarum Literarum | Familiari | Suo Hoc Mon | D.S.P.F.C.
Underneath, on the base :—Vetus (tate jam) Diu Deformatum | Refici curaverunt. | J. E. TYLER, Rector | GUL. PARKER, C. L. BIRCH, Eccles. Custod.

The following list of Rectors is painted up in the Large Vestry :—

Gulielmus Rowlandson, Cl., 20 April 1547.
Galfridus Evans, Cl., 8 Nov. 1551, per mort. G. R.
Gulielmus Steward, Cl., 3 Aug. 1579, per resig. G. E.
Nathaniel Baxter, Cl., 19 Aug. 1590, per mort. G. S.
Thomas Salisbury, Cl., 24 Dec. 1591, per resig. N. B.
Johannes Clarke, A.M., 16 Dec. 1592, per resig. T. S.
Rogerus Manwaring, A.M., 3 Jan. 1616, per resig. J. C.
Gilbertus Dillingham . . . .
Brianus Walton, A.M., 1 June ? 1635, per mort. G. D.
Gulielmus Heywood, S.T.P., ...
Robertus Bourman, Cl., 18 Nov. 1663, per mort. G. H.

Johannes Sharp, A.M., 3 Jan. 1675, per mort. R. B.
Johannes Scott, S.T.P., 7 Aug. 1691, prom. J. S. ad Archie Ebor.
Gulielmus Hayley, Cl., 24 April 1695, per mort. J. S.
Gulielmus Baker, D.D., ... 1715 . . . .
Henricus Gally, D.D., ... 1733 . . . .
Johannes Smyth, D.D., 24 Nov. 1769, per mort. H. G.
Johannes Buckner, L.D.D., 22 Mar. 1788, ... J. S. 1798, prom. Epi. Cicest.
Christopherus Benson, A.M., 29 Maii 1824, per mort. Episco. Cicest.
Jacobus Endell Tyler, S.T.P., 28 Oct. 1826, per resig. C. B.
Robertus Bickersteth, A.M., 29 Nov. 1851, per mort. J. E. T., Oct. 5, 1851.
Antonius Wilson Thorold, A.M., 20 Feb. 1857, per elect R. B., ad Episc. Ripon, S.T.P.
Johannes Majoribanks Nisbet, A.M., 28 Mar. 1867, per resig. A. W. T.
Henricus Gulielmus Parry Richards, A.M., 12 Nov. 1892, per mort. J. M. N.
Gulielmus Covington, A.M., 9 Nov. 1899, per resig. H. G. P. R.

FROM LANSDOWNE MS. 878.

[In this MS., among the inscriptions in some other London churches, are the following arms and inscriptions from St. Giles-in-the-Fields, most of which have now perished. The arms are tricked which are here given in blazon. In some cases towards the end, the shields have been drawn, but the arms partly or entirely omitted. The inscriptions are given line for line and spelt as in the MS. :—]

Arms : *A chevron between three fleurs-de-lis;* impaling [*blank*]. The "New View" gives the impalement as "a Lion Rampant," with a slight variation of the inscription, but adds "and Redeemer" before the last two words.

Here nere lyes the Bodyes of SUSAN WYNNE daughter of | FRANCIS DARRELL of Lillingstone Darrell in yᵉ county | of Bucks, Esq., and wife of THOMAS WYNNE of Bodvean | in the county of Carnarvan, Esq., & of BARBARA | WYNNE theire daughter who dyed in the begining of July | 1662 and were both examplary for their piety, goodness | and other Christian graces, which SUSAN dyed the 30ᵗʰ day | of May 1664 in full assurance of a Joyful resurrection at | the last day by the meritts of the Death and passion of our | blessed Lord and Saviour Jesus Christ.

Arms, at the top : *Azure, a maunche or,* CONYERS. Below the inscription : CONYERS, impaling . . . . *a cross and on a chief three bugle-horns,* LANGHORNE.

S. M.

Heic sita est | mulierum castissima ELIZABETHA CONYERS | GUILI' LANGHORNE ar. filia natu maxima uxorq3 | CHRISTOPHERI CONYERS ar. primogeniti Jo. CONYERS | de Horden in comit. Dunelm', Barᵗᵗ. | Prob dolor [puerpera obiit Aprilis 27ᵐᵒ Anno salvatoris 1654ᵗᵒ ætatis | suæ 24ᵗᵒ postquam marito filiam unicam filiosq3 duos pe- | perrisset quorum minor in partu ultimo moriens in com- | plexu matris filia MARIA dicta juxta matrem jacet | Hoc monumentum poni curavit Mastissimus conjux | ne forte per rigorem mortis sublato filio jam superstite me- | moria tam charæ uxoris oblivioni traderetur.

[The "New View" omits the last three lines and the impaled coat.]

Arms : *A chevron wavy.* Query an unfinished tricking. Below the inscription (in a lozenge) : *Argent, a mascle (sable) between three roundels (ogresses),* OSBALDESTON.

1659. | In memory of ARTHUR NEWMAN, gent., & ELIZABETH | his wife the fourth daughter of HENRY OSBASTON of | Hertfordshire, gent., and Theire issue, ANNE, HENRY, FRA- | NCES, MARY OSBASTON, ELIZABETH OSBASTON, and | ALICE, HENRY, & OSBASTON. The Two eldest sonns of | ARTHUR by ELIZABETH are deceased. HENRY lyes in- | terd in Sᵗ Andrew's, Holbourne, in the county of

Mid- | dlesex ; OSBASTON at Rickmeresworth in Hert- | fordsheire. ANNE & FRANCES, Theire two eldest | daughters, are likewise deceased and here lyes intered. | ARTHURE NEWMAN deceased in the .... yeare | of his age on the .... day of .... 16 .. | ELIZABETH his wife deceased the .... yeare of her age | on the .... day of .... 16 ..

In ANNAM GIFFORD sororem amantissimam quæ | migravit ex hac vita vicesimo septimo | die Januarii Anno D'ni 1632 | non quam diu sed quam bene | ANNA relicta DUCI GIFFORDI hic conditur arca | De quibus ANNÆ petis moribus illa capæ | Casta quidem Virgo mollis quoque nata parenti | Vixit condigno nupta benigna viro | Sed cito cum durum violavit vincula fatum | Sola sibi viduum possidet illa forum | Solatrix miseris nudis fuit altera Dorcas | Pauperibus cunctis alma Deoq3 pia | Carmine non opus hic neq3 marmore condida falis | Vita sibi carmen marmor & omne valæ.

In the MS. two shields are tricked : 1, *Ten roundels, in chief a crescent for difference,* GIFFORD ; impaling, *Per cross a bend.* 2, *Per cross a bend;* impaling, *A fesse.* Query unfinished. " These two coats should have bene borne quarterly."

Arms : *A mullet between three crescents ;* impaling [*blank*].

Here resteth the body of JOHN MONIN, Clarke | and Rector of the parish church of Evthorn in Kent | sonne of Sʳ WILLIAM MONINS of Waldershire in | the same county, Baronet, and of Dame JANE his wife | daughter of ROGER TWISDEN of Peckham, Esquire | who departed this life the 22 Novemb. Anno D'm'i 1650 | and in the 43 yeare of his age.

Arms : *Three palets ;* impaling, *A fesse, and in chief three lozenges.*
M. S.
GERTRUDIS eximia pietate fæmina uxor HENRICI | THIMELBY defuncti Hoc monumentum posuit supra | corpus suum cum corde suo.

Here lyeth REBECCA the daughter of JOSEPH LOYD | of This parish, gent., and of ELIONOR his wife, deceased | the 22 of May 1649.

Here the following shields are tricked, but without colours or stating if in glass, painted, or carved :—
1. The Arms of the City of London.
2. The Grocers Company.
3. The Fishmongers Company.
4. The Drapers Company.
5. The .... Company.
6. The Bakers Company.
7. *Three crescents, and over all on a canton a crest coronet,* HODGES.
8. ....
9. *On a cross between four fleurs-de-lis five roundels.*
10. *Ermine, three stags' heads erased ....;* impaling, *A fesse indented between three lions passant-guardant.*
11. *Per pale of three : I. Quarterly, 1 and 4, Between two bendlets engrailed, three covered cups,* BUTLER ; 2, *Three fish within a bordure engrailed ; 3, Three picks.* II. *On a pale the head of conger erect couped,* GASCOYNE. III. *A fesse counter-embattled between three escallop-shells.*

Arms, at the top : I. *Quarterly, 1, Or, on a chief sable two griffins' (wolves ?) heads erased argent ; 2, Gules, two lions passant or ; 3, Argent, a chevron (azure) between three eagles displayed sable ; 4, Or, on a cross (vert ?) a mullet gules* (HUSSEY). II. *Four lozenges conjoined in fesse.* III. *Three roundels, each charged with a talbot passant, on a chief a lion passant-guardant between two anchors erect.* IV. *Two chevronels, the lower one charged with three mullets, and in base a cinquefoil; over all on a canton a lion passant-guardant.* V. *On a chief two griffins' heads erased; impaling, Per pale a cross patée.* VI. *Sable, a cross fleury between four escallop-shells argent.*

Here before lyeth the body of WILLIAM STIDOLPH* | third sonne of JOHN STIDOLPH of Mickelham in the | county of Surrey, Esq. He had issue by his wife ELIZA- | BETH, daughter of JOHN FOXE of St John's in London | Gent., WILLIAM, JANE, MARY, THOMAS, and | ELIZABETH. He departed this life at the age of 55 | being the last of December Anno D'm'i 1660. | Here also before lyeth the body of the above named | ELIZABETH, who departed this life the 10th of Feb. | Anno D'm'i 1623.

[NOTE.—There must be an error in these dates. The wife cannot have had five children and died in 1623, her husband not dying until 1660, aged only 55; unless, indeed, the second date refers to the daughter without specifying that fact.]

The MS. does not give the colours of the arms, and has three heads on the chief in the first quarter of No. I., and two heads on the chief in the dexter coat of No. V. The colours are from the "New View," but that does not give the inscription, and only the quartered shield and No. VI. This book also calls it a spacious monument by the north-west door, adorned " with his Head and half-body, with a book in his right hand, and under his left a death's head." The author of the " New View " also says he was told this gentleman [*i.e.* William Stidolph] gave ground by which the churchyard was much enlarged southward, but it appeared to him not to be half big enough for this very spacious parish, " where they have often 8 Burials or upwards in an Evening."

Arms: *Three battle-axes erect in fesse, a chief ermine;* impaling, *A wyvern segreant with a lion attacking it from behind.*

This is over the inscription, and beneath it is the dexter coat; impaling, *On a fesse between three lions' heads erased as many pheons, all within a bordure.*

M. S.

Charissimæ matris ALICÆ uxoris venerabilis | olim viri ALEXANDRI SHEPPARD Legum Doctoris | nec non suavissimæ nuper conjugis ANNÆ ex antiqua | Daunteseyorum familia in agro Wilton oriundæ | pietatis & amoris ergo posuit THOMAS SHEPPARD | Hic loci juxta (quem si Deo videbitur) mortales suas ex- | uvias humandas designavit providus Anno D'm'i 1631.

Arms: . . . . *fretty, on a canton a sheldrake;* impaling, *Per bend three roses, two and one, counterchanged.*

Juxta requiescat Corpus NATHANIEL BRACKEN- | BURY hujus parochii Architecti ex ELIZABETHA uxore | plurimos suscepit filios superstites reliquit tantum duos | ELIZABETH & NATHANIEL obiit funebris illo Anno Dom' | 1665, Ætat. 43. | ELIZABETH ejus relicta postea nupta LEONARDO SOWERS- | BY ei peperit LUCIAM, PERCIVAL, & ALICIAM (super- | stites) præter alios prius mortuos obiit 29 die Novembris | Anno D'ni 1672 Ætatis 38° et corpus ejus in eodem tumulo | reconditur.

(*To be continued.*)

---

* For Pedigree, see "The Visitations of Surrey, 1530, 1572, and 1623." (Harl. Soc., vol. 43, p. 42.)

A GENEALOGICAL HISTORY

OF THE

Family of Adams of Cavan, etc.*

V.

THE DESCENDANTS OF BENJAMIN ADAMS, THE FIFTH SON OF ALLEN ADAMS AND MARTHA HIGENBOTHAM.

(1) THOMAS COOTE, D.L., of Raconnell House, co. Monaghan, born 28 November 1843 ; appointed 19 December 1859 Lieut. in the Monaghan Regiment ; Captain 10 December 1864 (" Army List ") ; married 28 April 1869 (St. Anne's, Dublin, Par. Reg.) Mary Alicia, daughter of Robert Adams, Esq., M.D., University Professor of Surgery, Trinity College, Dublin, and Surgeon in Ordinary to the Queen in Ireland, of 22 St. Stephen's Green, North Dublin. He died 18 January 1880, aged 36, and had issue as follows :—

    1. THOMAS COOTE, born 18 September 1870.

    2. MARY HORATIA ANNIE.

    3. KATHLEEN CHARLOTTE.

    4. NINA HELENA JOSEPHINE.

    5. MAUDE ALICIA.

        His widow married 6 September 1882 (Lisnadill Par. Reg.) James C. Wolfe, Esq., eldest son of the Ven. J. C. Wolfe, D.D., Archdeacon of Clogher.

(2) CHARLES WILLIAM MAXWELL COOTE, born 27 January 1845 ; entered the Army as Ensign 16 August 1864 in the 25th Regiment (King's Own Scottish Borderers) ; Lieut. 16 October 1867 ; sold out 2 April 1869 (" Army List ") ; married 1 July 1871 Maria Radcliffe, daughter of Captain J. S. Spencer, and granddaughter of the late Hon. Judge Radcliffe of the Supreme Court of New York (" Daily Express " Newspaper).

(3) WILLIAM B. COOTE, born 21 September 1847.

(4) REV. HENRY RICHARD ALBERT COOTE, born 16 April 1850 (Kilmore Par. Reg.) ; T.C.D., A.B. Hiem. 1873 ; entered Holy Orders 1874 ; was Curate of Castlerock, Diocese of Derry ; Rector of Fermoyle, Diocese of Derry, and afterwards, 1879, Rector of Donaghadee, Diocese of Down.

(5) ALBERT AUGUSTUS EYRE COOTE, born 12 September 1851 (Kilmore Par. Reg.) ; entered the Army as Lieut. in the Armagh Light Infantry (Royal Irish Fusiliers) 10 October 1874 ; Captain 15 September 1877 (" Army List ") ; married 9 August 1882 Mary Emily, daughter of the Ven. J. C. Wolfe, D.D., Archdeacon of Clogher (Armagh Par. Reg.).

* Communicated by MAXWELL ADAMS, Esq., Barrister-at-Law. From a MS. by the late Rev. B. W. ADAMS, D.D.—continued from p. 176.

(6) ANNE JANE, married 15 April 1874 George W. Hervey Alcock, Esq. (St. Anne's, Dublin, Par. Reg.).

(7) VICTORIA MARGARET MARY, married 15 June 1876 Thomas Ferdinand Richardson, Esq., of Carrahoe House, co. Monaghan.

5. ELIZABETH, married 18 November 1841 (St. Andrew's, Dublin, Par. Reg.) Rev. William Watkins Deering, A.M., T.C.D., who died 31 August 1870. She died 10 April 1888 at Newcastle, co. Down, aged 63 years, having had issue four sons and four daughters, viz. :—

(1) CHARLES LUCIUS HENRY DEERING, born 1844 ; entered the Army 3 April 1867 as Ensign in the 28th Regiment ; Lieut. 5 May 1869 ; sold out 8 August 1873 ("Army List") ; appointed Captain in the Royal Dublin City Militia 25 May 1875 ; married 26 February 1877 (St. Mary's, Dublin, Par. Reg.) Anna Louisa Soden, daughter of Francis Nesbitt Cullen, Esq., J.P., of Corry Lodge, co. Leitrim ; died 4 December 1878 at Corry Lodge, aged 34.

(2) WILLIAM STUART DEERING, born 1847 ; died 2 June 1858 at Clones, co. Monaghan.

(3) COSBY DEERING, born 4 April 1856 ; entered the Merchant Service 1872 from the "Conway" training ship, Liverpool, as Officer on board the "Flag of London," in which he was lost with the entire crew on his voyage from New York to London in January 1873.

(4) FREDERICK DEERING, born 6 February 1860 ; died 11 February 1867.

(5) HARRIET, born 1845 ; married 15 March 1871 at Ontario Lodge, Oakville, Ontario, Canada West, the residence of her uncle Edgar R. Bredin, Esq., J.P. (see below), John Dickenson, C.E., Resident Engineer of the Sincoe and Miskokee Junction Railway, of Toronto, and only child of Sir Drury Jones Dickenson, Knt., of 10 Mountjoy Place, Dublin ("Daily Express" Newspaper). She died s.p. 1 January 1872 at Orillia, Canada West, aged 26.

(6) CLARA SELINA MARGARET, born 1852 ; died unmarried 6 January 1874, aged 22, at Northlands, co. Cavan.

(7) ANNE JANE FOSTER, married 3 October 1872 Ambrose Going Adams, Esq., of Northlands (see p. 169).

(8) EDITH EMMA.

6. CAROLINE MARTHA, married 21 May 1851 (St. Mark's, Dublin, Par. Reg.) Edgar Robert Bredin, Esq., J.P., of Ontario Lodge, Oakville, Canada West, and J.P. for the County of Cavan, who died 28 April 1878. She died 25 June 1877, having had issue five sons and four daughters, viz. :—

(1) JOHN WILLIAM BREDIN, born 26 July 1852.

(2) CHARLES EUGENE ALLEN BREDIN, born 12 October 1853.

(3) EDGAR ATHELING HORATIO BREDIN, born 24 October 1855.

(4) ERNEST NOBLE BREDIN, born 28 February 1858.

(5) HENRY OSMUND BREDIN, born 16 May 1864.

(6) CONSTANCE EMILY ELIZABETH ADAMS.

(7) JOSEPHINE CAROLINE STUART.

(8) FLORENCE ANNE.

(9) HANNAH MARIA, born 25 September 1868; died 23 December 1868.

7. ANNE JANE, married 3 March 1853 (St. Mark's, Dublin, Par. Reg.) Rev. Stephen Radcliff, A.B., of Wilmount, Kells, co. Meath, and Rector of Lisnadill, Diocese of Armagh. She died 28 June 1900, aged 73, at Armagh, and was buried at Lisnadill, having had issue five sons and four daughters, viz. :—

(1) JOHN TRAVERS RADCLIFF, born 30 January 1857.

(2) CHARLES JAMES RADCLIFF, born 17 August 1860.

(3) THOMAS LIONEL RADCLIFF (twin with William Harold), born 24 January 1863, who died an infant.

(4) WILLIAM HAROLD RADCLIFF (a twin with Thomas Lionel), born 24 January 1863.

(5) STEPHEN RADCLIFF, born 5 November 1866.

(6) ANNE JANE WADE.

(7) CAROLINE ELEANOR.

(8) MABEL HORATIA GARNETT.

(9) FRANCES ADA.

v. ELIZABETH, born 26 April 1779 ; died 25 April 1780 (Family Register).

vi. ELIZABETH, born 21 October 1780 ; died 28 October 1780, aged 1 week (Family Register).

vii. AMELIA, born 22 April 1782 ; died 5 September 1782 (Family Register).

viii. CHARLOTTE, born 13 June 1789 ; died 26 August 1790 (Family Register).

ix. MATILDA, born 15 July 1794; died same day (Family Register).

x. CAROLINE, born 4 March 1796 (Family Register); married 1 January 1812 (Killersherdiny Par. Reg.) John James Archbold Leonard, Esq., of Claremont and Leamore Lodge, co. Wicklow, J.P. for the Counties of Wicklow and Carlow; died 22 June 1858 at Claremont, and was interred in Newcastle Churchyard, co. Wicklow (Newcastle, co. Wicklow, Par. Reg.), beside her husband, who had died 10 March 1858 at Claremont, aged 78, having had issue seven sons and three daughters, viz. : —

1. JOHN GEORGE BUNBURY LEONARD, baptized 7 January 1814 (Castle-dermot Par. Reg.), of Claremont House, Wicklow, and Captain in the 6th Carabineers ; married 12 July 1836 (Drumgoon Par. Reg.) Margaret, daughter of Major Thomas Coote of Fort William, Cootehill ; died 15 February 1847 at Rosscarbery, co. Cork, where he was interred (Ross Par. Reg.), having had issue three sons and two daughters, viz. :—

   (1) JOHN HENRY LEONARD.

   (2) THOMAS LEONARD, married, but died s.p. 5 September 1865.

   (3) BENJAMIN ADAMS LEONARD, surgeon, married 22 July 1893 at Holy Trinity Church, Glen Innes, Australia, Margaret Anna Eleanor, youngest daughter of George Alcock, Esq., of Cros-thwaite Park, Kingstown, Dublin.

   (4) CAROLINE.

   (5) ELIZABETH JOYCE, married September 1871 (St. Stephen's, Dublin, Par. Reg.) Robert Henry Robinson, Staff Assistant-Surgeon H.M.'s British Army, son of Thomas Robinson, Esq., of John's Mall, Parsonstown ("Daily Express" Newspaper).

2. BENJAMIN ADAMS LEONARD of Leamore Lodge, born 9 October 1816 ; married 8 June 1848 Frances, daughter of Captain Thomas Philips of Edergal and Castle Bagshaw, co. Cavan, and Ash Green, co. Meath. She died 27 January 1900 ("Irish Times" Newspaper) at Ballycarney, co. Wexford, having had issue three sons and three daughters, viz. :—

   (1) BENJAMIN SAMUEL LEONARD, born 22 April 1855 ; died 15 July 1883 of heart disease, at Le Mars, Iowa, U.S.A.

   (2) JOHN ARCHBOLD LEONARD, born 18 February 1857.

   (3) THOMAS PHILIPS LEONARD, born 8 October 1858 ; accidentally drowned while bathing 20 July 1869, and was interred in Ballycarney Churchyard (Ballycarney Par. Reg.).

   (4) CAROLINE JOCELYN, born 1 July 1849 ; died 24 December 1849 and was interred in Jersey.

   (5) HELENA MARY, born 5 November 1851 ; died 8 April 1868, aged 17 years, and was interred in Ballycarney (Ballycarney Par. Reg.).

   (6) CAROLINE ELIZABETH, born 21 May 1853 ; died 17 June 1866, aged 13 years, and was interred in Girly Churchyard, co. Meath (Girly Par. Reg.).

3. SAMUEL WILLIAM LEONARD, born 1824 ; entered the Customs 1847 ; died unmarried 13 July 1852 at Dominica, West Indies, when First Revenue Officer of that Island.

4. FRANCIS BERRY LEONARD, C.E., of Spring Hill, Ballyhooly, co. Cork, born 7 August 1827 (Newcastle, co. Wicklow, Par. Reg.) ; married 13 July 1861 Elizabeth, daughter of Edward Yates, Esq., of Leeds, England, and has issue one son and two daughters, viz. :—

(1) ERNEST EDWARD JOHN LEONARD, born 18 September 1863.

(2) BEATRICE.

(3) CONSTANCE.

5. CHARLES JAMES LEONARD of Claremont, born 6 April 1829 ; married 1 June 1860 Georgina Mary, daughter of Marcus Maingay, Esq., of Merry Meeting, co. Wicklow, and has issue two daughters, viz. :—

(1) CAROLINE FRANCES.

(2) GEORGINA EMILY.

6. RICHARD ADAMS LEONARD, born 27 September 1832 (Newcastle, co. Wicklow, Par. Reg.) ; died 28 March 1836, aged 3 years, and was interred in Newcastle Churchyard, co. Wicklow (*ibid.*). There is a mural tablet to his memory in Newcastle Church.

7. COSBY ADOLPHUS LEONARD, born 1833 ; entered the United States Navy, where he attained the rank of Lieutenant.

8. ELIZABETH, born 1818 ; died unmarried 16 November 1856, aged 38, and was interred in Newcastle Churchyard, co. Wicklow (Newcastle, co. Wicklow, Par. Reg.).

9. EMILY DEBORAH, born 1820 ; married 1 July 1852 Thomas Meredyth Archer, Esq., A.M., T.C.D., of Lower Bagot Street, Dublin ; died 30 August 1853, aged 33, at Claremont, and was interred in Newcastle Churchyard (Newcastle, co. Wicklow, Par. Reg.). Mr. Archer died 3 April 1866 at Queenstown, co. Cork (Saunder's " News Letter ").

10. CAROLINE, married 11 September 1862 (Christ Church, Cork, Par. Reg.) John Edwards, Esq., J.P., of Knockrobin, co. Wicklow ; died s.p. 7 September 1866 at Knockrobin.

VI.

MARGARET, ELDEST DAUGHTER OF ALLEN ADAMS AND MARTHA HIGENBOTHAM.

VI. MARGARET, married Foster Anderson, M.D., of Cootehill, co. Cavan, son of Samuel Anderson, Esq., of same place. Dr. Anderson died s.p. 1774. His will, signed 26 February 1771, was proved in Dublin 29 July 1774 (Probate Court, Dublin).

VII.

THE DESCENDANTS OF JANE, SECOND DAUGHTER OF ALLEN ADAMS AND MARTHA HIGENBOTHAM.

VII. JANE, married 1754 Thomas Bevan, Esq., of Cootehill, co. Cavan, cousin of the Right Hon. Henry Bevan, Lord Mayor of Dublin in 1776. Mrs. Bevan died about 1762, leaving issue two sons, viz. :—

I. THOMAS BEVAN, born about 1756; accidentally burned to death before 1762, and was interred at Cootehill.

II. REV. RICHARD BEVAN, T.C.D., A.B. Vern. 1779, Rector of Carne, Diocese of Ferns ; born 1758 ; married 8 November 1790 (St. Thomas's, Dublin, Par. Reg.) Charlotte, daughter of William Mussenden, Esq. He died 23 May 1842, aged 84, and was interred in Carne Churchyard, co. Wexford, beside his wife, who had died 3 June 1836, aged 73 (Carne Par. Reg.), having had issue, among others, two sons and two daughters, viz. :—

1. WILLIAM BEVAN, T.C.D., A.B. Vern. 1814, A.M. Hiem. 1832, M.B. Æst. 1845, F.R.C.S.I. ; born 2 December 1791 ; married 22 August 1820 Charlotte, daughter of Thomas Medlicott, Esq., of Rutland Square, Dublin, and died 26 January 1863. She died 7 March 1876 at Tuam, aged 74, having had issue one son and one daughter, viz. :—

(1) RICHARD BEVAN, born 2 March 1826.

(2) ANNE FRANCES, married 6 September 1866 Rev. William Richey Bailey, D.D., Rector of Clogher, Diocese of Clogher.

2. REV. RICHARD BEVAN, T.C.D., A.B. Vern. 1814, A.M. Hiem. 1832 ; Curate of Carne ; born 1793 ; died unmarried 24 February 1872 at Finglas, aged 78.

3. JANE, died unmarried 1815.

4. FRANCES, born 19 April 1805 ; married 14 April 1841 Rev. James Adams, A.B. (*vide* p. 84), Rector of Castlecor, Diocese of Meath ; died 30 December 1878, aged 73, and was buried in Mount Nugent Churchyard, co. Cavan (Castlecor or Kilbride Par. Reg.).

APPENDIX.

Extract from an anonymous MS. entitled "An Aphorismical Discovery of Treasonable Faction," preserved in the Library of Trinity College, Dublin, written between 1652 and 1660. Published in "Affairs in Ireland, 1641—1652." (Edited by J. Gilbert.)

1645. " Ormond and his faction examininge all theire witte, to invent a new scene, to frustrate this peere of this suposed comforte, to bringe this fatall design to the period of its wished end, had two strings in his bowe that one fayliegn the other could not misse, the Lord Leutenant therefore seriously adviced the Earle of Tomo(nd) (all this while behavinge himself neuter, and consequently not troubled by either partie) to be reconciled to his cossen Insichuyne (whoe alias were foes) and caused my lord of Muskry, Tomond's nephewe, to worke this attonment, not for any other intention, then to worke the distruction of the K(ing's) partie, the Catholicks, and to impower the Prespeteriants, which reconcelment was to be perfected conditiona(l) that Tomond did give upp Bonrattie to Insichuyne, upon the hands of some prime comaun(der) of his : whereby would mightily indure himself unto the Parliament, and would thereby prove most gratfull .... both did nominate for governor of Bonrattie Colonell Adams .... thither arrivinge with 600 men possessed himself of that brave house, and most comodious for the future trouble of the royallists."

Before giving up the castle of Bunratty to Colonel Adams the Earl of Thomond buried all his plate, etc., in the walls, but before he left some one told the soldiers that he had hidden it, and they made him shew where it was and took it all before his eyes.

Lord Muskerry marched to Bunratty and laid siege to the castle.

Extract from Richard Bellings' " History of the Irish Confederation and the War in Ireland, 1645-6." (Edited by J. Gilbert.)

" Thirdly, the Earl of Thomond, who before lived peaceably, without offending the country, in his castle of Bunratty, admitted into it at this time a garrison of eight hundred foot and threescore horse, most of them reformed officers, and, sayling into England, left that place, which was plentifully provided of victuals, and so seated, as the guarrison might from thence make excursions into the rich countryes which for threescore miles long bordered upon the Shannon in the hands of the Parliament, under the command of (Captain McAdam) a stout officer, who began immediately to raise works to strengthen the castle, that, by reason of the marshes with which it was environed, might in a short time be upon the matter impregnably fortified."

* * * * *

Lord Muskerry encamped in the park and laid siege to the castle, which was considered very strong.

* * * * *

" Wherefore it was resolved that the two pieces of cannon newly sent them from Limerick should be planted to batter the little castle, which we have described to have stood near upon the edge of the outworks which the besieged had raised for defence of the place ; the Irish being from thence much annoyed in their trenches, and their approaches retarded thereby. The battery was for two dayes continued against the side of the castle, which being thin, the bullets only peirced it, without shaking the fabrick ; and so undaunted did those intrusted with the guard of it maintaine it, that still as the cannon enlarged the breach, they at every shot poured forth a volley by the hole the bullets had made, until, towards the evening of the second day Captain McAdam, who commanded in Bunratty, coming to view the place, and to give order for drawing off his men in case he found it not tenable, received a shot about his hams from a feildpiece that was planted among the gabions, in some of the higher stages of the fences made upon the side of the hill, to incommodate the enemy on his sally, not with any designe to play upon the castle, where it could be of little use ; but the cannoneer taking the upper window of the castle for a mark to try his skill, made that shot, which by accident was fatal to McAdam, who then was in the room, to which that window gave light, and being carried thence dyed that night.

" Whereof the Lord Muskery being advertised by one that came off from the beseiged, and knowing how much they were discouraged at the loss of so valiant a person, and how little unanimous they were in the choyce of one to succeed him, he caused provision of fagotts to be made and resolved to take advantage of this their consternation and difference, and to assault them in their works."

* * * * *

After the attack the garrison capitulated for their lives, the officers retaining their swords, and they were allowed to return to Cork by sea.

(To be continued.)

Ray of Denston, Wickhambrook, and other places in Suffolk, together with Oakes of Nowton, Rawlinson of Stowlangtoft, Peigham of Dunston, Hasted, and other families, all of the said County.*

ARMS.—The Rays of Bury St. Edmunds bore: *Azure, on a chief or, three martlets gules.* CREST: *An ostrich gules.* MOTTO: ET JUSTE ET VRAY.—which were the arms of WRAY of Glentworth, and to which they evidently had no right. The same arms, crest, and motto were granted (8 March 1770) to RICHARD RAY of Haughley, Suffolk, with the difference that the chief was indented, and the ostrich held a horse-shoe azure in his beak.

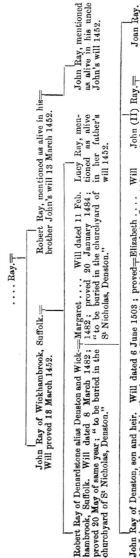

.... Ray.⊤

Robert Ray, mentioned as alive in his brother John's will 13 March 1452.

John Ray of Wickhambrook, Suffolk.⊤
Will proved 18 March 1452.

Margaret .... Will dated 11 Feb. 1482; proved 20 January 1484; "to be buried in the churchyard of St Nicholas, Denston."

Lucy Ray, mentioned as alive in her father's will 1452.

John Ray, mentioned as alive in his uncle John's will 1452.

Robert Ray of Denardstone alias Denston and Wickhambrook, Suffolk. Will dated 8 March 1482; proved 20 May of same year; "to be buried in the churchyard of St Nicholas, Denston."

Margaret.... Will dated 8 March 1482; proved 20 January 1484; "to be buried in the St Nicholas, Denston."

John Ray of Denston, son and heir. Will dated 6 June 1508; proved 16 July following; "to be buried in the church of Denston," to which he left "a cope of blewe velvett & connykelys of blewe velvett to be bowght accordyng to ye vesteament of blewe velvet yt is longyng to ye said cherche." Besides property in Denston and Wickhambrook, he also left his sons tenements in Stradishall and Clare and six shops in Newmarket, to be divided amongst them.

Elizabeth .... Will dated 27 Jan. 1521; proved 7 February following; "to be buried in the church of St Nicholas, Denston."

John (II) Ray, 2nd son.⊤ Joan Ray.

"Sir" Robert Ray, Priest, Canon of Newenham, co. Bedford; mentioned as alive in his uncle John Ray's will 1508, by whom he was left xд "for a trentall of Seynte Gregory for my soule to be song."

A

B 2

* Communicated by G. MILNER-GIBSON-CULLUM, ESQ., F.S.A.

A |

John Smith of Cavendish, Suffolk, gentleman. From Catherine Smith of this family, married to John Cavendish, descend the Dukes of Devonshire.

SMITH OF CAVENDISH, BACTON, AND THRANDESTON, which Pedigree see.

=Agnes Ray.

... Westropp,=Anne by whom John, Ray. Robert, and George Westropp in 1539.

... Sparrow, by whom there were several children, as=Catherine appears by their grandmother Elizabeth Ray's will Ray. 1521. One da., Agnes Sparrow, is mentioned in will of 1539. John Ray (6 June 1508) had left John Sparrow, "my godson, when he cometh to ye age of xx yeers, a tenement wᵗʰ ye appartenaunce lyeing in Wycke-h'mbrok be ye Bregge," evidently another of the children. Anthony Sparrow, Rector of the adjacent parish of Hawkedon, and successively Bishop of Exeter and Norwich (died 1685), was one of the Suffolk Sparrows. They bore *Argent, three roses gules.*

Thomas Ray, to whom his father left lands in Stradishall, Wickhambrook, Cowlinge, etc., 6 June 1508.

John Ray of Denston, yeoman, quit-claims=Agnes .... Will dated 19 June 1539; proved 16—[*sic*] 1540. She to Thomas Manwode of Glemsford land in died of the Plague before 23 August, 34 Henry VIII., as appears by a Glemsford 2 April, 27 Henry VIII.; he deposition in suit of John Cutter *v.* Ray ("Hunts," Series iii., p. 178); inherited a dwelling-house and lands in "to be bur. in Denston Church." She leaves "my soule to All mighti Denston on his mother's death 1521. Will God, to his blessed mother O' Ladye & to all the hoolye Seynts in dated 28 May 1589; proved 22 November Heaven & unto the Crosse wᵗʰ my husbande gave unto the churche of following; inq. p.m. 35 Henry VIII.; "to Denston à Crosse cloathe, pryse viˢ viiiᵈ." be bur. in Denston Church."

William Cracherode of Topsfield, Essex, gent.; died 10 January=Elizabeth 1685, after fifty-six years of wedlock, and was buried in Topsfield Ray, died Church; from which marriage Cracherode of Topsfield, Essex, 17 Feb. and of Cavendish, Suffolk. Of this family was Clayton Mor- 1687; daunt Cracherode, the celebrated Book and Print Collector, buried in whose collections were left to the British Museum 1799. Topsfield ARMS.—*Or, a saltire ermine between four lions' heads erased* Church, *sable.* (See Pedigree in "Visitation of Suffolk, 1612.") Essex.

Anne Ray, married .... =Alice Ray, mar. John Cutter, Scutt, by whom a da., complainant in case against 1558. In Agnes Ray's his three brothers-in-law Ray will, however (19 June 23 August, 34 Henry VIII. 1539), she leaves a legacy They had issue, as appears "to Roger *Strutt's* child- by will of John Ray (1539), ren," evidently her son- and Agnes Ray in the same in-law and grandchildren. year leaves a legacy to "my godson William Cutter."

B

[B

Robert Ray of Denston, son=Joan ....
and heir, æt. 32 in 1540.
Will dated 3 August 1550;
proved 9 January 1551; inq.
p.m. 5 Edward VI.; "to be
bur. in Denston Church."

John Ray of Cheveley, co. Cam-=Mar-
bridge, founder of the Grammar   garet
School there. Will dated 29   ....
December 1558; proved 23 Oct.
1560; died sans issue; "to be
buried at Cheveley."**

George Ray of Long Melford, Suffolk,=Elizabeth ....',
clothworker. Will dated 20 March   survived her hus-
1544; proved 19 June 1545. He left   band and proved
lands both in Suffolk and Essex, and his will 19 June
desired "to be bur. in Long Melford 1545.
Church."

William Ray, son
and heir, under
age 1544; devisee
of his uncle John
Ray 1558.

Robert Ray of Wickham-=Margery, da. of ... Bigg; married at Denston 18 June
brook, yeoman. Will   1567; proved her husband's will 25 Sep. 1598; buried at
dated 25 July 1598;   Wickhambrook 11 May 1612. [In entry of marriage 18
proved 25 September fol- June 1567 she is called Mary, but in the will she is called Margery.]
lowing.

(See PEDIGREE A, post.)

Elizabeth Ray, devisee
of her grandfather Ray
1539; alive and un-
married 1550.

John Ray of Denston, son and heir, æt. 22 in 1550.=Elizabeth .... [Eliza-
Will dated 22 October 1594; proved 18 May   beth Ray buried 28
1595; "to be buried in Denston Church under   January 1596-7, or does
my Grandfather's gravestone"; buried there   this entry refer to her
accordingly 18 April 1595.   sister-in-law?]

C

Richard Ray of Stradishall,=Mary ....,
Suffolk, yeoman; buried at   buried at
Stradishall 9 January 1610.   Stradishall
Will dated 1 February   27 February
1609; proved 25 February   1627.
1610.

Thomas Ray,
3rd son;
alive 1558.

D

* The Registers of Cheveley begin 19 January 1559, and make no mention of his burial, but in an account of Cheveley read at a meeting of the Bury and West Suffolk Archaeological Institute, 13 June 1860, it is stated : "In his will he mentions 'mie bodye to be buryed in ye chyrche of Seynt Marie of Heven at my stolis end.' The tomb of this man, the Founder, has been lately discovered in removing the old pewing of the nave. The inscription is almost worn out. The trustees had an intention of inserting a brass plate in the stone with the original inscription on it." [This was never carried out.] By this will he left a sum of money for the erection and endowment of a Free School in Cheveley—"The John Ray Grammar School." A grant was accordingly made, 6 July, 10 Eliz., appointing the following as first Governors and Trustees : Sir John Cotton, Knt., of Landwade, Cambridge; Thomas Everard, Christopher Bullett, Thomas Cadge, Thomas Norbery, and John Wymarke, all yeomen of Cheveley aforesaid.

D

C | | D

Robert Ray of King's Lynn, Norfolk, gentleman,=Ellen, da. of ...; proved will of her brother-in-law John Ray 30 June 1631 and of her husband 7 July 1631. Will dated 8 August 1633; codicil unoccupative 16 January 1634; proved 9 May 1635; mentions "cousin Margaret Coppin and her children, also cousin Elizabeth Parker."
baptized at Stradishall 5 January 1568-9; proved his father's will 25 February 1610; supervisor of his brother Henry Ray's will 21 January 1618-19. Will dated 9 May 1631; proved 7 July following; left lands in Stradishall and Wickhambrook to his wife and heirs for ever; "to be buried in St Nicholas's Chapel, King's Lynn."

Thomas Ray, baptized at Stradishall 17 March 1570-71; unmar. 1609; alive 31 Jan. 1630.

John Ray of Stradishall, yeoman, baptized there 7 August 1566; proved his father's will 25 Feb. 1610. Will dated 31 Jan. 1630; proved 30 June 1631.

Robert Ray, was living temp. of his mother's will, when she left him a house in Suffolk called "ffarlye House," and all her other lands with the exception of "Potters"; deceased before 25 October 1642, when his executors, John Arrowsmith and William Wright, surrendered land in Badmondisfield, Wickhambrook, to John Williamson.

Elizabeth Ray, married John Arrowsmith, by whom a son, John, alive 1633.

William White=Ellen Ray, to whom her mother left her house in King's Lynn for life and by codicil (16 Jan. 1634) for ever.
[? Wright], by whom Daniel, Elizabeth, and Mary White, all alive 1633.

Mary Ray, ex'trix to her mother's will (9 May 1635), by whom she was left ten acres of land in Suffolk called "Potters."

Anne Ray, ex'trix to her mother's will (9 May 1635), who left her a house and money.

Richard Ray of Stradishall, yeoman, baptized=Susan, da. of ....
at Stradishall 7 Feb. 1574-5. Will proved 28 April 1632; mentions "brother John Ray, lately deceased."

Susan Ray, baptized at Stradishall 1 Jun. 1615.

Sarah Ray, baptized 16 February 1618-19; bur. 20 February following, both at Stradishall.

Rev. John=... Benton, alive 1609 and 1630.

Ray (Anne or Bridget, see her sister).

Henry Ray of King's Lynn, Norfolk, "houseler," baptized at Stradishall 7 June 1572. Will dated 5 December 1618; proved 21 January following.=Mary, ex'trix of her husband's will 21 January 1618-19.

"Up-"=Mary,

Mary Ray, alive 5 December 1618.

John Ray, alive 1630.

Thomas Rowning.=Mary Ray, baptized at Stradishall 29 Nov. 1612; married there 7 May 1633.

Rev. John=... Rogers, alive 1609 and 1630.

Ray (Bridget, baptized at Stradishall 6 Jan. 1576-7, or Anne, baptized there 3 March 1581-2).

John Ray, admitted to Caius Coll., Cambridge, 1618, aged 16; B.A. 1618, M.A. 1621.

Ambrose Ray, baptized at Stradishall 9 August 1579; deceased before 1609.

Abraham Ray, baptized at Stradishall 4 Dec. 1580; alive 1609; deceased before 31 Jan. 1630.

Samuel Ray, baptized at Stradishall 11 December 1586.

C

John Ray, alive under age 1609; alive under the age of 24, 1680.

John Ray=Alice, da. of . . . Plume of Hawkedon; married at Denston 8 Oct. of Dens- 1578; buried there 28 January 1589-90. The Plumes of Hawke- ton, son don were descended from the Plumes of Great Yeldham and Maldon, and heir, Essex (see Sir John Cullum's "Suffolk Church Notes," p. 100, under men- 'Stansfield'), who bore *Argent, a bend vair or and gules, cottised vert,* tioned as yet on the tomb of Edmund Plume of Hawkedon at Stansfield the such coat is *Ermine, a bend vair or and gules, cottised sable.* For the Essex 1594. Plumes see "Visitation of Essex, 1634" (Harleian Soc. vol. xiii., p. 470). Dr. Thomas Plume, D.D., Vicar of Greenwich and Arch- deacon of Rochester (1630—1704), who founded the Plumian Professorship at Cambridge, was grandson of Thomas Plume of Yeldham, the brother of an Edmund Plume of Hawkedon.

George Ray, baptized at Dens-=Kathe- ton 6 February 1564-5; mar- rine, da. ried there 2 October 1590, on of . . . . same day as his sister Mar- Wright. garet. He is mentioned in his father's will 1594, when he was left a tenement called "Abel's" for life, to go after- wards to his son John and his heirs.

Charles Ray, bap- tized at Denston 28 Oct. 1567; de- visee of his father 22 Oct. 1594.

John Ray, mentioned in will 22 October 1594.

Elizabeth, da. of Clement Paman, gent, of Chevington,=John Ray of Denston, son=Mary, da. of William Suffolk, by Bridget, da. of Robert Kemp, gent., of Spains and heir, baptized at Wick- Hovey, gent., of Dens- Hall, Essex, by Elizabeth, da. of Sir Clement Heigham hambrook 12 February ston, and widow of of Barrow, Suffolk, Chief Baron of the Exchequer; 1595-6; devisee of his the Rev. Samuel New- married at Chevington 28 December 1607; probably the grandfather 1594; he was ton of Old Sandford, "John Ray's wife," buried at Denston 21 Feb. 1625-6. called "cousin" in the Essex; she was mar- For the Kemp—Heigham marriage see Howard's will of Robert Plume the ried to John Ray be- "Visitation of Suffolk," vol. ii., pp. 4 and 291. In the elder of Tilbury, Essex, fore 12 Sep. 1629, on Chevington Church Reeve's Book, 1513—34 (Hen- who made him supervisor which day her father's grave MS.), John and Robert Paman, ex'ors of the will thereof 21 July 1627; will is dated, and of Henry Paman the elder, hold two cows to pay yearly called "of Hunston, which was proved 15 to the common light of the Sepulchre, 2d; Isabella Pa- Suff.," by his son in the Feb. 1629-30 by relict man, widow, holds two cows, one to furnish one light latter's will, and still alive Mary. In it he men- before the Trinity, one before the Blessed Virgin, and 17 February 1635 - 6. tions "Granddaughter one before St John and St Edmund. In the finding of ? John Ray the elder, Elizabeth, da. of John arms for trained soldiers, 6 August 1595, are the entries: buried at Wickhambrook Ray, a minor." Will "Clement Paman, a corselet furnished; Henry Paman, 23 October 1644. dated 7 Dec. 1656; a calyver furnished." (Gage's "Suffolk," pp. 833, 384.) proved 1 Feb. follow- 1st wife. ing. 2nd wife.

Joseph Ray, baptized at Denston 16 Nov. 1689. Query, the Joseph Ray buried at Wickhambrook 27 October 1642.

Daniel Ray, devisee of his grandfather 1594.

Joseph Ray of Denston,=Grace, da. of . . . ; buried buried at Wickham- at Denston 21 February brook 10 June 1701. 1666-7.

. . . ffrench (?) "To my sister=Elizabeth Ray, "the granddau. of Wm Elizabeth ffrench a ring," Will Horey, a minor," mentioned in his will of John Ray 17 Feb. 1685-6. 12 September 1629.

Daniel=Sarah Ray, born at Rawlins. Denston 22 January 1654; married there 31 May 1675.

Elizabeth Ray, baptized at Chevington 20 December 1611; ? died young.

—

Sarah Ray, baptized at Chevington 17 June 1617.

Elizabeth Ray, baptized 23 April 1650; buried 31 October 1664, both at Denston.

Mary Ray, baptized at Denston 19 July 1650.

Grace Ray, baptized at Denston 6 June 1647.

Clement Ray, baptized 10 May 1666; buried 21 Feb. 1666-7 (same day as his mother), both at Denston.

John Ray, eldest son, born at Denston 14 Oct. 1658; alive 1655.

Rev. Clement Ray, Rector of Stansfield and subsequently of Denston, heir of his brother John; born 26 February, bapt. at Chevington 10 March 1618-19; Minister of Stansfield during the latter years of the Commonwealth, but conformed and instituted Rector 11 July 1661; resigned 26 January 1662 and was instituted Rector of Denston; bur. at Denston 6 April 1686.
=Mary, da. of .... Biggs; married at Wickhambrook 12 Sep. 1644; buried at Denston 22 September 1680.

Rev. Isaack Ray of Stansead, born 27 June and baptized 20 June 1654 [*sic*, it should evidently be *vice-versâ*] at Stansfield; Rector and Patron of Denston; B.A. Emmanuel College, Cambridge, 1675; M.A. 1679; heir to his brother Clement 1709; buried at Denston 21 April 1720. Will dated 15 July 1717; adm'on granted to brother Ambrose, the relict renouncing, 12 May 1720. Sans issue.
=...., da. of .... , who survived her husband and whoinherited the advowson of Stanstead.

Joseph Ray, bapt. at Stansfield 1 May 1653; buried at Denston 2 Feb. 1684.

John Ray of Denston, son and heir, baptized at Chevington 27 June 1618; died 7 March 1635-6; buried at Denston 9 March following. Will, in which he mentions "my brother-in-law Mr John Bennett," supervisor of the will, and "my sister Elizabeth ffrench," dated 17 February 1635-6; proved 25 March following; inq. p.m. 13 Charles I. Sans issue.
=Mary, da. of .... Bennett, and sister of John Bennett, gent.; married 1635; proved her husband's will 25 March 1635-6.

Clement Ray of Denston and Sudbury, gent., aged 40 and upwards on 15 June 1693 [Dep. at Colchester, Exchequer Dep., 3 William and Mary, Trin. 10]; buried at Denston 29 April 1709. Will dated 27 November 1708; proved 15 July 1709; he left lands in Denston, Wickhambrook, Hartest, Reed, Somerton, and Stradishall, Suffolk, to his brother Isaac. Sans issue.
=Anne, da. of .... bur. at Denston 23 Dec. 1700.

John Ray, born and baptized by his father at Denston 8 Dec. 1646-7.

Ambrose Ray of Bury St. Edmunds, baptized at Stansfield 7 Nov. 1650; mercer 1707; Churchwarden of Denston 1714; was "of Stanstead" at the time of his death; buried at Denston 9 Feb. 1727. Adm'on granted to Samuel Ray, Elizabeth Godfrey the ex'trix renouncing, 16 Sep. 1728. Sans issue.

G | 0

Richard=Mary Ray, baptized at Stansfield 2 May
Godfrey, 1651; married at Denston 6 April 1675.
gent. A Mary Godfrey married to William
Taylor at Denston 9 January 1699-
1700, and an Elizabeth Godfrey was
appointed ex'trix of Ambrose Ray's will
1727, both evidently daus. of Richard
and Mary Godfrey.

Elizabeth Ray, born 14 and baptized 17 November 1655 at Stansfield; buried there 23 November 1655.

John Last=Elizabeth Ray, bap-
of Chev- tized at Denston 26
ington. September 1686;
married at Cheving-
ton 17 February
1708-9.

Sarah Ray, baptized at Denston 9 June 1689.

Samuel Ray, born 7 Dec. and baptized 16 December 1660-61; bur. 17 May 1661, all at Stansfield.

Mary Ray, born 6 and baptized 14 May 1684; buried 5 Dec. 1708, all at Denston.

George Ray,=Mary, da. of
born 2 Dec. ....Wright;
1657; bap- married at
tized at Denston 9
Stansfield, September
Suffolk, 20 1683.
Dec. 1657.

Samuel Ray,=
baptized at
Stansfield,
Suffolk,1658;
buried at
Denston 4
Aug. 1729.

Clement Ray of Sudbury and Bury St. Edmunds, Suffolk, mercer,
born 5 and baptized 23 Nov. 1687 at Denston; buried there
26 May 1707. Will dated 23 April 1707; proved 15 July
1709; he left legacies to his uncles Clement, Ambrose, Samuel,
and Isaac Ray, which later he calls "of Stanstead," and makes
executor, leaving him an additional annuity, which was inherited from his "grandfather Clement Ray." Sans issue.

William Ray, baptized=Elizabeth ....,
at Denston 20 October survived her
1571; married before husband and
1594; he was owner administered
of lands in Thelnet- his estate.
ham, Suffolk. Adm'on
granted to widow 16
February 1634.

Richard Ray of Whepstead,=Elizabeth ....,
Suffolk, yeoman, baptized
at Denston 6 Jan. 1572-3;
bought lands in Denston
and Wickhambrook from
his nephew John Ray of Gosfield, son of Francis. Will
dated 1641.

mentioned in will of her husband. [Richard
Ray married at Wickhambrook, 20 December 1620, Elizabeth Overing. Is this the same? If it is and is also the
same as Elizabeth Ray, late of Whepstead, widow, who made
a nuncupative will 13 April 1648, proved 19 April following
by Peter Albon, then she was probably the step-mother of
her husband's children, as she mentions kinsmen and kins-
women but no issue.]

(See PEDIGREE B, post.)

Rev. Robert Ray, Rector of Hollesley, Suffolk. Will dated 21 December 1657; proved 9 July 1658; mentions "cousin=Anne, da.
Rewse." He was owner of lands in Thelnetham, Suffolk, and Market Harling and Blo Norton, Norfolk. of ....

H | 0

Edward=Catherine Ray, mentioned as alive and already married 21 December 1657.
Roberts, gent.

William Ray, born at Hollesley 16 April 1654; buried there 28 November following.

Robert Ray, alive 21 December 1657.

John Ray, alive 21 December 1657.

Frances Ray.

Anne Ray.

Lucy Ray.

Jane Ray.

Martha Ray.

Elizabeth Ray.

All alive 21 December 1657.

Rev. Robert Ray, Rector of Hawkedon, Suffolk.=Alice, da. of ... Webb; married at Denston 7 Feb. 1687; alive 1645.
Instituted 19 December 1584 (Ambrose Everard, Patron). He was succeeded in the living by Anthony Sparrow, afterwards Bishop of Norwich. Will dated 16 July 1645; proved 12 May 1647. Sans issue.

Elizabeth, da. of ...; married before 1595; buried 22 Feb. 1610-11. 1st wife.
=Francis Ray of Denston, buried there 15 Sep. 1611. Will dated 12 September 1611; proved 2 Oct. following.
=Frances, da. of ... Callowe, and sister of Thomas and Clement Callowe; married at Denston 6 Aug. 1611. Will dated 28 September 1630. 2nd wife.

Nathaniel Ray of Hawkedon, mercer, baptized at Cowlinge, Suffolk, 18 Dec. 1595. Will dated 24 October 1638; proved 5 Nov. following; left lands in Denston and Wickhambrook; mentions "goddau. Elizabeth Ray under age, Richard, Elizabeth, Mary, and Frances Evered," and he leaves his right and title to lands in Cavendish to "Thomas Ham'ond of Thurston End in Hawkedon." Sans issue.

Daniel Ray, baptized at Denston 25 April 1598; left land in Badmondisfield (Wickhambrook), Suffolk, by his father 1611; living in Stansfield 16 July 1645; dead before 6 October 1661. Adm'on of his goods granted to relict Hester 26 June 1661.
=Hester, da. of Thomas Hyndes by ...; married at Whepstead 4 October 1625; sister of Elizabeth, widow of ... Ray of Whepstead (who made nuncupative will 18 April 1648, proved by Peter Albon, residuary legatee, in which she left a legacy to her niece Hester), Adm'on of her goods granted as "of Stansfield, widow," 26 Nov. 1678 to her son Daniel.

Samuel Ray, baptized at Denston 1 May 1606; alive 1638.

Elizabeth Ray, bapt. at Denston 23 August 1601; alive 1611.

John Ray of Gosfield, Essex, yeoman, eldest son and heir; on 8 June 1629 he was plaintiff in a Chancery Suit; he sold his lands in Denston and Wickhambrook to his uncle Richard Ray.

Robert Ray, mentioned by his godfather and great-uncle 16 July 1645; admitted to lands in Badmondisfield (Wickhambrook) on the death of his father 6 October 1661; died before 15 July 1686.

Daniel Ray, administered his mother's goods 26 November 1678.

Robert Ray.

John Ray, son and heir (so declared 15 July 1686). As an infant of twelve years old admitted to High Bridge Field, Badmondisfield, 30 September 1686, his uncle William Lovett, guardian. (Badmondisfield Court Rolls.)

Thomas Ray of Denston, admitted to lands in Badmondisfield (Wickhambrook) 15 June, 1 James I. = Rose, da. of .... (so called 16 June 1608). She is probably the Rose Ray who died at Stradishall, and is stated in that register to have been buried at Denston 8 Nov. 1626; in the latter register there is no mention of her.

Robert Ray of Wickhambrook, baptized at Denston 12 October 1600; devisee of his uncle Robert Ray 1645; buried at Wickhambrook 9 July 1686. Will proved 30 September 1685 (Rev. Clement Ray of Denston a witness). = Mary, da. of ...; buried at Wickhambrook 2 July 1685.

Samuel Ray of Stansfield, ex'or to his brother's will 1685.

Richard Ray, baptized at Denston 16 June 1603.

Elizabeth Ray, baptized at Denston 6 May 1589; married there, 24 Oct. 1614, Edward Agas.

Martha Ray, baptized at Denston 18 September 1590.

Mirabel Ray, baptized at Denston 1 January 1591-2; buried there 13 Dec. 1611-12.

Rose Ray, baptized at Denston 16 June 1603. Twin with Richard.

Margaret Ray, baptized at Denston 8 February 1663-4; married there, 2 October 1690, Philip Parker. Her father (1694) left her the lease of a sheep-course in Icklingham, Suffolk. Ellen Ray of King's Lynn, Norfolk, widow, in her will dated 8 Aug. 1683, mentions "kinswoman Elizabeth Parker," probably a da. of Margaret.

Mirabel Ray, baptized at Denston 6 September 1566; alive and unmarried 1594.

John Ray, under age 1685.

Mary Ray, under age 1685.

Robert Rewse or Rous. = Elizabeth Ray, married at Denston 18 February 1574. Rev. Robert Ray, in will of 21 December 1657, mentions "cousin Rewse," evidently offspring of his aunt Elizabeth.

Ambrose Everard, gent, of Hawkedon, Adm'on of his effects granted to Martha his relict 25 March 1595, John Ray the younger her proctor. (See "Visitations of Suffolk.") ARMS.—Gules, three annulets engrailed or. = Martha Ray, married at Denston 31 Oct. 1576. Will dated 30 Oct. 1625; proved 18 Feb. 1632.

Ambrose Everard of Cavendish, devisee of cousin Nathaniel Ray 24 October 1638, and of his uncle Robert Ray 16 July 1645. = Martha ...; mentioned 16 July 1645.

1. Elizabeth Everard. 2. Martha Everard.

3. Dorothy Everard. 4. Sarah Everard.

Richard Everard of Hawkedon, gent. Will dated 11 March 1643; proved 18 October 1648; mentions brother-in-law Benjamin Lany, D.D., Chaplain to the King. = Catherine, da. of .....

John Everard, whom his father desired by will to be preferred to the Rectory of Hawkedon. This did not have effect.

1. Mary Everard.

2. Frances Everard.

Martha Everard, godda. of great-uncle Robert Ray, in whose will she is mentioned 16 July 1645.

Richard Everard of Hawkedon, gent, eldest son, ex'or of his father's will 18 October 1648. Presented the Rev. Stephen Newson to the living of Hawkedon 14 December 1665.

(To be continued.)

MARRIAGES OF PAINSWICK PEOPLE ENTERED IN THE REGISTERS
OF OTHER PARISHES.* †

GLOSTER, ST. MICHAEL.	Henry Aldridg & *Anne Aldridge*	17 May 1595.
GLOSTER, ST. MICHAEL.	Wyllyam Wokley & *Jane Rawlings*	23 January 1596.
CHELTENHAM.	*Jhon Poole* & Susan Mason, w.	7 March 1602.
GLOSTER, ST. MICHAEL.	*William Bub* & Joane [? Hall] of Dursly	4 September 1622.
GLOSTER, ST. MICHAEL.	*William Bubb* & Joane Clarcke	12 May 1623.
GLOSTER, ST. MICHAEL.	Edwardus Turner de Througham & *Elizabetha Fletcher*	21 April 1627.
GLOSTER, ST. MICHAEL.	Joh'es Tickle & *Maria Watkins*	9 June 1627.
OXFORD, SAINT MARTIN.	*Richard Seman* & Katherine Wryght	8 March 1649.
GLOSTER, ST. MICHAEL.	Henry Townsend, p'och de Bisleigh in Com' Glouc', & *Elizabetha Blisse*	25 March 1649.
BEVERSTONE.	*Francis Harris* & Sarah Brouning	10 July 1651.
GLOSTER, ST. MICHAEL.	Richardus Hooker, p'och de Stroud, & *Maria Osborne*	4 January 1651.
GLOSTER, ST. MICHAEL.	*John Andrews* & *Margaret Smith*	13 January 1651.
GLOSTER, ST. MICHAEL.	*Richard Collins* & Anne Gardiner of Bisleigh	13 August 1653.
GLOSTER, ST. MARY DE LODE.	*Daniel Webb* & Edith Wood of Matsonne Banns pub. 28 March, 4, 8 April 1657.
STANDISH.	*Thomas Clisol* & Mary Cleeve	18 May 1657.
GLOSTER, ST. MARY DE LODE.	*Giles Boyce* & *Sara Watkins* Banns pub. 6, 13, 20 August 1657.
STANDISH.	*Thomas Twining* & Hester Browne	26 September 1657.
GLOSTER, ST. MARY DE LODE.	William Hunt of Bislee & *Joanne Prichard* Banns pub. 9, 16, 23 March 1657.
GLOSTER, ST. JOHN.	*Giles Low* & *Margaret Charles*	4 January 1658.
GLOSTER, ST. MICHAEL.	*William Cooke* & Anne Farley	14 February 1658.
GLOSTER, ST. MICHAEL.	*William Packer* & *Sarah Rodway*	21 July 1659.
GLOSTER, ST. MARY DE CRYPT.	*Giles Smith* & Ann Tickel of St. John's	2 July 1663.
GLOSTER, ST. MICHAEL.	*George Dorwood*, Clerke, Vicar of Paynswick, & ffrancis Hodges	2 February 1664.
GLOSTER, ST. MICHAEL.	*Anthony Poole* & *Dorothy Davis*	21 July 1666.
GLOSTER CATHEDRAL.	*Johannes Dodwell* & Anne Chadwell de Stroud	19 December 1672.
GLOSTER, ST. JOHN.	Henry Shewall of Stroud & *Elinor Kinne*	11 May 1674.
GLOSTER, ST. MICHAEL.	Henrey Shewell de Stroud & *Eleanora Kynn*	11 May 1674.
QUEDGELEY.	*Samuel Smith* & *Elizabeth Tunley*	31 December 1674.
GLOSTER CATHEDRAL.	*Johannes Hastings* & *Margaretta Cowles*	4 October 1675.
QUEDGELEY.	Richard Layton of Longney & *Anne Wicke*	3 February 1675.
GLOSTER CATHEDRAL.	*Ambrosi' Hewett* & Anna Trindall de Edgeworth, wid'	10 June 1676.
GLOSTER CATHEDRAL.	Jacob Woodfield de Stroud & *Sarah Watkins*	5 September 1678.
GLOSTER CATHEDRAL.	Joh'es Adey de Rodburrow & *Jana More*	9 September 1678.
GLOSTER CATHEDRAL.	*Guilielmi Stephens* & *Hanna Cook*	20 February 1679.
GLOSTER CATHEDRAL.	*Arthur Long* & *Beata Watkins*	6 May 1680.

* Communicated by CECIL T. DAVIS, Esq.

† *Italics* are used for the names of those belonging to Painswick. I beg to express my thanks to the clergy for kindly allowing me to make the extracts.—C. T. D.

MISCELLANEA GENEALOGICA ET HERALDICA.

GLOSTER CATHEDRAL. *Thomas Smith* & *Anna Gardiner* 7 December 1680.
STONEHOUSE. *Daniel Heskins* & Sarah Smith 28 June 1681.
GLOSTER, ST. JOHN. *Gills Lowde* & *Hanna Smith* 1 June 1686.
GLOSTER, ST. JOHN. *William Tunly* & *Mary Land* 1 June 1686.
FRAMPTON-ON-SEVERN. *M*ʳ *John Webb* & Mʳˢ Ann Wheatcham of London ; lic.
 2 June 1687.
GLOSTER CATHEDRAL. Henric' Dimery & *Anna Renn* 21 January 1687.
GLOSTER CATHEDRAL. Rich' Bear de Stonhouse & *Sara Gardiner* 1 August 1688.
GLOSTER, ST. JOHN. Henry Averis of Cheltingham & *Eliona Heron*
 18 September 1688.
GLOSTER CATHEDRAL. Henric' Partridge de Stroud & *Eliz. Webb*
 19 December 1689.
CHELTENHAM. *Robert Vyner* & Bridget Warner of Harsvield 21 December 1689.
GLOSTER CATHEDRAL. *Egid' Holder* & Sarah Baylee de Upton St. Leonards
 24 April 1690.
GLOSTER, ST. JOHN. *Robert Hobbs* & Sarah Chedworth of Stroud 29 April 1690.
GLOSTER, ST. MICHAEL. Samuell Merrett & *Mary Hillman* 16 October 1690.
GLOSTER, ST. JOHN. John Frowd of Witcomb & *Elizabeth Gill*
 29 November 1690.
GLOSTER CATHEDRAL. *Henric' Brian* & *Hester Hewlings* 28 May 1691.
QUEDGELEY. John Garner & *Mary Castle* 6 June 1691.
GLOSTER, ST. MICHAEL. Rechard Tyler of Wootten-under-Hedge & *Anne Watkins*
 8 October 1691.
GLOSTER CATHEDRAL. *Stephan' West* & *Sarah Harding* 7 November 1691.
GLOSTER CATHEDRAL. *Carolus Hilman* & *Maria Lord* 20 March 1691.
GLOSTER, ST. JOHN. Richard Poole* of Elstone & Grace Perkin of Great Witcomb
 7 April 1692.
GLOSTER CATHEDRAL. *Joh'es Tunly* & Doroth' Blaxford de Pool, com' Wilts
 18 June 1692.
GLOSTER CATHEDRAL. *Georg' Smith* & Catharin Clissold de Pitchcumb
 30 June 1692.
WHADDON. *Stephen Hobbs* & *Elizabeth Cook* 7 July 1692.
WHADDON. *Jeremiah Walker* & Margaret Franklin of Lydiard, Wilts
 14 August 1692.
GLOSTER, ST. JOHN. Brian Branston of Vpton S. Leonard & *Mary White*
 2 November 1692.
GLOSTER CATHEDRAL. *Joh'es Webb* & *Cath' Webb* 8 November 1692.
GLOSTER CATHEDRAL. *Georg' White* & *Elizab' Beard* 16 November 1692.
GLOSTER, ST. MICHAEL. Robert Hayshard of Burley & *Elizab. Webley*
 11 March 1692.
GLOSTER, ST. MICHAEL. Robt. Hayward of Tetbury & *Elizabeth Weyley*
 30 December 1693.
GLOSTER, ST. JOHN. *William Renn* & *Margary Tunly ;* lic. 7 April 1694.
GLOSTER, ST. MICHAEL. John Dancer of Winstone & *Susannah Edwards*
 18 May 1695.
GLOSTER CATHEDRAL. Daniel Gardiner de Pitchcomb & *Eliz. Stephens*
 20 October 1695.
GLOSTER, ST. JOHN. John Wells of Stonehouse & *Ann White ;* lic.
 10 September 1696.
GLOSTER CATHEDRAL. Daniel Hawker de Stroud & *Margaretta Mansell*
 11 October 1696.
GLOSTER CATHEDRAL. *Johannes Wren* & Eliz. Arundell de Stroud
 15 October 1696.
MATSON. *William Mills* & Margaret Rogers 28 March 1696-7.
QUEDGELEY. *John King* & Maria Badger of Slymbridge 10 May 1697.

* Altar-tomb in Painswick Churchyard.

GLOSTER CATHEDRAL.   Robertus Mill de Haresfield & *Maria Buckle*
27 July 1697.
STONE.   *Joseph Russell* & Frances Bruton of Thornbury   25 December 1697.
STANDISH.   Richard Andrews & *Ann Palling*   28 September 1699.
STROUD.   Thomas Stephens & *Catherine Barnes*   28 September 1699.
STANDISH.   *Thomas Wathen* & Elizabeth Pocket   3 October 1699.
GLOSTER, ST. JOHN.   *Daniel Terrett* & Margery Dobbs of Upton Sᵗ Leonards ; lic.
21 September 1700.
GLOSTER, ST. JOHN.   *John Gardiner* & Sarah Hone of Upton Sᵗ Leonards. B.
2 August 1701.
GLOSTER, ST. MICHAEL.   Richard Cud & *Hester Knowles*   28 August 1701.
KING'S STANLEY.   Thomas Randle of Shurdington & *Martha Badger*
4 September 1701.
GLOSTER CATHEDRAL.   Egidius Watkyns & *Elizab. Loveday*   30 October 1701.
STROUD.   Edward Jones & *Mary Holder*   8 January 1701.
GLOSTER CATHEDRAL.   *Henricus Gardiner* & Dina Greening de Santhurst
3 February 1701.
GLOSTER, ST. JOHN.   *Laurence Rodway* & Hannah Gibbons of Elkstone; lic.
16 April 1702.
STROUD.   Henry West & *Anne Parry*   19 April 1702.
GLOSTER, ST. JOHN.   William Skinner of Preston in yᵉ Forest & *Mary Rogers ;* lic.
23 June 1702.
KING'S STANLEY.   *Richard Clark* & Deborah Moore   6 October 1702.
GLOSTER, ST. JOHN.   *Thomas Curtis* & Ann Belcher of Upton St. Leonards. B.
12 October 1702.
GLOSTER, ST. MICHAEL.   George Rogers of Bisley & *Anna Nibblet*
12 November 1702.
GLOSTER, ST. MICHAEL.   *Samuel Merrett* & Sarah Brown   26 December 1702.
GLOSTER, ST. MICHAEL.   Edward Nicholls Draper & *Elizabeth Dorwood*
7 March 1702.
GLOSTER CATHEDRAL.   Samuel Watkins & *Sarah Laud*   15 May 1703.
STROUD.   Tho. Webb & *Sarah Minstow*   12 October 1703.
STROUD.   Jon. Hasilton & *Mary Mower*   21 October 1703.
LONDON, ST. JAMES, DUKE'S PLACE.   *William Poole,* w., of Panswick in yᵉ county
of Gloucester, & Elizabeth Pope, w., of Sᵗ John's in Bristow
5 November 1703.
GLOSTER CATHEDRAL.   Edvardus Knight & *Anna Cordwell*   20 November 1703.
STONE.   *Philip Watkins* & Jane Russell   13 April 1704.
STROUD.   Richᵈ Stephen & *Mary Bayly*   28 April 1704.
STROUD.   Samuel Philips & Mary Wixey   13 June 1704.
STROUD.   Wᵐ Fryer & *Eliz. Knowles*   26 March 1705.
GLOSTER CATHEDRAL.   *Thomas West* & Elizabetha Kemore de Stroud
9 April 1705.
STROUD.   Jacob Mower & *Sharah Trotman*   1 October 1705.
BEVERSTONE.   *William Partridge* & Elizabeth Wicks of Tedbury   25 June 1706.
GLOSTER, ST. MICHAEL.   Bernard Ballinger of Cirencester & *Mary Dewzell*
28 October 1707.
KING'S STANLEY.   Sanuel Coal of Stroud & *Ann Hathaway*   3 December 1708.
STONEHOUSE.   *Maurice Clements* & Mary Andrews   15 June 1710.
GLOSTER, ST. MICHAEL.   Richard Jones of South-Cerney, Gent', & *Anne Pleydall*
1 August 1710.
GLOSTER CATHEDRAL.   *Egidius Lowther* & Maria Woadley de Upton St. Leonards
30 September 1710.
BEVERSTONE.   *Thomas Matthews* & Ann Webb   24 April 1712.
GLOSTER CATHEDRAL.   Gulielmus Harris & *Susanna Gyde*   14 May 1713.
GLOSTER CATHEDRAL.   *Mauritius Clements* & Elizabetha Laud de Standish
25 June 1713.

STANDISH. Joseph Brian & *Hannah Chapman*   18 September 1713.
GLOSTER, ST. MICHAEL. Daniel Gyde & *Mary Long*   27 October 1713.
PITCHCOMBE. Thomas Clarke & *Mary Smith;* lic.   21 December 1713.
PITCHCOMBE. Samuel Lewis & *Eliza Cook*   18 January 1713.
GLOSTER, ST. JOHN. *Walter Vyner* & *Sarah Freame;* lic.   30 March 1714.
GLOSTER, ST. JOHN. Samuel Beard of Upton St Leonards & *Sarah Jones;* lic.
          17 October 1715.
GLOSTER, ST. JOHN. Samuel Atwood of Upton St Leonards & *Elizabeth Tawney;*
   lic.   7 January 1715.
STONEHOUSE. *Emanuel Cook & Hanna White*   17 January 1715.
GLOSTER CATHEDRAL. Stephanus King & *Dorcas Wood*   2 February 1716.
PITCHCOMBE. John Harris of Moreton Valence & *Elizabeth King;* lic.
          2 February 1716.
GLOSTER CATHEDRAL. *Thomas Baylis* & Sarah Burdock de Miserdean
          18 February 1716.
GLOSTER, ST. JOHN. *Giles Barnwood* & Hanah Grimes of Upton St Leonards. B.
          21 April 1717.
DURSLEY. *Robert Holder* & Ann Trotman   25 April 1717.
GLOSTER, ST. MICHAEL. *William Bishop* & Sarah Dudbridg of Stroud
          17 September 1717.
BEVERSTONE. *Rowland Woode* & Elizebeth [. . . . poll ?]   25 September 1718.
PITCHCOMBE. *Daniel Jones* & Sarah Packer   6 January 1718.
GLOSTER, ST. MICHAEL. Nathaniel ffryer of Bisley & *Margaret Jones*
          30 March 1719.
GLOSTER, ST. MICHAEL. *Daniel Cook* & Anna Amos   17 September 1719.
PITCHCOMBE. *Richard Cooke* & Mrs Elizabeth Mitchell of ye Farm; lic.
          26 May 1720.
GLOSTER, ST. JOHN. Robert Gregory of Elkstone & *Deborah Kent;* lic.
          9 March 1720.
STANDISH. *William Banks* & Elizabeth Perry   9 April 1721.
STROUD. *Richard Cook* & Elizabeth Cole   31 January 1721.
GLOSTER, ST. JOHN. *Henry Bryan* & *Sarah Gardner*   6 February 1721.
GLOSTER, ST. JOHN. *James West* & *Beata Wessun;* lic.   26 May 1722.
FRAMPTON-ON-SEVERN. Wm Parker & *Bridgett Loveday*   19 October 1722.
GLOSTER, ST. MICHAEL. John Bossly & *Mary Bayly*   7 November 1722.
GLOSTER, ST. MICHAEL. Jacob Eigles & *Mary Alley*   28 August 1723.
GLOSTER, ST. JOHN. William Gardiner of Coberley & *Mary Hall;* lic.
          17 February 1723.
GLOSTER, ST. MICHAEL. Samuel ffoster & *Sarah Wrenn*   10 April 1724.
STANDISH. *George Winn* & Ann Rodway   20 September 1724.
GLOSTER, ST. MICHAEL. Tho. Cox of St Martins, Middlesex, & *Ann Barnefield*
          30 March 1725.
STANDISH. *Robert Ashelford* & Jane Carby of Randwick   25 May 1725.
STANDISH. *John Coock* & Mary Rodway   9 October 1726.
GLOSTER, ST. JOHN. *Benjamin Matthews* & *Mary Cullis*   6 August 1727.
GLOSTER, ST. MICHAEL. Richard Longford & *Abigail Turly*   7 October 1727.
GLOSTER, ST. MICHAEL. *John Rodway & Hannah Holder*   4 December 1727.
NEWINGTON BAGPATH. William Weaver of St Mary de Cript, Gloster, & *Ann
   Holder*   28 May 1729.
GLOSTER, ST. MICHAEL. John Batman & *Margaret Harmer*   2 January 1729.
GLOSTER, ST. MICHAEL. *Thomas Webb* & Margaret Showel of Stroud
          7 February 1729.
RENDCOMBE. *William Lidiard* & Anne Barnfield of Stroud; lic.   7 April 1730.
STROUD. *John Smith* & Olive Atkins   18 January 1730.
FROCESTER. *Robert Young* & Eleanor Knowles of Easington   14 August 1731.
GLOSTER, ST. MICHAEL. *Thomas Hulbert & Sarah Lodge*   28 September 1731.
CHELTENHAM. *John Hayard* & Martha Paker   19 June 1732.

GLOSTER, ST. MICHAEL.   *Richard Wakefield* & *Mary Evans*   10 May 1733.
STANDISH.   *Henry Terrett* & Ann Huggins   14 January 1733.
STROUD.   John Holder & [*blank*] of Painswick   18 April 1734.
GLOSTER, ST. MICHAEL.   Samuel Webb of Minchin Hampton & *Eliza Cull*
                                                             12 August 1735.
KEMERTON.   *John Cooks* & Anne Nicholson, wid., of Claynes, co. Worc.; lic.
                                                             16 August 1735.
STONEHOUSE.   *John Gardiner* & Martha Rickets   17 August 1735.
GLOSTER, ST. JOHN.   John Sollars of Charlton Kings & *Rachel King*; lic.
                                                              5 July 1736.
STONEHOUSE.   *John Clissold* & Mary Andrews   10 August 1737.
GLOSTER, ST. JOHN.   *William Gide* & Hannah Bubb   11 June 1739.
COALEY.   *Stephen Wood* & Sarah Cam   15 June 1739.
STROUD.   *Henry Clark* & Jane Halliday   24 August 1740.
PITCHCOMBE.   William Bates of Woodchester & *Mary Jeaks*; Banns
                                                              6 October 1740.
GLOSTER, ST. MICHAEL.   *Thos. Gardiner* & Sarah Trustrum of Upper Duntsborn
                                                             11 February 1740.
PITCHCOMBE.   *Daniel Packer* & Sarah Palling   5 November 1741.
GLOSTER, ST. JOHN.   Daniel Harding of Stroud, B., & *Sarah Harding*; lic.
                                                             17 September 1742.
FULHAM, MIDX.   *Thomas Grammatt*, B., & Hannah Prout of Fulham, S.; lic.
                                                             26 October 1742.
GLOSTER, ST. MICHAEL.   *Robert Hornett* & Mary Verringdon of Stroud
                                                             24 February 1742.
GLOSTER, ST. JOHN.   *John Wilkes* & *Sarah Holder*; lic.   4 April 1743.
GLOSTER, ST. JOHN.   *Jⁿ Holder* & Eliz^t Birch   6 November 1743.
GLOSTER, ST. MICHAEL.   *John Gardiner* & *Sarah Preston*   3 February 1743.
KING'S STANLEY.   *Samuel Cook* & Ann Rider   7 October 1744.
GLOSTER, ST. MICHAEL.   *Joseph Knowles* & Amy Allins of Cirencester
                                                             25 January 1744.
NIMPSFIELD.   *Nathaniel Frier* & Frances Dee; lic.   10 June 1745.
GLOSTER, ST. JOHN.   *Samuel Birt* & Hester Hooper   11 August 1745.
GLOSTER, ST. JOHN.   *Samuel Holder* & Anne Machin. B.   31 December 1745.
GLOSTER, ST. MICHAEL.   *Willm. Lydiats* & *Mary Hinton*   30 January 1745.
GLOSTER, ST. JOHN.   *William Gardner*, B., & Hannah Teal of Uphatherly. B.
                                                              2 December 1746.
STROUD.   Richard Young *alias* Twissell & *Hannah Poole*   31 January 1746.
GLOSTER, ST. MICHAEL.   Edward Randle of Ash-Church & *Sarah Beard*
                                                              2 September 1747.
GLOSTER, ST. MICHAEL.   James Osborne & *Elizabeth Cook*   28 March 1749.
GLOSTER, ST. MICHAEL.   *Samuel Beard* & Elizabth Banks of Upton St Leonard
                                                             10 July 1749.
GLOSTER, ST. MICHAEL.   John Scott & *Sarah Isles*   29 September 1749.
STROUD.   William Hare & *Mary Gardner*   9 April 1750.
STROUD.   John Copson, Vicar of Malmesbury, & *Mary Shipway* 18 October 1750.
STROUD.   Thomas Hyde & *Eliz. Poulson*   16 December 1750.
GLOSTER, ST. MICHAEL.   George Lander & *Anne Tippett*   24 September 1751.
HAMPNETT.   John Webb of North Cerney & *Sarah Boon*   1751.
GLOSTER, ST. MICHAEL.   *Job Stanley* & Elizabeth Excell of Rodborough
                                                              7 February 1753.
STROUD.   *Edward Poole* & Martha Nickolls   24 May 1753.
GLOSTER, ST. JOHN.   Thos. Ireland & *Hannah Garner*; lic.   20 June 1753.
STROUD.   *John Cook* & Mary King   27 September 1753.
GLOSTER, ST. MICHAEL.   William Pugh of Cayo in the Diocese of St David's &
     Martha Wrenn   9 October 1753.
GLOSTER, ST. JOHN.   *Benjamin Wager* & Anne Carter, wid. B. 24 October 1754.

HAMPNETT. John Haltone of Oaksey & *Elizabeth Cherington* 1754.
STROUD. *John Window* & Mary Land 14 October 1755.
NIMPSFIELD. *Thomas Gardiner*, clothworker, & Elizabeth Burfords
25 December 1757.
STROUD. *Richard Gardner* & Sarah Gainey 14 August 1759.
STROUD. *William Hughes* & *Anne Daniels* 5 November 1759.
STONEHOUSE. *Daniel Berry*, b., & Mary Jenner, s. 25 October 1761.
STROUD. *Stephen Ellis* & Mary Maycock 20 April 1762.
STONEHOUSE. *Thomas Merrey*, b., & Sarah Churches, s., of Rodborough
21 April 1762.
KING'S STANLEY. *Daniel Adey* & Margaret Clifford ; lic. 14 October 1762.
STROUD. *Samuel Lawrence* & Eleanor Cocks 5 January 1764.
STANDISH. *Thomas Hobbs* & Mary White ; lic. 23 September 1764.
STROUD. James Restall & *Anne Gardiner* 21 September 1766.
STROUD. *Edward Power* & Mary Morgan 19 February 1767.
STROUD. *Sam*[l] *Wood* & Lettice Hodgson 22 June 1769.
STANDISH. *Nicholas Olive* & Elizabeth Gardner ; lic. 30 July 1769.
GLOSTER, ST. MICHAEL. *Richard Packer* & Susanna Baylis 23 January 1770.
STROUD. *John Haines* & Hester Veysey 7 February 1771.
STROUD. *W*[m] *Rannells* & Hester Stephens 26 February 1771.
STANDISH. *Edward Mill* & Sarah Ridler 2 July 1771.
GLOSTER, ST. MICHAEL. *James Gastrell* & Sarah Carwardine ; lic.
10 November 1771.
STROUD. *John Marman* & Jane Pit 18 December 1771.
KING'S STANLEY. *Thomas Twining*, b., & Eliz. Cookes 8 February 1773.
STANDISH. *James Wood* & Mary Cook ; lic. 15 May 1774.
STROUD. William Fletcher of Stroud, son of Thomas Fletcher, & *Priscilla Kemble,*
Spinster, of Painswick, daughter of John Kemble 18 December 1774.
STANDISH. *Joseph Cook* & Patience Chamberlain [she signs " Chamberlayne "]
28 February 1775.
STROUD. *John Parker*, Bachelor, of Painswick, son of John Parker, & Jane
Clissold, Spinster, of Stroud, daughter of William Clissold 17 May 1775.
GLOSTER, ST. MICHAEL. *William Hamlett*, B., & Hannah Thomas, S. ; lic.
28 July 1784.
GLOSTER, ST. MICHAEL. *Daniel Ellis* & Sophia Ricketts ; lic. 10 August 1784.
QUEDGELEY. *Samuel Driver* & Jane Boulton 24 July 1785.
BISHOP'S CLEEVE. *John Parker* & Ann Pearce ; lic. 21 May 1788.
STONEHOUSE. *Charles Webb*, b., & Mary Caruthers, s. ; lic. 1 February 1790.
MATSON. Thomas Smith & *Sarah Greening ;* lic. 4 April 1792.
GLOSTER, ST. MICHAEL. *John Blackwell* & Elizabeth Welch ; lic. 2 July 1792.
FRAMPTON-ON-SEVERN. *Alexander Christie* & Mary Evans ; lic.
15 December 1793.
FRAMPTON-ON-SEVERN. *John King* & Mary Collins ; lic. 10 March 1796.
STONEHOUSE. *Samuel Niblett* & Anne Perkis, s. 28 March 1799.
CAM. *Timothy Stanley* & Joanna Hurlestone, this p. ; lic. 29 April 1799.
FRAMPTON-ON-SEVERN. *Joseph Denton* & Mary Carter ; lic. 8 July 1799.
STANDISH. *John Little* & Mary Anne Caruthers ; lic. 9 November 1806.
CHARLTON KINGS. *John Loveday* & Eliz. Greenwood ; lic.* 12 November 1807.
CAM. *William Webb* & Elizabeth Minett, this p. 16 October 1810.
DURSLEY. *John Jones*, b., & Mary Hill, s. 3 December 1810.
STONEHOUSE. *John Watts* & Mary Clissold ; lic. 22 August 1811.

(To be continued.)

---

* In "Glocester Journal": Mr. John Loveday of Oakham [Holcomb] to Miss Greening of Charlton Kings.

Monumental Inscriptions

AT

St. Mary's Church, Reading.*

IN SOUTH TRANSEPT.

On a white marble mural tablet, representing a woman, weeping, with a palm-branch in her hand:—

In Memory of
JOHN BERKELEY MONCK, Esqre
of Coley Park
who died December 12, 1834
in his 66th year.

In a three-light window of stained glass, representing (1) a mother dedicating her child in Holy Baptism; (2) a young man ministering to the sick; (3) the same giving a cup of cold water:—

In Memoriam GUL. STANLEY MONCK
Diaconi, pauperum Febre quibus eccles St Petri Leodiensis ministra-
bat, sublati A.D. Mater et familia
p.p. MDCCCXLVII, ætatis XXVI.

Below a marble mural tablet, representing a dying man, supported on a couch by a woman, with hand resting on Bible:—

In Memory of JOHN MONCK, Esqre
A descendant of the Monks of Potheridge
In Devonshire
who died the 12th of November 1809, aged 74
who was buried in Walcot
Church, Bath.

In a three-light window of stained glass, representing (1) Christ teaching; (2) the Crucifixion and Nativity; (3) the Last Supper:—

Erected by his late parishioners
& friends to perpetuate the memory
of the Revd SAMUEL WILDMAN YATES
M.A., for 25 years Vicar of this
parish. He resigned his pastorate
through bad health in October 1861
and died at Maperton House, Somerset
on the 7th day of May 1862, aged 67 years.
He was a faithful minister of Christ's
Gospel, a sincere friend & a true
gentleman. "The memory of the just
is blessed." Prov. x. 7.

* Communicated by Rev. G. P. CRAWFURD, sometime Curate in this parish, now Vicar of Bicester, Oxon—continued from p. 195.

In grateful
And affectionate remembrance
of her singular worth
This tablet
is erected to the Memory of
CHARLOTTE ANNE YATES
The daughter of JOHN PEEL, of Pastures House
In the County of Derby, Esquire
And the wife
of SAMUEL YATES, A.M.
Vicar of this parish.
In her
Whose name is here recorded
Were united in an eminent degree
Those qualities of the mind & principles of the heart
Which fitted her to adorn the Doctrine
Of God her Saviour
And by adorning to recommend it.
Among strangers
Her Kindness of manner & Affability of speech
Her uniform wish and power to please
Gave to her society a charm
And to her example an influence
Possessed by few.
While in all the Domestic relations of life
As a Wife, a Parent, a Friend
The meek & cheerful spirit
With which every duty was fulfilled
Her active sympathy with the distresses of others
Her benevolent consideration for the feelings of all
Rendered her
The Attraction, The Ornament, The Happiness
Of her Home.
After a life of Christian consistency
Which showed the Glory of God & the Good of man
To be alike her motive & her aim
She died on III day of April MDCCCXXXIX
Aged XLIV years
And was buried in the family vault
In the Cathedral Church of Worcester.

———

On a three-light window of stained glass, representing Our Lord and the emblems of the Evangelists :—
This window is dedicated to the
Mem. of WILLIAM WATLINGTON 1852.

———

Slab lying in passage of the nave (with coat of arms, worn smooth) :—
ROBERTUS BURD, M.D.
Ob^t 28 Dec^{bris} Anno $\begin{cases} \text{Dom. } 1742^{do} \\ \text{Æt. } 56^{to}. \end{cases}$
ELIZ. uxor. prædicti ROB^{ti} BURD
Ob. 31 Julii Anno $\begin{cases} \text{Dom. } 1748^{ro} \\ \text{Æt. } 59^{no}. \end{cases}$

On slab lying westwards of the last :—

> Here lyeth the Body of M^r
> JOHN FELLOW, late of London
> Merchant, who was born in this
> Parish and departed this life the
> 7th Day of September 1723 in
> the [84 ?] year of his age.

The following inscriptions are from tablets removed to the West Porch at the time of the restoration of the Church in 186– :—

On an oval tablet of white marble set in a border of green marble (with coat of arms) :—

> Sacred to the Memory of
> ELIZABETH
> the beloved & most affectionate Wife of
> HENRY ANNESLEY WOODHAM, Esquire
> Doctor of Laws, sometime Fellow
> of Jesus College, Cambridge
> & Daughter of CHARLES HUMFREY, Esquire
> of St. Andrew's Close in that Town.
> In full possession of all the most valued, & leaving a
> perfect sweetness of memory behind, she departed
> this life at Cambridge on the morning of
> Sunday the 12th of January 1851 &
> was buried in the vault belonging
> to her husband in the Cemetery
> of this Borough.

Round the border is inscribed :—Also in loving Memory of HENRY ANNESLEY WOODHAM, who died on the 16th of March 1875 at Cambridge, where he was buried. These words are inscribed by his sole surviving sister.

On a white marble urn set in slate :—

> Sacred to the Memory of
> PENELOPE READE
> who died May 5th, 1825
> Aged 17.

On a white marble tablet :—

> Sacred
> To The Memory Of
> JOHN SHERWOOD, Esqr
> of this parish
> Who died January 14th, 1831
> aged 53 years
> But whose remains are deposited
> In the family vault, in Purley Churchyard.

On a white marble tablet :—

> Sacred
> To The Memory of
> MARTHA OLIVER
> ob^t Jan^ry 14, 1820.
> She lived highly respected and with pious resignation
> Died deeply lamented by all who knew her.

On a white marble urn :—

To the Memory of
CHRISTIANA the wife of THOS. JESSE, Esqre
of Castle Hill House, in this parish
who died Feb^{ry} xxvth, A.D. MDCCCXXXI, Aged LXXV.
" In Life universally respected, in Death as sincerely lamented."
Also of THOMAS JESSE, Esqre
who died April VIIth, A.D. MDCCCXLVII, aged LXXXIV.
" Blessed are the dead which die in the Lord."

On a white marble tablet, set in grey marble, surmounted by an urn inscribed
VIMIERA, with sword and palm-branch crossed and a chaplet :—

To The Memory of
Lieut.-Col. CHARLES TAYLOR of the 20th Reg^t Light Dragoons
Who fell in the moment of Victory at the Battle of Vimiera
having obtained the love of his friends by his amiable qualities
The esteem of the British Army
and even the Admiration of the Enemy
by his Military Skill and Intrepidity.
This tablet is erected
to testify the Attachment of his native Town
and the Gratitude of his Country.

Beneath is coat of arms.

On a white marble tablet :—

In a Vault
Beneath this marble slab
Are deposited the remains of
JANE KETURAH HARRISON
aged 65
who died on the 26th day of January 1837
and
who was the second daughter of the
Reverend JOHN HARRISON
formerly
Rector of Bighton near Alresford, Hants.

On a white marble tablet surmounted by an urn :—

Sacred to the Memory
of Mr RICHARD SOWDON, of the Royal Navy
1 Son of THOMAS SOWDON, Esqr, Mayor of this Borough
Who fell at the early age of 21 in the ever memorable battle of Algiers
On board H.M.S. Leander August 27th, 1816
In the noble cause of releasing his fellow creatures from captivity.
His remains were consigned to the Bay of Algiers.
This gallant, enterprising, and courageous young Officer was selected
By his commander to execute a most important office
While the ship was in a perilous state of danger, and performed it
In a Manner which excited the utmost admiration
But had scarcely returned to receive the thanks of Captain Chetham
When he was mortally wounded by a cannon-shot, and was
The last victim to the ferocious enemy.

In his death he displayed as much patience, fortitude & resignation
As he evinced courage & bravery during the desperate conflict
And his country has to mourn the premature loss of one
Whose public and private endowments would doubtless
Have rendered him one of its greatest ornaments.
" For I will not trust in my bow, it is not my sword that shall
help me, But it is Thou that savest us from our enemies, O Lord
My Strength and My Redeemer.   Ps. xiv. 7, 8.
Beneath naval emblems, anchor, cannon, etc.

On a white marble tablet set in slate :—
M. S.
JOANNIS TAYLOR, M.D.
Qui in hoc oppido plusquam L annos vixit
Ob summam medicæ artis peritiam
Nemini non notus ;
Ob singularem O animi candorem
Urbanam morum simplicitatem, facilem colloquii suavitatem
Nemini non dilectus
Famam meresi quam appetere maluit :
Leni ergo lapsu ad extremam senectutem devenit :
Mentem, doctrinâ et literis
Græcis præcipue et Latinis, eximie adornatam
Ac sacrorum librorum studio diligenter excultam
Sonam ac integram usque ad LXXXIV^m annum servarit ;
Et e placidâ tandem vitâ placidé decessit
Spe fretus melioris et diuternæ.
Nat. A.D. MDCCXLI.   Ob. A.D. MDCCCXXV.

On a white marble tablet set in slate :—
Sacred to the Memory of
SARAH NOYES
and
ANN NOYES
the daughters & only children
of THOMAS BUCKERIDGE NOYES, Esquire
and SARAH his wife (formerly SARAH HUCKS)
who both died unmarried
ANN NOYES on the 9th of December 1841
in the 78th year of her age ;
and SARAH NOYES on the 19th of April 1842
in the 79th year of her age.

On a grey marble oval tablet :—
In the Church-yard
of this parish are interred the bodies
of JOHN & LYDIA MOORE
late of Wingham in the County of Kent.
They lived respected and died lamented
by all who knew them.
This tablet to their
Memory is erected by their only Son
in grateful remembrance of their
amiable qualities of Father, Mother,
and Friend.

On a white marble tablet set in slate :—
Sacred
to the Memory of
WILLIAM LYNE, Esqre
who died Novr 18th, 1799
Aged 79 years.
Also
MARY LYNE
Wife of the above
Died Augst 29th, 1803
Aged 78 years.
Their remains are deposited in a vault
In this Church on the south side.

(*To be continued.*)

Reviews.

*Paul Bush, the Last Rector of Edington and First Bishop of Bristol,*1490—1558. By ARTHUR SCHOMBERG. 1903. Devizes: "Gazette" Office.

THIS is a little *brochure* which will be very acceptable to Wiltshire men. Paul Bush was born in 1490, and his parents being fairly placed he aspired to studying at the Oxford house of the Bonhommes near the site of Wadham College. He soon acquired a position, taking his Bachelor's degree in 1518, at which time he was numbered among the celebrated poets of Oxford. In 1539 he was Canon Residentiary of Sarum and Chaplain to Henry VIII., and died in 1553, having been consecrated to the See of Bristol in 1542.

This little work gives his portrait, which now hangs in the Bishop's Palace at Bristol. By a lengthy deed (which is given in full) he surrenders Edington Monastery ; and his will, September 1558, is also given. His monument is shewn from a tracing of Bush's monument under a canopy of stone, but little can now be deciphered. In the sanctuary his arms were impaled with those of the See, and in the vestry can be seen an engraving of them.

The work is nicely got up, stitched in a coloured wrapper, and making 28 pp., and forms a neat monument to a worthy man and a devout Christian. Mr. Schomberg has done his best to immortalize the former history of one of our earliest bishops.

The Journal of the Ex Libris Society. Vol. XIII., Parts 3, 4, 5, and 6, for March, April, May, and June 1903. London : A. and C. Black, Soho Square, W.

THESE four Parts range as fair examples of the Work as it goes along. As frontispiece to the March Number is the plate of Mr. Arnold Greig, and as a separate plate it has that of Captain G. C. Swinton, March Pursuivant. Besides these are four legal bookplates, five designed by Mr. G. H. McCall—the one of Hermann Grünebaum being very artistic, a very neat sketch for Willesden Green Public Library, besides the arms chosen for the Grammar School, Tavistock. The whole forms a very good number.

The April Part has for frontispiece a very good library plate, engraved for W. A. Balaus by Martin Tyroff about 1760, and a plate by Vinycomb for Mr. Drew Appleby, done in that artist's delicate touch with scroll side ornamentation, and in the centre the beautiful spire of St. Nicholas Church, Belfast. There are two plates shewn by Mr. Graham Johnston, another giving the entrance to Gadshill of Dickens notoriety, with Pickwick fishing in pond, and one of Mr. Leonard Courtney shewing his house in Cheyne Walk, Old Chelsea, and also that of Mr. George Cave, giving a perspective view of his house. The plate designed by Mr. French for Mr. and Mrs. Burnham is well worthy of being shewn, the landscape with the mill and the library in front being very original ; another by Mr. French is for the Worcester Art Museum.

The May Part gives us three plates by Bruno Héroux, remarkably well done and original, the one shewing St. Peter's at Rome in the distance being very effective. Eight legal bookplates are a good accompaniment to the list of legal bookplates compiled by S. A. Grundy-Newman, which has been spread over the four Parts.

The Part for June has the bookplate of the Colquhoun Club, a dining club in connection with the Royal Society of Literature. It was designed by Philip H. Newman, and is well worth keeping as a sample of modern designing. There are four plates given of the Boston Public Library, three with portraits, viz.: John Adams, George Ticknor, and Longfellow; also the library plate of the King's Own Borderers, and that of the Taunton Castle Library. The plate of the Plymouth Proprietary Library is also shewn. The rough list of legal bookplates is still carried on, accompanied by four plates. These all combined form another good Part.

Fenland Notes and Queries. Vol. V., Part 57. April 1903. Peterborough : George C. Caster, Market Place.

WE have in the first place to wish the Reverend Editor a perfect recovery from his late illness, which had kept him away from his parish up to April last. The contents of the present Number are as usual interesting, one giving an account of the skating at Whittlesey Mere in 1845-6 being very amusing. There is a short account of Bishop Marsh being mobbed at Peterborough for taking the King's side against Queen Caroline. He prepared himself for the worst, for he was at the time represented as dressed in his sister-in-law's skirts, and he meant to beat a retreat into Hunts by means of a boat from the back of the palace. Feeling also ran high in London against him some years after. Mr. W. E. Foster gives a list of the Vicars of Moulton, Lincolnshire, from 1236 up to 1899, and there is also a list of the sons and daughters of inhabitants given in an inquisition made in Moulton. Although dates are not given, mention is made that "John Leland the antiquary had a brother John," who took care of him in his lunacy. This is corroborated by a Mr. William Cole, who dates from Milton July 8, 1772.

The Virginia Magazine of History and Biography. No. 4, Vol. X. April 1903. Virginia Historical Society, Richmond, U.S.A.

As usual local history forms the main articles of interest in this magazine, and for the present generation it must form most pleasing reading, as among other measures the "Two Penny Act" brought in by the clergy was entirely defeated, and strained the bond between "the King and the colonists, which was but the prelude to the combat that snapped the bond asunder."

John Brown's correspondence is still continued, although he is in prison and daily expecting the gallows, which, he says, appears "in more glorious and resplendent light than that which surrounds the throne of a king." As an uneducated man he has all the rhapsody of a fanatic, as he wished to say to his executors, " I am immortal ;" and so, we suppose, he died with the same conceit, for his last letter given is just before he expected execution. His case was like many other men before him—criminal for the sake of notoriety. The Part contains some excellent genealogical notices of the four families of John Minor and that of the Herndon family. It concludes with an ample Index, together with the Title to Vol. X. and Proceedings at the Annual Meeting in January 1903.

⁎ *Books for Review and Notices of Forthcoming Works should be addressed to Messrs. Mitchell and Hughes at the Publishing Office, 140 Wardour Street, London, W.*

𝔐onumental 𝔦nscriptions

IN THE

Church of St. Giles=in=the=Fields.*

Arms, at the top: *Argent, a fesse and in chief three lozenges sable,* ASTON.
Crest: *A bull's head couped or, mane sable, horns per fesse of the first and last;* helmet and mantling. Below the inscription these three shields: I. *Gules, a bend between three martlets or,* SLANEY ; impaling ASTON. II. *Gules, a chevron between three estoiles or,* CHITWIN ; impaling ASTON. III. *Argent, on a chevron azure between three roses gules, slipped and leaved vert, as many fleurs-de-lis or,* COPE ; impaling ASTON.

In hope of Resurrection to eternal life here resteth | The body of D. KATHERINE COPE, daughter to Sʳ ED- | WARD ASTON of Tixhall in the county of Stafford | Knᵗ. She was wife first to STEPHEN SLANY of London | Esq., To whome she bare one daughter only. Next to | Sʳ WILLIAM CHITWIN of Ingstree in the county of Staf- | ford, Knᵗ, and lastly to Sʳ EDWARD COPE of Cannons- | Ashby in the county of Northampton, Knᵗ, a virtuous | matron full of dayes abounding with all yᵉ emenent | graces of Charity, Piety, Religion, constancy & patience. | She departed this life Jan. XV in the yeare | of Redemption MDCXLVI, aged | LXXX.

The MS. says, "On the south side in ye chancell a small monument." The "New View" calls it "a plain black and white marble monument," and gives the inscription with a few variations : thus, "near" before "here resteth," Dame for D, and Knight instead of Knt. As the monument is gone we have no means of deciding which is correct.

The "New View" says of the next monument that it is on the south side of the chancel, westward from the Stanhope monument, being a handsome white marble monument adorned with cherubims, cornucopia, etc., and the copy of the inscription varies in some minor points.

"A monument hard by the former" (Arms: *Or, a lion rampant double-queued vert;* impaling *Argent, a fret gules*) :—To the liveing memory of CHRISTOPHER DUDLEY | of Yeanwith in Westmerland was this monument by | his sorrowfull wife for her deare husband here | erected.

> A Dudley lodgeth Here, peace Idle Fame
> It's Epitaph enough to have that name
> A Dudley too who in the basest time
> When to be just and loyall was a crime
> Was both : 'gainst Rebells bravely stood
> Unshaken and Undaunted with a flood
> Of Tyranny. Now his Tombes sole intent
> Shews he deserved But needs no monument
> When Rebells dye a tombe some life may give,
> He actuates the marble, makes it live.
>
> Shrines may portray our features on a wall
> But goodness crowns them ; that is all in all.
> Statues present lives, Families, and dayes.
> This shrine was rear'd by her whose love was such
> Her charge in his concerne was nere toe much
> So deare is nuptiall Zeale Though i'th' outward part
> Turne dust It holds impression in the heart.

---

* Communicated by ARTHUR F. G. LEVESON GOWER, Esq., assisted by ARTHUR J. JEWERS—continued from p. 211.

" On his gravestone [arms coloured in the MS.] under yᵉ Tombe are these arms
& verses " (Arms : *Or, a lion rampant double-queued*) :—Here lyeth yᵉ body of
CHRISTOPHER DUDLEY of Yenworth | in the county of Westmereland, Esq., who
dyed in yᵉ | Yeare of our Lord 1660, Septemb. 9ᵗʰ.

Upon CHRISTOPHER DUDLEY, Esq., obiit | Anno Domini 1660, Septemb. 9ᵗʰ :—

> Here lyes the body of a loyall one
> Who was a Friend to all a foe to none.
> Firme in affection in his actions just
> Which survive marble from a chest of Dust
> None in his spousall offices more deare
> Nor at his death stor'd with more christian feare
> Thus from the north he to this city came
> Leaving the world with a precious name.
> The King's approach gave spiritt to his wings
> And from that flight unto the King of Kings.

" This atchievement of arms hangs hard by the Tomb on the same south wall "
(tricked and coloured in the MS.) :—*Dexter, Quarterly of twelve:* 1, *Or, a lion
rampant double-queued vert ;* 2, *Gules, a cinquefoil ermine ;* 3, *Or, two lions passant
azure ;* 4, *Argent, a cross fleury azure ;* 5, *Per cross or and gules within a bordure
vair ;* 6, *Or, a cross sable ;* 7, *Barry of six or and azure, on a canton gules a cross
fleury argent ;* 8, *Or, a maunche gules ;* 9, *Sable, a bend fleury counter-fleury or ;*
10, *Vert, three lions rampant argent, crowned, collared, and chained or ;* 11, *Gules, a
fesse argent between three cushions of the last, tasselled or ;* 12, *Sable, a chevron between
three leopards' faces or ;* impaling, *Argent, a fret gules.*

" This atchievement of arms remains hard by yᵉ former," on a lozenge. The
Dexter, Quarterly of eight, arranged thus: One, one, two, two, one, one :—1, *Gules,
a chevron vair, the badge of a Baronet,* KNIVETON ; 2, *Ermine, on a chief indented
gules, three coronets or ;* 3, *Gules, a fesse and bordure ermine ;* 4, *Argent, a fesse
between six annulets gules ;* 5, *Gules, a lion rampant between three cross-crosslets
fitchée or ;* 6, *Paly of six, or and azure, a fesse ermine ;* 7, *Chequy or and azure, a
fesse gules, fretty or ;* 8, *as* 1; impaling, *Quarterly of sixteen,* viz.: 1, *Or, a lion rampant
double-queued vert ;* 2, *Gules, a cinquefoil ermine ;* 3, *Or, two lions passant azure ;*
4, *Argent, a cross fleury azure ;* 5, *Barry of six argent and azure, in chief three
torteaux ;* 6, *Or, a maunche gules ;* 7, *Barry of ten argent and azure, an orle of
martlets gules ;* 8, *Vair, or and gules ;* 9, *Gules, three lions rampant or ;* 10, *Azure,
three garbs or ;* 11, *Gules, a lion rampant or within a bordure engrailed of the second ;*
12, *Gules, a fesse between six cross-crosslets or ;* 13, *Chequy or and azure, a chevron
ermine ;* 14, *Gules, a chevron between ten crosses pattée argent ;* 15, *Gules, a lion
passant-guardant, crowned or ;* 16, *Or, a fesse between two chevronels sable.* This is
KNIVETON, impaling the well-known coat and quarterings of DUDLEY.

————

" A faire monument on the same south wall." Arms: *Quarterly of eighteen,*
viz. : 1, *Per cross ermine and gules ;* 2, *Azure, three lions passant or ;* 3, ... *a
bend between six cross-crosslets* . . . . ; 4, ... *a cross fleury* . . . . ; 5, *Argent, a
cross fleury azure ;* 6, *(Argent) three saltires couped (sable) ;* 7, *Azure, a fesse wavy
between three doves, each with a cross pattée fitchée in its beak, all or ;* 8, *(Argent) a
chief vair or and gules, over all a bend sable ;* 9, *Or, an eagle displayed azure ;*
10, *Ermine, on a bordure gules ten horse-shoes or ;* 11, *Gules, a bend engrailed between
six billets argent ;* 12, *Gules, three covered cups argent ;* 13, *Azure, four martlets in
saltire or, a canton ermine ;* 14, *Per fesse, a pall ;* 15, *A fret ;* 16, *A chevron ;* 17, *A
chevron* [these four are unfinished] ; 18, *as* 1.

At the foot of the inscription are two smaller shields : one, STANHOPE, impaling
Argent, a maunche sable, HASTINGS ; the other, *Per chevron sable and argent, in
chief three mullets or, and in base as many garbs gules.*

Of this monument the "New View" only says it is "a little westward from the Cornwallis monument on the south side of the choir, a large black and white monument with 'Pilasters and entablature of the composite order.' It has enrichments of seraphims, coronets, cartouches, &c.," but it does not give the inscription or arms, beyond that the latter has eighteen quarterings, which he has not room to blazon.

The inscription in the MS. is as follows :—

PHILIPE LORD STANHOPE OF SHELFORD & EARLE OF | CHESTERFIELD sonne and heire to Sr JOHN STANHOPE | K^t, by his wife, daughter & coheire of RICHARD ALLING- | TON, Esq., & JAINE his wife, sister & heire to Sr WILLIA' | CORDELL of Long Melford in the County of Suffolke | Kn^t, grandsonne and heire to Sr THOMAS STANHOPE of | Shelford com' Nott : K^t, by MARGARETT daughter and | coheire to Sr JOHN PORT of Etwall in com. Derb. K^t. | Departed this life the XII of Sept. 1656 aged LXXII | yeares, and lyeth under a black marble nere this place. | By his first wife KATHERINE (intered at Shelford) | daughter to FRANCIS LORD HASTINGS sonne of GEORGE | EARLE OF HUNTINGDON he had issue JOHN (who dyed young) | HENRY, THOMAS, EDMUND, CHARLES, FRANCIS, FAR | DINANDO, MICHAELL, PHILIPE, GEORGE, ARTHURE | SARAH and ELIZABETH, of whome MICHAELL & GEORGE | were intered in this church.

And by ANNE his second wife daughter to JOHN | PACKINGTON of Westwood in com. Wigorn, K^t, one sonne | viz. ALEXANDER.

HENRY by KATHERINE daughter and coheire to | THOMAS LORD WOTTON of Bocton in Kent had issue WOT- | TON who dyed young, PHILIPE now EARLE OF CHESTERFIELD | MARY & KATHERINE.

To the memory of his deare Father ARTHURE STANHOPE | erected this monument, which ARTHURE by ANNE his | wife, daughter to HENRY SALISBURY of Lawenney in | com. Denbigh, K^t & Barronett, & ELIZABETH daughter | to Sr JOHN VAUGHAN of Golden Grove in com. Car- | marthen, K^t, hath had issue PHILIP & HENRY intered | in this church, CHARLES & KATHERINE now liveing.

An° 1657.

" A table on ye south wall in ye chancel is this atchievement of Armes ":—

Arms, tricked : 1, *Per pale azure and gules three lions rampant argent; 2, Sable, a chevron argent between three spear-heads of the second embrued gules ; 3, Argent, three cocks gules ; 4, Gules, two bendlets, the upper or, the lower argent ; 5, Gules, five fusils conjoined in fesse or ; 6, Argent, on a cross gules five escallop-shells or ; 7, Per vale azure and sable three fleurs-de-lis or ; 8, Argent, a lion rampant sable.*

" On a gravestone in ye chancell hard by ye preceeding escotcheon."

Arms : *Per pale azure and gules three lions rampant argent,* HERBERT ; over the shield a baron's coronet.

Heic inhumatur corpus EDWARDI HERBERT Equitis | Balnei BARONUS DE CHERBURG & CASTLE-ISLAND | authoris Libri cui Titulus est De Veritate | Reddor ut Herbes | Vicessimo die Augusti Anno Dom. 1648.

" A faire monument of white marble on the south side of ye chancell."

Arms : *Per cross a bend, and in chief a crescent for difference ;* impaling, *Three bars gemells, over all a lion rampant.*

P.M.S.

Viator et si properes operæ erit sistere paulum | ut intellegas quantum pietatis depositum cippus | hic parvus habeat in quo puerpera cum prole | sua septima delitet integerrima | FRANCISCA WIDDRINGTON | THOMÆ viri desiderium | Matronarum (quantum est uspiam) | præstes in cultu numinis | Patre sata FARDINANDO D.

FAIRFAXIO, BARONE | DE CAMERON matre vero MARIA, EDMUNDI | COMITIS MUL-
GRAVII nec non Ordinis Garterii | militis è filiabus cæterum majora spirans |
Heroina postquam Illustre Genus | Innocentia morum & ingenti virtutum | cumulo
nobilitaverat Jamque æternis | vitæ ad Christi sui disciplinam institutæ | monu
mentis in arcem immortalitatis | sibi gradum fecisset mortalis esse dessiit | Ætat
suæ 36 pridie nonas Maii 1649. | Pudicitia Candore, fide, prudentia | atque religione
non minus quam sanguinæ | claræ incomparabili conjugi | THOMAS WIDDRINGTON
Eques Auratus | Dolens, mœrensque | sex liberis collactuci mantibus | Hoc marmor
debuit* | Si dolendi gratia viator adstes | nec lachrymarum quantum erat | FRAN-
CESCÆ funus exhausit | DOROTHEÆ te vocat | THOMÆ WIDDRINGTON, FRANCESQ;
sanguis | et utriusque Corculum | Cui sublimiora mundo muliebri quæri tanti |
Non formæ Decus, non Honoræ frontis apex | Denique nihil præter ætatem
deerat | at mentis sanctuarium si fas ingredi | ut ibi se jactat numen | ut fenello
lætatur pectore | quam interia parere mollis illa placere cerea tandem | ut christum
quem a cunis parturiit | virgo pareret | matrem cum Paterculo vix pollinctam
adhuc | repentino sequitur | eundem nacta Tumulum | 9 Cal. Julias A.D. 1649
Ætat suæ 12°.

"A small monument at the east end of yᵉ chancell."

Arms : *Argent, a tower triple-towered between three covered cups azure*, AMCOTTS ;
impaling, *Or, a cross vert*, HUSSEY.

Here lyeth intered the body of RHODA (widdow) the | relict of JOHN AMCOTTS
of Astrope in the county | of Lincolne, Esq., eldest daughter of THOMAS HUS- |
SEY of yᵉ same county, Knᵗ & Barronet (who left issue | RHODA Theire onely
daughter & heire). She departed this | life yᵉ 7ᵗʰ of March 1659.

> When two such fires met in one breast,
> What wonder, though she be deceas'd.
> The Feaver was enough to kill,
> But heavenly flames possest her will.

[Not in the "New View."]

"In a table at yᵉ east end of yᵉ chancell."

Arms: *Quarterly, 1 and 4, Argent, a lion rampant gules between six cross-
crosslets fitchée of the second; 2, Argent, two bars sable, and in chief three mullets of
the second pierced of the field; 3, Or, a saltire sable, in chief a mullet of the last;*
impaling, (1) *Sable, a fret argent*, HARINGTON ; (2) *Argent, three bars gules;*
(3) *Azure, fretty or, in each space a fleur-de-lis of the second ; (4) Argent, a chevron
between three billets gules.*

Nere this place lyeth intered the body of the LADYE | LUCIE FAWNT second
daughter of Sʳ JAMES HAR- | RINGTON of Ridlington in com. Suff., Knight &
Barᵗ | widow of Sʳ WILLIAM FAWNT of Foston in com. Leic. | Kᵗ, by whome she
had 3 sonns and six daughters where- | of two daughters are surviveing. She dyed
at her house in | . . . . street the 4ᵗʰ of Septemb. 1643.

"In a table on yᵉ north side of yᵉ chancell."

Arms: 1, *Sable, three mascles argent*, WHITAKER ; 2, *Argent, on a chevron
azure three garbs or ; 3, Ermine, on a chief indent sable three escallop-shells argent ;
4, Sable, a lion passant or between three pheons argent;* impaling, *Argent, a lion
rampant gules between three pheons sable*, EGERTON.

Insignia MARGARITÆ quæ stirpe paternâ | EGERTONORUM Cestrensium, maternâ
STAN- | LEIIORUM familiis nobilissimis prognatâ LAUREN- | TII WHITAKER armigeri
per annos plus viginti | uxor fidissima, amantissima, prudentissima : erga | Deum
pia, erga pauperes benigna, erga omnes humana | annos nata circiter 56 non tam

---

* The inscription from this point is omitted from the "New View."

ætate quam asthim- | nate confecta 1° Februarii 1636. Vitam cæducam langui- | dam, morbidam æternâ vegetâ salutiferâ commutavit, | et sub hoc pariete, altervin animæ corporisq3 connubium | in eoq3: beatificam Redemptoris visionem expectans | placide requiescit.

"On a gravestone in yᵉ chancell."
Arms : *Sable, three mascles argent.*
Here lyeth the Body of LAWRENCE WHITAKER | Esq., who dyed yᵉ 15ᵗʰ day of Aprill in yᵉ yeare of | our Lord 1654, Aged 76.

The two following shields of arms are on the next page of the MS. without any inscription or note :—

Arms, first shield : WHITAKER, *Quarterly of four as above;* impaling, *Per pale gules and azure a chevron engrailed or between three lions rampant argent,* HOSKINS. The second shield is : 1, *Azure, a lion rampant or a chief of the last,* DIXIE ; 2, *Argent, a saltire engrailed between four escallop-shells sable ; 3, Argent, on a cross gules five cross-crosslets or ; 4, Sable, a chevron between three mullets argent, over all the badge of a baronet;* impaling, (1) *Azure, semée-de-lis or a lion rampant of the second;* (2) *Azure, three garbs or,* EARLS OF CHESTER ; (3) *Azure, a wolf's head erased argent, langued gules,* LUPUS, EARL OF CHESTER ; (4) *Argent, a maunche sable,* HASTINGS.

The following abstract of the will of the Lawrence Whitaker, recorded above, is an interesting addition to the above memorials of his family :—

Lawrence Whitaker of Drury Lane in the parish of St. Giles-in-the-Fields, co. Midd., Esq. Will dated 20 September 1646. To be buried in the chancel of St. Giles-in-the-Fields near former wife Margaret. Now wife Dorothy, by whom up to this time he has had no children, has settled on her testator's fee farm rents, of the Rectory of St. Botolph Without, Aldgate, London ; of the manors of Walton, Cheddar, and Stowes in Somersetshire ; of the Rectory of Hockslowe, co. Lincoln, being £42 12s. 2d. per ann. and the profits, all his lands and tenements for her life. Cousin George Cox of Lambeth, Surrey, Gent., who married testator's former wife's niece Mary, and to their issue all copyhold lands in the manor of Kennington in the parish of Lambeth. The above rents, with lands in the parish of Chiswick, after wife's death to testator's two sisters Elizabeth Daynes, widow, and Rebecca Parkyn, wife of . . . . Parkyn, for their lives and then to their children ; also £1500 to each of said sisters. To . . . . wife of . . . . Allen of Gravesend, wheelwright, £10 and two tenements in Milford Lane in the parish of St. Clement Danes without the Temple Barr, London, for her life after the death of said wife Dorothy, but if they trouble said executor or sisters and are not contented then the said Allen to have nothing. Mistress Elizabeth Batch £5 for a ring. Mistress Frances Riche 40s. for a ring. Residue of estate, household goods, plate, coach-horses, etc., to wife, and she to be executrix. Overseers: Brother-in-law Sir Thomas Bedingfield, Knt., Attorney of His Maggesties Court of the Dutchie of Lancaster, and brother-in-law Master Thomas Hoskyns. £5 to the parish of Chiswick and £5 to the parish of St. Giles-in-the-Fields.

Codicil dated 13 November 1650. The brick house, outhouses, orchards, garden, etc., with two acres of ground where testator lives, to go to wife absolutely, and she to leave it by her will.

Proved 9 May 1654. (P.C.C., 44, Alchin.)

(To be continued.)

Ray of Denston, Wickhambrook, and other places in Suffolk, together with Oakes of Nowton, Rawlinson of Stowlangtoft, Heigham of Dunston, Hasted, and other families, all of the said County.*

PEDIGREE A. (See page 221.)

Robert Ray of Wickhambrook, yeoman=Margery, da. of . . . . Bigg.

John Ray, eldest son, baptized at Denston 21 February 1567-8; paid arrears of customary rents in Wickhambrook 26 October 1615; mentioned as lately deceased 12 June 1632.

Thomas Ray, baptized at Denston 6 April 1578; mentioned as under age 1598; was of Mildenhall, Suffolk, 12 June 1632, when he inherited a house there and a tenement in Stoke, Suffolk. The former he had sold by October 1644 to his nephew John Ray.=Elizabeth Houghton, married at Wickhambrook 4 December 1600 (same day as Henry Houghton married Elizabeth Ray).

Anne Ray, baptized at Wickhambrook 26 December 1593.

Mary Ray, baptized at Wickhambrook 3 August 1598.

Elizabeth Ray, baptized at Wickhambrook 18 May 1602.

Sarah Ray, baptized at Wickhambrook 12 August 1618.

John Ray, baptized at Wickhambrook 12 February 1595-6; ex'or of his uncle Matthew Ray's will 8 July 1633.
    Is this the John Ray of Aldersfield or Asfield Hall in Wickhambrook, who in his will, dated 17 October 1644, proved 16 May 1651, mentions wife Martha, Daniel Wade his brother-in-law, brother Richard Ray, John Ray his eldest son, and Thomas Ray his uncle, from whom he has lately bought a house in Mildenhall?=[Martha Owers, sister of Charles Owers of Gifford in Wickhambrook; married at Wickhambrook 10 October 1621; mentioned as having issue in her brother Charles Owers' will 4 August 1638.]

Rev. Clement Ray of Wattisfield, Suffolk, baptized at Wickhambrook 1 May 1600; inducted 14 July 1626; buried at Wattisfield 5 Nov. 1658. "Famous for Preaching and Conversation" (Wattisfield Register).

Samuel Ray, baptized at Wickhambrook 8 June 1607; a legatee of his uncle Matthew 12 June 1682.

John Ray, baptized at Wickhambrook 12 January 1594-5; died an infant.

Robert Ray, baptized at Denston 5 June 1606; devisee of uncle Matthew 1632.

Samuel Ray, baptized at Wickhambrook 4 June 1612; devisee of uncle Matthew 1632; [of Whepstead, and buried there 9 August 1670].=?Marian, da. of . . . Will dated 20 January 1699-1700, "of Whepstead," widow," proved 11 June 1701.

Daniel Ray, baptized at Wickhambrook 21 April 1616; buried there 13 February 1616-17.

Elizabeth Ray, baptized at Denston 4 May 1602.

Judith Ray, baptized at Denston 19 June 1608.

Mary Ray, baptized at Denston 1 January 1606-7.

Anne Ray, buried at Wickhambrook 18 March 1611-12.

Audrey Ray, bapt. at Wickhambrook 10 November 1614; bur. there 17 February 1629-30.

* Communicated by G. MILNER-GIBSON-CULLUM, Esq., F.S.A.—continued from p. 227.

A :

B

Samuel Ray, son of Samuel and Marian, baptized at Whepstead 18 March 1665-6; buried there 5 January 1667-8.

Elizabeth Ray, da. of Samuel and Marian, baptized at Whepstead 2 October 1649.

Mary Ray, married at Whepstead, 25 September 1695, John Fenton, called "son-in-law", in Marian Ray's will.

Marian Ray, baptized at Wickhambrook 13 April 1651; married John Isbell.

...Edgley. [From 1701 to 1728 the Registers of Wickhambrook are signed by the Rev. William Edgley, Curate.]

[From 1701=Sarah Ray, baptized at Wickhambrook 21 July 1660.

Frances Ray.

Ambrose Ray of Sudbury, Suffolk, mercer, bapt. at Denston 8 Sep. 1578; left a messuage in Wickhambrook by brother Matthew 12 June 1632, and proved his will 3 July 1633. Will dated 14 June 1652; proved 15 Nov. 1655 by relict. = Anne, da. of .... ; proved her husband's will 15 November 1655.

William Ray, left lands in Wickhambrook by father 1598; legacee of brother Matthew Ray 12 June 1632. = Joan Rowninge, married at Stradishall 28 August 1592; buried there 28 October 1628.

Charles Ray, left lands in Wickhambrook 1598 by father, and a messuage in Stansfield, Suffolk, by brother Matthew 12 June 1632.

Charles Ray the younger, devisee of his uncle Matthew 12 June 1682.

Richard Ray, baptized at Stradishall 18 Nov. 1610.

Martha Ray, baptized at Stradishall 4 March 1601-2.

Mary Ray, baptized at Stradishall 3 March 1604-5.

Anne Ray, baptized at Stradishall 28 May 1607.

Stephen Ray, baptized at Wickhambrook 11 August 1608; devisee of uncle Matthew Ray 1632; buried at Wickhambrook 20 March 1640-41.

Samuel Ray, baptized at Wickhambrook 11 July 1624.

Daniel Ray, "son of Ambrose Ray of Sudbury"; admitted to St. John's College, Cambridge, 1652, æt. 16. Evidently the Daniel Ray, M.A., of Burstall, Suffolk, whose will, dated 17 January 1677-8, was proved 9 February following by relict Elizabeth, and mentions son Daniel and daus. Elizabeth and Anne.

Nathaniel Ray, to whom his father left a messuage in Wickhambrook, "now in the occupation of Samuel Ray, mercer," 1652.

John Ray, under age 1652.

Elizabeth Ray, baptized at Wickhambrook 15 July 1606; buried there 21 July 1636.

Mary Ray, baptized at Wickhambrook 6 May 1613.

Esther Ray, baptized at Wickhambrook 1 October 1615; buried there 20 March 1636-7.

Helen Ray, baptized at Wickhambrook 21 March 1618-19.

Abigail Ray, baptized at Wickhambrook 28 August 1621.

Sarah Ray, baptized at Wickhambrook 25 August 1627.

Simon Ray, left lands in Wickhambrook by father 1598; deceased before 8 September 1680. = Sarah, du. of ....

Matthew Ray of Wickhambrook, yeoman, baptized at Denston 19 February 1580-81; buried at Wickhambrook 24 May 1633. Will dated 12 June 1632; proved 3 July 1688; mentions "Mary Raye, wife of Daniel Wade," "nieces Judith and Martha Ray and nephew Charles Ray the younger."

Henry=Elizabeth Ray, Houghton, married at Wickhambrook 4 December 1600.

Elizabeth Ray, baptized at Denston 28 December 1582; mentioned as under age 1598. She is mentioned as Elizabeth Haulkes in Matthew Ray's will 1632 (? a second marriage).

Judith Ray, baptized at Denston 1 August 1585; under age 1598; married at Wickhambrook, 5 May 1608, William Hasell.

o |

Richard Ray of Hundon, Suffolk, "single man," baptized at Cowlinge 14 February 1618-19. Will dated 17 July 1637; proved 8 November following; "no lands."

Dennis Ray, baptized at Cowlinge 7 Feb. 1621-2.

Anne Ray, baptized at Cowlinge 12 Jan. 1608-4.

Mark Balles (or Bates), mentioned in will 17 July 1637. = Judith Ray, baptized at Cowlinge 4 March 1605-6; married at Hundon 23 January 1638-4.

Richard Neave of Cavendish, Suffolk, mentioned in will 17 July 1637. = Mary Ray, baptized at Cowlinge 17 August 1608; married before 17 July 1637.

Sarah Ray, buried at Cowlinge 17 June 1622.

Margaret Ray, baptized at Cowlinge 3 June 1624.

John Ray, baptized at Cowlinge 25 March 1615; buried there 9 June 1640.

Simon Ray, baptized at Cowlinge, Suffolk, 1 November 1610; returned as son and heir to father and as of full age at a Court held 5 October 1636 (manor of Wickhambrook); returned as deceased at a Court held 25 May 1657, next heir unknown.

Philemon Ray, baptized at Cowlinge 9 December 1612; buried at Clare 4 October 1679. Will, "of Clare, Suffolk, yeoman," dated 18 September 1679; proved 16 October following.

Elizabeth ...., devisee of her husband of land called "Lankford Marsh" 1679. Will, "of Hundon, widow," dated 30 December 1702; proved 1706.

Robert Ray, baptized at Cowlinge 21 Sep. 1614; buried there 4 August 1618.

Daniel Ray, baptized at Hundon 9 August 1652; devisee of land in Cowlinge under his father's will 1679.

Samuel Ray of Clare. = Elizabeth Hart, married at Clare 24 March 1679-80.

Mary Ray, devisee of her grandmother Ray 30 December 1702, who left her "my little hanging cupboard."

Simon Ray of Hundon, Suffolk, devisee of lands in Wickhambrook under his father's will 1679. Adm'on of his goods granted to his widow 5 October 1682. = Martha Last, married at Hundon 26 February 1678-4; devisee of her mother-in-law 30 December 1702.

Samuel Ray, baptized at Clare 6 August 1681.

Daniel Ray, baptized at Clare 12 Feb. 1688-4. = ? Mary ....

John Ray, baptized at Clare 24 March 1686-7; buried there 12 May 1709.

Philemon Ray, baptized at Clare 24 March 1686-7.

Elizabeth Ray, baptized at Clare 5 December 1685.

John Ling. = Elizabeth Ray, da. of Daniel and Mary, baptized at Hundon 9 June 1730; married there 25 December 1751.

Simon Ray, baptized at Hundon 2 May 1676.

Samuel Ray, baptized at Hundon 14 April 1678.

Elizabeth Ray, baptized at Hundon 11 Feb. 1674-5.

John Argent of Hundon. = Mary Ray, da. of Daniel and Mary, baptized at Hundon 1728; married there 6 October 1748.

Daniel Ray, son of Daniel and Mary, baptized at Hundon 22 September 1738.

Mary Ray, da. of Daniel and Mary, baptized at Hundon end of March 1748.

(To be continued.)

Walmoden Countess and Baroness
of Yarmouth in the County of Norfolk

Bookplate of Amelia Sophia, Countess of Yarmouth.*

AMELIA SOPHIA DE WALMODEN, sometimes called AMELIA SOPHIA MARY ANNE, Baroness von Walmoden in Germany, wife or widow of Adam Gotlieb, Baron von Walmoden, a Hanoverian noble (by whom she had male issue), and daughter of Lieut.-Gen. von Wendt, the presumed mistress of George II. during one of his visits to Hanover (in his wife's lifetime), came to England in 1738, soon after the Queen Consort's death, and, after having been naturalized, Feb. 1740, was created, 24 March 1740, Baroness Yarmouth, co. Norfolk, and Countess of Yarmouth, for the term of her life. She died at Hanover 20 Oct. 1765, aged about 56, when the peerage became extinct. This is the last case of a British peerage conferred on a Royal favourite. She had one son, who was not acknowledged, and who was commonly called about the Court "Master Louis." The King is said to have left her £12,000.

ARMS.—*Or, three morions per pale argent and azure, banded gules.*

The Registers of Inkberrow, co. Worcester.† ‡

THE TRANSCRIPT OF YE PARISH OF INKBERROW FOR YE YEAR 1667.

[*Burials.*]

April	5	Alice ye wife of Edw. Opplebee.
May	24	Rob. Heynes of Dormston.
May	31	Margaret ye wife of John Ganderton.
June	20	John ye son of John Gower, gent.
July	4	Richard Johns.
July	4	William Chandler of Kington.
July	20	Willia' ye son of Rob. Weaver.
July	23	Edward Eaton.
July	25	Richard Merrill.
July	26	Mary ye daugh. of Tho. Lambe.
Aug.	9	Alice ye wife of Tho. Edwards.
Aug.	19	Jerome Rise.
Aug.	31	William Poole of Dormston.
Sep.	7	Mary ye daugh. of Rob. Steward.
Sep.	15	John Whoman.
Sep.	18	Ann ye wife of Tho. Laite.
Sep.	16	Margaret ye daugh. of Mr Whipham.
Oct.	2	Tho. Chandler of Kington.
Oct.	2	Richard Hunt.
Oct.	2	Ann ye daughter of Anthony Juggins.

* The illustration is taken from a bookplate in the collection of Mr. HARRY SOANE.
† From the Transcripts in "Edgar Tower," Bishop's Register.
‡ Communicated by WILLIAM BRADBROOK, M.R.C.S.—continued from p. 190.

Nov. 1   Margaret Page.
Nov. 2   Tho. ye son' of John Bradley.
Nov. 3   Shusanna ye daughter of Rob. Rise.
Nov. 4   Willia' Hunt.
Nov. 27   Elizabeth ye wife of Richard Farr.
Jan. 24   Alice ye wife of John Whoman of Dormstone.
Feb.· 2   Christopher Clifford.
Feb. 3   Margret ye daugh. of John Heming of Kington.
Feb. 6   Simon Kingly.
Feb. 17   Arthur ye son'e of Arthur Bagshaw, jun., gent.
Mar. 1   The Wid. Buggins.
Feb. 20   Ursula ye wife of Richard Perkes.
Mar. 15   John Freeman.
Mar. 15   Tho. Dance [?], sen.
Mar. 23   Alice ye daughter of Jo. Harbach.

JOHN BELLETT, } Churchwardens, *ibid.*
JOHN REYNOLDS, }

THE TRANSCRIPT OF YE PARISH OF INKBERROW AN' D'M' 1668.

[Baptisms.]

Mar. 25   Francis ye daughter of Anthony Baylis.
May 31   Issabell ye daughter of Joseph Moore of Rouslench.
June 18   Alexander ye son'e of John Wedgberry.
July   5   Joshua filius populi begotten off Ann Benett.
July   9   Sarah ye daughter of Tho. Bellett.
Aug. 2   Edward ye son of Morrice Jubick.
Aug. 2   Hester ye daughter of Thomas Ceare.
Sep. 13   Francis ye daught. of Nathaniel Hem'ing of Rous Lench.
Oct.   4   Augustine ye son'e of Edward Steevens.
Oct. 18   Willia' ye soun of Will. Hill.
Oct. 21   Ralph ye son'e of Walter Steward.
Oct. 24   Willia' ye son'e of John Steward.
Oct. 27   John ye son'e of John Shepwey.
Dec.   6   Elizabeth ye daughter of John Dowley.
Dec. 10   Mary ye daughter of Thomas Yate.
Dec. 20   Joane ye daughter of Thomas Dyson.
Dec. 26   Steephen ye son'e of Francis Mogg.
Dec. 31   Elizabeth ye daughter of Arthur Bagshaw, gent.
Jan. 17   Jane ye daughter of Will. Goore.
Feb. 3   George ye son'e of John Hunt.
Feb. 4   Jane ye daughter of Francis Freeman.
Feb. 10   Sarah ye daughter of William Figgett.
Feb. 21   Elizabeth ye daughter of Roger Tandy.
Feb. 21   Mary ye daughter of John Harbage.
Mar. 7   Francis ye daughter of Francis Hale.

Marriages.

Sep. 29   Thomas Hunt & Ann Griffin.
Nov. 2   John Bellett & Elizab. Steward.
Nov. 2   Richard Goddard & Elizab. Grasier.
Jan. 16   Willia' Edwards & Mary Smith.

[*Burials.*]

April 7 Francis Heynes of Dormstone.
April 11 Francis Figgett.
May 22 Isabell Lewes, widd., of Dormstone.
June 24 Richard Huggins.
July 1 Elizabeth ye daughter of Jarvis Camden.
July 15 Thomas Bartlett.
July 16 Margret ye daughter of Thomas Figgett.
July 19 John ye son'e of John Wilson.
Aug. 14 Elizabeth ye wife of Robert Dyson, junr
Aug. 19 Will. Keene, a servant in Dormstone.
Aug. 20 Ursula ye wife of John Blick.
Sep. 19 Mary ye wife of Robert Weaver.
Sep. 22 Will' ffarr of Kington.
Jan. 1 Anne ffarr, widd., of Dormstone.
Jan. 26 Anne Rawlins, widd.
Feb. 14 A child of John Brinton's of Kington.
Mar. 15 Ursula Pearce, widd.

WALTER STEWARD, } Church-
WIL. WALFORD,   } Wardens.

THE TRANSCRIPT OF YE PARISH OF INCKBERROWE AN' D'M' 166(9) [?].

[*Baptisms.*]

—   — Alice ye daughter of . . . .
—   — . . . . ye son'e of John Freeman.
May — Elizabeth ye daughter of Tho. . . . .
Aug. — . . . . ye daughter of Robt. . . . .
Aug. — . . . . ye daughter of George . . . .
Aug. 24 . . . . ye daughter of Will. Bartholmew.
Sep. 2 Thomas ye son'e of [? Tho.] Lamb.
Sep. 19 Mary ye daughter of John . . . . olly [?].
Sep. 26 Willia' ye son'e of Richard . . . . ard [?].
Oct. 7 Alice ye daughter of Thomas Parker.
Oct. 28 Willia' [?] ye son'e of Anthony Juggins.
Oct. 28 Mary ye daughter of Tho. Buggin.
Nov. 1 [? John] ye son'e of Christopher Robberts.
Nov. 16 Martin [?] ye son'e of Henry Jackson, Clerke.
Nov. 20 Francis ye daughter of Henry Ellins.
Dec. 9 Henry ye son' of Will. Harvey.
Dec. 9 Thomas ye son'e of Tho. Marshall of Bolts.
Dec. 19 Jane ye daughter of Rich. Hobday.
Dec. 19 Jane ye daughter of John' ffrancis.
Dec. 23 Mary ye daughter of Will. Steward.
Jan. 2 John ye son'e of John Ganderton.
Jan. 27 Joseph ye son'e of Jarvis or James Hem'ing.
Feb. 6 Joseph ye son'e of Will. Hill.
Feb. 17 Alice [?] ye daughter of Humfrey D . . . .
Feb. 18 Lawrence ye son'e of John Rainolls.
Feb. 19 Elizabeth ye daughter of John Steward.
Mar. — John ye son'e of John Bowes.
Mar. 13 Elizabeth ye daughter of Tho. [? Higgins].
Mar. 20 Margret. ye daughter of John Steevens.

Marriages.

April — .... & Joan Chare [?].
 —   — Robert Weaver ....
 —   — Thomas James & Ann [? Harbach].
 —   — John Bow .... A ....
June — Richard ffar & [? Sarah ....].
 —   — Thomas ....
 —   — Richard Shekle & Jone N ....

[*Burials.*]

April 5   Isabell ye wife of Jarvis Camden.
April 22   Elizabeth ye daughter of Mr Bagshaw.
April 25   Mary ye daughter of James Heming.
May   6   Alice ye daughter of Tho. Browne.
May   7   Willia' Webb.
May 28   A daughter of Henry Simons.
June 10   Arthur Bagshawe, gent.
June 11   Willia' Parsons.
June 19   Thomas Sabell.
July 9   Willia' ye son'e of Will. Heynes of Kington.
July 25   Alice Harrit, widd.
Aug. 4   Frances ye daughter of Rich. Glouer.
Sep. 17   John Opplebee.
Sep. 26   Thomas ye son'e of Will. Davis of Dormstone.
Sep. 27   Richard ffrancis.
Sep. 29   A son'e of Jo. Bellett of Cladsall.
Oct. 11   Thomas Ingra'.
Oct. 18   Mary ye wife of Richard Shekell.
Nov. 8   George Windle.
Nov. 11   Mary ye wife of Francis Smith.
Nov. 12   Leonard Morris.
Dec. 26   John Harvey of Egioke.
Dec. 30   Willia' Rann.
Dec. 31   Elinor Bradford.
Jan. 16   Mary ye wife of Tho. Harbach.
Jan. 18   Henry Goore.
Jan. 21   Francis Smith.
Feb. 4   The wife of Arthur Hemus.
Feb. 13   Thomas Boults.
Feb. 27   Francis Taylor of Dormstone.
Mar. 16   Peter Shouler.
Mar. 18   A daughter of James Hem'ing.
Mar. 22   Richard Hobday.

Jo. Dyson, ⎫
Ed. Huband, ⎬ Churchwardens.

(*To be continued.*)

Monumental Inscriptions

AT

St. Mary's Church, Reading.*

On a slab in the floor of the West Porch :—
Here lieth the body of MARY
RICHARDS, the wife of
RICHARD RICHARDS
of the Parish of S^t [Mary's ?],
who departed this life May
17, 1733, in the . . . . [*Four lines illegible.*]
Here also lyeth the Body of
the aforesaid RICHARD RICHARDS.
He was three times Mayor of this
Corporation And dyed January
ye 6th, 1745, Aged 74 years.

On a white marble slab :—
To the Memory of JOHN DREDGE, Esq., who was thrice Mayor
of this Corporation.   He died on the 4th of June A.D. 1771 in the 70th
Year of his age.
FRANCES his wife died the 11th of March A.D. 1761 in
the 63rd year of her age.
FRANCES daughter of the above JOHN
& FRANCES DREDGE died the 7th of Jan. A.D. 1752
aged 21 Years.
Three of their Children died in their Minority.

On a slab in the floor :—
To the Memory of
Mr ADAM SMITH . . . .
who dep . . . .

On a white marble tablet set in slate :—
In Memory of
The Revd CHARLES STURGES, Junr, M.A.
Fellow of King's College, Cambridge
And Curate of this Parish.
He died at Worthing Aug. the 26th, 1802
In the 27th year of his age
And lies buried in the Parish Church
of Broadwater, Sussex.
Near this tablet are deposited
The remains of SARAH STURGES
One of the daughters of the late
Revd CHARLES STURGES
Formerly Vicar of this parish
And sister of the above
Revd CHARLES STURGES, Junr.
She died on the 21st February 1846
Aged 78.

* Communicated by Rev. G. P. CRAWFURD, sometime Curate in this parish, now Vicar of
Bicester, Oxon—continued from p. 239,

On a white marble slab :—

Sacred
To the Memory
of the Revd CHARLES STURGES, A.M.
Formerly Fellow of King's College
Cambridge
42 years Vicar of this parish
and sometime Rector
of St. Luke's, Chelsea
who was most pious & faithful
in the discharge of all his duties.
He died April 22nd, 1805,
Aged 66 years
and was buried
in the Church of Loddington
Northamptonshire.
Near this tablet
Are deposited the remains
of PENELOPE, the wife of
The Revd CHARLES STURGES,
Aged 77.
Died July 16th, 1818.

On a white marble urn :—

Sacred to the Memory
of the
Revd WILLIAM ROMAINE, D.D.
Who died March 11th, 1826, aged 69 years.
Also
MARTHA ROMAINE
his widow
Who died Decr 31st, 1852
Aged 97 years.

IN CHURCHYARD, BEGINNING AT NORTH EAST DOOR.

On a slab close to South East door :—Sacred to the Memory of THOMAS CHILD who departed this life Oct. 31, 1830, aged 60 years, ... ELIANOR .... who departed this life .... 1841, ... of THOMAS & ELIANOR CHILD.

On adjoining slab:—Sacred to the memory of WILLIAM FRANCIS who died April 6, 18 . .

On a recumbent slab:—In memory of M^r .... COOPER .... [*Rest illegible.*]

On headstone, now recumbent :—Sacred to the Memory of JOHN WILLINGTON, Esqre, who departed this life January 16th, 1812, aged 47 years.

On headstone:—Sacred to the Memory of Mr THOS. FULKES who died 23rd Aug. 1824, aged 57 years ; also of HARIOT daughter of the above, who died 16th March 1825, aged 15 years ; also of ELIZA daughter of the above, who died March 18th, 1825, aged 4 years ; also HENRY son of the above, who died Dec. 19,

1830, aged 23 years.   On reverse: Sacred to the Memory of Mrs HARIOT FULKES who died Feb. 16th, 1822, aged 43 years ; also CHARLES FULKES, son of the above, who died Dec. 24th, 1812, aged 14 months ; also SARAH FULKES, daughter of the above, who died Feb. 26th, 1818, aged 11 weeks.
On foot-stone :—T. F., 1821.   On reverse : H. F., 1822 ; C. F., 1812.

On recumbent headstone :—Sacred to the memory of Mrs ELIZA CLISSOLD who died . . . . aged 71 years.

On recumbent headstone :—In memory of ANN BIGOT, wife of ANTHONY BIGOT, Gent., who departed this life the 16th of Feb. 1801, aged 46 years ; also died on 20th June 1809 Mr ANTHONY BIGOT, aged 42 years.

On headstone :—Sacred to the Memory of SARAH SIMONS, late of Thame Oxon, who died April 23rd, 1810, aged 56 years.   "The Lord is Just."   Also of her grandson JAS. WAY SIMONS REYNARD, who died Dec. 13th, 1827, aged 14 years ; also FRANCIS REYNARD, born at Knaresborough, York, March 16th, 1777, died at Andover Nov. 21st, 1810 ; also of CLARISSA REYNARD, relict of the said FRANCIS REYNARD, who died at Kensington . . . .   [*One line illegible.*]
On foot-stone :—S. S., 1810 ; J. R., 1827 ; F. R., 1840 ; C. R., 1845.

On recumbent headstone :—Sacred to the Memory of ANN wife of JAMES SWALLOW, who died Oct. 14, 1810, aged 66 years ; also MARY daughter of the above, who died Nov. . . 1820, aged 31 years ; also of JAMES SWALLOW, who died Nov. . . 1829, aged 87 years.

On a wooden rail :—To the Memory of LUCY COOPER, wife of W^{M} COOPER, who died Feb. 24, 1818, aged 51 years.

A recumbent tomb, surmounted by cross :—In Memoriam TIMOTHY TYRRELL, Gent., of this parish, who died April 20th, 1766, aged 73, and ELIZABETH TYRRELL his widow, who died August 2nd, 1787, aged 67 years ; also of RICHARD TYRRELL (Surgeon) his brother, who died Nov. 18th, 1787.

On tomb :—Sacred to the Memory of Mr JOHN MACE who died June 29, 1833, aged 55 years.

On tomb :—Sacred to the Memory of MARGARET BEAN (relict of the Revd PETER BEAN, late of Tottenham, Middlesex) who died 5th Sept. 1838, aged 73 years.

On tomb :—In Memory of ANN BRAIN who died 19th Dec. 1803, aged 7 years ; also SUSAN BRAIN who died 6th March 1807, aged 2 years ; SAM^L BRAIN who died 19th Jan. 1812, aged 2 years ; THOMAS BRAIN, father of the above, died 4th March 1835, aged 72 years ; ANN, relict of the above, died 29th . . . . 1845, aged 73 years ; JOSEPH their son died 19th April 1836, aged 29 years ; WILLIAM BENNETT who died Oct. 15, 1846, aged 58 years ; HARRIET BENNETT who died April 27th, 1846, aged 52 years ; MARY BURNHAM who died 10th Jan. 1825, aged 88 years.

On recumbent headstone :—Sacred to the Memory of ANNE ELIZA PENDERED who died June . . 1833, aged 44 years.

On recumbent tomb :—Sacred to the Memory of Mr THOMAS SMITH (Solicitor of this town) who died Dec. 29th, 1825, aged 42 years.   On other side : Sacred to the Memory of SARAH wife of THOMAS SMITH . . . . aged 60 years.

On recumbent bar of stone :—In Memory of Thomas son of John & Jane Shuttle, who died Oct. 12, 1825, aged 20 years ; also John Shuttle who died Jan. 26, 1827, aged 17 years ; also Francis Shuttle who died Dec. 23rd, 1839, aged 32 years.

On similar stone :—Sacred to the Memory of George Shuttle, died April 17, 1834, aged 21 years. On reverse : Sacred to the Memory of John Shuttle who died Sept. 16, 1842, aged 68 years ; also Jane wife of John Shuttle, who died Jan. 17 . . . . aged 7(7 ?) years.

On stone tomb :—Sacred to the Memory of Mary Adelaide daughter of Richard & Grace Munt, who died 19 May 184(5 ?), aged 14 years ; also in memory of Grace Munt the beloved mother of the above, who died 9 June 18 . . [*Rest illegible.*]

On recumbent stone :—Sacred to the memory of Mary wife of Richard Chipperfield, who departed this life May 6th, 1830, in the 37th year of her age. Resting in hope. On reverse : Sacred to the memory of Richard Chipperfield who died June 25th, 1831, aged 65.

On recumbent slab :—Sacred to the memory of Mrs Sarah Carver who departed this life Nov. . . 1829.

On side of stone tomb within rails :—Sacred to the memory of Colonel Robt. Blane who died Jan. 18, 1798, aged . . On west side : In memory of Mrs Margaret Blane who died Nov. 21, 1810, aged 80 years. On east side : In memory of Mrs Elizabeth Blane who died Nov. 24th, 1825, aged 81.

On recumbent stone :—Sacred to the Memory of John Treacher who departed this life Feb. 23, 1836, aged 76 years ; Sacred to the memory of Elizth wife of John Treacher, who departed this life Octr 11th, 1835, in her 71st year. On reverse : Sacred to the memory of James son of John & Elizabeth Treacher, who departed this life May 30th, 1854, aged 45 years.

On recumbent stone :—In memory of Letitia Maria Bennett who died Dec. 31st, 1830, aged 27 years ; Sacred to the memory of Mr William Bennett who died Dec. 2nd, 1835, aged 78 years. On reverse : Sacred to the memory of Mrs Sarah wife of Mr William Bennett, who died June 12, 1845, aged 63 years.

On recumbent stone :—Sacred to the memory of James Mogridge, Esqre, of Broad St. in this parish, who died Nov. 15, 1830, ætat. 43. On reverse : To the memory of Eliza Foster, relict of James Mogridge, who died Dec. 14, 1830.

On recumbent headstone :—Sacred to the memory of Bethier Bradford who departed this life Feb. 5th, 1833, aged 32 years.

On recumbent headstone :—Sacred to the memory of Francis Hamlin who died Dec. 8th, 1847, aged 40 years ; also Ann his daughter, who died Sept. 28, 1833, aged 8 months.

(*To be continued.*)

A GENEALOGICAL HISTORY

OF THE

Family of Adams of Cavan, etc.*

The Family of Magennis, Viscount Iveagh.†

The Magennises were from a very early period the territorial Lords of Clan Aodha under the O'Haugheys, Chiefs of Iveagh in the County of Down, claiming descent from the famous warrior Connall Ceanach, and ranking as the head of the Clanna Rory. Morris McLoughlin, King of Ireland (1150—68), granted, about 1160, a Charter to the Abbey of Newry, among the witnesses to which is Aodh (Hugh), the great Magennis, Chief of the Clan Aodha in O'Neach Uladh, now the Baronies of Upper and Lower Iveagh, County Down.

In 1172 Mulmurry Macmurrough, Lord of Muintir Birn, was slain by Hugh Magennis and the Clan Aodha of Uí Eathach Uladh. Muintir Birn was a part of Tyrone on the borders of Monaghan.

In 1173 Hugh Magennis and the Clan Aodha invaded and plundered the third part of Armagh, and about three months afterwards the said Hugh was slain.

In 1208 Duvinnis Magennis, Lord of Clan Aodha, was slain by the son of Donslevy O'Haughy, Chief of Iveagh. Subsequently the Magennises extended their territory and became Lords of Iveagh.

In 1314, when Edward II. sought the aid of the magnates of Ireland, he directed an especial letter to Admillis MacAnegus, "Duci Hiberniorum et Onenagh," he being then "The Magennis."

In 1349 Murtough Riaganagh Magennis was slain by his own kinsmen, or as the Annals of Clanmacnois state, by his brothers, and under the date 1348.

In 1359 Art, the son of Auliffe O'Rourke, was slain by Magennis.

In 1360 Art, son of Gillareagh Magennis, was treacherously slain by the sons of Savadge, a family who inhabited the territory now called "The Ards" in the east of the County Down.

In 1374 Senicin (Jenkin) Savadge was slain by Magennis.

In 1376 John O'Rooney, chief poet to "The Magennis," died.

In 1380 Art Magennis defeated the English and the people of Orior (part of Armagh) in a battle in which O'Hanlon, Chief of Orior, and many of the English were slain. Subsequently Edmund Mortimer, who had married the granddaughter of Edward III., came over as Lord Lieutenant of Ireland, when Magennis, who with various native chiefs had waited upon him, was treacherously taken prisoner in Mortimer's house. After this the Irish, and many of the English, became afraid to place any confidence in Mortimer, or trust themselves in his power. This Art Magennis, "sole prop of the hospitality of Ireland in his time," died in 1383 of the plague at Trim, where he was imprisoned.

In 1396 Cu-Uladh-Magennis, heir to the Lordship of Iveagh, was slain by the English.

In 1399 Murtough Magennis, son of Murtough More, Lord of Iveagh, was slain by his own tribe.

---

* Communicated by MAXWELL ADAMS, Esq., Barrister-at-Law. From a MS. by the late Rev. B. W. ADAMS, D.D.—continued from p. 218.
† Compiled from "The Annals of the IV. Masters"; John D'Alton's "Illustrations, Historical and Genealogical, of King James the Second's Army List, 1689"; Lodge's "Peerage"; Burke's "Extinct Peerage"; "Charta Abbatiæ de Newry"; Clarendon MSS., British Museum; and Ware's "Prelates of Ireland."

In 1400 Rory Magennis, the son of Art ("The Magennis"), was slain by the sons of Cu-Uladh-O'Neill, assisted by Caffar Magennis, his own brother.

In 1418 Sir John Talbot, Baron Furnival, Lord Chief Justice of Ireland, having made a foray on Iveagh, sustained a severe defeat, in which an immense number of the English were slain or taken prisoners by Hugh Magennis ("The Magennis"), assisted by Mac-j-Neill Boy, Chief of Clannaboy.

In 1420 the Earl of Ormond, Lord Deputy, waging war with the Ultonians to obtain dominion for O'Neill, reduced Magennis under submission to O'Neill and delivered up his hostages to him.

In 1422 Niall Garv O'Donnell, Lord of Tirconnell, invaded Iveagh and subjugated Magennis, who subsequently assisted him in his expedition into Connaught against the MacDonoughs.

In 1424 the Earl of Ormond, Lord Deputy, made an excursion against Magennis and demolished his castle of Lough Bricrenn (now Lough Brickland, County Down), killed the Constable of his gallowglasses, and almost the whole ward of the Castle. Soon afterwards Hugh Magennis died of the plague, and his son Rory succeeded him as " The Magennis," and was slain in 1426, in his own house, by Brian Magennis.

In 1453 Cu-Uladh, a son of Cuthbhan Magennis, heir to the Lordship of Iveagh, with Hugh Magennis and several other chiefs, fell in the battle of Ardglass, fighting for Henry Mac-j-Neill Boy, Chief of Clannaboy, against the Savadges of Ards, assisted by the English of Dublin, when the latter were victorious, the Chief of Clannaboy being taken prisoner.

In 1488 Brian Magennis ("The Magennis"), son of Art, died, and his brother Hugh was inaugurated in his place.

In 1491 Echmily, son of Hugh, son of Art Magennis, was slain in his own house in a nocturnal assault by the sons of Melaghlin, the son of Murtough, son of Owen O'Neill.

In 1493 Hugh, son of Art, son of Hugh Magennis, assisted Henry Oge O'Neill against Hugh Roe O'Donnell at the battle of Beanna-Boircha (part of the Mourne Mountains), where the latter was victorious.

In 1495 he again assisted O'Neill in invading Fermanagh, but they had to agree to Maguire's terms for peace.

In 1501 Rory McMahon, son of Brian, son of Redmond, was slain by the sons of Magennis.

In 1504 (15 August) Donnell Magennis, with several other Irish chiefs, assisted the Lord Justice (Garrett, son of Thomas, Earl of Kildare) against MacWilliam Burke of Clanricard, Turlough O'Brien, etc., at the battle of Cnoc-Tuagh (now Knockdoc, a hill near Galway), where MacWilliam Burke and his allies were defeated.

In 1520 Donnell, the son of Hugh, the son of Art Magennis ("The Magennis"), died, and his brother Phelim the Hospitable was inaugurated in his place. He also died, and Edmond Boy Magennis was styled "The Magennis."

In 1526 Glasney, the son of Hugh Magennis, Abbot of the Monks of Newry and Prior of Down and Saul, was slain by the sons of Donnell Magennis, namely Donnell Oge and his kinsmen.

In 1539 Murtough Magennis was taken prisoner by the men of Oriel after the defeat of the northern forces by Lord Leonard, the Lord Justice, at the battle of Bel-atha-hoa (now Belahoe, Barony of Farney, County Monaghan), and after some time was put to death by them at the instigation of his own tribe, who bribed them to commit the deed.

In 1550 Arthur Magennis swore fidelity to Edward VI., and was by him confirmed in the bishopric of Dromore, while Eugene (Owen) Magennis was about the same time Bishop of Derry.

In 1566 Mary, the daughter of Manus, son of Hugh Duv, son of Hugh Roe O'Donnell, Prince of Tirconnell, and wife of "The Magennis," died on 8 October. At the Parliament, which met in Dublin 26 April 1585 under Sir John Perrott, the

Lord Deputy, the Magennises were represented by Hugh, the son of Donnell Oge, the son of Donnell Duv *alias* Ciar (of the dark brown hair) Magennis.

In 1595 Hugh, son of Hugh, son of Donnell Oge Magennis, a man of his patrimony of greatest name and renown among the English and Irish of Ireland, died penitently.

In 1607 Catherine Magennis, daughter of "The Magennis," who had married Hugh O'Neill, Earl of Tyrone, left Ireland, on board a vessel from Lough Swilly, for Normandy. On the Plantation of Ulster, Bryan Oge Mac Rory Magennis of Edenticallow, County Down, having surrendered all his lordship, precinct, or circuit of Killwarlin, with all the townlands within the said territory, obtained a re-grant thereof in 1611 to hold the same henceforth free from Royal Composition. Other members of the family obtained grants of estates in the same county. Sir Arthur Magennis, Knt., also releasing to the King all his claim and right to the territory of Iveagh, had, in 1613, a grant of various and extensive townlands of his old inheritance within Iveagh, the extent of which was soon after directed to be ascertained on inquisition. He was raised to the Peerage of Ireland as Viscount Magennis of Iveagh, County Down, by a patent dated at Westminster 18 July 1623. He married Sarah, daughter of Hugh O'Neill, Earl of Tyrone, and had issue Hugh, his heir ; Evelyn, married Sir James MacSorly Boy MacDonnell, Knt., ancestor of the present Earl of Antrim ; Catherine, married Colonel Adams (*vide* p. 8) ; and another daughter, married to Bryan O'Neill of Edinduff, Carrick, ancestor of the late Viscount O'Neill. Viscount Iveagh, dying 21 May 1629, was succeeded by his son Hugh Magennis as second Viscount, who married Mary, eldest daughter of Sir John Bellew of Bellew's Town, and dying, was succeeded by his son Arthur Magennis as third Viscount, who with Daniel Magennis of Angerstown, County Meath, was attainted in 1642. At the Supreme Council in 1646 sat Arthur Magennis, Roman Catholic Bishop of Down and Connor, as one of the Spiritual Peers, while of the Commons were five of the family. Oliver Cromwell's Act of 1652 excepted from pardon for life and estate Viscount Iveagh, Sir Con Magennis, Knt., of the County of Down, and five others of the name. The declaration of Royal thanks in the Act of Settlement includes Captain Phelim Magennis and Lieutenant Bryan Magennis, of the Province of Ulster, with Lieutenant Con "Mac Gennis" of Iveagh, County Down. Lord Iveagh, dying 1683, was interred 1 May in St. Catherine's Church, Dublin (Lodge's "Peerage," vol. iv., p. 170), and was succeeded by either his brother or uncle, Bryan Magennis, as fourth Viscount, who appears in the Pension List of the Establishment for 1687-88 under the name of "Arthur, Viscount Iveagh" for a pension of £300 [see original vellum manuscript in the Library of Trinity College, Dublin, marked MS. E.I.I., dated 3 February at Whitehall, and signed by the Council in England]. Besides Colonel Lord Iveagh, the name of Magennis is commissioned on five other regiments. Lord Iveagh and his sept furnished James II. with a Regiment of Dragoons and another of Infantry. This nobleman sat in the Parliament of 1689 ; while in the Commons, Murtough Magennis of Green Castle and Eiver Magennis of Castlewellan represented the County Down, and Bernard Magennis of Bally-gorionbeg was one of the members for the Borough of Killileagh. Lord Iveagh was appointed Governor (*i.e.* Lord Lieutenant) of the County of Down, while two other members of the family were his deputy-governors.

In 1690 Lord Iveagh was Governor of Drogheda with a garrison of 1500 men. On the day succeeding the Battle of the Boyne, King William sent Brigadier de la Mellonière with a thousand horse and a party of foot to summon the town to surrender, and on their hesitation to inform the garrison that he should bring up his cannon, when they must expect no quarter. Lord Iveagh surrendered on condition that he and his garrison should be conveyed to Athlone, the nearest garrisoned town, with their baggage, leaving behind them their stores, ammunition and arms, except the officers' swords.

In June 1691 two officers of this sept were killed in Athlone, and at the battle of Aughrim 12 July 1691 was taken prisoner Lieut.-Colonel Murtough Magennis (for to that rank had a Captain of Sir Neill O'Neill's Dragoons arrived by reason of the slaughter of that gallant regiment at the Battle of the Boyne). When Galway surrendered, 26 July 1691, Lady Iveagh and her daughter, being then resident in the town, had an especial protection for themselves in the Articles of Capitulation. She had been Lady Margaret De Burgh, daughter of William, the seventh Earl of Clanricarde, and had married 1689 Viscount Iveagh. At the close of the campaign he did not accompany the Irish Army to France, but entered the Austrian Service with a choice battalion of 500 men, part of the 2000 Irish troops of King James's old army, who were landed from Cork at Hamburg in June 1692. He employed them against the Turks, by whom they were so severely handled that the remnant was drafted into other corps of the Imperial Army. The attainders of 1691 present twelve of the name of Magennis. Lord Iveagh died in 1692 without an heir, when the title became extinct.

    Lady Iveagh married secondly Colonel Thomas Butler of Kilcash, and died 19 July 1744, leaving issue three sons and five daughters.

    A Captain Murtough Magennis of Bulkeley's Brigade was wounded at Lauffield in 1747.

The Family of O'Neill.

    The family of O'Neill descend from Niall Glumdubh, Monarch of Ireland, who was killed in battle A.D. 954 against the Danes. Their title was "The O'Neill." One of them, Henry Mac Owen O'Neill, married Eleanor, eldest daughter of Thomas, seventh Earl of Kildare; their son Con More O'Neill married a daughter of Gerald, eighth Earl of Kildare, and had issue two sons, Con Baccagh O'Neill, or "The Lame," and Art Oge O'Neill, ancestor of Sir Phelim Roe O'Neill (*vide* p. 8). The elder son Con, on relinquishing the title of "The O'Neill," was in 1552 created by Henry VIII. Earl of Tyrone, with remainder to his son Matthew, created Baron of Dungannon, who was killed during his father's lifetime by his brother Shane, leaving three sons, Brian, Hugh, and Cormac. The eldest, Brian, became second Earl of Tyrone, but was soon murdered by his brother Hugh, who became in 1585 the third Earl of Tyrone, but throwing off his allegiance to England he assumed the ancient title of "The O'Neill," and engaged in a war against the English, which, for a time, was successful, gaining several victories over the armies sent against him; but after the siege of Kinsale in 1603, finding his cause hopeless, he fled to Spain. He was attainted in 1612 by James I., when his title, Earl of Tyrone, became forfeited. He died 20 July 1616 at Rome, having had issue five sons : (1) Hugh O'Neill, died s.p. in Italy. (2) Henry O'Neill, a Lieut.-General in the Spanish Army, where he was called El Conde de Tyrone. He died leaving issue, which became extinct in the male line in the second generation. (3) Shane O'Neill,* remained in Ireland. (4) Con O'Neill, fled to Spain. (5) Bryan O'Neill, hanged at Brussels in 1617 for high treason against James I.

---

* In 1895 the death occurred in Paris of the Comte O'Neill de Tyrone (as he was known in that city), who claimed to be a descendant of this Shane O'Neill, and hereditary head of the family. Although his family had long been settled in France, he kept up his interest in Ireland, and was well known to Irishmen visiting Paris. During the Franco-German War he identified himself with the Irish Ambulance.

English Inscriptions in the Cemetery, Ostend, and at Ghistelles (Belgium).*

At the Cemetery, the first "parc" on the right, behind the Superintendent's lodge, is devoted to the burials of English people, only a very few of other nationalities being interred in the same plot. The epitaphs in this plot are as follows :—

Them that sleep in Jesus | will GOD bring with him.
[Nothing else on cross at head or on ledger.]

Sacred to the Memory | of | ELIZA HELEN BETTCHER | née APPLEYARD | the beloved wife of | JULES BETTCHER, Esq. | Born at Teignmouth, county Devon | February 21ˢᵗ, 1858 | She departed this life at Ostend | September 14ᵗʰ, 1882 | Deeply regretted by her husband and child.
[She was fourth daughter of the late F. N. Appleyard.]

In Memory of | Colonel CORNELIUS BOWYER, C.B. | in the Honᵇˡᵉ E.I.C.S. | who died at Ostend | Feb. 12, 1855 | Aged 68 years.
[He retired in 1829.]

To the | Memory of | Mᵉʳ J. CAVALIER | Professor in the | Navigation School | Born at Hackney | England | 17 7ᵇᵉʳ, 1818 | Died at Ostend 6ᵗʰ 8ᵇʳᵉ, 1882 | R.I.P.

Sacred | to the Memory of | Dame ROSINA | wife of | WILLIAM DODD COPE, Esq. | deceased at Sas-Slykens | 30 Augᵗ 1882 | aged 47 years. | Sacred | to the Memory of | WILLIAM DODD COPE | deceased at Sas-Slykens 11 March | 1892, Aged 57 years | Dius id vult.

Sacred | to the Memory of | JULIA, widow of the Honᵇˡᵉ | WILLIAM LIONEL DAWSON DAMER | who died Decᵇᵉʳ 23ʳᵈ, 1877 | aged 56.
[She was youngest daughter of the late Capt. S. Hopkinson, R.N., and became the Hon. W. L. D. Damer's third wife 20 May 1856. He died 16 Feb. 1859.]

In Memory of MERCY EAGLES | née ROBINSON, widow of the | late Captain E. B. EAGLES, R.N. | who died at Ostend | 19ᵗʰ April 1870 | in her 80ᵗʰ year | Deeply lamented by her son and two daughters | R.I.P.
In Memory of | MARIA EAGLES | Daughter of the late Captⁿ E. B. EAGLES, R.N. | who departed this life Janʸ 13, 1869 | at Ostend | Deeply lamented by her mother | brother and sisters, who pay this | tribute to her many virtues | with a firm belief of meeting | hereafter in a better world.

Sacred | to the Memory of | WILLIAM DAVIS EVANS, formerly Commander in the Post Office | on the Milford and Waterford Station, and Peninsular and Oriental Steam Services | Superintendent in the Royal Mail Steam Company | their agent at Porto Grande | Also well known in the Chess World as the author of "Evans Gambit" | Died at Ostende 3ʳᵈ August 1872, aged eighty three years | and six months.

FRANCES JANE FLETCHER | died January 1ˢᵗ, 1881, Aged 44 | years. | LOUISA SYDNEY FLETCHER | died August 20ᵗʰ, 1885 | Aged 20 years.

* Communicated by CECIL T. DAVIS, Esq. Copied Whitsuntide, 1903.

To the beloved Memory | of | CHARLOTTE GATES | who departed this life | on the 14th Decber 1881 | Aged 36 years. | This stone was erected by a sorrowing mother | in memory of a devoted daughter | BARBARA HENSTBACH | aged 70 years | widow of the late JOHN GATES and mother of the above-named CHARLOTTE GATES | She departed this life on the 20th February 1882 | deeply regretted | for ever.

In Memory | of | JOHN GATES | aged 42 | died at Beauvais (France) April 6th, 1882 | Buried at Ostend | son of BARBARA and JOHN GATES | deeply regretted.

To the Memory of | EMILY SARAH | wife of | CHARLES BOWATER HARRING-TON | died 28 March 1876, aged 34 years | Also of LUCY her mother | the beloved wife of JOHN MALLESON | died 13 April 1876, aged 69 years.
Also of the above | JOHN MALLESON | died 12 May 1878, aged 81 years.
[Formerly of Wimbledon.]

Sacred | to the Memory | of | CHRISTOPHER ATWELL HARRIS | Royal Navy | died July 24, 1855 | Aged 69 years | Deeply lamented by his wife and children.

ΕΚ ΠΙΣΤΕΩΣ | Sacred | to | the Memory of | Captain ALEXANDER HAWTREY | late of H.M. IX Royal Lancers | sixth son of the late Rev. C. S. HAWTREY, M.A. | Vicar of Whiston, Monmouthshire | and of HARRIET his wife | Born Oct. x., 1819, died Feb. xi., 1857.
[He suffered for many years from long exposure on the field after the Battle of Chillianwalla.]

Sacred | to the Memory of | HANNAH RIDDLESDALE | Relict of the late Captain | S. HOPKINSON, Royal Navy | who died at Ostend | 19 September 1869 | aged 80 years.

In Memory | of | CAROLINE LAVINIA | MITCHELL | beloved wife of | ERNEST HOUSMANN | born in Launceston (Tasmania) Janry 28th, 1859 | died in Ostend May 17th, 1879 | R.I.P.

In Memory of | ARCHIBALD DOUGLAS | the beloved son of JAMES and ELLEN HUGHES | who died at Ostend June 2 | 1867 | in his fifth year | R.I.P.

To the Memory | of | Rev. SALUSBURY HUMPHREYS | died at Ostend | 13 April 1855 | Aged 48 years.
[He was eldest son of the late Admiral Sir Salusbury Humphreys (afterwards Davenport) of Bramhall Hall, Cheshire. He was of Brasenose College, Oxford, B.A. 1830, also a Licentiate in Theology of Durham 1840, and Rector of Fleet Marston in Suffolk, on his own presentation.]

Sacred | to the Memory of | CHRISTIANIA MARIA HUXLEY | who died at Ostend on the 17th October 1854 | Also of THOMAS HUXLEY, Esqre | husband of the above, who departed this life | on the 1 August 1875.

Here resteth the body of | WILLIAM MASTERMAN IRVING | Born 15th April 1853 | died 14th January 1872.
[Younger surviving son of John Irving of East India Road, London.]

Sacred | to the Memory of | GEORGE KILLICK, Esqre | who died Jany 13th, 1872 | in the 72 year of his age.
[He was of Kirby Hall, Melton Mowbray, Leicestershire.]

Sacred | to the Memory of | GEORGE LOVELL | Born at . . . ., Hampshire | died at Ostend aged 72 years.

ARTHUR DUFF MORISON | died June 10th, 1894 | Ostend.

Sacred | to the beloved memory of | JOHN MORSE | who died September 23rd, 1854 | Aged 44 years. | Also of | MARTHA | widow of the above and wife of | HENRY HALIDAY | who died January 30th, 1877 | Aged 63 years.

In Memory of | MARY ELIZA | the dearly beloved child | of JOHN and MARTHA | MORSE | who died Jany 18th, 1857 | Aged 8½ years | She lived beloved and | died deeply lamented.

Sacred | to the | Memory | of | JOSEPH NEYNOE | 5th R. Vetn Batn | who departed this life | at Ostend Nov. 6th, 1857 | Aged 71 years.

To the Memory | of | AGNES daughter of | J. T. PARES of Narborough | Leicestershire | who died August 9, 1859 | aged 34 years.

To the Memory of | MARY Widow of | JOHN T. PARES, Esq. | of | Narborough, Leicestershire | who died May 11, 1861 | Aged 64 years.
[1831, Nov. 20. At Gloucester Terrace, Regent's Park, John Tylson Pares, Esq.]

Sacred | to the Memory | of | ALEXANDER | died at Bruges 4 December 1849 | aged 2 years | VICTORIA | died at Ostend 26 April 1852 | Aged 8 years | ARTHUR WELLESLEY | died at Oudinbourg 2 January 1857 | the dearly beloved children | of | JAMES HAMMOND PARKS | and | HARRIOT DEAN PARKS | his wife.

Sacred | to the Memory | of | HENRY PARRY, Esqre | Surgeon | who was born at Belmont | in Monmouthshire | Novber 7th, 1806 | And died at Ostend on the 6th of | January 1853. | He was a generous friend to the poor.

In | Memory | of | JAMES PELLING, Esqr | who died at Ostend | December 19, 1881 | aged 68 years.

Sacred to the Memory of | JOHN THOMAS PENICHE | who died at Ostend on the 20th March 1873, aged 77 years.
Sacred to the Memory of | MARY ALICIA PRENDERGAST wife of JOHN THOMAS PENICHE | Born 6th November 1807, died at Ostend 24th March 1894, aged 86 years.

Sacred | to the Memory of | RICHD Sr AMOUR, Esqre | born at | Hammersmith 16 Jan. 1784 | died at | Ostend 9 June 1858.
[Formerly of Pimlico.]

To | the dear | Memory of | MARGARETTE BUTLER ANDERSON SCOTT | who died | at Ostend | 23 August 1896.

Sacred to the Memory of | MARGARET relict of the late H. A. SEYMOUR, Esqre | who died at Ostend 31st August 1867, aged 82 | Also of ISABELLA ANNE | eldest daughter of the above | who died at Brussells 6th of September 1867, aged 56.

Sacred | to the | Memory | of | Revd GEORGE SLOPER | Rector of West Wood-hay, Berkshire | who departed this life at Ostend, Belgium | 9th Jany 1855 in his 81st year | Universally Lamented by his numerous Friends | and Relatives. The Poor have lost a generous Benefactor | and his Widow pays this Tribute | to his many Virtues with a firm Belief | of meeting hereafter in a better World.

> Kind, courteous, upright, prompt to succour woe,
> He sleeps in death, let tears of sorrow flow.
> How sweet the exchange to him, his fetter'd soul
> Has scap'd its Prison holds, and reach'd the Heavenly Goal.

[He was of Emmanuel College, Cambridge, B.A. 1795, M.A. 1798, Vicar of West Woodhay 1798.]

To the | Memory | of | JOHN STEPHENS, Esqre | Born at Coventry | the 28th March 1782 | Died at | Ostend | 4 February 1853 | R.I.P.

Sacred | to the Memory of | MARGARET HELEN | beloved daughter of | Colonel STEPHENS | who died 7th January 1874.

In Memory of | HELEN STEVENS | who died at Ostend 4th Feb. 1869 | Aged 44 years. | This slab is placed by | her sorrowing husband, children, and sisters.

Sacred | to the Memory | of | JANE STRANACK | born at Margate 4 9^ber | 1822 | died at Ostend 2^d January | 1882.
[She was a daughter of J. Stranack of Ostend.]

In Memory of | Lt Col. HENRY C. | STREATFIELD, 87 Royal | Irish Fusileers, who | died at Ostend 25 Decr 1860 | Aged 76 years.

Beneath repose | the remains of | THOMAS SWEETLOVE | born at Ashford in Kent | died Jan. 6, 1859, aged 60 | CATHERINE SWEETLOVE | born at Charing in Kent | died December 30th, 1884, aged 91 | THOMAS SWEETLOVE | born at Ashford in Kent | died Dec. 26, 1879, aged 63 | GEORGE SWEETLOVE | born at Ashford in Kent | died Sept. 25, 1861, aged 43 | HARRIET GOLDER | born at Ashford in Kent | died March 2, 1896, aged 75 | ALFRED SWEETLOVE | born at Ashford in Kent | died Sept. 22, 1839 [? 59], aged 36 | SIMMONDS SWEETLOVE | born at Ashford in Kent | died Jan. 6, 1839 [? 59], aged 34.

Sacred | to the Memory | of | G. W. T. | who died on the | 15th April 1858 | Aged 71 years.

Sacred | to the Memory | of | Mrs REBECCA VARNEY | who died at Ostend | July 25th, 1859 | aged 74 years.

EMILY ALICE WADE | born Decr 24, 1844 | Died Feby 18, 1852 | aged 7 years | Irreparable.

ELIZABETH WALSH | Born December 21st, 1822 | Died at Ostend Jan. 15, 1863.

I.H.S. | In | memory | of | ARTHUR VASSALL WEBSTER, Esqre | who died at Ostend 5th May 1868 | Aged | 46 years.

I.H.S. | In | memory | of | GUY VASSALL WEBSTER, Esqre | who died at Ostend 14 April 1868 | Aged 36 years.

A la Mémoire | de | Dame MYRA KATHERINE MARIE WILKINSON | décédée à Ostende | . . . . de 8bre, 1866 | agée de 82 ans | et 10 mois.

In Memory of | ALICE FLETCHER | wife of HENRY WINDSOR, Esqre | Born at Clifton House, Lancashire | died at Ostend | on the 9th August 1870 | Aged 40 years.

Ici repose | Me CATHERINE WOOD | Epouse de | Mr THOMAS WOOD | Née à Sandwich, Kent | Angleterre | Décédée à Ostende | le 6 7bre, 1854 | à l'Age de | 34 ans et 6 mois | R.I.P.

A la Mémoire | de Monsieur | LOUIS DE WYNTER | époux de Madame | ADÈLE SWEETLOVE | né à Bruges | le 7 Janvier 1835 | et décédé à Ostende | le 9 Octobre 1894.

Inscriptions scattered in different parts of the cemetery. I am indebted to Mons. Ivo Wittevrongel, Meester Grafmaker, for learning their positions:—

Arms: *Gules, a lion rampant; impaling, Argent, a bend sable.* Crest: *Pelican in piety.* Motto: TRIUMPHO MORTE TAM VITA :—Sacred to the Memory | of | HARRIET WALSH PORTER ALLEN | (*née* SEMPER) | the beloved wife | of | WILLIAM ALEXANDER ALLEN, Esquire | Born in Montserrat | West Indies | & departed this life at Ostend 11th July 1878 | Deeply regretted by her Husband | Children and Friends. | Sacred to the Memory | of | WILLIAM ALEXANDER ALLEN, Esquire | Husband of the above | Born in Saint Croix (West Indies) on the 14th March 1814 | Died in Brussels 26 August 1900.

MARGARET HANRIET SOPHIE | BORTHWICK | Beloved daughter of | General and Mrs BORTHWICK | died at Ostend 30th | January 1893 | Aged 8.

In loving memory of | ADAH CATHERINE BOUCH | third daughter of JOHN THOMPSON | and MARY BOUCH | Born at Liverpool 1st September 1871 | died at Middelkerke 7th October 1886.

In Loving Memory | of | ANNA CULMER ADDIS KEENE | wife of FRITZ GABBÉ | who died January | 5th, 1897, aged | 29 years.

A Dieu gloire! amour! reconnaissance! In loving memory of | NATHANIEL WATTS GRANT-DALTON | who died at Ostend March 23rd, 1890 | Also of | MARTHA ANNA MARIE BURRILL | wife of the above | who died at Ostend September 20th, 1882 | Also in Memory of | ALICE MARY GRANT-DALTON | who died [*blank*] | And of ELOËY MARTHA GRANT-DALTON | who died [*blank*] | daughters of the above | R.I.P.
Also in Memory of | Mrs ATWELL KING *née* EDITH GRANT-DALTON, who died at Mount Lehmann | October 21st, 1892, and was buried at Vancouver, B.C., Canada | Daughter of the above.

In loving Memory of | THOMAS HENRY GRYLLS | died at Ostende December 18th, 1882 | Aged 31 years.

In loving Memory | of | Captain CHARLES HORROCKS | Born at Edinburgh June 29th, 1816 | Died at Ostend May 12th, 1885.

ARCHIBALD MACKAY.
[Written in pencil on a wooden cross.]

WILLIAM JOHN MAYNE | Born April 21st | 1846 | Died August 20th, 1902.
[Last surviving son of the late Sir Richard Mayne, K.C.B. (1796—1868), and his wife Georgiana Marianne Catherine, eldest daughter of Thomas Carvick of Wyke, Yorkshire.]

Sacred to the Memory | of ROBERT PATRICK O'HARA | of Raheen, co. Galway | Born 17th March 1836 | Died 21st Sept' 1885.

Sacred | to the Memory | of GEORGE D. H. PHILLIPS | son of Major General G. B. PHILLIPS | of the British Army | He was drowned at | Blankenberghe on the | 4th of September 1884.

In loveing memory | of ELVESTONE ALFRED DAISH | son of ALFRED and LOUISE WEBB | of Sea View, Isle of Wight | Born June 4, 1868 | accidentally drowned at | Ostende | September 27th, 1894.

[Photograph beneath, and his last letter to his mother received by her on day of his death.]

ENGLISH CHURCH.

In the English Church is one inscription on the north wall not far from the Vestry door.

Tablet on north wall:—In . loving . Memory . of | JOHN . CRANMER . CAMBRIDGE | Aged . 23 . who was . drowned | at . Ostend . Aug. 8 . 1901 . while | rescuing . a . stranger.

[In the cemetery a wooden cross is erected on his grave and on it is: JOHN C. CAMBRIDGE | Born Avg. 18 | 1877 | Drowned Avg. 8 | 1901.

He was son of E. Cambridge, Mus. Bac., of Croydon.]

GHISTELLES (GISTEL).

The following epitaphs were copied from tombs in the churchyard adjoining the Parish Church (St. Mary) of Ghistelles. The tombs are arranged along the eastern boundary wall of the churchyard, on the south side of the church :—

Sacred | to the memory of | EDWARD THOMPSON CURRY, Esq. | Her Britannic Majesty's Consul | at Ostend | Born the 8th of August 1792 | Died the 4th of January 1874 | Aged 81 years | And of CHARLOTTE his wife | daughter of Lieut. Colonel HEYLAND | She died at Ostend | the 10th of April 1844 | Aged 42 years.

Here are interred | the Remains | of | CAROLINE | spouse of JOHN FINLAISON, Esq' | Actuary of the National Debt | of England | She departed this life at Ostend on the 19th | of May A.D. 1832, aged 27 | And | here also is interred the body of | LEOPOLD THOMAS FINLAISON | their infant son | who died at Ostend the 17th day of February preceding.

> Stay Passenger, and if thy heart can feel
> For sorrow not thine own, let Pity steal
> For him who raised this stone a transient tear,
> Whose wife and infant all he loved lie here.
> God was his Guide, his Comfort and a Stay,
> When toil and care beset life's dreary way.
> The babe alas was claim'd by heaven,
> While spotless save the stain by Adam giv'n.
> So pure, so meet for mansions of the Blest,
> In these precincts may the survivor rest.

[Second daughter of the late Mr. Thomas Davis of Waltham Abbey.]

[John Finlaison (1783—1860) " was removed on 1 Jan. 1822 from the Admiralty to the Treasury, and appointed Actuary and Principal Accountant of the Check Department of the National Debt Office, the duties of which position he performed for twenty-nine years."—D. N. B.]

Sacred | to the Memory of | Colonel LANGFORD HEYLAND | many years British Consul at Ostend | He died 1st November 1829 | Aged 61 years, and his remains were at his own request interred on this spot | Also | to the Memory of | CHARLOTTE Relict | of the late Colonel HEYLAND | who died .... 1833.

On head-stone:—Sacred to the Memory of | Lᵗ Colonel LANGFORD HEYLAND | Many years | His Britannic Majesty's Consul | at Ostend | He died on the 1ˢᵗ Nov. 1829 | aged 61 years | and his remains were | at his own request interred | near this spot.

Sacred | to the Memory of THOMAS PHILLIPSON, Esq. | born in London | .. July 1759 .... [*Rest broken away.*]

Sacred | to the Memory of | GEORGE [NEVILE*], Esq. | of | Skelbrook Park | Yorkshire, Died at Ostend | 9 of March 1843 | Aged 64 years.

𝔖𝔦𝔯𝔯, 𝔖𝔢𝔯𝔰, 𝔖𝔢𝔥𝔯𝔰, 𝔖𝔢𝔢𝔯, 𝔖𝔢𝔢𝔯𝔰.†

WILLS.

WILL OF CHRISTOPHER SURR. DATED 1668. DIOCESE OF TUAM.

In the name of God, Amen. I Christopher Surr nowe one of the sheriffs of the towne of Galway doe make this my last will and testament in manner followinge ffirst bequeathinge my soule unto God Almighty that gave it & body decently to bee buried I order and dispose of my worldly substance my money and debts first accompted that my plate Juells Corne housholduffe brasse pewter and what else soever belongeth and appertaineth unto mee beeinge duely appraized by two indifferrent appraizoʳˢ the whole beinge cast into a Just sume I give and bequeath unto my beloved wife Marrian over and above the thirds thereof of right belonginge unto her the sum'e of twenty pounds sterʳ and the remainder of all my worldly substance I give and bequeath unto my son ffrancis and Daughter Elizabeth equally to bee divided betweene them wᶜʰ I desire my brother in lawe Mʳ John Barrett to take into his care and Custody & to mannage & imploy for the best advantage of my said children and to pay the same with the advantage thereout accrewinge the one moiety unto my said sonne ffrancis at the accomplishmᵗ of his age of twenty one yeres or sooner as occaceo' & discreceo' will require & the other moity thereof unto my daughter at her age of eighteene yeares or sooner if shee shall dispose of herselfe in marriage with the advice & consent of my said wife & brother And in case either of my said Children shall dye before the accomplishing the fore said p'ticulers then the share or moity of the Child soe dyeing to goe & appertaine unto the Child surviveinge and in case both dye before the accomplishemᵗ as aforesaid then the whole to bee & enure unto my said beloved wife Marrian And of this my last will & testamᵗ I nominate and appointe my said wife Marian & John Barrett Joynt executoʳˢ And my Loveinge freind Richard Walcot Overseere desireinge him to take care that this my will bee duely p'formd. In wittnes whereof I the said Christopher Surr unto this my last will & testament have hereunto sett my hand & seale the twentieth day of July Anno d'ni 1668 in the 20ᵗʰ yere of his Maᵗⁱᵉˢ reigne that now is.

CHRISTO. C. S. SURR. [*L.S.*]

P'sons p'sent when the within Christopher Surr beinge in p'fect mynd & memory yett not able to signe his name by reason of his weakenesse but signed his Marke & sealed the within as his last will & testamᵗ & published & declared the same to bee soe, John Davies, Ellinor Barrett, Rich. Walcott.

---

* See Burke's "Landed Gentry," and "Gent. Mag.," vol. xix., N.S., 558.—C. T. D.
† Communicated by H. SIRR, Esq.—continued from p. 205.

WILL OF FRANCIS SIRR, 1735. PREROGATIVE COURT, CANTERBURY.

In the name of God, Amen. I ffrancis Sirr of the Parish of S⁺ Clements Danes in the County of Middlesex Mercer being of Sound and disposing mind and memory but very weak in body do therefore make this my last Will and Testament for disposing all the worldly estate wherewith God hath blessed me in manner following In the first place I do recommend my Soul into the hands of Almighty God hoping for a pardon of all my faults by the merits of Jesus Christ my Saviour and I desire that my funeral may be without pomp requesting only a walking burial and Pall Bearers and that I may be interred in S⁺ Clements Church Yard as near my dear wife deceased as possible And as to my estate of what kind soever the same doth consist I give devise and bequeath as follows first I give and bequeath unto my niece and serv⁺ Maid Anne Sirr now living with me the sum of fifty pounds of lawfull money of Great Britain over and above the wages that I now owe her I do also give unto my nephew Roger Sirr the sum of ten pounds of like money and I do give unto my niece Catherine Sirr the sum of ten pounds of like money And after payment of my funeral expenses just debts and the above legacies I give devise and bequeath all the rest residue and remainder of my estate consisting of ready moneys stock in trade moneys out on any sort of securitys goods and chattels of any sort real or personal outstanding debts or other estate and personalitys whatsoever unto my two dear children ffrances Sirr and Joseph Sirr to be equally divided between them share and share alike To hold to them their executors and administrators for ever in equally Moieties but having been informed that M⁺ Stone of Lyons Inne who was Clerk to M⁺ Challis of the same Inne has made his addresses in the Matrimonial way unto my said daughter which intended match is entirely against my inclination therefore the bequest of one moiety of the residuum of my estate unto my said daughter ffrances Sirr is only conditional that in case my said daughter do not marry the said M⁺ Stone within four years next after my death for if she doth marry the said M⁺ Stone within that compass time then and not otherwise I do hereby revoke the above mentioned bequest of a moiety of the residuum of my estate hereby given unto my said daughter and do give and bequeath the same to my son Joseph Sirr his executors and administrators Ordering and directing my said son and his assigns to place out the said moiety or half part of my estate intended for my daughter in case she did not marry said M⁺ Stone at interest in government or other good securities and other good securities and from the produce thereof to pay my said daughter the sum of one hundred pounds yearly during her life by quarterly payments and her own receipt shall be a sufficient discharge for the same for my Will is that the said annuity shall in no wise be subject to the incumbrances or control of said M⁺ Stone in case my daughter should indiscreetly marry him And I do appoint my said daughter ffrances Sirr and son Joseph Sirr joint Executors of this my Will revoking all former Wills declaring this to be my last Will. In Witness whereof I have hereto set my hand and seal this first day of December 1735.

FRANCIS SIRR.

Signed sealed published and declared by the said Francis Sirr the testator as and for his last Will and Testament in the presence of us who have in his presence and at his request set our names as witnesses hereto, James Singer, Cha. Hore.
Proved P.C.C. 11 February 1735. (42, Derby.)

WILL OF MAJOR JOSEPH SIRR. 1800. DIOCESE OF DUBLIN.

In the name of God, Amen. I Joseph Sirr of the City of Dublin being of sound mind & body do make this my last will & testament after paying my just debts and funeral expenses which I request may be very private at a small expense I leave to my daughter Catherine Frances Minchin the interest of a house in Bride Street now in the possession of Michael Lacy Grocer and also one hundred pound due to me by note in my pockett book from Henry Charles Sirr dated Sept⁺ 1791

In consideration of Mr Minchin having paid me eighteen pounds p^r annum from the day of his marriage to my daughter being the interest of £300 which at that time I was not able to spare without receiving the Inst towards my support. Given under my hand & seal this eleventh day of March 1794.

JOSEPH SIRR.   [Seal.]

Witnesses : Eliza Minchin, Mich^l McDermott.

3 day of Decr 1799. On which day Catherine Francy Minchin the universal legatee named in this will of Joseph Sir dec^d was sworn as well to her belief of the truth of s^d will as well & faithfully to administer the goods, etc., of s^d Dec. accord^g to the contents thereof no Ex^r being named therein, before me,

JOHN LEAHY, Surrogate.

WILL OF MAJOR HENRY CHARLES SIRR. 1841. PREROGATIVE COURT, DUBLIN.

Dublin Castle, 2 May 1832. In the name of God, Amen. After paying all just debts I bequeath my effects as follows, viz.: My paintings prints minerals shells books & furniture to be sold as may be deemed most advisable to the best advantage for to pay off Alicia Orpen my beloved daughter & Catherine my dear child their fortunes as by me settled on each of their marriages Out of the amount of sale of my property as above I bequeath to my dear son Henry Chas Sirr two thousand pounds sterling and to my beloved Christian friend Doct' Chas Orpen as a token of my esteem the sum of two hundred pounds. I bequeath all my plate & residue of what my paintings minerals shells, etc., bring by sale & after paying all above demands to my dearly beloved son Joseph D'Arcy Sirr I also leave to the said Joseph D'Arcy Sirr my antiquities should it be found unnecessary to sell them to make up any demand against me my precious & cut stones I consider as part of my mineral collection. May the God of all mercies be with you all & remain with each of you and each of yours and may all your hearts be continually looking up to Our Saviour Jesus Christ who died for you & me and I do trust & hope that we will meet in that Kingdom where Christ reigneth.

HENRY CHA^s SIRR.

The hour of my departure's come,
I hear the voice that calls me home.
At last O Lord let troubles cease
And let thy servant die in peace.
The race appointed I have run,
The combats o'er, the prize is won.
And now my witness is on high
And now my records in the sky.
Not in my innocence I trust
I bow before thee in the dust
And through my Saviour's blood alone
I look for mercy at thy throne.
I leave the world without a tear
Save for the friends I held so dear.
To heal their sorrows Lord descend
And to the friendless prove a friend.
I come, I come at thy command,
I give my spirit to thy hands.
Stretch forth thy everlasting arms
And shield me in the last alarms.
The hour of my departure's come,
I hear the voice that calls me home.
Now, O my God, let troubles cease,
Now let thy servant die in peace.

H. C. S.

PUBLIC RECORD OFFICE, IRELAND.

ENTRY BOOK OF MILITARY COMMISSIONS, 1796—1806, p. 75.   RECORD TOWER
COLLECTION.

Henry Char^s Sirr, Esqre, Town Major of the Garrison of Dublin.

GEORGE R.

George the third by the Grace of God King of Great Britain France and Ireland
Defender of the Faith &c. To our Trusty and well beloved Henry Charles Sirr
Esqre Greeting We do by these Presents constitute and appoint you to be Town
Major of the Garrison of Dublin in our Kingdom of Ireland in the room of Gustavus
Nicolls Esqre. You are therefore carefully and diligently to discharge the Duty of
Town Major by doing and performing all and all manner of things thereunto
belonging. And you are to observe and follow such Orders and Directions from
time to time as you shall receive from us, our Chief Governor or Governors of our
said Kingdom for the Time being, or any other your superior Officer, according to
the rules and Discipline of War. Given at our Court at St James's the tenth day
of November 1798, In the Thirty ninth Year of our Reign.

By His Majesty's Command,

PORTLAND.

LIEUTENANTS' CERTIFICATES, 1795. VOL. XIX.

ADMIRALTY OFFICE, 9th October 1795.

Gent^m

Mr William Whiteway Sirr having represented to Us that he lost his
Journals & Captains Certificates for His Majestys Ship Jason, when the Bush
Revenue Cutter was wrecked on the Coast of Ireland, of which he was Commander,
and requested they may be dispensed with, when he is examined touching his
Qualifications to be a Lieutenant in the Royal Navy ; We do hereby desire And
direct You to cause his request to be complied with, upon his making Oath that he
Actually did keep Journals of the said Ships proceedings, And that they, with his
Captains Certificates, were lost as he hath set forth. We are

Your affectionate Friends,

ARDEN.
CHA^s MIDDLETON.
H. SEYMOUR.
NAVY BOARD.   J. GAMBIER.

I Wm Whiteway Sirr of His Majestys Ship Amyhurst [Amethyst] Do hereby
voluntary make Oath & swear that being Commander of His Majestys Revenue
Cutter Bush on the 18th of January in the Year of our Lord one Thousand Seven
Hundred & Eighty Six was Cast away in Balinakill on the Coast of Ireland at which
time he the said Wm Whiteway Sirr Lost all his Journals of his Servitude in His
Majestys Ship Jason, James Pigott Commander, at the time he was Cast away in
Balinakill Bay.

W^M WHITEWAY SIRR.

Sworn before me this — Day of October 1795.

THOMAS THINNE [?], Mayor.

Middlesex to wit.

I William Whitney [*sic*] Sirr do hereby make oath that he was born on the 10 day of May in the year of our Lord 1766 in the Parrish of Werburgh in the Citty of Dublin in the Kingdom of Ireland as he had been informed and Verily Believes.

W^M WHITEWAY SIRR.

Sworn before me at the Office, Bow street,
the 7 of Oct. 1795.

[Signature illegible.]

SHIPS.	ENTRY.	QUALITY.	DISCHARGE.	TIME.			
				Y.	M.	W.	D.
Jason	31 March 1779	Capt^s Sc^r	18 April 1780	1	—	2	5
D^o	19 April 1780	Able	28 February 1782	1	11	1	1
D^o	1 March 1782	Mid.	14 Decem^r 1782	—	10	1	2
D^o	15 Decem^r 1782	Able	30 July 1783	—	8	—	4
Tremendous	6 Decem^r 1793	Able	13 January 1794	—	1	1	4
D^o	14 January 1794	Mas^{rs} Mte	30 June 1795 last Book	1	6	—	—
Amethyst No Books	20 July 1795	Ma^s Mte	30 Septem^r 1795 last Book	—	2	2	3
				6	1	1	5

NAVY OFFICE. 5th October 1795.

These are to Certify, that Mr William Whiteway Sirr is borne on the Books of His Majesty's Ships above-mentioned, the Time, and in the Qualities there expressed, being Six years one month one week and five days.

P. HYATT.

For a Lieutenant.

DUBLIN CORPORATION JOURNALS, ETC.

MAJOR HENRY CHARLES SIRR.

Extract from Commons Journal (No. 186), pp. 92 and 236 :—

> *Michaelmas Assembly*, 1798.—A Member moved the following Resolution : " Resolved that the thanks of the Sheriffs & Commons be returned to Charles Henry Sirr, Esq., for his exertions in bringing to justice a number of traitors and United Irishmen." Question & allowed.

> *Michaelmas Assembly*, 1803.—Petition of certain of the Commons for thanks to Major Sirr and order thereon agreeing, and that same be engrossed and presented by the Town Clerks. Read and allowed.

Extract from Assembly Book (No. 182), pp. 136, 327, 342 :—

Michaelmas Assembly, 1803.—Right Hon. Henry Hutton, Lord Mayor. Petition of certain of the Commons praying to confer some mark of approbation on Major Cha' Sirr, *Town Major,* for his eminent and essential services to his Majesty, the Constitution and this City: whereupon it was ordered that the thanks of this Corporation be given to Major Cha' Sirr for the above reasons in the said petition ; that same be engrossed and presented by the Town Clerks.

> *Easter Assembly*, 1807.—John Claudius Beresford and Henry Charles Sirr of Dawson Street, merchant, elected Sheriffs for ensuing year commencing Michaelmas next.*

> *Post Assembly, 8th May* 1807.—Henry Charles Sirr, Esq., praying to be excused from serving the office of Sheriff: whereupon it was ordered that the within named Henry Charles Sirr be excused from serving the office of Sheriff for the ensuing year commencing, etc., he having paid a fine of three hundred guineas.

CASTLEREAGH CORRESPONDENCE.

(Vol. i., p. 423.)

Lord Castlereagh (Chief Secretary of Ireland) to Mr. Wickham (Under Secretary to the Duke of Portland, Prime Minister).

DUBLIN CASTLE,

Secret.]   *November* 3, 1798.

SIR, I understand from Captain Taylor that Lord Cornwallis† has been pleased to recommend an arrangement in favour of Major Sirr, highly advantageous to his interest. The services Major Sirr has rendered to the King's Government, since I have been in office, are such as to make me feel it an incumbent duty to bear testimony, in the strongest terms, to his merits.

From the want of any efficient system of police in this city, he has been constantly employed by Government, on every occasion which called for great personal exertions, discretion, & courage ; his life has frequently been exposed, particularly in the arrest of Lord Edward Fitzgerald. I can truly state that, during the most trying period of public danger, the metropolis was peculiarly indebted for its tranquility to the unceasing activity of Major Sirr, assisted by Mr Swan, who so nearly lost his life in that same struggle, which proved fatal to Mr Ryan, & in which Major Sirr was exposed to very imminent danger.

Permit me to request that you will communicate the above to the Duke of Portland, and assure his Grace that the King has not a more faithful officer than Major Sirr in his service.

I have the honour to be, etc.,

CASTLEREAGH.

---

* Major H. C. Sirr was a Member of the Guild of Merchants, or Holy Trinity Guild, who elected him their representative in the Corporation of Dublin in 1794.
    † Lord Lieutenant.

COMMISSION BOOK, IRISH RECORD OFFICE.

WHITEHALL,

29 *November* 1798.

His Excellency The Lord Lieutenant.

MY LORD,

Having laid before the King your Excellency's letter of the 10th Instant enclosing a list of successions, which you propose for the army in Ireland, I am Commanded to acquaint your Excellency that his Majesty is graciously pleased to approve of all of them except as to the appointment of Town Major of Dublin, which it would be highly objectionable to have sold, but his Majesty has been pleased to say that a Lieutenant Colonelcy on the Irish Establishment or a troop of Cavalry may hereafter be sold to reimburse the present Town Major, and that Major Sirr shall be now appointed to that situation without purchase. The necessary Commissions will be immediately prepared for the Royal Signature & transmitted to your Excellency in the usual manner.

I am, etc.,

PORTLAND.

_____

The Lord Lieutenant having recommended him, Sirr lodged Three Thousand Guineas for the Commission (the pay of Town Major then being less than subsequently). Sirr was gazetted to a majority of Dragoons, and the purchase of the Town Majority effected by the sale of that Commission. The Town Majority was unexpectedly presented without purchase in acknowledgment of great and voluntary services beyond mere duty, and the office created into a very active and confidential one.

_____

Monumental Inscriptions
IN
Wandsworth Parish Church.*

A nameless brass (*temp.* Henry V.) of a Serjeant-at-Arms, with mace instead of dagger :—✠ **Hic jacet Richüs** .... [**serbiens Regis Henrici quinti post conquestum ad] arma qui obijt bicesimo sexto die Januar' anno dñi mill'io CCCCo XXo Cujus anime .... amen Pater noster.**
Now on north wall of chancel aisle, formerly on floor in front of Communion rails.

Mural, east end of south aisle. Arms : *Barry of six argent and sable, in chief two eagles displayed and the golden fleece alternating with three mill-rinds :*—In Memory of | ROBERT WILDMAN BARCHARD, | of Wandsworth, Esquire, | a deputy lieutenant for | the County of Surrey, | and one of the churchwardens | of this parish, | who died 13th January, 1848, | in the 55th year of his age. | This tablet is erected | by subscriptions from the | inhabitants of Wandsworth | as a tribute | to his public, private, | and social worth. | Virtutibus instructos et ornatos | bonos veros decimus. (Cic. *Tusc.* 5, 10.)
Robert Wildman Barchard, B., of St Mary, Lambeth, and Charlotte Barchard, S., of this parish [Wandsworth], mar.; lic. 16 Sep. 1823.
Robert Wildman Barchard, Wandsworth, January 20th [1848], 54 years, [buried by] Edwd Robt Pemberton, Vicar. [He died at East Hill.]

_____

* Communicated by CECIL T. DAVIS, Esq.

Mural, west end of north aisle :—Near this place was laid in earth | the body of EDW. BARKER, Esq., | one of the Barons of His Majesty's | Court of Exchequer, | who was born in this parish the 19ᵗʰ | day of December 1671, and departed | this life the 10ᵗʰ of June, 1759. | Reader, if you would inquire | how he lived and died, | be content with this answer : | Not without faults | by the frailty of man ; | not without repentance | by the grace of God. | He was the son of JAMES and nephew | of EDWARD by goodness to him a second | father, sons of EDWARD the elder, | all whose remains with others of the | family were deposited | in this church.

1671   Dec. 21   Edward son of James Barker, gent., bapt.
1759   June 16   Edward Barker, Esq., 86, bur.

BARKER, Edward, born at Wandsworth 19 December 1671. He was the son of James Barker and grandson of Edward Barker. He was baptized two days afterwards in Wandsworth Church. His father died next year, and was buried on 13 January 1672-3 in the Church. His grandmother (Mrs. Barker, sen.) paid the churchwardens 13s. 4d. for "her husband's and sonnes grave in the church." His grandfather was buried on 23 January in the same year, ten days after his father's burial. He had a posthumous brother, whose entry of baptism reads : " 1673. April 10, James son of Mʳ James Barker, lately deceased." His uncle Edward adopted and educated him. He was admitted to the Inner Temple in 1690. In 1729 he was made Reader, Treasurer in 1732, and he was appointed Cursitor Baron of the Exchequer on 9 May 1743. He resigned office on 19 April 1755, and four years after he died on 10 June, and was buried on 16 June in the family vault in Wandsworth Church. His age in the Burial Register is given as 86, but he was in his 88th year.
He married Dorothy . . . . and had several children, of whom Dorothy the eldest only grew up. Mrs. Dorothy Barker died on the 13th and was buried on the 19th April 1749, but her name does not appear on the Barker tomb.
Manning and Bray chronicle :—" His dau. Dorothy marᵈ Abraham Tucker, Esq., of Betchworth Castle in this co. on 3 Feb. 1736.* By her he had 3 daus., Dorothy, who died under 3 yrs. old. Judith, & Dorothea Maria, who on 27 Oct. 1763 marᵈ Sir Hen. Paulett Sᵗ John, Bart., & died on 5 May 1768, leaving one son. Mʳˢ Tucker died 7 May 1754, aged 48. Her husband collected all the letters wh. passed betn. them whenever they happened to be absent from each other, wh. he copied in books twice over under the title of ' The Picture of Artless Love.' One copy he gave to her father, who survived her five years, & the other he kept to read over to his dau's frequently. He died 20 Nov. 1774. Judith inherited ; she died 26 Nov. 1794, her only nephew Sir Henry Paulet Sᵗ John Mildmay, who sold Betchworth estate in 1798." (Vol. i., p. 558.)
Monumental Inscription at Dorking.

Mʳ Stephen J. Tucker, Rouge Croix, Pursuivant of Arms on December 4, 1874, exhibited " Dame Tucker's Shoe," being the dress shoe and clog of Dorothy, wife of Abraham Tucker of Betchworth Castle. (" Archæological Journal," vol. xxxii., p. 111.)

1711   Oct. 20   Dorothy daughter of Edward Barker, Esq., bapt.
17⅟₄   Feb. 24   Edward son of Mʳ Edward Barker, Esq., bapt.
1719   Nov. 19   Edward son of Edward Barker, Esqr., bapt.
1712-13   *Church Receipts.*—Receued for yᵉ Intermᵗ of an Infant of Edward
        Barker, Esqr.   00   07
1749   April 19   Dorothy Barker, bur.

BARKER FAMILY.

ARMS.—*Or, a bend between six billets sable.*

Edward Barker, buried 23 January 1672-3⊤. . . .

| James Barker, baptized 11 April 1642 ; buried 13 January 1672-3. | Anne, baptized 5 July 1643 ; buried 14 Nov. 1644.

Edward Barker, baptized 16 Sep. 1644. | James Barker, baptized 14 February 1646-7 ; buried 2 December 1652.

William Barker, baptized 14 June 1649. | John Barker, baptized 27 June 1650 ; buried 4 November 1650.

Joseph Barker, baptized 7 Oct. 1651.

John Barker, baptized 30 Nov. 1652. |

A

---

* When this marriage took place Edward Barker is described as of East Betchworth.

A |

Edward Barker (Judge), born 19 December 1671 ;=Dorothy . . . ., died 13   James Barker, bap-
baptized 21 December 1671 ; died 10 June 1759; | April 1749 ; buried   tized 10 April 1673.
buried 16 June 1759. | 19 April 1749.

Dorothy, baptized 20=Abraham Tucker,   Edward Bar-   Eliza-   Edward Bar-   Benjamin
October 1711 ; mar- | born 2 September ker, baptized beth.   ker, baptized Barker.
ried 3 Feb. 1736-7 ; | 1705 ; died 20   24 February   19 November   —
died 7 May 1754. | November 1774.   1713-14.   1719.   A dau.

Dorothy, died   Judith, died 26 Novem-   Dorothea Maria, married 27 October=Sir Henry Paulet
3 years old.   ber 1794, unmarried.   1763 ; died 5 May 1768. | St. John, Bart.,
                                                                          | died 1784.

Sir Henry Paulet St. John Mildmay, Bart.,=Jane, eldest dau. and coheir of Carew Mildmay,
died 11 November 1808. | married 1786 ; died 6 May 1857.

(Present possessor of title, Sir Henry Paulet St. John Mildmay, Bart., succeeded 1902.)

Ledger, north aisle :—Beneath this Stone | are deposited the Remains of | HARRIOT BARLOW, Wife of | WILLIAM BARLOW, Esq. | of this Parish, who departed | this Life, Decr 26th, 1801 | Aged 36 years.
1802 Jan. 2 Harriot Barlow, 36, bur.

Mural, west end of north aisle. Arms : *Argent, a chevron between three bears' heads couped sable, muzzled or :*—To the memory of | THOMAS BARWIS | of Wandsworth | in the county of Surry, Esquire | who died January 26th, 1815 | In the 89th year of his age.
Ledger, north aisle :—T. B. | died Jany 26th, 1815 | Aged 89 years.
1815 Feb. 2 Thomas Barwis, Wandsworth, 89, bur. P. Allwood.

"On a fair stone before the Table is this inscription in a Brass Plate" (Stowe). No trace now remains:—" Hic jacet RICHARDUS BREAME, Gen., oriundus de Comitat Suffolciæ : qui diu et fideliter infervivit Dominæ Elizabethæ, Reginæ et postea domino Jacobo Regi. Et deinde Senectute provectus et multis morbis gravatus, placidè et quiete de vita, mortali in immortalem, emigravit Anno ætatis suæ 62, et Salutis humanæ 1610, Jan. 2. RICHARDUS filius posuit pietatis ergo."
16⅔₉ Jan. 6 Rich. Breame, gent., bur.
163⅔ Jan. 1 Mrs Joane Breame, widowe [? his widow], bur.
160⅘ Feb. 4 Richard Breame, son of Richard Breame of Wasenworth [?], Surrey, Gent.
1611 Dec. 17 Thomas son of Richard Breame, gent., bur.
   In an indenture, dated 9 January 1625, is the name *inter alios* Richard Breame, son and heir of Richard Breame, deceased, parishioners of Wandsworth.

On east wall, with two busts (removed in 1900 to Peperbarow Church) :— THOMAS BRODRICK, Militis, e Richmondiâ Angliæ ad Septent' | antiqua proavorum serie traducti, qui pictate non fictâ, morum comitate | et Benevolentiâ singulari, sibi fœlix, suis charus et a quam plurimis | optimè fuit meritus, vitæ quidem si quis alius integer cœlum pro patria | agnovit . . . . et Morbi tedio fractus excessit tantium atque istub quod | caducum (aliquondo resumpturus) sub hoc sole deposuit anno consistentis | ultimo ætatis suæ 46 salutis humanæ 1641. Veré lugendus et semper | desideratus. Katherine, stirpe Nicholaiorum et S. Johannis in agro | Wiltoniense Nobili oriunda quæ convixit Uxor marito, liberis Mater | optuma ; nemo magis prudentiam civilem excoluit, nemo fœlicius charitatem | exercuit ; relicta quinetiam in mediâ ætate viduitatem ad extremam | usque senectutum (memor conjugii) affectavit. Non enim nisi exactis | a natali octies decem annis mariti in consortium (amicâ mortalitatis lege) | denno reddita spousa sed exanimis heic a'dlatus decubuit anno D'ni, 1678.

1641 Dec.   4   Sir Thomas Brodrick, Knt., bur.
1632 April   5   Margaret daughter of Sir Thomas Brodrick, Knt., bapt.
1633 Sep.   21   Willm. son of Sir Thos. Brodrick, knight, bapt.
1635 May   25   Henry son of Sir Thom. Brodrick, knt.

    Sir Thomas Brodrick of Wandsworth married Catherine daughter of Robert Nicholas, Esq., of Manningford Bruce. His eldest son was Sir Alan Brodrick, Knt., who died unmarried 25 November 1680. His brother, Sir St. John Brodrick, married Alice daughter of Sir Randal Clayton, Knt., of Thelwall, co. Chester. His second was created Viscount Midleton 15 August 1717, and is ancestor of the present Viscount Midleton.
    In the Constitution of Vestry in 1627 Sir Thomas Broderick, Knt., is one of those appointed to be Vestrymen. His name also occurs in an indenture dated 30 January 1631-2.

    Mural, west end of north aisle :—Near this place | lye the remains of | ROBERT BUCK of London, | Gent., who died November 3ᵈ, 1769, | aged 66 years. | Also of | SUSANNAH, his wife, who | died July 14, 1767 | aged 42 years. | This monument was | erected to their memory | by ELIZABETH BUCK, | their sister, | in the year | 1774.
    The following inscription to their memory is in Mount Nod :—In memory of SUSANNA | the wife of ROBERT BUCK, mercer | in King Street, Covent Garden, | and of this Parish, | who died the 17ᵗʰ of July 1767 | Aged 4[4] years. | Also of the said ROBERT BUCK, | who died the 10ᵗʰ November, | 1769, Aged 66 years.

1769 Nov. 10   Robt. Buck, bur.
1767 July 17   Susannah wife of Robert Buck, bur.

    To the Glory of God, | in loving memory of | JOHN BUCKMASTER, B.A., Oxon, | Vicar of Wandsworth, 1856—1884, | who departed this life 28th Aug., 1884, aged 64. | " I am the Resurrection and the Life ; he that | believeth in Me, though he die, yet shall he live." | Erected by his family.
    To the Glory of God, | in affectionate remembrance of | Rev. RALPH NEVILL BUCKMASTER, B.A., Oxon, | 1819—1897. | His life, the last 25 years of which were spent in this | Parish, was one of voluntary service for his Saviour. | " My flesh shall rest in hope." | Erected by his sister.

    Both memorials are placed on part of the old east wall of the Church, over the arch leading to the older monuments formerly on the east wall.

    Mural, north wall :—Sacred to the memory of | the Revᵈ ROBERT HOLT BUTCHER, LL.B. | Forty-four years vicar of this parish | rector of Chesham Bois and vicar of Chesham Wooburn | in the county of Buckingham. | He died on the 31ˢᵗ day of August 1822 | In the 79ᵗʰ year of his age. | Also of FRANCES ELIZABETH BUTCHER | Daughter of the above and ANN his wife | who died on the 19ᵗʰ of August 1830 | in the 60ᵗʰ year of her age. | And of ANN relict of | the said Revᵈ ROBERT HOLT BUTCHER | who departed this life April 25ᵗʰ, 1831 | in the 86ᵗʰ year of her age.
    Ledger, north aisle :—Revᵈ ROBERT HOLT BUTCHER | LL.B., who was 44 years | Vicar of Wandsworth | Died 31ˢᵗ day of August 1822 | Aged 79 years. | Also FRANCES ELIZABETH BUTCHER | Daughter of the above | and ANN his wife | Died the 19ᵗʰ of August 1830 | Aged 59 years. | Also of | Mʳˢ ANN BUTCHER | Relict of the above | who died April 25ᵗʰ, 1831 | in the 86ᵗʰ year of her age.

1822 Sep.   7   The Revᵈ Robert Holt Butcher, LL.B., forty-four years Vicar of this Parish, 79, bur. ; he died on the 31ˢᵗ of August; by the Rev. T. L. Strong, as by the Certificate.
1830 Aug.   27   Frances Elizabeth Butcher, Wandsworth, 59 years, bur. P. Allwood.
1831 April 30   Ann Butcher, Wandsworth, 85 years, bur. Philip Allwood.

    He was presented to the Vicarage of Wandsworth in 1778 by Mr. T. A. Ackworth, and to the Vicarage of Chesham in 1780 by the Duke of Bedford. He was also Chairman of the Bench of Magistrates of the West Half Hundred of Brixton. He graduated at Trinity College, Cambridge, in 1770.

Here lieth the body of Mʳ ROBERT CRANSTON, late | mercer of Round Court in the Strand, who died the 30ᵗʰ | of September 1751, aged 51 years.

1751 Oct.   5 Robert Cranston, 50, bur.

Mural, near Vestry door :—Near this place are deposited the remains of | Mʳ SOMERSET DRAPER, who departed | this Life, greatly lamented January 31ˢᵗ, 1756, | aged 49 years. In the year 1742 he married ELIZABETH | youngest sister to the friend of his heart, | JAMES CLUTTERBUCK, Esq., who in | grateful remembrance of his affection to her, | & of his other truly amiable qualities, | hath caused this monument to be erected to his memory.

1706 April 1 Somerset son of Mʳ Draper, bapt.
1756 Feb.   7 Somerset Draper, bur.

He was a partner of Messrs. Tonson, booksellers in the Strand.

Somerset Draper⹃Ann Thompson.

Anne.	Geffery Draper.	Somerset=Elizabeth Clutter- Draper. buck.	Jeffery Draper.	Nightingale.	Mary.

Mural, south wall. Arms : *Argent, five fusils in cross or.* Crest : *A hand proper holding a fusil or.* Motto : TRIA JUNCTA IN UNO :—In the family vault near this spot | are deposited the remains | of Vice-Admiral Sir WILLᴹ ESSINGTON, K.C.B. | who departed this Life July 12ᵗʰ, 1816 | Aged 63 years | And on the north side of this church were interred | the remains of his mother | ANN ESSINGTON | who died May 20ᵗʰ, 1774, Aged 46 years.

1774 July   2 Ann Essington, 46, bur. [? married to Claphamton Essington, at Clapham, 1 May 1750.]

Ledger, south aisle :—Sacred | to the memory of | Vice-Admiral | Sir Wᴹ ESSINGTON, K.C.B.

1816 July 20 Vice-Admiral Sir William Essington, K.C.B., of the Parish of Sᵗ Mary-le-Bone, London, 63, bur ; by the Rev. R. H. Butcher the Vicar, as by the Voucher. [He died at Nottingham Place, Marylebone.]

"On 3rd August 1796 Vice-Admiral Sir George Keith Elphinstone was lying in Simon's Bay, South Africa, and in his fleet was the ' Sceptre,' Captain William Essington." (James's "Naval History," vol. i., p. 535.)

"On the 17th August the Dutch squadron of nine vessels, under Admiral Lucas, capitulated." (*Ibid.*, p. 536.)

"On 9th October 1797 Captain William Essington commanded the ' Triumph,' one of the British North Sea fleet, under Admiral Adam Duncan. On 11th they engaged with the Dutch fleet, under De Winter. The ' Triumph ' had for opponent the ' Wassenaer,' which she compelled to strike. With others she attacked the Dutch flagship the ' Vryheid,' which at length struck. The ' Wassenaer,' although she had struck to the ' Triumph,' was fired at by a Dutch brig that followed her out of the line, and which brig actually compelled her to rehoist her colours. The ' Russel ' soon afterwards coming up, the ' Wassenaer ' again struck them, and was taken possession of. (Battle of Camperdown.) The ' Triumph ' had 25 seamen, 3 marines, and 1 boy killed ; her captain, 1st and 3rd lieutenants (Patrick Chapman and George Trollope), master (James Read), 1 midshipman (Mr. Jones), and 50 seamen and marines wounded. Captain Holland of the ' Wassenaer ' was mortally wounded early in the action. Gold medals were struck and presented to the admirals and captains to be worn. Richard Power was 1st lieutenant of ' Triumph.' " (*Ibid.*, vol. ii.)

He was presented at Court 30 Oct. 1801, when he was made one of the Knights Commanders of the Most Honourable Military Order of the Bath, and was present with Lord Nelson (who wore the diamond aigrette in his hat presented to him for his services by the Court of Naples), Admiral Edward Hughes, and others, at the Palace.

"On 7th August 1807 Rear-Admiral William Essington joined Lord Gambier at Copenhagen." (*Ibid.*, vol. iv., p. 412.)

"On a plate in the south aisle was this inscription" (Strype), now wholly disappeared :—" Of your charity pray for the sowle of ELIZABETH GALE, widow, the which decessed in the paryth the 21ˢᵗ day of January MᵛᶜxLV. Upon whose soule and al christen sowles Jhesu have mercy. Amen."

278 MISCELLANEA GENEALOGICA ET HERALDICA.

Mural, south wall :—Sacred | to the memory of | ANN, the wife of HENRY GARDINER, | of this parish | who departed this life November 11th, 1810 | Aged 65 years. | Also the above-named HENRY GARDINER, | died at Farnham in this county, July 15th, 1839 | aged 95 years, | and was buried there.

1774 Feb. 21 Kirkman son of Henry and Ann Gardner, bapt.
1775 April 6 Ann Holmes daughter of Henry and Ann Gardner, bapt.
1775 May 4 Ann Holmes, inf. dau. of Henry Gardiner, bur.
1776 Mar. 7 Henry son of Henry and Anne Gardiner, bapt.; born Feb. 8.
1776 May 8 Henry Gardiner, inf., bur.
1777 Aug. 25 Mary Anne daughter of Henry and Anne Gardiner, bapt.; born July 28.
1779 Mar. 28 Henry son of Henry and Ann Gardiner, bapt.; born Mar. 1.
1781 Jan. 20 Henry Gardiner, inf., bur.
1780 Aug. 27 Sophia daughter of Henry and Ann Gardiner, bapt.; born Aug. 3.
1781 Sep. 30 Caroline daughter of Henry and Ann Gardiner, bapt.; born Sep. 8.
1783 Sep. 29 Lucy daughter of Henry and Ann Gardiner, bapt.; born Sep. 5.
1785 Nov. 16 Henry William son of Henry and Ann Gardiner, bapt.; born Oct. 8.
1810 Nov. 19 Ann Gardiner, 65, bur.

July 14. At Farnham, aged 96, Henry Gardiner, Esq., formerly of Wandsworth. ("Gent. Mag.," Aug. 1839.)

"A little child shall lead them." | In sweet memory ETHELFLŒDA BERTHON | HOWELL, 8 Nov. 1899—24 May 1901.

Chancel, south-east window :—Subject as above.

In Wandsworth Cemetery is this inscription :—ETHELFLŒDA BERTHON HOWELL, 24 May 1901.

Daughter of Thomas Arthur Ives Howell, M.R.C.S.

Brass plate on ledger, nave :—HIC IACET SEPVLTVS ROB'TVS KNARESBROVGH | GEN'OSVS NVP' SERVVS SERENISSIME | D'NE NVP' R'NE ELIZABETHE & OLIM | HVIVS ECCLESIE PATRONATVS QVI OBIIT | VNDECIMO DIE JANVARII ANNO SALVTIS 1611.

1584, Oct. 21. Robert [? Sarisbroughe], yeoman, and Anne Glascocke, widow, of the City of London, relict of William Glascocke, of Wandsworth, Surrey; at St Sepulchre's. (Marriage Licences : Bishop of London.)

16½½ Jan. 12 Robert Knarisborough, bur.
1619 July 10 Anne Knarisborough, bur.

As Patron of this Church he presented Jerom Shepherd, B.A., to the Vicarage on 1 May 1585, vice John Edwyn, deceased.

In a deed, dated 10 October 1610, is the name of Robert Knarisborough the elder, and in a deed poll, dated 28 October 1611, occurs Robert Knarisborough, jun., gentleman, and again in an indenture of 30 January 1631-2 is Rob. Knarisborough.

On north wall :—TO THE MEMORY OF | CHARLES EDWARD LAWES, | ELDEST SON OF | HENRY AND ELIZABETH LAWES, | OF THIS PARISH, | WHO DIED ON BOARD THE ORWELL | ON HIS PASSAGE TO MELBOURNE, | THE 13th OCTOBER, 1856, | IN THE 19th YEAR OF HIS AGE. | THIS TABLET WAS ERECTED BY HIS FRIENDS | AS A TOKEN OF THE HIGH ESTEEM AND RESPECT | IN WHICH HE WAS HELD BY THEM.

(*Doncaster, Wandsworth.*)

Mural, west end of north aisle :—Hereby lieth the body of | THOMAS MOSELEY, reader of this | parish, and his sonn in law WM TATON | and his grandchild, he departed ye 13 | day of June 1681.

Pd Mr Moseley for reading Service Severall times when Mr Acworth (Vicar) was Sicke, 10s.
(Churchwardens' Accounts, 1671.)

At a Generall meeting of ye Minister, Churchwardens, and other Inhabitants then present ye first day of January 1672-3—
Mr Thomas Moseley was chosen Clerke of ye parish of Wandsworth in ye Countie of Surrey ye same day by and with ye consent of ye p'sons [hereunder *erased*] whose names are hereunder

mentioned. Then it was ordered that y⁰ said Thomas Moseley should neuer require or demand any allowance from y⁰ minister or y⁰ p'ishioners besides y⁰ accustomed dues of the Clerke :—

Allyn Acworth, Vic' Jb.	George Streete.	Ralph George.
Miles Poole, } churchwardens.	Wᵐ Bentley.	Robert Hansloe.
John Best, }	John Bigsby.	George Coswell.
Joshua Monger.	Giles Goose.	Robt. Roades.
Abraham Hubbert.	Richard Coswell.	Thomas Jenkes.
Som'set Draper.	William Roades.	Richard Pillett.

I, Thomas Mosely, do vnder my hand promise to the minister and Parishion's of Wandsworth that I will never require or demand from the minʳ or any of the Parishioners of Wandsworth any allowance besides the accustomed dues of the Clarke for any assistance of the minister in any service of the Church, by me THO. MOSELEY.

Payd Mᵉʳ Holbrooke for cleaning y⁰ Church Plate and washing y⁰ Church Linnen from our Lady 1672 to Christmas following 0 15 0
Payd Mʳ Moseley for Cleaning y⁰ Church Plate and washing the Church Linnen froᵐ Christmas to our Lady Day 1673 . . . . 0 5 0
Payd Mᵉʳ Moseley and Mʳ Holebrooke for schooling 4 parish boyes, vizᵗ, Mathew Waxham, James Stephens, Will. Danson, & Will. Bull 02 0 0
(Churchwardens' Accounts, 1672.)
Payd Mʳ Moseley for washing y⁰ Church Linnen and Clean. y⁰ Plate ffor one year's Broomes for y⁰ Church, as appeares by bill 1 06 04
Payd Mʳ Moseley for Schooling of four poor boyes, vizᵗ, Michafare Alfrey,* James Stephens, William Bull, and John Deane 002 00 00
(Ibid., 1673.)
Payd Mʳ Moseley for Cleaning y⁰ Plate and washing y⁰ Church Linnen 001 00 00
Payd Mʳ Moseley for baptizing And buring severall poor people 000 10 00
Payd Mʳ Moseley by y⁰ hands of Mʳ Osborne and Ed. Athew for looking to y⁰ clock and find in oyle 002 00 00
Payd Mʳ Moseley for Schooling of 4 parish boyes for one year ending at our Lady Day last '76. vizᵗ, James Stephens, John Deane, Francis Poole, and William Bull 002 00 00
[Vicar Acworth buried 10 July 1674.] (Ibid., 1675.)
Rec'd of Mʳ John & Mʳ Thomas Moseley for the intermᵗ of severall in the Church, as per note from the 20ᵗʰ of Aprill '81 to Aprill '82 . . . . . 004 02 10
Paid Mʳˢ Moseley for cleaning y⁰ plate & washing y⁰ Linne' 001 00 00
Paid Mʳ Moseley, clark, for looking to the clock for y⁰ year '80, which was omitted in the last accompt, & Mʳ John Moseley for eighty one, each fourty shilling . 004 00 00
Paid Mʳ Moseley for writing & returning y⁰ Annual Register 000 05 00
Paid Mʳ Moseley for writing a poores Booke 000 02 06
Paid Mʳ Moseley for 4 poore Boyes Schooling for one year ending at our Lady Day last, vizᵗ, John Wright, John Shipway, Smuin Dee, & John Franklin . . . 002 00 00
(Ibid., 1681.)
1665 May 6 Elizabeth daughter of Thomas Mosely, Cler. [bapt.].
1668 July 8 Elizabeth dau. of Mʳ Thomas Moseley [bur.].
166⁴⁄₇ Feb. 5 John son of Thomas Moseley, Cler. [bapt.]
1681 Nov. 13 John Moseley of Wandsworth, Deacon, & Mary Houghton of Sᵗ Olives, Southwark ; Banns.

John Moseley elected Clarke of Wandsworth post fratrem, June y⁰ 24ᵗʰ, 1681. The entries are now in the " Clarke's " handwriting.

(To be continued.)

Reviews.

The Journal of the Ex Libris Society. Vol. XIII., Parts 7 and 8, for July and August 1903.
London : A. and C. Black, Soho Square, W.

THE July Part has for frontispiece the bookplate of Arthur Hopton, of Clements Inn, 1611 ; it is all in outline, and unusually large. A long account of the family from 1470 is given by the Rev. Wickham M. Birch, with five smaller arms. Another one of George Frederick Bodley of Bridgefoot is large, but has some good mantling about it. Mr. Jewers gives an account of the

---

* A descendant of the ancient royal family of Russia. (See " Wandsworth Notes and Queries.")

bookplate of General Sir Reginald Pole-Carew, which is carefully drawn by Mr. G. W. Eve. There are four bookplates designed by the Hon. Frances Wolseley, that of the Field-Marshal Viscount having a mantling very artistically arranged. The bookplate of Mr. A. Price Haig, as designed by Mr. Graham Johnston, is well done.

The August Part has the plate of Chelsea Public Library, the figures rather roughly drawn, and five bookplates engraved by Mr. F. G. House, and inserted as a supplement by Messrs. Truslove and Hanson ; each plate is well delineated, particularly the one for Miss Fetherston-haugh Frampton. The old plates and the improved new bookplate is shewn by Mr. J. Rogers Rees, who has a little Paper on the subject, and illustrates it by shewing the title of a "New Dictionary " by William Walker, B.D., in 1691.

The New York Genealogical and Biographical Record. Vol. XXXIV., Nos. 2 and 3, April and July 1903. Society's Office : 226 West 58th Street, New York, U.S.A.

THIS is the best of the genealogical periodicals which come to England, and the Part for April has an excellent portrait of Mr. Heber Reginald Bishop, one of America's Railway Directors, and celebrated as the largest collector of jade, which he finally presented to the Metropolitan Museum of Art, New York, shortly afterwards dying of heart disease.

The next article with a plate is the Jumel Mansion, at Manhattan Island. It was used at times by General Washington and by the officers of the British Army, and went through many vicissitudes, and finally became the head-quarters of the war party. Of Church Records, those of the Corporation of Zion in New Germantown, and Registers of Marriages, Baptisms, and Deaths in East Hampton are next given, followed by the family history of Edward Fuller, and inscriptions from Gilead Cemetery, Carmel, N.Y., and a general Obituary, etc., complete the April Number, which must be interesting to many Americans.

The July Part has a portrait of Mr. Asa Fitch, Physician and Naturalist, who for fifty years had made the latter a study, and was created State Entomologist in 1854. Several of the papers in the April Part are continued, and an account is given of the Dumont Family and John de Witt, with his portrait. An Obituary and Book Notices close the Part.

Fenland Notes and Queries. Vol. V., Part 58. July 1903. Peterborough : George C. Caster, Market Place.

THIS Part begins with a good account of Dr. Richard Howland, Bishop of Peterborough in 1584. It is embellished, too, with his portrait, autograph, and seal ; he had it when he was ordained. His father was a Salter of London, and he was one among ten other sons and one daughter. His seventh brother was knighted as Sir Giles, and was a Grocer of London. A Paper on Charteris Church Notes, written in 1745, is interesting. There are excellent accounts given again of the drainage of the Fens in Charles the First's time, and a company of noblemen was formed to carry it out.

The Virginia Magazine of History and Biography. Vol. XI., No. 1. July 1903. Virginia Historical Society, Richmond, U.S.A.

THE Virginia Committee of Correspondence, the Surrender of Virginia in 1651-2, and an account of Virginia in 1638-9, occupy a fair amount of this Part, and John Brown's letters are continued. Isle of Wight County Records and Virginia Gleanings in England, and the Militia in the Revolution, are interesting locally, and the genealogy of the Brooke Family and the Herndon Family, besides several others, and the usual historical Notes and Queries, complete the Part.

LITERARY ANNOUNCEMENT.

THE HARLEIAN SOCIETY have just issued Vol. II. of "Lincolnshire Pedigrees" to its Members.

** Books for Review and Notices of Forthcoming Works should be addressed to Messrs. Mitchell Hughes and Clarke at the Publishing Office, 140 Wardour Street, London, W.

Pedigree of Holdich of Wadenhoe, co. Northampton.*

ARMS (as recorded in the Heralds' College).—*Or, on a chevron sable, cottised gules, three martlets of the field, a chief vair.*
CREST.—*A martlet sable in front of a cross pattée fitchée between two palm-branches or.*

John Holdeche of Wadenhoe, co. Northampton, 1545—48. Will proved at Northampton. (Book I, p. 180.)

John Hedich of Lilford, co. Northants. Will proved at Northampton 1524—27. (Book C.)

Symon Holdich of⹂=Margaret..... Thrapston aforesaid ; died 1602. M.I.
died 1619. M.I.

John Holdich.

Joseph Holdich of Wadenhoe aforesaid ; buried there 14 Sep. 1573. Will dated ....; proved at Northampton. (Book T, p. 98.)

Elizabeth, baptized 21 November 1572; married at Wadenhoe, 2 Oct. 1598, John Willymote.

John Holdich of Wadenhoe=⹂Alice, da. of aforesaid and of Thrapstone in said county of Northampton, 1540—66 ; buried at Wadenhoe aforesaid 1 August 1591.
....; buried at Wadenhoe 2 April 1598.

John=⹂Elizabeth, baptized 30 June 1563 ; West. married at Wadenhoe 5 Oct. 1569.

Thomas Holdich of Thrapston ; died 17 August 1638. M.I.

Eleanor, baptized at Wadenhoe 25 Oct. 1570.

Robert Holdich, 2nd son, baptized at Wadenhoe 26 Sep. 1568 and buried there 5 Nov. 1572. 1st wife.

John Holdich, baptized at Wadenhoe 16 May 1578.

Robert Holdich, baptized at Wadenhoe 18 December 1580.

Nicholas Holdich, baptized at Wadenhoe 6 November 1583.

Thomas Holdich, baptized at Wadenhoe 3 November 1586.

Dorothy, buried at Wadenhoe 24 March 1638-9.

Agnes Webster, married at=⹂Jeffery Holdich of Wadenhoe aforesaid, baptized there=⹂Margery Cowper, mar. at Waden-=⹂Eleanor Wadenhoe aforesaid 18 Sep. 17 November 1566 ; died Monday 16 October and buried 1592 and buried there 27 at same 17 October 1638. M.I. Will dated — October March 1598. 1st wife. 1637 and proved at Peterborough. (Lib. O, 74.)
hoe aforesaid 4 August 1602 ; buried there 14 July 1625, as "Marg. Hollidge." 2nd wife.
...: 3rd wife.

A

B

* Communicated by EVERARD GREEN, Esq., *Rouge Dragon*, F.S.A.

A |

B |

John Holdich, baptized at Wadenhoe 16 Sep. 1598.

Anna, baptized at Wadenhoe 9 March 1594-5.

Rev. Theodore Holdich, of Lynn, co. Norfolk, born at Wadenhoe 31 May and baptized there 1 July 1604; died 1658.

Jeffrey Holdyche, baptized at Wadenhoe 29 Sep. 1605 and buried there 26 March 1606.

Francis Holdich of Wadenhoe aforesaid, baptized there 14 Oct. 1610 and buried there 8 October 1658.

Johan Saunderson, married at Wadenhoe 28 November 1638 and bur. there 15 March 1696-7.

Thomas Holdich, baptized at Wadenhoe 6 April 1697; living 1637 and buried there 17 Jan. 1657-8.

Jeffrey Holditche, baptized at Wadenhoe 20 November 1606 and buried there 20 November 1691.

See PEDIGREE A, page 283.

Ann, 6th da., 1637.

Joane, eldest da., baptized 26 March 1608; buried 1608.

Joane, 2nd da., baptized 11 June 1609; married at Wadenhoe, 22 Nov. 1636, Thomas Dison (or Dysonn). Living 1637.

Margery, 3rd da., bapt. at Wadenhoe 15 Dec. 1611. Living 1637.

Prudence, 4th da., bapt. at Wadenhoe 20 Dec. 1614.

Elizabeth, 5th da., baptized 23 June 1616. Living 1637.

... Wade, dead before Oct. 1637.

... = Gatonby.

Thomas Gatonby, 1637.

John Wade, 1637.

James Houldich, bapt. at Wadenhoe 6 October 1613. Living 1637.

Sarah, baptized at Wadenhoe 12 October 1659.

Adam Holditch of Lynn, co. Norfolk, baptized 7 January 1641-2; = Sarah ..., 1696; died 1709.

Seth Holditch of Lynn aforesaid and of Walsoken (near Wisbech), co. Norfolk, 1709—14.

Adam Holditch of Lynn aforesaid; died 1713.

Adam Holditch of Lynn aforesaid; died 1754, aged 69. = Mary ...; baptized at Narborough 1742, æt. 50. Mary ...; died 1692.

Adam Holditch of Lynn aforesaid, born 27 June 1720 and died 1784, aged 64. = Mary ..., born at Galway in Ireland 26 October 1729; died 1781, æt. 52. Had fourteen children; seven survived.

C

c |

Adam Holditch of King's Lynn, born 9 June 1752 and died 7 May 1818, aged 66. = Mary Barnsley, born at Brampton, co. Hunts, 12 March 1753 and married there 29 March 1773.

Hamnett Holditch.

John Holditch. William Holditch.

1. Isabella. 2. Mary.

3. Elizabeth.

George Holditch of King's Lynn aforesaid, "Pilot," = Mary Wilkinson. born 5 March 1774.

Adam Holditch of King's Lynn.

Elizabeth.

Hamnett Holditch, President of Caius College, Cambridge, 1835 to 1867; born at King's Lynn; baptized, as an adult, at St. Michael's, Cambridge, 17 March 1823; admitted Pentioner at Gonville and Caius College 16 February 1818, then aged 18; B.A. 1822; M.A. 1825; Senior Wrangler and Smith's Prizeman; died in College 12 December 1867 and buried at North Wootton, co. Norfolk. Presented with the Freedom of King's Lynn. In 1850 he gave £100 to the new College Buildings of Caius.

PEDIGREE A. (See page 282.)

Francis Holditch of Wadenhoe = Johan Saunderson.

Benjamin Holditch, baptized at Wadenhoe 24 November 1658.

Rebecca, baptized at Wadenhoe 4 April 1650; buried there 26 September 1675.

Hannah, baptized 9 Sep. 1654.

Elizabeth, baptized at Wadenhoe 12 August 1656.

Francis Hollidge of Aldwincle St. Peter, co. Northants, born 3 August and baptized at Wadenhoe aforesaid 31 August 1654; bur. there 6 May 1726. = Katharine ....

Elizabeth, baptized at Aldwincle aforesaid 9 March 1683-4.

Rebecca, baptized at Aldwincle aforesaid 1 March 1688-9.

Joana, baptized at Aldwincle aforesaid 28 April 1678.

A

┌ A

Jeffrey Holdich, baptized at Wadenhoe 5 April 1640; buried there 9 April 1640 as "Godfrey."

Edward Holdich of Wadenhoe, baptized there 24 February 1641-2; died 18 April and buried there 21 April 1705. M.I. == Mary, dau. of ...; buried at Wadenhoe 19 November 1688. 1st wife. == Sarah, dau. of ...; died at Thrapston aforesaid 2 April and buried at Wadenhoe aforesaid 5 April 1729. M.I. 2nd wife.

Francis Holdich, eldest son, baptized at Thrapston [? Wadenhoe] 23 December 1681.

Edward Holdich of Sidney-Sussex College, Cambridge, 2nd son, baptized at Wadenhoe 23 December 1681; B.A. 1703; died s.p.

Thomas Holdich of Thrapston aforesaid, 3rd son, baptized at Wadenhoe 29 March 1697; died intestate 1752; buried at Thrapston, in the nave. == Susanna, dau. of Thomas (toadfellow of Denford, co. Northants, by Susannah Baxter; married in 1723 at Cranford or Cransley, co. Northampton. Will dated 7 Oct. 1754; proved 24 Feb. 1755.

... da. == Geoffrey (Jeffery) Holdich, Rector of Stibbington, co. Hunts, 4th son, baptized at Wadenhoe 1 Nov. 1701; bred at Clare College, Cambridge, B.A. 1723; M.A. 17—; died 7 July 1779, aged 80, and buried at Stibbington aforesaid. M.I. == Mary Gray of Titchmarsh, co. Northampton, born about 1710; died 19 Feb. 1796, aged 86. M.I. at Stibbington aforesaid.

... de Rippe of Wakerley, co. Northampton. 1st wife.

John Holdich, buried at Wadenhoe aforesaid 2 January 1692-3.

Sarah, buried at Wadenhoe aforesaid 2 May 1700.

See PEDIGREE B, page 287.

Thomas Holdich, sole ex'or of his mother's will 24 February 1755. == Sibyl ...., ob. 21 June 1776, aged 39. M.I. at Aldwincle St. Peter.

Edward Holdich.
—
Anne.

Edward Holdich, ob. 17 July 1824, aged 66. M.I. at Aldwincle St. Peter.

Thomas Holdich, died 10 January 1838, aged 70. M.I. at same.

Edward Holdich of Farndon, co. Northants; a deed executed 1789; died 17 Aug. 1806, aged 88, and buried at Farndon aforesaid. M.I. == Anne, eldest da. of Thomas Peach of Gretton, co. Northants; married 17 August 1756; died 17 February 1791, aged 50, and buried at Farndon aforesaid. M.I.

Joseph Keep of Boughton Lodge, Banker and Farmer at Boughton and Kettering. == Elizabeth, youngest da. died 27 January 1822, aged 44. M.I. in Farndon Church, co. Northants.

...., a da., wife of William Ashby.
—

...., a da., wife of William Lee, and had two sons.

...., a da., wife of David Oswin, and had a son William Oswin.

John Keep, an infant in 1822.   Joseph Keep, an infant in 1822.   .... Tresham == ...., a da., an infant in 1822.

B

B |

Edward Holdich of Great Addington, co. Northampton, "a confirmed old bachelor"; died s.p. about 1842.

William Holdich of Market- or Husbands-Bosworth, Leicester. = Charlotte Busswell.

John Peach Holdich, died 13 October 1774, aged 12. M.I. in Farndon Church aforesaid.

Jeffrey Holdich of Oundle, died ob. s.p. in 1800; buried at Oundle, co. Northants. M.I. = Elizabeth . . . .

William Holdich, ob. s.p. | Charles Holdich, ob. s.p. | Daus., ob. s.p.

Rev. Thomas Holdich, fifty-eight years Rector of Maidwell and twenty-five years Rector of Draughton, co. Northants, and Rector of Burton Overy, co. Leicester, 16 September 1801 to 1822; born at Thrapston aforesaid 14 Oct. 1771; bred at Clare College, Cambridge, A.B. 1794; A.M. 1797; died 15 April 1866, aged 94, and buried at Maidwell aforesaid. M.I. = Anne, da. of Henry Haynes of Whittlesea Hall, co. Cambridge; married in 1802; died 20 February 1806, aged 35. M.I. at Maidwell aforesaid and in St. Mary's, Whittlesea. 1st wife.

Eliza Laura, da. and coheir of Henry Laurence Maidwell of Whittlesea aforesaid; born 22 September 1782; married 1808; died at Maidwell aforesaid 30 March 1863, aged 80, and buried there 4 April. M.I. 2nd wife.

For issue see Θ, page 288.

Henry Hungerford Holdich-Hungerford of Dingley Park and Maidwell Hall, co. Northants, J.P. and D.L. co. Northants, son and heir, born at Burton Overy, co. Leicester, 9 January 1803; entered at Harrow 1815 (left 1820) and at Oriel Coll., Oxford; matriculated 22 March 1820; then aged 17; B.A. 1823; High Sheriff of Northants 1828; assumed, by Royal Licence dated 11 Feb. 1824, additional N. and A.; mar. at St. George, Hanover Square, 4 Aug. 1846; died in St. James's Place, London, 2 Dec. and buried at Dingley aforesaid 7 Dec. 1872. M.I. = Augusta Louisa, da. of Arthur Ward of Calverley, Tunbridge Wells; married 14 July 1875. 1st wife.

Mildred Georgina, da. of Ramson Reid of Stratford Place, London. 2nd wife.

Thomas Thornhill of Fixby Hall, co. York, and of Riddlesworth, co. Norfolk, born 15 December 1780; died 29 May 1844, aged 64, and buried at Riddlesworth, co. Norfolk. M.I. Will dated 18 November 1839, and proved, with three codicils, 12 July 1844, in P.C.C. = Honoria Louisa, younger da. of Major Francis Forester by Lady Louisa Catherine Barbara his wife, eldest da. of Henry Vane, Duke of Cleveland, K.G.; born 20 January 1817; died at Pau, Basses Pyrenees, in France, 16 July 1859, aged 43; buried in Dingley Church aforesaid — August. M.I.

Henry Vane Forester Holdich-Hungerford of Dingley Park and Maidwell Hall aforesaid, son and heir, J.P. and D.L., born 8 May 1852; entered at Harrow 1867 (left 1869); High Sheriff of Northants 1879.

Honoria Louisa, married at St. James's, Westminster, 7 April 1864, Lieut.-Colonel Thomas Harvey Brampton of Skreens, co. Essex.

Eleanor Frances, married at St. George, Hanover Square, 3 August 1865, Arthur Watson de Capel Brooke of Loddington Hall, co. Northants.

O | D

σ | D

Powlett Henry Edward Holdich-Hungerford, 2nd son, born in Lowndes Square 5 July 1853; Lieut. R.N.; died unmarried in London 22 June 1885 and buried in Brompton Cemetery. M.I.

Edward Lytton Holdich-Hungerford, 3rd son, born in London 15 August 1855 and baptized at Dingley; died unmarried in Norland Square, London, 14 June and buried in Brompton Cemetery 17 June 1881. M.I.

Julia Mary Ann, eldest da., living 1903 and unmarried married.

Louisa Erica, 2nd da., married at St. George, Hanover Square aforesaid, 4 November 1875, Arthur Francis Pennell, younger son of Sir Charles Henry Pennell, Kt.

Clara Constance, 3rd da., died unmarried at Boulogne-sur-Mer in France 15 January and buried at Dingley aforesaid 25 February 1859. M.I.

Catharine, eldest da. of Rev. Francis Thomas Corrance, Rector of Great Glen, co. Leicester; married there 25 November 1830; died s.p. at Bath, co. Somerset, 28 February 1834 and buried at Foxton, co. Leicester. M.I. 1st wife.

Rev. Thomas Peach Holdich, 2nd son, Rector of St. James's, Dingley 1841—54, then Vicar of St. James's, Notting Hill, and afterwards Rector of Lynwood, co. Lincoln, from 1869; born 21 Dec. 1804; entered at Harrow 1817, Monitor 1821, Head of the School 1822 (left 1823), and at Balliol College, Oxford; matriculated 4 Dec. 1822, aged 17; B.A. 1826, M.A. 1829; built the Schools at St. James's, Notting Hill; died at Lynwood aforesaid and buried there. M.I.

Susan, 4th da. of W. Garrard of Carisbrooke, Isle of Wight; married there 29 January 1889; died at Redruth, co. Cornwall, 20 November 1848 and buried at Lynwood aforesaid. M.I. 2nd wife.

Mary Anne, eldest da., born 29 Dec. 1803; married, 16 November 1836, Charles Boultbee of Whittlesea aforesaid, Surgeon; died s.p. 8 May and buried at Whittlesea aforesaid 14 May 1879.

Edward Holdich, twin with Edgar, born Jan. 1806; died Feb. 1806.

Edgar Holdich, died February 1806.

Sir Thomas Hungerford Holdich of the Royal Engineers, K.C.I.E., born at Dingley aforesaid 13 February 1843.

Ada Maria, da. of Captain John H. Vanrenen, H.E.I.C.S.; married in India 17 June 1878.

John Peach Holdich, twin with elder brother, born 18 Feb. 1843.

Bella, 2nd da. of Lieut.-Colonel Henry Morland; married at Bedford 12 December 1872.

Augustus Henry Holdich, 3rd son, born 10 April 1846; married Annie Sullivan; died s.p.

Harold Adrian Holdich, son and heir, born 20 March 1874.

John Edward Holdich, 2nd son; died an infant.

Godfrey William Vanrenen Holdich, 3rd but 2nd surviving son, born 30 September 1882.

Ida Laura, eldest da., married Captain E. Peach.

Joan Alice Hungerford, younger da.

Mary Alice, eldest da., born at Newport, Isle of Wight.

Charlotte Eliza, 2nd da., married, 11 Oct. 1866, Rev. James Augustus Leicester of Market Rasen, co. Lincoln.

Constance Jane, 3rd da., married Rev. W. W. Cooper, Vicar of West Rasen, co. Lincoln.

Bernard Stephen Ward of Dresden and Maidenhead.

Susan Theresa Davey, 4th da., married at All Saints', Dresden, 30 April 1879.

PEDIGREE B. (See page 284.)

Geoffrey (Jeffery) Holdich, Rector of Stibbington, co. Hunts═Mary Gray of Titchmarsh, co. Northampton.

Edward Holdich of Chelsea, co. Middlesex, son and heir, Surgeon to H.R.H. the Duke of Cumberland, and attended his Grace at Culloden, and Apothecary to the household of H.M. King George III. ; born 10 March 1786-7; married Catharine . . . . ; died s.p. in Chelsea aforesaid 16 April 1814 or 1818, and buried there.

Jeffrey (Godfrey) Holdich═Anne....; bur. of Hornchurch, co. Essex, at Hornchurch Surgeon, 2nd son, born 7 aforesaid 12 April 1738 and buried August 1769, there 21 November 1790. aged 27.

A son and two daughters.

Thomas Holdich of Reading, co. Berks, 3rd son, born 20 Feb, 1740-41; died at Reading 1814, leaving a son and two daughters.

Elizabeth, 3rd da. of Thomas Peach of═Robert Holdich of Holdich═Sarah Cockle Gretton aforesaid, and great-niece of Thomas Peach of Dingley Park aforesaid; married at Thrapston aforesaid in 1768; died at Spalding aforesaid 11 July 1807. M.I. 1st wife.

House in Spalding, co. Lincoln, J.P. and D.L., 4th son, born 6 April 1747; died 28 March 1828; buried at Spalding.

of Lincoln, died s.p. 2nd wife.

Sarah, born 2 May 1783; married Abraham de Rippie; died 7 September 1759, aged 26. M.I. at Stibbington.

...Baines═Mary, born of Ramsey, 30 March co. Hunts. 1785.

....Copeland of Horncastle,═....Baines. co. Lincoln.

....Baines of Ramsey, in the Admiralty; had a pension of £500═Mrs. Brightley, a year; "a very handsome man;" died at Ramsey. a widow.

Edward Copeland of Boston, M.D.═

Rev.....Copeland.

A

Charles Martin Dinham Green of the Manor House, Spalding aforesaid, Captain-Commandant of the Volunteers, born 11 June and baptized at Spalding aforesaid 13 July 1763; died 13 September 1837, aged 74, and buried 18 Sep. in the Green-aisle, Spalding Church. M.I. Will dated 23 November 1833, and proved at Lincoln 20 January 1888. === Mary Holdich, da. and sole heir, born 12 August and baptized at Spalding aforesaid 20 September 1770; married there 9 March 1799; died 16 October 1833, aged 63, and buried there, in the Green-aisle aforesaid, 23 October. M.I. Adm'on granted at Lincoln 30 May 1849.

B

Rev. Thomas Holdich, Rector of Maidwell. (See ⊕, page 285.) === Eliza Laura, da. and coheir of Henry Laurence Maidwell of Whittlesea.

William Hungerford Holdich === Georgiana, 4th da., born at Spalding 19 December 1806, and there baptized with her brother Charles 11 July 1810; married at Spalding 26 September 1832; died s.p. at Sleaford aforesaid 24 April 1874, aged 68, and buried there 29 April. M.I.

William Hungerford Holdich, of Sleaford, co. Lincoln, 5th son, Solicitor, born at Burton Overy, co. Leicester, 2 June 1809; entered at Harrow at Westcotes 1823, left 1826; died s.p. at Sleaford 30 Jan. 1880, aged 70, and buried there. M.I.

Rev. Martin Johnson Green, Rector of Winterbourne Abbey-cum-Steepleton, co. Dorset, and Prebend of Salisbury (Alton Borealis), and Rural Dean of Bridport; sometime Fellow of Lincoln College, Oxford, and Junior Proctor; born at Spalding 28 December 1813, and baptized there 30 December; B.A. 1 December 1836, M.A. 25 October 1838, and B.D. 11 May 1848; died 17 September 1889, and buried at Steepleton aforesaid 20 September. M.I. === Elizabeth Laura Catharine, 2nd da., born at Kibworth, co. Leicester, 7 September 1812; married at Maidwell aforesaid 6 September 1848; died at "Winterbourne," Polstead Road, Oxford, 26 January 1908, aged 91, and bur. at Oxford. M.I.

Martin Holdich Green, Fellow of Trinity College, Oxford, living unmarried 1903.

Laura Georgiana, eldest da., living 1903.

Jane Elizabeth, 2nd da., living 1903.

Edith Mary, 3rd da., living 1903.

Anne Cecilia, 4th da., living 1903.

Charles Green of Holditch House, Spalding aforesaid, born at the Manor House, Spalding, 8 July 1810, and baptized there 11 July following; educated at Shrewsbury; died at Gosforth, co. Northumberland, 21 June 1885 and buried there. M.I. Adm'on granted in June 1885. === Mary, 4th da. and coheir of Henry Everard of Croyland-Postland and Spalding, co. Lincoln, by Anne, da. of George Toynbee of Waddington, co. Lincoln; born at Everard House, Postland aforesaid, 20 July 1811, and baptized at Croyland Abbey 22 July; married at Spalding 27 June 1838; died 22 Dec. 1869; buried at Hollington, co. Sussex. M.I.

Rev. John Henry Green, son and heir, Rector of Mowsley, co. Leicester; M.A. Oxon.

Charles Martin Green, 2nd son, sometime of Richmond, co. Surrey.

Mary Elizabeth, living unmarried 1903.

Everard Green, 3rd son, Rouge Dragon in H.M.'s Heralds' College, F.S.A. The Compiler of this pedigree 1903.

B

Edward Lawrence Holdich, 6th son, died an infant at Burton Overy aforesaid in 1810.

Anna Maria, eldest da. of George Wartnaby; married at Market Harboro' 13 November 1845; died s.p. at Deane Rectory 20 June 1854. 1st wife. = Rev. John Henry Holdich, 7th son, Rector of Bulwick, co. Northampton (instituted 1861), and of Clare College, Cambridge; born at Burton Overy aforesaid 3 April 1811; A.B. 1834, A.M. 1837; bur. at Stibbington. M.I. = Catharine Jane, youngest da. of Barnard Smith of Rickinghall, co. Suffolk; married at Glaston, co. Rutland, 22 November 1870; buried at Stibbington. 2nd wife. M.I.

George Maydwell Holdich, 8th son, born at Maidwell Hall aforesaid 14 August 1816; died s.p. at Forest Hill, co. Surrey, 30 July 1896, aged 80.

Alfred Henry Dashwood of Stibbington House, co. Hunts, son of .... Dashwood of Stamford Hall, co. Leicester. = Evelyn Maydwell Holdich, only da. and sole heir, born 2 April 1872; married in London May 1892.

John Dashwood, born June 1893.

Charles Walter Holdich of Slenford and then of Peterborough, 10th son, born at Maidwell Hall 6 Jan. 1820; died at Werrington 18 April and buried there 23 April 1908. M.I. = Eleanor Anne, da. of John Stona Smith of Whittlesea aforesaid, brother of General Sir Harry Smith, Bart.; born 3 June 1819; mar. at Whittlesea.

George Goodwin Buckston of Bradbourne, co. Derby, 1st husband. = Emily Hallward, da. of Rev. Crosbie Morgell, Vicar of East Knoyle, co. Wilts. = General Sir Edward Alan Holdich, K.C.B. (1875), 11th son, born at Maidwell aforesaid 10 May 1822; C.B. 1858; Colonel 57th Foot (West Middx.); mar. at St. George, Hanover Square, 18 November 1880.

Mary Juana, "a Sister" at Brighton 1903.

Annie Florence, died unmarried 1861.

Eleanor, unmar. 1903.

Alice Ground, unmarried 1908.

Robert Walter Holdich, 9th son, died an infant at Maidwell Hall in 1819.

Laurence Maydwell Holdich, 2nd son, born 28 June 1845; Sergt.-Major of the Frontier Light Horse; ob. s.p. at Homglia, South Africa, 30 July 1878, aged 33.

Thomas Hinman Holdich of Sleaford, 3rd son, born 14 October 1851; a Solicitor at Sleaford 1903.

Rev. Charles Walter Holdich, son and heir, Vicar of Werrington, co. Northants, M.A. born 24 March 1813; at Northampton 1908.

Rev. Thomas Farebrother, sometime Perpetual Curate of St. Margaret's, Wardend, co. Warwick; sometime Curate of Aston-juxta-Birmingham; Rector of Whilton, co. Northants, 1854—56, and of Weston-on-Trent, co. Derby, 1857—63; matriculated at Oxford (Queen's Coll.) aged 17, B.A. 1829, M.A. 1834; died at Oxford 30 July 1896 and buried there. M.I. = Jane Susanna Holdich, 3rd da., born at Maidwell aforesaid 10 Feb. 1824; married there 3 June 1856.

Anna Maria Holdich, 4th and youngest da., born at Maidwell Hall aforesaid 29 March 1825; died unmarried at Dorchester, co. Dorset, ... 1899 and buried there. M.I.

Mary Jane Frances Farebrother, da. and sole heir, born 4 August 1865 and baptized at Maidwell aforesaid.

𝕸𝖔𝖓𝖚𝖒𝖊𝖓𝖙𝖆𝖑 𝕴𝖓𝖘𝖈𝖗𝖎𝖕𝖙𝖎𝖔𝖓𝖘

IN

𝖂𝖆𝖓𝖉𝖘𝖜𝖔𝖗𝖙𝖍 𝕻𝖆𝖗𝖎𝖘𝖍 𝕮𝖍𝖚𝖗𝖈𝖍.*

Ledger, nave:—Under this stone lieth the body of Mr MARTIN NEW- | PORT, of this parish, who departed this life the 16th day | of February, 1734, aged 60 years; and of PENELOPE, his | loving and beloved wife, who departed this life the 26th | day of June 1754, aged 72.

1704 May 24 Martin Newport, Merchant in Wandsworth, Surrey=Penelope Hall ; married
              by Mr Edgeley, Vicar of Wandsworth. (Gray's Inn Chapel Register.)
1705 Sep. 2 Penelope daughter of Mr Martin Newport, Mercht., bapt.
17⅘ Feb. 28 John son of Mr Martin Newport and Penelope his wife, bapt.
173⅘ Feb. 23 Mr Martin Newport, Merchant, 65, bur.
1754 July 3 Penelope, Widow of Martin Newport, 72, bur.
1723-4 R^d for the Interment of Mr Newport's Child 7 4
                                                    (Churchwardens' Accounts.)

Chancel, central window. *Subject:* Virgin Mary holding infant Jesus, and three angels:—In Memory of | GEORGE NIND | obiit 26 Jan. 1897.

A great benefactor to the parish.

On one of the Benefaction Boards is the following :—

The Chancel of this Church was erected A.D. 1900, at a cost of £2450, a legacy of £2000 having been left to the Vicar and Churchwardens of Wandsworth for that purpose by a Parishioner, Mr George Nind.

A large cross is erected over his grave in Wandsworth Cemetery. On it is : . IN . MEMORY . OF . | . GEORGE . NIND . | . MEMBER . OF . THE . PHARMA- | CEUTICAL . SOCIETY . AN . OLD . | . INHABITANT . OF . WANDSWORTH . | . AND . A . GREAT . BENEFACTOR . | . TO . THE . CHURCH . OF . ENGLAND . | . AND . THE . POOR . OF . THIS . PARISH . | . BORN . 16th . MAY . 1818 . | . DIED . 26th . JAN. . 1897.

(W. E. Buchanan, Trinity Road.)

The total gross yearly income of Nind's Wandsworth Church Trust is £1840 13*s.* 11*d.*

Mural, west end of north aisle. Arms : *Argent, a chevron between three palmers' scrips sable, tassels and buckles or :*—To the Memory | of SAMUEL PALMER, Esqr. | Many Years one of the Surgeons | And afterwards Treasurer | of St. Bartholomew's Hospital, | and Fellow of the | Royal Society. | Born Ian. 5, 1670. | Dyed April 20, 1738.

1738 April 28 Mr Samuel Palmer, 68, bur.

His eldest daughter Frances married Peter Sainthill, Esq. She died 21 February 1766, and lies buried with her husband outside east end of north aisle of Wandsworth Church. She inherited £50,000 from her father.

SAINTHILL FAMILY.

ARMS.—*Or, on a fesse engrailed azure between three leopards' heads gules as many bezants, each charged with a fleur-de-lis of the second ; on a pile in chief azure three demi fleurs-de-lis per pale attached to the top and sides of the front.*

```
                        William Sainthill of Devon⊤. . . .
              ┌─────────────────────────────────┴──────────────────────────┐
      Peter Sainthill⊤Margaret Upton.                        Samuel Palmer⊤. . . .
      ┌───────┴──────────────────────────────────────────────────────┴───┐
Peter Sainthill, Surgeon, Wandsworth⊤ffrances Palmer (dau. of Samuel Palmer, see above).
                        A |
```

* Communicated by CECIL T. DAVIS, Esq.—continued from p. 279.

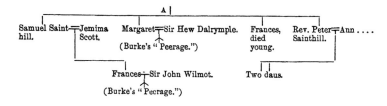

Mural, east end of south aisle :—**Ịn | Ạemory | of | Ạilliam Ạlank,** |
FATHER AND FOR FIFTY-TWO YEARS A MEMBER | OF THE COURT OF ASSISTANTS |
OF THE WORSHIPFUL COMPANY OF SALTERS; | AND FOR 78 YEARS A LIVERYMAN | OF
THE SAME COMPANY AND A FREEMAN OF THE | CITY OF LONDON. | BORN AT WANDS-
WORTH, | 7ᵀᴴ NOVEMBER, A.D. 1767, AT 3 P.M. ; | DIED AT HARROW ON THE HILL, |
(WHERE HE HAD RESIDED FIFTY-SIX YEARS) | 20ᵀᴴ NOVEMBER A.D. 1867, AT
5.10 A.M., | AGED 100 YEARS AND 12 DAYS. | INTERRED AT HARROW, IN THE OLD
CHURCHYARD. | "**Ạod is love.**"
1767 Nov. 29 William son of James and Hannah Plank, bapt.
His parents were buried in the churchyard.

Ledger, south aisle :—Here lyeth the body of | Mʳˢ ELIZABETH PLUME who |
departed this life Iune yᵉ 17ᵗʰ, 1703 | in yᵉ 72 year of her Age.

Brass plate on ledger in nave :—IOHN POWELL GENTLEMAN SERVANT BOTH
TO QVEENE | ELIZABETH, AS ALSO TO KINGE IAMES BEING 74 YEARES | OLDE,
DEPARTED OVT OF THIS WORLD Yᴱ 26 OF IVNE 1611 | HIS BODY RESTETH VNDER
THIS STONE IN | EXPECTATION OF A BLESSED AND GLORIOVS | RESVRRECTION.

On the north side of the chancel on a monument was this inscription (much
perished) and now on east end of north aisle.   Arms: POWELL *impaling* HAY-
WARD :—

> Under a stone within this place
> Doth lie JOHN POWELL, who for the space
> Of thirty yeres before his death
> Did serve the Queene Elizabeth :
> And to King James of worthy fame,
> For nine yeres more he did the same :
> And when the yeres of seaventy-foure,
>   Were now come to an end,
> Into the hands of God above
>   His soul he did commend.
>   Obiit 26 die Junii
>   Anno Dom. 1611.

1611 June 30 John Powell, gent., bur.
Recᵈ of Mʳ Edmund Powell for a Legacie geven by the last will of Mʳ John Powell, Esq.,
    deceased, xxˢ.   (Churchwardens' Accounts, 1610-11.)

Mural with effigy, north chancel aisle :—" SUSANNA POWELL, late of Wands-
worth, widow, daughter of THOMAS HAYWARD, of Wandsworth, Yeoman of the
Guard unto King Henry the VIII., King Edward the VI., to Queene Mary, and to
Queene Elizabeth (of ever precious memory), and wife unto JOHN POWELL, of
Wandsworth, gentleman, who was servant to Queene Elizabeth. This SUSANNA
POWELL was a gracious benefactor unto this Towne of Wandsworth.   She lived
a widow the space (almost) of twenty yeeres, deceased the 19 day of February,
1630, and at her death bequeath'd by her will unto 24 poore widowes of this

Towne of Wandsworth, for ever, four pence in money, to be distributed every Lord's Day, 12 on one Sabbath, and 12 another, for ever, at the North Doore of the Church at Wandsworth. She also bequeathed 40 shillings every yeere for ever, to put forth a poore man's child an apprentice, with divers other loving Remembrances unto her good friends and neighbours. These aforesaid donations are to issue out of the Benefit and Profits of the Rectory of Wandsworth. This was desired to be recorded, that God might be glorified, the memorial of the just might be blessed, and the living stirred up to such like good Workes of Piety and Compassion. More, to this Church for the Communion Table, two Flaggon Pots of Silver, price XX*l*. and upwards. To release poore prisoners out of prison on the day of her burial, XX. pounds. To the Poore of the Parish of Putney, long before she deceased, 50 pounds. To the poore Householders of Wandsworth, for many yeeres before her death, towards payment of their rent, per annum 5 Pounds."

The foregoing is the inscription as it is preserved in the county histories. It now reads thus :—

Svsanna Powel, late of Wandsworth, widdow, davghter of | Thomas Hayward, of Wandswth, Yeoman of ye Gvard vnto | King Henry ye 8, King Edward ye 6, to Qveen Mary, | and to Qveen Elizabeth (of ever preciovs memory), | and wife vnto John Powel, of Wandsworth, gent., who | was servant to Qveen Elizabth & King James. This Svsann Powel was a graciovs benefactor vnto this | Town of Wandsowth. She lived a widdow ye space almost | of 20 yeeres, deceased ye 19th day of Febry, 1630, and at | her death beqeathed by her will vnto 24 poore widdows | of this Town of Wandsworth, for evr 4^d in bread & 4^d mony to be distribvted every Lord's Day, 12 one Sabbth, and 12 | another, for ever, at ye North Doore of ye Chvrch at Wandswth. | She also beqeathed 40^s every year for ever, to pvt forth | a poore man child an apprentice, with diver other loving | Remembrances vnto her good friends and neighbours. These aforesaid donations | are to issve ovt of the Benefit and Profits of the Rectory of Wandsw'th. This was desired to be recorded, that God might be glorified, | the memorial of the just might be blessed, and the living stirred vp | to svch like good Workes of Piety and Compassion.

Above is a lozenge, on which is :—*Argent, a double-queued lion rampant-guardant sable.*

The rent charge of £22 16*s.* a year issuing out of the rectorial tithes of Wandsworth is still paid to the Trustees.

Rec'd for a graue in the Church for Mrs Powell	6	8
P'd the Coppie of Mr Powells will	2	6

(Churchwardens' Accounts, 1630-31.)

163$\frac{0}{1}$ Mar. 1 Mrs Susanna Powell, widowe, bur.

Her will (17 St. John) was proved 23 February 1630-31 by Sibil Sturdevant.

Brass plate on ledger in nave :—Depositvm Henr. Smith, | Senatoris Londinensis | Mole sub hac quæris ? Quis conditur ? Optime lector | Cuias et Qualis ? Qnantus in orbe fuit ? | A dextris muri statuam tu cernere possis | Oranti similem marmore de pario, | Subter quam statuam cernatur tabula sculpta | Auratis verbis quæ tibi cuncta notant.

Mural, with effigy, north chancel aisle. Arms: Quarterly, 1 *and* 4, *Sable, a fesse between three saltires or, for* Smith ; *2 and* 3, *Barry of six gules and argent, on a chief of the last three wolves' heads erased of the first, for* . . . . Here Lyeth the Body of Henry Smyth Esquire Sometime Citizen and | Alderman of London, who departed this Life the 3rd day of January | A^o Dni. 1627, being then near the Age of 79 years, Whom While he | lived gave unto these Severall Townes in Surry following ; One | Thousand Pounds a piece to buy Lands for perpetuity for ye Reliefe | and setting the poor People aworke in the said townes, Viz. To | the Towne of Croydon, one thousand pounds, to the Towne of | Kingston, one thousand pounds, to the Towne of Guilford, one thou- | sand pounds, to the Towne of Darkin, one thousand pounds, to the | Towne of Farneham, one thousand pounds, & by his last Will & Testament | did further give & devise to buy Lands for perpetuity for the | Reliefe & setting their poor aworke ; unto the Town of Ryegate | one thousand pounds, and unto the Towne of Richmond one especyaltye | or debt of a thousand pounds, and unto this Towne of Wandsworth | wherein he was born, the sum of five hundred pounds for yᵉ same uses | as before, & did further Will & Bequeath one Thousand to buy Lands | for perpetuity to redeeme poor Captives & Prisoners from yᵉ Turkish | Tyranie, & not here stinting his charity & bounty, did also give | and bequeath the most Part of his Estate being to a great Value | for the Purchasing Lands of Inheritance for ever, for yᵉ reliefe | of the poor and setting them aworke. A pattern worthy the | imitation of those whome God hath Blessed with the Abundance of | the Goods of this Life to follow him herein.

Rec'd for the bells at Mʳ Smith's buriall .   .   .   .   0 ᵛ 0
Pᵈ for mending of two baldricks against Mʳ Smiths funerall .   .   .   .   .   0 j iiij
(Churchwardens' Accounts, 1627-8.)

Recᵈ of Mʳ Smiths executors   .   .   .   .   1 ℔ 0 0
(Ibid., 1629-30.)

Pᵈ Gaunnon for chousing Mʳ Smithe Monument 0 2 0
(Ibid., 1645-6.)

Pᵈ chousing Mʳ Smithe toombe 00 01 06
(Ibid., 1646-7.)

Wandsworth receives over £170 annually from this charity.

In the Burial Register for 1627-8 are these two entries :—
Feb. 7   Henry Smith of London, gent.
Feb. 14   Henrie Smith, Esq.

The Funeral Certificate in the College of Arms records Smith was buried on 7th day of February, "being of the age of 79 years at May next."
His will is dated 24 April 1627, and proved 23 January 1627-8.
In the Churchwardens' Accounts for 1549 the name of Walter Smith is mentioned. He possibly was Henry's father.

———

On a monument on the south side was this inscription :—" Here lieth the Body of EDWARD SNOW, of Chicksands in the County of Bedford, Esquire, in memory of whom EMMA his wife, daughter to WILLIAM BYNE, in the County of Sussex, Esquire, erected this monument. He had issue ELIZABETH, ALICE, and SARAH. He deceased at the Mannor of Alfarthing, Anno Dom. 1587."

———

SNOW FAMILY OF WANDSWORTH.

ARMS.—*Per fesse embattled azure and argent three antelopes' heads erased counterchanged, horned or*, SNOW.

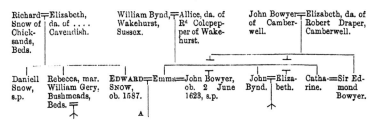

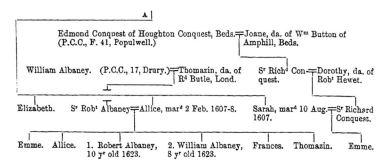

Aubrey, in his "Natural History of Surrey," gave a transcript of an inscription at Wandsworth, Surrey, now lost :—

"Here lieth the Body of Edward Snow, of Chicksands in the county of Bedford, esquire, in memory of whom Emma his wife, daughter to William Byne, in the County of Sussex, esquire, erected this monument. He had issue Elizabeth, Alice, and Sarah. He deceased at the Mannor of Alfarthing Anno Dom. 1587."

Edward Snow was second son of Richard Snow (Will proved P.C.C. 1554, 18, More) of Chicksands, co. Bedford, and his wife Elizabeth (Will proved P.C.C. 1587, 17, Spencer), a gentlewoman of the Privy Chamber to Queen Elizabeth, and daughter of . . . . Cavendish, aunt to the old Countess of Shrewsbury. He married Emma, daughter of William Bynd of Wakeherst, Sussex, and his wife "Allice," daughter of Richard Colepeper of Wakeherst. After her husband's death in 1587 she married John Bowyer, J.P., second son of John Bowyer of Camberwell, Surrey, who died 2 June 1623, s.p.

As the Parish Registers as well as the Churchwardens' Accounts for the parish of Wandsworth are missing for 1587, there is no record locally of Edward Snow. His name does not occur in the parish deeds, though in 1608 Cecily Riche assigns a lease of certain lands belonging to the church to John Bowyar, who was Lord of the Manor of Alfarthing in 1598. He appears to have received this manor from his grandfather Robert Draper, and Edward Snow was his tenant.

The will of Edwarde Snowe of Alfarthing, par. Wansworthe, Surrey, is in P.C.C., 73, Spencer (1587).

Edward and Emma Snow had three daughters, Elizabeth, Alice, and Sarah.

160⅘ Feb. 2 Sir Robert Albany, Knight, married Mʳˢ Alce Snow ; at Wandsworth. (Wandsworth Parish Registers.)

Sir Robert was son of William Albaney of London and his wife Thomazin, daughter of Richard Butle.

Sir Robert and Alice had issue, Emme, Allice, Robert (æt. 10 in 1623), William (æt. 8 in 1623), Frances, and Thomazin.

1607 Aug. 10 Sir Richard Conquest, Knight, married Mʳˢ Sara Snowe ; at Wandsworth. (Wandsworth Parish Registers.)

Sir Richard was second son of Sir Richard Conquest of Houghton, Beds, by Dorothy, daughter of Robert Hewet of Ampthill, Beds, Esq.

Sir Richard and Sarah had one child, Emma.

The family of William Bynd intermarried with that of John and Elizabeth Bowyer : John Bynd was first husband of Elizabeth Bowyer ; Catharine Bynd was married to Sir Edmond Bowyer ; and Emma Bynd was married to Edward Snow and afterwards to John Bowyer.

(See the pedigrees printed by the Harleian Society : "Visitations of Bedfordshire," pp. 97, 110 ; "Visitations of Surrey," pp. 26, 32, 116.)

———

Here lyeth interred the body of Thomas Tayer, Senior, | Aged 101 years, buried the 30ᵗʰ December 1653. Also the body | of Thomas Tayer his son, aged 78, buried the 14ᵗʰ January | 1662. Both of Rants in Northamptonshire, Esquires.

1653 Dec. 30 Mʳ Thomas Tayer, aged 101, bur.
166¼ Jan. 14 Thomas Tayer, Esq., bur.

On a small brass plate on the south side of the rails was the following :—Pray for the sowle of Mr WHEDDON, who dessessed the | xxiiij of . . . . in the year of our Lord God MCCCCCXX | Upon whose sowle Jesu have mercy.   Amen.

Marble tablet, south wall of south aisle :—✠ . IN . MEMORY . OF | JEMIMA ("MIME") | THE . BELOVED . WIFE . OF . JAMES . WHITE | OF . THIS . TOWN | WHO . DIED . 30th . NOV. 1902 | AGED . 43 . YEARS. | "HE . GIVETH . HIS . BELOVED . SLEEP."   (Buchanan.)
[Daughter of George Dolling of Aldenham, Herts.]

Mural, west end of nave:—Under this Stone | In a Vault is Deposited the | Remains of JOSEPH WIGHT, Esqr | who died the 18th of November 1770, | Aged 74 years | Also lies Inter'd in the same Vault | the Remains of his Niece | Mrs MARTHA DUNWELL | who Died Augst ye 13th, 1773 | Aged 63.

1770 Nov. 26   Joseph White, Esq., 74, bur.
1773 Aug. 19   Martha Dunwell, in ye church, 60, bur.

Ledger, north aisle :—

A. W.
S. C.
I. W.

On tablets :—Part of this | Church was rebuilt | and Beautified A.D. 1780 | The Revd ROBERT HOLT BUTCHER, Vicar | Mr JAMES OLIVER | Mr HENRY GARDINER | Churchwardens.

In the year of our Lord 1859 | extensive repairs, alterations | and embellishments were made | in and to this Church | chiefly by improving the Chancel and | introducing a stained glass window* | Re-pewing the galleries to obtain | additional accomodation and lighting | the church with gas | The Revd JOHN BUCKMASTER, A.M., Vicar | Wm THOS. MACKRELL | SIGISMUND RÜCKER | Churchwardens.

To the Glory of God and for the Welfare of | the Parishioners this Church was | restored and enlarged in the last year of the | 19th Century at a cost of £4505 : 10 : 3 | The Chancel, Organ chamber and Choir Vestry were added and a New Roof provided for the Nave.

Wm REED, M.A. { HARRY FEW } Churchwardens.
Vicar.   { Jas WILLCOX }

On south wall (exterior) of tower:—This Tower | was repaired and heightened | in the year of our Lord | MDCCCXLI | D. C. DELAFOSSE, A.M., Vicar | THOMAS ALLEN & JOHN DORMAY | Churchwardens.

---

* Representing the Transfiguration.

Bookplate of John Hervey, Esq.*

JOHN HERVEY, Esq., a distinguished member of the House of Commons, Hereditary High Steward of Bury St. Edmunds, was elevated to the Peerage, 23 March 1703, as *Baron Hervey of Ickworth, co. Suffolk*, and created, 19 Oct. 1714, EARL OF BRISTOL. He married 1st, 1 Nov. 1688, Isabella, daughter and sole heir of the Right Hon. Sir Robert Carr, Bart., of Sleaford, co. Lincoln, Chancellor of the Duchy of Lancaster, and granddaughter (maternally) of Lord Arlington, by whom (who died 7 March 1692-3) he had a son CARR, *Lord Hervey* (who died unmarried 15 Nov. 1723), and two daughters. The Earl married 2ndly, 25 July 1695, Elizabeth, daughter and coheir of Sir Thomas Felton, Bart., of Playford, co. Suffolk (by his wife Lady Elizabeth Howard, daughter and coheir of James, 3rd Earl of Suffolk), by whom (who died 2 May 1741) he had eleven sons and six daughters. (*Vide* Burke's " Peerage.")

For two other varieties of John Hervey's Bookplates, respectively dated " 1698 " and " 23 March 1702," see " Visitation of the County of Suffolk, 1561," by the late Dr. Howard, F.S.A.

A Heraldic and Physiological Curiosity.†

In July 1698 Thomas Greenhill, chirurgeon of London, petitioned the Earl Marshall, that, being the thirty-ninth child and seventh son of one father by one mother, he might be allowed a difference in his Arms to be borne by him in commemoration thereof.

This was transmitted by the hands of Blanche Lyon, who was at this time the Duke's private pursuivant.

At the College of Heralds [Original Grants, vol. iv., fols. 276-9] is the grant which resulted and in these words:—

" To all and singular to whom these presentes shall come Sir Thomas St George Knight, Principall King of Armes, and Sir Henry St George Knight, Clarenceux King of Armes, send Greeting. *Whereas* Thomas Greenhill of the City of London, Chirurgion [thirty-ninth child and seventh son of William Greenhill of Greenhill in ye County of Middlesex by his only wife Elizabeth Daughter of John Jones of London], has made application to his Grace Henry Duke of Norfolk, Earl Marshall of England, yt the Arms born and used, under the hand of William Ryley, by his said Father—scilicet, Vert 2 Barrs Argent, in chief a Leopard passant or—may be allowed and confirmed to be born by him wth ye Alterations of ye Barrs from Argent to Ermine, and whereas they have borne for their Crests in seals and otherwise a Demi-Griphon, he may be allowed to bear ye same Gules, powdered with thirty-nine Mullets or. *And* forasmuch as ye said Earl Marshall, being well satisfyed of the Qualifications of ye said Thomas Greenhill, and in consideration of his Services to his Grace and his Family, did by Warrant or Order under his Hand

JE NOBLIERA JAMAIS

John Hervey of Ickworth in
Com. Suff. Esq. 1698.

and Seal of his Office of Earl Marshall, bearing Date y[e] Eight day of August last past, Order and appoint Us to Grant Allow and Confirm y[e] said Arms and Crest so differenced as abovesaid.

Know ye therefore y[t] We y[e] said Garter and Clarenceux, in Pursuance of y[e] said Earl Marshall's Order, and by Virtue of y[e] Letters Pattents of o[r] Offices, to each of us respectively Granted, under y[e] Great Seal of England, have allowed and confirmed and by these Presents do Grant allow and Confirm unto the said Thomas Greenhill y[e] said Arms and Crest with the Alterations and Additions abovesaid, as in y[e] Margin hereof is more plainly depicted. To be borne and used for ever hereafter by him the said Thomas Greenhill and y[e] Heirs and other Descendents off his Body lawfully begotten, in Shield, Coat-armour, Penon, Seal, or otherwise according to y[e] Law of Armes, withoutt Lett or Interruption of any Person or Persons whatsoever. *In Wittness* whereof We y[e] said Garter and Clarenceux Kings of Armes have to these Presents subscribed our Names and affixed y[e] Seals of our Respective Offices y[e] first Day of September, in y[e] Tenth year of the Reigne of o[r] Sovereigne Lord William y[e] Third, by y[e] Grace of GOD King of England, Scotland, France and Ireland, Defender of the Faith, Annoque Domini 1698.

"Thomas S[r] George, Garter,   "Henry S[r] George,
    "Principall King of Armes.   "Clarenceux King of Armes."

I would draw attention to several interesting points: The William Ryley mentioned was called Norroy by the Parliament, and advanced to be Clarenceux on the death of Arthur Squibb in May 1646, after which Edward Byshe, who was named Garter in 1646, and Ryley seem to have constituted the whole staff of the Heralds' College and took all the fees they could make. The proclamation 4 September 1660, addressed to Sir Edward Walker (he had been deposed in 1645 and was recreated Garter 1660), declares, "Whereas Edward Bish, Arthur Squibb, and W[m] Ryley have for divers years usurped," etc. It then enacts that all grants of Arms made by them be null and void, and orders them to be destroyed and defaced. (The original is at the College—see my "Earl Marshal's Court in England," pp. 58-9.) Therefore Thomas Greenhill's father's grant was null and void! Among the Papers at the Heralds' College there is a note that a drawing on vellum of the Arms, as altered and sought for, had been submitted by Thomas. No doubt this was the work of his friend Blanche Lyon; and the wording, "in consideration of his services to his Grace and his Family," shewing that Thomas was and had been for some time their medical attendant, readily accounts for the friendly relations of these two—Thomas Greenhill and Blanche Lyon—who put forward and aided Greenhill's application. I think it is extremely rare to get so strong a concurrence of proof. We have (1) Thomas declaring the most unusual and startling fact of the family in which he was thirty-ninth, and on that plea asking its heraldic recognition! (2) Blanche Lyon, the Earl Marshall's own Herald, who had ready means of verifying that extraordinary statement, risks his future career in placing before his Master a statement which the Medical profession declares to be now impossible. (3) The Earl Marshall knew him as his medical attendant, and was willing to testify to such an extraordinary event by ordering the thirty-nine Mullets as desired to be placed on the Crest in demonstration thereof. (4) The Kings of Arms, jealous of the honour of the Earl Marshall and their own dignity, must have satisfied themselves by evidences—before they would carry to completion what, if not exactly true, would have been a transparent and conspicuous farce—easily disproved, and entailing disgrace and shame on all implicated! I would not have considered all this as at all necessary, except to prove that whatever limit to the extent of families may *now* prevail, we have here an indisputable case in 1698, and physiological changes must have come since !

Among the Papers preserved at the Heralds' College is a volume of much later date, entitled "Pingo MSS.," where, at fols. 276-9, are collections for the Greenhill Pedigree—from William Greenhill of Greenhill, the father of Thomas—after whose name appears "39 children, 7 of which were sons," but only the names of the six sons who survived are entered ; all the rest died young. William, the father, is described as Secretary to General Monk (created Duke of Albemarle in 1660 ; died 3 January 1670) and of Hyde in Abbots Langley, Herts, as well as of Greenhill in Harrow, Middlesex. Cussans, in his "History of Hertfordshire," helps us here, as he notes (vol. iii., p. 88) the conveyance of the Manor of Hyde in 1612 by Lawrence Greene of London to Henry Greenhill of Greenhill Grove in the parish of Harrow, from whose son* William it descended to another William, the father of our Thomas, "chirurgion." Henry, the eldest son of this William and brother of Thomas, sold the Manor in 1714 to Edward Strong, a noted Mason of London. Cussans, when writing his work, had never seen the original grant to Thomas ; at p. 97 he gives the date 1698, but quotes from an incorrect copy among the Stow MSS., No. 670, in British Museum, fol. 73.

It is mentioned (Pingo MSS.) that the children were all at single births except one, and that seven only of the thirty-nine were surviving in 1698.

In "Gent. Mag." for 1805, Part I., p. 405, "Chris. Johnson" communicates that a small portrait of Mrs. Greenhill—at Wallingwells, the residence of Sir Thomas Woollaston White, Bart.—has a MS. note on the back: "she had 39 children by one husband. They were all born alive and baptized, and all Single births save one. The last child, who was born after his father's death, was a chirurgeon in King Street, Bloomsbury, and wrote Νεκροκηδεια.

(Signed)   "RICH. ASHBY, a clergyman."

As no family connection seems at all probable, I think this picture must have been purchased and hung up at Wallingwells as a curiosity in natural history (?).

In " Notes and Queries" for September 1852 (First Series, vol. vi., p. 303) is given a MS. note written in a copy of Νεκροκηδεια and sent by E. D.: " Mrs Greenhill, mother of the author, had 39 children," etc., just as above, and almost word for word up to " Bloomsbury."

"Νεκροκηδεια or the Art of embalming, wherein is shewn the right [*sic*] of burial, the funeral ceremonies, and the several ways of preserving the dead bodies in most nations of the world," etc., 4to, London, 1705 [British Museum Press Mark 454, A. 22], was written by our Thomas Greenhill. Among the subscribers are William Greenhill, Esq. (three copies), and Mr. John Greenhill (one copy). In an allegorical frontispiece, on the left hand top corner, is a curtain against which hangs a shield of Arms and Crest as granted in 1698, but the artist has failed to get thirty-nine mullets into the limited space on the Crest. The work consists of three letters, viz.: (*a*) To Chas Bernard, Serj.-Surgeon to her Ma^ty & present Master of the Surgeons Company & one of the Surgeons to St Bart^s Hosp^l ; (*b*) To Dr John Lawson, sometime president of the Coll. of Physicians, London ;

---

* It is not within the scope of this paper, but I think it likely that if Mr. Cussans had consulted the will of Henry Greenhill of Greenhill in the parish of Harrow, proved at P.C.C. 21 August 1630 by his *brother* William Greenhill, he might have hesitated to write *son*. The reference is 69, Scroope.

and (c) To Dr Hans Sloane, Sec^y to the Royal Society and F.C.P., London. The second and third letters are quite interesting reading, and contain accounts of Egypt, the Nile, Pyramids, etc., with many illustrations, culled from the works of travel published at that date.

I would warn my readers against the inaccurate account given in the "Dictionary of National Biography," vol. xxiii., pub. 1890, of Thomas Greenhill (1681—1740?). The writer cannot have seen the original grant of Arms, 1698—"born 1681." Are we to suppose that a young surgeon ætatis 17 (if he could hold a diploma at that age) could venture to apply for such a distinction! and could thus, still an infant, have earned that the Earl Marshall should be "well satisfyed of his Qualifications," and "in consideration of his Services to his Grace and his Family," etc.? Such language could only apply to the experienced medical attendant upon such an illustrious household. Nor does it seem probable that a young man of 24 could have published the book in 1705 and addressed his letters to such distinguished heads of the profession. That may be possible. The other case pointed out is not. *If* William the father died in 1681, Thomas cannot have been a posthumous child! The grant is absolutely exact evidence, and was given to this Thomas and his descendants. Again, it seems to me that the, I am glad to say anonymous, writer never saw the original grant, or he would not have said that the lady's maiden name was White ; she was daughter of John Jones.

The Greenhills have been at Harrow for many generations—I suppose they may be found even as early as the thirteenth century—and there were several branches. The Abbots Langley Registers of Births, Marriages, and Deaths from 1653 to 1680 have been missing for many years, as noted in the Register Census Act Report of 1830 ("Middlesex and Herts Notes and Queries," vol. iii., p. 11). But in the Subsidy Rolls for Harrow we find the following [see "Middlesex and Herts Notes and Queries," vol. iii., p. 136, and iv., p. 187] :—

1642. Subsidy Roll.
  In Roxeth—Thomas Greenhill, in lands xx^s.
      William Greenhill, in lands xx^s.
      John Greenhill, in lands xx^s.
  In Greenhill—William Greenhill, gent., in lands iij^{li}.

1675. Hearth Tax.
  In Roxeth—William Greenhill pays for 7 chimnies.
      John Greenhill, for 5 chimnies.
  In Greenhill—Mr Greenhill, for 6 chimnies.

The last shews that Mr. Greenhill held his house in Greenhill ; had it been let the tenant's name would have appeared. I think it likely that the anonymous writer has given the date of the death of another William Greenhill and not the father of Thomas, who was of Greenhill and of Hyde in Abbots Langley.

I have given a picture of the Arms as in the margin, because there is much confusion as to the term "Leopard." In James Coat's "New Dictionary of Heraldry, 1739," is this explanation : French Heralds laid it down that Lions passant-guardant were to be called "Leopards," but English Heralds declined· to follow so absurd a distinction. It is thus that we sometimes meet with "the Leopards of England"! Even Papworth, at p. 19, blazons the Greenhill Arms granted 1698 as "Vert 2 bars erm., in chief a lion pass. guard. or," and so it seemed desirable to give the original picture shewing the ordinary "Felis Leopardus."

I, too, found it impossible to get distinctly the important thirty-nine mullets on the Crest ! and so have left it, like the original office copy, merely an uncoloured sketch. It will be noticed that the gryphon is disposed with wings addorsed, so as to leave the greatest possible space for these mullets, but the artist abandoned the attempt to shew them there !

Monumental Inscriptions

IN THE

Church of St. Giles=in=the=Fields.*

"A faire monument on yᵉ north side of yᵉ chancell."

Arms : Dexter [*blank*] ; impaling, *On a chevron three mullets.*

Resurgam.

Nere to this place intered lyes the body of the much | Lamented WILLIAM THOROLD, Esq., sonne and heire | apparent of Sʳ WILLIAM THOROLD of Marston com. | Lincoln, Barronet, who departed this life on the fourth | of 9ᵇʳⁱˢ ætatis suæ 30ᵗʰ, 1649. To whose deare memory | his beloved wife erected this monument.

> Spectators of this solemn monument
> Behold how senseless marble doth relent,
> In sympatbizing feares a verdant age,
> Here shrin'd for Heaven, too good for this sad stage
> Of Tragicke wooes ; a soule that whilst on earth
> It liv'd, dy'd unto sinne, quick to its birth
> Above three Tryumphs This exalted sunne.
> Such onely bare the prize who thus have runne.
> Here rest, sweete urne ; let Friends no more bemoane
> Thy hopefull (blossom'd) fruite, Thy Buds are flowne
> With thee to Eden, fructifying there,
> Till that grand day of Christ assize drawe neare,
> When trumpets shall Thee rowse from slumbering night,
> Sounding good morrow To thy endless light.
>
>   *John Marshall, Sculptor.*

The "New View" says of this monument, it is "By the N. doorcase opening into the chancel, a very neat marble monument." The inscription is only given as far as "Baronet," because "being uncivilly eclipsed from view by the interposing Cornish [*sic*] of the Doorcase." But it gives the arms : *Sable, three goats springing argent ;* impaling, *Gules, on a chevron argent three mullets sable.*

"On a gravestone in yᵉ chancell " :—Here rests hopefull of a glourious resurrection The LADY | ALICE The eldest daughter of HENRY, LORD HASTINGS | EARLE OF HUNTINGDON & relict of Sʳ GERVAS CLIFTON | Knight & Baronet, whose constant pietye assures her | happiness. Obiit 12° Martii 1666, ætatis 61.

"This atchevement of arms hang on yᵉ north wall of yᵉ chancell immediately over his gravestone " :—

Arms : I. *Azure, on a chief or three martlets gules, in the field a crescent of the third for difference,* WRAY. II. *Argent, on a chevron between three hawks' heads sable as many cinquefoils of the field,* JACKSON. III. *Argent, on a chief vert a tau cross between two mullets or,* DRURY. IV. *Argent, six cross-crosslets sable, a chief indent azure.* V. *Sable, six cinquefoils argent.* VI. *Chequy argent and gules, on a fesse azure three . . . . or.* VII. *Azure, two lions passant-guardant or.* VIII. *Gules, an eagle displayed argent.* IX. *Azure, four lozenges conjoined in fesse or, each charged with an escallop-shell gules.* X. *Azure, a fesse argent between six lions rampant or.* XI. *Bendy of eight argent and gules.* XII. *Gules, a fesse or between three saltires couped argent.* XIII. *Argent, a fesse between three horse-shoes gules.* XIV. *Argent, three lozenges conjoined in fesse, barry wavy of six argent and sable.* XV. *Sable, a bend between six escallop-shells or.* XVI. *Gules, two bars or, over all a bend sable.* On an escutcheon of pretence : I. *and 4, Barry of ten argent and azure, six inescutcheons sable, each charged with a lion rampant or,* CECILL ; 2 *and 3, Gules, on a saltire argent an annulet of the field,* NEVILL.

---

* Communicated by ARTHUR F. G. LEVESON GOWER, Esq., assisted by ARTHUR J. JEWERS—concluded from p. 245.

" On a gravestone of black marble, inlade round the superficies with white, in which is this inscription ":—

Arms : *Azure, on a chief or, three martlets gules,* WRAY ; impaling, *Argent, on a chief vert a tau cross or between two mullets of the last pierced of the chief,* DRURY. Also this shield : CECIL, as above, impaling *Or, fretty gules, a canton ermine.*

Here lyes Sr CHRISTOPHER WRAY of Ashby in | Lincolnesheire who dyed the 6th of February 1645 | in ye 44th Yeare of his age, and in his last will and Tes- | tament desired this inscription following. | Christ Jesus came into the world to save sinners | of whome I am cheife.—The 1 Tim. i. 15.

" There is a table hard by the former containeing onely the arms of WRAY," viz., *Azure, on a chief or three martlets gules.*

" On a gravestone part covered by ye railes of ye communion Table " (A shield divided quarterly of four ; in the third quarter a chevron only is tricked) :—

" Here lyeth interred the body of an accomplished Gentle- | man by name RICHARD HOLFORD, Esq., he was extracted | out of that most ancient family of the HOLFORDS in | the county of Chester . . . . | deserves an honorable esteeme & perpetual memory of | his meritts to all posterity. He dyed the 23 Aprill in the | Yeare of our Lord 1663, Aged . ."

This monument is not given in the "New View." In " The Visitation of Cheshire, 1580 " (Harl. Soc.), the arms are given as 1, *Argent, a greyhound passant sable,* HOLFORD ; 2, *Argent, three bulls' heads caboshed sable,* BULKELEY ; 3, *Argent, a chevron between three text ᙻ's sable,* TOFT ; 4, *as* 1. Crest : *A greyhound's head couped sable.* This agrees with the chevron in the third quarter of the tricked coat. The accompanying abstract of his will is valuable, as although the inscription says he was of the Cheshire family, his will shews he did not come directly from there, but from Cambridgeshire.

Richard Holford of Drury Lane in the parish of St. Giles-in-the-Fields, gent. Will dated 20 April 1661. To the parish of Long Stanton, co. Cambridge, £50, to be invested in land the profitts for the relief of the poor there, being the place where he was born. Daughter Bulstrode £100, and to her husband £5. Grand-child Mary Hall £20. Boy Edward Mellon £40 to bind him apprentice. Parish of Okington, co. Cambridge, £30 to purchase a revenue to relieve the poor. Son Charles £100 beside the house already given him. Residue between four sons, viz., Henry, John, Stephen, and Charles Holford, and daughter Sarah Holford. Names late wife's will and her children, viz., John Webb, Jane Webb, and Katherine Webb the wife of James Tomlinson, £5 each. Mr Holford, a shoemaker in White Fryers, London, £5. Will of Mr Webb, late wife's first husband. Friend Mr Watts of Mitcham in Surrey. Late wife's son Robert Webb £100 beside what he had from his father and mother, when he is 21. To the masters of the parish of S. Clement's Danes £10 above the £10 already given, to buy a yearly rent to be given each Christmas day before eight o'clock to poor people, each 12^d. £160 to S. Giles, Criplegate, to buy a yearly rent for the relief of the poor there. Thomas Hall of Long Stanton £5 for a horse testator borrowed for a journey and it died. Residue of lands and tenements to son Henry Holford. Mrs Smith, widow, of the " Mayremaid " in Holborne, £10, and the children she had by her husband Mr Burton £10.

Proved 30 April 1661. (P.C.C., 58, May.)

" On a grave stone in the chancel ":—

Arms : *A cross engrailed,* uncoloured, and no doubt unfinished, like some others in this MS.

Cubat hic inhumatus JUSTINIANUS PAGITT, arm. | Custos Brevium & Recordo-rum de Banco Regis, clausit | ille diem extremum anno orbis redempti 1668 | mense decemb. die 29°.

" On a grave stone in the chancell ":—

Arms, on a lozenge: *A cross engrailed, in the first canton an escallop-shell,* PAGITT ; impaling *A chief vaire.* This shield is not coloured in the MS. and is unfinished. The impalement should be : *Argent, a lion rampant between three crescents sable, a chief vaire,* WILCOCKS.

Here resteth the body of DORCAS PAGITT, widdowe | daughter of RICHARD WILCOX, citizen & haberdasher | of London, & late wife of JUSTINIAN PAGITT, Esq. | Custos Brevium et Recordorum of the King's Bench, by | whome he had 3 sonns & 2 daughters, JUSTINIAN, THO- | MAS, LEWIN, DORCAS, & MARY. She departed this | life the 14 day of September anno salutis 1669.

The above JUSTINIAN PAGITT died intestate, administration being granted of his effects, but the following short abtract of the will of his widow supplies the names of their surviving children, and shews the eldest son was still unmarried.

Dorcas Pagitt of Holberne in the par. of St Giles, widow. Will dated 6 Sept. 1669. The jewell she had from her husband to her son Justinian for his wife when he has one. Three leases in or near Peterborough to her five children Justinian, Thomas, Mary, Dorcas, and Lewin. Money due from cousin Huxley. Son Justinian residuary legatee and executor. Witnesses: Rich. Pagitt, Tho. Maydwell, Ab. Pagitt.

Proved 18 Sept. 1669. (P.C.C., 107, Coke.)

" These arms are depicted in severall windows of the chancell, viz." :—

I. *Argent, on a bend between two lions rampant sable, three boars' heads couped or ;* impaling *Gules, a fesse ermine, within a bordure engrailed of the second,* SPECKART and ACTON. II. *Gules, a fesse between three hedgehogs argent ;* impaling *Sable, guttée de l'eau on a fesse argent three Cornish choughs proper,* CLAXTON, impaling CORN- WALLIS. III. *Ermine, two chevronels gules, in chief a crescent of the last for difference ;* impaling *Sable, a lion rampant or, guttée de poix, a canton of the second,* FENNER, impaling . . . . IV. *Quarterly* : 1 *and* 4, *Paly of six argent and azure a bend gules ;* 2 *and* 3, *Or, a pile gules,* CHANDOS ; *over all the badge of a baronet,* ANNESLEY, LORD MOUNTMORRES. V. *Per saltire argent and gules,* SHELBURY. VI. The same, impaling *Argent, on a bend sable three lions' heads erased argent, crowned or,* SHELBURY, impaling WROTH. VII. *Quarterly* : 1 *and* 4, *Argent, a cross between four Passion- nails gules ;* 2 *and* 3, *Per pale* [? *wavy*] *argent and gules a lion rampant sable,* PYLE and ELFORD.

HENRICUS FARRER | de | Thowood in comitatu Eboracensi | Armig : mortuuis in Domino Junii | 28 Anno Dom. 1610 anno ætat | 74 beatorum resurrectio- | nem hic expectat.

Here | lyeth the bodies of WILLIAM SMITH | Baker & JOANE his wife. Hee departed | this life Decemb. the first 1656. She | Aug. the 25, 1651. With them lye | two daughters ANN & MARGA- | RET SMITH.

Here | lyeth the body of THOMAS FOWNES | second sonn of THOMAS FOWNES, Esq., of | Stapleton in the county of Dorsett who | deceased the 27 of March 1655 being | one yeare & seven months old.

A blank shield :—Here | lyeth interred the body of MARGARET | JOHNSTONE alias SMITH the wife | of JOHN JOHNSTONE of Newbye, merchant | in London, by whome she had 6 sonns | & 7 daughters & deceased the | 12 of Aprill 1652, aged 53.

Here | lyeth interred the body of EDWARD | BIRKHEAD, Esq., serjeant att | armes, who departed this life | the 14 day of October in the | Yeare of Our Lord 1662, aged | 59 yeares.

A blank shield :—In memoriam .... | conjugis posuit mæstissemus obiit |
5 May 1650 ....

A blank shield :—Here | lyes interred the body of Coll. HENRY | SIBTHORPE of
the privy chamber | in ordinary to K. CHARLES THE FIRST | who departed this life
the 8 of | Decemb. 1672, aged 84.
Henry Sibthorpe of London, Esq. Will dated 13 Dec. 1670. Cousin Mrs. Barbara
West £100, and her brother Mr. George West £10. Cousin Elizabeth Crosby £10.
Cousin Anne Crosby £10. Cousin John Crosby £10. Friend Col. Edward Gray
of Gray's Inn £50. Friend Mrs. Anne Francklyn, widow, £10; her daughter Alice
Francklyn, widow [sic], £5. Landlord Mr. Bryan Sharpe and Mrs. Frances his
wife each £5. Mr. John Cooke, Attorney of the Common Pleas, living in Sheere
Lane, £20. Friend Mr. Charles Francklyn of the "Utlary Office" in Lincoln's
Inn, gent., executor and residuary legatee.
Proved 16 Dec. 1672. (P.C.C., 154, Eure.)

A blank shield :—Under | the gravestone att the end of the 3rd pew in the | next
Alley lyeth the body of THOMAS GARRETT | Esq., & grandchild to Sr GEORGE
GARRETT, Kt & | Alderman of London, aged 5 yeares, dyed | 1669.

A blank shield :—Here | lyeth the body of EDWARD THORNE | gent. who dyed
the 18 day of May | 1670, aged 54 yeares.

Here | lyeth interred the body of ALEXANDER | DAVIES of Ebury in the county
of | Middlesex, Esquire, who departed | this life the 2d of July Anno | Dom. 1665,
ætat suæ 30.

[Here the account of the Monuments in this Church ends, as far as Lansdowne
MS. 878 gives them. Several of these it will be seen are not given in the "New
View." On the other hand, the latter work gives some which were put up after the
manuscript account was made ; and having done so much, it may perhaps be not
unacceptable if we complete our account of the Monuments in the Church of
St. Giles-in-the-Fields by adding those in the "New View" not in the above MS.
or among those still existing.]

[The inscriptions following are from the "New View of London," printed in
1708.]
The "New View of London," p. 259, says "a little way from the last
(Widdrington's), on the south side of the chancel, is a neat blue-veined marble
monument with this inscription :—
Underneath lyeth the Body of THOMAS CORNWALLIS, Esq., son of Sir FRANCIS
CORNWALLIS | and ELIZABETH his wife, sole Daughter and Heir to Sir HENRY
JONES, Baronet | of Abermarless in the county of Caermarthen. He married
EMMA Daughter | of Sir JOHN CHARLETON, Knight and Baronet, by whom he had
4 Sons and 5 | Daughters ; three sons died before him and one son and five
Daughters survived. | His person was graceful, and his Soul sublime ; Virtue
Honour, | and Complacency guided all his Actions ; a Lover of his Country ;
most | tender and indulgent to his Wife and Children ; obliging and serviceable |
to his Friends ; hospitable and generous to his Neighbours, just, charitable | and
courteous to all he conversed with. He lived beloved and | died much lamented
by them all the 16th of July A.D. 1703. His | Noon was Night, being made perfect
in 33 years. His Grandfather | CHARLES, his Father Sir FRANCIS, and his Brother
CHARLES lye buried in this church, near the Pulpit. | His disconsolate Widow
caused this Monument to be erected in | memory of her dear Husband, and his
Relations.
His Armes here are 8 Coats quarterly : I. *Sable, gutté de l'eau, on a Fess
Argent 3 black birds.* II. *Sable, 3 Bars gemells Argent, on a canton or a crescent*

Gules. III. *Or, a Lion Rampant Gules.* IV. *Gules, 10 Bezants, 4, 3, 2, and 1.* V. *Sable, a cross flory or.* VI. *Argent, a chevron sable betn. 3 black birds within a Bordure engrayled Gules, charged with Entoir 11 Bazants.* VII. *Azure, on a mount proper a lion passant guardant or.* VIII. *As the third; and the crest a Buck lodged (or Cumbant) Argent attired or."*

[The peculiarities of the blazon are those in the "New View," and it will be observed that the arms of Charleton and Jones are both given as quarterings, but it may be that the arms were incorrectly marshalled on the monument.

A manuscript note in the British Museum copy of the "New View" says that when the church was destroyed his body was taken up and removed into the vault of Bishop Robinson in the east end of the churchyard at Fulham, and buried with his sister Lætitia, as a stone there states.]

"On the N. side of the chancel near the E. end, a pretty white marble monument with this Inscription :—

> Hospes si longam spem inchoas, allucinaris
> Sis licet in paucis, æqui leoniq ; tenax,
> Sis & Juris & sanctioris Minervæ consultus
> Nec fari nescius etiam in foro regnes
> Tamen is quod es ante fuit insigniterq ;
> Hocre Jam de sub Lapide cinis.

D. THOMÆ WIDDRINGTONI serv. ad legem & Eq. aurat. Quem | Northumbria mundo Middlesexia cœlo dedit postquam virin dicendo cælestis. | Non solum innocentem bactenus illustrem Togæ quoq ; Decus primulum | intulisset, verum etiam omne fere nomen Britannicum humanitate, | consilio, fide sibi devinxisset nusquam non interim & vulgo | cluens causarum. Tam patronus quam arbiter incorruptissimus, | nec unius Regionis aut Urbis columen sed & Berwici præsidium | & Oraculum Dunelmiæ & mens Eboraci & pauperum (quæ Pater Anglia) Lingua.

M.S.

Parenti suo longe indulgentissimo natæ quatuor (quas unice | delexit) FRANCIS, CATHERINA, MARIA, URSULA, MARMOR hoc | posuere, 3 non Aprilis MDCLXXIV.

Arms : *Per cross over all a bend, with a crescent for difference."*

"On one of the S. pillars fronting N.W. is a very curious tho' small monument, in memory of FRANCIS BACON and his children by ELIZABETH his wife. Under which are these words, in gold characters : 'For of such is the Kingdom of God '—St Mark, chap. 10 ; and these arms : *Gu., on a chief arg. two mullets sa.,* 'quartered with ' *Sa., three laurel-leaves or betw. two bendlets arg., a crescent for diff."* [The book gives this coat as *Sable, on a bend cotised,* so that it is quite likely the two coats were impaled.]

On the same pillar was a "neat small white marble monument ":—To the pious memory of JOHN and ALICE PEARSON and their son | JOHN, late of this parish. She died the 13th of April 1682 and the son | March the 30th, 1695.

Arms : *Per fess embattled azure and gules, three suns or.*

"Near the S.E. corner of the church is a neat, small, white marble monument, with this Inscription :—

P.M.S.

Hic prope inhumatum Jacet (prouz. loquitur Saxum sepulcrale infra | positum) in spe fælicis Resurrectionis quod mortale fuit MARGARETÆ | BEAW uxoris GULIELMI BEAW Legum Doctoris com. Essexiæ, Suffolciæ | & Norfolciæ Admiralitat Judicis, Regii & filii natu maximi Gul. | Episcopi Landaveus, hæc soboles fuit natu maxima RICHARDI LYSTER | de Rowton in agro Salopiensi Ar. Familia generosa & vetusta, matrem | habuit ELIZABETHAM fil natu maximam THOMÆ

EYTON de Eyton de | Wilmores in Agro prædic. mil. Familia Domini Equestris & per vetusta | hæc peperit mæstissimo suo marito quinque filios duasq ; filias, quorum | quatuor filii & filia, matrem charissimam ad lugend. Supervixerunt | liberi parentem indulgentissimam. Conjux conjugem sine pare | amantissimam pariter ac adamatam. Matrem familias sine | avaritia providam & nunquam satis dolend perdidit Fæminam | hanc Delectissimam, tum animi tum formæ dotibus excellentem | pustulæ puerperio confederatæ Fato heu ! nimis festino è terris | rapuerunt simulq à marito in re ardua fidissimum consiliarium | & ultra sexum perspicacem, in anxietatibus consolatricem alacrem | & promptam ultroque & perlubenter participem diveilserunt animam | vero ad cœlum in Dei & Angelor, consortium transtulerunt, ab hac | luce transmigravit, 29 Decemb. Anno sal. 1694 & 33 Ætatis suæ anno.

It is adorned with cherub and urn, under which are these words : ' vivit post Funera virtus,' and these arms : *Azure, a lion Rampant or* [written above ' *maned proper* '] ; impaled with *Ermine, on a fess sable 3 mullets or.* The crest is a *Dexter hand holding a curtelax (or cutlas) proper.*" [Doubtless the lion maned proper was only extra shading on the mane, taken by mistake to mean proper.]

" At the W. end of the church a small stone monument with this inscription :— Huic juxta dormit prænobilis HEROINA FR. COTTON, vid. | Domina de Boscobell (loco ob Rege conservatum Celebri) serenissimæ | Reginæ a privatioribus cubiculis, Fæmina, vitæ innocentia, morum | suavitate pietate in Deum, Charitate in proximum planè admirabilis. | Animam placide efflavit die Sept. Novemb. Anno Dom. 1677. Ætat suæ 63.

"Arms over the inscription : *An eagle displ., with a crescent for diff. ; imp. Three stirrups.* Higher up : *4 Eescucheons crossways, each charged with as many amulets* [*sic*] *within a Border bearing 7 castles.*"

" On a small monument on one of the S. pillars of the church this Inscription, fronting North :— Here under resteth the Body of JANE late wife of | WILLIAM WHETSTONE of this parish who departed | this life the 11th of April 1653 being 23 years of age.

Earth hath possess'd her Ashes, Clay, and Dust,
And Heaven contains her soul among the just.
Favour is deceitful and Beauty is Vain ; but a Woman
That feareth the Lord she shall be praised."

" On one of the N. pillars towards the W. end and fronting S.E. a very small but neat white marble monument, inscribed :—

H. S. E.
PLEYDELL HALE, gent. THO. & ELIZAB. | E. Fam. Pleydelorum de Shrivenham in Agro Bercheriensi | Quem è Schola Ventæ Belgarumq ; Literas | Regis secretas vocatum intercipiunt | Variolæ & hoc cordunt sepulchro | O mortem nimis invidam | Quæ ex eadem manu rapuit | Calamum Poetæ, Oratoris, & Secretarii | O Fatum tamen non Infaustum | Quod Juveni cui nihil plus ultræ | Datur vel Literaturæ, vel Ingeni | Vitam dedit nunquam morituram | ob. 4 Octob. 1694, Ætat 18.

Arms : *Three arrows, points in base* " [*Gules, three arrows, points in base or, headed and feathered argent*].

" On a pretty small white marble monument on a south pillar, almost fronting the Pulpit, this Inscription :—

Near to this marble JUDITH BAYLEY lies,
Who was both modest, sober, chast, and wise.
Religion was her study, Zeal her care,
A fervant Lover of the House of Prayer ;
Her Parents had her Duty and her Love,
Who now are pleas'd in hope she's blest above.

> Virtue was still her Guide, her End, and Aim,
> Her Zeal was constant to her as her name ;
> Near 18 years of Age, who can forbear
> To read her character without a Tear ?
> She departed this life the 18th of October 1683.
> Her brother JOHN 14 days after dy'd,
> Aged 7 years, lyes by his Sister's side.

She was the eldest Daughter, and he the only Son of | JOHN and JUDITH BAYLEY, of this Parish.

> SARAH another Daughter sleeps in mould.
> She left this Life when almost 6 years old :
> She that was filled with Duty, Wit and Love
> Is surely happy with the Saints above.
> November 24 in Eighty five
> She dy'd to us to be with Christ alive.

The said Mr JOHN BAYLEY their Father died January the 7th, 1696, in the 63d year of his age.   The monument is adorned with Urns, Leaves, Fruit, etc.

———

" On a plated Grave stone in the middle Ile, near the Pulpit, this Inscription, tho' somewhat worn out :—

> Interr'd the corps of BARON BYRCH lyes here
> Of Gray's Inn sometime, by degree Esquire :
> In Chequer 18 years a Judge he was
> Till Soul from aged Body his did pass.
> Alive his wife ELIZA doth remain,
> Of Stydfolk stock one Son and Daughters twain
> She bare by him ; the eldest in his Life
> He gave to THOMAS BOWYER for his Wife.
> His body sleeps till Angel trump shall sound.
> God grant we all may ready then be found.

JOHANNES BYRCH, Obiit Anno D. 1581, Maii 30, Ætat suæ 66."

Arms, on a brass plate : *A chevron wavy between three eagles displayed.*

———

" In the Cemetery or churchyard, close to the wall on the South side and near the West end, on a Tombstone :—

JOHANNES THORNTON in memoria Charissimæ Uxoris | MARGARITÆ Filiæ GEORGIÆ COLLINS hujus Parochiæ Sancti | Ægidii in Campis hoc monumentum posuit.

> Under this sad marble sleeps
> She for whom even Marble weeps ;
> Her Praise lives still, tho' here she lyes
> Seeming dead that never dies.
> Religion, Love in suffering Breast,
> Her Charity, Mildness, and the rest,
> Have crown'd her soul ; all mourn with Fame
> Her Husband's loss and Midwife's blame.
> She dy'd in Child-bed, 70 times blest and seven,
> Her child and she deliver'd both in Heaven.
> Ob. 8 Jan. 1611.

Round the Margent of the stone these words :

> Full South this stone four Foot doth lye
> His Father JOHN and Grandsire HENRY
> THORNTON of Thornton in Yorkshire bred,
> Where lives the fame of THORNTONS being dead."

[The transcript of this is mistaken in Mr. Stow's " Survey."]

"On a marble stone, somewhat raised, on the S. side of the church in the yard :—

Here lyes the Body of ROBERT HOPE of this parish, Gent. who | departed this Life the 22ⁿᵈ Septemb. 1651, being aged 71 years. | To whose Memory his loving wife JANE HOPE caused this | Monument to be erected.

> Reader, it grieves me that I cannot bring
> A sea of Tears to drown my sorrows in,
> For the lamented Death of my dear Father,
> Whose Soul God to himself did lately gather.
> His Life was ever holy, and last Breath
> Was full of Goodness, pious at his Death ;
> Which confidently makes me hope and trust
> His Fame takes Wing from his so hopeful Dust.
> Oh ! Grief stops my Eye-streams ; pray, Reader, then
> Lend me some Tears till I can weep agen.
> Memoria Pii Æterna.

Here also lyes the Body of Mʳˢ JANE HOPE, Wife of the above | named ROBERT HOPE, who departed this life the 18ᵗʰ of | December 1675, in the 77ᵗʰ year of her age."

Arms: *A chevron between three roundels.*

" On a stone on the S. side of the church :—

> Here lyes the best of Men, whose Life is at an end,
> The best of Husbands and the truest Friend ;
> Who rests I hope as I do hope to be
> Happy with him in all Eternity.
> JOHN HENSHAM, who died 17 Dec. 1695."

" Close by the Hope stone is a marble inscribed :—

Anicitiæ Pignus | Felici memoriæ MARIÆ HOPE, obiit | Anno Salut 1670. Ætatis suæ 27.

> All the rare Qualities the Poets fam'd
> On those they most ador'd, she justly claim'd
> Wit, Vertue, Wisdom, all in Hope are gone,
> To meet a glorious Resurrection.
> Mourn wisely then, Hope does not truly die,
> But change Her Being for Eternity."

" On a Tombstone close to the south side near the East end of the church :—

Here lyes expecting the coming of our Lord and Saviour, | the Body of JOHN HEARNDON, PRUDENCE his Wife and | WILLIAM their Son, all of this Parish. JAMES died Aug. 1653 | PRUDENCE Oct. 1656, and WILLIAM Octob. 1662.

> Reader, let thy Reason know
> We were once as thou art now.
> Whilst we lived we wrought in Stone,
> And now attend the Corner one ;
> And in health did this prepare
> For us our Wives and children here.
> Death's only by the Wicked fear'd,
> The Righteous 'gainst his sting's prepar'd.
> Then, Reader, let thy Care in Life be such
> Earth may thy Body, not thy Spirit touch."

" On a grey marble Tombstone, sd. from the Chancel in the churchyard :—

Here lies the Bodies of JOHN, ANN, and OBEDIAH, | children of JOHN and ANN EASTON of this Parish.

> The ravenous Eagle Death, greedy of Prey,
> Whose piercing Eye found where these infants lay,
> He crush'd them with his Tallons, and convey'd
> Their Souls to Heaven, and here's their Ashes laid
> Where now they rest in Providences Store
> Till Time and Death and Tears shall be no more.

Also ANN the Wife of the said JOHN EASTON, died August | 1679.

> " Earth hath possess'd their ashes, Clay, and Dust,
> And Heaven contains their Souls among the Just."

" At the E. of the S. Ile, in the wall without the church, this Inscription :—
Here under resteth the Body of JOHN the son of ROBERT | and CONSTANCE
WIGHT, who died the 10th of July, Anno Dom. | 1678, aged 4 Years and 10
months.

> " My Time is short, the longer is my Rest.
> God called me hence because he thought it best."

" In the wall close by the last :—
M. S.
Near this place lyeth buried the Body of FRANCIS HARROWELL, | who died the 12th
of April 1652 aged 73 Years, and bequeathed | to the poor of this Parish £5 a
year for 20 years and upward, | beginning in the year 1652."

MARY PERKINS 1703. [Query if part of the above.]

" On a Tombstone close to the N.E. corner of the N. Ile and in the churchyard :—
Solus Christus mihi sola Salus | In Camera sub hoc Lapide Jacet corpus |
MARIÆ charissimæ amate uxoris | EDWARDI BRISCO, Lond. gen' sola proles
nuperrime vivens | plusquam quadriginta annos post cæteras CAROLI SOUTHWELL |
hujus Parochiæ Gen. erat Deo devotissima, marito amantissima, | & Fidessima
prudens & modestissimæ pauperibus amica | & perpetua memoria dignæ, cum aman-
tissimo marito in matrimonio | dilecto vixit annos 39, current ob. 24 Martii 1689 |
Ætat Current 63.

> " Mitis, Amans, prudens humilis, pia, fida, modesta,
> Uxor eras sponsæ chara MARIÆ tuo,
> Mæstissimus maritus Charissimæ uxoris amori
> Hanc terram emit & monumentum posuit."

Arms : *Three greyhounds courant in pale;* impaling, *Three cinquefoils with a
mullet for difference.*

[This ends the monumental inscriptions given in the " New View."]

The Registers of Inkberrow, co. Worcester.* †

THE TRANSCRIPT OF YE PARISH OF INCKBERROW FOR YE YEARE 1671.

[*Baptisms.*]

April 6	Mercy ye daughter of Henry Jackson, Cler.
April 23	Mary ye daughter of Arthur Davis.
April 24	George ye son'e of Walter Hill.
May 21	Jane ye daughter of Rich. Dewes.
June 18	Samuell ye son'e of Francis Hale.
June 25	Mary ye daughter of Willia' Goore.
June 25	Anthony ye son'e of John Younge.
Aug. 6	Jone ye daughter of John Hichcocke.
Aug. 20	Henry ye son'e of Henry Smith.

* From the Transcripts in "Edgar Tower," Bishop's Register.
† Communicated by WILLIAM BRADBROOK, M.R.C.S.—concluded from p. 252.

Aug. 20   Elizabeth ye daughter of Rich. Mogg.
Aug. 27   Arthur ye son'e of Arthur Bagshawe, gent.
Aug. 31   George ye son'e of Rich. Collins.
Sep.   7   Frances ye daughter of Willia' Edwards.
Sep. 24   Henry ye son'e of Tho. Dyson.
Oct. 19   Thomas ye son'e of Francis Foord.
Nov. 27   Robert ye son'e of Rob. Wheyha'.
Dec. 27   John ye son'e of John Ganderton.
Jan.   7   Frances ye daughter of George Horne.
Jan. 13   Elizabeth ye daughter of John Rannolds.
Mar. 21   John ye son'e of Henry Brerely.
Mar. 24   Elizabeth ye daughter of Tho. Bennett.

[Married.]

Feb.   3   Tho. Dolfin & Eliz. Robbinson.

[Burials.]

May   1   Willia' Hunt.
May   1   John Haynes of Dormstone.
May   5   The wife of Christopher Dyson.
May 15   Thomas Grasier.
May 21   The wife of William Em's of Kington.
May 22   Elizabeth ye daughter of Tho. Cere [?].
June   3   Roger Sale.
June 12   Frances ye wife of Bartholomew Redding.
June 17   Bridget ye daughter of Tho. Laugher.
June 22   Willia' y' son'e of ye Wid. Poole of Dormstone.
June 29   Mary ye daughter of John Francis.
July 16   Edward Opplebee.
July 19   Willia' ye son'e of John Rand.
Aug. 13   Anne Sale.
Aug. 15   John Sheppy.
Sep. 11   Anne ye wife of Willia' Harvey.
Sep. 28   Alice Harbidg, widd.
Oct. 30   Thomas Bellett.
Nov. 15   Elizabeth Groues, wid.
Nov. 26   A son'e of Henry Grasier.
Nov.   3   George ye son'e of Rich. Collins.
Jan. 27   John Laugher.
Jan. 27   Alice Goore, widd.
Jan. 27   Isabell ye daughter of Tho. Cere.
Feb. 12   Elizabeth ye wife of Rich. Goddard.
Feb. 17   Elizabeth ye wife of Willia' Farr of Dormstone.
Feb. 21   Mary ye wife of Willia' Edwards.

JOHN HUNT,   } Church-Wardens.
JOHN HARRIS, }

A TRANSCRIPT OF YE PARISH OF INCKBERROW FOR YE YEARE 1672.

[Baptisms.]

April 14   Henry ye son'e of Francis Freeman.
April   2   Willia' ye son'e of Willia' Figgett.
June   9   Hester ye daughter of Anthony Baylis.
Aug.   7   Thomas ye son'e of Tho. Poole.
Aug. 11   Robert ye son'e of Tho. Marshall.
Aug. 11   Willia' ye son'e of Walter Hill.

Aug. 18   Sarah ye daughter of John Harrit.
Sep. 22   Joseph ye son'e of John Bellet, jun^r.
Sep. 22   Ursula ye daughter of Tho. Ganderton.
Oct. 8   Willia' ye son'e of Tho. Fairfax.
Oct. 10   Elizabeth ye daughter of Rich. Perkes.
Oct. 16   Rachell ye daughter of Tho. Parker.
Nov. 1   Alice ye daughter of Joyce Stuard.
Nov. 17   John ye son'e of Tho. Dowfen.
Nov. 17   Thomas ye son'e of Will. Harvey.
Nov. 21   Robert ye son'e of Rob. Sorrill.
Nov. 24   Mary ye daughter of Rich. Ben'ett.
Nov. 29   Oliva ye daughter of Caleb Charles.
Dec. 22   Thomas ye son'e of John Boes.
Dec. 26   Robert ye son'e of Rob. Small.
Jan. 1   John ye son'e of Rich. Shekell.
Jan. 8   Alice ye daughter of Henry James.
Jan. 9   William ye son'e of Thomas Ceare.
Jan. 12   Edward ye son'e of John Francis.
Feb. 20   Henry ye son'e of Willia' Raven.
Feb. 23   Arthur ye son'e of Arthur Davis.
Feb. 26   Catherine ye daughter of James Hem'ing, sen.
Sep. 8   Richard ye son'e of Willia' Walford.

Marriages.

April 18   Richard Edward & Issabell Browne.
April 23   Francis Small & Ann Raven.
July 23   Willia' Edwards & Elinor Lacy.
Nov.   4   John Tayler & Eliz. Cresser.
Jan. 25   Robert Marshall & Sarah Ealis.
Feb.   7   Lawrence Hughes & An' Opplebee.

[Burials.]

April 13   Elizabeth Ballard, wid.
April 14   The wife of Rich. Bradford.
May   5   John Steward.
May   23   Alice ye wife of Willia' Heynes of Kington.
June   6   Mary ye wife of Nicholas Farr.
June 11   Ann Mathews, wid., of Dormstone.
June 13   Elizabeth ye daughter of Ric. Ben'ett.
July   2   Christopher Savage, gent.
July 18   Mary Page.
July 24   Ann ye wife of Christopher Roberts.
Aug. 14   . . . . ye daughter of Henry Grasier.
Aug. 24   Willia' ye son'e of Willia' Willis of Dormston.
Oct.   8   Catherine Ellins.
Oct. 16   Francis Smyth of Alcester.
Oct.   8   Martha ye wife of John Bradford.
Dec. 15   Willia' Poole.
Jan.   —   Mary ye wife of Willia' Willis.
Mar.   5   Margery Day.

                              Jo. Harbach, } Church
                              Tho. Laugher, } Wardens.

THE TRANSCRIPT OF THE PARISH OF INCKBERROW FOR THE YEAR OF OUR
LORD 1674.

[Baptisms.]

May	—	Ann ye daughter of Tho. Dyson.
May	25	Han'ah ye daughter of Will. Walford.
May	31	Francis ye son'e of George Court.
July	16	Elizabeth ye daughter of Rich. Walford or Stafford.
July	25	Phinees ye son'e of Henry Jackson, Cler.
Aug.	16	Ann ye daughter of Tho. Webb.
Oct.	1	Thomas ye son'e of George Harris.
Nov.	1	John ye son'e of Rich. Mogg.
Dec.	15	Thomas ye son'e of Tho. Bellett.
Dec.	27	Elizabeth ye daughter of John Latha'.
Jan.	2	Mary ye daughter of John Netherton.
June	10	Mary ye daughter of Tho. Laite.
June	10	Mary ye daughter of Tim. Collis [?].
Feb.	21	John ye son'e of John Laite.

Marriages.

April	30	. . . . & Ann Poole.
May	9	. . . . [? Millard] & Joane Edwards.
June	17	Henry Johnson [?], gent., & Mary ye daughter of And. Baker [?], gent.

[Burials.]

April	3	Ann ye daughter of John Westwood.
April	29	. . . . Holford.
May	12	Willia' ye son'e of James Hem'ing, jun.
May	21	Mary ye daughter of Francis Hale.
May	23	Frances ye daughter of Arthur Davis.
June	16	Elizabeth Ten'ant, wid.
June	17	Ann ye wife of John Wedgberry.
July	29	Thomas Poole of Egioke.
Sep.	24	James ye son'e of James Hunt of Kington.
Oct.	24	Edward Phillips.
Nov.	—	Francis ye son'e of Christopher Robberts [?].
Nov.	23	Anthony Phillipps.
Nov.	29	Ann ye daughter of Simon Baker.
Dec.	—	Thomas ye son'e of Tho. Savage, gent.
Dec.	6	Mary ye daughter of Arthur Davis.
Jan.	28	Frances ye daughter of Will. Edwards.
Feb.	10	Rob. Parsons.
Feb.	13	The Widdow Harvey.
Feb.	14	John Bunde.
Feb.	21	Mary ye daughter of John Netherton.
Mar.	20	Katherine ye wife of Tho. James.
Mar.	21	Humfrey Hem'ing of Kington.

BARTHOLOMEW READING, } Churchwardens.
RICH. GROUES,

[Baptism.]

1615   Mar. 28   John son of Sir Francis Edgeiocke, Knight.

[Married.]

1660   Nov. 2   John Savage, gen., & Elizabeth Hunt, widdow, both of Bradley in
the co. of Worcester. (From a transcript without parish name.)

The following Burials and Weddings are not in the existing Parish Register but are found in the Bishop's Transcripts for the years 1689 and 1690 :—

Burials, 1689.

April 4	Margery wife of George Eeds.
April 27	Tho⁵ Dyson.
May 18	Jone, bastard of Eliz. Huntley.
June 9	Oliver Dolphin.
June 22	Richard Hunt ; Kington.
July 10	John Wilson.
July 11	Joseph Dilloth.
July 14	Christian Sale.
July 24	Jone wife of William Hunt ; Kington.
Aug. 11	William Hunt ; Kington.
Aug. 17	John son of John Brown.
Aug. 23	Mary Baskefield.
Aug. 27	John son of John Bennett.
Sep. 24	Mary Bennett, widow.
Sep. 26	Eliz. dau. of Tho⁵ Dyson.
Oct. 13	Thomas son of Richard Sowly.
Oct. 20	Eliz. Harritt.
Nov. 18	Isabell Harritt.
Dec. 3	Tho⁵ Dison, junʳ.
Dec. 18	John Gore.
Dec. 19	Anne Pool.
Dec. 28	Henry Hunt.
Jan. 11	Thomas ffoard.
Jan. 24	Thomas Pool.
Feb. 3	John son of Richard Chandler ; Dormstone.
Mar. 14	John Glover.
Mar. 20	Hannah, dau. of John Willis.
Mar. 21	Anne wife of William Buggins.

Weddings, 1689.

June 27	Edward Harriss of Norton & Alice Stewart ; by Lic.
Oct. 6	Thomas Yate & Alice Claybrook.
Jan. 13	Anthony Baylis & Anne Bennett.

Burials, 1690.

Mar. 29	Tho⁵ Adams.
May 6	John Steward.
May 19	Eliz. Huntley.
June 16	Mary dau. of [John] Netherton.
June 19	Philip son of Mʳ John Apletree.
June 24	Robert Wheyham.
June 25	Olive dau. of Tho⁵ Lewis ; Dormstone.
July 15	William Huet of Kington.
July 23	Arthur Davies.
Aug. 19	John son of William Harvey.
Sep. 3	Joseph Sermon.
Sep. 26	Sarah dau. of Tho⁵ Peters.
Sep. 26	Ann wife of Tho⁵ Hunt.
Oct. 9	William Farre ; Kington.
Oct. 18	William Farre ; Dormstone.
Nov. 20	Tho⁵ son of Tho⁵ [Teuaal].

Nov. 20 Henry son of Henry Spearpoint.
Nov. 24 William Heming.
Nov. 26 Margery Redding.
Dec. 27 Sarah Heming.
Jan. 29 Frances wife of John Sheldon.
Jan. 30 George son of Richard Wigget.
Feb. 16 [? 10] Richard Marshall.
Feb. 18 Giles son of Giles Ganderton.

Monumental Inscriptions

AT

St. Mary's Church, Reading.*

On recumbent headstone :—Sacred to the memory of ELIZA d'r of JOSEPH & HANNAH RAWLINS, who died Nov. 10, 1833, aged 11 months ; also JOSEPH RAWLINS who died July 26th, 1834, aged 35 years.

On recumbent headstone :—Sacred to the memory of MARY ANNE the beloved child of JOHN & FANNY RAWLINS, who died July 11, 1830, aged 9 months.

On recumbent headstone :—Sacred to the memory of JAMES WILKINSON who died Jan. 16, 18[30], aged 42 years ; also ELEANOR wife of the above, who died Feb. 20, 1837.

On block of stone :—WILLIAM RUSHER died March 8, 1819, aged 90 ; MARY wife of WILLIAM RUSHER died March 7, 1837, aged 81.

On recumbent headstone :—In memory of JOSEPH DAVIES who died March 23, 1841, aged 52 ; also LUCY relict of the above, who died . . . . 18[52].

On recumbent headstone :—Sacred to the memory of MARY TAYLOR, the wife of WILLIAM TAYLOR, who died June 14, 1809, aged 74 years ; also of WILLIAM TAYLOR who died . . . . aged 81 years.

On recumbent headstone :—Sacred to the memory of WILLIAM HIGHAM who departed this life Jan. 26th, 180[?], aged 46 years.

On block of stone :—Sacred to the memory of JOHN NORTH who died Aug. 2nd, 1842, aged 66 years ; also ANN wife of JOHN NORTH, who died Sept. 28, 1839, aged 79 years. On reverse : Sacred to the memory of SARAH NORTH who died Aug. 9, 1843, aged 65 years ; Sacred to the memory of ELIZTH GURNELL who died Sept. 30th, 1840, aged 60 years.

On block :—Sacred to the memory of ANN wife of RICHARD WAKEFIELD, who died June 16th, 1839, aged 33 years. On reverse : Sacred to the memory of ROB. WAKEFIELD . . . . [rest illegible] ; also MARY wife of ROBT. WAKEFIELD, who died Feb. 7, . . . 8, aged 82 years.

* Communicated by Rev. G. P. CRAWFURD, sometime Curate in this parish, now Vicar of Bicester, Oxon—concluded from p. 256.

On stone slab within rails :—Sacred to the memory of HARRIET HANNAH PARSONS, wife of WILLIAM PARSONS, Esqʳᵉ, of the Hon. East India Company's service, who died Feb. 13, 1840, aged 46.

On block :—Sacred to the memory of MARGARET HODSON who died Dec. 8ᵗʰ, 1832, aged 40 years.

On block :—Sacred to the memory of Mʳ JOHN MACE who died June 29, 1833, aged 55 years.

On tomb within rails :—Sacred to the memory of TEMPERANCE WAGSTAFFE, wife of JOHN WAGSTAFFE, who died June 23, 1780, aged 65 years ; Sacred to the memory of JOHN WAGSTAFFE who died Oct. . . 1782, aged 70 years.

On side of tomb within iron rails :—Sacred to the memory of Mʳ DAVID BLISSETT who died Nov. 8, 1777, aged 42 years ; also SARAH his wife who died May 9, 1786, aged 44 years ; and of his children ANN who died Nov. 5, 1767, aged 8 months ; ANN who died Nov. 17ᵗʰ, 1776, aged 9 weeks ; WILLIAM who died Nov. 27, 1777, aged 2 years & 5 months. On reverse : In memory of MARY CUMBER who died Aug. 3, 1775, aged 70 years.

On wooden rail :—Sacred to the memory of SARAH wife of ROGER WILLIAMS. On reverse : Sacred to the memory of ANN WILLIAMS who died April 4, 1842.

On recumbent headstone :—Sacred to the memory of JAMES BARKER who died Jan. 29, 1847, aged 65 years ; also MARTHA wife of the above, who died Jan. 25, 1837 ; also MARY their daughter who died Jan. 27, 1823, aged 20 years.

On block :—In memory of MARTIN BAYLIE who died Sept. 28, 1765, aged 49 years ; also of MARTIN WILLIAM son of MARTIN BAYLIE, who died May 20, 1790, aged 30 years ; also of SARAH BAYLIE, daughter of MARTIN BAYLIE, who died Dec. 13, 1837, aged 77 years. On reverse : In Memory of ANN HATTON who departed this life Oct. 12, 1777, aged 75 years.

On recumbent headstone :—CHARLES STEWART BROMLEY died March 17, 1836, in 40ᵗʰ year of his age ; CHARLES BROMLEY, eldest son of CHARLES BROMLEY of Fort St. George . . . . died Feb. 14, 18 . ., aged 69.

On block :—In Memory of MARY HUNT, died May 16, 1786, aged 67 years ; HANNAH HUNT her daughter, died Sept. 15, 1824, aged 67 years. On reverse : In Memory of JAMES ADAMS, died Feb. 10, 1841, aged 65 years.

On block :—Sacred to the memory of ANN JAMES who departed this life Jan. 19, 1842, aged 43 years.

On tomb within rails :—Sacred to the memory of Mʳˢ MARY BELL who died July 7, 1771, aged 50 ; MATHEW BELL who died Jan. 2, 1772, aged 30 ; ROBERT BELL who died Sept. 5, 1772, aged 23 ; and MARY BELL who died Sept. 1, 1777, aged . . . . On west side : In memory of ISABELLA Relict of Mʳ JOHN ROBINSON & afterwards wife of Mʳ WELCH of . . . . On south side : JOHN ROBINSON of London, Merchant, died Dec. 24, 1769, aged 49.

On block :—JOHN READ, died March 18, 1824, aged 37 years. On reverse : Also SARAH his wife, died Sept. 21, 1849, aged 65 years.

On block :—Sacred to the memory of JAMES son of JOHN & SARAH READ, died March 2, 1828, aged 9 years & 3 months,

On recumbent headstone :—In memory of ELIZABETH the wife of WILLIAM PAGE, who departed this life March 30, 1801 ; also of WILLIAM PAGE who died Feb. 11, 1826, aged 69 years ; also of CHARLES & MARY, children of RICHARD & ANN SIMONS, who died in their Infancy.

On tomb within rails :—On surface of mensa : Sacred to the memory of THO. NEWBERY, Esqre, son of THOMAS & MARTHA ANN, who died Jan. 8, 1829, aged 39 years. On north side : Sacred to the memory of MARTHA ANN NEWBERY, relict of THOS. NEWBERY, Esqre, who died May 14, 1821, aged 61 years ; M.S. JACOBO PATEY, Equiti, qui rem privatam summa prudentia, probitate, felicitate publicam, mira integritate, diligentia, gravitate administravit, mareito optimo patri cariss bene merenti uxsor, et filiam . . . . [rest illegible]. On west side : Sacred to the memory of Mr RICH^D SMITH of this Parish who died Oct. 2, 1775, aged 42. On south side : Sacred to the memory of Mrs MARTHA SMITH, wife of ADAM SMITH, Gent., of this parish, who died April 23, 1771, aged 64. [Another inscription in Latin illegible.]

On tomb within rails :—On north side : In hoc mausoleo conduntur exuviæ JOHANNIS DEANE, qui plurimos annos in hac Parochia, cum summa egit laude, Maritorum, Parentum, Amicorum, Magistratum, optimus obiit Aug^st 30 Anno ætatis 62. Salutis 1780. Memoriam ipsius pie prosequere ; exemplum imitare. Also on north side : In memory of ANNE DEANE, relict of JOHN DEANE, Esqre, Ob^t 24 Novr 1785, Æt. 65. On south side : JOHN DEANE, Esqre, Ob^t 8 Jany 1814, Aged 66. Also on south side : SARAH ANNE DEANE, relict of JOHN DEANE, Esqre, Ob^t 26th Feb. 1818, Aged 70.

On tomb within rails :—On south side : Sacred to the memory of THOMAS SOWDON, Senr, Esqre, who died April 13th, 1791, in the 73^d year of his age ; also THOMAS SOWDON, Esqre (Senior Alderman of this borough, and a magistrate of the County of Berks), who died Novr 23^d, 1829, Aged 69 years ; also ELEANOR, relict of the last named THOMAS SOWDON, who died 13th April 1839, Aged 75 years. At west end : ELEANOR SOWDON, died Feb. 13th, 1792, Aged 11 months ; MARY ANN SOWDON, died Jany. 12th, 1802, Aged 15 years ; ARTHUR SOWDON, died 6th Novr 1831, Aged 30 years.

The Sirr Family.—FURTHER MEMORANDUM.

Entry in Catalogue of MSS., Trinity College Library, Dublin :—
Major Henry C. Sirr's Papers, relating chiefly to the Rebellion, 1798 to 1804. 9 vols. folio, with Portfolio. Including Letters, Informations, Warrants, etc. ; also other Papers concerning matters of Police of various dates up to 1831. The Portfolio contains the " Declaration of the Catholics of Ireland," 1792, as sent to Dublin from different localities ; some copies on parchment, some on paper, with all the original signatures.

CORRECTION TO NOTES, PAGE 204.

The note as to Peter Sers of Gedney, Lincolnshire, whose will was proved 23 March 1812 (P.C.C.), should read :—
His wife, whom he married in 1798, was included in a Grant of Arms to her brother Sir George Nayler, York Herald (afterwards Garter).

In Memoriam.

The Rev. FRANCIS JOHN POYNTON, M.A., died at the Rectory, Kelston, Somerset, on the 22nd of November, aged 76. He was born at Chew Magna, Somerset, 16th June 1827, and was educated at Shrewsbury School and Exeter College, Oxford. Elected to the Symes Scholarship in 1849 he was ordained Priest in 1851, and having served as Curate of Ducklington (Oxon), Slapton (Bucks), and Burmington (Warwick), he was presented to the living of Kelston in 1858. In 1874 he contributed to this Magazine " Genealogical Memoranda relating to the Family of Blackburne," and a few years later he wrote and privately printed a History of Kelston, a work of great research, and containing many details of the Families of Harrington, Huddleston, Hawkins, etc. He was a friend of the late Col. J. Lemuel Chester, and was elected a member of the Harleian Society in 1875. Mr. Poynton had a very extensive knowledge of the antiquarian and family history of his neighbourhood, and contributed papers to the Bristol and Gloucestershire Archæological Society, the Somersetshire Archæological Society, and to the " Genealogist." He became a member of the Record Society of Somerset ; and having been for many of the early years of his life a member of the Palæontological Society, he formed an extensive collection of fossils, but outside the field of genealogy his most valuable collection was one of Roman coins.

Genealogical Notes and Queries.

HERCY OF NETTLEBED, OXON.

TO THE EDITOR OF " MISCELLANEA GENEALOGICA ET HERALDICA."

SIR,

    I have found a very curious point about this family, viz., they lived in Sonning, Berks, 1602—59. The Visitations of Berks and Oxon ignore nearly all dates. I find them at Nettlebed 1586—1666, i.e., later than the pedigree in the 1634 Visitation of Oxon. I send you particulars, to save them from being lost. Some time ago you printed several items from Shottesbrook Registers—Hercy, Weldon, Calverley.

    I have also found a very bad mistake in the descent of Rev. Thomas Warton of Oxford, 1728—90. His ancestor, Rev. Anthony Warton, came from Walton, Lancs, 1596, to Lincoln College, Oxford. He was born at Walton 1581, and died at Breamore, Hants, 1661. Will in the P.C.C.

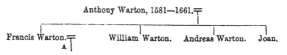

Anthony Warton, 1581—1661.⨯

Francis Warton.⨯   William Warton.   Andreas Warton.   Joan.

A

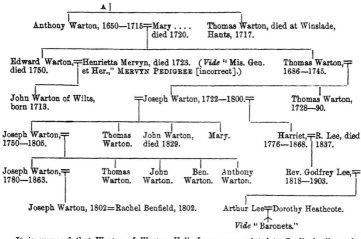

It is supposed that Warton of Warton Hall, Lancs, was related to Cardinal Allen, who founded Douay College. I should think that these Wartons were also of the same county and dates.

William Warton of Warton Hall, Lancs, 1586.⊤

Thomas Warton.

Thomas Wharton of Walton on the Hill, Lancs.⊤

Anthony Wharton, born 1623 ; died 1623.

Probably nephew of the other Anthony. Unfortunately the registers are gone in 1581.

42 Dennington Park Road, West Hampstead,
London, N.W.   CHAS. JAS. HERSEY.

Reviews.

The Ancestry of Randall Thomas Davidson, D.D., Archbishop of Canterbury. By Rev. ADAM PHILIP, M.A., Longforgan. London : Elliot Stock, 62 Paternoster Row, E.C.

THE Author of this tastefully got-up book begins his history of our Primate by narrating how a worthy old lady nearly 80 years old in 1750 had bitterly complained of a Mr. David Randall, a merchant, who had been entrusted with a valuable MS. given to her by John Livingstone of Ancrum, explicatory of the Bible, on the promise that he would get it printed in Holland. This was about 1728, and more than twenty years after she was still bewailing its loss. This Mr. Randall had a son Thomas, who was taken to Edinburgh, where he graduated as an M.A. in 1730, and was ordained at Inchture in Perthshire when he was about forty years old. Here he brought home his bride, Mary Davidson, daughter of a minister of Dundee. Like a prudent Scot he did not incur the happiness of marriage before he was fairly situated ; a fine marble tablet in the wall of the Church records that he died on 18th November 1760, aged 62. He was charitably inclined, as he left £300 for the benefit of the poor. His wife, who was widow of Mr. Thomas Elliot when he married her (another trait of his Scotch tact), had a son John Elliot, who became an apothecary, and went out as a surgeon on board a privateer, and having acquired a large amount of prize-money, he settled and graduated at St. Andrew's University in 1750 as a physician, and three years after became a Licentiate of the College of Physicians and was soon celebrated in London, and was knighted in 1776, and finally became a baronet, having been Physician to the Prince of Wales ; it is said his fees were £5000 a year. Sir John Elliot married a Miss Grace Dalrymple, but got a divorce from her and £12,000 damages, and finally died at the seat of his friend Lord Melbourne ; his uncle, the merchant of Rotterdam, put up a tablet to his memory in the Church of Dundee.

Our minister at Inchture proved to be a man of great force, publishing several papers on the laxity in the observance of the Lord's Supper. He was besides a busy man in his parish, which had a population in 1755 of 893, and on Saturday nights he would go round the village to see that the people were housed and at rest, and he was not slow to rebuke those trespassing on the early Sabbath. It was surmised that he had met John Wesley, who had been more than once in the neighbourhood, but he had his misgivings of his zeal. He wrote several tracts, some of which were against patronage, which he considered was injurious. After a very active life he died in 1780, in his seventieth year and forty-second of his ministry. Thus passed away the ancestor of the present Archbishop of Canterbury.

Mr. Thomas Randall left a son Thomas, who was born in 1747. There is a remarkable story told at Inchture, how that a parishioner had dreamt that her boy had fallen into the well used by the Manse and the village, and early in the morning she went direct to it, and found not her boy, but the minister's boy in it. Thus the child saved became the distinguished Dr. Thomas Randall Davidson.

This son's early life was at Inchture, but having an uncle in Holland, who like his grandfather had been there and prospered, after he had taken his college course in Glasgow young Randall was sent to Holland, and studied at Utrecht and Leyden, where he attended the Scotch Church, and found as a companion his tutor, Dr. William Thomson, a man of exceptional knowledge, and who left a long list of writings behind him.

He became a preacher at Rotterdam in 1769, and preached his first sermon in Amsterdam ; he then returned to Scotland, and was appointed his father's successor at Inchture, when he was removed to Stirling. His stay here was not long, for he went to Glasgow, where he made his mark, and then went to Edinburgh, where he laboured from 1785 till his death in 1827, receiving the degree of D.D. from Harvard University in 1793, and adopting the surname of Davidson from his uncle at Rotterdam, he inheriting his uncle's property at Muirhouse, Midlothian, as Dr. Thomas Randall Davidson, the present Primate his grandson being Dr. Randall Thomas Davidson. The enconium passed upon him by Dr. Mason of New York, the Chalmers of America, was "Rev. Dr. Davidson—Gentle, placid, pure, spiritual ; talents moderate ; zeal and diligence great ; affectionate, tender, beloved by the good," etc.

It suffices now for us to come to Dr. Davidson's sons. William, the eldest, succeeded to the estate at Muirhouse, and then it was associated with the fortunes of his fourth son Henry, who was a partner in a firm of timber merchants. There was another son, who was distinguished as an engineer. Mr. Henry Davidson married the daughter of a well-known Border laird, Mr. Swinton of Kimmerghame, and had three sons and a daughter—Randall Thomas, John Henry, Ernest Archibald, and Mary Catherine, and the eldest is the Primate, "for whom no better prayer can arise than that a double portion of the spirit of his forefathers may be upon him," as our Author concludes his history with.

His Grace married Edith, the second daughter of Archbishop Tait, in 1878, and was Private Secretary to his father-in-law, whose name is reverenced by many in London. He was also the Secretary to Archbishop Benson in 1882-3. He became Bishop of Rochester in 1891—95 and Bishop of Winchester in 1895—1903, his predecessor at each place being also well known in London as Dr. Thorold, formerly of St. Giles's and St. Pancras.

In these days of confederation, when thousands of miles do not prevent our colonists " across the seas " from according to us their lives and friendship, and where our good old friend Dr. Nicolson lived very many years in Tasmania, his Church being the first built there, ministering as a Scotch clergyman since 1851 to a diocese equal in size to many a minor European State, and passing away to his heavenly rest in his 94th year, what would not the British nationalities gain by an amalgamation brought about by the Primate between the English and the Scotch Churches. Their services are nearly alike, in many cases they sing the same hymns, and both are above pandering to notoriety. We mooted the same to an eminent Scotch clergyman who preaches in London, pointing out the advantages of one Church, but he gave no reply beyond his invite to come to his Church and hear him.

The Work is illustrated by twelve excellent engravings, and its price of 3s. 6d. is too low for its worth.

A Way of his Own: An Autobiography. By A. KNOTCUTTER. London : Henry J. Deane, Salisbury Square, Fleet Street. 1903.

THIS is a well printed book of 256 pp., dedicated " to all the Mudies and the Smiths of the present time," but we doubt if they will move an inch out of their chosen way to enhance the circulation of the book. We are introduced to the boy who had "a way of his own " in his conversation with an old soldier, and the book recalls Hughes's " Tom Brown's School-days," except that the hero is under the control of the Lord Chancellor, and was possessed of fair wealth, was reckoned the best bowler and the " cock of the school " in the summer for the coming season ; besides which he almost won a scholarship in Divinity, but the question about the " march of the Jews in the wilderness " floored him. He put an extreme case to the Lord Chancellor by asking what could he do if a revolution broke out and his estates were seized ; how could he earn his livelihood ?

Little episodes are given shewing how his sympathy would be given to animals. At a battue given by a sporting friend our hero was reckoned the best shot, and was accordingly invited, and had the head gamekeeper to attend to him. To the latter's disgust, when a trembling hare at fifteen paces off looked up plaintively and caught his eye, he took no notice of it, although several gamekeepers were waiting to see what a shot he was, as he had struck the running deer ninety-nine times out of a hundred at a private gallery. The fearful eye of the hare was a shock to him, and he spared it, much to the beater's disgust, and so his character as a good shot was ascribed to " Mad Leverett," as he was called.

This shews us how the hero's sympathies were with animals. He found life too monotonous on his estates with three houses, so he sailed for Australia at a friend's invite. Here he helped him by taking up a banker's advance, and so saved his friend, and eventually the estates he himself acquired while there proved to be a gold mine to him.

Our Author gives an account of a racing establishment, and among the horses he had reared when he returned to England, and had entered for the great Olympia race, was Mayflower. Greatly to the Squire's horror, his jockey came to him quite ill, saying he had been " got at " and could not ride the mare, and, driven to a great extremity, he sought advice of the head of the racing Committee, General Grouse, who acquiesced in his riding the mare himself, but being a man six feet high and clearing eleven stone, the bystanders gave a faint cheer, whilst the racing ring exclaimed "just like Leverett," when they saw him jump into the saddle, having on " white knee-breeches and silk stockings, but neither boots nor whip nor spurs." The upshot was, Mayflower shot ahead at once, after a cheering whisper from her master riding her, and despite all efforts of the riders against him she came in two lengths ahead of a colt not in the betting, but whose owner would not support an objection, as he said Leverett had been " a friend to the Turf that day." Where the Author got his account from of his hero's dress without his boots or whip was certainly not reported by any racing journal !

Our Author next pushes him forward for Parliament, and he got in. Having by an accident been enabled to help Lord Regibus when he had a fit in the Park, he got acquainted with his sister, who by her charming manner impressed our hero so much that he gave her Mayflower, and she finally gave him her hand. A merry wedding party of Lord Regibus and his bride and Squire Leverett, of Hare Park and Leverett Paddocks and the Overtun Run in Australia, with Lady Victoria his bride, the daughter of the Duke of Ataris, all started together for Spain on their honeymoon.

Having thus written a pleasing account of an eligible young man, who, because "he had a way of his own" was set upon by Society, our Author has to be congratulated upon the strict observance of not pandering to sensation or suicides or broken vows, and has always kept his readers in good society, from the Lord Chancellor, who was the hero's guardian, down to the old soldier who first spoke to him as to all being working men, anxious to do something, from the Prime Minister to the policeman. He has produced a book which would be as great an attraction to boys as " Sandford and Merton," and ought to be in the hands of schoolmasters and others as a fit prize for a steady boy. Its price is only 3s. 6d.

The History of Friar Lane Baptist Church, Nottingham, being a contribution towards the History of the Baptists in Nottingham. By JOHN T. GODFREY and JAMES WARD. Nottingham : Henry A. Saxton, King Street. 1903.

THIS is a handsome royal 8vo volume, the first of its kind for publishing the Registers of a leading Nonconformist Church. Besides giving a full history of the Friar Lane Baptist Church, it gives fourteen pedigrees of the most notable families, well drawn up and printed, some dated from the early part of 1700, one later of William Vickers being born in 1797 and his wife in 1799, and she living till January 1891. The Church was built in 1724, and was sold for £100 as the third place of worship of the Baptists in Nottingham, the earlier records of the body being lost. Like many other congregations they soon split up, seven members going from Park Street and establishing another Church, the George Street Baptist, Mr. Thomas Morley being the first Pastor in 1742.

The "Declaration of Faith," dated 2 November 1769, began : " We, a small handful of the unworthy dust of Zion, assembled together for the worship of God in Friar Lane," etc.; and " in obedience to the command of God, we being now met together, again to make a fresh surrendour of ourselves to the Lord." The Rev. Richard Copper was the Pastor in 1769, and he had come from Kingston-upon-Hull, and in the book of the Declaration he had a list of all the regular members from 1770 to 1802, containing seventy-eight entries, but another list was there containing " those who had been excluded and for what," and numbering eighty-seven names from 1770 to 1818, so that sixteen years later there were nine more members excluded than what formed the first congregation. Why the "unworthy dust of Zion" should be thus " excluded " is not given, but it certainly was not the behaviour of Christians who " love one another " to rebel so soon and in such numbers. In this early period the sum devoted to the Pastor in quarterly collections amounted to £44 8s. 9d. for ten months, about £1 2s. 2d. a week, so that possibly those who did not subscribe were those " excluded." However, those who followed were not better, for " Mr. Hopper's income from the Church averaged about £1 0s. 0d. per week " only. In 1784 half-a-crown was paid for " Engraving Cup," but after this extravagance some one stole it, and no trace of it could be found.

In this small way the Church began, each year adding but little, until in 1810 £1144 were raised for the erection of a Chapel, the sums " varying from seven shillings down to two pence monthly." Wherever " Providence opened a door " a Brother would go and preach, but in 1812-13 several members were excluded for impropriety, and two women for telling falsehoods, and in 1815 a Mr. Hood was excluded for being an " irreclaimable Antinamian," who contended that " faith alone would insure salvation."

The earliest known burial-ground was formed in 1724, and was a place of worship originally. The earliest head-stone is to the memory of John Walkley, who died in 1757, and the last interment was that of Miss Elizabeth Aldknow, who died in November 1876, aged 64 years. A list of eighty inscriptions is given.

The Register of Births and Burials is given from 1742 to 1837, and was " taken from the original volume in the custody of the Registrar General, Somerset House," and the names occupy 40 pp., and that is followed by Biographical Notes in alphabetical order, including that of their first minister, the Rev. Richard Hopper, who began his ministry with fifteen members meeting in a cottage before he went to Nottingham. There are twenty-four biographies and nineteen portraits, the Rev. Samuel Ward dying in January 1840. A list of members from 1769 to 1815, including women, is next given, occupying 11 pp., and contains the names of fifty-eight persons "dismissed," several to London and neighbouring places, the last name given being William Vickers, who was of humble origin, getting his education from the Church's Sunday School. He was apprenticed in 1810 to a lace manufacturer, and afterwards in 1818 he is described as in the lace trade, and had entered into partnership with a Mr. Frearson; they prospered, and had several agencies in South America, etc. In 1815 Mr. Vickers joined the Baptist Church, and was in his prime in the days of Chartists and the Anti-Corn League. He afterwards became Alderman, and finally Mayor, when Her late Majesty visited Nottingham with the Prince Consort in 1843. To the Nottingham High School he devoted a great amount of time. He died in May 1882 and his wife in January 1891, and the book gives both their portraits. He seems to have been the most successful man among the Baptists in Nottingham, and had seven children, some of his great-grandchildren being born up to 1892 according to the pedigree. All the pedigrees are drawn out in a very excellent manner, and each folded within the book. The volume is a great credit to both the Authors, and ought to be supported by Baptists generally as an earnest monument to the history of their body. It is excellently printed by the Choroton Press, and altogether worthy of patronage.

How to Decipher and Study Old Manuscripts: Being a guide to the reading of Ancient Manuscripts. Second Edition. By E. E. THOYTS, with an introduction by C. PRICE MARTIN. London: Elliot Stock, 62 Paternoster Row. 1903.

WE are very glad to welcome a second edition of Miss Thoyts' excellent guide to the decipherment of ancient documents, because the inference is that the work has paid its expenses at least. Mr. Martin has written an introduction, and some amusing blunders he gives, though to an unpractised reader of old documents the mistakes might not have been understood.

In the Authoress's "hints to beginners" there are some excellent remarks about writing. This as a rule has deteriorated very much during the last thirty years. The pretty Italian handwriting taught in schools then to young ladies has drifted down to a coarseness which can be done equally well with a pointed piece of wood instead of with a delicate pen, and the young ladies of the day have degenerated in their writing to a large and awkward hand which a butcher boy would excel in. In a similar way our boys in going into examinations at Sandhurst and elsewhere are more often plucked for bad spelling, because the Universities, and after them other public and private schools, have thought spelling to be beneath their notice. The beautiful examples of writing we have among our Grants of Arms and similar documents are a proof of what writing was during 1400 and 1500. The deed of the Wax Chandlers' Company has a beautiful inscription at the foot which is a fair sample, and the Italians or Monks who did that no doubt wrote the inscription on other companies' grants. In the same way the Italian ornamentations adopted in many churches and colleges and private houses in Elizabethan days were done by the same Italian workmen, travelling from Westminster to Oxford and Wales and other parts.

The Authoress considers that the decline or alteration in writing, dated from the introduction of the art of printing, is superseding the labour of the large class of men who had formerly earned their living as professional writers. But against these we must place the labour of love which the monks adopted in their beautiful designed initial letters running down a page in gold and blue, along with the text, examples of which are so rich in those shewn at the British Museum.

It is rare we come across erasures or mistakes in the lettering of old charters, but any one versed in copying out wills, etc., will find the testator's name spelt differently throughout, as we have seen a will where the testator's name was spelt in seventeen different ways, and last of all he signed the will with a different spelling than what he began the deed with.

A good knowledge of Latin is indispensable to a transcriber, whether the deed be in Latin or Norman-French, to which modern French is a great assistant; but it is only by experience that he can decipher or interpret the multitudinous contractions and signs so generally adopted in the older documents.

Even in our own days Sir Walter Scott and Charles Dickens' hands were charming, whereas Lord Brougham and other leading men had such execrable writing to decipher that it was stated that only one compositor could *translate* his lordship's meaning in the printing office where his work was done.

The work is embellished with examples of writing, some of Fines and Court Rolls, such as the Sheriffs' Roll among the Neville MSS., and two photographic copies of the Reading Abbey Chartulary, besides giving some examples of quaint signs from old Parish Registers. The Author spares no pains in shewing the student what abbreviations he may come across, and her motto, as she finishes her agreeable task, is " Persevere and Practise." The work is published at 4s. 6d., and we would recommend every student of antiquarian taste to secure a copy.

Ball Records. No. 1. *Index to Wills of Ball, Balle, or Balls in the Prerogative Court of Canterbury, Somerset House,* 1445—1802. Bishops Stortford : A Boardman and Son. 1903.

WE must congratulate Mr. H. Houston Ball upon getting together a mass of information concerning the families of the redoubtable Balls from 1445 to 1802. Why such a name should be immortalized by the assiduity of a Ball living in 1903 is alone known to the compiler, who is, however, a member of the Royal Society of Antiquaries of Ireland, and that may account for his eccentricity, for he threatens his readers that if his efforts are supported he will deal with the calendars of the Bishop of London's Courts, and that may be a preliminary to the publications of the wills themselves. Such a catastrophe we trust we may be spared to see, much more to read ; and as among the gentlemen who take matters easy finding life is not long enough for chess, what is to be said of the future generation of readers who likewise take life easy, but will have to encounter the volumes of wills of the Balls families ? Out of 536 persons given in the book there are a few clergymen, gentlemen, and mariners, and the rest belong to the ordinary public, including 100 women, the best placed of them apparently being the third wife of Dean Alexander Nowell of St. Paul's, who was married twice before to Thomas Ball and Laurence Ball. There are about eighty Balls given in Kelly's " Commercial Directory," but we only find one Ball even among the knights.

The pamphlet is undoubtedly a labour of love, and is a monument of painstaking industry. The Author does not affix any price to the book, which makes 22 pp. demy 8vo.

The Virginia Magazine of History and Biography. Vol. XI., No. 2. October 1903. Virginia Historical Society, Richmond, U.S.A.

THE present Part gives an excellent account of the passing of the Moravians through Virginia in 1749, from a diary kept by Leonhard Schnell and John Brandmueller, who went from the settlements founded by Germans, preaching as they journeyed, and sometimes travelling for thirty-five miles without seeing a house, and climbing high mountains, living only on Johnny cakes. They were always allowed to share in whatever was ready ; one, a miller, however, had not a bit of bread in the house. The two travellers were received everywhere very cheerfully, and their host generally got together a company of neighbours to hear them preach and baptize the children.

The proceedings of the Virginia Committee of Correspondence, 1750—67, were concerned in acts for relief of debtors, the liberty to import salt rather than ballast, and also to exchange coin. In Virginia "Gleanings in England " are published the wills of many merchants and others, several requesting to be buried in the old country, and many leaving all they had to relations there. In some Virginia Records are petitions of various kinds : one for taking off a fine of 500 lbs. of tobacco against the petitioner for burning " one Anthony Parre," as he had already paid 4000 lbs. on account of the action.

In genealogy the Bruce family is amply given, likewise that of the Brookes and Herndon families, besides several others ; and the Part ends with historical notes and queries of various kinds, some of which are very quaint.

The Journal of the Ex Libris Society. Vol. XIII., Parts 9, 10, and 11, September, October, and November. London : A. and C. Black, Soho Square, W.

THE Part for September has a plate as a frontispiece dated at top 1603 and 1793, and is inscribed " Ex Bibliotheca Abbatiæ Sti. Gregorii Magni de Downside," beautifully engraved. There are two examples of bookplates designed by Mr. Graham Johnson of the Lyon Office, Edinburgh, one of the arms of David MacRitchie of Logie, Perth, and the other of Sir John Ure Primrose, Lord Provost of Glasgow, recently granted by Lyon Court, well drawn on similar lines. There is another bookplate of a very different character to these designed by Mr. C. E. Eldred, who is a Naval Officer but a delicate draughtsman, as the plate of " Mary E. Harvey " shews. The Franks' collection of bookplates is ably referred to by Mr. Alfred A. Bethune Baker, F.S.A., who refers to the first volume of the catalogue of the British and American bookplates bequeathed to the British Museum by Sir Wollaston Franks being published ; and as he says that before the end of the year the rest of the catalogue will be printed, comprising nearly 4000 bookplates, it is very gratifying to know that the Museum has so soon completed a catalogue of the collection nobly bequeathed to the institution which was graced for so many years by the presence and assiduous study of the kind donor. The Museum is thus the first public institution possessing a representative collection of bookplates, thus adding a great interest to the members of the Ex Libris Society. Such a collection as that of the late Dr. Howard's would have made another good addition had it not been so carelessly sent for sale, and many valuable plates distributed amongst buyers without any regard to the value of them. The Part ends with a further list of legal bookplates and also of a list of Chippendale plates.

The October Part has a Hebrew bookplate of Elkah Nathan Adler as a frontispiece with a Hebrew inscription at the top of it ; it merely displays the outstretched eagle with an inscription running round the coat. There is a good account of Jewish bookplates written by Israel Solomons. Some single legal bookplates are also given, besides one of Mr. Henry Lawrance, originally designed by Miss F. R. Sarg and engraved by Will. Foster of Plymouth.

The November Part, which reaches us as we are going to press, has two plates for the Frontispiece, one of Daniel Parsons and the other Robert Lovell's, some notes upon which will be found. That of Mr. Parsons is described as " a paternal coat quartering a maternal one, and impaling conjugal arms," an excellent and concise description. The selection of Legal bookplates include those of the Lord Chief Baron and Lord Penzance. There is also an illustration of the plate of Pratt Institute, Brooklyn—truly American. Some notes on Designing and Designers, a criticism of a recent American work on that subject, leaves us satisfied that the bookplate of the future will not want for able men to ensure at least artistic merit, which after all, it must be admitted, should be the principal feature of a bookplate.

The New York Genealogical and Biographical Record. Vol. XXXIV., No. 4. October 1903. Society's Office : 226 West 58th Street, New York, U.S.A.

THIS Part begins with a sketch of Anthony Bleecker of New York, and his portrait forms the frontispiece plate. The history of Old White Church in Salem is mentioned in an address delivered by Dr. A. Fitch, and the account given of it concludes with the record that it was 116 years old, 100 of which was settled in the present place, and it can claim to be the oldest religious society in Washington County, and the Author finishes with the exhortation, " Long live the Old White Church in Salem ! and when the last of its members shall lie beneath the sod, may it be the lot of a future chronicler to record with truth that we were worthy of the precious heritage it was our privilege to enjoy." There are the Records of Marriages, Baptisms, and Deaths in Easthampton from 1696 to 1746, occupying several pages. A review of disbanded soldiers mustered at Bear River on 25 January 1784, and also a muster roll of officers, soldiers, and loyalists taken at Gulliver's Hole, etc., also in June 1784. There are full accounts given of the family of Edward Fuller, also of the Waring family of co. Salop, England, with arms, and the Freer family of New Paltz, New York. An interesting Paper is given of Southampton, England, with a couple of illustrations of the Bar Gate, including a good account of objects of interest there. The Part winds up with Editorial accounts of several families, among them that of Mr. Rufus King, a late member of the Harleian Society of England, and the Part gives ample indices of names and subjects in Vol. XXXIV., with title, etc,

Fenland Notes and Queries. Vol. V., Part 59. October 1903. Peterborough: George C. Caster, Market Place.

THIS Part contains an interesting account of De Foe, the author of Robinson Crusoe, whose family it appears was at Etton in Northamptonshire, not Elton as generally supposed. Mr. Thomas Wright, who published De Foe's life in 1894, holds that Foe. Faux, Vaux, and Devereux are variations of the same name, and that his family came from Flanders. Daniel died in 1631, leaving a small estate.

There is an interesting account of the French register at Thorney. The Huguenot settlers who came over here were engaged in the reclamation of the land on the Bedford estate. and in twelve years 40,000 acres of land had been brought under cultivation. Cromwell in 1630 issued an ordinance granting to foreigners full rights of English citizenship, thus inducing many Protestant refugees from Flanders to betake themselves here. It was a hard life. hard even for them, for those who invested their money lost it, and in many cases it was forfeited for arrears of rates and taxes.

The Part contains an account of two extensive fires occurring, one at Woodwalton Fen, where ten acres of bracken and turf were one blaze, and it required the Huntingdon and Ramsey fire brigades to put it out. The other was at Wicken Fen, a resort of the wild fowl and scarce butterflies which frequented the neighbourhood. Twenty acres were destroyed of this last piece of fenland of Old England, and it was the home of considerable numbers of English plants and insects and some rare birds which are found in no other part of England. All were destroyed through the carelessness of four University men from Cambridge in throwing away unspent matches in the usual custom of smokers ; they saw the sedge catch fire, and when alight " they lost their heads and ran away." They honestly owned it, so the proprietor forgave them.

There are other interesting Papers all worth reading, and the Part keeps up its useful purpose in publishing anything pertaining to Fenland, and its drainage from 1637, great opposition being shewn to it by the commoners, who commenced riots in several towns. Cromwell besides was opposed to the drainage, which had been going on for years, and he abetted the malcontents.

** Books for Review and Notices of Forthcoming Works should be addressed to Messrs. Mitchell Hughes and Clarke at the Publishing Office, 140 Wardour Street, London, W.

End of Volume V., Third Series.

INDEX OF NAMES.

Names in *Italics* have their Arms given.
pl. signifies reference to a Plate.

A

Baxter, Rev. Nathaniel, 208; Susannah, 284.
Baylee, Sarah, 229.
Bayley, John, 306; Judith, 305, 306.
Baylie, Eleanor, 196; Martin, 314; Martin William, 314; Sarah, 314.
Baylis, Anne, 312; Anthony, 190, 250, 309. 312; Francis, 250; Hester, 190, 309; Margaret, 58; Sarah, 231; Stephens, 157; Susanna, 233; Thomas, 231; Will., 25.
Bayly, Rev. Anselm, 138; Mary, 230, 231.
Bayons or *Bayous*, 129.
Bayons or Bayous, Sir Walter, 129.
Beacham, Mary, 141.
Beale (Beal *or* Bele), Ann, 40; Elizabeth, 31, 40; Fanny, 31; Hannah. 31; Hester. 31; John, 31; Rev. John, 40; Mary, 31; Richard, 31; Sarah, 31; Susanna, 31; William, 31.
Bean, Margaret, 255; Rev. Peter, 255.
Bear, Elizabeth, 140; Rich., 229; Sara, 229; Savage. 140.
Beard, Edward, 56; Elizab., 229; Elizabeth, 232; ffortuna, 56; Samuel, 231, 232; Sarah, 231, 232.
Beath, Jemima, 136.
Beatty, Catherine Selina. 45; Charlotte Elizabeth Frederica, 46; David, 85; Adjutant David, 45; David William, 46; Edward, 45; Elizabeth, 124; Elizabeth Sophia, 46; Dr. Foster, 124; Henrietta Loftus, 46; Horace Edward, 46; Jeanetta Letitia Katherine, 46; Letitia Eleanor, 46; Letitia Eva Geraldine, 46; Letitia Thomasina, 45, 85; Mary Frances, 46, 85; Olivia Constance, 46; Captain Richard Carden Allen, 46; Captain Thomas Charles Edward, 46; William John, 46.
Beaupree, Dorathie, 54; Edmond, 54.
Beauvais, Anne Louise, 12; Françoise, 12; Louis, 12; Simon, 12; Susannah (? Ourry), 12.
Beaw, 305.
Beaw, Gulielmi, 304; Margaretæ, 304.
Bedborough, Charlotte, 165; Daniel, 165.
Beddow, Ann, 57; Mary, 106; Tho., 57; Thomas, 106.
Beddowe, John, 103; Thomas, 103.
Beddowes, Thomas, 158.
Bedford, Earl of. 200; Duke of, 79, 276; John, Duke of, 201, 205.
Bedingfield. Sir Thomas, 245.
Beele, Grisill, 57.
Beels, John, 64.
Beeseley, Ann, 158; John, 158.
Begley, Elianor, 157.
Belcher, Ann, 230.
Bell, Mary, 314; Mathew, 314; Pat., 146; Robert, 314; Rev. Robert, 146.
Bellases or *Belasyse*, 185, 186 *pl.*
Bellasis *or* Belasyse, Ann, 185, 186; Lady Ann, 183, 184, 185, 186; Lady Ann (Powlet), 183, 184, 185, 186; Barbara. 183; Catherine, 183; Elizabeth. 185, 186; Frances, 183, 184, 186; Francis, 185; Sir Henry, 183, 184, 185, 186; Honnora *or* Honora, 183; Isabella, 183; Lady Jane, 183, 184, 185, 186; John, 185, 186; John (Lord), 182, 183, 184, 185, 186 *pl.*, and Baron Worlaby, 184, 185, 186; Mary, 183, 184, 185, 186; Mary Ann, 186; Rogersa, 186; Svsana, 186; Thomas, 186.
Bellet, John, 310; Joseph, 310.
Bellett, Alice, 189; Elizabeth, 250; Jo., 252; John, 250; Sarah, 190, 250; Tho., 189, 190, 250, 311; Thomas, 309.

Bellew, Sir John, 259; Mary, 259.
Bellings, Richard, 218.
Bendyshe, Caroline, 198; Ireton, 198; Thomas, 198.
Benett, Ann, 250; Joshua, 250.
Benfield, Rachel, 317.
Bennet, Anne, 103, 104; Richard, 57, 103.
Bennett *or* Ben'ett, Ann, 91; Anne, 312; Elizabeth, 105, 309, 310; Harriet, 255; John, 224, 312; Letitia Maria, 256; Mary, 224, 310, 312; Ric., 310; Rich., 310; Richard, 187; Sarah, 142, 256; Tho., 309; Thomas, 105; William, 255, 256.
Bennitt, Alice, 157; Thomas, 157.
Benson, Archbishop, 318; Rev. Christopherus, 209.
Bentlee, Elizabeth, 53; Robart, 53.
Bentley, Elizabeth, 166; William, 279.
Benton, Anne *or* Bridget, 222; Rev. John, 222.
Beresford, Anne Jane, 22; Henry Barre, 22; Rt. Hon. John, 22; John Claudius, 272.
Bergavenny, George, Lord, 183; Lady Honnora, 183.
Bernard, Dr. Chas., 298.
Berry, Alicia, 87; Allen Noble, 85; Daniel, 233; Dorothea, 86; Elizabeth Bury, 88; Frances, 87; Francis, 87; Isabella Adams, 85; John, 88; Louisa, 85; Marlborough Parsons, 85; Martha, 85; Mary, 233; Smith Massey, 85; Sterling, 86; Thomas, 85.
Bertie, Hon. Robert, 130; Rt. Hon. Robert, Earl of Lindsey, 130.
Bertodano, *see* De Bertodano.
Best, Beata, 231; James, 231; John, 279.
Betham, Sir William, Ulster King of Arms, 205.
Bethune-Baker, Alfred A., 38.
Bettcher, Eliza Helen, 261; Jules, 261.
Betts, Mary, 140; Willm., 140.
Beuzeville, Elizabeth, 12, 15; Elizabeth Charity, 15; Rev. Samuel, 12, 15.
Bevan, Anne Frances, 217; Charlotte. 217; Frances, 84, 217; Rt. Hon. Henry, 217; Jane, 217; Richard, 217; Rev. Richard, 84, 217; Thomas, 217; William, 217.
Beytoun, Jon., 145.
Bickersteth, Rev. Robertus. 209.
Bidell, Mary, 24; Robert, 24.
Bigg, Margery, 221; —, 221.
Biggs, Anne, 102; Harry, 102; Mary, 234; —, 234.
Bigot, Ann. 255; Anthony, 255.
Bigsby, John, 279.
Biles, Ann, 143.
Birch, C. L., 208; Elizt., 232; Rev. Wickham M., 279.
Birchall, Charles. 164.
Bird, Charlotte, 139, 140; Elizabeth, 57; John, 139, 140; Mary, 139, 140; William, 39.
Birkhead, Edward, 302.
Birt, Hester, 232; Samuel, 232.
Biscat *or* Bisket, Jon., 144.
Bishet, Ann, 148.
Bishop, Emily, 22; Heber Reginald, 280; James, 22; Sarah, 231; William, 231.
Bishop of London (1607), 119.
Bisset, Isabel, 8; John *or* Jon., 145; Marie, 145.
Black, A. and C., 38, 79, 120, 160, 199, 239, 279, 323; B. E., 128; Jane Cannon, 128.
Blackburn, George, 29; Jane, 29.

294; Elizabeth, 293, 294; Emma, 293, 294; John, 293, 294; William, 293, 294.
Byrch, 305.
Byrch, Baron (Judge), 306; Eliza, 306; Johannes, 306.
Byrne, Alice, 116; Catherine, 116; Charles, 116; Christian, 116; Christopher, 116; Gregory, 116; Sir Gregory, Bart., 116; Henry, 116; Margaret, 116; Mary Ann, 116; Sarah, 116.
Byset, *see* Bisset.
Byshe *or* Bish, Edward, "named" Garter King of Arms, 297.
Byshopp, Thomas, "Capellani," 64.
Bysshe, Sir Edward, 43; Sir Edward, Clarencieux King of Armes, 137.

C

Cadge, Thomas, 221.
Calandrini, Francis, 112; Magdalen, 112. 114.
Caldwell, Captain Arthur James, 21; Baylie, 147; Major-General Sir James L., 21.
Callowe, Clement, 226; Frances, 226; Thomas, 226; —, 226.
Calthrope, Anne. 54; Sir Martin, 54.
Calverley family, 316.
Cam, Sarah, 232.
Cambridge. E., 266; John Cranmer, 266.
Camden, Elizabeth, 251; Isabell, 252; Jarvis, 251, 252.
Cammalt, Mr., 72.
Campbell, Rev. Adderley, 122; Alexander, 122; Major Alexander, 19; Dona Maria Brigida do Faria e Lacerda, 18; Elizabeth, 151; Elizabeth Dancer, 122; Isabella Verling, 122; James. 145, 195; Lieut.-Colonel Sir John, 18; John David, 18; Jon., 146; Lilias, 145; Lucy. 19; Mary, 19; Peter, 151; Sarah, 151.
Camperdown, Earl of, 174.
Campion, Ann, 28; Henry, 28.
Cannon, James, 182.
Canterbury *or* Cant., Benson, Dr., Archbishop of, 318; Davidson, Dr. Randall Thomas, Archbishop of, 318; (Sancroft), Archbishop of (1688), 70, 71; Tait, Dr., Archbishop of, 318.
Carbery, John, 5th Lord, 169.
Carby, Jane, 231.
Care, John, 190; Mary, 190.
Carew, *see* Pole-Carew.
Carnac, Henrietta, 20; James Rivett, 20.
Carnarvon, Henry, Earl of, 16.
Caroline, Queen of England, 71.
Carpenter, John, 14; Lucy, 14.
Carr, Isabella, 296; Rt. Hon. Sir Robert, Bart., 296.
Carruthers, David, M.P., 20, 22; Elizabeth, 139; Fanny Elizabeth, 20; Laws, 139; Mary, 20, 22.
Carte, Prebendary Samuel, 68.
Carter, Anne, 232; Joane, 28; John, 28, 30; Mary, 233; Rebecca, 30; Robert, 28; Sarah, 150.
Cartwright, Anne, 103; Dorothy, 151; Joan, 60; Martha, 60; Mary, 106; Ric., 98; Rich., 106; William, 103, 151; Will'm, 60.
Caruthers, Mary, 233; Mary Anne, 233.
Carver, Sarah, 256.
Carvick, Georgiana Marianne Catherine, 265; Thomas, 265.
Carwardine, Sarah, 233.

Casineto, *see* De Casineto.
Castelfranc, Rev. Mr., 77.
Caster, George C., 39, 79, 120, 160, 199, 240, 280, 324.
Castle, Mary. 229.
Castleman, Dorothy, 152; Henry, 152.
Castlereagh, Lord, Chief Secretary of Ireland, 272.
Castle-Rosse, Viscount, 178.
Cathcart, Rt. Hon. Chas., Lord, 141; Hon. Louisa, 141; Lord, 125.
Cattell, Hannah, 102; Hewens, 102.
Cavalier, J., 261.
Cave, Anne, 30; George, 239; Ralph, 30.
Cavendish, Catherine, 220; Dukes of Devonshire, 220; Elizabeth, 293, 294; John, 220; —, 293, 294.
Cawley, Anne *or* Ann, 33; Elisabeth, 33; John, 33; Rev. Mr., 74, 75, 76, 77; Rev. Thomas, 32, 33.
Ceanach, Connall, 257.
Ceare, Hester, 250; Thomas, 250, 310; William, 310.
Cecill or *Cecil*, 300, 301.
Cere, Elizabeth, 309; Isabell, 309; Tho., 309.
Cha . . ., Edward, 163; Elizabeth, 163; James, 163.
Chadwell, Anne, 228.
Challis, Mr., 268.
Chamberlain *or* Chamberlayne, Patience, 233.
Chamberlen, Isabella, 3.
Chamberlin, Ann, 143; John, 143.
Chambers, Edward, 58.
Champion, George, 150.
Chance, Isabell, 190; Tho., 190; William, 107.
Chandler, John, 312; Richard, 312; Tho., 249; William, 249.
Chandos, 302.
Chapman, Georgius, 208; Hannah, 231; Lieut. Patrick, 277.
Chare, Joan, 252.
Chares, Edward, 103; Jane. 103; Robert, 103; Thom.. 103; Thomas, 103.
Charke, —, 108.
Charles, Caleb, 310; Margaret, 228; Oliva, 310.
Charles I., King of England, 132, 139, 182, 183, 184, 185, 186, 303.
Charles II., King of England, 71, 132, 182, 183, 184, 185, 186, 208.
Charleton, 304.
Charleton, Emma, 303; Sir John, Bart., 303.
Charleville, Earl of, 88.
Charlotte, Queen of England, 15.
Cheap, Rev. And., 140.
Chebsey, Hester, 68; John, 68.
Chedworth, Sarah, 229.
Cheek, Lady Essex, 62.
Cheeseman, Mary, 162.
Cherington, Elizabeth, 233.
Chester, Earls of, 245.
Chester, Lupus, Earl of, 245.
Chester, Sir Anthony, 199; Colonel, 42, 101; Colonel J. Lemuel, 216; Rev. W., 141.
Chesterfield, Earl of, 243; Philipe, Earl of. 243.
Chetham, Captain, 237.
Child *or* Chiles, Anne, 29; Elianor, 254; Lawrence, 29; Thomas, 29, 254.
Childs, Phebe, 93.
Chilton, Emily Georgina, 180; George, 180; George Robert Comyn, 180; Matty Wolff, 180; Rosalind Elizabeth, 180.

Edwards, Alice, 249 ; Caroline, 216 ; Elinor, 310 ; Emma, 127 ; ffrancis, 105 ; Frances, 31, 309, 311 ; Grace, 133 ; James, 157 ; Jno., 71 ; Joane, 311 ; John, 216 ; Mary, 250, 309 ; Susannah, 229 ; Tho., 249 ; Thom., 103 ; Thomas, 103, 133, 153, 157, 158, 159 ; Will., 311 ; Willia', 250, 309, 310 ; William, 153.
Eeds, George, 312 ; Margery, 312.
Egerton, 244.
Egerton, Margaritæ, 244 ; —, 244.
Egiocke, George, 104.
Egioke, John, 187.
Eglintoune, Heugh, 144.
Eigles, Jacob, 231 ; Mary, 231.
Eldred, C.E., 323.
Eleanor (of Castile), Queen of England, 199.
Eley *or* Ely, Thomas Green, Bishop of, 72.
Elford, 302.
Eliott, Archibald, 201 ; ffrances, 201 ; General, 205 ; Sir Gilbert, Bart., 201 ; Vernon, 201 ; —, Lord Heathfield, 201.
Elizabeth, Queen of England, 9, 291, 292, 294.
Ellets, Anne, 55 ; Ellenora, 59 ; Hen., 26 ; Henr., 59 ; Joan, 26 ; Johanna, 23 ; Tabitha, 59.
Ellett, Henry, 188.
Elletts, Anne, 106 ; Henry, 106 ; Johane, 188.
Ellins, Anne, 55 ; Arthur, 24 ; Catherine, 310 ; ffrancis, 57 ; ffraunces, 188 ; Francis, 251 ; Hen., 189 ; Henry, 187, 188, 251 ; Humfrey, 105 ; John, 55, 104, 187 ; Judith, 57 ; Margaret, 158 ; Mary, 189 ; Thomas, 104.
Elliot, Giles, 4 ; Grace, 318 ; Sir John, Bart., 318 ; Margaret, 4 ; Mary, 318 ; Thomas, 318.
Elliotts, Henrici, 156.
Ellis, Daniel, 233 ; Edward, 166 ; Elizabeth, 166 ; Elizabeth Hurst, 49 ; Henry, 49 ; Mary, 233 ; Sophia, 166, 233 ; Stephen, 233.
Elly, Anne, 32 ; Benjamin, 32 ; Brigid, 32 ; Elisabeth, 32 ; Jame-Slater, 32 ; Joseph, 32 ; Mary, 32 ; Widow, 32.
Elmer, Selina Clayton, 126.
Elphinstone, Andro., 147; Captain Charles, R.N., 19 ; Elizabeth, 19 ; Elizabeth Fullerton, 18 ; Vice-Admiral Sir George Keith, 277 ; Hon. William Fullerton, 18, 19.
Elton, Mary, 150 ; William, 150.
Emmett, —, 202.
Emperor Francis Josef of Austria, 173.
Empress Frederick of Germany, 38.
Em's, Alce, 105 ; Richard, 105 ; Richd., 105 ; William, 309.
English, Mr., 71 ; Mrs., 36, 71.
Eresby, Sir Anthony, 54 ; Elizabeth, 54.
Essington, 277.
Essington, Ann, 77, 277 ; Anne, 77 ; Claphamson, 77, 277 ; Elizabeth, 74, 77 ; John, 74, 77 ; Vice-Admiral Sir William, 277.
Estrange, *see* L'Estrange.
Eustace, Catherine, 116 ; Eleanor, 116 ; James, 116 ; —, 116.
Evans, Eliz., 140 ; Hon. Frances Dorothea, 169 ; Rev. Gulfridus, 208 ; John, Lord Carbery, 169 ; Margaret *or* Margret, 140 ; Mary, 232, 233 ; Robert, 150 ; Thos., 140 ; William Davis, 261.
Eve. George W., 80, 280.
Evelyn, Charles. 77 ; Edward, 77, 78 ; Edward Rutter. 78 ; George Rutter, 78 ; John, 38, 77, 78 ; Phebe, 77, 78 ; Phœbe, 77, 78.

Everard, 227.
Everard, Ambrose, 226, 227 ; Anne, 288 ; Catherine, 227 ; Dorothy, 227 ; Elizabeth, 227 ; Frances, 227 ; Henry, 288 ; John, 227 ; Martha, 227.; Mary, 227, 288 ; Richard, 227 ; Sarah, 227 ; Thomas, 221.
Evered. Elizabeth, 226 ; Frances, 226 ; Mary, 226 ; Richard, 226.
Evets, John, 97.
Evett, John, 188 ; Margaret, 188 ; Mary, 188 ; William, 188.
Ewbank, Frances, 23 ; Margaretta, 23 ; Rev. Thomas, 23.
Ewing, W., 202.
Exail, Elizabeth, 33.
Excell, Elizabeth, 232.
Exeter, Anthony Sparrow, Bishop of, 220.
Exmouth, Lord, 48.
Eydes, John, 66 ; Margaret, 66.
Eyres, 99.
Eyres, Anne, 102 ; Daniel, 66, 101 ; Henry, 102 ; Jane, 99 ; John, 69, 99 ; Thomas, 99.
Eyton, Elizabetham, 304 ; Thomæ, 304.

F

Fairfax, Anne, 162 ; Lord, 182, 185 ; Tho., 310 ; Willia', 310 ; William, 162.
Fairfaxio, Ferdinando D., Barone de Cameron, 244 ; Maria, 244.
Fairlie, Alexander, 77 ; Anne, 77.
Falconbridge, Viscount, *see* Fauconberg.
Faldoe, William, 130.
Fallon, Amy, 48 ; Dr., 48.
Farebrother, Jane Susanna, 289 ; Mary Jane Frances, 289 ; Rev. Thomas, 289.
Farie, James, 145.
Farley, Anne, 228.
Farr, Elizabeth, 250, 309 ; Mary, 310 ; Nicholas, 310 ; Richard, 250 ; Willia', 309.
Farre, William, 312.
Farrer, Henricus, 312.
Fauconberg *or* Falconbridge, Thomas, Viscount, 182, 183, 184, 185.
Faukener (Faulkener *or* Fawkener), Alice, 66, 96, 97, 101 ; Marye, 66 ; William, 66, 96, 101 ; Wm., 66.
Fawnt, Lady Lucie, 244 ; Sr. William, 244.
Feild, Agnes, 109 ; Francis, 109.
Fellow, John, 236.
Felton, Elizabeth, 296 ; Lady Elizabeth, 296 ; Sir Thomas, Bart., 296.
Fenner, 302.
Fenton, John, 247 ; Mary, 247.
Ferguson, Margaret, 8.
Fergusson, Barbara, 149 ; George, 149 ; T. Colyer, 81.
Ferrard, Viscount, 175.
Fetherstonhaugh, Alicia, 87 ; Alicia Frances, 87 ; Anna Maria, 87 ; Frances Maria, 87 ; Francis Henry, 87 ; Louisa Maria Jane, 87 ; Susanna, 87 ; Thomas Orme, 87 ; William, 87.
Few, Harry, 295.
ffar, Richard, 252 ; Sarah, 252.
ffarr, Anne, 251 ; ffrancis, 25 ; Margery, 190 ; Rich., 25 ; Rich'us, 157 ; Thomas, 158 ; Will', 251 ; William, 158.
ffarre, Anne, 103 ; John, 58 ; Marie, 103 ; Mary, 106 ; Nicholas, 103, 106 ; Richard, 27.
ffarwood, Elizabeth, 158 ; Richard, 158.

G

Gabbé, Anna Culmer Addis Keene, 265 ; Fritz, 265.
Gainey, Sarah, 233.
Gale, Elizabeth, 277.
Gally, Rev. Henricus, D.D., 209.
Gambell, Alicia Frances, 87 ; Arthur, 87 ; Susanna Olive, 87.
Gambier, J., 270 ; Lord, 277.
Ganderton, Ægidius (Giles), 59 ; Giles, 313 ; Joh'is, 59 ; John, 106, 249, 251, 309 ; Margaret, 249 ; Tho., 310 ; Thomas, 106 ; Ursula, 310.
Ganerton, John, 153.
Garde, see De la Garde.
Gardener, Michl., 98.
Gardiner, Anna, 229 ; Anne, 228, 233 ; Daniel, 229 ; Dina, 230 ; Eliz., 229 ; Elizabeth, 233 ; Henricus, 230 ; Henry, 295 ; John, 230, 232 ; Martha, 232 ; Mary, 231 : Sara, 229 ; Sarah, 230, 232 ; Thomas, 233 ; Thos., 232 ; William, 231.
Gardiner or Gardner, Ann or Anne, 278 ; Ann Holmes, 278 ; Caroline, 278 ; Henry, 278 ; Kirkman, 278 ; Lucy, 278 ; Mary Anne, 278 ; Sophia, 278.
Gardner, Elizabeth, 233 ; Hannah, 232 ; Mary, 232 ; Richard, 233 ; Sarah, 231, 233 ; William, 232.
Garey (Gearey or Geary), Anne, 77 ; Charles, 77 ; Elizabeth, 77 ; Frances. 77 ; Francis, 77 ; Mary, 77 ; Philip, 77 ; Phillip, 77 ; Sarah, 77.
Garner, Ann, 190 : Elizabeth, 149 ; Hannah, 232 ; John, 229 ; Mary, 229.
Garnier, Lady Harriet, 14 ; Lucy, 14 ; Rev. William, 14.
Garnishe, Margaret, 52 ; Thomas, 52.
Garrard, Susan, 286 ; W., 286.
Garrett, Sir George, 303 ; Lord Justice, 258 ; Thomas, 106, 303 ; Thomas, Earl of Kildare, 258.
Gascadon, Lady Agnes, 148.
Gascoygne, 210.
Gaston, Christopher, 142 ; Elizabeth, 142 ; Henry, 142.
Gastrell, James, 233 ; Sarah, 233.
Gates, Barbara, 262 ; Charlotte, 262 ; John, 262.
Gatonby, Ann, 282 ; Thomas, 282 ; —, 282.
Gaunnon, —, 293.
Gay, Fanny Michell, 126 ; William, 126.
Gazzard, Louisa, 178 ; William, 178 ; William Richard, 178.
George, Alice, 30 ; Edward, 30, 138 ; Elizabeth, 29, 30, 138 ; Henry, 138 ; Jane. 29 ; John, 30 ; Mary, 29 ; Mr., 144 ; Nathaniel, 30 ; Ralph, 29, 279 ; Rebecca, 29, 30 ; Rebeccah, 138 ; Susanna, 138 ; Susannah, 138 ; William, 29, 30, 138 ; see also St. George.
George I., King of England, 71.
George II., King of England, 71, 249.
George III., King of England, 287.
George IV., King of England, 240.
Gernoone or Gernon, John, 52 ; Margaret, 52.
Gerrard, Mary Anne, 49 ; Thomas, 49.
Gery, Rebecca, 293 ; William, 293.
Gerying, Elizabeth, 107.
Gibbons, Hannah, 230 ; Johanna, 64 ; Richard, 64.
Gibbs, Mary, 189.
Gibson, David Thomas, 149 ; Joh., " Blewmantle," 129.

Gidding (? Hidding), Barthol., 155.
Gide, Hannah, 232 ; William, 232.
Gifford, 210.
Gifford, Anna, 210 ; Duci, 210.
Gilbart, " Widdow," 106.
Gilbayre, Margret, 147.
Gilbert, Elizabeth, 140 ; J., 217, 218.
Gill, Elizabeth, 229.
Ginner, Joane, 106 ; John, 107 ; Symon, 106.
Gipps, Elizabeth, 179 ; George, 179.
Glascocke, Anne, 278 ; William, 278.
Glass, Mary, 72.
Glenton, Margaret, 94 ; Robert, 94.
Gloucester, William, Duke of, 71.
Glover or Glouer, Elizabeth, 60, 104, 159 ; Frances, 252 ; Francis, 190 ; Henry, 188 ; Rev. Hugh or Hugone, 23, 24, 25, 26, 55, 56, 57, 58, 59, 60, 104, 105, 155 ; John, 189, 312 ; Rich., 189, 252 ; Richard, 159, 188, 190 ; —, 156.
Goar, Alice, 55 ; Hen., 24 ; Henry, 55, 60 ; Sarah, 60 ; —, 26.
Goare, Sarah, 188.
Goddard, Elizabeth, 250, 309 ; James, 138 ; Mary, 138 ; Rich., 309 ; Richard, 250.
Godfrey, Elizabeth, 224, 225 ; John T., 320 ; Mary, 225 ; Richard, 225.
Godin, Peter, 22 ; Sophia, 22.
Godwin, Charlotte, 119.
Godwyn, John, 25.
Goffe, Mr., 62.
Going, Ambrose, 169 ; Elizabeth Frances, 169.
Golder, Elizabeth, 188 ; Harriet, 264.
Goldicote, Isabell, 60 ; Nicholas, 60 ; Phillip, 60.
Goldsmith, James, 139 ; Mary, 139.
Gonin, Anne, 15 ; Major John, 15.
Goodfellow, Susanna, 284 ; Susannah, 284 ; Thomas, 284.
Goodsherry (?), Jane, 103.
Goodwin, Rev. Mr., 33.
" Goodwyfe " of Craigalen, 145.
Goore, Alice, 309 ; Ann, 159 ; . . . . lielmi, 157 ; Henry, 55, 252 ; Jane, 250 ; John, 159 ; Mary, 308 ; Will., 250 ; Willia', 308 ; William, 188.
Goose, Giles, 279.
Gordon, Captain Alexander, R.N., 49.
Gore, John, 312.
Goss, Henry, 153 ; Mary, 153.
Goswell, Anne, 29 ; Richard, 29.
Goulburn, Henry, 177 ; Sarah, 177.
Govan, Alexander, 195 ; Bessie, 195 ; Jon., 148 ; Marie, 148.
Gower, Arthur F. G. Leveson, 18, 130, 177, 206, 241. 300 ; John, 249 ; Mary, 26 ; Willia', 26.
Gowld [Alice], 55 ; Thomas, 55.
Graham, Captain Edward Loyd, 175 ; Hannah, 77 ; Mary, 142 ; Wm., 145.
Graine, Sir Robert, 186 ; see also Crane.
Grammatt, Hannah, 232 ; Thomas, 232.
Granger, Alice, 1.
Grant-Dalton, Alice Mary, 265 ; Edith, 265 ; Eloëy Martha, 265 ; Martha Anna Marie Burrill, 265 ; Nathaniel Watts, 265.
Grantham, Elizabeth, 143 ; Joane, 52 ; Nicholas, 52.
Granville, Catherine, 112, 114 ; George, 112 ; —, Marquis of Buckingham, 112.
Grasier, Elizab., 250 ; Elizabeth, 56 ; Elizabetha, 156 ; ffrancis, 104, 106 ; Gratiamus, 59 ; Henri, 59 ; Henry, 56, 104, 106, 156, 309, 310 ; Sibell, 56 ; Thomas, 309.

Stephen, 301; Tho., "Windsor," 129; —, 311.
Holland, Captain, R.N., 277; Rt. Hon. the Earl of, 62; Lady, 62.
Hollidge. Margaret, 281.
Holton, Henry, 153.
Home, Elizabeth Evarina S., 47; Dr. William Luis, 47.
Hone, Sarah, 230.
Honeywood *or* Honywood, Arthur, 76; Elizabeth, 76; Mary, 76.
Hood, Mr., 320.
Hooker, Maria, 228; Mr., 62; Richardus, 228.
Hooman, Ann, 188; John, 188; Widdowe, 188.
Hooper, Hester, 232.
Hope, 307.
Hope, Jane, 307; Mariæ, 307; Robert, 307.
Hopkins, Alice, 188; Anne, 80; George, 94; Sir John, 80; Sarah, 94; Thomas, 156, 158, 187, 188.
Hopkinson, Hannah Riddlesdale, 262; Julia, 261; Captain S., R.N., 261, 262.
Hopper, Rev. —, 320.
Hopton, Arthur, 279.
Hore, Cha., 268.
Horne, Frances, 309; George, 309; Richard, 159; Thomas, 159.
Hornett, Mary, 232; Robert, 232.
Horrocks, Captain Charles, 265.
Horton, Rebecca, 152.
Horwood, Ann, 103; Ellenor, 57; Hugh, 27, 57, 58, 59; Hugo', 25; Jane, 25; Margeria, 58; Margery, 27; Robert, 58; Tho., 59.
Hoskins, 245.
Hoskyns, Thomas, 245.
Hotspur, Harry (Sir Henry Percy), 7.
Hotton, William, 143.
Houghton, Elizabeth, 246, 247; Henry, 246, 247; Mary, 279.
House, F. G., 280.
Housmann, Caroline Lavinia Mitchell, 262; Ernest, 262.
Hovenden, Robert, 43.
Hovey, Mary, 223; William, 223.
How, Sarah, 91.
Howard, 41 *pl.*
Howard, Dr. A. Dashwood, 41; Rev. Adderley Bernhard, 172; Lady Elizabeth, 296; Ellen Clara, 41; Georgiana Roberts, 172; James, 3rd Earl of Suffolk, 296; Joseph Jackson, LL.D., F.S.A., Maltravers Herald Extraordinary, 41, 42, 43, 296, 323; Peter, 41.
Howard de Walden, Lord, *see* Griffin-Whitwell.
Howell, Dorothy, 138; Ethelflœdo Berthon, 278; Dr. Thomas Arthur Ives, 278; William, 138.
Howes, Edward, 24.
Howland, Sir Giles, 280; Dr. Richard, Bishop of Peterborough, 280.
Howse, Edward, 187.
Huband, Alice, 158; An'e, 189; Anne, 158; Ed., 252; Edward, 105, 106; Isabell, 105; Tho., 189; Thomas, 106, 155.
Huband *alius* Hibbots, Ann, 57; Richard, 57; Thomas, 57.
Hubande, Edward, 189; Frances, 189.
Hubbert, Abraham, 279.
Huckley, Anne, 32.
Hucks, Sarah, 238.
Hudson, Edmond, 266.
Huet, William, 312.

Huggeford, William, 99.
Huggins, Ann, 232; Richard, 251.
Hugh, Robert, 99.
Hughan, Alexander, 154; Robert, 154.
Hughes, Alice, 26; An', 310; Archibald Douglas, 262; Charles Robert, 164; Charlotte, 164; Admiral Edward, 277; Eleanor, 233; Elizabeth, 74; Ellen, 262; Emma, 164; Rev. Herbert Maxwell Carlyle, 171; Irene Gwendoline, 171; James, 262; Jane, 44; Lawrence, 310; Richard, 74; Rev. S. C., LL.D., 171; Thomas, 74; William, 233.
Hulbert, Mrs., 71; Sarah, 231; "Sister," 71; Thomas, 231.
Hull, Anne, 32; Edward, 141; Margrett, 93; Rebecca, 141; Sarah Eleanor *or* Elizabeth, 141; William, 32, 141.
Hulls, —, 70.
Hume, Adolphus Willm., 194; Alexander, 193; Ann, 193; Frederick, 194.
Humfrey, Charles, 234; Elizabeth, 234.
Humphrey, Catherine, 136; John, 136.
Humphreys or *Humphrey*, or *Heylyn*, 135.
Humphreys, Admiral Sir Salusbury (afterwards Davenport), 262; Rev. Salusbury, 262.
Hungerford, *see* Holdich-Hungerford.
Hunsdon, Elizabeth, Lady, 52; Lord, 52.
Hunt, Alice, 158; Ann, 159, 187, 250, 312; Anna, 155; Anne, 104; Armel, 56; Armell, 156; Armill, 59, 105; Elizabeth, 311; Elizath., 69; Ellenor, 27; ffrancis, 60, 103; George, 250; Hannah, 314; Henrici, 57; Henry, 55, 60, 104, 159, 188, 312; Isabel, 24; James, 311; Joane, 106; Joanne, 228; Johannis, 156; Joh'es, 59, 155; John, 27, 57, 59, 103, 106, 188, 189, 250, 309; Jone, 312; Laricke, 156; Margareta, 155; Margery, 158; Martha, 105; Mary, 106, 314; Mary Ann, 164; Mr., 69; Raphael, 187; Richard, 27, 106, 249, 312; Robert, 56, 57; Samuell, 60; Tho., 24, 60, 155, 189; Thomas, 27, 55, 104, 105, 158, 189, 250; Thos., 312; Ursula, 158; Willia', 250, 309; William, 158, 164, 228, 312.
Huntbac, Elianora, 156.
Hunte, *see* Le Hunt.
Hunter, Issobell, 148.
Huntingdon, George, Earl of, 243; Henry, Lord Hastings and Earl of, 300.
Huntingford, Elizabeth, 31.
Huntley, Dorathy, 106; Eliz., 312; Ellenor, 24; Joh'es, 155; Jone, 312; Thomas, 106.
Hunt-page, Elenor, 104; Richard, 104; Widdow, 104.
Hurlestone, Joanna, 233.
Hurley, Charlotte, 151; Edward, 151; Eleanor, 151; Emma, 151; William, 151.
Hussey, 210, 244.
Hussey, Rhoda, 244; Sir Thomas. Bart., 244.
Hutchinson, —, D.D., 70.
Hutchossonn, James, 145.
Hutson *or* Hudson, Elisabeth, 95; Eliz., 95; Elizabeth, 95; Isaac, 95; Lucy, 95; Mary, 95; Sarah, 95; William, 95.
Hutton, Rt. Hon. Henry, 272.
Huxley, Christiania Maria, 262; Thomas, 262; —, 262.
Hyatt. P., 271.
Hyde, Eliz., 232; Elizabeth, 52; John, 52; Lawrance, 54; Mary, 54; Thomas, 232.
Hyudes, Elizabeth, 226; Hester, 226; Thomas, 226.

Murphy, Catherine Selina, 45, 46; Daniel, 117; Henry Charles B. MacMurrogh, 45, 46; Joanna, 117.
Murray, Major Charles, 141; Rt. Hon. David, Viscount Stormont, 141; Ja., 146; James, 196; Jo., 146; Hon. Louisa, Viscountess Stormont, 141.
Muskerry (Muskry), Lord, 217, 218.
Mussenden, Charles, 217; William, 217.
Muston, Anne, 161; Hugh, 161.

N

N . . . ., Jone, 252.
Nale, Isabel, 25; Joh'es, 25.
Nayler, 204.
Nayler, Sir George, "Garter," 204; —, 204; *see also* "correction," p. 315.
Naylor. Isabella, 126; James Richard, 126.
Neale, Isabell, 60; John, 142; Mary, 142.
Neave, Mary, 248; Richard, 248.
Neill *and* Co., 197.
Nelson, Fanny, 74; Lord, 80, 277; Mary, 32, 74; Richd., 71; Thomas, 74; William, 74; Rev. —, 36.
Netherton, Anne, 27; Joanna, 155; John, 311, 312; Margaret, 27; Mary, 311, 312; Nicholai, 155; —, 24, 59.
Nettleton, Robert, 135.
Neue, *see* Le Neue.
Nevil, Lady, 70.
Nevile, George, 267.
Nevill, 300.
Nevill, Sir Henry, 110.
Neville, Ann, 114; Catharine, 112, 114; Elizabeth, 114; Henry, 112, 114; Katherine, 114; Richard, 112, 114.
Neville-Aldworth, Magdalen, 114; Richard, M.P., afterwards Aldworth-Neville, 112.
Newbery, Martha Ann, 315; Tho., 315; Thomas, 315; Thos., 315.
Newman, Alice, 209; Anne, 209, 210; Arthur, 209, 210; Edward, 30; Elizabeth, 30, 32, 209, 210; Elizabeth Osbaston, 209; Frances, 209, 210; Henry, 56, 209; Mary Osbaston, 209; Osbaston, 209, 210; Philip H., 240; Richard, 30; *see also* Grundy-Newman.
Newport, John, 290; Martin, 290; Penelope, 290.
Newson, Rev. Stephen, 227.
Newton, Rt. Hon. Sir Alfred, Bart., 178; Amelia, 15; Mary, 223; Rev. Samuel, 223; —, 15.
Neynoe, Joseph, 263.
Niall Glumdubb, Monarch of Ireland, ancestor of the O'Neill family, 260.
Nibblet, Anna, 230.
Niblet, Alice, 55; Georg., 55.
Niblett, Anne, 233; Samuel, 233.
Nicholas, Catherine, 275, 276; Robert, 276.
Nicholson, Anne, 232.
Nickolls, Martha, 232.
Nicolls, Gustavus, 270.
Nicolson, Rev. Dr., 318.
Nind, George, 290.
Nisbet, Henry Kingscote, 181; Rev. Johannes Majoribanks, 209; Rev. Canon John Marjoribanks, 181.
Norbery, Thomas, 221.
Norffolke, Hugh Bygod, Earle of, 51.
Norfolk, Henry, Earl Marshal, Duke of, 296.

Norris, Ellen, 101; John, 98, 99, 101, 102.
North, Andrew, 44; Ann, 313; Eliz., 29; John, 313; Sarah, 313; William, 29, 93.
Nortier, Madelaine, 29.
Norwich, Anthony Sparrow, Bishop of, 220, 226.
Notier, Nurse, 70.
Nowell, Alexander, Dean of St. Paul's, 322.
Noxon, Ellenor, 24; Thomas, 24.
Noyes, Ann, 238; Sarah, 238; Thomas Buckeridge, 238.
Nugent, Anne, Lady Delvin, 115; Christopher, Lord Delvin, 115.
Nurse, Sarah, 32.

O

Oake, ffu (?), 56.
Oakes, Elizabeth, 27; Jane, 55; John, 27, 55; Thomas Alexander, 23.
Oakey, Henry, 163; Mary, 163; Mary Ann, 163.
O'Brien, Arthur Percival, 123; Edward, 123; Eleanor Sarah, 123; Emily Grace, 123; Frederick, 123; Henry Acheson, 123; Robert Francis, 123; Robert Irwin, 123; Turlough, 258; William Francis, 123.
O'Donnell, Hugh Duv, 258; Hugh Roe, 258; Hugh Roe, Prince of Tirconnell, 258; Manus, 258; Mary, 258; Niall Gary, Lord of Tirconnell, 258.
O'Donovan, Anne Melian, 89; The, 89.
O'Hanlon, Chief of Orior, 257.
O'Hara, Robert Patrick, 266.
O'Haugheys, The, Chiefs of the Iveagh, 257.
O'Haughy, Donslevy, Chief of Iveagh, 257.
Oke, Catherine Mary, 127; Dr. Robert Rouby, 127.
Okeley, John, 55.
Olive, Elizabeth, 233; Nicholas, 233.
Oliver, James, 295; Martha, 192, 236.
Olney, 99.
Olney, Abraham, 101; John, 64, 99; Susan, 101; Thomas, 64.
O'Neile, Lady Alice, 115; Hugh, Earl of Tyrone, 115.
O'Neill, Art Oge, 260; Brian, 2nd Earl of Tyrone, 260; Bryan, 259, 260; Con, 256; Con Baccagh, afterwards 1st Earl of Tyrone, 260; Con More, 260; Cormac, 260; Cu-Uladh-, 258; Eleanor, 260; Henry, Spanish Lieut.-General, 260; Henry MacOwen, 260; Henry Oge, 258; Hugh, 260; Hugh, 3rd Earl of Tyrone, 260; Matthew, Baron of Dungannon, 260; Melaghlin, 258; Murtough, 258; Sir Neill, 260; Owen, 258; Sir Phelim Roe, 8, 260; Lady Sarah, 8, 259; Shane, 260; Viscount, 259; *see also* Niall Glumdubb.
Opplebee, Alice, 249; An', 310; Edw., 249; Edward, 309; John, 252.
Orford, Margery, 161; Nicholas, 161.
Ormond, Earl of, Lord Deputy of Ireland, 258; James, 9th Earl of, 115; —, 217.
Ormsby, Lieut.-Colonel Owen Lloyd, 170; Sarah Mary, 170.
O'Rooney, John, 257.
O'Rourke, Art, 257; Auliffe, 257.
Orpen, Alicia, 202, 269; Alicia Frances, 203; Dr. Charles, 202; Charles E. Herbert, 203; Dr. Chas., 269.
Orr, Jon, 145.
Osbaldeston, 209.

S

Sabell, Thomas, 252.

Sadler, Henry, 164 ; Sarah, 164.

St. George, Sir Henry, 42 ; Sir Henry, Clarenceux King of Arms, 296, 297 ; Tho., "Garter." 129 ; Sir Thomas, Garter King of Arms, 296, 297.

Sainthill, 290.

Sainthill, ffrances, 290 ; Frances, 290, 291 ; Jemima, 291 ; Margaret, 290, 291 ; Peter, 290 ; Dr. Peter, 290 ; Rev. Peter, 291 ; Samuel, 291 ; William, 290.

St. John, Dorothea Maria, 274, 275 ; Sir Hen. Paulett, Bart., 274, 275.

Sale, Anne, 155, 309 ; Christian, 312 ; Guilmus, 155 ; John, 155 ; Margaret, 3, 60 ; Roger, 60, 309 ; Thomas, 3 ; William, 158.

Salisbury, Anne, 243 ; Elizabeth, 243 ; Sir Henry, Bart., 243 ; Rev. Thomas, 208.

Salle, Anne, 118.

Salter, Mrs., 37.

Sampson, Rev. Mr., 33.

Sanders, Agnes. 196.

Sandys, Rev. Geo., 2.

Sarg, F. R., 323.

Sarum, R. Ro. Benjamo Hoadly. Episc., 37.

Sault, Margaret, 153 ; Mary. 153 ; Obedience. 153 ; William, 153.

Saunders, Ann, 141 ; Rev. E., 141 ; Elizabeth. 142 ; Mary, 141 ; Nathaniel, 141 ; Nathaniel James, 141 ; Sarah, 141.

Saunderson, Carolus, 98 ; Johan, 282, 283.

Savadge, Senecin (Jenkin), 257.

Savadges of Ards, The, an old Irish family, 257, 258.

Savage, 1, 99. 100 (*with coat of arms and seals*).

Savage (Savddg, Savadge, Savag, Savidge, *or* Savig), Agnes, 2, 65, 100 ; Alice, 3, 4, 65, 66, 67, 68, 100, 101 ; Alicia, 2 ; Alis, 4 ; Ann, 98 ; Anne, 2, 3, 4, 32, 67, 98, 100, 101, 102 ; Annis, 1 ; Arthur, 166 ; Benedict, 64 ; Blachea, 3 ; Blanch, 3 ; Blanche, 4 ; Cath., 2 ; Cathe., 4 ; Charles, 67, 68, 98, 100, 101, 102, 166 ; Christopher, 2, 4, 310 ; Deborah, 3 ; Dority, 3 ; Edmond, 2, 4 ; Edmund, 3 ; Edward, 3, 4, 65, 67, 100 ; Elinor, 2 ; Elisabeth, 4 ; Elisth., 4 ; Eliz., 3 ; Elizabeth, 3, 4, 67, 94, 98, 99, 100, 101, 102, 311 ; Elizth., 3 ; Ellen, 65, 101 ; Ezechiell, 3 ; Francis, 2 ; Geo., 3 ; George, 3, 4 ; Hannah, 3, 68, 101, 102 ; Henery, 4 ; Henry, 3, 100 ; Hester, 3, 4, 68, 101 ; Hope, 2, 68, 69, 96, 97 ; Humphry, 3 ; Isabella. 3 ; Jane, 3, 65, 100 ; Jhon, 3, 4 ; Joan, 68, 100 ; Joane, 3 ; Johannes, 26 ; John, 1, 2, 3, 65, 66, 68, 96, 97, 98, 99, 100, 101, 102, 311 ; Jonah, 3 ; Juliana, 64 ; Kathe., 2, 3 ; Laurence, 65 ; Lawrence, 65 ; Leonard, 2, 3, 4, 65 ; Mabel, 101 ; Mabell, 67 ; Margaret, 3, 4, 64, 65, 100, 101 ; Margery, 4 ; Maria, 1, 2, 3, 4, 66, 101 ; Mary, 3, 4, 66, 67, 68, 98, 101, 102, 158 ; Matilda, 64, 65, 68 ; Michael, 32, 100 ; Moses, 3 ; Patience, 2 ; Prudence, 2, 4 ; Rebecca, 101 ; Rebecka, 3 ; Ric., 99 ; Ricd., 64 ; Rich., 99 ; Richard, 2, 3, 4, 64, 65, 66, 67, 68, 69, 97, 98, 99, 100, 101, 102 ; Richardson, 3, 4 ; Richd., 4, 64 ; Robert, 64, 65 ; Robt., 99 ; Roger, 97, 100, 101 ; Samuel, 101 ; Sarah, 1, 3, 68, 101 ; Susannah, 3, 68, 102 ; Tho., 311 ; Thomas, 2, 3, 4, 64, 65, 66, 67, 68, 97, 99, 100, 101, 311 ; Thos., 2, 64, 66, 68, 69, 96, 97 ;

Walter, 2, 100 ; Widow, 4 ; William, 2, 3, 4, 64, 65, 66, 67, 68, 97, 98, 100, 101, 102 ; Sir William, 100 ; Willm., 2 ; Wm., 3, 4, 65, 66, 67, 68, 69, 96, 97.

Savill. Ann, 190 ; Rob., 190.

Sawndes, John, 24.

Saxton, Henry A., 320.

Scarman, George, 163 ; Mary, 163 ; Sarah, 163.

Schaw, 203.

Schaw, Catharine Louisa, 203 ; Major George Henry, 203 ; John Sauchie, 203.

Schnell, Leonhard, 322.

Schomberg, Mr., 239.

Scot, Andro, 143.

Scott, Hon. Abraham, 122 ; Allen Stewart, 124 ; Anna, 123 ; Anne, 124 ; Anne, mother of Sir Walter, the celebrated poet and novelist, 203 ; Lieut. Benjamin. 123 ; Benjamin James, 124 ; David, 13 ; David, M.P., 115 ; Edward Forde, 124 ; Elizabeth. 124, 150 ; Helena, 122 ; Rev. Henry, 124 ; James, 150 ; Jane, 124 ; Jemima, 291 ; Rev. Johannes, 209 ; John, 232 ; John Blundell, 123 ; Louisa, 124 ; Margarette Butler Anderson, 263 ; Mr., 80 ; Robert, 150 ; Samuel Baird, 124 ; Sarah, 232 ; Walter, 322 ; Sir Walter, 7.

Scutt, Anne, 220 ; —. 220 (? Roger Strutt).

Seagood, John, 206.

Seaward, Lucy, 152 ; Thomas, 152.

Sebright, Captain, 201, 205.

Seers (? *Sehrs*), 204.

Seman, Katherine, 228 ; Richard, 228.

Semer, *see* Seymour.

Sermon, Joseph. 312.

Sers. 204 pl.

Setten. Margery, 28.

Sewell, Thomas, 68 ; Thos., 68, 69.

Seymour, Edward, Duke of Somerset, 53 ; H., 270 ; H. A., 263 ; Isabella Anne, 263 ; Margaret, 263 ; Mary, 53.

Shacle. Edward, 60.

Shailer, John, 60 ; Martha, 60.

Shakle, Mary, 105.

Shank. Anna Maria, 20 ; Diana Henrietta, 20 ; Henry, 20.

Sharp, David, 146 ; Rev. Johannes, 209.

Sharpe, Ann, 82 ; Bryan, 303 ; Charles, 163 ; Frances, 303 ; Rev. Isaac, 82 ; Rev. John, 142 ; Mary, 163 ; Sutton, 19.

Sharpus, Jane, 149 ; Richard, 149.

Sharratt, Anne, 77.

Shaw, Ann, 33 ; James, 33.

Shaxton, Richard, 108 ; —, 108.

Sheehy, Father Nicholas, 201.

Sheffils, Catherine, 75.

Shekell, Jacobus, 156 ; John, 310 ; Mary, 252 ; Rich., 310 ; Richard, 252 ; Richi., 156.

Shekle, Jone, 252 ; Richard, 252.

Shelbury, 302.

Sheldon, Frances. 313 ; John, 313.

Shelton, Johane, 188 ; Walter, 188.

Shepard, Catherine, 10 ; Elizabeth, 10 ; Richard, 10 ; William, 10.

Shepherd, Elizabeth, 154 ; Henry, 154 ; Jerom, 278 ; Mary, 154.

Sheppard, 211 ; Alexandri, 211 ; Alicæ, 211 ; Annæ, 211 ; Joan, 29 ; Mary, 93 ; Thomas, 211.

Sheppey, Elizabeth, 27.

Sheppy, John, 309.

Shepray, John, 188.

Shepwey, John, 250.

Sherborn, C. W., 296.
Sherwood, John, 236.
Shewall, Elinor or Eleanora, 228 ; Henry, 228.
Sheward, Samuel, 167 ; Sophia, 167.
Shilton, Cicily, 189 ; Walter, 189.
Shipton, Mr., 70.
Shipway, John, 279 ; Mary, 232.
Shore, George, 14 ; Helen, 14.
Shouler, Peter, 252 ; Widdow, 157.
Showel, Margaret, 231.
Showler, Elizabeth, 158 ; John, 26 ; Katherine, 106 ; Nathaniel, 106.
Shrewsbury, Countess of, 294.
Shuldam, Major-General Thomas, 136.
Shuttle, Francis, 256 ; George, 256 ; Jane, 256 ; John, 256 ; Thomas, 256.
Shuttleworth, Hannah, 134.
Sibbald, Elizabeth, 15 ; Sir James, Bart., 15.
Sibthorpe, Coll. Henry, 303.
Sidmouth, Rev. William Leonard, Viscount, 14.
Silverwood, Jacob, 72 ; —, 35.
Simkins, 80.
Simkins or Simkin, Anne, 80 ; Charles, 80 ; Dorothy, 80 ; Elizabeth, 142 ; Jane, 142 ; Thomas, 142.
Simm, Bessie, 195.
Simon, Catherine, 192 ; J. E., 192.
Simonds or Symonds, Jane, 31 ; William, 31.
Sim'ons, Alce, 105.
Simons, Ann, 314 ; Charles, 314 ; Rev. Edw., 138 ; Henry, 252 ; Mary, 314 ; Richard, 314 ; Sarah, 255.
Simpson, Anne, 124 ; Henry, 154 ; —, 124.
Singer, James, 268.
Sinnot, Christian, 116 ; —, 116.
Sirr, 203, 204.
Sirr (Seer, Seers, Sehrs, Sers, Serse, Sir, or Surr), A. E. J., 201, 202 ; Agnes, 202 ; Alfred John Orpen, 202 ; Alicia, 202, 269 ; Alicia Catherine, 202 ; Alicia Frances, 203 ; Anne, 201, 204, 268 ; Catherine, 201, 202, 204, 268, 269 ; Catherine Ann, 204 ; Catherine Frances, 201, 203 ; Catherine Louisa, 203 ; Celia, 204 ; Charlotte Henrietta, 202 ; Christo. C. S., 267 ; Christopher, 267 ; Dunne, 202 ; Edward Hoare, 202 ; Edward Joseph Arthur, 202 ; Eliza Dorothea, 203 ; Elizabeth, 201, 202, 267 ; Elizabeth Lucinda, 202 ; Elizabeth M. A., 203 ; Elizabeth Martha Mory, 203 ; ffrances, 201, 268 ; ffrancis, 267, 268 ; Frances Elizabeth, 203 ; Francis, 201, 204, 268 ; Francis Pole, 202 ; Frederick Purefoy Augustus, 202 ; Gervais, 202 ; H., 201, 202, 267 ; Harry, 202 ; Henry Charles, 268, 269, 270 ; Major Henry Charles, 201, 202, 205, 269, 271, 272, 273, 315 ; Hubert Hoare Francis, 202 ; Isabella Anne, 202 ; Jane, 203 ; John, 204, 205 ; Joseph, 202, 268, 269 ; Major Joseph, 201, 205 ; Joseph D'Arcy, 202, 269 ; Joseph D'Arcy, D.D., 202, 205 ; Loth, 205 ; Louisa, 202 ; Louisa Catherine, 202 ; Louisa Frances, 202 ; Margaret Theodosia, 202 ; Marrian or Marian, 267 ; Mary, 205 ; Mary Jane, 205 ; Patrick, 204 ; Peter, 201 ; Peter (of Gedney), 204, 315 ; General Peter, 205 ; General Peter von, 204 ; General Philip Loth, 205 ; Pierre, 204 ; Captain Richard Theodore Howard, 202 ; Roger, 201, 204, 268 ; Samuell, 204 ; Sophia Priscilla, 202 ; Thomas, 205 ; William, 204 ; Rev. William, 202 ; William Shepherd, 202 ; Lieut. William Whiteway, R.N., 203, 205, 270, 271.

Siseager or Iseager, Mary, 28 ; Richard, 28.
Skinner, Elisabeth, 90 ; Elizabeth, 90 ; John, 98 ; Joseph, 90 ; Mary, 230 ; William, 230.
Skrimsher, Frances, 132 ; —, 132.
Slane, Charles, Randal, and William, Barons of, 115 ; *see also* Fleming.
Slaney, 241.
Slany, D. Katherine, 241 ; Stephen, 241.
Slarke, Eliza Jane, 119 ; Emily Ann, 119.
Slawter, Joane, 28.
Sloane, Dr. Hans, 299.
Sloper, Rev. George, 264.
Small, Ann, 310 ; Francis, 310 ; Rob., 310 ; Robert, 310.
Smart, Sir George Thomas, 177 ; Margaret Rose, 177.
Smibert, Thomas, 7.
Smith, 292.
Smith, Adam, 253, 315 ; Agnes, 220 ; Alice, 59 ; Ann, 105, 158, 228, 302 ; Anna, 58, 124, 229 ; Barnard, 289 ; Carrington, 198 ; Cath., 2 ; Catharin, 229 ; Catharine Jane, 289 ; Catherine, 179, 220 ; Dr. Charles, 47 ; Dr., 70 ; Edward, 59, 106 ; Eleanor Anne, 289 ; Elizabeth, 58, 76, 228 ; Elizabeth Evarina S., 47 ; ffrances, 106 ; ffrancis, 55, 58, 106 ; Georg', 229 ; Giles, 228 ; Hanna, 229 ; Hannah or Johanna, 95 ; General Sir Harry, Bart., 289 ; Helen Mary, 86 ; Henry, 308 ; Henry Scott, 47 ; James, 58 ; Rev. James, 47 ; Joan, 100 ; Joane, 302 ; Johanna, 95 ; John, 55, 104, 105, 179, 220, 231 ; Sir John, 61 ; John Stona, 289 ; Margaret, 228, 302 ; Margareta, 23 ; Martha, 315 ; Martha Jane Sophia, 47 ; Mary, 86, 105, 231, 250, 252 ; Michael, 86 ; Mrs., 301 ; Olive, 231 ; Rebecca, 76 ; Rebeccah, 76 ; Rebekah, 76 ; Richd., 315 ; Robert, 124 ; Samuel, 228 ; Sarah, 1, 229, 233 ; Simon, 76 ; Susannah, 138 ; Tho., 58, 59 ; Thomas, 105, 106, 229, 233, 255 ; Rev. Thomas, 86 ; William, 95, 302 ; Will'm, 2, 138.
Smith (Smithe or Smyth), Henr., 292 ; Henrie, 293 ; Henry, 292, 293 ; Walter, 293.
Smyth, Alice, 27 ; An., 57 ; Ann, 188 ; Anne, 25 ; Caroline, 198 ; Edward, 27 ; Edwardi, 23 ; Family, of Colkirk, 198 ; of Elkington Hall, 199 ; ffrancis, 56, 57 ; Francis, 310 ; Henry, 27 ; Jane, 58 ; Joan, 56 ; Rev. Johannes, D.D., 209 ; Joh'is, 26 ; John, 56 ; Katherine, 26 ; Margaret, 26, 58 ; Rob'ti, 58 ; Tabitha, 58 ; Thomas, 27, 58, 188 ; Ursula, 27 ; Will., 25 ; Willimus, 26 ; Willm., 64 ; *see also* Johnson-Smyth.
Snell, F. S., 149, 162.
Snelling, Jane, 30.
Snow, 293.
Snow or Snowe, Alce, 294 ; Alice, 293, 294 ; Daniell, 293, 294 ; Edward, 293, 294 ; Edwarde, 294 ; Elizabeth, 293, 294 ; Emma, 293, 294 ; Rebecca, 293, 294 ; Richard, 293, 294 ; Sarah, 293, 294.
Snowdon or Snowden, Eliz., 138 ; George, 138.
Soane, Harry, 249.
Sollars, John, 232 ; Rachel, 232.
Solomons, Israel, 323.
Soltau, Florence, 14 ; John Thomas, 14.
Somersett, Edward Semer (Seymour), Duke of, 53.
Sommers, C. G., 92.
Sorrill, Rob., 310 ; Robert, 310.
Sorsby, Sarah, 140.

London : Mitchell Hughes and Clarke, Printers, 140 Wardour Street, W.